FOREIGN COMMERCE

FOREIGN COMMERCE

HAROLD J. HECK

Professor, College of Business Administration
Tulane University

New York   Toronto   London

McGRAW-HILL BOOK COMPANY, INC.

1953

FOREIGN COMMERCE

THE MAPLE PRESS COMPANY, YORK, PA.

To

Suzanne Holt Heck

Preface

This book was designed primarily for use as a text in college courses in foreign trade or in international economics, if the latter is taught with emphasis on or purposeful consideration of private-business aspects. The title *Foreign Commerce* was selected because foreign *trade*, as such, cannot be studied adequately without continued reference to transactions other than those in merchandise. They are all related through the foreign-exchange market.

Internally, the study is an integration into one volume of practical and theoretical aspects of international economics. Theoretical discussions are interspersed with practical considerations and applications. Practical phases have been broadened, where possible, to represent a view beyond that of vocational study. But, because of the objective, it was not considered advisable to present the study along lines of the detailed architectural structure of forms and documents. These forms change very often, and the details mean something to the student only when he has had, is having, or very soon will have experience in working with them. They belong in a more specialized text or a handbook. However, it is not feasible to eliminate discussion of use of documents from any study of foreign commerce because of their functional role in the conduct of commerce.

The first two parts of the book deal with such topics as the importance of foreign commerce to the student and the citizen, the types of international transactions, the patterns of trade between nations, the organizational structure for conducting foreign commerce, and financial and marketing practice.

There were two reasons for covering this material. One is that such a study enables the student to see what the *business* of foreign commerce is about. He is thereby introduced to the specific types of activity which he would go into if he went into foreign commerce at all. The other reason is an assumption that the student will have had as a prerequisite at least a year's work in economic principles. Hence he will already have been introduced to some of the theoretical aspects, and a factual or anatomical study at this point will orient him better for the more intensive theoretical discussion and analysis which follow.

The third and fourth parts are concerned with theoretical and policy aspects of a broad, yet specialized, nature. The student with a background of economic principles and with some knowledge of the "industry" he is now studying in detail should be in a position to benefit most fully from economic and policy discussions at this stage. These will constitute a good part of his interest in foreign commerce throughout life, either as a practitioner or as a well-informed citizen. Policies, especially, can be better understood and evaluated if we know the problem which they are intended to cope with, both in the broader and in the narrower sense, and the economic structure through which they are mechanically to be accomplished.

The fifth section deals largely with postwar developments at *inter*governmental level. It is the most international section in character, whereas the earlier parts are primarily either national or individual, though in an international field.

On completing a book, an author finds himself indebted to many people. The obligation may rest on a discussion, a critical review, a suggestion here or there—some of these quite informal or casual. This author finds the list of friends and colleagues with whom he has discussed particular parts of this work to be extensive. However, several whose interest served as an aid and a source of encouragement can be singled out, although listing them in order of indebtedness is not possible. Identification is not intended to imply responsibility or liability to any of them.

In this perspective, the author wishes to acknowledge his gratitude to the following:

From the business community, Howard C. Gary, Department of Economics, McGraw-Hill Publishing Company, Inc.; Adolfo E. Hegewisch, foreign freight forwarder and former President, International House, New Orleans; Percy L. McCay, Vice President, Whitney National Bank, New Orleans; Morris S. Rosenthal, President, Stein-Hall and Company, Inc., New York; George E. Roper, Jr., International House, New Orleans; and George L. Sawicki, International House, New Orleans.

From the government, Robert L. Sammons, U.S. Department of Commerce; F. Preston Forbes, U.S. Department of Commerce; Nathan Ostroff, U.S. Department of Commerce; Prentice N. Dean, U.S. Department of Defense; and Harold F. Linder, Deputy Assistant Secretary for Economic Affairs, U.S. Department of State.

From the university community, W. H. Baughn, Louisiana State University; Francis J. Kennedy, Loyola University of the South; Henry T. Owen, University of Texas; H. B. Carnes, Tulane University; Marvin L. Fair, Tulane University; Robert W. French, Tulane University; A. B. Hillabold, Tulane University; Harry A. Mitchell, Tulane University; and F. Santry Reed, Tulane University.

Harold J. Heck

NEW ORLEANS, LA.
JANUARY, 1953

Contents

PART ONE

Significance and Background

CHAPTER 1

Why Study Foreign Commerce

Foreign commerce may be defined as the international exchanging of goods and services of all types, whether on the part of individuals or of governments. The foreign commerce of the United States therefore involves considerably more than trade in merchandise. However, trade in goods is of more direct interest and understanding to a greater number of citizens than is any other single type of international transaction.

Merchandise trade is unavoidably and consistently influenced by all transactions making up our foreign commerce. Because of its volume, however, it bears more weight on the other elements than they do on it. These other elements include transactions in services, capital movements, interest and dividends, gold, travel expenditures, gifts and donations—all the things comprising the movement of goods, funds, services, or claims between the people and government of one country and those of another.

The subject of foreign commerce is timely—perhaps of greater immediate interest than ever before. This calls for clear and thorough understanding on the part of informed citizens of its theories, mechanisms, and impacts.

Foreign commerce is of importance to all of us, but of direct importance to many segments of the population for a number of reasons. Students, businessmen, and many others will find the study of more or less direct applicability depending on their interest, occupation, and residence.

Interest of Students May Be Professional or Academic. Students in business and economics may profitably study foreign commerce, not only for cultural reasons, but because of their direct interest in finding employment in the field—in trade, transport, finance, the Foreign Service of the United States, or any of the other activities connected with foreign trade. If such employment is not to be had, or if better opportunities arise in domestic commerce, perhaps students will find employment with a company a significant part of whose domestic eco-

3

nomic activity is linked with foreign activity, either in importing or in exporting. It may be that its immediate customers are interested in or dependent on some phase of foreign commerce. It will be seen later that large percentages of the production of certain items are exported. Not only are those engaged directly in these activities vitally interested in foreign commerce, but others who make their living by rendering services to those directly engaged are no less dependent than the former on a reasonably good knowledge of foreign commerce—the underlying activity providing their livelihood. Furthermore, students interested in almost any aspect of international relations will need a foundation in foreign commerce, which is, actually, the applied phase of international economic affairs.

Several Businesses Are Part of Foreign-commerce "Industry." To the businessman who is engaged in some phase of foreign commerce, directly or indirectly, study of the subject will offer a broader view of his own specific activity as it fits into the over-all picture. Whether he pursues a formal course of study or not, he will benefit by being better informed on other functional activities serving him or served by him. Thus, he has a fuller appreciation of the industrial sphere or spheres surrounding his daily business interests.

Well-informed Citizens Realize Foreign-commerce Influences throughout the Country. Whether he falls within these two groups or not, any well-informed citizen needs to know about foreign commerce. The impact and cost of foreign aid bring the subject close to everyone in the mid-twentieth century. For example, United States international finance and aid expenditures during the fiscal years 1946 to 1952 amounted to over $32,000,000,000, or about $213 for every man, woman, and child in the nation. As citizens, we find domestic governmental and economic policies being developed in the light of their relationship to foreign commercial affairs. Furthermore, we are becoming more aware that almost all cities, towns, and regions are influenced to some degree by foreign commerce. Leading testimony on this is the existence and functioning of foreign-trade bureaus of chambers of commerce in small and large cities throughout the United States. Interest is by no means confined to port cities or areas.

It can thus be seen that the study of foreign commerce is of substantial interest to the producer, consumer, financier, transporter, freight forwarder, port operator, insurer or provider of other services, government employee, and students undertaking formal educational programs.

Similarity to Domestic Commerce. The functional operations comprising commerce, whether foreign or domestic, are the same. Both call for producing, selling, financing, transporting, storing, insuring, and otherwise attending to goods and services reaching the ultimate consumer.

Accordingly, the study of foreign commerce rests on the standard business disciplines of marketing, transportation, finance, insurance, business law, accounting, and statistics.

From a broader point of view, foreign commerce is similar to domestic in that it provides employment comparable to solely domestic activities. Thus, foreign commerce has an effect on income and taxation similar to that of domestic business. Also, as in domestic commerce, there is a continual interrelationship among all functional activities. In this regard, foreign commerce simply means a broadened market for domestic production and wider competition for the domestic market.

Differences between Foreign and Domestic Commerce. In view of many functional parallels and links between foreign and domestic commerce via individual products and foreign exchange, the differences narrow down pretty much to the workings of people, geography, and time. Or one may choose to look on differences between foreign and domestic commerce as being the reflection of differences in human resources and physical resources within respective national boundaries. However, in some large countries, great differences are found in the conduct of business in one part of the country as compared with another; in any country, different "trade" customs can be found to prevail as between different lines of business. From either view, human and physical resources are the cumulative results of people and geography and their working together over a period of time.

PEOPLE. In most cosmopolitan countries, different types of people meet, enjoy social contacts, absorb each others' culture, transact business together, and in general overcome many of the difficulties found when great distances separate them. Provincial characteristics, resulting in different languages, customs, and laws, as well as national and racial traits, bring about significant differences between domestic and foreign commerce.

Not only completely different languages must be overcome; the meaning of words or terms sometimes differs. In some countries, for instance, a billion is one million million; in others, it is one thousand million. Internationally, for example, one must make sure of the meaning of the term "ton." Not only are there a long and a short ton, as in the United States; common reference in other countries may mean a metric ton. A hundredweight (cwt) in Canada is 100 pounds, while in other commonwealth countries it is 112 pounds. Furthermore, different money and monetary systems are used, giving rise to foreign-exchange problems.

Customs in different countries have a bearing on the preparation, color, display, and other features of certain products. In Latin countries, the religious influence is quite apparent; use of sacred names may be found in connection with everyday items, such as cigars. Customs and traits have to do as well with methods of transacting business. The subtle as against the aggressive; the suave as against the brusque; the apparent placing of business before pleasure or vice versa—all have their place in making up a difference between domestic and foreign business. One of the most valued characteristics a foreigner may possess in some Latin-American countries is to be *simpatico*. This intangible, indefinable, one-of-us-in-understanding attribute may at times be the difference between success and failure in internatioal business negotiations.

More specifically, foreign and domestic commerce differ because of the different laws pertaining to their undertakings. These may vary from packing and marking regulations to rights and remedies of creditors in different countries. Types of taxes, regulations, and court procedures vary from country to country; this is especially significant in that each party to the transaction may prefer his own country's legal structure and would like to have it hold in case of difficulty.

GEOGRAPHY. The physical problems faced by exporters and importers some distances apart are more than a lessened opportunity to visit each other. Greater distances increase the possibility of differing terrain and climate. This may mean modification in packing or in the size of the unit which can be handled by the weakest of a number of transporting facilities. Danger from rough handling, water, sun, salt air, or temperature changes presents some exporters and importers with problems not faced by businessmen engaged in a good part of domestic trade, especially that near at hand. Furthermore, the geographic factors of distance and terrain may present different problems with regard to financing, insurance and documents than are normally found in domestic commerce. Some of these operating differences are, as indicated before, due to laws or customs, but others rest on problems posed by physical factors which are relatively permanent in their influence on commerce.

TIME. Closely related to geographic differences is the time element, although time differences within a country as large as the United States may be greater than those between parts of the United States and other countries. This pertains both to communication and to transportation. As to the former, undertaking foreign commerce between, say, the United States and Europe, the time differences may be so substantial that use of telephone or radio is restricted to only an hour or two each day if it is to be within regular business hours. This is, of course, overcome by arranging for someone to be in each place during the same hours. In some cases, this difference may be put to advantage.

The standard time difference between New York and Rio de Janeiro is two hours, and all of South America is some time ahead of most of the United States in time zones. This can be seen by looking at a map, which will show that if one were to move due north from the Panama Canal he would touch Charleston, S.C.; if he were to travel due south from New Orleans, he would not touch South America at all. He would, after crossing Central America, strike around the Galápagos Islands, far off the coast of Ecuador. South America is practically east of North America, and this accounts for the fact that the East coast of South America is several hundred miles nearer New York than New Orleans.

Another aspect of time is that it may be looked on as simply a dimension of distance. But since finance, storage, and insurance costs are measured in units of time, both geographic distances and time zones are often a matter of concern in foreign commerce while relatively less significant in domestic.

From a longer point of view, time over the years may be said to have been an influence in the stages of economic development of various countries of the world. Application of human resources to physical factors of production, out of which capital resources evolve, give rise to different stages of national economic development over a period of time; these, in turn, contribute to differences between foreign and domestic commerce.

Price System Is Basic Link between Foreign and Domestic Commerce. Possibly the most important link with domestic commerce is to be found in the price system, which resolves itself through the various countries' monetary and banking structures. As demand for goods, services, or investments payable in foreign currencies exceeds at any time foreign demand for goods, services, or investments payable in the domestic currency, the result is that the price of foreign exchange is driven upward.

When driven sufficiently high, individuals or business turn to the central bank or the government for gold or for foreign exchange, itself, to settle accounts abroad. Loss of gold or of monetary reserves affects the monetary and credit structure of the "debtor" country; this, in turn, tends to affect the price level and individual prices which represent the various types of economic activity of that country, whether or not directly engaged in foreign commerce. Reciprocal effect may be expected in the country increasing its holdings of gold or of monetary reserves.

This indirect but strong link between foreign and domestic commerce makes a knowledge of foreign commerce of some interest to the business community at large, even though, as said before, there is no direct engagement in foreign commercial activities.

Growing Importance of Foreign Commerce. The importance of foreign commerce may be appraised from several viewpoints. One is in absolute dollar or physical volumes. Another is in relation to some other measure of economic activity, such as employment or national income.

Secular growth will account for a large part of the dollar or physical volume, and there is no doubt of the substantial increase in total foreign commerce over several decades. Ordinarily, there would seem to be no reason to expect foreign commerce to increase or decrease in relative position in the economy. Nor is there a very satisfactory basis for measuring the changing importance of this commerce. However, war or significant political changes may alter this somewhat.

It may properly be said that foreign commerce has come into greater prominence because the world seems to have become smaller. One need only consider transportation and communication facilities to see how much nearer we are to other countries than we were some few decades ago, even though there are many obstacles preventing fuller gains from technical progress. Nevertheless, these facilities can make the undertaking of foreign commerce considerably easier and more certain because of the opportunity for buyer and seller to know each other better. Basically, it has become easier to obtain up-to-date and complete economic intelligence on an international scale.

If the man-made barriers to world commerce can be reduced, as have the physical barriers, it would seem that foreign commerce may play an increasingly apparent and immediate part in our daily lives.

International Stature of United States Has Grown. By its own effort, and partly by default on the part of other countries, the United States has come to enjoy an economic and political stature which has tremendously increased in the first half of the twentieth century. Such enjoyment, though, carries with it responsibilities, both for citizens and for their government. This means that individually and nationally we shall have to be increasingly aware and informed of the international economy and its functioning, and especially of the part played in it by the United States. This development imposes a responsibility on many segments of the population to become students, formal or informal, of foreign commerce.

International Economic Organization Has Grown. The ill-fated League of Nations, established after the First World War, followed by a larger scale and more detailed attempt at international organization along economic as well as political lines, after the Second World War, are good reasons to expect a wider interest in international economic affairs. International economic organization and cooperation are a vital phase of the subject of foreign commerce. Their existence and rapid growth are further evidence of the need for more people to be better informed about the subject matter under consideration.

Actually, few people can say that they have no interest in foreign commerce and need to know no more about it. To the extent that one needs to know about the domestic economy, he will also find it to advantage and of interest to know about the international economy. The students' future, the businessmen's present and future, and the taxpayers' pocketbook are all tied in to some extent with foreign as well as domestic commerce.

As will be evident throughout this study, the subject covers more than trade in merchandise. Accordingly, the text deals not only with international transactions in goods but also in investments and in services of several types. Moreover, because of the importance of finance in international economic relations, this aspect has been especially emphasized.

It is hoped that the student will find the subject not only interesting but also beneficial in business and academic undertakings, and that study of the subject will be particularly helpful in making him or her a better informed and more responsible citizen.

REVIEW QUESTIONS

1. What economic activities comprise the foreign-commerce industry?

2. What interest does or should the study of foreign commerce have for (*a*) college students, (*b*) businessmen, and (*c*) citizens in any walk of life?

3. In what way is foreign commerce similar to domestic commerce?

4. How does foreign commerce differ from domestic commerce?

5. Explain how the price system is the basic link between foreign and domestic commerce.

6. Is there any obvious basis for expecting that foreign commerce may increase or decrease in relative position in any nation's economy? What could bring such a change about? What forces tend to prevent such changes? Discuss.

CHAPTER 2

Types of International Transactions

Foreign commerce, in the broad sense, comprises trade in goods and services, travel expenditures, gifts, foreign philanthropic or charitable activities, loans and other investments, gold movements between countries, international military expenditures, and other intergovernmental dealings—in fact, everything moving across national boundaries and making up what may be termed the international economy.

Not all such transactions are recorded, but most are summarized by countries in their "balances of international payments." Chapter 13 deals with analysis of balances of payments in broader terms. The present chapter is intended to review in some detail the entire field of foreign commerce, as recorded in balances of payments, and to describe the accounts representing various types of transactions, their relative importance and, where appropriate, the source of statistical data thereon. Data used here will pertain primarily to the United States, which officially publishes the material under the titles *International Transactions of the United States during——*, and *The United States Balance of International Payments*.[1] Only a few countries publish as many data on their foreign transactions as does the United States. For some years, the League of Nations issued balance-of-payment estimates for about thirty countries, and in 1938 its Committee of Statistical Experts began studying the classification of international business transactions with a view to framing a new model scheme. The last publication issued in the series of reports was *Balances of Payments, 1939–1945,* published by the United Nations in 1948. The International Monetary Fund has undertaken the postwar responsibility and now issues a *Balance of Payments Yearbook* with reasonably comparable data for several of the major countries.

Whichever report form is used, it is designed to show the monetary approximation of international transactions effected within a specified

[1] *The United States in the World Economy* (1943), and *International Transactions of the United States during the War,* 1940–45 (1948), include tabular presentations of balances of payment going back to 1919. Quarterly and annual reports appear in *Survey of Current Business*. All are issued by the U.S. Department of Commerce.

period of time. It does not represent actual payments made or received; whether merchandise sold abroad is ever paid for is not revealed in this tabulation. It does not necessarily represent actual invoice amounts covering the underlying transactions; they may be more or less than the amount included in the tabulation. It does not indicate whether the transactions summarized were quoted in dollars, pounds, francs, or pesos. Some of its inclusions are at best estimates. And, despite its *balancing* implication, or title, there is no real balancing as of any one time except that which results from residual entries for the purpose of forcing a balance.

Inasmuch as the tabular presentation followed since 1940 appears to have replaced the format formerly used in the arrangement known as "Balance of International Payments," this chapter will be set up accordingly; it is probably the form most likely to be used by students in the next few years. The several groupings reported include both private and public transactions (some figures are segregated because of the growing importance of public transactions), and they include what are ordinarily termed "visible" and "invisible" imports and exports. Some of the accounts consistently show an excess of exports or of imports; this is brought out in the sections that follow.

Table 1 shows summary tabulations for the years 1921 through 1951. From it,[2] the following main groupings of transactions may be studied:

1. Exports and imports of goods and services
2. Unilateral transfers
3. Long-term capital
4. Gold and short-term capital (net)
5. Errors and omissions

Relative Importance of Recorded Items. In order to point up the relative importance of these items, Tables 2 and 3 have been prepared. Table 2 shows the proportions comprising the first three main groupings listed above. It covers all transactions except movements of gold and short-term capital and items included in Errors and Omissions. A more detailed breakdown, for a shorter period of time, is given in Table 3, but the figures are not entirely comparable with those of Table 2; capital movements are excluded from the former, while similarly designated accounts, coming from different publications, are not exactly in the same amounts. Because some figures are reported on a cumulative basis while others are the reflection of net changes during the period, it is not possible to reduce the total tabulation (Table 1) to meaningful percentages.

[2] The table itself is divided into four main sections, which encompass the five groupings listed.

Table 1. International Transactions of the United States, 1921–1951
(In millions of dollars)

Item	1921–1925 average	1926–1930 average	1931–1935 average	1936–1940 average	1941–1945 average	1946–1950 average	1951
Receipts, total	$6,107	$7,244	$3,394	$4,902	$17,255	$18,093	$21,517
A. Goods and services, total	5,647	6,438	2,951	4,443	15,102	16,381	20,140
1. Goods	4,505	4,886	2,108	3,351	11,818	12,798	15,424
2. Income on investments	726	1,039	537	567	545	1,296	1,905
3. Other services	416	513	306	525	2,739	2,287	2,811
B. Unilateral transfers	62	68	22	38	1,702	264	*
C. Long-term capital, total	398	738	421	421	451	1,448	1,377
1. United States capital	213	526	301	201	352	1,121	1,072
2. Foreign capital	185	212	120	220	99	327	305
Payments, total	$5,729	$7,106	$2,978	$3,937	$18,367	$18,312	$22,862
A. Goods and services, total	4,376	5,356	2,563	3,558	7,431	9,473	15,111
1. Goods	3,519	4,093	1,840	2,604	4,827	7,110	11,663
2. Income on investments	130	268	152	241	179	303	400
3. Other services	727	995	571	713	2,425	2,060	3,048
B. Unilateral transfers	451	423	233	227	10,029	4,435	4,939*
C. Long-term capital, total	902	1,327	182	152	916	4,404	2,812
1. United States capital	882	1,301	164	76	737	4,174	1,993
2. Foreign capital	20	26	18	76	179	230	819
Net inflow (+) or outflow (−) of funds on gold and short-term capital account	−$299	−$ 4	−$617	−$1,544	+$1,026	−$433	+$ 834
A. Net increase (−) or decrease (+) in United States gold stock	− 295	− 39	− 575	− 2,370	+ 392	− 547	− 53
B. Net movement of United States short-term capital abroad	− 47	− 201	+ 282	+ 103	− 106	− 111	− 132
C. Net movement of foreign short-term capital to United States	+ 43	+ 236	− 324	+ 723	+ 740	+ 225	+ 1,019
Errors and omissions	− 79	− 133	+ 202	+ 579	+ 95	+ 652	+ 511

* Not fully comparable with preceding periods because reported net.
Source: U.S. Department of Commerce.

Table 2. International Transactions* of the United States, 1921–1951
(In per cent)

Item	1921–1925 average	1926–1930 average	1931–1935 average	1936–1940 average	1941–1945 average	1946–1950 average	1951
Receipts, total............	100	100	100	100	100	100	100
Goods and services, total.....	93	89	87	90	88	91	94
Goods.................	74	68	62	68	69	71	72
Income on investments....	12	14	16	12	3	7	9
Other services...........	7	7	9	10	16	13	13
Unilateral transfers........	1	1	1	1	9	1	†
Long-term capital movements.	6	10	12	9	3	8	6
United States capital.....	3	7	9	4	2	6	5
Foreign capital.........	3	3	3	5	1	2	1
Payments, total...........	100	100	100	100	100	100	100
Goods and services, total.....	76	75	86	90	40	52	66
Goods.................	61	57	62	66	26	39	51
Income on investments....	2	4	5	6	1	2	2
Other services...........	13	14	19	18	13	11	13
Unilateral transfers........	8	6	8	6	55	24	22†
Long-term capital movements.	16	19	6	4	5	24	12
United States capital.....	16	18	5	2	4	23	9
Foreign capital.........	‡	1	1	2	1	1	3

* Except gold and short-term capital.
† Not fully comparable with preceding periods because reported net.
‡ Less than 0.5 of 1 per cent.
SOURCE OF BASIC DATA: U.S. Department of Commerce.

Table 3. "Current" International Transactions of the United States, 1921–1939
(In per cent)

Item	1921–1925 average	1926–1930 average	1931–1935 average	1936–1939 average
Receipts, total....................	100	100	100	100
Merchandise......................	77	73	69	73
Shipping and freight..............	6	6	5	6
Travel expenditures...............	1	2	3	3
Personal remittances..............	1	1	1	1
Institutional contributions.........	...	...	...	
Interest and dividends............	11	13	17	14
Government aid and settlements....	3	4	2	
Other government items...........	...	...	1	1
Silver...........................	1	1	1	
Miscellaneous adjustments and services..........................	...	...	1	2
Payments, total...................	100	100	100	100
Merchandise......................	71	69	62	65
Shipping and freight..............	7	8	9	9
Travel expenditures...............	6	8	9	8
Personal remittances..............	7	6	7	4
Institutional contributions.........	2	1	1	1
Interest and dividends............	3	5	5	7
Government aid and settlements....	1	1	...	
Other government items...........	1	1	3	2
Silver...........................	1	1	4	4
Miscellaneous adjustments and services..........................	1	...	...	
% of payments to receipts.........	84	89	96	92

SOURCE OF BASIC DATA: U.S. Department of Commerce.

Pertinent factors relating to each section (main grouping) are discussed in the remainder of this chapter. Before moving on to detailed considerations, however, it should be specifically noted that data on goods and services are usually reported gross, with net balances being derived from them. Other transactions are often reported net, but partial gross data are available.

EXPORTS AND IMPORTS OF GOODS AND SERVICES

This main grouping embraces both visible and invisible items and includes practically all transactions except those of gifts, investments, and gold movements. It comprises five subgroupings, titled:

1. Merchandise
2. Transportation
3. Travel
4. Miscellaneous services
5. Income on investment

Significant facts relating to each are presented in the next few paragraphs.

Merchandise

This group is normally the largest of all those shown. It discloses the estimated value of the merchandise exported from and imported into the United States. Both extent of coverage and recognized inaccuracies in the raw data make a number of adjustments advisable, but lack of complete information makes all necessary adjustments impossible. For example, in the total for exports, a distinction may be desired between exports of domestic origin and reexports; for imports, it may be desirable to know the total of imports for consumption as well as general imports. Moreover, for balance-of-payments purposes, certain adjustments may have to be made, with the result that all series on exports and imports do not exactly agree.

The Meaning of "Favorable" Balance of Trade. When exports exceed imports, it is commonly said that a country enjoys a favorable balance of trade; if imports exceed exports, the balance of trade is said to be unfavorable. Data reported in the *Statistical Abstract of the United States,* selected because of length of series, and extended to more recent date, show that total exports have exceeded general imports in every year since 1900; the cumulative excess of exports over imports between 1900 and 1951, inclusive, amounted to around $100,000,000,000.[3] One may well pause to consider what is so favorable about our having shipped abroad this large amount of merchandise, bearing in mind that some of it represents nonreplaceable minerals.

Some efforts have been made by writers to abandon the use of the terms "favorable" and "unfavorable" balance of trade and to substitute for these some other terms which would more accurately reflect the meaning of the disparity between exports and imports of merchandise. Among the suggestions are "excess of exports," or "credit balance."

Merchandise Is Generally the Largest Account. In point of relative importance in current international transactions, Tables 3 and 4 show that merchandise accounted generally for about 70 to 75 per cent of the annual current commercial export transactions, for the periods indicated, and for a somewhat smaller and less regular proportion of current import

[3] *Statistical Abstract of the United States, 1949,* U.S. Bureau of the Census, 1949, p. 855; *Survey of Current Business,* June, 1951, and March, 1952.

transactions. But this percentage relationship is apt to be misleading. Different bases (totals) are used for computing the percentages, so the proportion of exports to imports is shown in the last column of Table 4. Although they are not detailed by individual years in the table, exports were over 50 per cent larger than imports in thirteen years since 1921 and less than 10 per cent larger in only four.

Table 4. Percentage of Current International Transactions Represented by Merchandise, 1921–1951

Period	Exports	Imports	% of exports to imports
1921–1925	77	71	128
1926–1930	73	69	119
1931–1935	69	62	115
1936–1940	75	69	129
1941–1945	71	28	245
1946–1950	77	51	180
1951	77	58	132

Reporting and Valuations Prescribed by Law. Before commercial shipments of merchandise are permitted to enter or leave the United States, a certain amount of recording and reporting is prescribed by law. The official agency for gathering and publishing foreign-trade statistics is the Bureau of the Census, U.S. Department of Commerce. Both exports and imports are valued by customs rules on a basis that excludes ocean freight. Thus, items exported and imported are reported at their values at the border or port of lading of the exporting country. Official prescription for valuation of imports is found in Sec. 402 of the Tariff Act of 1930, as amended, which reads, in part:[4]

[4] By definition, the "foreign value" represents the market value or the price, at the time of exportation of such merchandise to the United States, at which such or similar merchandise is freely offered for sale for home consumption in the principal markets of the country from which exported, including expenses incident to placing the merchandise in condition for shipment to the United States. The "export value" is the market value or price at which such or similar merchandise is offered for sale for exportation to the United States.

The "United States value" represents the price at which such or similar imported merchandise is offered for sale for domestic consumption, at the time of exportation of the imported merchandise, with allowance made for necessary expenses from the place of shipment to the place of delivery (duty, transportation, insurance, etc.). The "cost of production" represents the cost of producing such or similar merchandise and placing it in condition for shipment to the United States, including ordinary profits. The "American selling price" is the price at which such an article is offered for sale for domestic consumption in the principal market of the United States, or the price which the owner would have received or was willing to receive, at the

For the purposes of this Act the value of imported merchandise shall be—

(1) The foreign value or the export value, whichever is higher;

(2) If the appraiser determines that neither the foreign value nor the export value can be satisfactorily ascertained, then the United States value;

(3) If the appraiser determines that neither foreign value, the export value, nor the United States value can be satisfactorily ascertained, then the cost of production;

(4) In the case of an article with respect to which there is in effect under section 336 a rate of duty based upon the American selling price of a domestic article, then the American selling price of such article.

The value most commonly shown on import entries is the foreign value.[5]

In the case of exports, the value in the Shippers' Export Declaration[6] must be the actual selling price, or cost, if not sold, including inland freight, insurance, and other charges at the port of exportation. Freight and other charges from the United States port of departure to the foreign country are not included.

Valuations Not Necessarily Invoice Amounts. Mention was made earlier that the summary of international transactions does not necessarily represent actual invoice amounts covering the underlying transactions. In an interesting article titled "The Dollar Value in United States Import Statistics,"[7] the point is well developed that the tariff value is not necessarily the same as the amount actually paid in the case of individual shipments. In the case of exports, the two values are possibly more apt to be the same. Both the fact that export declarations are for statistical and not for duty purposes and the relative lack of necessity for conversion of values stated in other currencies would appear to work toward bringing the customs valuations and the invoices more closely together. In addition, the penalties involved under export-licensing procedures serve as a strong deterrent to dissimilarity between the actual and statistical values.

Not only are basic figures considered inadequate for balance-of-payments purposes, but they must be recognized as somewhat inaccurate because of physical difficulties in their collection. Types of errors which

---

time of exportation of the imported article. The American selling price pertains only to articles produced in the United States, and is to be used only upon proclamation by the President for the purpose of "equalizing costs of production," as provided in Sec. 336 of the Tariff Act of 1930.

A proposed customs-simplification bill, introduced in the 81st Congress (H.R.-8304), would amend the Tariff Act of 1930 to provide for a different basis of valuation, designations being export value, United States value, comparative value, and constructed value. Each of these values, in turn, is defined in detail.

[5] *Foreign Commerce Weekly*, U.S. Department of Commerce, Aug. 14, 1948, p. 8.

[6] Must be filed with collector of customs on all commercial exports.

[7] *Foreign Commerce Weekly*, Aug. 14, 1948, p. 37.

creep in are those relating to valuation at the port of exportation, as required by customs regulations. Occasionally, declared values exclude
charges such as inland freight, which by definition is a component of
the f.o.b. port-of-exportation value. On shipments through parcel-post
channels, aside from correctness as to valuation, there is the problem
of incorporating them into the final report even though they are not
included in the data collected by collectors of customs.[8] There is also
the possibility of difference between invoice price and official statistics
owing to valuations in U.S. dollars for official statistics, while invoices
may actually be in other currencies. This difficulty is further complicated
by the existence of multiple exchange rates, which makes valuation of
exchanges somewhat arbitrary. As of April, 1949, for example, imports
from France were valued using an exchange rate reflecting 50 per cent
"free" and 50 per cent "official" quotations. The official rate was 214
francs to the dollar; the free rate was about 330.[9]

Countries Use Different Methods for Valuing Imports. All countries
do not employ the same basis for valuing imports and exports of merchandise in their tabulations of international transactions. A major difference pertains to valuation of imports. The standard scheme employed
by the United Nations (superseding the League of Nations) in its
publication *Balances of Payments, 1939–1945* calls for valuing merchandise exports f.o.b. and valuing merchandise imports c.i.f.[10] Thus
the valuation scheme employed by the U.S. Department of Commerce
shows imports to be valued at less than they would be were we to use
the scheme employed by the United Nations; the difference is the amount
of freight and insurance involved. This "undervaluation" of imports
affects the so-called favorability in the balance of trade which appears
generally to be an annual feature of United States statistics. It obviously
makes our balance of trade appear more favorable than it is as calculated
by the United Nations.

Table 5, constructed from page 168 of *Balances of Payments, 1939–
1945,* and from Table I of Appendix to *The United States in the World
Economy,* shows the excess of exports (+) or of imports (−) under the
respective arrangements. It is interesting to note that in four of the years,
the United States is considered by the United Nations report to have
had an "unfavorable" trade balance, and, of course, the extent of being
"favorable" in the other years is substantially lessened. There are
defensible arguments for favoring either method, mainly depending on

[8] For a complete discussion of these problems, see *International Transactions of
the United States during the War, 1940–45,* U.S. Department of Commerce Economic Series 65, 1948, pp. 172–174.
[9] *American Import and Export Bulletin,* June, 1949, p. 428.
[10] See Chap. 8 for description of terms.

Table 5. United States Trade in Merchandise, 1919–1939
[Excess of exports (+) or of imports (−)]

Year	United States basis (f.a.s.)	League of Nations basis (c.i.f.)
1919	+$4,016	+$2,854
1920	+ 2,950	+ 1,604
1921	+ 1,976	+ 1,495
1922	+ 719	+ 324
1923	+ 375	+ 46
1924	+ 981	+ 648
1925	+ 683	+ 340
1926	+ 378	+ 9
1927	+ 680	+ 307
1928	+ 1,037	+ 610
1929	+ 842	+ 388
1930	+ 782	+ 355
1931	+ 333	− 9
1932	+ 288	+ 40
1933	+ 225	+ 81
1934	+ 478	+ 264
1935	+ 236	− 299
1936	+ 33	− 242
1937	+ 265	− 88
1938	+ 1,134	+ 720
1939	+ 859	+ 483

the purpose intended, but it should be more obvious than ever that loose use of the terms "favorable" and "unfavorable" may be meaningless and at the same time quite misleading or damaging in public acceptance.

Transportation

This is a rather important account in our total of international transactions, and ordinarily one in which our purchases from abroad exceed our sales abroad, thus making possible in part the maintenance of an excess of exports over imports of merchandise. By definition, the account includes

all international payments and receipts arising out of the international movements of goods and persons, specifically: (1) freight and passenger revenues paid by Americans to foreign air and ocean carriers and similar revenues received by American carriers from foreigners, (2) expenditures of American carriers in foreign ports and foreign carriers in American ports, (3) revenues and expenditures in Canada of American railroads operating in that country, and (4) revenues received by American railroads for hauling foreign goods (but not passengers) in transit through the United States.[11]

Transportation Purchases Normally Larger than Sales. In point of importance, transportation accounted for about 5 to 6 per cent of our current "sales" abroad and about 6 to 8 per cent of our current "purchases" during the interwar period. Postwar experience has modified this noticeably. Table 6 shows the relative position of this account over several years.

Table 6. Percentage of Current International Transactions Represented by Transportation (Freight and Shipping), 1921–1951

Period	Exports	Imports	% of exports to imports
1921–1925	6	7	92
1926–1930	6	8	80
1931–1935	5	9	68
1936–1940	6	9	84
1941–1945	6	2	281
1946–1950	8	5	181
1951	7	5	163

Details of this account will suggest some of the difficulties in collecting all necessary data. As reported by the U.S. Department of Commerce, the summary account comprises the following activities:[12]

ITEMS INCLUDED IN THE INTERNATIONAL TRANSPORTATION ACCOUNT RECEIPTS

Freight, ocean, Great Lakes, and air (earned from foreign residents by United States carriers on United States exports).

Passenger fares, ocean and air (earned by United States vessels and airplanes carrying foreign residents).

Port expenditures, ocean, Great Lakes, and air (received from foreign lines for fuel, provisions, stevedoring, etc., at United States ports).

Railway operations:

In-transit freight (earned on foreign goods carried through the United States).

Earnings of United States railroads in Canada (on Canadian goods and United States exports to Canada).

PAYMENTS

Freight, ocean, Great Lakes, and air (earned from United States residents by foreign carriers on United States imports).

[11] *International Transactions of the United States during the War, 1940–45*, p. 168.
[12] *Foreign Commerce Weekly,* June 19, 1948, p .5.

Passenger fares, ocean and air (paid by United States residents to foreign vessel or air-line operators for transportation to and from the United States).

Port expenditures, ocean, Great Lakes, and air (paid by United States lines for fuel, provisions, stevedoring, etc., at foreign ports).

Railway operations:

In-transit freight (paid by United States residents to Canadian railroads on United States imports from countries other than Canada).

Expenditures of United States railroads in Canada (for maintenance of way, repairs, rentals, etc.).

Import vs. Export; United States vs. Foreign-flag Influences. It will be recalled that merchandise is valued at the port of exportation. Accordingly, freight on exports is considered to be paid by the foreign purchaser, while ocean freight on imports is ascribed to the account of the United States importer. Thus, on exports, if carried in United States bottoms, an international transaction is calculated to have been entered, but if carried on foreign-flag vessels, foreigners are considered to have paid themselves for performing the service. On imports, if carried in United States bottoms, an international transaction is not considered to have occurred; it is looked on as an intra-United States payment. But if the imports are brought in on a foreign-flag vessel, even though freight is paid in advance by the shipper, the statistical system records an international purchase by the United States of a foreign service. When, in practice, imports and exports are billed with freight charges included, they are valued by Customs exclusive of the transportation costs, which are then transferred in the compilation of the international balance of payments to the transportation account.

Transportation Account Has Economic and National-defense Aspects. Of very great interest and importance is the question of whether the United States should strive to maintain an excess of sales over purchases in the transportation account. This is stating the question rather indirectly, for it ties in most obviously with the maintenance of a large merchant marine. If we persist in the view that we should do so because of national-defense requirements, it will mean a net demand for U.S. dollars with which to cover this account. Yet the reconversion of some European countries contemplates a return to their position of net exporters of freight and shipping services, for one thing, as a means of paying for their imports of merchandise. Thus a certain conflict appears between the economic and the national-defense aspects of this account— the activities which it represents—in our total of international transactions. It will be seen later (Chapter 4) that to some countries sales of freight and shipping services represent a much greater proportion of total sales abroad than do such sales for the United States, or, in some cases, a larger amount than sales of merchandise.

Travel Expenditures

Ordinarily an account representing about 2 to 3 per cent of our current foreign sales and 8 or 9 per cent of our purchases abroad, travel expenditures decreased to insignificant proportions during the war. But this item has since begun to resume its important position. This type of transaction is one in which our "purchases" from abroad have for many years been greater than our "sales," or foreign purchases from us, and the disparity is increasing rather steadily. Table 7 shows the percentage of current transactions accounted for by travel expenditures in the period 1921 to 1951.

Table 7. Percentage of Current International Transactions Represented by Travel Expenditures, 1921–1951

Period	Exports	Imports	% of exports to imports
1921–1925	1	6	27
1926–1930	2	8	28
1931–1935	3	9	32
1936–1940	3	8	43
1941–1945	1	1	48
1946–1950	2	4	54
1951	2	4	61

It will be noted that not only does our export of this activity represent a smaller portion of total current exports than does import activity of total current imports; in each year shown we have imported considerably more than we have recorded as exports. In many years we have spent abroad about three dollars for every dollar spent in this country by foreign travelers.

At a recent National Foreign Trade Convention, tourist expenditures abroad were classed by a speaker as our largest single import.[13] Our excess expenditures on this item (import) help make possible, in part, the maintenance of an excess of exports in the merchandise account.

It should be noted that this account does not include passenger fares covering ocean and air travel to and from the United States. But it does include Great Lakes and rail travel, if an international payment is involved.[14] If the fares for ocean and air travel were paid by United States residents to foreign-line operators, or if paid by foreign residents to United States ocean and air lines, the amount of such fares enters the

[13] E. A. Emerson, "Our Greatest Import—What Is It?" *Report of the Thirty-fourth National Foreign Trade Convention*, National Foreign Trade Council, Inc., New York, 1948, pp. 214–226.

[14] *International Transactions of the United States during the War, 1940–45*, p. 51.

Balance of International Payments in the *transportation* account; if paid by a United States resident to a United States line, even for travel abroad, it does not involve a transfer of funds to foreign hands, and thus does not enter the international accounts. The travel account, therefore, represents amounts spent in traveling abroad, or spent here by foreign travelers for other than the originating and terminal fares, except when they were fares via Great Lakes or rail.

Collection of Data Is by Questionnaire on Sample Basis. Even the simplest picturization of the mechanics involved in collecting figures for this account leaves the reader with considerable reservation as to accuracy of the figures. This view is obvious from the following partial description of the manner in which some of the figures are derived:[15]

In 1941 and prior years, questionnaires were mailed to a group of United States citizens selected at random from lists of passport applicants . . . similar questionnaires were distributed to holders of (alien) re-entry permits. . . . For each year, average per capita expenditures were computed for citizens and for alien residents of the United States, by class of steamship accommodation utilized and by geographic areas visited.

Questionnaires are distributed by United States Customs officers on a random basis to approximately one United States resident out of every seven who return to the United States over the Canadian border by rail, boat, plane or long-distance bus. Canadian authorities sample the travel of United States residents who enter Canada by automobile by means of questionnaires printed on the reverse of the Vehicle Permits. . . .

In 1944 the Bank of Mexico conducted a survey by means of questionnaires handed to the United States tourists visiting Mexico City who stayed in hotels and lodging houses and to students who pursued courses of study in that city. . . .

The foregoing should remind the reader that the Balance of International Payments is not a true, recorded summary of international transactions; it is the best available indication of the magnitude of our foreign transactions, most of which have resulted in or will result in a demand for or a supply of foreign exchange.

Miscellaneous Services

This subgroup includes both private and governmental services. The private category covers such items as insurance, royalties, home-office expenses, motion-picture rentals, communications, advertising, and sales and purchases of gas and electric power. The government category includes expenditures and receipts of federal agencies and their personnel abroad for the purchase of services. For the years 1941 to 1945, lend-

---

[15] *Ibid.*, pp. 178–180.

lease *services* were also included, both as services rendered and as
services received (reverse lend-lease). Ordinarily this account is not
large, but the lend-lease services during the war transformed an otherwise minor account into one of important proportions.[16]

Income on Investments

Of much, and perhaps most, immediate significance in the status of
a creditor nation is the continuing impact of interest and dividend
receipts. This means a net demand by foreign debtors for its exchange
with which to meet their obligations. Thus the effect is the same as that
of a country's having a favorable balance of trade in goods. Both, in the
case of the United States, call for a net settlement in U. S. dollars; the
realization seems to be increasing that this dual "net-receipts" position
must eventually break down. It is argued that, now being a creditor
nation, we must revise our policies toward the importation of goods and
encourage more imports to permit us to maintain our creditor position
without harm to other countries.

In view of the absolute and relative size of these accounts and the
large postwar increases in foreign loans and other investments, both
private and public, it is very possible that this segment of our economy
will play an increasingly important role in our future foreign commerce.
Table 3 shows these accounts to be usually next in importance to merchandise among all current transactions. From 1921 through 1939, over
10 per cent of our current exports represented the "sale" of the use of our
capital abroad, while the comparable figure for imports was generally
between 2 and 5 per cent. With the greatly expanded volume of imports
and exports of merchandise and of government unilateral transfers, this
percentage declined somewhat in the postwar period, but, as is shown
in Table 8, the importance of this account is steadily mounting.

Increasing "Dollar Gap" in Interest-and-dividends Account. Table 8
shows the status of our interest-and-dividends account in dollars and in
percentages of current transactions. Then, for comparative purposes, it
records receipts for the use of our capital abroad as a percentage of merchandise exports. The figures show that in some years foreign requirements for dollars to pay interest and dividends is a goodly percentage
of the demand for dollars for the payment of merchandise; it reached a
high of 32 per cent in 1932. Of particular importance is the prospect of
an increasing dollar gap in the account. Actually, the net difference (net
receipts) increased in each postwar year. It was $594,000,000 in 1946 and
$1,505,000,000 in 1951. Increasing foreign investments by United States
interests should hold these net receipts to well over $1,000,000,000 for
many years.

[16] *Ibid.*, pp. 84–85.

Table 8. Income on International Investments, 1921–1951

Period	Average receipts (000,000 omitted)	Average payments (000,000 omitted)	Percentage relationships		% of receipts to merchandise exports
			% of current transactions		
			Receipts	Payments	
1921–1925	$ 726	$130	11	3	16
1926–1930	1,039	268	13	5	21
1931–1935	537	152	17	5	25
1936–1940	567	241	13	6	17
1941–1945	545	179	3	1	5
1946–1950	1,296	303	8	2	10
1951	1,905	400	9	2	12

Creditor Status Not Uniform with All Countries. Of importance and interest regarding the item of income on investments is that while a nation may be a creditor nation over all, its investment status as compared with the several other countries need not be uniformly that of creditor or debtor; it may be a creditor to one and a debtor to another. For example, Table 9 shows the income from investments account by regions.

Table 9. Receipts and Payments of Interest and Dividends, by Area, 1946–1951
(In millions of dollars)

Area	1946–1950 average		1951	
	Receipts	Payments	Receipts	Payments
OEEC countries	$ 175	$220	$ 303	$273
OEEC dependencies	59	2	99	3
Other Europe	10	1	12	*
Canada and Newfoundland	332	55	396	84
Latin-American republics	504	12	688	16
All other countries	212	14	400	16
International institutions	4	4	7	8
Total	$1,296	$308	$1,905	$400

* Less than $500,000.
Source: *Survey of Current Business*, June, 1950; June, 1951; March, 1952.

If the data on merchandise exports and imports are recalled, it will be clear that, while foreign investments may be suggested at times as the answer to balancing trade between the United States and foreign countries, we should carefully consider the several other balance-of-payments accounts. In the case of any given country or area, we may maintain an excess of exports of goods and at the same time experience an excess of receipts over payments of investment income. In others, we may buy more merchandise from them than we sell them, and at the same time we may be paying more interest and dividends to the people of those countries than they pay us. Accordingly, in studying world commerce, the whole view must generally be maintained; transactions between one particular country and another may result in more distortions than appear overall.

As in the case of other elements of our international transactions, knowledge of the method of obtaining data on international interest and dividend payments is valuable. Estimates of income *receipts* are derived from questionnaires to large companies, information filed with the Securities and Exchange Commission, questionnaires to fiscal and paying agents of foreign dollar bonds, corporate income-tax returns, and (for 1942) the Treasury Department *Census of American Property in Foreign Countries.* The basis for data on income *payments* is withholding-tax returns and income-tax returns filed with the Bureau of Internal Revenue. Estimates are also made for payments abroad on government bonds and short-term paper.[17]

UNILATERAL TRANSFERS

Unilateral transfers may be defined as those not requiring reimbursement, such as gifts, or those in which the conditions of reimbursement are not sufficiently clear to justify recognition of the creation of a capital asset.[18] These may be private or public, the former consisting of personal and institutional remittances. Public, or government, transfers include a wide variety of transactions, such as the cost of diplomatic and consular representation, maintenance of military establishments abroad, lend-lease and reciprocal aid, reparations, and civilian supplies furnished the occupied areas.

Ordinarily, this section is not a large part of the total of transactions reported, but during the recent war and in immediate postwar years, it has made up a rather sizable sum. In *The United States in the World Economy,*[19] the ordinary transactions are tabulated as Other Government Items, and transactions arising out of special circumstances are tabulated under the heading Government Aid and Settlements.

Population Changes Influence Unilateral Transfer Account. Over the years, personal remittances have been the source of a substantial excess of payments to foreigners over receipts. They represent noncommercial payments between individuals and may be either in cash or in kind. A

[17] *Ibid.,* pp. 181–182.
[18] *Ibid.,* p. 170.
[19] U.S. Department of Commerce Economic Series 23, 1943.

noticeable secular decline in personal remittances from this country to others is observable. The publication *The United States in the World Economy* states:[20]

The basic factor determining the long-run trend of personal remittances to foreigners is the size and character of the remitting group in this country, which is believed to consist almost solely of foreign-born residents. The number of foreign-born residents declined from 14,200,000 in 1930 to 11,800,000 in 1940. Not only was the number of potential remitters in the United States declining, but their ties with the old country were growing continually more remote and their average remittances smaller. By 1940 about 55 per cent of the foreign-born white population was over 50 years of age, and as early as 1930 over 60 per cent of this group had been in the country for more than 20 years.

Institutional remittances include noncommercial transfers of funds and materials by philanthropic, religious, educational, and scientific organizations. These organizations assist in the support of hospitals, missions, churches, schools, and scientific undertakings abroad.

As in the case of other main segments of the tabulation of international transactions, the methodology of collecting data on unilateral transfers is such as to impress the student with the necessity for caution in using the figures. For the period 1940 to 1945, estimates of total contributions of individuals in the United States to foreign countries were composed of separate estimates of contributions forwarded through various agencies such as banks, steamship and travel companies, and communications companies, and by postal money orders. In addition, there were special deductions from the wages of imported workers which were made by the Department of Agriculture and the Department of Labor under their work programs. In the same period of time, the value of gift parcels was estimated by applying an average rate of 60 cents per pound. Postal-money-order data, both payments and receipts, were obtained from the annual reports of the postmaster general, and in the matter of receipts other than postal money orders, it was assumed that postal money orders represented the same proportion of the total on both sides of the account.[21]

Sources of data on institutional remittances were replies to an annual letter from the Department of Commerce sent to religious, charitable, educational, and scientific organizations and reports to the President's War Relief Control Board (now the Advisory Committee on Voluntary Foreign Aid of the United States Government) by war-relief agencies registered with that organization.

[20] P. 78.

[21] *International Transactions of the United States during the War, 1940–45*, pp. 186–187.

The source of data on United States government transactions was the appropriate government agency, either direct or through the Clearing Office for Foreign Transactions.[22]

TRANSACTIONS IN FOREIGN INVESTMENTS AND GOLD

In the section titled Income on Investments, the figures reported were those of distributed earnings or interest. This section deals with the movements of the *principal* amounts, which are the base to which income in investments must be related.

Foreign investments are usually separated into long-term and short-term categories. Basic data on international transactions in securities are therefore arranged in the same way. However, the short-term totals are included with gold, and the long-term transactions are the subject of separate compilations.

Long-term Investments

These investments may be both private and public, and they include what are generally identified as "direct" and "portfolio" investments. In recent years, the specter of a rapidly growing public or governmental area of foreign investment has shown itself, and, interestingly, some reports suggest that the borrowers may prefer to have the investments made (loans extended) by the United States government rather than by private United States investors. Many times in the postwar years, the proposal to "make investment attractive" has been offered as a necessary step toward economic expansion of less developed countries. This means making investment attractive to private investors rather than government, through assurances regarding taxation, discrimination, convertibility of exchange, and occasional expropriation.

How Much of a Creditor Nation Is the United States? Be these points as they are, any student of foreign commerce will probably hear at an early stage that the United States is a creditor nation, and that such a position calls for a change in policy from that which we followed as a debtor nation. The international investment position of the United States at the end of 1951 showed us to be a net creditor in the amount of $14,-900,000,000. In 1945, we were a net debtor by $548,000,000[23] (see Chapter 15 for discussion).

Comparative Significance of Transactions in Securities. In order to illustrate the importance of transactions in securities between the United States and foreign countries, which have the same effect on international

[22] *Ibid.*, pp. 188–189.
[23] *The Balance of International Payments of the United States, 1946–48*, U.S. Department of Commerce, 1950, p. 162.

financial balance or dislocation as do transactions in goods, Table 10 has been prepared. It was developed from data presented in *The United States in the World Economy,* supplemented by postwar figures appearing in the *Survey of Current Business* and the *United States Treasury Bulletin.* This table is of special significance because transactions in securities are usually reported *net,* which obscures their impact on total commercial transactions.

Table 10. International Transactions in Merchandise and in Long-term Securities*

(Dollar figures in millions)

Year	Sales (exports)			Purchases (imports)		
	Securities	Merchandise	% of securities to merchandise	Securities	Merchandise	% of securities to merchandise
1935–1939	$10,980	$14,359	76	$9,646	$11,832	82
1946	1,603	11,672	14	1,672	5,168	32
1947	1,287	15,977	8	1,337	6,100	22
1948	945	13,427	7	1,233	7,833	16
1949	1,194	12,337	10	1,091	7,144	15
1950	2,774	10,658	26	1,975	9,315	21
1951	2,336	15,424	15	3,247	11,663	28

* Excluding capital transactions of the United States government.

It may be noted that in several years our international sales or purchases of securities amounted to almost as much as our sales and purchases of goods. Actually, in 1936, both our purchases and our sales of securities exceeded either imports or exports of goods; for the ten-year period 1930 to 1939, for every $100 in goods that we sold abroad we sold about $64 in securities (mostly outstanding domestic); for every $100 in goods that foreigners sold us, they sold us about $66 in securities.[24] It would be difficult to find more striking evidence that the foreign commerce of the United States involves considerably more than trade in merchandise and that governmental policies thus require development of an economic atmosphere which will do far more than merely close the gap between exports and imports of merchandise. Even new foreign investments may not be the answer, in view of the very impressive volume of transactions in outstanding long-term securities, and assuming a sincere effort to maintain and sponsor wider recognition of

[24] This computation does not include short-term capital movements, but some of the transactions in outstanding securities could easily have been of short-term intent. Nor does it include direct investments.

the freedom of the individual to take steps which to him appear in his best interest.

Perhaps the reader may profitably recognize that the impelling motives in long-term capital movements are not always the same as those involved in transactions in goods, although an international movement of goods, such as machinery, might very well result from (be the reciprocal of) investment abroad.

Detailed explanation of the methodology employed in tabulating data for long-term investments may be found in *The United States in the World Economy*[25] and in *International Transactions of the United States during the War, 1940–45*.[26] Generally, the main source of data on transactions in outstanding securities is compiled by the Federal Reserve Bank of New York from reports of banks, brokers, and dealers located in the United States. Data on new issues are compiled primarily from information obtained from underwriters and financial services. Questionnaires and fragmentary data provide the basis for other elements making up the total of long-term capital movements.

Short-term Capital Movements

By definition, the short-term capital account includes all international claims payable within the year. As in the case of long-term investments, short-term accounts may be private or governmental. There is no need to break this segment down between direct and portfolio investment, as is evident from the following explanation of the composition of the account:[27]

Private short-term claims comprise bank deposits, bill acceptances, commercial paper, short-term state and municipal obligations, brokerage balances, commercial deposits abroad for the direct account of United States firms, advance payments for merchandise, and United States currency and coins held abroad. Foreign short-term claims on the United States government include holdings of United States government short-term obligations, deposits with the Treasury, and various claims arising out of the provision of currency for expenditures by our armed forces. United States government short-term claims on foreigners, include holdings of foreign currencies, deposits abroad, and various advances and settlements.

Thus, it is apparent that it should probably be one of the more widely fluctuating accounts. Unfortunately, data on gross short-term movements are not available, but the net movement of United States short-term capital abroad and the net movement of foreign short-term capital in the United States indicate that the volume is impressive and important. In

[25] Pp. 213–215.
[26] Pp. 188–191.
[27] *Ibid.*, p. 170.

the twenty-two years from 1930 through 1951, net movements were as shown in Table 11.

Table 11. Net Changes in Short-term Capital Accounts, 1930–1951
(In millions of dollars)

Year	United States short-term capital abroad	Foreign short-term capital in United States	Total
1930	−$191	−$ 288	−$ 479
1931	+ 628	− 1,265	− 637
1932	+ 227	− 673	− 446
1933	+ 35	− 454	− 419
1934	+ 96	+ 126	+ 222
1935	+ 424	+ 648	+ 1,072
1936	+ 55	+ 376	+ 431
1937	+ 45	+ 311	+ 356
1938	+ 27	+ 317	+ 344
1939	+ 211	+ 1,259	+ 1,470
1940	+ 177	+ 1,353	+ 1,530
1941	+ 11	− 400	− 389
1942	− 115	+ 182	+ 67
1943	+ 3	+ 1,222	+ 1,225
1944	− 153	+ 509	+ 356
1945	− 274	+ 2,189	+ 1,915
1946	− 60	− 639	− 699
1947	− 297	+ 339	+ 42
1948	− 24	+ 549	+ 525
1949	+ 14	− 37	− 23
1950	− 186	+ 912	+ 726
1951	− 132	+ 1,019	+ 887

SOURCE: 1930–1945: *The Balance of International Payments of the United States, 1946–48*, U.S. Department of Commerce, 1950, pp. 152, 274; 1946–1948: *Survey of Current Business*, June, 1950; 1949–50: *Ibid.*, June, 1951; 1951: *Ibid.*, March, 1952.

Net Changes as Large as in Merchandise Account. Comparison with merchandise transactions for the same period indicates that, in seven of the twenty-two years, the net difference in this account was greater than the net difference in the account covering either goods alone or goods and services combined. And in 1935, 1939, and 1940, the *net* difference in the short-term-capital account was more than half the *gross* amount of our imports of goods from abroad.

As significant as is this item of short-term capital in our over-all foreign commerce, collection of data is of recent origin. The earliest available calendar-year short-term data relate to 1923, and data relating

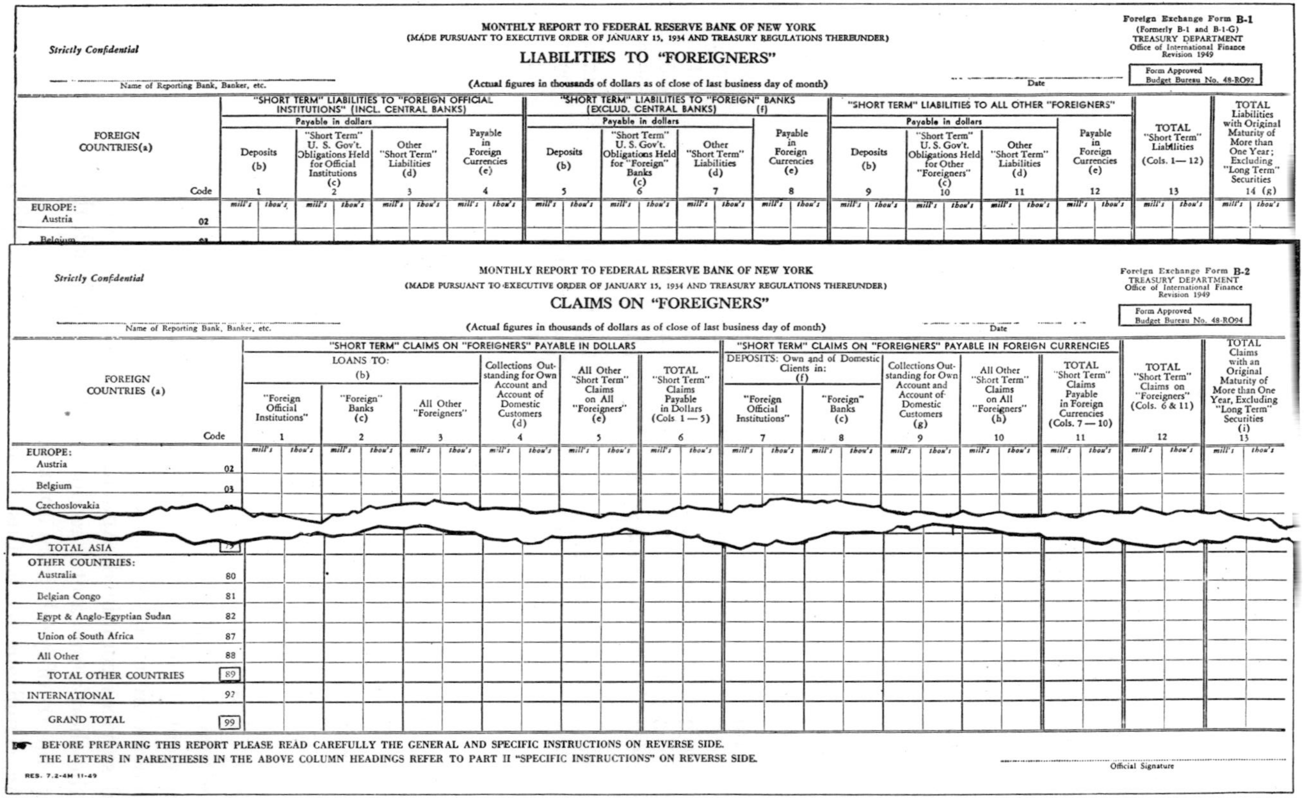

Strictly Confidential

MONTHLY REPORT TO FEDERAL RESERVE BANK OF NEW YORK
(MADE PURSUANT TO EXECUTIVE ORDER OF JANUARY 15, 1934 AND TREASURY REGULATIONS THEREUNDER)

LIABILITIES TO "FOREIGNERS"

Foreign Exchange Form B-1
(Formerly B-1 and B-1-G)
TREASURY DEPARTMENT
Office of International Finance
Revision 1949

Form Approved
Budget Bureau No. 48-RO92

Name of Reporting Bank, Banker, etc.

(Actual figures in thousands of dollars as of close of last business day of month)

Date

FOREIGN COUNTRIES (a)	Code	"SHORT TERM" LIABILITIES TO "FOREIGN OFFICIAL INSTITUTIONS" (INCL. CENTRAL BANKS) — Payable in dollars: Deposits (b) 1	"Short Term" U. S. Gov't. Obligations Held for Official Institutions (c) 2	Other "Short Term" Liabilities (d) 3	Payable in Foreign Currencies (e) 4	"SHORT TERM" LIABILITIES TO "FOREIGN" BANKS (EXCLUD. CENTRAL BANKS) (f) — Payable in dollars: Deposits (b) 5	"Short Term" U. S. Gov't. Obligations Held for "Foreign" Banks (c) 6	Other "Short Term" Liabilities (d) 7	Payable in Foreign Currencies (e) 8	"SHORT TERM" LIABILITIES TO ALL OTHER "FOREIGNERS" — Payable in dollars: Deposits (b) 9	"Short Term" U. S. Gov't. Obligations Held for Other "Foreigners" (c) 10	Other "Short Term" Liabilities (d) 11	Payable in Foreign Currencies (e) 12	TOTAL "Short Term" Liabilities (Cols. 1—12) 13	TOTAL Liabilities with Original Maturity of More than One Year; Excluding "Long Term" Securities 14 (g)
		mill's thou's	mill's thou's	mill's thou's	mill's thou's	mill's thou's	mill's thou's	mill's thou's	mill's thou's	mill's thou's	mill's thou's	mill's thou's	mill's thou's	mill's thou's	mill's thou's
EUROPE:															
Austria	02														
Belgium	03														

Strictly Confidential

MONTHLY REPORT TO FEDERAL RESERVE BANK OF NEW YORK
(MADE PURSUANT TO EXECUTIVE ORDER OF JANUARY 15, 1934 AND TREASURY REGULATIONS THEREUNDER)

CLAIMS ON "FOREIGNERS"

Foreign Exchange Form B-2
TREASURY DEPARTMENT
Office of International Finance
Revision 1949

Form Approved
Budget Bureau No. 48-RO94

Name of Reporting Bank, Banker, etc.

(Actual figures in thousands of dollars as of close of last business day of month)

Date

FOREIGN COUNTRIES (a)	Code	"SHORT TERM" CLAIMS ON "FOREIGNERS" PAYABLE IN DOLLARS — LOANS TO: (b) "Foreign Official Institutions" 1	"Foreign" Banks (c) 2	All Other "Foreigners" 3	Collections Outstanding for Own Account and Account of Domestic Customers (d) 4	All Other "Short Term" Claims on All "Foreigners" (e) 5	TOTAL "Short Term" Claims Payable in Dollars (Cols 1—5) 6	"SHORT TERM" CLAIMS ON "FOREIGNERS" PAYABLE IN FOREIGN CURRENCIES — DEPOSITS: Own and of Domestic Clients in: (f) "Foreign Official Institutions" 7	"Foreign" Banks (c) 8	Collections Outstanding for Own Account and Account of Domestic Customers (g) 9	All Other "Short Term" Claims on All "Foreigners" (h) 10	TOTAL "Short Term" Claims Payable in Foreign Currencies (Cols. 7—10) 11	TOTAL "Short Term" Claims on "Foreigners" (Cols. 6 & 11) 12	TOTAL Claims with an Original Maturity of More than One Year, Excluding "Long Term" Securities (i) 13
		mill's thou's	mill's thou's	mill's thou's	mill's thou's	mill's thou's	mill's thou's	mill's thou's	mill's thou's	mill's thou's	mill's thou's	mill's thou's	mill's thou's	mill's thou's
EUROPE:														
Austria	02													
Belgium	03													
Czechoslovakia														
TOTAL ASIA	79													
OTHER COUNTRIES:														
Australia	80													
Belgian Congo	81													
Egypt & Anglo-Egyptian Sudan	82													
Union of South Africa	87													
All Other	88													
TOTAL OTHER COUNTRIES	89													
INTERNATIONAL	97													
GRAND TOTAL	99													

BEFORE PREPARING THIS REPORT PLEASE READ CAREFULLY THE GENERAL AND SPECIFIC INSTRUCTIONS ON REVERSE SIDE.
THE LETTERS IN PARENTHESIS IN THE ABOVE COLUMN HEADINGS REFER TO PART II "SPECIFIC INSTRUCTIONS" ON REVERSE SIDE.

Official Signature

RES. 7.2-4M 11-49

FIG. 1. Monthly report by banks on liabilities to and claims on "foreigners."

to American banking balances abroad were not obtained until 1925. Beginning with 1935, weekly data from banks and brokers have been collected by the Federal Reserve Bank of New York,[28] and under Executive Order of January 15, 1934, and Treasury regulations thereunder, bankers and banking institutions in the United States are required to report monthly on the form shown in Fig. 1.

This report is on a geographic basis and must be filed by all banks if the sum total of either its claims on or liabilities to foreigners averages $100,000 or over in the six months ending with and including the reporting date, computed by averaging the monthly closing balances. By definition, foreigners include several categories of persons, organizations, and governments, including citizens of the United States domiciled outside the United States or its territories and possessions.

Gold Movements

Gold movements, while included in the tabulation of international transactions representing the total of foreign commerce, are not of similar meaning and importance to all countries. Some countries have included gold in their merchandise exports or have treated it in similar fashion, for to them gold is a principal export item. In so far as the United States is concerned, the inflow or outflow of gold has been the reflection not only of trade developments but also of political uncertainties, either here or abroad. At times, gold movements may be attributed to the lack of balance between dollars supplied by and required for transactions in goods, services, and investments. But gold does not move for monetary purposes if exchange is otherwise available at a competitive cost.[29]

Even before the Second World War, however, the development of special forces led to tremendous movements of gold, especially into the United States. Among the major reasons for this movement were probably devaluation of the dollar (bidding up the price of gold) some time after several other countries had devalued or departed from their respective types of gold standards, combined with the relative certainty of property ownership in the United States as compared with ownership in many other countries.

It is interesting to note that the Subcommittee on Balance of Payments Statistics of the League of Nations recommended a standard treatment of gold in statements of the various countries. This is necessary because of difficulty in collecting full information in all countries and also because of the international movement of nonmonetary as well as monetary gold. Details of the proposed scheme may be found in

[28] *Ibid*, p. 215.
[29] Unless a government buys gold as such to build up its reserves at home.

Notes on Balances of Payments, published by the League of Nations at Geneva in 1947.

ERRORS AND OMISSIONS

The foregoing discussion of the several groups of items making up a country's international transactions, both commercial and noncommercial, public and private, current and long-term, and the brief mention of the practical difficulties in collecting reliable data—sometimes because of changes in exchange rates, inaccurate valuations, inadequate data, and numerous other difficulties—leads to the realization that a "forced" entry must be made in order to bring about an apparent balance in these transactions during any period. Thus, it must be understood that there is never any such thing as a balancing of payments as of any one time or ever and that the U.S. Department of Commerce, which is charged with preparing summary statistics on our total of international transactions, must force a balance through this account, labeled, properly, Errors and Omissions. Another designation used at times is Unexplained Items.

The relatively small size of this account, however designated, tends to lend a little more credence to the other figures in the summary, but the entry itself serves no purpose except to bring about a balance between our total recorded exports of "sales" abroad, of all types, and our total recorded imports or "purchases" abroad, of all types.

REVIEW QUESTIONS

1. What is the relative importance of the following types of international transactions in our (*a*) export and (*b*) import trade:
   (1) Merchandise
   (2) Income on investments
   (3) Freight and shipping
   (4) Travel
2. What is the basis for valuation of merchandise imports for customs purposes?
3. What is the relationship between customs valuation and valuation on commercial invoices?
4. Do the following accounts normally show an excess of exports or of imports in United States foreign commerce:
   a. Merchandise
   b. Income on investments
   c. Freight and shipping
   d. Travel
5. The ABC Company imports coffee from Brazil, bringing it in on Lloyd Brasileiro.

a. Which accounts in the balance of payments are affected—export or import —and in what way?

b. The same purchase is made, but the coffee is brought in on the Delta Line (United States flag). Which accounts in the balance of payments are affected, and how?

c. The International Harvester Company exports agricultural machinery to France, with shipment via Lykes Lines (United States flag). Which accounts in the balance of payments are affected, and how?

6. Contrast the economic and the national defense aspects of our merchant marine.

7. How important are our exports of the use of our capital as compared with our exports of merchandise?

8. What are unilateral transfers?

9. Compare our transactions in long-term securities with our transactions in merchandise.

10. Discuss the favorable and the unfavorable aspects of our having exported about $100,000,000,000 more in goods than we imported in the past half century.

11. Of what does the short-term-capital account consist?

12. Why are gold movements recorded differently in the balances of payment of some countries than they are in others?

CHAPTER 3

Patterns of World Trade: The United States

Few economic subjects have come into such prominence in recent years as the foreign trade of the United States has. The position of the United States in world trade changed materially during the First World War; since then, we have become probably the most important economic power in the world.

This chapter surveys and analyzes the composition of United States foreign commerce. Parts of it may appear to be somewhat repetitious of Chapter 2 in certain aspects, especially with regard to references to our total international transactions. It is felt, however, that detailed analysis of over-all volumes and trends is an important part of any study. Furthermore, comparisons made between our trade in merchandise and our trade in other balance-sheet accounts will again serve to emphasize that foreign commerce is an all-inclusive subject and that it is well not to attempt a clean segregation between trade in goods and trade or transactions in the other accounts, all of which pour dollars into or pull dollars from the common pool of foreign exchange.

MERCHANDISE TRANSACTIONS

It was shown in Chapter 2 that the foreign commerce of the United States in merchandise is characterized by rather wide fluctuations, measured in terms of dollar value. Normally, the sum total of exports exceeds the sum total of imports, at times by substantial amounts. As we look into the details of this trade, it will be of interest to notice shifts in the types of items exported and imported, and shifts in the relative importance of supplier and customer nations.

Many groupings of export and import trade can be found in the statistical data of the U.S. Department of Commerce; two of these are available in sufficient detail and over a long enough period of time to be mentioned specifically. The first classifies all trade into five broad economic classes, along lines of degree of processing: crude materials, crude foodstuffs, manufactured foodstuffs, semimanufactures, and fin-

36

ished manufactures. The second classifies the items into nine broad commodity groups, depending on their origin or nature rather than on the degree of processing.

Trade, by Economic Class

As illustrated in Fig. 2, the merchandise export trade of the United States over the last century is characterized principally by a noticeable proportionate increase in our exports of finished manufactures and semi-manufactures and by proportionate decreases in exports of manufactured foodstuffs, crude foodstuffs, and crude materials. The chart is arranged to show each class as a portion of a 100-per-cent total; accordingly, the relative changes alone do not indicate whether there may have been an absolute increase or decrease in each class. This may be determined by reference to Table 1 or to any of the official tabulations reporting absolute amounts of exports and imports. However, it will suffice here to note that both exports and imports have been at all-time highs since 1941. The peak years for exports were 1944 and 1947; for imports they were 1951 and 1950.

During the same over-all period, our imports of crude materials increased proportionally until 1916 to 1920, since which time they have declined somewhat. Finished manufactures generally trended downward in relative importance, but for two decades they have remained fairly constant, percentagewise. There were no outstanding changes relatively in our imports of manufactured foodstuffs, crude foodstuffs, and semi-manufactures, but the latter two classes do show some growth. Despite any relative decline, though, total import volumes increased significantly, and all economic classes of imports increased in absolute amounts, with the greater increases being shown for crude materials, obviously, and the smallest for finished manufactures.

Trade, by Commodity Group

For some purposes, it may be found more desirable to consider the structure of our merchandise exports and imports in terms of types of commodities rather than the stage of processing. Therefore, the statistical arrangement pictured in Fig. 3 may mean more to some readers.

Outstanding Increases in Exports of Machinery and Vehicles. In the period covered by Fig. 3, machinery and vehicles have accounted for an increasing proportion of total exports, with a relative decrease in almost every other commodity group. The decrease is most noticeable in textiles and nonmetallic minerals; these two groups include, respectively, cotton and petroleum and petroleum products. While these facts are not offered as a full explanation, the reader might recall our reduction in cotton production by government direction and the substantial reduction in cotton

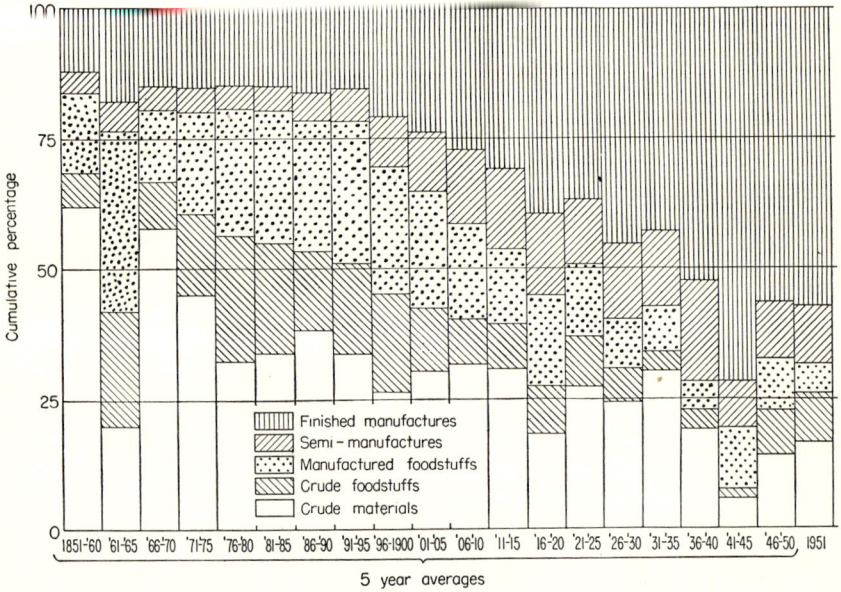

FIG. 2A. United States exports of merchandise, by economic class.

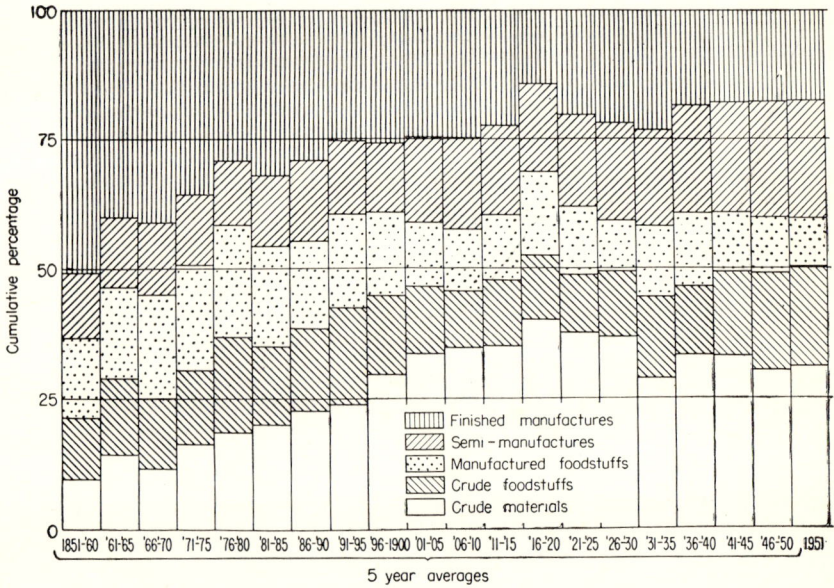

FIG. 2B. United States imports of merchandise, by economic class.

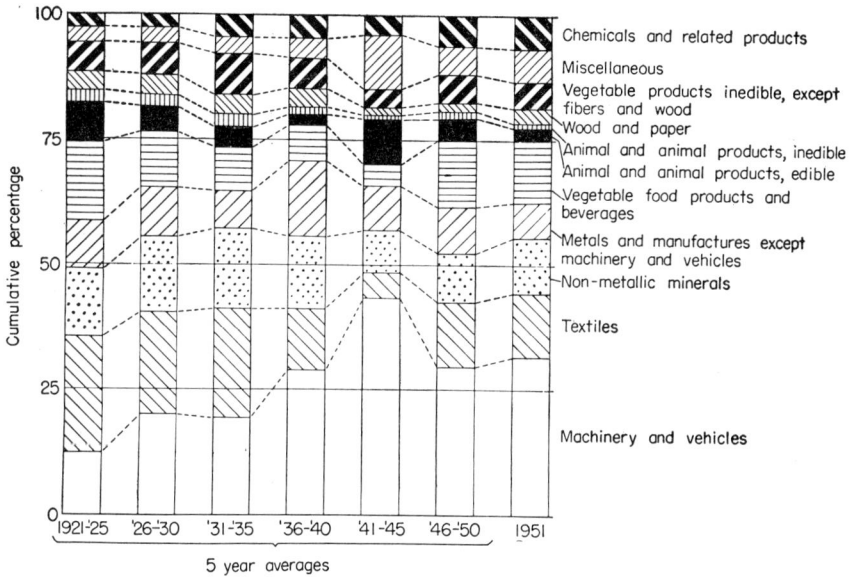

FIG. 3A. United States exports of merchandise, by commodity group.

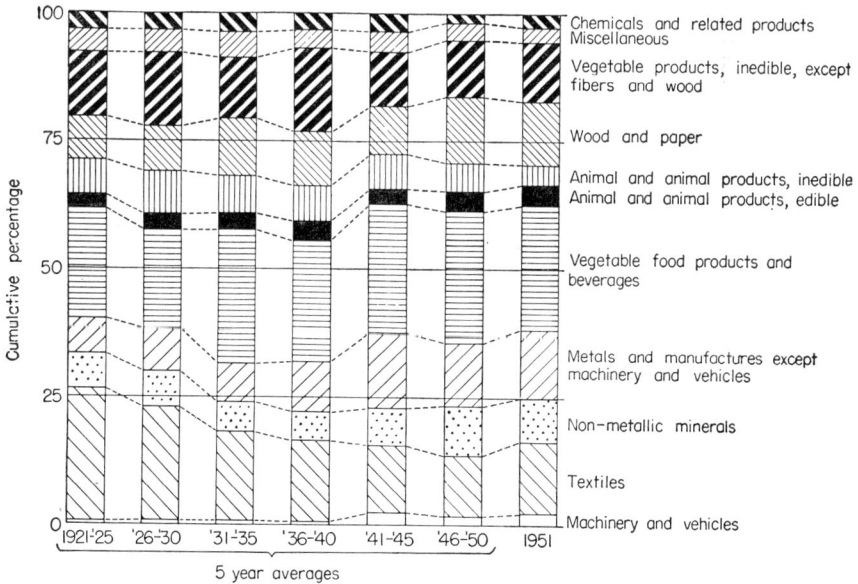

FIG. 3B. United States imports of merchandise, by commodity group.

exports relative to total production. During the same period the petroleum industry was faced with increased production abroad and exchange difficulties which, in many cases, resulted in reduced foreign consumption of petroleum except for official or approved purposes. In addition—and this is probably the single most important explanation—our exports of machinery and vehicles for the war effort brought that group of exports into maximum prominence; for the period 1941 to 1945 it accounted for 43 per cent of our total exports.

No Outstanding Intergroup Changes in Imports. The only striking change to be noted in the structure of imports by commodity groups was the decline in proportionate importance of textiles. For this, probably the most obvious explanation is the effect of our rayon and nylon industry on silk imports. There was a slight increase in the relative importance of imports of vegetable food products and beverages and, in the war years, of metals and manufactures besides machinery and vehicles.

From the point of view of volume, rather than trend, our major export trade is in finished manufactures, mainly of machinery and vehicles, while our least important is in crude foodstuffs. Our next most important export class is that of crude materials, such as cotton and petroleum, while commodity groups of substantial importance are nonmetallic minerals (petroleum products), metals and manufactures (iron and steel, and nonferrous), and textile (cotton).

With regard to imports, our major import trade, by economic class, has been in crude materials (rubber, oilseeds, tobacco, and furs), with important volumes also shown for all the other economic classes. By commodity groups, our most important import trade is in vegetable food products and beverages (cocoa, coffee, sugar, tea), inedible vegetable products (rubber), and textiles (wool and jute).[1] We also import large volumes of wood and paper (mainly paper and manufactures) and metals and manufactures, except machinery and vehicles (principally nonferrous metals).

Our Leading Import and Export Items

Following consideration of the over-all and group changes in our merchandise trade, we should go into more detail and study the trade volumes by specific items or more compact groups in order to ascertain just which ones comprise the major part of our total trade.

As would be expected from the underlying circumstances, some of these leading items come into more or less prominence from time to time. Depending on the degree of economic activity, its peculiarities, the

[1] Raw silk, one of our major prewar imports, has declined materially in importance. In 1946, imports were about at immediate prewar levels, but in 1950 and 1951, the dollar volume imported was less than one-fifth the 1946 amount.

state of war or preparation for war, and other such circumstances, certain types of exports and imports become exceptionally prominent at one time or another. Or they may become unavailable, as rubber and silk did during the Second World War. However, barring major changes in world conditions, the same items are rather consistently in the leading 5, 10, or even 20 items of export and import trade, although they are not in the same relative position from one period to another. It should also be noted that classification of exports and imports presents another difficulty in that some single items are of sufficient importance and uniformity to comprise one classification, such as coffee, cane sugar, and unmanufactured cotton. Others represent a more general grouping, such as types of machinery, iron- and steel-mill products, chemicals, fruits, and nuts.

Tables 12 and 13 list the most important export and import items, in

Table 12. Leading Products in United States Export Trade
(Dollar figures in millions)

Product	1950 Amount	1950 Rank	1951 Amount	1951 Rank
Raw cotton	$ 1,017.0	(1)	$ 1,138.4	(2)
Automobiles, parts, and accessories	723.1	(2)	1,187.6	(1)
Petroleum and products thereof	499.5	(3)	783.0	(5)
Wheat and wheat flour	488.6	(4)	996.6	(4)
Other machinery and vehicles	488.2	(5)	1,003.1	(3)
Iron- and steel-mill products	472.5	(6)	611.6	(7)
Electrical machinery and apparatus	438.8	(7)	632.2	(6)
Tobacco and manufactures thereof	298.6	(8)	382.3	(10)
Coal and related products	277.8	(9)	606.2	(8)
Tractors, parts, and accessories	244.7	(10)	310.2	(12)
Coarse grains	229.6	(11)	349.7	(11)
Cotton manufactures	226.9	(12)	390.4	(9)
Medicinals and pharmaceuticals	210.7	(13)	281.4	(13)
Metal-working machinery	202.7	(14)	192.4	(19)
Construction and conveying machinery	186.6	(15)	259.3	(15)
Chemical specialties	178.7	(16)	271.9	(14)
Synthetic textiles	176.7	(17)	226.4	(16)
Advanced manufactures of iron and steel	149.8	(18)	196.2	(17)
Mining, well, and pumping machinery	143.0	(19)	195.8	(18)
Vegetable oils and oilseeds	126.2	(20)	187.1	(20)
Total for year	$10,142.5		$14,867.6	
Leading 5 items, % of total	31.6		34.4	
Leading 10 items, % of total	48.6		52.1	
Leading 20 items, % of total	66.6		68.7	

SOURCE: *Business Information Service,* International Trade Statistics Series, U.S. Department of Commerce, February, 1952.

Table 13 Leading Products in United States Import Trade
(Dollar figures in millions)

Product	1950 Amount	Rank	1951 Amount	Rank
Coffee..	$1,092.0	(1)	$ 1,361.3	(1)
Petroleum and products thereof..............	591.9	(2)	601.3	(4)
Paper and paper manufactures................	472.8	(3)	544.0	(5)
Rubber, crude...............................	458.0	(4)	807.5	(2)
Wool, unmanufactured........................	427.8	(5)	713.6	(3)
Sugar, cane.................................	381.2	(6)	386.9	(7)
Paper base stocks...........................	273.8	(7)	413.7	(6)
Sawmill products............................	265.2	(8)	229.2	(10)
Copper......................................	242.8	(9)	278.5	(9)
Vegetable oils, inedible, and oilseeds..........	208.2	(10)	220.2	(11)
Tin...	202.3	(11)	157.6	(16)
Cocoa or cacao beans........................	167.3	(12)	196.8	(12)
Fish, including shellfish......................	157.0	(13)	187.4	(13)
Diamonds...................................	139.2	(14)	156.9	(17)
Lead..	136.1	(15)	80.1	
Hides and skins.............................	118.7	(16)	132.7	(20)
Iron- and steel-mill products.................	113.6	(17)	329.1	(8)
Meat products..............................	113.0	(18)	187.4	(14)
Fruits and preparations......................	112.9	(19)	111.7	
Ferroalloys, ores, and metals.................	111.9	(20)	132.8	(19)
Grains, fodders, feeds, and manufactures.......	111.8		173.4	(15)
Sisal and similar vegetable fibers..............	87.9		154.1	(18)
Total for year............................	$8,743.1		$10,813.0	
Leading 5 items, % of total................	34.8		37.3	
Leading 10 items, % of total................	50.5		52.4	
Leading 20 items, % of total................	66.3		67.8	

SOURCE: *Business Information Service,* International Trade Series, U.S. Department of Commerce, February, 1952.

terms of dollar value, during 1950 and 1951. The totals shown for exports and imports are not identical with merchandise totals in Table 1. The reason is that the figures come from different reports, one of which may have been more fully adjusted or may have been able to incorporate more complete coverage.

Among the 10 leading export groups, 9 are included both years, with the leading 5 the same in both years. The import schedule is similarly characterized by appearance of the same leading 9 groups during each period, and with the same 5 groups in the lead in each year. Compared with prewar tabulations, several products were of top importance then but, for 1950–1951 at least, were not in the 20 leading groups. These were:

Exports	Imports
Copper	Silk
Fruits and nuts	Furs
Lumber	Burlaps
Meat products	Fertilizers
Rubber manufactures	Cotton manufactures

Leading 5 Items Account for Large Percentage of Total. For exports, the leading 5 items accounted for 32 and 34 per cent of our total trade in 1950 and 1951; the leading 10 made up about half of our total volume in each year. The import schedule reflects a shade greater concentration, as the 5 leading items represent 35 and 37 per cent of the total, in respective years, while the 10 leading items accounted for over 50 per cent each year. Our foreign trade in merchandise is thus rather concentrated into a few quite important leading groups, but aside from these leading groups, there is a wide variety of less important volumes. Many of these, however, represent monetary values running into several million dollars. This is quite a different picture from that presented by several smaller countries (see Chapter 4) in which a very large part of their total export trade, especially, is represented by from one to three items or groups.

Trade, by Geographic Area

Some students choose to emphasize the pattern of our trade in merchandise according to geographic area rather than commodity. This view seems to come more often to public notice because of the "dollar" difficulties experienced by most countries in recent years. As part of their efforts to overcome this difficulty, they have focused attention on ways and means by which specific countries may bring their merchandise balances more closely together. In fact, some countries have attempted to effect a closer balance between imports and exports by limiting the volume of imports from the United States (or from the dollar area) to the volume of exports to the United States. In theory, and if interchangeable and sound currencies were available, this problem should not present itself, for multilateral-trade possibilities should effect the necessary adjustments. At the same time, while trade in goods is important, trade in services is also of considerable importance to many countries. Thus, to the extent that transactions other than in merchandise do not balance, the transactions in merchandise must also not balance by approximately the same amount, but on the opposite side of the ledger.

Trade, by Continent. A convenient method of studying United States trade on a geographic basis is first by continent, then by individual country. Also, in order to avoid possible misinterpretation if only very recent years are considered, the figures used for analysis are those for a rather long time. In the case of trade by continent, data presented cover about eighty years. For obvious reasons, the U.S. Department of

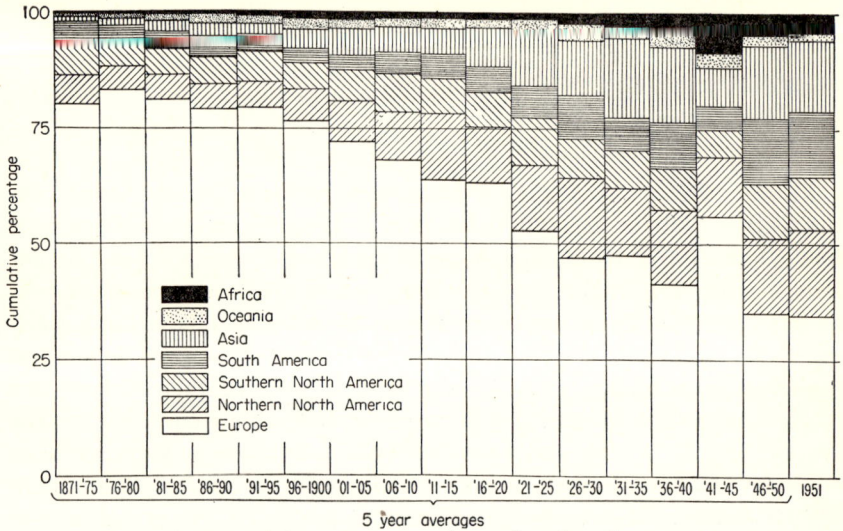

FIG. 4A. United States exports of merchandise, by continent.

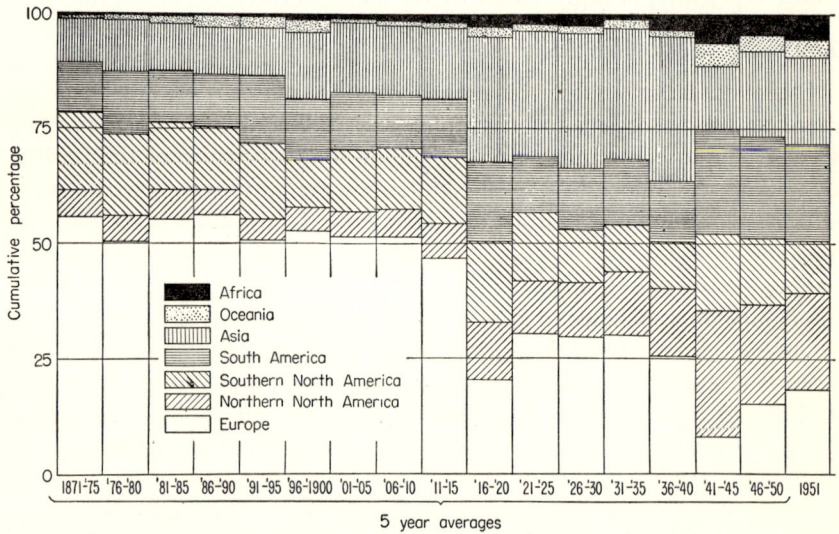

FIG. 4B. United States imports of merchandise, by continent.

Commerce has broken down our North American trade between northern North America and southern North America. Fig. 4 shows on a percentage basis the relative importance of our trade with different major geographic areas of the world.

Europe Declines Relatively as Purchaser and Supplier. What appears to be most striking in both the upper (export) section and the lower (import) section is the decline in relative importance of Europe, both as a purchaser and as a supplier in our foreign merchandise activities, and the relative increase in importance indicated by our trade with Asia and with northern North America (Canada and Newfoundland). As late as the 1921 to 1925 period, Europe was the market for over half of total United States exports; while its percentage shows a decline ever since that time, Europe is still our major geographic market, by far. In the most recent prewar period shown, 1936 to 1940, 41 per cent of our total exports went to Europe. This percentage stepped up to 56 during the war, but in 1951, it dropped to around 35, a good part of which was made possible by grants or loans through the Economic Cooperation Administration.[2] On the import side, Europe has not been so important, relatively, as in exports. As recently as 1911 to 1915, over 45 per cent of our imports came from Europe. But with the occurrence of the First World War, there was a sharp drop in Europe's portion of foreign sales in the United States, from which decline only small recovery took place. During the Second World War, Europe supplied only 8 per cent of our imports; in the postwar years of 1946 to 1950, this percentage rose to 15, then to 19 in 1951.

As Europe's percentage of our trade has declined, the record shows that the principal gainers, in both our export and our import trade, have been Asia and northern North America. On the import side, a large part of this is undoubtedly to be accounted for by substantial increases in our imports of three items purchased abroad in large amounts—rubber, silk, and petroleum. These come mainly from Asia, not from Europe. Also, our much larger purchases of wood pulp, paper, and certain minerals from Canada have served to increase noticeably the portion of our total purchases abroad provided by northern North America. On the export side of the ledger, the great increase in our exports of several types of machinery and of vehicles was an outstanding development of the past few decades. Since Asia and northern North America are not so heavily industralized as Europe, it appears logical that these areas would be more likely to absorb the products of an industrial United States than would Europe, which in significant degree is a competitor.

Merchandise-dollar Flows Not Reconcilable. A point which should not be overlooked is that although the merchandise is shown as having moved between Asia and northern North America and the United States, the entrepreneurial interest may well have been European. This is because of dominion or colony control or because of investment. Hence, if one were to deduce that the flow of dollars was in accordance with the charted movement of merchandise, he might well be in error, not only because of entrepreneurial interest but also because a large part of the trade may have been carried on in pounds sterling, guilders, francs or

[2] Succeeded by Mutual Security Agency.

some other currency than that of the countries between which the goods moved.

Trade, by Country. Most statistics being maintained on a national basis, and international dealings being at national rather than continental level, it is to be expected that a most important analysis of our foreign commerce would be by country. Some difficulty arises when national boundaries change, as when Germany absorbed areas formerly identified as Austria, Czechoslovakia, and Poland, in the 1930s, and as will be observed from the partition of India and other realignments in Asia, especially with regard to Japan and China. However, the occurrence of these instances is relatively rare, and it is possible to find dependable statistics going back over many years and reflecting our trade with the various countries. Table 14 shows the relative standing of all countries accounting for as much as 1 per cent of our export and import trade in the years included.

A Few Countries Dominant. In all three periods covered, only two countries account for as much as 10 per cent of either our export or our import trade. These were Canada, for both exports and imports in all periods, and the United Kingdom, for our exports in the period 1936 to 1940. However, available statistics do not disclose the true position of the United Kingdom and several other countries as export markets in 1950 and 1951. The data by country exclude "special-category" exports, such information being withheld for security reasons. Moreover, only six countries accounted for as much as 5 per cent of total trade in exports at any time shown, while only five provided as much as 5 per cent of our total imports during any of the periods covered.

Subject to the exclusion of "special-category" exports, the United Kingdom, Canada, Mexico, Brazil, Germany, France, and Japan were our leading markets consistently. Both Germany and Italy were more important markets in the prewar period. Our principal sources of imports as measured in dollars were Canada, the United Kingdom, Brazil, British Malaya, and Cuba. Japan was a very important supplier until 1941, but up to 1951 had not recaptured its United States markets. All the figures reflect war-induced activity in the 1936 to 1940 period and the United States postwar foreign-aid programs.

An interesting observation is that Canada, with a population of around 14,000,000, accounts for a larger part of our export trade than does all of South America, with a population about seven times larger. Also, Canada supplies about as large a volume of our import trade as does South America.

Trade, by Commodity and Country

Thus far, data presented have been from the viewpoint of either geography or commodity, without relation between the two. A survey of

Table 14. United States Trade with Selected Countries
(Per cent of total exports and imports)

Country	Exports			Imports		
	1936–1940	1950	1951	1936–1940	1950	1951
Argentina..................	2.6	1.5	1.7	3.1	2.3	2.0
Australia...................	2.1	1.0	1.3	....	1.6	3.2
Belgium-Luxembourg.........	2.0	2.8	2.8	2.2	1.6	2.0
Brazil......................	2.3	3.6	5.2	4.3	8.1	8.3
British Malaya..............	....	0.2	0.4	7.6	3.5	3.9
Canada....................	15.9	20.7	19.2	14.4	22.1	20.8
Chile......................	....	0.7	1.2	1.6	1.8	1.9
China.....................	1.6	0.4	....	3.0	1.6	0.4
Colombia..................	1.3	2.4	1.7	1.9	3.5	3.3
Cuba......................	2.5	4.7	4.0	4.7	4.6	3.8
France....................	5.3	3.5	3.2	2.4	1.5	2.4
Germany..................	2.4	4.6	3.9	2.4	1.2	2.1
India.....................	1.3	2.2	3.4	3.2	2.9	2.7
Italy......................	1.9	3.5	3.4	1.6	1.2	1.3
Japan.....................	7.4	4.3	4.4	6.6	2.1	1.9
Mexico....................	2.7	5.3	5.3	2.3	3.6	3.0
Netherlands...............	2.3	2.3	2.1	1.4	1.0	1.1
Indonesia..................	....	0.8	1.2	4.1*	1.8	2.4
Philippine Republic..........	2.6	2.4	2.6	4.1	2.7	2.6
Spain.....................	....	0.5	0.8	....	0.6	0.5
Sweden....................	1.9	1.0	1.0	1.7	0.8	1.0
Switzerland................	....	1.3	1.4	1.0	1.2	1.2
Union of South Africa........	2.5	1.2	1.8	....	1.6	1.2
U.S.S.R...................	1.8	0.3	....	....	0.9	0.6
United Kingdom............	18.7	5.3	0.7	6.6	3.8	4.2
Venezuela..................	1.6	4.1	3.4	1.1	3.7	3.0
Total for countries listed....	82.7	80.6	76.1	81.3	81.4	80.8
Leading 5 countries..........	50.0	40.6	38.1	39.9	42.3	41.0
Leading 10 countries.........	62.6	59.6	55.3	58.7	58.5	56.2

* Netherlands Indies.
SOURCE OF BASIC DATA: U.S. Department of Commerce.

our foreign commerce should also indicate the principal goods we sell to
and buy from different countries; for this purpose, Tables 15 and 16
have been prepared.[3]

They list countries buying or selling at least 5 per cent of selected
product volumes. Some countries are among our leading customers in

[3] The commodity breakdown is not in exact accord with that used in Tables 12
and 13. This is because the selected groupings showing data by country were not
all-inclusive. But their over-all significance is indicated in the fact that the export
groups listed accounted for 69 per cent of total comparable exports and the import
groups accounted for 73 per cent of total imports.

Table 15. Principal Markets for Selected United States Exports, 1950
(Per cent of total of respective products)

Market	Grains and preparations	Fruits and preparations	Vegetable oils and oilseeds	Tobacco and manufactures	Cotton, raw	Cotton manufactures	Synthetic fibers and manufactures	Coal and related products	Petroleum and products thereof	Steel-mill products	Iron and steel manufactures	Electrical machinery	Construction machinery	Mining, well, and pumping machinery	Metalworking machinery	Other industrial machinery	Tractors and parts	Automobiles and parts	Medicinals and pharmaceuticals	Chemical specialties
Canada	6	42	20	..	6	16	8	91	32	26	30	19	21	18	12	24	36	23	7	24
Mexico									6	8	8	7	6	11	..	10	6	9	8	11
Cuba	9	10				11	15				7	6						6	6	5
Colombia											6							6	6	
Venezuela		8				7	7				11	7	6	9				8	5	5
Brazil										7	12	5				6	7	10	10	6
Argentina																			5	
United Kingdom	7	7		28	10				6							7				6
Netherlands	6		11																	
Belgium-Luxembourg		7	6				5									12			5	
France			5		11										5	17				
Germany	14		23	11	11															
Austria	5															9				
Switzerland						6														
Italy			5		10										11	5				
Greece																	10			
India						7														
Indonesia							10													
Philippine Republic						11	7				5								5	
Hong Kong																				9
Japan	11		10		21															
Australia				5													5			
Union of South Africa																5				

several export groups (Canada, Mexico, Venezuela, Cuba, Brazil, and United Kingdom); others are relatively big markets for only one or two groups of products.

Medicinal and pharmaceutical products, machinery, cotton, and grains are sold in volume in several countries, while other important export groups, such as tobacco, steel-mill products, and petroleum products, find less concentrated national markets. If the measure for inclusion in the

Table 16. Principal Sources of Selected United States Imports, 1950
(Per cent of total of respective products)

Source	Meat and meat products	Fish and fish products	Hides and skins	Grains and preparations	Fruits and preparations	Cocoa, coffee, and tea	Sugar and sugar products	Rubber and rubber products	Vegetable oils and seeds	Jute, sisal, and similar fibers	Wool, raw	Sawmill products	Paper base stocks	Paper and manufactures	Petroleum and products thereof	Precious stones	Iron- and steel-mill products	Ferroalloys	Copper and manufactures thereof	Lead	Tin	Furs and fur manufactures
Canada	37	46	8	81	10							85	76	95			17	10	16	22		18
Mexico		14		6	8					9		7			5				7	40		
Cuba					5		83															
Colombia					5	20									6							
Brazil			8			46					21											
Uruguay	6										20											
Argentina	27		16								22											
United Kingdom											9						7					8
Belgium-Luxembourg											6					19	21					8
Netherlands																		9				7
Norway		5																9				
India			10							35								15				
British Malaya								44													48	
Indonesia								23													7	
Philippine Republic					5		12		50	8												
China									10									6				5
Japan		13																	7			
Australia				15							25									5		5
New Zealand			13								9											
Union of South Africa																50		11		5		9

table were to be 1 per cent instead of 5, many more countries would have to be brought in; many of those already included would appear as important markets for several additional groups of products.

Some Countries Are Important Markets for Several Items. From the tabulation, as arranged, one can also note the relative concentration of export and import trade for each group. For example, about 42 per cent of our exports of fruits and fruit preparations went to Canada. So did 91 per cent of our coal exports, and over 25 per cent of our exports of petroleum and petroleum products, steel-mill products, iron and steel manufactures, and tractors and parts. Rather large percentages of export trade in certain products went to 8 or 10 other countries.

If the data for the two leading countries in each case were to be combined, we would find that these two countries account for over one-third of our export trade in 12 of the 20 groups listed, and for over 20 per cent in 19 of these groups. Looking across the table by countries, we see that only 3 appear in at least 10 of the 20 groups as very important markets for exports of those groups (Canada, Mexico, and Venezuela), but four more (Cuba, Brazil, the United Kingdom, and Belgium) appear in 5 of the 20 groups, and several more would be found in the list of those countries taking 1 per cent or more of our exports in each group. The position of the United Kingdom is of interest in this respect. As already indicated, certain exports to the United Kingdom and other countries are classed as "special category," so are excluded from the table. A similar computation for 1938 showed the United Kingdom to be the principal export market for 6 of the groups of products and the second most important for 4 more.

Imports Are More Concentrated as to Source. The import pattern is quite different, with a greater concentration of suppliers in fewer countries. Considering first the pattern by product, we see that over 40 per cent of our total imports of several products came from only one

Import	Country	% of total imports
Fruits and preparations..........	Ecuador	6
	Honduras	11
	Panama	5
	Spain	17
Petroleum and products thereof...	Kuwait	7
	Netherlands Antilles	27
	Venezuela	49
Tin.........................	Bolivia	13
Copper......................	Chile	47
	Northern Rhodesia	7
Lead........................	Peru	9
	Yugoslavia	8
Paper base stocks.............	Finland	6
	Sweden	14
Iron- and steel-mill products......	France	13
	Germany	20
Furs and manufactures thereof....	U.S.S.R.	19
Ferroalloys...................	Gold Coast	7
	Turkey	7
Jute, sisal, hemp, etc...........	Pakistan	7
Rubber and rubber products......	Ceylon	9
	Siam	13
Precious stones................	Nigeria	7

country. Examples are fish, grains, sawmill products, paper base stocks and paper, and manufactures from Canada; sugar and related products from Cuba; lead from Mexico; copper from Chile; petroleum from Venezuela; rubber and tin from British Malaya; coffee from Brazil; and vegetable oils from the Philippines. Most groups listed were acquired in some degree from several countries, but the concentration of sources is very noticeable.

The importance of Canada as a source of our imports is also indicated by the very high percentages of several groups of imports which came in from Canada. If we look across the lines, we see that only one country—Canada—supplied as much as 5 per cent of our total imports in as many as half of the groups shown. The nearest to this figure was Mexico, which provided at least 5 per cent in eight of the groups; no other country supplied this percentage for more than four of the groups. Many countries supplied at least 5 per cent of only one of the selected groups. These were as shown in the table on page 50.

TRADE IN SERVICES

It was pointed out in Chapter 2 that international transactions in services are an important element in our total foreign commerce. Sales of miscellaneous services are commonly from 30 to 35 per cent as large as our sales of merchandise, and have been as high as 44 per cent. Our purchases of services from other countries are often over 40 per cent as large as our purchases of goods, and in 1932 the percentage was as high as 65.

Reference to Table 1 will serve to recall that the most important service transactions, in terms of dollars, are shipping and freight, travel expenditures, personal remittances, and interest and dividends. At times, government transactions have appeared as of paramount importance; it would seem safe to predict that in the future the value of government transactions will bear a substantially higher ratio to the total than it has consistently done in the past.

Freight and Shipping Services

This account may be subdivided into four main sections: port expenditures, water-borne freight, rail receipts, and passenger fares. Since the problem of collecting and reporting accurate data relating to these items has already been pointed out in Chapter 2, the discussion will not be repeated here. Table 17 illustrates the importance of these items in terms of dollar volume and in relation to each other.

Our principal sales abroad have been of ocean freight and services to foreign vessels in United States ports. Port-expenditure receipts are those costs which foreign vessels find it necessary to incur while in United

Table 17. Freight- and Shipping-services Account, 1946–1948
(In millions of dollars)

Item	Sales			Purchases		
	1946	1947	1948	1946	1947	1948
Port expenditures..............	$ 192	$ 367	$ 284	$258	$304	$288
Water-borne and air freight......	1,082	1,208	806	211	303	431
Rail receipts...................	44	40	37	42	41	45
Passenger fares................	57	94	106	23	53	75
Total......................	$1,375	$1,709	$1,233	$534	$701	$839

SOURCE: *The Balance of International Payments of the United States, 1946–48*, U.S. Department of Commerce, 1950, p. 63.

States ports, and cover such items as fuel, provisions, dockage, stevedoring, and other goods and services. Geographically, our activity in this field must be related to our trade in merchandise, but it is materially affected by the nationality of the vessel transporting the merchandise (our rail and Great Lakes trade with Canada is almost entirely to be excepted). Goods may be imported from Brazil, as an illustration, but transported in a Swedish vessel. Our geographic purchases and sales of goods and of freight and shipping services would therefore not follow identical patterns. Also, the major part of our trade in goods with any one or more countries may be carried in United States bottoms, with practically none under the flags of vessels of these countries. Table 18 presents a summation of our transactions in freight and shipping services (the transportation account) with various areas of the world from 1946 to 1951.

Table 18. Freight- and Shipping-services Account, by Area, 1946–1951
(In millions of dollars)

Area	Purchases from (payments)		Sales to (receipts)	
	1946–1950 average	1951	1946–1950 average	1951
OEEC countries.....................	$341	$454	$680	$738
OEEC dependencies..................	22	19	57	60
Other Europe.......................	12	6	34	19
Canada and Newfoundland............	98	106	63	74
Latin-American republics..............	187	261	263	333
Others.............................	58	71	240	271

SOURCE: *Survey of Current Business*, June, 1950; June, 1951; March, 1952.

Travel Expenditures

To some countries, as to some cities in the United States, tourist trade is a very important element in their economies. One need only observe the travel section of papers like *The New York Times,* or the travel advertisements of several popular magazines, to find a good indication of the importance which foreign countries attach to the tourist trade of United States citizens. Several countries have established tourist bureaus in various cities of the United States, and many issue appealing and elaborate travel circulars. After all, $100 spent abroad by a traveler from the United States has the same effect on a foreign country's dollar earnings as has $100 spent by a United States importer in bringing in merchandise (excluding duty and services purchased from United States interests).

As with other "services," travel expenditures represent a respectable percentage of current international transactions. The volume of business officially reported as arising from this activity over the period 1921 to 1951 is shown in Table 19.

Table 19. International Travel Account, 1921–1951
(In millions of dollars)

Year	Receipts	Payments
1921–1925	$ 368	$ 1,353
1926–1930	613	2,166
1931–1935	407	1,262
1936–1940	612	1,428
1941–1945	511	1,075
1946–1950	1,633	3,006
1951	444	733
Total........	$4,588	$11,023
Average......	148	356

Significance Indicated by Comparison with Merchandise. Comparison of our travel expenditures with total purchases of some of the leading import items shows it to be a very substantial element in our over-all international purchases. Another indication of the significance of this item in our purchases from abroad is that in the thirty-one-year period covered, travel abroad created about $11,000,000,000 in dollar exchange; for every $100 recorded as merchandise imports, travel "imports" were almost $9.

While so important to us, especially as "purchasers," tourism is even more significant to many other countries as "sellers." For instance, in Switzerland, one-seventh of the national income is derived from tourism; in Great Britain, tourism has at times been a leading dollar earner; and tourists are of great economic importance to several other countries, such as France, Italy, and Belgium.[4]

Not only is travel of such importance commercially, but it also has a spectacular appeal to which most people respond where possible. The selling of this feature of an economy is pursued with as much organized effort as is that of merchandise. Tourism means the possibility of sale to foreigners of hotel and restaurant accommodations and all the other services *and goods* which the traveler is able and willing to buy. Sometimes proposed as an effective instrument for alleviation of the dollar shortage is the promotion and encouragement of travel abroad by residents of the United States. In this connection, a recent change in the duty-free limit which each traveler is permitted to bring into the United States has been acclaimed as a positive step, or contribution.[5]

Table 20. International Travel Account of the United States, by Area,
1946–1951
(In millions of dollars)

Area	Imports (by United States travelers abroad)		Exports (by foreigners in United States)	
	1946–1950 average	1951	1946–1950 average	1951
Canada..............................	$249	$262	$146	$236
Latin-American republics...............	175	213	106	122
OEEC countries......................	134	191	45	49
OEEC dependencies..................	24	47	8	10
Other Europe........................	5	3	4	3
Other foreign countries...............	15	17	19	24

Geographic Pattern Differs. Another aspect of this important element in our foreign commerce is the geographic distribution of our travel expenditures and receipts. Overseas travel is commonly the first which comes to mind in picturing the ruminations of our international travelers, for it is probably the most enticing. But, as shown in Table 20, our most important source of this "import" is Canada, with Latin America (mainly Mexico) second. European countries rank third. This is probably due to the fact that Canada and Latin America are immediate neighbors of the United States, with Canada quite near our greatest concentrations of

[4] *Foreign Commerce Weekly,* July 25, 1949, p. 3.

[5] In 1948, the duty-free limit was raised from $100 to $400 per person. This duty-free volume can be exercised only once every six months and is subject to certain other conditions, such as duration of stay abroad. Taxes must still be paid on certain imported articles when brought in by travelers.

population. This proximity permits numerous trips of short duration and, possibly, the reporting system may be more accurate in view of arrangements existing among Canada, Mexico, and the United States. From the "export" side, Canada is also our first customer, with Mexico second as an independent country.

Personal and Institutional Remittances

Personal remittances are defined for this purpose as any noncommercial payments between individuals. They may be either in cash or in kind. Institutional remittances include noncommercial transfers of funds and materials by philanthropic, religious, educational, and scientific organizations. These organizations assist in the support of hospitals, churches, schools, and scientific undertakings abroad. While these international transfers can hardly be classed as commerce, they are mentioned as having some significance in the sum total of our international shipments and receipts of goods and funds. Personal remittances, while declining in recent years, have often provided well over $100,000,000 annually, some part of which was usable in the purchase of other goods and services from the United States.

Interest and Dividends

An item certain to be of increasing importance and influence in our foreign commerce is the servicing of foreign investments, particularly the payment of interest and dividends (excluding amortization and repayment). As Table 3 indicates, recorded receipts of interest and dividends are the second most important account in our total current transactions. Even in the interwar period, foreign demand for dollars with which to cover interest and dividends payable to United States investors was equal to a high percentage of their demand for dollars with which to pay for our exports of goods.

In some years, as was brought out in Chapter 2, the volume of our "sales" of the use of our capital abroad is over 25 per cent as large as the volume of our foreign sales of goods. In 1931 and 1932, for instance, for every $100 foreigners expended for the purchase of our goods, they spent about $30 for the use of our investment abroad. With the revival and expansion of foreign investment following the Second World War, and with the continued encouragement of foreign investment through guarantees as to convertibility and such, the outlook would appear to be for an increase in our receipts of interest and dividends from abroad. But increased exports of merchandise keep the percentage relationship lower than in the late 1920s and early 1930s.

Just as with the other principal elements comprising our total of international transactions, the geographic source and destination of interest and dividend payments and receipts vary widely This will be shown in Chapter 15, which will go into more detail with regard to foreign investments on which interest and dividends are received or paid. It will be seen that our principal investments are of the "direct" type and are in Canada and the Latin-American countries; this accounts for the high proportion of interest and dividends received from these areas. On the payments side, the summation regarding OEEC countries (Western Europe), will show that from 1946 through 1950, payments were larger than receipts from these countries.[6]

TRANSACTIONS IN OUTSTANDING SECURITIES

A prime consideration in connection with foreign investment is whether an investment, once made, is forever made or whether the investor has the right to decide that he wishes to dispose of an investment in one country and either buy another in that same country or transfer his funds to some "healthier" location, politically and/or geographically. In recent years, there has been a widespread restriction on the transfer of capital from one country to another, largely through control over foreign exchange. During the war, some countries saw fit to inventory foreign holdings of their nationals and, where necessary to the war effort, to vest and dispose of such assets.

Several Motives May Impel Transactions in Securities. Where it is possible, it would seem natural to expect to find a considerable amount of activity in international transfers of outstanding securities, either for trading advantages, for repatriation of funds, or for the safety or increased income to be found in certain foreign rather than domestic securities.

The usual summaries of international transactions show capital movements as a net rather than a gross amount. However, gross figures have been published for several years. The volume of international transactions in securities is quite high at times. While postwar exchange restrictions have not permitted free movement of investments, a sizable volume is carried on, as evidenced by reported international transactions by United States interests, shown on page 57.

Transactions at Times as Large as Mercantile Volume. At times, as indicated in Chapter 2, security transactions are about as large as our purchases and sales of merchandise—sometimes greater in volume. Possibly this type of transaction represents an investment which is essentially short-term rather than long-term in character, and an important motivat-

---

[6] The same would hold for 1951, were it not for payment of interest by governments of these countries, especially the United Kingdom, to the government of the United States.

ing factor may be capital appreciation or speculation. Accordingly, it must be expected that transfers of a very large volume of these securities may impose their weight on the exchanges of a country at one time; this may be a rather embarrasing time from the viewpoint of the government in power. The Department of Commerce reports, further, that typically the international-securities movement has been between creditor countries, and the movement into and out of the United States has involved chiefly the United Kingdom, Switzerland, the Netherlands, and Canada, although nationals of other countries may have operated extensively through agents in those countries.

Transaction	1946–1950 average (000,000 omitted)	1951 (000,000 omitted)
Sales of domestic securities.............	$962	$1,563
Sales of foreign securities...............	600	773
Purchases of domestic securities.........	879	2,125
Purchases of foreign securities...........	582	1,122

SOURCE: *United States Treasury Bulletin*, January, 1952, p. 54; March, 1952, p. 58.

Table 10 will be helpful here. It is obvious from the tabulation that a very substantial inflow of foreign capital to the United States occurred in many years, although the United States has for some time been classed · as a creditor nation, and it should thus probably not have to *seek* foreign capital. What these figures reflect, of course, is the activity of individual owners of foreign capital seeking something more desirable— either safety or income—in the United States. One should not overlook the events of history in connection with these capital movements; universal financial, political, and military crises provide some advance evidence of occurrences before the public realizes what is happening, and generally cause large-scale flights of capital.

REVIEW QUESTIONS

1. What have been the principal changes in the pattern of United States export and import trade by:
    a. Economic class
    b. Commodity group
Can you reconcile this with the economic history of the United States?

2. Name five of our leading export and five of our leading import items.

3. What is the extent of concentration of our export and import trade by product?

4. What have been the principal changes in our trade by continent? Can you explain the basis for these trends?

5. Name five leading export and five leading import markets (annually) for United States trade.

6. To what extent is our trade by country rather concentrated?

7. How does Canada compare with Latin-American countries as a market for our exports and as a source of our imports?

8. Describe the pattern of our export and import trade, by commodity and country.

9. Describe the structure of our international-freight-and-shipping-services account, by type of activity and by geographic area.

10. Describe the geographic pattern of our international travel account.

CHAPTER 4

Patterns of World Trade: The World

The preceding chapter indicated the impressive volume of foreign commerce of the United States and its importance in the trade of several other countries. But a study of foreign commerce would be incomplete if it did not survey total world international commerce. This chapter shows how important the United States is in the total picture, what the principal trading nations are, what the principal items entering world trade are, and the network of services which to some countries are almost as important in business volume as any other element of their foreign commerce.

At the outset, one must recognize the difficulty of finding totally satisfactory data for comparisons; balance of-payment schemes are not uniform, data may be irregularly or apparently unscientifically collected, the same dates for reporting are not used by all countries, and a very practical difficulty arises in reducing the figures to a common denominator—dollars. Many of the figures represent a year's accumulation, perhaps more, and to convert these by use of an exchange value which may not have held during the period can easily lead to a distortion of values. Yet it is the only manner in which some comparison can be made, and it is impossible to know whether the figures are underestimated or overestimated, or to what extent.

Another point to note is that the figures are to a large extent influenced by contemporary international troubles; the war and its repercussions have left no choice in the matter.

MAGNITUDE OF WORLD TRADE

Both the League of Nations and the U.S. Department of Commerce have published data from time to time on the magnitude of world trade in merchandise. A League of Nations study, *The Network of World Trade* (1942), lists the volume of world trade in old gold dollars, in new gold dollars, and simply in dollars; the Department of Commerce, in

Significance and Background

Foreign Commerce Yearbook (1939) reports international trade in terms of gold dollars.

More recently, the International Monetary Fund has kept such figures up to date. The tabulation below shows the dollar volume of exports and imports for selected years.

Year	Exports (f.o.b.) (000,000,000 omitted)	Imports (c.i.f.) (000,000,000 omitted)
1928	$33,209	$36,103
1938	22,137	24,863
1947	50,785	56,298
1948	56,780	64,042
1949	58,000	64,000
1950	56,710*	59,606*

* Excludes U.S.S.R., China, and certain countries of Eastern Europe.

SOURCE: *International Financial Statistics*, International Monetary Fund, September, 1950, pp. 18–19; January, 1952, pp. xxii–xxiii.

The decline of the 1930s from high volumes of the late 1920s is reflected, but perhaps the outstanding change is the very great increase in the value of postwar trade. Most of this is due to inflated prices, the price indexes for principal export and import goods having more than doubled between 1938–1939 and 1946–1948.[1]

Total Exports Not Equal to Total Imports. It will be noted, also, that exports and imports do not balance. Theoretically, it would appear that they should. But among reasons for the lack of exact balance are differences in methods of valuation. Most countries include ocean transportation and insurance in the value of their imports, imports being valued c.i.f. port of importation, while exports are valued f.o.b. port of exit. Thus, imports always exceed exports in value, although it could happen that an unusually large volume was exported in the few days preceding the end of the reporting period and was en route prior to being picked up in the import statistics of the receiving country.

The figures just presented should not be interpreted as indicating the magnitude of total *commerce internationally.* In addition to trade in merchandise, which alone is shown, there are, in each case, transactions involving services, capital movements, gold shipments, and other activities providing or requiring certain types of foreign exchange.

Uniform Reporting System Proposed. Unfortunately, there is no summary tabulation of balances of payments of all nations of the world. Steps were taken by the League of Nations toward uniform reporting

[1] *International Financial Statistics*, International Monetary Fund, September, 1950, p. 22.

as early as 1938, and a draft classification titled *Notes on Balance of Payments Statistics* was communicated to governments for observation and comments in early 1946. As work of this sort progresses, the result will be more dependable, complete, and up-to-date data on international transactions. The International Monetary Fund has now taken over this program for the United Nations. In 1949 it published a *Balance of Payments Yearbook*, covering data usually for 1938, 1946, and 1947. Later editions were published in 1950 and 1951, the latter including data for 1949 and, in some cases, 1950, for 59 countries.

Significance of Transactions Other than Merchandise. Figures are shown in the currency of the country in question in most cases and have not been reduced to a common currency unit. Accordingly, the most satisfactory way to indicate the significance of all items is by a percentage reduction based on current transaction totals, and then by a comparison of the volume of dealings in services and other current transactions (travel, interest and dividends, transportation, etc.) with the total for merchandise.

On the import side, these other current items amount in some cases to over half as much as the trade in merchandise. Examples of countries with this experience are Argentina in 1943 and 1944, Bolivia in 1939, Peru in 1938 and 1939, the United States in 1946 and 1947, and Canada in every year from 1926 to 1944. In 1932 and 1933, these "invisible" imports exceeded the imports of merchandise into Canada.

On the export side, also, sales of services, including interest and dividends received, at times and for some countries will equal or exceed sales of merchandise. This situation held for Norway in 1938, 1939, and 1946, Ireland in 1946 and 1947, and Finland in 1940. In other instances, they amount to over half of the volume of sales of merchandise, as in the case of the Netherlands and the United Kingdom.

These comparisons are intended to point up the fact that, although there are no satisfactory tabulations to indicate the volume of total world commerce, it is obviously quite a bit larger than the trade in merchandise. This deduction has an even stronger base when it is recalled that capital transactions and gold movements are excluded from the comparisons made.

As would almost necessarily be inferred from the foregoing comments pertaining to the significance of other items than merchandise in the total foreign-commerce picture, the importance of these items varies from country to country. It has already been mentioned that it is difficult to compare balance-of-payment tabulations for the various countries, for several reasons. It will serve the purpose, though, to consider a few countries as illustrative of the differing significance of the various items making up recorded current transactions. These transactions, as indicated above, exclude gold and capital movements. Table 21 shows some of these proportions for selected countries.

Table 21. International Current Transactions of Selected Countries, 1949
(Percentage represented by various accounts)

Transaction	Argentina	Canada	Mexico	Norway	Venezuela
Exports:					
Merchandise................	94.9	76.7	64.1	40.8	95.6
Interest and dividends.......	.....	2.0	.....	0.4	
Services..................	5.1	18.9	32.2	45.2	4.4
Transportation..........	3.2	3.7	0.1	36.7	1.4
Travel.................	.....	7.0	27.1	1.5	0.7
Miscellaneous..........	1.9	8.2	5.0	7.0	2.3
Other current transactions...	.....	2.4	3.7	13.6	
Total current transactions.	100.0	100.0	100.0	100.0	100.0
Imports:					
Merchandise................	95.9	73.1	80.4	65.7	60.6
Interest and dividends.......	0.9	9.9	10.3	1.4	22.9
Services..................	.....	14.2	9.3	31.5	15.0
Transportation..........	.....	2.5	0.3	22.4	7.3
Travel.................	.....	4.9	7.6	2.3	2.0
Miscellaneous..........	3.2	6.8	1.4	6.8	5.7
Other current transactions...	.....	2.8	.....	1.4	1.5
Total current transactions.	100.0	100.0	100.0	100.0	100.0

Wide Variation in Importance of Various Accounts. Of particular interest is that, of the countries shown, the highest proportion of current export transactions accounted for by merchandise is 95.6 per cent and the lowest 40.8; for imports, the highest percentage representation by merchandise is 95.9 and the lowest 60.6 Interest and dividends received represent a high of 2.0 per cent of current export transactions (for the United States the figure is 8.6 per cent), while interest and dividends paid amount to as much as 22.9 per cent of current import transactions.[2] Exportation of services in the year under observation (1949) amount to as much as 45.2 per cent of total current transactions, and on the import side the high figure shown is 31.5 per cent of the base. Thus the economic structure, the productivity, the location, the size, and all other factors influencing world commerce reflect their influence on the foreign commerce of the several countries.

Relation of Imports to National Income. Another interesting computation suggesting the impact of its foreign commerce on the respective

[2] An unusual experience was reported for Iran in 1948–1949, when merchandise accounted for only 29.4 per cent of its total current imports. Interest and dividends paid (importation of the use of foreign capital) accounted for 68.1 per cent.

Table 22. Percentage relationship of Imports to National Income, 1922–1939

Year	New Zealand	Australia	United Kingdom	Canada	Netherlands	Sweden	Denmark	Norway	Japan	France	Germany	Total
1922	19.9	20.9	19.2	20.3	37.6	17.5	40.8	36.2	17.7	18.1	9.5	17.9
1923	27.1	22.5	22.8	22.9	37.8	20.3	52.1	39.0	18.7	21.9	10.9	20.6
1924	24.0	22.0	26.0	21.0	42.8	21.7	56.4	43.9	21.3	23.2	13.2	22.3
1925	31.6	21.7	24.8	21.4	45.2	21.3	50.8	39.3	20.8	23.3	20.0	24.0
1926	30.9	22.1	24.7	22.4	43.6	21.5	43.8	36.3	19.7	25.5	15.5	22.9
1927	26.0	21.0	23.2	23.2	43.7	22.4	47.4	34.8	18.1	22.3	19.5	22.8
1928	24.5	19.1	22.8	23.8	43.7	23.7	49.7	37.3	17.7	20.9	18.0	22.1
1929	26.9	18.3	23.3	25.2	43.8	23.1	48.7	37.9	18.6	21.2	17.2	22.2
1930	26.7	15.6	20.4	23.3	40.7	21.0	46.1	37.7	14.5	19.0	14.3	19.6
1931	17.8	11.7	18.7	18.0	35.4	20.8	41.3	35.8	12.6	15.8	11.3	16.9
1932	17.6	11.8	15.5	15.6	27.0	18.2	33.6	28.6	14.4	12.9	10.0	14.4
1933	16.8	12.6	14.4	14.4	25.5	17.1	35.6	27.6	15.9	12.7	8.7	13.6
1934	19.6	13.3	14.4	16.2	22.1	18.1	35.1	30.4	17.5	11.4	7.9	13.0
1935	21.0	14.6	14.1	16.3	20.3	18.7	32.8	31.5	16.6	11.0	6.5	12.1
1936	22.3	14.8	14.7	16.6	21.5	19.3	35.4	30.7	16.9	12.2	5.8	12.3
1937	25.7	16.0	16.5	18.6	30.9	22.2	38.7	37.7	18.5	18.1	6.8	14.6
1938	22.2	16.7	15.7	16.0	27.0	20.9	35.4	31.7	11.8	18.4	6.4	13.1
1939	17.6	15.2	13.6	17.0	27.7	23.3	35.2	33.8	11.9	17.3	6.0	12.3

SOURCE: Data provided by Office of Business Economics, U.S. Department of Commerce.

countries is the percentage relationship of imports to national income (see Chapter 12 for discussion). For several important countries, the U.S. Department of Commerce has made such computations, and they are reported in Table 22. For the countries shown, imports generally declined relative to national income in the 1930s as compared with the 1920s. This probably resulted from the wave of import barriers which became so widespread at that time as well as from lowered living standards during the years of adjustment to the depression. Based on these figures, also, it would seem that imports are more vital to Denmark, the Netherlands, and Norway than to Australia and Canada.

Per Capita Trade in Merchandise. This differing importance may also be sensed from Table 23, which shows the per capita trade in merchandise for several countries. In view of the fact that per capita in-

Table 23. Per Capita Foreign Trade, 1939 and 1948

Country	1939*		1948	
	Imports	Exports	Imports	Exports
New Zealand................	$109	$128	$241	$278
Norway....................	109	64	234	130
Switzerland................	101	70	252	173
Denmark...................	94	85	169	135
Netherlands................	93	59	272	103
Sweden....................	83	74	198	160
United Kingdom............	83	41	167	132
Belgium-Luxembourg........	75	84	228	193
Ireland....................	69	40	184	64
Australia..................	67	64	142†	171†
Canada....................	64	78	204	239
Finland....................	48	47	119	102
Union of South Africa.......	37	13	76	33
Panama....................	36	6	86	20
Germany...................	32	31	30	14
France....................	32	21	80	48
Venezuela..................	29	81	151	228
Argentina..................	26	30	93	101
Cuba......................	25	35	102	137
United States..............	18	24	49	86
Italy......................	13	13	33	23
Japan.....................	10	13	8	3
Mexico....................	6	6	21	19
Brazil.....................	6	7	23	24
U.S.S.R...................	1	1	‡	‡

* Figures are for 1939 except for a few countries for which 1938 data are used.
† Year ending June 30.
‡ Not available.
SOURCE: *Foreign Commerce Yearbook*, 1939 and 1949.

come varies widely among countries, a low or high figure for imports and exports of merchandise does not of itself indicate the importance of foreign trade to each country. One hundred dollars of exports for the average Italian, for instance, does not mean the same as would $100 of exports to the average United States citizen, whose per capita income is much higher. Also, since the table is reduced to a common denominator—dollars per capita—it is clear that some countries show an excess of imports (unfavorable balance of trade) while others show an excess of exports. This lack of balance in merchandise transactions alone is offset, in each instance, by transactions in the other items making up the sum total of foreign commerce. Selecting individual countries for passing comment, it will be seen that Panama, for instance, imported four to six times as much as was exported per capita; the comparable ratio was also high for Norway, the United Kingdom, and the Union of South Africa. On the opposite side, exports of merchandise were about three times as high as imports per capita for Venezuela in 1939, although not as high in 1948. Other countries showing high ratios of exports to imports were Argentina, Canada, Cuba, and the United States.

It may be noted, further, that some of the countries listed experienced an excess of exports in 1939 and of imports in 1948 (or a much smaller excess of exports). This was due, most likely, to the effect of loss of productive facilities during the war, to reconstruction requirements, and to the impact of pent-up demand which carried over from war years.

While not shown on the table, it is interesting that out of 59 countries for which tabulations were made in 1947, 17 had favorable balances of trade and the remaining 42 reported unfavorable balances.[3]

GEOGRAPHIC PATTERNS OF TRADE

Trade, by Continent

As an indication of the over-all importance of some geographic areas in world trade, attention will first be given to continental divisions. Arrangement by continent is a very broad generalization and is intended only to afford a rough approximation of the importance of these areas in world trade. Importance of each is determined by, among other things, population, productivity, and national boundaries within each.

On a continental basis, the summation of the foreign trade of each country is the sum total of that continent's world trade. Thus the world trade of a continent, in the figures developed in this manner, include not only the trade of the group with the rest of the world but also the trade between its constituent parts. The large volume of world trade was indicted on page 60. Now, in order to emphasize proportionate rather

[3] *Foreign Commerce Yearbook,* 1948, p. 590.

than absolute importance of continental volumes, Table 24 has been prepared. It shows the percentage of world total exports and imports, by continent.

Table 24. Continental Shares of International Exports and Imports
(Percentage of world totals)

Continent	1913	1926–1930	1938	1948	1949	1950
Exports:						
North America......	16.9	22.6	21.1	32.0	29.7	27.3
South America......	6.1	6.5	6.5	9.0	7.4	8.9
Europe.............	60.1	48.5	48.6	38.3	40.1	37.9
Asia...............	11.4	15.9	16.0	12.5	13.2	13.2
Oceania............	2.4	2.8	3.5	3.4	4.3	3.7
Africa.............	3.1	3.7	4.3	4.8	5.3	9.0
Imports:						
North America......	13.1	18.0	13.9	21.2	20.0	26.5
South America......	5.2	5.2	5.0	7.3	6.5	6.2
Europe.............	65.5	55.9	58.3	47.5	47.7	43.6
Asia...............	10.5	13.7	13.9	14.2	15.4	11.4
Oceania............	2.3	2.8	3.1	2.8	3.3	3.6
Africa.............	3.4	4.4	5.8	7.0	7.1	8.7

SOURCE: *Foreign Commerce Yearbook*, 1939, p. 316; *International Financial Statistics*, August, 1950, and January, 1952.

Europe is clearly the most important continent in world trade, as it accounts for close to half of the total export and import volumes in most of the periods reported. But its relative importance appears to be decreasing as other areas, especially North America, make up a larger proportion of the total. It is significant to note, also, the rather steady growth of Africa as a factor in world commerce.

The Directions of Continental Trade. Viewing the subject more analytically, we should consider intra- as well as intercontinental trade. Table 25 depicts the directional flow of merchandise exports and imports by continent or broad continental subdivision. Close study of the table will offer perhaps the best means of obtaining a perspective of the movement of world trade *within* as well as between the areas shown; they are reasonably reconcilable as continental references.

Large Volumes of Intracontinental Trade. It will be noted that, while Europe is the most important continent in world trade, a very large part of its trade is among the countries comprising that area. Of Northwestern Europe's imports, for example, about 36 per cent came from other counties in Northwestern Europe. Thirty-six per cent of Southern Europe's imports came from Northwestern Europe, and the comparable figure for Eastern Europe was 57 per cent. Between 44 and 61

Table 25. Directional Flow of Continental or Regional Trade, 1950–1951
(Per cent of total for each area)

Exported by \ To	North America	Central America and Antilles	South America	North-western Europe	Southern Europe	Eastern Europe and U.S.S.R.	Middle East	Other Asia	Oceania	Africa, other than Middle East	Other	Total
North America	33	6	11	21	4	1	2	10	2	3	7	100
Central America and Antilles	53	2	8	30	2	1	*	1	*	2	1	100
South America	48	1	9	32	5	1	1	2	*	1	*	100
Northwestern Europe	9	2	6	44	6	4	4	8	6	11	*	100
Southern Europe	12	1	6	47	5	5	6	5	2	10	1	100
Eastern Europe and U.S.S.R.	8	*	3	61	7	12	5	2	1	1	*	100
Middle East	8	*	*	46	11	5	7	15	4	3	1	100
Other Asia	21	1	2	24	2	1	2	38	4	3	2	100
Oceania	14	*	*	57	4	2	2	11	3	*	7	100
Africa, other than Middle East	10	*	*	63	3	1	2	2	1	11	4	100

Imported by \ From	North America	Central America and Antilles	South America	North-western Europe	Southern Europe	Eastern Europe and U.S.S.R.	Middle East	Other Asia	Oceania	Africa, other than Middle East	Other	Total
North America	58	7	17	14	2	1	2	13	3	3	...	100
Central America and Antilles	72	3	5	15	1	*	*	3	1	*	...	100
South America	45	3	10	32	4	2	*	3	*	*	1	100
Northwestern Europe	16	3	6	36	5	4	6	8	6	13	*	100
Southern Europe	23	1	7	36	3	4	9	5	4	7	1	100
Eastern Europe and U.S.S.R.	6	1	4	57	7	12	3	6	3	1	*	100
Middle East	21	1	2	39	7	6	8	8	3	3	2	100
Other Asia	23	*	1	22	2	1	5	40	4	1	1	100
Oceania	10	*	*	59	2	*	3	15	3	1	7	100
Africa, other than Middle East	13	1	1	62	3	1	2	6	*	9	2	100

* Less than 0.5 per cent.

SOURCE: Developed from *Direction of International Trade*, Series T, Vol. 2, No. 12, January–December, 1951. Joint publication of Statistical Office of United Nations, International Monetary Fund, and International Bank for Reconstruction and Development, April, 1952.

per cent of exports from Northwestern, Southern, and Eastern Europe were destined for Northwestern Europe.

Consolidation of the basic figures from which the percentage table was developed reveals that about 45 per cent of Europe's imports came from Europe, and 55 per cent of Europe's exports went to other European countries. This is less than prewar experience and is probably due to destruction of productive facilities and as well to the ECA- and MSA-financed imports from the United States.

The importance of Europe to Africa's total trade is also outstanding; over 65 per cent of Africa's imports came from Europe, while 70 per cent of African exports went to Europe. Another interesting feature is the high proportion of intra-Asian trade. About 40 per cent of Asia's imports were from Asian countries, while about 38 per cent of exports were within the continent. Some of the principal imported items in United States total trade come from Asia, yet North America is shown as having been a market for only 21 per cent of Asia's total exports. The pattern of North American trade appears somewhat better balanced, geographically, than that of other areas. In only one category, imports from within itself, is there more than a 35-per-cent concentration. Trade between Latin America and Africa, Asia, and Oceania appeared negligible, in proportion to the total, while North American trade with Africa and Oceania was relatively small. Eastern Europe and the U.S.S.R. do not appear to be important purchasers or suppliers in the trade totals of other geographic areas of the world, but statistics on this trade are not satisfactory. In fact, the basic report was compiled in part by using statistics of other (partner) countries in the transactions.

Imports into Latin America were mainly from North America, which was also a principal export market, although Europe took about 35 per cent of the exports of Latin America.

Trade, by Country

After the important grand areas in world trade have been considered, it is interesting to reduce the areas to more meaningful size, and this is by country.

United States and Great Britain Dominant. It is commonly understood, and correctly so, that the United States and Great Britain are the principal countries in world trade. This is indicated in Table 26, which also points up the fact that several other countries are important in the over-all picture. Germany, for instance, was a close third in some of the periods shown, and Canada is gaining in importance. While such a tabulation as Table 26 can suggest no trend, several important changes are observable, all of which are of much more significance to the coun-

Table 26. Exports and Imports of Leading Countries
(Per cent of world total)

Country	Exports				Imports			
	1911–1913	1938	1949	1950	1911–1913	1938	1949	1950
Argentina.............	2.4	2.1	1.7	1.9	2.2	1.9	1.7	1.4
Australia.............	1.8	2.5	3.1	2.6	1.7	2.2	2.4	2.6
Belgium...............	3.8	3.4	3.1	2.9	4.3	3.2	2.9	3.2
Brazil................	1.8	1.4	1.9	2.4	1.5	1.2	1.8	1.8
Canada...............	2.0	3.9	5.4	5.4	2.9	2.8	4.7	5.4
Chile.................	0.7	0.7	0.5	0.5	0.6	0.4	0.5	0.4
China................	1.5	0.8	....	....	1.8	1.1		
Colombia.............	0.2	0.4	0.5	0.7	0.1	0.4	0.4	0.6
Cuba.................	0.8	0.7	1.0	1.1	0.6	0.4	0.8	0.9
Czechoslovakia.........	....	1.7	1.4	1.4	....	1.2	1.3	1.2
Denmark..............	1.0	1.6	1.2	1.2	1.0	1.5	1.3	1.4
France...............	6.7	4.1	4.7	5.4	7.8	5.6	5.2	5.1
Germany..............	11.4	9.7	2.0	3.5	12.1	9.2	3.6	4.5
India.................	4.1	2.9	2.2	2.2	2.5	2.4	2.5	2.1
Italy.................	2.4	2.6	1.9	2.1	3.4	2.5	2.4	2.4
Japan................	1.4	3.6	0.9	1.4	1.5	3.2	1.4	1.5
British Malaya.........	1.0	1.5	1.3	2.3	1.0	1.3	1.3	1.6
Mexico...............	0.8	0.9	0.8	0.8	0.5	0.5	0.7	0.9
New Zealand...........	0.5	1.1	1.0	0.9	0.5	0.9	0.7	0.8
Netherlands...........	4.2	2.7	2.3	2.5	4.7	3.3	3.0	3.5
Netherlands Indies......	1.1	1.7	0.9*	1.4*	0.8	1.1	0.8*	0.7*
Norway...............	0.5	0.9	0.7	0.7	0.7	1.2	1.2	1.1
Poland................	....	1.1	1.2	.....	....	1.0	1.0	
Spain................	1.0	0.6	0.7	0.7	1.0	0.7	0.7	0.7
Sweden...............	1.1	2.2	2.2	1.9	1.0	2.2	1.9	2.8
Switzerland...........	1.3	1.4	1.4	1.6	1.7	1.5	1.4	1.8
U.S.S.R..............	4.2	1.3	.....	.....	3.1	1.2		
Union of South Africa...	0.6	0.8	1.0	1.3	0.9	1.7	2.1	1.6
United Kingdom........	15.3	11.9	11.9	11.1	17.4	18.9	13.4	12.2
United States..........	12.4	14 1	21.0	18.1	8.4	8.2	12.0	16.9
Uruguay..............	0.3	0.3	0.3	0.4	0.2	0.2	0.3	0.3
Venezuela.............	0.1	1.3	1.8	2.2	0.1	0.4	1.2	1.0

* Indonesia.

Source: *Foreign Commerce Yearbook*, 1939, p. 316; *International Financial Statistics*, August, 1950, and January, 1952.

tries concerned than to total world trade. Examples are reductions in the proportions which British exports and imports bear to the total, the reduction in "German" trade following the world wars, the declines in relative importance of France as an exporter and importer, and the outstanding increase of both Canada and the United States in both exports and imports.

Table 27. Directional Flow of Export Trade between Selected Countries (1950–1951 average, in millions of dollars)

From \ To	United States	Canada	Mexico	Cuba	Argentina	Brazil	United Kingdom	Belgium-Luxembourg	Denmark	France	Germany	Netherlands	Norway	Sweden	Switzerland	Italy	Spain	Czechoslovakia	Finland	India	Japan	Malaya and Singapore	Australia	New Zealand	Union of South Africa
United States		$2,292	$610	$498	$188	$521	$706	$321	$60	$380	$479	$256	$79	$115	$161	$398	$77	$6	$27	$338	$507	$39	$139	$42	$83
Canada	$2,036		22	1ᶜ			516	75		30	22	16	9	30	24	30	3	1	2	31	44	7	8	15	1
Mexicoᵃ	449	22		15			11	6		10	9	5			9	3	4ᵇᶜ			1					
Cubaᶜ	399	1ᶜ	15				115	28		92	23	32	7	28	23	3	10								
Argentinaᵃ	213	3	16			110	254	34	7	83	83	45	15	44	15	77	15		21						3
Brazilᶜ	734	16	6		76		112	170	21	64	163	32	32	251	81	24	32	8	21		25				8
United Kingdom	393	376	11	15	95	138		9	175	179	163	216	32	76	210	43	9	8	76	298	11	199	816	277	23
Belgium-Luxembourg	177	29	6	9	23	51	197		9	198	140	423	30	42	165	53	12	12	24	15	20	12	36	8ᵇ	1
Denmark	15	2	1	1	4	11	300	9		31	128	11	30	78	43	20	36	18	29	3	11	16	2		
France	188	18	3	5	98	69	332	220	50		220	109	43	179	210ᵇ	90	20	5	30	21	10	14	38	3	26
Germany	170	17	16	9	54	74	148	197	105	235		312	43	61	165	137	36	19	41	34	9	16	43	5	5
Netherlandsᵃ	82	7	6	3	25	74	246	226	24	25	51		35	25	15	23	20	33	19	27	2	14	16	3	33
Norway	41	2	2	2	16	16	96	9	72	74	167	22		35	12	21	9	23	7	9		3	13	2	
Sweden	80	7	1	1	26	55	247	19	41	88	117	82	35		20	99	7	21	28	18		6	40	4	
Switzerland	128	1	9	9	50	41	171	19	15	117	21	35	9	21		5	14	20	24	5	8	3	16	12ᵇ	2
Italyᵃ	90	6	10	3	19	33	41	19	30	29	117	25	6	18	17ᶜ		3	5	6	4	25	6	10	4	7
Spainᵈ	60	8	8ᵇᶜ		52	16	58	19	4	33	40	15	9	21	21	17		bc		2	6		12		
Czechoslovakia	24	b					25	19	10	12	57	12ᶜ	7	18	5	21	2			6	63		2		
Finlandᵉ	44	1			28	10	157	19	10	79	79	33	4	21	8	6	1			4	92	5ᵇ	7		2
Indiaᵈ	251	2			33	10	325	9	6	155	155	19	9	18	2	63	5		1		30	58	10	12	3
Japanᵈ	168	9	1	19	31	8	33	86	3	28	54	27	3	21	5ᵇᶜ	92	bc	12		30		42	78	44	4
Malaya and Singapore	366	44	3		23		288	9		155	16	25		21		6	b		b	31	50		71	12	5
Australiaᵈ	244	7		1			610	25		28	16	27		18		6	5		5	52	110	42		58	9
New Zealandᵉ	41	5					280	9		28	28	25		21		6				2	3	5	12		5
Union of South Africa	76	4	1		2	4	202	25	2	101	28	33	1	6	38	30	2	b	2	3	4		9	3	

ᵃ January–November, 1951.
ᵇ Less than $500,000.
ᶜ 1950 only.
ᵈ January–October, 1951.
ᵉ January–June, 1951.

SOURCE: Developed from *Direction of International Trade*, January–December, 1951. Joint publication of Statistical Office of United Nations, International Monetary Fund, and International Bank for Reconstruction and Development, April, 1952. Some data are derived from statistics of partner trading countries.

Table 28. Directional Flow of Import Trade between Selected Countries
(1950–1951 average, in millions of dollars)

Into \ From	United States	Canada	Mexico	Cuba	Argentina	Brazil	United Kingdom	Belgium-Luxembourg	Denmark	France	Germany	Netherlands	Norway	Sweden	Switzerland	Italy	Spain	Czechoslovakia	Finland	India	Japan	Malaya and Singapore	Australia	New Zealand	Union of South Africa
United States		$2,116	$22	$414	$213	$812	$400	$178	$16	$197	$166	$102	$45	$88	$122	$125	$55	$24	$45	$278	$194	$367	$245	$81	$139
Canada	$2,320		24	6	12	32	386	29	2	18	20	12	2	9	14	11	4	5	1	36	12	41	37	20	5
Mexico	542	12		2	1ᶜ		13	7		10	11	1ᶜ	1	3	6	4	5	1		22	1ᶜ	2	5	1	1
Cuba	474	17	7ᶜ			76ᶜ	15	8	ᵃ		8ᵒ	8ᵒ	2		3	3ᶜ	7ᶜ	1ᶜ		33	21ᶜ	6			ᵃ
Argentina	188	10					135	23	8	98	54	8	6	50	3	64ᶜ	6ᵒ	8ᵒ	28		35	23	1		1
Brazil	379	13	1		110	149	200	63	301	51	19	25	14	48	19	14	8	25	6	352		285	661	418	162
United Kingdom	830	617	32	1	254	39	265	189	11	343	167	302	106	285	17	188	91	10	187	23	5	2	3	11	21
Belgium-Luxembourg	358	37	16	120	28	19	138	31	32	242	193	237	16	77	46	35	14	4	21	31	11	79	163	41	112
Denmark	93	31	1		7	71	200	178	109	65	122	34	34	76	67	18	10	12	34	26	12	69	74	23	33
France	449	16	24	17	92	48	175	121	29		243	83	25	171	19	122	32	21	37	13	8	9	22	5	28
Germany	539	22	15	1	83	23	200	406	29	200		270	55	81	87	125	12	18	41	4	7	4	24	3	9
Netherlands	248	33	4	3	44	16	262	75	14	101	280		21	102	86	24	18	6	38	7	9	20	9	3	28
Norway	96	25	1	2	1	46	88	50	23	42	195	34		22	34	14	12	21	12	6	3	5	85	1	19
Sweden	135	2	9	1	28	19	75	11	7	80	163	69	46		2	40	4	18	17	17	8	41	3	7	28
Switzerland	182	8	10	9	23	27	26	18	1	11	129	42	12	34	25	83	3	13	11	5	3	12		2	2
Italy	375	10	11	2	87	7	12	27	7	30	16	20	7	7	55		4	ᵃ	4	1		1	8	4	2ᶜ
Spain	51	11	1	4	9	18	80	26	5	20	20	7	5	23	8	3ᵒ		7	1	2	31	44	64	1	4
Czechoslovakia	6	1		ᵃ		16	273	20		13	48	36	8	29	23	16	3	6	ᵃ	38		45	102	6	5
Finland	32		1			7	18	31ᵉ		10	35	12	6	12	18	33	4	3		66	55	64	41		11
India	317	34	1		21	18	211		5	40	12	16	2	7	16	5		8	6		49			12	2ᵃ
Japan	521	43	55	26	42	16ᶜ	836	21		3	16	17	1	3	11	19		ᵃ		86	ᵃ		64		4
Malaya and Singapore	50	8				1ᶜ	200			40	40	21	1	37	16	44	ᵃ	3	ᵃ	85	55		36		5
Australia	145	38	1			7	211	31ᵈ		3			4	3	11	44		8		5	49	64			11
New Zealand	25	4		ᵃ			836	3ᵇ		18	30	21	1	23	6	33	1		6	9	ᵃ	23	36		5
Union of South Africa	196	43	1		3	9	410	21	1		30	12	4	23	6	33	1	4			29	23	8	1	2

ᵃ Less than $500,000.
ᵇ January–November, 1951.
ᶜ 1950 only.
ᵈ January–October, 1951.
ᵉ January–June, 1951.

SOURCE: Developed from *Direction of International Trade*, January–December, 1951. Joint publication of Statistical Office of United Nations, International Monetary Fund, and International Bank for Reconstruction and Development, April, 1952. Some data are derived from statistics of partner trading countries.

Table 29 Principal Exporters and Importers of Selected Items, 1948
(Percentage of world trade in each item accomplished by respective countries)

Commodity	Principal exporters		Principal importers	
Foodstuffs:				
Butter..............	New Zealand..............	31	United Kingdom...	71
	Denmark.................	27		
	Australia.................	21		
Cacao..............	Gold Coast and Togo......	39	United States......	43
	Nigeria and Cameroons.....	16	United Kingdom...	19
	Brazil...................	12		
Coconut oil..........	Ceylon...................	43	United Kingdom...	39
	Malaya..................	27	United States......	25
	Philippines...............	24		
Coffee..............	Brazil...................	55	United States......	54
	Colombia................	18		
Copra..............	Philippines...............	54	United States......	36
	Indonesia................	21		
Rice................	Burma...................	31		
	Thailand.................	20		
	United States............	10		
Sugar, raw...........	Cuba....................	49	United States......	36
Tea................	India....................	49	United Kingdom...	49
	Ceylon..................	36	United States......	11
Wheat..............	United States............	51	United Kingdom...	22
	Canada..................	23	Italy..............	10
	Australia.................	13		
Textiles:				
Cordage fibers........	British East Africa.........	37	United States......	45
	Philippines...............	19	United Kingdom...	20
	Mexico..................	16		
Cotton..............	United States............	34	United Kingdom...	18
	Egypt...................	17	France............	10
	Brazil...................	10		
Cotton yarn..........	Italy....................	27		
	United Kingdom..........	21		
	United States............	10		
Jute................	Pakistan.................	87	India.............	46
Silk................	Japan...................	74	United States......	38
	Italy....................	20	United Kingdom...	10
Wool (greasy).........	Australia.................	43	United States......	31
	Argentina................	17		
	New Zealand.............	17		
Metals:				
Copper..............	Chile....................	33	United Kingdom...	29
	Rhodesia................	18	United States......	29
	Belgian Congo............	13		

Table 29. Principal Exporters and Importers of Selected Items, 1948
(Continued)
(Percentage of world trade in each item accomplished by respective countries)

Commodity	Principal exporters	Principal importers
Lead..................	Mexico................... 35	United States...... 38
	Australia................. 24	United Kingdom... 27
	Canada.................. 15	
Steel.................	Belgium.................. 34	
	United States............. 32	
	United Kingdom.......... 12	
Tin..................	Malaya................... 58	United States...... 60
	Netherlands.............. 15	
	Belgium.................. 12	
Zinc.................	Canada.................. 29	United Kingdom... 38
	Belgium 16	United States...... 19
	Mexico.................. 10	
Other materials:		
Coal.................	United States............. 37	France............ 15
	Poland................... 20	
	Germany (Bizone)......... 18	
Fuel oil..............	United States............. 19	United Kingdom... 11
Gasoline.............	Netherlands West Indies... 35	United Kingdom... 25
	United States............. 24	
Linseed oil...........	Argentina................. 41	United Kingdom... 36
	Uruguay.................. 21	France............ 12
	Canada.................. 16	
	United States............. 10	
Newsprint............	Canada.................. 85	United States...... 80
Rubber..............	Malaya................... 47	United States...... 51
	Indonesia................ 30	United Kingdom... 15
Tobacco.............	United States............. 44	
	Turkey................... 11	
Wood pulp...........	Sweden.................. 36	United States...... 42
	Canada.................. 34	
	Finland.................. 18	

SOURCE: *International Financial Statistics*, August, 1950, pp. 30–33; March, 1952, pp. xxxii–xxxvi.

Also, with the advance of the machine age, there has been a substantial increase in importance of certain areas producing the raw materials needed for satisfactory functioning of the machinery in use. The products are petroleum and rubber; the areas are, as an example, British Malaya, the Netherlands Indies, and Venezuela.

Directional Flow of Trade between Countries. The directional flow of merchandise trade between the principal foreign-trading countries is shown in Tables 27 and 28. Being reduced to a common denominator (millions of dollars), the tables show not only the importance of trade

Table 30 Exports of Selected Countries
(Major products as per cent of total exports)

Country	Product	1937	1948	1950
Argentina.................	Wheat and corn	47	40	17
	Meats	14	12	11
	Oilseeds	12	8	17
	Wool	7	7	16
	Hides and skins	6	8	13
Australia.................	Wool	42	37	51
	Wheat	13	13	10
Bolivia...................	Tin	61	65	64
	Silver	10	4	5
Brazil....................	Coffee	42	42	64
	Cotton	19	16	8
	Cacao beans	5	5	6
Chile.....................	Copper bars	56	60	50
	Nitrates	19	16	25
Colombia.................	Coffee	65	78	76
	Crude petroleum	23	16	16
Costa Rica...............	Coffee	53	45	35
	Bananas	26	25	38
	Cacao beans	12	11	7
Cuba.....................	Sugar and molasses	78	90	89
Denmark..................	Dairy products	33	37	33
	Meat and meat products	26	10	22
Dominican Republic........	Sugar	60	51	47
	Cacao beans	14	21	17
	Coffee	10	7	15
Ecuador..................	Rice	..	29	13
	Cacao beans	34	29	29
	Coffee	17	15	30
El Salvador...............	Coffee	95	92	87*
Finland..................	Wood and manufactures	45	36	44
	Wood pulp	25	25	23
	Paper and products	14	20	20
Guatemala................	Coffee	68	62	78
	Bananas	25	31	11
Iceland...................	Fish and fish products	81	93	90
India.....................	Jute and jute manufactures	16	35	20
	Tea	13	15	14
	Cotton manufactures	5	10	24
Iran......................	Petroleum and products thereof	73	90	†
Mexico...................	Lead, zinc, and copper	34	26	22
	Henequen and cotton	5	10	21
Nicaragua................	Coffee	50	45	65
	Sesame	16	3	2
Panama...................	Bananas	68	49	58
	Cacao beans	20	20	13
Peru.....................	Petroleum	34	18	13
	Cotton	25	26	35
	Sugar	9	22	15
Philippine Republic........	Copra and coconut oil	24	57	48
	Sugar	35	7	14
	Abaca	14	9	13
Thailand.................	Rice	46	53	52
	Rubber	14	14	22
Venezuela................	Petroleum	89	97	97

* 1949.
† Not available.
Source: *International Financial Statistics*, January, 1952.

to each of the partner countries involved; they indicate the importance to any single country of others in the table to which it exports or from which it imports. For example, Table 27 reveals not only the dollar amount of Canadian exports to, say, France; the size of this volume indicates the relative importance of France among other principal Canadian export markets. The same type of comparison on imports may be seen from Table 28. In interpreting the tables, it should be noted that United States exports by country exclude special-category products, details of which have been withheld for security reasons. Furthermore, the data for some countries are not for the full twelve months of 1951; for these countries, no attempt was made to adjust the volumes to a proportionate basis.

High Degree of National Specialization. Export trade shows a high degree of national specialization on particular commodities and a consequential interdependence of the groups of nations on each other. Evidence of this high degree of commodity-by-country specialization is to be found in Table 29, which lists the principal exporters and importers of selected large-volume items entering world trade.

Some Countries' Exports Concentrated in Two or Three Products. The noticeable degree of national specialization in the export of many products is reflected by a reliance on only a few products for the major export volumes of several countries. This lack of diversification and consequent susceptibility to fluctuations in only a narrow segment of the world's economy have encouraged some governments to press for industrialization and have fostered an international interest in general economic development.

Table 30 shows, for selected countries, the extent to which a few products dominate their total export trade. For many of these countries, one product accounts for well over half of the total of exports, while two or three products account, in most instances, for over 75 per cent of the total.

MERCHANDISE TRADE

A survey of trade by country is interesting in that it reveals the broad geographic movement of varied goods. It also has some meaning, but not of major significance, in connection with the demand for and supply of foreign exchanges. The trade figures reveal the countries of export and import; no indication is given as to whether they were quoted in one currency or another or whether a third currency may have been used.

For some purposes, a survey by commodity is of special significance, as is evidenced by the international arrangements, both private and gov-

ernmental, having to do with international trade in goods. Several commodities or groups of foreign-traded products represent a very substantial part of the total demand for and supply of foreign exchange.
Some, because of seasonal production, result in seasonal pressures on
the exchanges; some, because of their importance to individual countries, have great effect on the economic well-being of the countries
concerned.

Trade, by Economic Class. In the preceding chapter, reviewing United
States trade, the initial broad classification of merchandise was in five
economic classes. For the purpose of world comparisons, however, such
a classification is unavailable. Owing to difficulties of classification and
especially of converting statistics from one currency into others, neither
the U.S. Department of Commerce nor the United Nations had made
a tabulation of the principal items entering world trade, by value, up
to 1950. The International Institute of Agriculture (absorbed by the
Food and Agriculture Organization of the United Nations in 1948) did
maintain for some years detailed data on world trade in agricultural
products, but these did not cover manufactured goods and raw materials. However, it was estimated by the League of Nations, in its *1937
Review of World Trade,* that around 25 per cent of world trade involved
foodstuffs, around 37 or 38 per cent consisted of raw materials, and
about the same proportion was made up of manufactured articles. This
estimate classified live animals as foodstuffs, and "materials, partly
manufactured" as raw materials. Accordingly, manufactured articles
might more closely approximate half the total in value.

Trade, by Commodity. Turning now to individual items or groups,
we see that the major products in the following tabulation accounted
for about one-third of total world exports in 1938. The reader may wish

Product	Export (000,000 omitted)	Product	Export (000,000 omitted)
Cotton	$600	Beef, lamb, and mutton	$ 222
Coal	530	Maize	220
Crude petroleum	448	Pork	216
Wheat	442	Tea	202
Wool	435	Rice	197
Petrol	394	Iron ore	149
Tobacco	359	Silk	124
Sugar	340	Wheat flour	127
Copper	325	Tin (metal)	123
Butter	304	Citrus fruit	103
Gas and fuel oil	298	Total	$ 6,708
Rubber	287	Exports of all goods	$21,824
Coffee	263		

SOURCE: *The Network of World Trade,* League of Nations, 1942, p. 30.

to question the reported valuations or rankings when compared with exports for the United States alone, as shown in Tables 12 and 13. Some differences are obviously due to coverage within each classification; for example, the figures above show separate amounts for crude petroleum, petrol, and gas and fuel oil. United States data, on the other hand, show only "refined oils" and crude petroleum separately.

As an indication of some of the other important products entering world trade, export data of the United States for the same year, 1938, may be used. In that year, the principal export in terms of value was industrial machinery, valued at $270,000,000.[4] This group is not included in the list given above. Nor are iron- and steel-mill products (U.S. exports of $184,000,000), passenger cars and trucks (U.S. exports of $172,-000,000), electrical machinery and apparatus (U.S. exports of $102,000-000), metal-working machinery (U.S. exports of $102,000,000), and chemicals (U.S. exports of $80,000,000).

More complete data on trade, by commodities, is in process of development by the statistical office of the United Nations. This series is designed to provide, by quarter year, figures on world commodity trade by countries of provenance and destination, classified according to the Standard International Trade Classification. The second issue was released in December, 1951, for 14 reporting countries.

IMPORTANCE OF UNITED STATES IN TRADE OF
OTHER COUNTRIES

Table 25 indicates the direction of trade as between 10 important geographic areas. One of these is North America, which represents largely the trade of the United States and Canada. It will be well to consider now the position which the United States plays in the total trade of the other countries of the world. Table 31 includes both prewar and postwar data on the part played by the United States as a supplier of and purchaser from other countries. The postwar volumes reflect the phenomenal production and consumption of the United States economic system. However, even in the prewar period, the United States was by far the dominant nation in the commerce of many others.

The United States was the market for over half of the total exports of 8 of the 46 countries listed in 1938 and of 15 in 1950. The United States supplied over half of the imports of 9 of the countries in 1938, of 17 in 1949, and of 14 in 1950. Another significant indication of the importance of the United States in the trade of the 46 countries listed is that this one country was the market for over 10 per cent of the total exports of 23 others in 1938 and of at least 28 in 1950. It provided over 10 per cent of the total imports of 38 of the countries in 1938 and of at

[4] This is a *group* of products; the largest single commodity export of the United States was raw cotton, valued at $229,000,000.

Significance and Background

Table 31. Merchandise Trade with United States
(Per cent of total of respective countries)

Country	Exports				Imports			
	1937	1938	1949	1950	1937	1938	1949	1950
Argentina	13	9	11	20	11	17	15	16
Australia	7	2	6	8	15	16	10	10
Belgium	8	7	5	8	9	11	18	16
Bolivia	6	5	45	52	28	26	52	47
Brazil	36	34	40	55	24	25	42	34
Canada	36	31	50	65	61	63	71	67
Ceylon	15	13	11	21	3	2	7	3
Chile	23	16	49	52	29	28	54	48
China	28	11	20*	†	20	17	48*	†
Colombia	57	53	81	82	47	50	78	70
Costa Rica	45	46	76	71	42	49	73	67
Cuba	81	76	64	59	69	71	83	79
Czechoslovakia	9	6	3*	†	9	10	5*	†
Denmark	2	1	1	3	5	8	16	9
Dominican Republic	35	32	35	44	52	54	75	73
Ecuador	25	21	55	55	39	35	71	67
Egypt	7	2	3	9	6	7	8	6
El Salvador	60	61	84	86	40	47	72	67
Finland	8	9	6	9	9	10	7	6
France	6	6	2	4	9	11	18	12
Guatemala	63	69	92	89	45	45	73	68
Honduras	90	82	78	69	58	62	79	78
Iceland	8	9	6	13	1	1	17	20
India	10	8	16	18	6	7	15	19
Indonesia	19	14	16	16	10	13	25	21
Iran	2	2	4*	†	9	5	30*	†
Iraq	7	3	8*	†	8	9	8*	†
Ireland	1	1	1	2	7	11	14	13
Italy	8	7	4	6	11	12	34	23
Japan	21	16	16	22	34	34	64	44
Mexico	51	62	74	86	62	58	87	88
Netherlands	5	4	3	4	9	11	17	12
New Zealand	7	2	4	10	12	12	10	7
Nicaragua	49	56	47	77	54	60	79	82
Norway	10	8	7	10	9	10	13	12
Paraguay	8	12	1	3	8	10	33	25
Peru	22	27	29	26	36	35	63	53
Philippines	80	78	72	73	58	68	81	75
Spain	9	10	6	15	17	17	9	13
Sweden	11	9	6	6	14	16	10	9
Switzerland	9	7	12	13	7	8	20	14
Turkey	14	12	14	17	15	11	20	25
Union of South Africa	3	2	8	8	21	19	26	16
United Kingdom	7	5	3	6	11	13	10	8
Uruguay	14	4	26	51	14	12	21	20
Venezuela	14	13	29	†	53	57	74	68
50% or more	7	8	10	15	8	9	17	14
40% or more	9	9	14	16	12	12	19	14
33% or more	12	12	15	16	15	15	21	17

* 1948.

† Not available.

SOURCE: *International Financial Statistics*, September, 1950; January, 1951; January, 1952; February, 1952.

least 35 in 1950. Think of the weight of such an economic giant in the world's economy!

The influence it can bear throughout the world places a responsibility on each of us to choose carefully the men on whose shoulders its guidance rests. Yet there are some who would change this multiheaded business effort for one of bureaucratic control which would nullify the impelling drive of a competitive, insecure economic system.

For some countries, also, the United States is a principal, or a very important, supplier *and* purchaser. Bolivia, Brazil, Canada, Colombia, Cuba, Guatemala, Mexico, and the Philippine Republic are examples. But for others, the United States may only be an important purchaser *or* an important supplier.

SERVICES

In several places in this and the preceding chapters, emphasis has been placed on the importance in international commerce of transactions in things other than merchandise. Some data can be had for a few countries but, owing to inadequacy of uniform balance-of-payments schemes, it is not possible to present a statement showing the magnitude of world commerce in these various fields. Enough data are available, though, to enable the student to recognize the most important nations in these activities; it is a shortcoming, however, not to be able to state positively that international dealings in interest and dividends, for example, are so much larger or smaller than dealings in freight and shipping or than travel expenditures, etc. Reference to Table 21 will serve to recall how these accounts are of varying importance from one country to another.

In some countries, such as Great Britain, Ireland, the United States, and the Netherlands, income from foreign investments is ordinarily a large part of total "sales" abroad; while in others, such as Australia, Chile, Cuba, Iran, the Dominican Republic, Canada, Bolivia, and Peru, the payment of interest and dividends constitutes a substantial proportion of "purchases" from abroad.

Mention has already been made of the importance of tourists or travel expenditures to several countries, such as Canada, France, Ireland, Great Britain, and Italy, and the fact that the United States is a principal purchaser of these services. Other countries reporting substantial expenditures for tourist or travel purposes are Canada, Cuba, Mexico, the Netherlands, New Zealand, and several European countries, although exchange control has interfered seriously with this in recent years.

Freight and shipping expenditures are closely related to national trade in merchandise, whether large trade volumes induce foreign vessels to call or whether the same nation is supporting a large merchant marine (port expenditures are included in the transportation account). Chief among the countries showing large sales of freight and shipping services are Great Britain and the United States. But this type of international commerce is also of considerable importance as an "export" item to the Netherlands, Canada, Denmark, Norway, Sweden, and a few other countries. On the "import" side, the United States and Canada are quite important purchasers; others, either in total value or in relative importance to the country concerned, are Argentina, Australia, Brazil, the Dominican Republic, Ethiopia, Great Britain, the Netherlands, Norway, Peru, and Sweden. Some of these, to repeat, reflect purchases of freight and shipping services, others of port expenditures by their merchant marines while in foreign ports.

Owing to inadequate statistical data for many countries, no attempt will be made to indicate volumes of other items which enter foreign commerce, such as gold and silver, which are considered as merchandise by some countries, emigrant remittances, and government expenditures of various sorts. Possibly in a few years sufficient data will have been collected and will be available for a more thorough analysis of these very important elements making up the total of the world's foreign commerce.

REVIEW QUESTIONS

1. Why do recorded world exports not equal recorded world imports?
2. What is the significance of international transactions other than in merchandise in the balances of payment of Mexico? Of Norway?
3. What is the pattern of world trade by continent, *i.e.*, how important is each continent relatively in world trade and in trade with each other?
4. Name the 10 leading countries in export and import merchandise trade.
5. What is the economic significance of the concentration of some countries' export trade in two or three products?
6. Name several of the leading commodities or products in world trade.
7. Describe briefly the importance of the United States in the trade of other countries.
8. Name several countries which export over 50 per cent of their total exports to the United States.
9. Name several countries which obtain over 50 per cent of their total imports from the United States.
10. Name three countries in which:
   a. Interest and dividend receipts represent a substantial part of "sales" abroad
   b. Interest and dividend payments represent a substantial part of "purchases" abroad
   c. The international travel account represents a significant part of exports
   d. Sales of freight and shipping services represent a significant part of exports

PART TWO

Organizational Structure and Practice

CHAPTER 5

Organizational Structure: The Exporter and the Importer

The Exporter

In simplest terms, the export problem is the job of getting the goods from here to there—from John to Juan or Jean. The goods must get there on time, in good condition, at a satisfactory price, with the seller being paid per agreement, and with title protected as long as desired or required. One authority states: "Export business is the orderly, methodical, somewhat technical process of adapting American merchandising and marketing methods to conditions in countries outside the continental United States."[1]

Several types of organization for export by producers may be found, depending largely on the job to be done. One type may be set up for one or several markets; two arrangements may be used by the same producer at the same time but in different markets, or for different products. The organization adopted is dictated by requirements of the situation.

FACTORS DETERMINING EXPORT ORGANIZATION

Among factors which determine the organization for export are type of product, financial factors, ability to sell abroad, volume expected, intent of the manufacturer, customs of the trade, and laws of foreign countries. Each of these factors involves details deserving attention.

Type of Product. This is perhaps the most important factor determining the type of export organization to be adopted. If a certain type of sales organization is suitable domestically, one close to it is probably the best to use internationally, provided that it is reasonably close to established methods of distribution for that product in the foreign coun-

---

[1] E. E. Pratt, *Foreign Trade Handbook* (Chicago and London, The Dartnell Corporation, 1949), p. 42.

tries in question. Characteristics of the product or the market for such products will have significant influence on the producer's decision as to the best method of reaching foreign markets. Among these are:

1. Whether the product is crude, semimanufactured, or manufactured
2. Whether the product is easy or hard to sell
3. Seasonality of production and consumption
4. Frequency and size of sales
5. Whether it is a high- or low-unit-value item
6. Whether servicing or attention after sale is required
7. Whether a spare-parts supply is necessary
8. Foreign marks-of-origin regulations
9. Whether advertising is advisable or necessary

To describe each of these characteristics at some length and relate them to export organization would unduly expand the size of this volume. However, a little thought on each and on the type of organization found necessary to reach and hold the domestic market will almost mark certain types of organization as the only suitable ones for distributing certain products.

Financial Factors. This aspect relates to both the producer in the United States and the channels through which his goods reach foreign markets. It is to be expected that funds will have to be tied up longer in foreign sales than in domestic. The longer transportation time and, quite often, the longer credit terms and collection period mean that financial engagements call for more funds than would comparable sales volume domestically. Adequate banking facilities for opening or servicing credits may also enter the picture, although many metropolitan banks in the United States serve customers in practically every section of the country as well as abroad. The financial strength and facilities of foreign distributors and purchasers can also determine the selection of distribution channels.

Ability to Sell Abroad. Successful foreign distribution calls basically for a knowledge of foreign markets and the necessary contacts to enter those markets on favorable terms. These may often take years to acquire, and many of the most desirable contacts may be reached more easily through middlemen than directly. Furthermore, an organization of specialists as to product or area may, by reason of volume and past experience, be a much more suitable channel for foreign sales than a small export department spread thinly over several markets.

Volume Expected. The size and potentiality of the market will be a limiting factor on the size of any organization for export. If the volume in any one or several markets is sufficient to permit the necessary specialization, then an export organization may be supported. If the volume anticipated is rather small, a different type of distribution system may be advisable. In this connection, the point to be emphasized is not so much physical size of the organization as stature in ability, which can arise most easily from a sufficient volume of business to afford adequate specialization in knowledge and interest.

Intent of the Manufacturer. By this is meant the nature of the manufacturer's interest in export trade. If he is an in-and-outer, desiring to dispose of occasional surpluses abroad, one type of organization or channel of distribution may be used; if he intends to stay in the export market and aggressively cultivate it, another type is indicated. Part of the decision may rest on plant capacity and on the need to seek new markets and, once found, to supply the potential demand. Some companies export only a small part of their production—say 5 per cent— while others may find export markets absorbing as much as 25 to 30 per cent of production. For the in-and-outer, it would not be a wise decision to build up an export organization geared to an aggressive sales policy.

Customs of the Trade. If wholesalers habitually buy a product from importers, or if the product is typically imported by the wholesalers, the pattern for distribution thus set may have a decisive influence on the method of export organization adopted. Different practices for the same product are not uncommon, though, depending on such circumstances as availability of transportation, communications, and financing and, in general, the degree of economic development of the respective countries.

Laws of Foreign Countries. Because of the differing laws in various countries relative to distributors or agents, foreign corporations or businesses, trade-marks and patents, customs duties and taxes on business, a thorough study of applicable laws is to be advised in considering the type of organization which may be used for selling abroad. This is also a reason for the occasional use of different types of organization for different markets.

TYPES OF EXPORT ORGANIZATIONS

The simplest classification of exporting practice is the direct and the indirect. The difference seems to be the extent of control retained by the producer over foreign sales functions rather than the performance of specific actions in accomplishing a sale. Thus there is no clear line. If a producer sells to an export merchant, the latter running all subsequent risks and setting his sales price, it is an open case of indirect export selling. But if the producer engages in certain other methods of distribution, with something to say about price or area in which sold, he can be called a direct exporter.

Several fairly distinct types of export organization are to be found.

However, it should be noted that a producer may employ one type for one product or market and a different type for another. Similarly, one of the independent organizations to be listed may act as such for one product or account and in a different capacity for another product or account. These organizations fall into three broad groupings:

DOMESTIC (INDIRECT)

1. Export merchant
2. Export commission house
3. Foreign buying agent
4. Export broker

DOMESTIC (DIRECT)

5. Built-in export function
6. Separate export department
7. Export sales company
8. Export associations
9. Combination export managers

FOREIGN

10. Branches or subsidiaries (sales, assembly, or manufacturing)
11. Licensing arrangements
12. Foreign representatives (agents, distributors, or dealers)
13. Traveling salesmen and mail-order selling

If these are considered in order, the following observations may be made.

Domestic (Indirect)

1. EXPORT MERCHANT. This is the man who buys and sells for his own account. He pays the producer an agreed price and runs the expense and risk of storage, insurance, transportation, financing, and price changes. He is free to set his own selling price without interference from the producer. The merchant's activities may be said to be opportunistic, in that if the chance arises to turn a trade in almost any product he is in business to do. He is the man who can advertise himself as willing to handle any product in almost any market. Export trade through merchants is limited, however, by the nature of products and by the development of other merchandising methods. Brokers, commission houses, and direct dealings between foreign buyers and producers bypass the merchant as a separate function. Then, in the exportation of machinery requiring spare parts and servicing or technical assistance in installation or adaptation, the merchant can find little field from which to draw business. Also, to be discussed later, if special marks of origin or other modifications are best done during the manufacturing process, the merchant, as such, is at a disadvantage. He normally would be used most advantageously for agricultural products such as cotton, but would not

be used extensively for branded products, especially if the producer wished to cultivate a market aggressively. The merchant might be an excellent outlet for temporary surpluses or out-of-date inventory. Also, he might have the best entree into new markets for the producer, particularly in less developed countries.

2. EXPORT COMMISSION HOUSE. Acting for either buyer or seller, but ordinarily in the interest of the foreign buyer, the export commission house draws a fee for service to its principal. As the buyer's purchasing agent in the exporting country, it is the commission house's business to shop around and obtain the most advantageous deal for its principal. Naturally, the type of activity calling for this function would be that in which a buyer seeks a supplier, which means that intensive foreign-market cultivation could not be accomplished under the arrangement. If the export commission house acts in the interest of the seller, and is paid by the seller, it may request an exclusive territory and, in effect, the nature of its activities changes to another of the types of organization listed.

3. FOREIGN BUYING AGENT. In addition to purchases made by commission houses under instruction from abroad, some export business is also done through foreign buying agents, who approach producers for the requirements of their principals. These foreign buyers may be stationed rather permanently in the exporting country or they may make seasonal visits or buying missions of short duration. They may act for foreign governments or for large purchasers such as transportation and public-utility companies.

4. EXPORT BROKER. By widely accepted definition, a broker is one who serves to bring two principals together. He does not take title to merchandise, and the sale is *through*, not *to*, him. In the export trade, brokers are said to be characteristically good channels of distribution in such fields as canned goods, packaged foodstuffs, and dried fruits, in which fields there are several small producers who are not in a position to export for themselves.[2]

Domestic (Direct)

5. BUILT-IN EXPORT FUNCTION. The built-in arrangement simply means that foreign sales are in specialized hands but that other activities incidental to foreign sales are performed by personnel in the regular company organization. Foreign orders usually call for special treatment in the matter of packaging, labeling, financing, invoicing, and documentation, and the coordination of shipment calls for close following by someone responsible. Yet the volume of business done may not justify employee specialization on these functions. Accordingly, one of the com-

[2] *Ibid.*, p. 166.

mon criticisms of the built-in function is the continual possibility of friction between the domestic- and the foreign-sales functions in their de
mands on other employees and functions in the business. Not only may
the service departments delay export orders because they are somewhat
more involved than the routine, but the fact that export business accounts for usually a small percentage of total business also serves to place
it second in importance in the eyes of many.

To overcome this, the export manager must be a diplomat as well as
an aggressive salesman and capable executive.

6. SEPARATE EXPORT DEPARTMENT. When volume justifies, setting up
all or the principal export functions into a separate department may be
a very advantageous practice. In this manner, there is opportunity for
specializaton, with personnel becoming better skilled in the special
procedures involved. The separate export department means, then, not
only the segregation of sales personnel, but also several "servicing" employees. Of course, the export function is no less under company direction, but the administrative jurisdiction does not filter down through
all departments as is the practice when a built-in function is employed.
Several functions, such as credit and finance, can still be carried under
the company's principal credit or financial officer, but even this may at
times be under the export department itself.

Recognition of the export function on a departmental basis, organizationally, opens the question of location of the department, physically.
It may be at the factory or at seaboard if the factory is inland. Both
arrangements have advantages. For example, if the department is located
at the factory, inland, the export manager can exercise closer supervision over preparation and packaging of orders, and the export function
may, in turn, be more effectively supervised by appropriate company
officials. The manager is perhaps in a little better position to ship through
two or more ports if advisable. Being with the company and its other
executives, he is more a part of the organization, which may have a
bearing at times when domestic orders threaten to cut into available
production, thus causing delay in the export business.

There are, though, several advantages to being located at seaboard,
if in a very important port. One is closer contact with other export executives and banks, through whom more frequent and up-to-date information on foreign markets and customers may be had. Another is
the possibility of easier meetings with buyers or foreign visitors. A third
is the greater ease of making close steamship conections with documents and correspondence, although this may be offset, by an export
department located in the interior, through the services of a capable
forwarder. A fourth is that some or all of the work which would have to
be farmed out to a forwarder (see Chapter 6) may be done by the

company's own export office. Whether it can be done more economically would seem to be the deciding factor. Many manufacturers operate more than one plant; if foreign orders call for production from more than one, or from different warehouses, the coordination and consolidation might be more satisfactorily handled by an officer on the spot at the port. This, too, is a service which a capable forwarder may offer. Finally, some exporters feel that the prestige of a New York office, for example, is a substantial competitive asset, especially in its impression on foreign buyers.

Many Export Departments Are Inland. The number of export departments at seaboard is no doubt considerable, but the number of export managers in such interior cities as Chicago, St. Louis, Memphis, Minneapolis, and Milwaukee points to the conclusion that the greater number of export managers work at their factories or main offices.

Further evidence of the location of exporters is to be found in a survey completed in early 1950 by the Economic Cooperation Administration with the assistance of the Department of Commerce. In order to render European (ECA) markets somewhat more available to small United States exporters, a directory of American small-business firms interested in export trade was compiled, primarily for distribution in Europe. It was based on questionnaires distributed all over the United States by the 42 field offices of the Department of Commerce.[3] The published directory listed 15,255 names, spread geographically as shown in Table 32. Not only does the list show a relatively small concentration in seaboard states, except for New York, but the evidence proves a nationwide activity, with several interior states showing large numbers of businesses so interested. Some of the firms listed are for services (banking, advertising, forwarding) rather than for merchandise.

7. EXPORT SALES COMPANY. Little difference can exist in operating methods between the separate export department and the export sales company. Both are primarily part of a larger organization with the difference that the separate company is legally a person in itself, although owned by the parent. Among the reasons offered for choosing the separate company are taxes and legal advantages, in matters of price or market division, and the possibility of smoother handling of products of other companies if this is to be done. With regard to taxes, an advantage may be found in setting up a separate company because of the impact of either foreign or domestic taxes. This is so when size of the company or volume of total company earnings affects the rate of tax, or when tax relief may be obtained under provisions such as those applicable

---

[3] By definition, a small business is one which does not occupy a dominant position in the trade or industry of which it is a part, the number of whose employees does not exceed 500, and which is independently owned and operated.

to Western Hemisphere trade corporations. Domestically, if the sales office is in a different state than the factory or the head office, some advantage may be found in incorporating in the state from which the principal export sales business is done.

Table 32. American Small Business Firms Interested in Exporting
(By Location, as of early 1950)

State	Number of Businesses	State	Number of Businesses
Alabama	70	New Hampshire	34
Arizona	30	New Jersey	632
Arkansas	34	New Mexico	6
California	1,040	New York	4,756
Colorado	61	North Carolina	108
Connecticut	360	North Dakota	6
Delaware	17	Ohio	990
Florida	123	Oklahoma	87
Georgia	117	Oregon	160
Idaho	11	Pennsylvania	965
Illinois	1,147	Rhode Island	173
Indiana	251	South Carolina	42
Iowa	143	South Dakota	9
Kansas	74	Tennessee	145
Kentucky	91	Texas	284
Louisiana	129	Utah	17
Maine	32	Vermont	34
Maryland	242	Virginia	157
Massachusetts	816	Washington	169
Michigan	465	West Virginia	33
Minnesota	301	Wisconsin	307
Mississippi	40	Wyoming	3
Missouri	327	Washington, D.C.	89
Montana	8	Hawaii	2
Nebraska	112	Puerto Rico	1
Nevada	3	Virgin Islands	2

SOURCE: Economic Cooperation Administration.

Another significant factor in deciding the department or company question is the possibility of relief from antitrust action if advantage is taken of the Webb-Pomerene provisions. Formation of a separate export company is considered by some as reducing the possibility of accusation that price and market agreements internationally are also agreements affecting domestic activities.

Owing to varying volumes in different markets and in different seasons, a separate export company may find it advantageous to handle noncompeting products or other manufactures going to the same general trade. Conversely, a manufacturer may handle some of his foreign business in certain products or certain markets through export facilities of other companies under an arrangement described by Pratt as "allied export selling company."[4]

8. EXPORT ASSOCIATIONS. In order to enable United States exporters to enter into international agreements with each other or with foreign competitors in matters of price or markets, an export trade act (Webb-Pomerene Act) was passed by Congress in April, 1918. This law permits association by contract or otherwise between United States exporters in a prescribed manner which would be illegal if applied to domestic activities. Under the Act, exemptions are granted from certain provisions of the Clayton Act and the Sherman Act if (*a*) the agreements are not in restraint of trade within the United States and (*b*) are not in restraint of the export trade of any domestic competitor of such association, and provided (*c*) the agreements do not artificially or intentionally enhance or depress prices within the United States of commodities of the class exported by such association.

Reports of such association or agreement must be filed with the Federal Trade Commission at the time of activation and annually thereafter. In one of the most thorough discussions to be found on the subject of export associations, Pratt states that, in general, semimanufactured products have lent themselves more readily to agreements relating to exports,[5] but that some specialized products have been so sold advantageously.

The number of associations has varied from 43 in 1920 to 57 in 1929, 1930, and 1931. One hundred and fifty-two such associations were formed during the period 1918 to 1950, representing 2,575 companies in the United States. Exports by these associations averaged around 6 per cent of United States totals in the period 1920 to 1948, rising as high as 17 per cent in 1930.[6] While these percentages may not be impressive as an over-all figure, the importance varies according to groups of products.

In his interesting discussion of the subject, Pratt says that export associations offer opportunities which have by no means been sufficiently exploited.[7] Several advantages are to be found in such cooperative effort, through which the associations may serve as a selling agent for members, may buy members' products and resell them, or may set up policies leaving it up to the members to carry on as before but within the agreed policy framework.

9. COMBINATION EXPORT MANAGERS. There can be little doubt that an efficient export department, with good overseas connections, is an asset,

---

[4] *Op. cit.,* p. 195.

[5] Since they may be standardized and sold under general rules as to quality and quantity (*op. cit.,* p. 153).

[6] Data from Federal Trade Commission.

[7] Pratt, *op. cit.,* p. 166.

but one which requires time to develop and volume to support. Many exporters are unable to meet adequately these limiting requirements. For them, the answer may be the combination export manager.

Sometimes referred to as the manufacturer's export agent, who becomes a combination export manager when he serves two or more exporters, this person serves an independent function in foreign trade. The combination export manager (or company) logically attempts to handle related but noncompeting lines, serving each company in the same manner as would its own export manager.

Business may be done in the name of the producers, using their letterheads but with the address of the combination export manager or company as that of the producer's export department, or it may be done in the name of the combination export company itself.

Ordinarily, orders are taken subject to acceptance by the manufacturer, and the manufacturer may be expected to take care of functions other than selling and perhaps documenting. But numerous variations are possible, depending on the individual contract. Prices are normally set by the manufacturer, but the combination export manager's views would carry due weight.

Since the combination export manager holds himself out to be somewhat of a specialist—or more of a specialist than the manufacturer can support on his volume, its seasonal characteristics, or its geographic spread—he often confines his activities to certain products or certain areas. His location may be at seaboard or inland, depending on his accounts and the advantages of being in one locality over another. One such manager known to the author operates out of a city in Iowa, acting as the export department for 19 companies located as far away as New Jersey and the Pacific coast.

These organizations may function through agencies abroad, through traveling salesmen, or by mail. Depending on their location, they may perform some of the functions ordinarily done by freight forwarders. Compensation is usually by commission, but instances are reported in which a retainer arrangement is made. Commissions are said to range from 2½ to 15 per cent.

Among the principal advantages to the manufacturer are expert service, ability to function with little delay, and contacts and facilities already established. All these must be reduced to terms of relative cost, but it is generally admitted that direct selling methods are likely to be more expensive. In effect, the manufacturer is sharing the expense of this service with others.

One must not overlook some possible disadvantages, though. First, the combination export manager may be spread so thin, as to product or area, that his attention to each manufacturer's situation may be less than desired. Second, more effort may be made to further the sale of goods whose volume or commission may work to the combination manager's advantage. Third, foreign sales activity is practically out of the manufacturer's hands, and if the combination manager is not pursuing as aggressive or thorough a program as the manufacturer would like to see, there may be little relief to be had during the life of the contract. This aspect would be of special significance if the manufacturer were seeking rather intensive development of his foreign markets.

Foreign Sales Organizations or Channels

Up to this point, all export organizations mentioned would be located in the exporter's country. Whether the producer employs a direct or an indirect method of selling abroad, a person or business is needed in the foreign country to serve as another link in the distribution chain between producer and retailer or ultimate consumer. In some cases, the producer's direct selling effort goes so far as to call for a branch sales office; in others, a branch plant or assembly unit is used. In either of these cases, the manufacturer in the United States would normally operate through a separate export department or an export sales company. Foreign distributors (sometimes called agents or dealers) are also a popular export-sales link, with probably less use being made of commission representatives, traveling salesmen, and mail-order selling. The product and the size, ability, and intent of the producer are deciding factors in determining foreign organization or channels, just as they are in domestic organization.

10. BRANCHES OR SUBSIDIARIES. The initial distinction between a branch and a subsidiary is that the latter is a separate organization usually set up under the laws of the country in which it is located. A branch, on the other hand, is an installation which is not a business entity in itself but a component of the parent company in some other country. Foreign branches and subsidiaries constitute the "direct" investments of American business abroad, and there appears to be an inclination to favor the local-subsidiary-corporation method in preference to registering a branch of an American corporation.[8]

The function of either a branch or a subsidiary may be sales alone, assembly and sales, or manufacturing and sales. To these may be added customer service and the carrying of inventory to accomplish fast action on orders.

Branches or subsidiaries offer the best means of intensive cultivation of any foreign market, but they call for a substantial sales volume to justify and support their operations. The large sales volume must be

---

[8] Joseph S. Cardinale, "Methods of Manufacturing Abroad," *Exporters' Digest*, March, 1951, p. 30.

on the part of each branch or subsidiary and must be sufficient, even in poor years, to justify support. Through such establishments abroad, American sales programs may be developed and pursued most satisfactorily, with managers selected and trained in the home office.

As one of the advantages of branches, the increased control over marketing policies and activities has already been mentioned. Besides this, there are possible savings to be derived through taxation and, significantly, a substantial element of good will may be obtained, especially if the branch or subsidiary does any assembly or manufacturing. Local manufacturers may at times have a real advantage in consumer acceptance. A very important consideration in arriving at a decision regarding type of overseas activity is the extent of restrictions on imports imposed by foreign countries. Because of customs duties, quotas, or exchange controls, the United States exporter may effectively be blocked out of any country, in spite of the fact that it is the objective of our government's policy to assure nondiscrimination against United States interests. Customs duties are often higher on finished or assembled goods than on those calling for some labor in the importing country. On this point, some saving in transportation cost may also be experienced. At the same time, costs of assembly or production may be lower abroad than in the United States. Even if they are higher, the added production cost may more than offset the extra duty applicable to finished goods.

One of the principal deterrents to expansion of foreign branches and subsidiaries is the widespread use of exchange controls which prevent or materially limit repatriation of foreign earnings. In this connection, one of the promotional methods in foreign commerce is the idea of industrial guarantee, which assures foreign investors of the ability to convert earnings and perhaps principal for a period of time.

Laws on patents and trade-marks are another source of possible disadvantage to be derived from operation of a branch or subsidiary in preference to exporting through other channels.

11. LICENSING ARRANGEMENTS. Closely related to branch or subsidiary participation in foreign markets is an arrangement whereby a producer in one country licenses a producer in another to manufacture his product in the second country. In this situation, the "exporting" manufacturer may be said to be exporting his *know how*—the use of his industrial techniques, patents, processes, and, in some cases, special equipment. In return he receives a royalty on the products sold, while still retaining control and ownership of the trade-marks and patents.[9]

An arrangement of this type may be particularly appropriate in coping with trade barriers which make exporting of merchandise difficult or unprofitable. This is the case in many countries employing exchange

[9] *Ibid.*

controls and import quotas, and the Economic Cooperation Administration took aggressive steps to acquaint United States companies with licensing opportunities in Europe in the postwar period.

In addition to use as a vehicle for overcoming trade barriers, the owner of the patent or trade-mark may also find it advantageous to enter into a licensing arrangement when, because of his financial position, he cannot well undertake the necessary capital investment to establish a plant abroad or when the market is not large enough or sufficiently developed to attract the required investment.

The licensing rights may be for limited manufacturing only, say an amount sufficient for the domestic market of the licensee or for one or more additional foreign markets. Of course, the right to manufacture under license would not ordinarily go so far as to invite competition for the owner of the patent or trade-mark in his own country or other selected markets.

In setting up the licensing arrangement, prudence calls for wise selection of the licensee, as to both character and ability, and for appropriate protection as to the quality and amount of production. The continuing arrangement may be via inspections and audits and, in the case of production techniques, via provision of technical advisers.

12. FOREIGN REPRESENTATIVES (AGENTS, DISTRIBUTORS, OR DEALERS). By accepted definition, an agent is one who works on a salary or commission but does not buy or sell for his own account; prices and marketing practices are largely dictated by the exporter. Distributors and dealers, on the contrary, usually buy on their own account and may sell for prices considered most advisable by them. The distributor is primarily a wholesaler, while the dealer is a retailer. The agent and the distributor appear to be much more widely used in export distribution than is the foreign dealer, or retailer.

Agents perform many functions for an exporter, and the agency method of foreign selling is said by Pratt to be a compromise between the manufacturer's or exporter's desire to have his own personal representative on the spot and the overhead expense entailed in having a representative dispatched from the United States.[10]

Among the services performed by the agent, in addition to selling, are:

a. Supplying information on the types of goods which can be sold in his area and on design, packing, and pricing
b. Settlement of claims and making of collections
c. Credit guarantees (if this is done, the agent is known as a *del credere* agent)
d. Advertising and publicity.
e. Servicing, if necessary

[10] Pratt, *op. cit.*, p. 219.

Depending on the contract, these services may be reduced or increased, with rate of remuneration adjusted accordingly.

It is common practice for an agent to request exclusive representation
in a certain territory, and this arrangement seems to work satisfactorily
in many cases. Some points of caution are to be noted, though. These
pertain primarily to the laws of the respective foreign countries. In
matters of registration of trade-marks, the question of who shall register them arises, and in some countries a company's ability to terminate
its agency contract is seriously limited. Cuba was a case in point when,
in 1947, it proposed a decree which would have made it virtually impossible to dismiss an agent except for gross inability or negligence, and
then only after long notice of intent. It is not to be inferred that agencies
are always so frequently canceled. Many run for decades and, as a matter of fact, the logical step from an agency (or a distributorship) is a
branch sales office—not simply a change in the agent. However, it is
stated by H. Lyman Smith, manager of the foreign-trade bureau of the
St. Louis Chamber of Commerce, that the reason many representatives
demand an exclusive contract, and for a long period, is because they
have seen instances in which exporters have changed representatives
for one reason or another and sometimes for no apparent reason.[11]

The relationship between a principal in the exporting country and
his foreign representative is such that a clear and thorough understanding must exist between the two. It is obvious that there must be mutual
trust and respect, for both men are in business for themselves, even
though working together for this purpose. They have something to sell
to each other, and each stands to gain or lose according to the actions
of the other.

Since the representation is likely to be of considerable duration, and
since distance may render impracticable frequent visits with each other,
more than usual caution is required in selecting the agent. His most
important asset is, of course, his selling ability; the entire purpose in
having foreign representation is to expand sales. But since the agency
may well be exclusive, the exporter will need to satisfy himself also as
to a proposed agent's character, business ability, and financial strength.
These may be generally compared with the three basic features of credit
investigation—character, capacity, and capital.

The exporter may obtain references from the prospective agent himself or from his bank, his competitors, the Foreign Service of the United
States (through the Department of Commerce), or a credit-rating and
reporting agency. However, the source of information considered by
many to be the best is other exporters who are using or have used the

---

[11] "Organization and Functions of the Export Department," address at Fourth
Institute of Foreign Trade, St. Louis, October, 1946.

foreign prospect. The basis for this information's being available is that the active agent will probably represent, or will endeavor to represent, several related but noncompeting lines.

Inquiry regarding the prospective agent covers the points mentioned above, the matter of competing products, estimates as to anticipated volume, and the like. If there is agreement between the two parties, the understanding is normally reduced to written contract form covering points such as the following:[12]

1. Clauses involving concessions granted and obligations assumed by the manufacturer: The naming of the agent and his appointment to exclusive or restricted representation; specifications as to territory, duration, compensation, advertising allowance, and similar arrangements.
2. Clauses involving principal concessions and obligations on the part of the agent: The handling of competitive goods; efforts to be made by him; advertising responsibilities; arrangements respecting registration of trade-marks; and other functions undertaken such as credit guarantees.
3. Clauses covering concessions and obligations of a mutual bearing or nature: Points such as quotas, stocks to be provided and carried, price changes, approval of orders, understandings as to direct sales into the territory by the exporter, indirect sales into the territory by other agents, and extraterritorial sales into other territories by the agent; and, very importantly, the cancellation clause.

Some companies employ a printed contract form, but others find individual letter contracts preferable because of variations in detail regarding agents, products, methods of compensation, basis of compensation, and dissimilarities in laws under which different agents operate.

Distributors are given the right to sell specified products in a specified area, on either an exclusive or a nonexclusive basis. They buy the goods outright, and are said to be widely used by automobile manufacturers, makers of various types of machinery and specialties, and producers of branded and labeled merchandise.[13] When a foreign market is turned over to a distributor, he should be one with sufficient standing, finance, and organization to do the most desirable job for the exporter. Functions listed for the agent are not exactly those performed by the distributor, mainly because the distributor *purchases* the merchandise from the exporter, who no longer has as much detailed interest in matters of finance, credit, and prices as in dealing through an agent. Distributors

---

[12] Points drawn especially from Grover G. Huebner and Roland L. Kramer, *Foreign Trade Principles and Practices*, rev. ed. (New York, Appleton-Century-Crofts, Inc., 1942), pp. 248–249.

[13] Pratt, *op. cit.*, p. 220.

must set up their own servicing organizations, and the exporter to attain best results, may have to assist distributors in such activities as advertising, service and sales training, and even price and administrative recommendations.

Contracts assigning agencies and distributorships must go into many details for mutual protection, as both the exporter and the foreign representative are investing time and funds in a business undertaking which is expected to run for some time. It is constantly stressed that most careful screening be made of applicants for foreign representation, most of whom are citizens of the country in which they request representation privileges.

Dealers, since they are mainly retailers, are ordinarily of interest in narrower markets, in which a leading retailer is in effect as satisfactory a distribution outlet as is the smaller wholesaler operating locally.

13. TRAVELING SALESMEN AND MAIL-ORDER SELLING. Either through a traveling salesman or through a resident, who may handle one line or several, the traveling-salesman method of foreign selling is of recognized importance.

Some products, mainly branded and advertised, lend themselves to sale abroad by mail order. Several companies in St. Louis, for example, do considerable overseas business by this method. Naturally, this calls for advertising and a reasonably good reputation on the part of the exporter.

Other avenues of distribution may be found, such as importers (wholesalers or jobbers) abroad, foreign governments, and the larger private buyers such as large industrial or agricultural concerns and transportation and public utilities companies.

Summarizing, it should be noted that even with a fairly clear line of classification for export organizations and methods, a company may operate as several at one and the same time—for different products and in different markets. The International General Electric Company is reported to use "almost every type of distribution channel and every form of remuneration, varying them to meet the volume of business and the local circumstances."[14] Methods used will change with time as the volume changes. The natural progression is, in the manufacturer's country, from indirect to direct selling, from a built-in to a separate department; abroad, from foreign representation (agent or distributor) to a branch sales office or subsidiary.

THE IMPORTER

By the mental process of reversing the movement of goods, handling of which was described in the preceding pages on export methods and

[14] *Ibid.,* p. 191, quoting letter from W. V. B. van Dyke, assistant to the president.

organization, one might expect to blanket automatically the methods and organization for import. To a considerable extent this holds true, for just as the export operation ranges from indirect to direct, so does the import. But what may appear to be simple "buying" operations of some importers actually call for a more complex business process than does much exporting. Aside from the act of purchasing, and depending on the stage in the marketing process at which the individual importer enters the picture, he may be faced with any or all of the following functions:[15]

1. Assembly of goods in foreign market or shipping center
2. Grading, sorting, and warehousing in foreign market
3. Arranging for transportation and insurance
4. Receiving and entering the goods through customs in the United States
5. Drayage and warehousing of the goods at the port of entry
6. Cleaning, grading, sorting, repacking, and so forth, for redistribution
7. Resale of the imported goods to domestic distributors or consumers or to foreign buyers
8. Forwarding goods to final destinations
9. Making financial arrangements in connection with payments, collections, and credits

Depending on the characteristics of the imported item and on the nature of the foreign and domestic marketing structure, some of these marketing functions may not have to be performed and, even if they are called for, the importer may engage the services of some specialist in performing them. Or additional functions, such as inspection abroad and in the United States, may be required by law or called for as a matter of protection to the importer. His organization for doing business would be modified accordingly.

Difference between Importer and Buyer of Imported Products. Before considering the types of organization, it would be well to draw a distinction between the importer, as such, and the buyer of imported products. There is, to be sure, a close connection between organization for export (in the exporting and importing country) and for import (in the importing and exporting country). But for our purpose, the term "importer" will mean the person or firm doing the physical importing into the country, and questions of organization will follow the distinction. By this definition, then, an importer into the United States may be a foreign sales branch located in the United States.

Importer May Be Merchant or Agent. Basically, an importer's activities

[15] George B. Roorbach, *Import Purchasing* (New York, McGraw-Hill Book Company, Inc., 1927), p. 42.

may be grouped under two headings, (1) as a merchant, when he buys for his own account, and (2) as an agent, when he imports merchandise as representative of a foreign seller.

A third, and closely related, marketing activity is that of the broker, who acts as an intermediary between merchants or between producers and buyers. In foreign trade, the broker does not normally act as the intermediary between the shipper abroad and the buyer in this market; he acts as the intermediary between operators in this market, whether they are merchants trading with each other or a merchant and a consuming buyer.

The broker operates between companies dealing in imported commodities; he does not have the representation of a specific buyer or seller. He works with many buyers or many sellers in trying to bring them together on specific lots either on the spot, already afloat, or to be shipped from abroad. While the seller pays the broker's commission, the broker, unlike the agent and as indicated above, does not normally have exclusive sales representation for any particular seller. However, there is overlapping in activity. Some agents also act as brokers and some brokers may represent specific accounts in addition to doing their general brokerage business.

When acting as a merchant, the importer naturally runs the risk of price or style changes, of spoilage or deterioration, of having the merchandise arrive too late for a season or in damaged condition, and of having the merchandise lack some desired degree of uniformity or not conform exactly to samples. Some of these risks may be protected by insurance or by having the exporter eventually make good, but the lost opportunity to turn a profit and the disappointment to expectant users are sizable risks to be borne by an import merchant. In raw or semiprocessed commodities, part of the import merchant's function may be collecting, sorting, and grading to meet requirements of the trade.

In the light of these indicated risks, and the probability that a purchaser, no more than a seller, can well afford to have all his eggs in one basket, the position of some manufacturers and retail merchants becomes clear. Both the manufacturer and the retail merchant may often need a specified product at a specified time. They cannot afford to take the risk of price fluctuations, of disputes over quality, quantity, or price, or of loss of all or part of a shipment. For, even though he is covered by insurance, the chance of inconvenience or disruption of production or marketing plans may compel use of an import merchant, and may make the buyer of the product not an importer at all.

Organization May Depend on Whether Seller Seeks Out Buyer or Vice Versa. Selling either to the industrial user or to the wholesale or retail trade, the import merchant may buy direct from abroad or he may buy from foreign sales offices located in the United States. In both cases, though, the import merchant would do the physical importing. In the importation of raw materials, the buyer often seeks out sellers, while in the case of manufactured goods, the seller attempts to develop his markets. Thus it is that in the purchase of coffee, tea, mahogany, and numerous raw products, the importing organizations frequently send buyers abroad or employ buying agents. Some large distributors or processors, as in the case of coffee, sugar, and petroleum, buy direct from abroad. These naturally make up a goodly portion of total United States imports. Large retailers, such as leading department stores, chain stores, or jewelry stores, import some products direct. In the make-up of this structure, it must be recognized that many raw materials are produced by numerous small companies or by individuals, and the initial steps of collecting, sorting, and grading for foreign markets may result in rather concentrated marketing facilities. Furthermore, sales effected through auctions in some lines, or commodity exchanges in others, will determine to a great extent the type of organization needed for obtaining imported goods. Of course, the user of such goods should choose to buy them on the same basis as domestic competitive products, meaning that his total costs must be compared.

Furthermore, the need for knowing several international markets intimately, and for knowing grades and qualities, makes possible and practically compels the functioning of importers specializing in some one or a few items. They may be merchants, agents, or brokers concentrating on one or a few products. Among the products in which trade is specialized are cotton, wool, silk, hides and skins, furs, lumber, coffee, sugar, vegetable oils, and spices. A high degree of specialization is also found in manufactured goods such as tool steel, chinaware, cutlery, laces, and toys.

Organization May Depend on Size and Number of Producers. In importing manufactured or consumer goods, the organization or method may also vary depending on whether the producers are numerous and small or few and large, and depending on the type of product. Automobiles imported from abroad—say, the Renault—call for a distributor in major United States markets. Each such distributor may be designated by the foreign exporter, or subagencies may be established in important localities.

Much emphasis has been placed in postwar years on increasing United States imports of foreign, mainly European, products. These are mostly manufactured articles. It will be pointed out in a later chapter that some European governments or business interests have divided the United States into regional markets, in each of which the first requisite is to set up satisfactory representation for the foreign producer. In view of potential volumes, these will probably for some time be American distributors adding a line or two of some foreign producer or producer's association. These distributors may be wholesalers or jobbers or, for certain specialty goods, large retailers. Of interest is the fact that many retailers are willing to handle foreign products but do not wish to act as importers themselves. This was brought out in a survey conducted by International House (New Orleans) in early 1950, based on several cities in the Mississippi Valley area. Also to be considered in organization for import is the fact that several articles of import interest are under cartel or foreign-government control, with sales offices located in the United States.

United States Markets Not Intensively Developed by Exporters Located Abroad. There are few branch sales offices or subsidiaries of foreign companies in the United States, and intensive United States market development by foreigners has not generally occurred. It may be that the size of the American market and the relatively small size of foreign producers is a forbidding influence in the lack of development. Added to this is the fact that purchasing of raw materials is largely by or for industrial users, which are relatively few in number as compared with consumers and, buying to specification, the buyer seeking out the seller may tap several world sources. Not to be overlooked is domestic ownership of foreign supply sources in such products as sugar, bananas, petroleum, and several other agricultural and mineral products.

Import Businesses Generally Small in Size. In general, it can be said that many import merchants are rather small in size and specialize in only a few products. Their purchasing and selling establishments can in no way compare in size with domestic businesses which employ thousands in the various phases of production and distribution. Import brokers and agents are also small businesses; all one need do is visit several companies to observe how many are one- or two-man operations and how few have as many as 10 or 20 employees. It is, nevertheless, dangerous to generalize, as organization for import depends on the type of product, size and financial strength of foreign producers and American middlemen, extent of cultivation of the United States market by foreign sellers, and regional or world-wide trade practice in each product. Importers of some raw materials or big-volume commodities are very large companies, indeed; on the other hand, many buyers conduct their importation of foreign products as an adjunct to their principal business, in domestic products, and require as little as half of one man's time.

Importer Must Sell, and May Have to Finance. The discussion of import organization should not be closed without mentioning that two important functions of the importer are *selling* his merchandise, either before or after acquisition, and financing and accounting. The method of selling depends largely on customs of the trade. For instance, furniture buyers for department stores look forward to annual buying trips to New York or Chicago, both for the trip and for the opportunity to observe new lines and shop around with competing sellers. Some, but not all, purchases are made on this basis, and the displayers follow up with personal calls at the buyers' places of business. Thus import organization calls not only for meeting the customs of foreign sellers; it must also conform to buying customs and habits within the country of import. A recent development in this connection is the concept of regional marketing facilities for imported products.

The extent of financing required of the importer may also affect, at least be materially affected by, his marketing function and aim. If he buys direct from abroad, operations may go so far as to involve advances on production or on the primary collection of a commodity from several small producers. At the other extereme, he may be sold on convenient credit, with the exporter providing credit for him. In the importing country, the character of the importer's organization will naturally depend on the extent to which he tries to reach the ultimate purchaser, and on the extent his product must be manipulated or processed for resale.

REVIEW QUESTIONS

1. How does the type of product handled influence the type of export organization to be adopted?

2. How does volume expected influence the type of export organization to be adopted?

3. Distinguish between direct and indirect types of export organization.

4. Distinguish between the built-in and the separate export department. What advantages does each offer over the other?

5. Where should the export office be located? Why?

6. What are the benefits to be derived from entering into export associations under the Webb-Pomerene Act? What are the principal disadvantages? Do these offer any particular benefit to the producers of one type of product as compared with others?

7. Why is it so necessary to use the most careful judgment in the selection of a foreign agent?

8. What are the marketing functions which may have to be performed by the importer?

9. Distinguish between import merchant, import agent, and import broker.

10. How does the possibility that the importer must sell, and may have to finance, influence the type of import organization employed?

CHAPTER 6

Organizational Structure: Services

In earlier chapters it was pointed out that foreign commerce is fundamentally the same as domestic commerce—both involve production, marketing, financing, transporting, storing, insuring, and otherwise attending to goods and services reaching the ultimate consumer. In foreign commerce, however, these operations are complicated by time, distance, customs, language and monetary differences, and many varied national regulations pertaining to, or placing restrictions on, the movement of goods, services, and investments. The study of foreign commerce must therefore be broader than is selling alone, finance, transportation, insurance, or any of the other recognized fields of commerce and business administration. Because of this, also, specialized functions have developed and are available to the exporter or importer as a service ranging from physical handling of the goods to financing and insuring, and to coordination of the merchandise movement with required documents and shipping schedules.

It is the purpose of this chapter to discuss these various activities, which are all part of the general field of foreign commerce. Many of the functions may be performed by the shipper or importer himself. Such jobs as marking, packing, labeling, or otherwise readying the goods for export may better be done by the shipper himself. If not, the work can be let out on contract to specialists. Some functions, however, can almost certainly be done better by specialists—not only because of the high degree of training needed, but also because of the necessity of having established international and trade connections.

Many Specialized Functions. Among the specialized institutions and functions to be covered in this chapter are financing, transportation, foreign freight forwarding, customhouse brokerage, packaging and cooperage, warehousing, marine insurance, communications, public weighing and inspecting, and arbitration facilities.

FINANCING

Since financial aspects of foreign commerce are discussed in detail in later chapters, it will suffice here merely to point out the principal functions of the banking system as a service to exporters and importers. Major attention will be given the foreign department of a commercial bank, which is the principal, though not the only, banking activity of interest to foreign traders. In brief, banks perform two main functions for foreign commerce—financing and providing a market for converting foreign exchanges. The financing aspect may be direct, through issuance of credit, or it may be the nature of an "assist," when serving as a collection mechanism, sometimes without but often with advances on the drafts being collected. Also to be included in the financing service is the development of credit information for its own use and for the benefit of its customers. Credit accommodation may be through the foreign department, by means of acceptance financing or advances against drafts being collected, or through the regular loan department, by means of a commercial loan.

In performing its service identified as a market for converting foreign exchange, the commercial-banking system buys and sells foreign exchange and currency, thus acting as a dealer. Maintenance of balances abroad and the holding of deposits for foreign banks provide the daily working structure through which this service is accomplished.

Commercial Banks Perform Several Services for Foreign Commerce. Services to the exporter and importer by the commercial banks may, accordingly, be classified as follows:

Financing:
Granting of commercial loans, similar to domestic credits
Issuance of letters of credit and execution of bank acceptances covering import, export, or storage of merchandise
Purchases of or advances against bills drawn on foreign buyers
Provision of credit information
Foreign-exchange conversion:
Purchase and sale of mail or cable transfers
Purchase and sale of foreign currencies
Purchases and sale of foreign-exchange futures contracts
Purchase of drafts or acceptances payable in foreign currencies
Other:
Issuance of traveler's checks and travel letters of credit
Collection of foreign securities or other obligations
In some cases, compilation of foreign economic information

No accurate count of the banks in the United States with formal foreign department has been made, but the total is known to be over 100. Organizationally, foreign departments are set up according to the job to be done and the number and capabilities of personnel. A bank in Memphis, for instance, has a foreign and cotton department. Another, with a foreign department of approximately 20 employees, functions without formal specialization, while larger departments may be organized on a geographic basis.

Services Are Provided by Federal Reserve Banks. Services to foreign commerce are also provided by the Federal Reserve banks, which played a major role in the development of a bank-acceptance market and which are authorized to deal in foreign exchange, to maintain foreign balances, and to establish correspondent relationships for conduct of business abroad. These activities come under supervision of the Board of Governors and, in certain areas, under jurisdiction of the Open Market Committee. Acting as a depository for foreign banks and governments, the 12 Federal Reserve banks reported deposit liabilities on foreign account of around $577,000,000 in early 1952. Amounts due them from foreign banks at the same time totaled about $28,000. Every Federal Reserve bank reported accounts on both sides of the ledger with foreign customers, but operations are carried out through the Federal Reserve Bank of New York.

Investment Banking Also Plays Role. The investment-banking system for some years provided an important service to foreign commerce. But the Johnson Act (1934) prohibited public offerings of securities of governments which were in default on their debts to the United States government. In 1945, however, this Act was amended so as not to apply to countries holding membership in the International Monetary Fund and the International Bank for Reconstruction and Development. This practically nullified the Johnson Act, but the public sale in the United States of foreign-government securities had not resumed on a large scale, because the principal postwar source of United States funds to foreign governments has been our own government's foreign credits or gifts. Sale of foreign securities in the United States has also been rendered difficult by the world-wide weakness of money and exchange defaults and restriction.

Activities of the Export-Import Bank, also an important service institution, will be discussed in Chapter 7.

TRANSPORTATION

A convenient grouping of services in this field is ocean, inland, and air. These may be further subdivided.

Ocean

Physically, this service may be said to include steamship lines and stevedoring companies. Stevedoring covers the physical movement of merchandise into and out of vessels, in the performance of which longshoremen are employed. Sometimes this movement may be direct from or to railroad cars, but ordinarily the placing of goods in or removal of goods from railroad cars is handled by carloading or unloading employees or companies engaged by railroads.

Steamship lines, in some cases, serve both foreign and coastwise shipping. Since coastwise traffic is reserved to domestic lines, our view of foreign transportation service may be confined to three types—scheduled, tramp, and industrial lines. The first, as the name implies, operate on an established schedule between designated ports. The vessels

Trade-route Number	Ports Served
1. U.S. Atlantic	East coast South America
2. U.S. Atlantic	West coast South America
3. U.S. Atlantic	East coast Mexico
4. U.S. Atlantic	Caribbean ports
5. U.S. North Atlantic	United Kingdom and Ireland
6. U.S. North Atlantic	Baltic and Scandinavian ports
7. U.S. North Atlantic	German North Sea ports
8. U.S. North Atlantic	Belgium and the Netherlands
9. U.S. North Atlantic	Atlantic France and Northern Spain
10. U.S. North Atlantic	Mediterranean and Black Sea
11. U.S. South Atlantic	United Kingdom and Europe north of Spain
12. U.S. Atlantic	Far East
13. U.S. Gulf and South Atlantic	Mediterranean and Black Sea
14. U.S. Atlantic and Gulf	West coast of Africa
15A. U.S. Atlantic	South and East Africa and Madagascar
15B. U.S. Gulf	South and East Africa and Madagascar
16. U.S. Atlantic and Gulf	Australasia
17. U.S. Atlantic and Gulf	Straits settlements and Netherlands East Indies
18. U.S. Atlantic and Gulf	India, Persian Gulf, and Red Sea
19. U.S. Gulf	Caribbean
20. U.S. Gulf	East coast South America
21. U.S. Gulf	United Kingdom, Continent, Baltic, and Scandinavia
22. U.S. Gulf	Far East
23. U.S. Pacific	Caribbean
24. U.S. Pacific	East coast South America
25. U.S. Pacific	West coast South America, Central America, and Mexico
26A. U.S. Pacific	United Kingdom and Ireland
26B. U.S. Pacific	Le Havre–Hamburg range
27. U.S. Pacific	Australasia
28. U.S. Pacific	Straits settlements, Netherlands East Indies, India, Burma, Persian Gulf, and Red Sea
29. California ports	Far East
30. Washington and Oregon ports	Far East
31. U.S. Gulf ports	West coast South America

SOURCE: *Essential Foreign Trade Routes of the American Merchant Marine,* United States Maritime Commission, May, 1949.

move whether each trip is a full or a partial load. They may carry either cargo only or cargo and passengers; a few vessels are passenger liners.

Essential Trade Routes Designated. Scheduled lines operate principally on what the United States Maritime Administration of the Department of Commerce (formerly Maritime Commission) has designated as essential routes for the maintenance of adequate merchant-marine service. As of 1949, 31 such routes had been designated, as shown in the table on page 107.

Tramp steamers move generally as cargo beckons, usually under charter for a full load. Industrial vessels are those whose employment and ownership are usually the same—tankers for the larger oil companies and some freighters for such bulk products as bauxite and iron ore. Some industrial vessels run scheduled services.

The importance of transportation in our over-all purchases and sales abroad is discussed in Chapter 3, and treatment of the transportation account in the summary of international transactions is covered in Chapter 2.

Steamship lines employ solicitors at inland points to call on prospective shippers and consignees within those areas. These solicitors are also employed at principal ports; abroad, the usual practice is to appoint agents. For the same reason, agents are appointed in the United States for certain foreign lines.

While the entire organization of an ocean-steamship line may be said to exist for the exporter or the importer, those organizational functions of most direct interest are the traffic, solicitation, and operations departments.

Stevedoring Functions. Stevedoring companies, located at ports, sell their services to steamship lines, and the cost is included in rates paid by shippers. Longshoremen are employed by stevedoring companies, which may be either independent contract companies or "house" companies, owned by and performing their work for their parent steamship line.

Inland: Rail

Inland transportation service, feeding ocean lines, is usually by rail, truck, or water, although pipelines may be used for some products and air shipments may be necessary to catch a close schedule. Some major railroads have foreign freight departments, with personnel especially trained in this phase. But regardless of whether a foreign department is formally organized, as in the case of the Illinois Central System, Missouri Pacific, New York Central, or Pennsylvania Railroad, the function of transporting merchandise for export or import is of interest to any railroad serving a port. Accordingly, representatives are employed to solicit business and to provide better service to shippers.

Inland: Truck

Truck lines appear to be playing an increasingly important role in foreign shipments, especially in the case of less-than-carload movements from reasonably proximate points of origin. Some truck lines have developed such a large volume of this business that they have established foreign departments, employing solicitors to engage further business for them. This particular activity appears to have developed more extensively in the East and on the West coast than in the South.

Inland: Water

Inland-water transportation service to foreign commerce is mainly by barge line along streams like the Mississippi and other great rivers. In the case of barge service on the Mississippi, a significant proportion of traffic on the lower section of the river is of foreign origin or destination.

Significance of Foreign-freight Differential. An important feature of inland transportation service to foreign commerce is the import and export freight differential, whereby shipments moving between, say, Chicago and New Orleans, or Chicago and New York, move at one rate if either port city is the destination and at another rate if the goods are for export or were imported. These differentials hold for rail traffic to both coasts and the Gulf of Mexico and for some truck lines on some products. Lower Mississippi River barge rates generally follow the rail pattern.

Air

Growing rapidly in the postwar period, air service in foreign commerce has grown to giant proportions. Its first appeal is, of course, to the traveler; over half of the international departures and arrivals from the United States (excluding Canada and Mexico) are by air. Caribbean travel accounts for a large part of this movement. About 30 per cent of travelers between the United States and Europe and the Mediterranean area move by air. In the movement of freight, also, air service is quite significant.

In early 1949, 65 international air carriers were reported in operation, serving more than 2,000 cities in over 200 countries on some 500,000 miles of airways.[1] Scheduled air-freight service was available on a common-carrier basis over the routes of 22 United States lines, some with direct

---

[1] William F. Muller, "Air Cargo and the International Forwarder," *The International Trader*, 1949, p. 49.

and others with foreign interchange facilities for goods moving internationally.

Almost any type of merchandise can be shipped by air except those whose reactions to altitude would be dangerous to the passengers, crew, or other cargo. It is reported that four-engine cargo aircraft can normally accommodate pieces as large as 60 by 80 by 90 inches, that two-engine planes can normally accommodate pieces as large as 53 by 57 by 60 inches and that all other commercial planes will handle cargo as large as 20 by 24 by 44 inches. There are, of course, weight limitations as well.

Advantages Offered by Air Shipment. Among the principal features offering advantages to shippers, which can be reduced to cost, are:

1. Lower packing costs. Packaging requirements for air shipments may be simpler than those of surface carriers. Generally speaking, the damage from load shifting through bumping and swaying is reduced. Use of lighter packing material can thus result in lower packing and shipping costs, but adequate packing must be used for any surface transportation at origin or destination. In connection with packing costs, another possible saving may be found in those instances in which duty payable includes weight of the container in its computation; the use of lighter material may result in lower duties, provided the material used is itself dutiable.
2. Reduction of inventories. Since stocks can be replenished more rapidly, larger inventories need not be held to offset transportation time. The volume in the transportation "pipeline" is reduced, also, with consequent potential reduction in interest, storage, and insurance costs—in all, lowered distribution costs.
3. Reduction of spoilage losses in perishables and increased sales appeal due to freshness. This feature is of particular applicability in the matter of fresh fruits and vegetables, fish and lobsters, and flowers.
4. Competitive timeliness in publications, fashions, novelties, etc.

FOREIGN FREIGHT FORWARDERS

This extremely vital link in the movement of goods for exporters is a highly specialized and technical field. Services offered shippers are manifold and the arrangement between them may be for full or partial use of the facilities of the forwarder, depending on the requirements of the individual exporter or importer. Many forwarders also act as licensed customhouse brokers and provide or arrange for export packaging and other services required by shippers.

Forwarder Performs Many Services. When it is recalled that the forwarder's prime arena of activity is at the port and that his work involves the problems of booking space, execution and clearing of documents, coordination between the movement of goods and of documents, and the arrangement of insurance and financing, his ordinary functions may be listed as follows:[2]

1. Arranging for steamer or air-cargo space for the shipment.
2. Preparation and clearance of the U.S. Export Declaration.
3. Securing of steamship delivery permit and arranging for delivery by truck or lighter and preparation of dock receipt; in case of air shipments, delivery to air-cargo terminal or airport.
4. Preparation of steamer bill of lading, or air waybill, arranging payment of freight charges, picking up the signed ladings.
5. Covering shipment with marine and war insurance, as instructed.
6. Preparation of consular invoice, certificate of origin, or other documents required by laws of the country of destination, presentation to foreign consul and paying of consular fees.
7. Disposition of the completed documents in accord with the financial arrangements made between buyer and seller. On draft collections it may mean the preparation of drafts and bank instructions; where a letter of credit is involved, presentation of all documents that the credit requires.

As requirements pertaining to shipments change, these functions are accordingly modified. For example, the forwarder is at times called on in such matters as obtaining export licenses and ascertaining that import permits required by foreign countries are in order. Prior to quotation, also, the forwarder may perform an important service for the shipper in advising him about the preparation of price estimates and about letter-of-credit specifications. A number of incidental tasks to assist his shipper clients also accompanies performance of the principal services of the forwarder. These may cover such details as checking routes and rates and arranging for and checking final documents. Goods may also be consigned to correspondents of the forwarder abroad, for clearance through customs and shipment to an interior point. However, the importer may designate the forwarder in his country which he desires to have used.

While the term "foreign freight forwarder" may point principally to export trade, the forwarder performs a vital service in import trade as well. A close connection exists between the activities of customhouse brokers, described below, and freight forwarders. The former attend to the formalities of clearing a shipment through customs, the latter to the distribution and forwarding of the shipment to interior points if destination is inland. As indicated above, some companies are set up to perform both services.

[2] E. G. Hinrichs, "Functions of the Foreign Freight Forwarder," *The International Trader*, 1949, p. 127.

Income Derived from Shipper and Carrier. The forwarder sells his services to exporters and, in most instances, also derives income from steamship and air lines in the form of freight brokerage or commissions. These commissions are included in, and constitute a percentage of, freight charges—about 1¼ per cent in the case of ocean freight and about 5 per cent in the case of air freight, depending on destination. In booking cargo space, which represents the sale of part of the capacity of a vessel to a shipper for one voyage, the forwarder acts in the capacity of a freight broker, but the freight rate includes brokerage even though freight is booked direct by the shipper.

Business Characterized by Small Units. Some forwarders operate only in a single port; others have several branches, domestic and foreign With no license having been required to engage in business (up to early 1952) and no absolute need for heavy financial investment, the activity has been characterized by a number of small, independent operators, although there are several large national concerns. Many forwarders have as few as 5 employees; those with over 35 employees seem to be uncommon. Internally, the organization is arranged to suit individual needs. Functions are practically the same for all, and, when volume permits, job specialization on the basis of geographic distribution or commodity is possible.

Mention of the small size of many forwarding concerns is not intended to imply that the task is easy and does not call for a high degree of skill and care. On the contrary, it is one of minute detail and exacting coordination. For this reason, the forwarder with wide knowledge and experience has much more to sell to the shipper than merely services. As an example, a forwarder may act as freight broker and engage ship's space under the most advantageous conditions of freight rates, time in transit, and delivery at foreign ports. He should therefore be intimately acquainted with freighting conditions to enable his principals to quote in a competitive market on the most favorable basis.

Forwarders Subject to Government Regulation, 1950. For some time, forwarders have been threatened with regulation by some government agency—in this case, the Federal Maritime Board (formerly United States Maritime Commission). Under the Bland Act of 1942, the Maritime Commission was charged with coordinating

. . . the functions and facilities of public and private agencies engaged in the forwarding and similar servicing of water-borne export and import foreign commerce of the United States, for . . . the maintenance and development of present and post-war foreign trade, and the preservation of forwarding facilities and services for the post-war restoration of foreign commerce.[3]

[3] Pub. L. 498, 77th Cong., approved Mar. 14, 1942.

General Order 72 of the United States Maritime Commission, published in the *Federal Register* of May 24, 1950, provides for a permanent register of all foreign freight forwarders dispatching shipments by ocean-going vessels, registration to have been accomplished within 60 days after June 1, 1950. Each forwarder filing the required information is assigned a registration number which must be used on all his "letterheads, invoices, advertising and all other documents relating to his forwarding business." Failure to use his registration number subjects the forwarder to its possible suspension or cancellation.

The registration form calls for data on type of organization, date of establishment, relationship to other businesses or activities, ownership interest and citizenship of officers, number of employees, and extent of

Table 33. Freight Forwarders Registered with Federal Maritime Board
(Number and location as of Nov. 27, 1950)

State	Main offices	Branches	State	Main offices	Branches
Alabama	9	6	New Jersey	4	5
Arizona	0	0	New Mexico	0	0
Arkansas	0	0	New York	719	46
California	93	47	North Carolina	2	0
Colorado	1	0	North Dakota	0	1
Connecticut	2	2	Ohio	4	9
Delaware	0	0	Oklahoma	0	0
District of Columbia	2	12	Oregon	10	5
Florida	62	24	Pennsylvania	22	12
Georgia	6	4	Rhode Island	2	0
Idaho	0	0	South Carolina	5	2
Illinois	18	20	South Dakota	0	0
Indiana	0	1	Tennessee	0	4
Iowa	0	1	Texas	36	50
Kansas	0	1	Utah	0	1
Kentucky	0	0	Vermont	0	0
Louisiana	76	34	Virginia	9	9
Maine	4	0	Washington	22	10
Maryland	20	20	West Virginia	0	0
Massachusetts	25	9	Wisconsin	2	4
Michigan	0	6	Wyoming	0	0
Minnesota	2	6	Hawaii	6	3
Mississippi	2	7	Puerto Rico	4	8
Missouri	4	11	Foreign	2	39
Montana	0	0	Total	1,175	419
Nebraska	0	0			
Nevada	0	0			
New Hampshire	0	0			

SOURCE: Federal Maritime Board, U.S. Department of Commerce.

specialization. Accordingly, it does not include much usable information which could serve as criteria to determine that a forwarder is capable of carrying on such a business. Nor does assignment of a number indicate a certification of the forwarder's capabilities. The order specifies billing practices which must be followed, making it necessary for forwarders to list specific charges for specific services rendered, including freight, insurance, and consular costs incurred by the forwarder for account of the shipper.

While some indication has been given that regulation of rates might be advisable, there had been no such vital regulation in force up to early 1952. The order does, however, provide that only registered forwarders shall accept brokerage from ocean carriers and that such brokerage shall not be shared with a shipper or consignee.

Wide Geographic Representation. As a result of the listing of forwarders, it is possible to have a geographic tabulation as to location. This is shown in Table 33. Numerical figures, of course, do not take into account the volumes of business done by each forwarder; as a result, the listing should not be interpreted as indicating the relative importance of trade of the localities shown. However, the geographic spread of both main and branch offices is an indication that exports and imports, are of interest to many sections of the United States, both at ports and in the interior.

International Air-cargo Forwarders. Specialization is found in international air-cargo forwarding as distinct from ocean-freight forwarding. Functionally, as in ocean-freight forwarding, the organization may also offer service as a customhouse broker. Functions of the international air-cargo forwarder when serving in this capacity have been listed by an outstanding authority as follows:[4]

EXPORT

1. Domestic routing and forwarding through agents in United States cities
2. Warehousing for consolidation of shipments from client's branches and/or suppliers
3. Crating, repacking, and marking advice and facilities
4. Routing via fastest and most economical carrier
5. Space booking and aircraft chartering
6. Complete documentation and banking service
7. Insurance coverage
8. Advancement of foreign and domestic charges
9. Foreign customs clearance and reforwarding by foreign branches or agents

[4] Muller, *op. cit.*, pp. 49, 53.

10. Credit, collection, and C.O.D. service through foreign branches or agents
11. Consultation service for shippers on United States and foreign policies, decisions, rules, and regulations affecting air transport, currency, and customs formalities

1. Consolidation of shipments by foreign branches or agents
2. United States Customs inspection, appraisal, and clearance services
3. Documentation services for clearance
4. Advancement of freight charges, custom duties, and C.O.D.s
5. Bonded storage for in-transit shipment
6. Domestic reforwarding and transshipment services
7. Consultation service for consignees on United States policies, decisions, rules, and regulations affecting air transport, currencies, and customs formalities

CUSTOMHOUSE BROKERS

The function of the customhouse broker is to clear his client's imported merchandise through customs. As with all specialized services, the customhouse broker also serves as an adviser to the importer in considerations affecting landed costs.

Brief reference to Chapters 16 and 17, dealing with restrictions on imports, will indicate the detailed and current knowledge one must have in order to clear merchandise with the least delay and smallest over-all expense. Tariff rates are listed in the Tariff act of 1930, as modified by several reciprocal trade agreements, and a summary thereof, *United States Import Duties*, was published in 1948 and again in 1950 by the United States Tariff Commission. The 1950 study is about 350 pages in length and shows the 1930 rates, modifications thereof under various agreements, and the reference for such modification. Supplements to this 1950 study will keep the publication up to date until any revision is issued.

In the importation of any one product, the principal factors which determine duties are classification—determining just exactly what an item is—valuation, and applicable rate. Then such matters enter as marking of the goods, use of certain packing materials, quota restrictions, and other applicable taxes. Any person is free to make his own entries, but time limitations, routine delays, and the high penalty for errors render this activity more than usually specialized.

Customs Procedure Calls for Specialized Knowledge. When a customs entry is made, an estimated duty is paid by the importer. It is only a deposit, for when liquidation of duty is made, the official amount of duty is established. This may take several months, and the importer is liable for additional duties then determined, even though the merchandise may long since have left his inventory. It thus behooves the importer to exercise best judgment in entering merchandise through customs. This best judgment is probably evidenced by engaging the specialized service of a customhouse broker; informal estimates are that well over 90 per cent of the importers in the United States use customhouse brokers.

Customhouse Brokers Are Licensed. By Sec. 641 of the Tariff Act of 1930, customhouse brokers must be licensed by the Secretary of the Treasury. No license is required, though, for a person to transact business with a customhouse if it pertains to his own importations. Individuals, partnerships, or corporations may be so licensed and the Secretary of the Treasury may require, as a condition to granting of a license, the "showing of such facts as he may deem advisable as to the qualifications of the applicant to render valuable service to the importers and exporters."[5] This calls for an examination, a high standard of knowledge of customs law, and the possession of satisfactory character and good reputation in the trade.[6]

Licenses may be revoked or suspended by the Secretary of the Treasury if the broker is shown to be incompetent, disreputable, or to have refused to comply with rules and regulations of Sec. 641 of the Tariff Act of 1930 or if he has "with intent to defraud, in any manner wilfully and knowingly deceived, misled or threatened any importer, exporter, claimant, or client, or prospective importer, exporter, claimant, or client, by word, circular, letter or by advertisement."

In carrying out this regulatory power, the Secretary of the Treasury is authorized to prescribe rules and regulations which may require the keeping of books, records, documents, and correspondence by customhouse brokers, the inspection thereof, and the furnishing by them of information relating to their business to any duly accredited agent of the United States.

As of July, 1950, there were about 2,000 licensed customhouse brokers in the United States.

Indication of the keen interest customhouse brokers have in preserving their position as sole authorized representatives of importers is the opposition reported to have developed in early 1950 as the result of the proposal by overseas airlines whereby these airlines would handle the customs entries on imports shipments valued at $100 or less.

[5] Sec. 641(a), Tariff Act of 1930.

[6] Winslow Manly, "Import Customs Clearance," *The International Trader*, 1949, p. 126.

PACKAGING AND COOPERAGE FIRMS

Although many exporters are in a position to pack for export through their own facilities, the volume of business is such that a number of firms have been established to provide specialized service of this type, especially at ports. Importance of the function can best be seen by considering the job to be done.

All cumulative expense and effort on any shipment are wasted if the merchandise does not reach destination in good condition. Because of many hazards or risks, the only satisfactory means of avoiding this waste is by proper precaution in the form of protection. This is the job of packaging, and principal risks which are overcome or significantly reduced by proper packaging are pilferage, rust or corrosion, water damage, breakage, and concealed damage. Pilferage is theft of part of the contents from a package. Concealed damage is internal breakage or injury not apparent on the surface. Distance, time, heat, rain or spray, sunshine, open storage, several handlings, and a few other factors arising in various ports of the world all contribute to these hazards.

Packaging Influences Transportation Costs and Duties. The problem of protection against these risks must be weighed against more than merely cost of packaging, which in itself is an item of importance.[7] Because of the influence of ocean-shipping rates and customs duties, export packaging presents a problem somewhat different from that of domestic packaging. Ocean rates are usually based on weight or cubic measurement, at ship's option. This means that the rate charged will be the higher of the two. Accordingly, it behooves the shipper to pack his goods so as to reduce them to the smallest occupancy of space. Physical weight cannot be reduced; shape or size may be changed under certain conditions. Thus, type of packing or crating affords an opportunity to pay either more or less in transportation costs. Packing or crating must be able to withstand stowage patterns, including stacking.

Overpacking may itself be unwise, for in some countries customs duties are based on the gross weight of a shipment, including packing. At the same time, there is not much wisdom in crating a case of canned goods or crackers with protection called for by the weight or shape of a piece of heavy and valuable machinery. Loss experience also affects insurance rates.

In meeting these requirements, then, the packaging that is adopted must assure that outside containers are well closed and will remain so; that the package has been reduced in size to permit application of weight as a basis for rate charges if possible, that the interior packing, wrapping,

[7] Export-packaging costs are said to range from about 3 to 20 per cent of the value of the goods shipped.

and bracing are sufficient for the purpose; and that the package can stand the strain imposed by the stacking or palletizing of others over it.

Losses Due to Faulty Packing Are High in Some Lines. At an export-packing panel of the Propeller Club Convention in New York, in 1949, it was disclosed that export-packing losses are highest in the glassware, textiles, and hard-goods fields. A great part of the damage seems to occur even before the goods are loaded aboard ship, and estimates of annual losses as high as $1,000,000,000 due to faulty packing have been suggested. There has been no accurate tally made of these total losses, and it is felt by some that the assertions may be exaggerated. In connection with the belief that a great part of the damage occurs during handling and even before being loaded aboard ship, a report of the Westinghouse Electric Corporation, compiled in 1950, illustrates the damage to porcelain-enameled refrigerators when moved by various types of carriers and at various stages of their movement. This information was developed by attaching an electric shock recorder to a conventionally crated refrigerator to measure the degree of shock at various stages. It was found that relatively little shock was experienced while the shipment was en route and that impact reached its highest stages during handling, during the switching and car shifting of railroad freight, and while moving over rough streets and bridges when transported by truck. Air, truck, railroad express, and railroad freight were the means of transit tested, and the type of transportation used offered little significant difference in the bumping or jolting received by the package.[8] The survey did not include steamships or other water carriers, nor did it cover the varied handling facilities at foreign ports, but there seems to be no reason to suspect that experience would be any different. In any case, practically all shipments must move by two or more means of transportation, and the purpose of the survey was to measure the degree of shock, as well as the timing. The results of the survey make it easier to determine the type of packaging necessary to afford protection.

Many Losses Are Preventable. One insurance underwriter states that, although in a ten-year average period before the war about 53 per cent of all his company's losses were preventable, this figure rose to 68 per cent in 1946 and to 79 per cent in 1947. Losses from theft and pilferage, which were 8 per cent in the ten-year average period, were 35 per cent of total preventable loss in 1946 and 43 per cent in 1947.[9]

Packaging and cooperage firms sell their services to shippers or to forwarders; their service include such activities as picking up, crating, waterproofing, storing, shipping, marking, and preparing packing lists. In general, these firms attend to the physical preparation and handling of

---

[8] *Business Week,* June 24, 1950, pp. 42–44.
[9] *Export Trade and Shipper,* Feb. 7, 1949, p. 9.

the merchandise, as contrasted with the forwarder, who arranges for this function (unless he should have such facilities available) and deals with documents, schedules, insurance, financing, and coordination of all these operations.

MARINE INSURANCE

A principal difference between domestic- and foreign-transportation service is to be found in the risk assumed by the common carrier.

Ocean Carriers' Responsibility Limited by Law. In foreign shipping, the ocean bill of lading greatly limits the shipping company's responsibility; by law (Harter Act of 1893 and Carriage of Goods by Sea Act of 1936), the shipping company's responsibilty is also limited. The Carriage of Goods by Sea Act reads, in part:

Neither the carrier nor the ship shall be responsible for loss or damage arising or resulting from—

Act, neglect, or default of the master, mariner, pilot, or the servants of the carrier in the navigation or in the management of the ship;
Perils, dangers, and accidents of the sea or other navigable waters;
Act of God;
Act of war;
Act of public enemies;
Arrest or restraint of princes, rulers, or people, or seizure under legal process;
Strikes or lockouts or stoppage or restaint of labor from whatever cause, whether partial or general: Provided, that nothing herein contained shall be construed to relieve a carrier from responsibility for the carrier's own acts;
Riots and civil commotions;
Saving or attempting to save life or property at sea.

Several other situations are outlined which excuse the carrier from liability. On the other hand, the same Act provides that the carrier must make the ship seaworthy, must properly man, equip, and supply the ship, and must make the holds, refrigerating and cool chambers, and all other parts of the ship in which goods are carried "fit and safe for their reception, carriage and preservation."

It is seen that a fine line may have to be drawn at times to determine whether the carrier has exercised due diligence in these responsibilities. In any case, the exceptions to liability on the part of the shipping company require that these risks be borne and covered elsewhere.

Terms Commonly Used. The marine-insurance policy covers basically the perils of the sea such as stranding, sinking, burning of the vessel, and collision. Coverage can be extended to "all risks," which include loss from unusual and unforeseen hazards as well as the perils named

above. They do not mean loss of markets, deterioration, and inherent vice
(some characteristic of the merchandise which will bring destruction
from within). These risks all imply loss or damage to the specific merchandise, in the coverage of which certain terms are used:

1. FREE OF PARTICULAR AVERAGE (F.P.A.). This may be interpreted as
"free of partial loss." In this sense, *average* means loss or damage.
Particular refers to the specific goods insured. This clause bears two
standard qualifications—F.P.A., A.C. (American conditions) and F.P.A.,
E.C. (European conditions). Under the former, the damage, to be covered, must be *caused* by the vessel's being stranded, sunk, burned, or in
collision. The latter is more liberal, reading: "Free of Particular Average
unless the vessel, craft or lighter be stranded, sunk, burned or in collision." Under American conditions, then, the loss must be the direct
result of the named perils, while under European conditions, it is not
necessary that the loss be the direct result of the named perils, provided
one of these perils did befall the vessel during the voyage.

2. 3% PARTICULAR AVERAGE. This clause reads "subject to," and not
"free of," particular average unless caused by stranding, sinking, fire, or
collision. In case any of the named perils occurs, coverage will be by the
F.P.A. clause; in case the named perils do not occur, coverage will be
by this clause, provided the loss amounts to 3 per cent or more, in which
case the loss is paid in full.[10]

In this connection, it may be specified that each package be separately
insured, which is a little broader coverage than if the 3 per cent applies
to the whole shipment. For example, if two packages are shipped,
each worth $1,000, and each package is separately insured, a loss of any-
thing over $30 on either package will render insurance payable; if the
whole shipment is covered, the loss will have to be $60 before insurance
can be collected. This loss or damage could occur by shifting in heavy
seas, by water entering the hold, or by some other act not related to
the four basic perils.

3. WITH AVERAGE. This clause covers all loss by perils of the sea, regardless of amount. Sometimes called "average irrespective of percentage," this type of insurance is more expensive than are either of the types
listed so far. It covers general average contribution, if one should be
necessary, and offers particular average protection as well.

Shipment Considered a Joint Venture. The term "general average" is
very significant, since risk attaches to the merchandise from causes other
than loss or damage to that particular merchandise. The voyage may be

---

[10] This feature may be contrasted with the $50-deductible clause common in auto-
mobile insurance. Under the deductible clause, only losses above that sum are
covered. Under the 3% particular average clause, no loss is covered unless it amounts
to at least 3 per cent, but if the loss is that high, the total loss is covered.

compared to a joint venture by all shippers and the carrier, in which loss or damage to any one shipper's goods *for the common benefit of all* must be borne by all and not only by the shipper whose goods were damaged. For example, if it became necessary to throw overboard cargo to lighten the ship, and thus to save the ship and other cargo, the shipper whose goods were lost would be reimbursed, with all contributing on a pro rata basis according to over-all valuation of the cargo and ship. Or a vessel may be on fire; water and steam used to extinguish the fire may damage other cargo not touched by the fire. This would be a "voluntary" damage to save the entire ship, from which the ship and the undamaged cargo would have benefited. Another example would be the expense of floating a vessel when stranded.

Joint Risk Is Designated "General Average." This risk is called "general average," and all marine policies include such coverage. In order for general average loss to be declared, the peril must be such as to endanger the entire venture, a voluntary sacrifice or extraordinary expenditure must be incurred to conquer the peril, and there must be a remainder or preserved part of the venture to which part of the loss may be assigned. The carrier holds a lien on cargo pending settlement of general average loss, and the goods will be released on posting of a bond by the underwriter, if the goods are insured, or of a cash deposit by the owner, if the goods are not insured.

As an illustration of the operation of a general average contribution, assume that a fire occurs, destroying or damaging some cargo. In putting out the fire, water damage occurs to other cargo. The destruction or damage by fire is not a voluntary sacrifice, so the loss resulting from this cause constitutes a particular average claim against the cargo underwriters. But water damage to the other cargo was due to a voluntary act on the part of the master of the vessel, in the common interest of all, and would constitute a basis for general average contribution. In determining the contribution, the party whose merchandise was so damaged by fire would not be reimbursed in full; he, too, would have to stand a proportionate loss.

The three types of clauses explained above pertain to perils of the sea. But there are also other risks arising from external causes which may and should be insured against, such as theft, pilferage, breakage, leakage, and nondelivery. For each additional risk covered, the premium naturally must increase. As completeness of coverage increases, the type of clause reads: "average *plus* theft, pilferage, breakage," etc.

4. ALL-RISK CLAUSE. Finally, the most extensive, and most expensive, coverage is identified as the "all-risk clause." This reads as follows: "To cover all risks of physical loss or damage from any external cause, irrespective of percentage, including theft, pilferage and non-delivery."

This clause is widely used in connection with manufactured goods and clearly offers the most complete coverage. However, the underwriter will wish to satisfy himself as to the commodity and packing before covering with this clause.

Distinction between Underwriter and Broker. Two specific functional elements must be recognized in marine insurance. One is the underwriter, the other the broker. The underwriter is the company which insures the specific risks (the term may also be used to designate the individual who selects risks for his company to insure). The broker is the link between the shipper (or shipper's agent) and the underwriter. He acts on behalf of the shipper in placing the insurance in the company offering most advantageous terms or conditions. The underwriter may employ or appoint agents, who are paid by the underwriter for seeking out risks and in doing so, agents act for their principals (the underwriters), while brokers act for their principals (the shippers).

COMMUNICATIONS

One of the most important services to the exporter and the importer in the entering of international transactions is the communications network. These services may be grouped under the four general headings of mail, cable, telephone, and radio, each of which deserves detailed attention.

Mail

Starting with ordinary steamer mail, written communications now make wide use of air service, through which a letter, picture, or catalogue may now reach any part of the world in just a few days. Postal service is also available for the shipment of certain types of merchandise, through use of the same facilities as those which carry written communications.

In the United States, the postal system is arranged into seven international mail ports officially known as mail-exchange offices. Mail originating in different parts of the country, which is organized into 15 railway-mail-service divisions, is forwarded for overseas transmittal to these designated mail ports. These mail ports are New York, New Orleans, San Francisco, Philadelphia, Miami, Seattle, and San Pedro. One mail port may be designated for all United States mail or parcel post going to a certain country, or mail originating in different parts of the United States may be sent to a designated port. Similarly, some are designated to handle mail only, while others handle parcel post only for named foreign destinations.

Incoming parcel post is funneled to mail-exchange offices at which customs service is available.

Universal Postal Union. To permit a more adequate international mail service, several conferences have been held in the past, and there is now in force a Universal Postal Union, dating from 1874, and a Postal Union of the Americas and Spain, the first convention being signed in 1911. The former has codified a body of regulations which governs the international exchange of mail matter within the postal territory of the Union. Each member is obligated to permit foreign mail to circulate within its territory as freely as its own and, for a just and reasonable compensation, to forward such mail matter to its destination by the most rapid means available. Practically all nations of the world are members of the Universal Postal Union.

Under provisions of the Universal Postal Union, regional organizations are authorized for the purpose of reducing postal rates or otherwise improving postal relations. The United States is a member of one of these —the Postal Union of the Americas and Spain. Under a recent convention (Rio de Janeiro, 1946), each member is guaranteed free transit of its mail across the territories and by the ships of the registry or flag of other member states. The convention also provides that domestic rates will be applicable to regular mail exchanged between the member states, and generous franking privileges are granted to diplomatic, consular, official, and cultural correspondence.

Cable

Cable services are available from any telegraph station in the United States to practically any city in the world. Service is classed as (1) ordinary, which may be full worded or in code, (2) deferred, which moves at reduced rates but is transmitted after ordinary full rate and code messages have cleared, and (3) night letter, which is delayed in transmission until all other services have cleared and which is not delivered until the day after filing. In cable service, the address is charged for at the scheduled rate per word, and the full rate has no minimum number of words in the message. Code and deferred service require 5 words minimum rate, and night-letter charges are based on messages allowing 25 words, with an extra charge for each additional word. Selected rates are shown in Table 34.

Of 20 transatlantic cables in operation in early 1951, 16 were owned and operated by United States interests (Western Union Telegraph Company and International Telephone and Telegraph Company) and the remainder by foreign interests, mainly British and French.[11]

[11] *Business Week,* Jan. 20, 1951, p. 39.

For many years cable service to many parts of the world, developed and operated by British interests, imposed discriminatory treatment on United States interests in matters of cost and time. But in 1945, a British–United States conference held in Bermuda considered the problem; some but not all of the difficulties were eliminated by agreement. Further international conferences are indicated as likely to resolve the problems to an acceptable solution.

Codes may be commercial or private, but both the sender and the receiver must have a key to the code. On many letterheads or other correspondence forms, the code or codes used are shown and, in the case of commercial codes, ciphering and deciphering catalogues are provided. Among the well-known commercial codes are Western Union Telegraphic, A.B.C. (sixth edition), Acme, Bentley's, and Lieber's. Other commercial codes designated especially for certain trades or industries may be used. The purpose of the commercial code is not secrecy, but merely the reduction of communications to fewer words—economy in transmission.

Private codes, on the other hand, are specially designed for more restricted use and may be either for the purpose of economizing on cable expense (beyond what the commercial code offers) or for greater secrecy in communications.

Radio

With the commercial application of wireless telegraphy and the subsequent transmission by voice, this type of communication opened a new facility to the foreign trader. Communication between ship and shore, plane and land, and points on the earth not connected by wire have brought distance down to a negligible factor in business negotiations.

Radio-message and cable rates are competitive in price, and each seems to have some advantage over the other. Radio can reach places not linked by cable, and such troubles as line breakages are no problem. On the other hand, cable transmission is not so susceptible to weather conditions, and the transmission facility may offer some advantages through code messages which are directed to one point only; the possibility of interception is minimized. About two-thirds of transatlantic messages move via cable; radio carries the rest.[12]

The important part played in foreign commerce by communications can hardly be exaggerated. Services offered are substantially the same as in domestic communications, and a degree of standardization is brought about through control of both facilities by some of the same large companies or governments.

[12] *Ibid.*

Telephone

Through radio-telephone link,[13] it is possible for a businessman in the United States to reach most of the important cities of the world from his own telephone. This feature is expensive, but cost is sometimes offset by the advantages of speaking with another person rather than sending a message through third hands and waiting for a reply. Overseas telephone service from the United States is routed through New York, San Francisco, Seattle, and Miami. Typical of rates prevailing in late 1950 are those shown in Table 34.

Table 34. Selected Radio, Cable, and Telephone Rates*
(As of November, 1950)

| Country | Radio and cable from United States | | | | Telephone (New York City) first three minutes |
| | Full rate | | Letter rate | | |
	Minimum 5 words	Additional per word	Minimum 22 words	Additional per word	
Argentina	$1.35	27¢	$2.97	9.5¢	$12.00
Belgian Congo	1.50	30	3.30	15.0	15.00
Cuba	0.95	19	2.09	9.5	5.25
Egypt	1.50	30	3.30	15.0	12.00
France	1.15	23	2.53	11.5	12.00
India	1.15	23	2.53	11.5	15.00
Japan	1.50	30	3.30	15.0	12.00
United Kingdom	0.95	19	2.09	9.5	12.00
Union of South Africa	1.15	23	2.53	11.5	15.00

* Radio and cable messages subject to 10-per-cent federal tax; telephone rates subject to 25-per-cent federal tax.

SOURCE: *Exporters' Digest*, November, 1950, p. 48A.

INSPECTORS AND WEIGHERS

When a shipment is ordered, especially by sample or classification, with payment to be made based on documentary evidence, a survey is sometimes required to assure that the merchandise is as ordered. Among features which may be the subject of coverage by a certificate or inspection are condition, quantity, quality, and packing. Inspection may be required by law, as in the case of grain or other animal and plant shipments. At other times, staple commodities sold by designation, such as raw cotton, may call for inspection or warehouse certification of the

[13] Wire connection reaches Canada, Cuba, and Mexico.

goods before shipment to assure that the type ordered is that delivered.

Another service to the exporter and importer pertains to weights, especially those which change in transit because of the absorption of moisture or the process of drying out. Also, commodities such as coffee shipped in bags may not only change in weight during a lengthy voyage, but some of the merchandise may be lost through openings in the bags; at times the losses of several bags will be swept up and resacked.

These inspecting and weighing services may be performed by the exporter or importer himself, to the satisfaction of all concerned, but at other times the inspection or weighing may have to take place where no direct representation is advisable, or where an independent survey is desired by one or both parties to the transaction. In major ports, public weighers and public inspectors or laboratories are to be found as a specialized service to foreign commerce.

WAREHOUSEMEN

In the synchronization of production-marketing-shipping schedules, merchandise must be stored in a safe place. This is the job of the warehouseman, who is an important factor in foreign commerce. Storage space may be at dockside, in the interior of the port, or even inland. Field warehousing is widely practiced. The warehouses may be bonded, for the purpose of storing imports pending their entry for consumption or reexport, or pending seasoning or processing. A special type of warehouse of particular interest to foreign commerce is the "free zone," discussed in Chapter 19, which may be publicly or privately operated.

Only a limited free time is allowed shipments in railroad cars before demurrage becomes applicable. The storage of such a commodity as cotton in Southern ports pending export is a usual practice in this trade.

It can be seen that, while one may not ordinarily consider a warehouseman in, say, New Orleans to be in foreign trade, the larger part of his business may be in goods whose last or next steps pertain to import or export.

LEGAL AND ARBITRATION SERVICES

International and maritime lawyers are specialists in this aspect of foreign commerce and relations. Their field of activity is naturally in large cities or ports and, in conjunction with established arbitration facilities, constitutes an important service to foreign commercial interests.

Owing to the expense, delay, and probable damage to good will involved in court settlement of disputes, a promising development has been

the rapid growth of arbitration as the most satisfactory means of reconciling differences. The idea of arbitration is merely the prior agreement
that any dispute will be settled by submission of the issue to a third
party. This third party may be one person or more—occasionally three,
with one representative named by each principal and the third selected
by these two representatives. Formal organization may be provided for
in advance, as indicated below. Arbitration findings are binding, by prior
agreement and legal support, and a number of facilities have been established to render the procedure more widely used.

American Arbitration Association. The American Arbitration Association was formed in 1926 as a nonprofit group. It has been the center of
United States activities of the Inter-American Commercial Arbitration
Commission, the Canadian-American, the Chinese-American, and the
Philippine-American Commissions. Reciprocal relationships are also
maintained with other groups interested in facilitating arbitration, such
as the International Chamber of Commerce, the London Court of Arbitration, the Manchester (England) Chamber of Commerce, the American Chamber of Commerce in London, and the Netherlands Chamber
of Commerce in New York.

It is emphasized by authorities that the proper time to arrange for
arbitration is when the contract is first drawn, for at that time good will
is high and the possibility of a dispute can be looked on as something
remote—something that may happen, and not something which already
has occurred.

Lists are maintained of qualified arbitrators who are specialists in
various lines of trade. The procedure is for each party to look over the
list and cross off the names of any arbitrator not acceptable to him.
No reason need be given for doing so. The remaining names are then
numbered in order of preference and the arbitrators having the highest
degree of joint preference become the ones to arbitrate the controversy.[14]

It is also emphasized that the only satisfactory agreement calls not
only for the act of arbitration but also for a clear statement as to how
arbitration is to take place, if necessary, and when and where. Recommended clauses have been drawn up by the American Arbitration Association to cover arbitration in countries other than in the Western
Hemisphere, in the United States, and in Latin-American contracts. The
latter reads as follows:[15]

Any controversy or claim arising out of or relating to this contract or the
breach thereof, shall be settled by arbitration, in accordance with the Rules,
then obtaining, of the Inter-American Commercial Arbitration Commission.

[14] George N. Butler, "Arbitration's Tested Techniques Smooth World-trade Paths,"
Foreign Commerce Weekly, June 5, 1948, p. 5.
[15] *Ibid.,* p. 4.

This agreement shall be enforceable, and judgment upon any award rendered by all or a majority of the arbitrators may be entered in any court having jurisdiction. The arbitration shall be held in_____ or wherever jurisdiction may be obtained over the parties.

REVIEW QUESTIONS

1. List the principal services comprising the foreign-commerce "fraternity."
2. What services do commercial banks perform for foreign commerce?
3. What is the role of Federal Reserve banks and of investment banking in the conduct of foreign commerce?
4. What are "essential" trade routes?
5. What are the advantages offered by air shipment over surface transport?
6. List the principal functions of a foreign freight forwarder.
7. In what way are forwarders subject to government regulations?
8. Where are foreign freight forwarders located?
9. What is a customhouse broker?
10. Why is packaging so important in foreign commerce?
11. Distinguish between general average and particular average. Is there a difference between marine insurance and insurance against theft, pilferage, breakage, etc., while the goods are on a vessel on the high seas?
12. What is the Universal Postal Union?
13. Why are weighers and inspectors important in the conduct of foreign commerce?
14. What are the benefits to be derived through arbitration rather than through courts of law?

CHAPTER 7

Organizational Structure: Government Agencies

There are many government institutions and activities in the field of foreign commerce necessitated by the variety of restrictions on imports and exports and, at the same time, by public efforts to promote foreign commerce. They are needed, also, to care for administrative and operational responsibilities deriving from laws relating to foreign commerce of the United States.

Several Governmental Departments Are Active in Foreign Commerce. Among federal government departments or agencies having an interest in foreign commerce or its conduct, and their specific responsibilities, are:

National Advisory Council: Coordination of policies and operations of representatives of the United States on International Monetary Fund, International Bank for Reconstruction and Development, Export-Import Bank, and all other government agencies engaged in foreign lending and financial, exchange, and monetary transactions.

Department of State: Basic economic aspects of over-all United States foreign economic policy; the Foreign Service of the United States; Reciprocal Trade Agreements program; passports and immigration (with Department of Justice); intergovernmental commodity arrangements; international monetary problems.

Treasury Department: Administration of customs laws; collection of duties and certain import taxes; international monetary problems.

Department of Commerce: Link between United States business and the Foreign Service of the United States; collection of official statistics on foreign commerce; educational activities; administration of export-control program; administration of import-quota program (with Department of Agriculture); administration of Foreign Trade Zones Act; administration of Federal Maritime Board; administration of government rubber program; publication of such periodicals as *Foreign*

129

Commerce Weekly, Foreign Commerce Yearbook, Survey of Current Dusiness, and Foreign Commerce and Navigation of the United States.

Department of Agriculture: Inspection of certain imports to prevent spread of diseases; control over exports of tobacco plants and seeds; through Office of Foreign Agricultural Relations, acting for farm interests in foreign agricultural matters in somewhat similar capacity as does Department of Commerce in business matters; through Production and Marketing Administration, administration of commodity-export programs; determination of import quotas on certain agricultural products; indirectly, interested in effect of imports on agricultural price-support programs; under the Insecticide Act, joins with Treasury Department and Department of Commerce in enforcement of this law; under Federal Seed Act, joins with Treasury Department in enforcement.

Department of Defense: Determination of list of strategic and critical materials and administration of stock-piling program; with other appropriate departments and agencies (State, Commerce, Treasury, Mutual Security Agency, etc.) participates in formulation of government policy regarding foreign economic defense measures.

Department of Labor: Primary responsibility for United States participation in International Labour Organisation; statutory membership on Board of Foreign Service.

Post Office Department: Administration of international mail ports and interest in international postal matters.

United States Tariff Commission: Investigatory and advisory functions regarding tariff matters and economic effect of foreign commerce.

Federal Trade Commission: Administration and enforcement of Webb-Pomerene Export Trade Act.

Federal Security Agency: Through Food and Drug Administration, issuance of regulations governing importation of teas; administration of Federal Food, Drug and Cosmetic Act.

Securities and Exchange Commission: Jurisdiction over public distribution of certain foreign securities.

Department of Justice: Jurisdiction over alien property; representation of government in proceedings brought by importers in United States Customs Court.

Director of Mutual Security: On behalf of the President directs, supervises, and coordinates the programs of military, economic, and technical assistance without, however, infringing on the powers or functions of the Secretaries of State and Defense. The Mutual Security Agency, newly created in 1951, succeeded the Economic Cooperation Administration on Dec. 31, 1951, and exercises the functions formerly vested in that organization in administering the European Recovery Program, as modified and expanded.[1]

United States Public Health Service: Administration of quarantine regulations and regulations pertaining to importation of disease organisms and vectors.

Export-Import Bank: Credits to facilitate exports and imports.

In addition to federal departments or agencies, state and municipal interest is based on the establishment and operation of ports and other services to attract the routing of commerce through them.

These varied and extended interests and their detailed organizational position and coordination within government could be the subject of a study in itself. For purposes of this text, however, attention can be restricted to certain organizations selected because of their wide or direct influence on the conduct of foreign commerce. These are:

The Department of State
The Department of Commerce
The Department of Agriculture
The Customs Service
The United States Tariff Commission
The Export-Import Bank
Foreign Consular offices
Ports

Only those aspects of organization and activity pertaining to foreign commerce will be described.

U.S. DEPARTMENT OF STATE

In the implementation of foreign economic policy, principal responsibility for intergovernmental negotiation rests with the Department of State. Since many of the underlying problems involve foreign commerce, it is proper to pay considerable attention to this unit of government in the study of foreign commerce. Moreover, the Department is active in interdepartmental coordination bearing on foreign commercial policy because of the political implications of major commercial questions.

The Department is under the direction of the Secretary of State, who is a member of the President's Cabinet and his principal adviser in the determination and execution of American foreign policy. His top assistant is the Under Secretary of State. There are 10 assistant secretaries,

[1] There is a Mutual Assistance Advisory Committee composed of representatives of the Office of the Director for Mutual Security, the Bureau of the Budget, the Departments of State, Treasury, and Defense, the Mutual Security Agency, and the Office of Defense Mobilization.

2 of whom have been designated Deputy Under Secretary. One of the latter is interested in coordination and policy; the other is Deputy Under Secretary for Administration. The remaining 8 assistant secretaries have jurisdiction in the following areas:

Congressional relations
United Nations affairs
Inter-American affairs
European affairs
Far Eastern affairs
Near Eastern, South Asian, and African affairs
Public affairs
Economic affairs

On the same organizational level as the assistant secretaries are the Legal Adviser, Counselor, a Special Assistant for Intelligence, the Administrator of the Technical Cooperation Administration, and the Administrator of the United States International Information Administration.

Almost all major organizational units have some bearing on foreign economic activities. For example, the Administrator of the Technical Cooperation Administration manages the programs for international development known as the Point Four programs. But major interest for the student of foreign commerce is found in two principal offices: the Assistant Secretary for Economic Affairs and the Foreign Service of the United States, which functions under the Deputy Under Secretary for Administration.

Assistant Secretary for Economic Affairs

This official is charged with responsibility for the development of basic economic aspects of over-all United States foreign policy and for assuring consistency among the various components of such policy.[2] To carry out his duties, his bureau is divided into four offices. Each of these is subdivided into functional staffs.

The Office of International Materials Policy is concerned with harmonizing domestic and foreign emergency economic controls; with international measures to stimulate production of basic materials in short supply; with availability for export from the United States and Western European countries of goods essential to meet minimum civilian requirements of other parts of the free world; with availability to the United States of adequate supplies of basic materials; and with promoting multilateral international allocation, if necessary, of materials in short supply.

The Office of Economic Defense and Trade Policy, in collaboration

[2] *United States Government Organization Manual, 1951–52,* 1951, p. 79.

with other governmental departments and agencies, deals with programs and policies for economic defense measures. This includes reconciliation of domestic price control and stabilization policies with levels of import and export trade in relation to foreign policy objectives, and consistency of domestic and foreign conservation measures. In matters of trade policy, it endeavors to promote the maximum flow of trade in items not subject to specific allocation or control. Internationally, it encourages action to eliminate restrictive business practices which prevent increased output.

The Office of Financial and Development Policy is primarily interested in policies with respect to finance, investment, and economic development. These involve, among other things, exchange rates, exchange controls, foreign loans and grants, investment- and property-protection policies, and investment and economic-development programs and policies of foreign countries. Negotiations and administration of the lend-lease and surplus-property agreements are under jurisdiction of this Office.

The Office of Transport and Communications Policy collaborates with other government agencies on transport problems having foreign-policy implications, such as intergovernmental measures for the control of shipping, the international United States civil-air-route pattern, allocation of routes and planes to specific United States carriers, mobilization of foreign facilities and services, and international air priorities.

The Foreign Service of the United States

In American constitutional practice, the President is charged with responsibility for administering the official foreign relations of the United States. The Secretary of State is his agent, the Department of State is the staff, and the Foreign Service is the field agency.[3]

It was not until 1924 that the diplomatic and consular services (until then separate) were combined into a unified Foreign Service. Even after 1924, Congress provided for a foreign-commerce service under the Department of Commerce (1927) and for a foreign-agricultural service under the Department of Agriculture (1930). However, this multiple representation abroad was resolved in 1939, when the two new services were incorporated into the Foreign Service. Although the Foreign Service is administered by the Department of State, the Departments of Agriculture, Commerce, and Labor participate actively in its administration.

Organizationally, the Foreign Service is administered through the Deputy Under Secretary of State for Administration, who is advised on

[3] *Some Facts about the Foreign Service,* U.S. Department of State, Publication 3789, April, 1950, p. 4.

policies governing administration of the Foreign Service by the Director
General of the Foreign Service. Other key functional offices pertaining
to the Foreign Service are the Office of Personnel, the Foreign Service
Inspection Corps, the Office of Security and Consular Affairs, and the
Division of Foreign Reporting. This latter division coordinates the
reporting demands on Foreign Service posts and establishes standards
for economic and politico-economic reporting. The Office of International
Trade, Department of Commerce, is the channel through which the
business community in the United States is normally served in the promotion and protection of foreign trade by the Foreign Service.

The Foreign Service of the United States numbered about 19,000
people in April, 1952. These people were classified as ambassadors,
ministers, Foreign Service officers, Foreign Service reserve officers,
Foreign Service staff officers and employees, consular agents, and local
employees. Prerequisites for appointment to these groups (in addition
to requirements with respect to citizenship, age, physical and mental fit-
ness, loyalty, and security) vary from the highly competitive written and
oral examinations for Foreign Service officers to informal reviews of
qualifications used in selecting Foreign Service reserve officers (who are
appointed for nonconsecutive periods of not more than four years each)
and aptitude tests given to clerks. Ambassadors, ministers, and Foreign
Service officers are appointed by the President, by and with the advice
and consent of the Senate. Other appointments are made by the Secretary
of State.

Foreign Service Has Political and Economic Responsibilities. A distinction should be made between the political and the economic responsibilities of Foreign Service personnel. The former is mainly concerned
with governmental contacts and activities. The latter is the one in which
foreign traders of the United States have most immediate interest, for
work done by the Foreign Service (especially consular officers) in this
sphere is for the benefit of commercial elements in the United States
which are engaged in foreign trade.

Commercial activities of the Foreign Service are varied. Some arise
from the administration of laws and regulations. Others are in the nature
of promotion of commerce and the gathering and interpretation of economic intelligence. Typical of the former are:

1. The issuance of passports to citizens and visas to aliens
2. Documentation of merchandise shipped to the United States
3. Implementation of food and drug laws affecting imports
4. Entries and clearances of United States vessels
5. Protection of American seamen

6. Legal, protective, and advisory services to United States residents and travelers
7. Supplying of information desired by the several departments and agencies of the United States government

While these may all affect the full execution of foreign commercial transactions in some degree, none of them serves to encourage or protect trade as such, except possibly the item having to do with the supplying of information.

Some Activities Are Directly Concerned with Trade Promotion. More specifically, in the field of assisting the foreign trader, the Foreign Service performs a number of services that are of inestimable value and which are obviously expensive to accomplish. These services fall into two broad categories, namely, trade promotion and trade protection, and may be summarized as follows:

Trade promotion:

1. Reporting on concrete trade opportunities for the benefit of American importers and exporters, as well as opportunities for the employment of American techniques, engineering and production skills and other professional skills and services.
2. Reporting on the potentialities of overseas areas and districts as markets for American products and as sources of supply to the American economy.
3. Submitting trade lists of commercial firms (see Fig. 14).
4. Investigating and submitting World Trade Directory Reports on the general standing and distributing capacity of foreign firms (see Fig. 15).
5. Facilitating and reporting in advance on proposed visits of alien professional men and businessmen to the United States so that interested firms and agencies may have the opportunity to meet them.
6. Maintaining commercial reading rooms which contain current copies of American daily newspapers, trade journals, and catalogues for the use of local businessmen.
7. Lending direct assistance to American businessmen abroad, including salesmen, buyers, and other representatives of American manufacturers, exporters, and importers, by supplying appropriate information and by facilitating their legitimate business.
8. Encouraging the establishment of, and supporting, American chambers of commerce.
9. Performing trade conference work, when in the United States, not only for the federal government but for chambers of commerce,

foreign-trade associations, exporters, importers, and other business-men or organizations having trade problems or an interest in conditions abroad.

Trade protection:

1. Observing and reporting on discriminations against American business interests in other countries.
2. Guarding against infringement of rights of American citizens in matters relating to commerce and navigation, including patents and copyrights.
3. Furnishing information regarding national and local laws and administrative regulations serving to restrict trade, and monopolies operating in restraint of trade.
4. Investigating and reporting on restrictions on commercial travel.
5. Endeavoring to adjust and obtain settlement of trade complaints filed against American exporters.
6. Assisting in the appointments of boards of survey to examine and report on the condition of American merchandise imported into foreign countries when complaints are made by importers.
7. Aiding the arbitration of trade disputes by submitting names of individuals considered competent to act as arbitrators (but Foreign Service officers may not act as such arbitrators).

Some of the types of information listed are obviously of only limited interest, while others are of sufficient interest or applicability to be made public at little or no direct cost to the individual receiving the information. The economic intelligence so collected is the basis for and appears in several publications, which are described in Chapter 19.

Consular Offices Are Maintained All over the World. Generally speaking, practically all foreign areas of sufficient economic importance to United States government and business interests are covered by consular officers assigned to diplomatic missions (embassy or legation) at foreign capitals or to separate consular posts at other places in foreign countries.

We find consular representation in practically every United States mission at foreign capitals and in a great many cities and towns outside the capitals throughout the rest of the world. Commercial attachés, however, are assigned only to missions. In April, 1952, there were 178 separate United States consular offices, exclusive of consular sections of the 73 missions and the 29 consular agencies. The countries having the greatest number of consular offices are Mexico, Canada, and Brazil. In many countries, such as the Soviet Union, Ceylon, Iceland, and Afghanistan, there are no consular offices other than those in the missions.

The highest ranking consular office is the consulate general. In April, 1952, there were 52 offices of this rank. Next in rank is the consulate, of which there were 126. In past years there were a few vice-consulates, but there are none at present. At one time the United States had a few honorary consuls, but there are none of these at present.

The lowest ranking consular office abroad is the American consular agency, of which there were 29 in early 1952, all but 3 of which were in Latin-American countries. Consular agents are part-time employees, many of whom are foreign nationals. The duties of an agent are primarily of a routine consular nature. They certify consular invoices and perform certain shipping and protection-of-seamen services. A permanent agent also performs notarial services, but an acting agent is not legally authorized to perform notarial services. Consular agents are appointed at places where the volume of consular work does not warrant establishment of a higher ranking consular office. They are valuable in representing the interests of the United States, and some assist supervising consular offices by reporting economic and commercial data.

UNITED STATES DEPARTMENT OF COMMERCE

Several times thus far, mention has been made of activities of the U.S. Department of Commerce in foreign commerce. These cannot well be presented in detail, by organizational and functional chart, because they are subject to occasional change and because some of the activities have only an indirect or casual bearing on the subject. However, it will be of value to outline rather generally where direct interest in foreign commerce rests in the Department of Commerce.

About a dozen bureaus, administrations, and offices comprise the top organizational structure of the Department. Three of these, the Bureau of Foreign and Domestic Commerce, the Bureau of the Census, and the Maritime Administration appear to have most to do directly with foreign commerce. But others, like the National Production Authority, the Civil Aeronautics Administration, the Coast and Geodetic Survey, and the National Bureau of Standards, also have some interest in the subject. In addition, the Foreign Trade Zones Board, which is charged with administering the Foreign Trade Zones Act, is lodged administratively in the Department of Commerce. The Census Bureau compiles and reports monthly and annual tabulations of official foreign-trade statistics. The Maritime Administration has jurisdiction over the merchant marine and foreign freight forwarders.

Bureau of Foreign and Domestic Commerce

This Bureau consists of four offices. They are the Office of International Trade, Office of Business Economics, Office of Industry and Commerce, and Office of Field Service.

In carrying out its functions, the Bureau of Foreign and Domestic Commerce offers the United States businessman personal and published aids in the fields of international and domestic commerce and industry. These aids are based on (1) an intimate knowledge of business both at home and abroad; (2) a storehouse of information and statistics of interest and value to business which are evaluated, interpreted, and analyzed for easy assimilation; and (3) a constant scrutiny of trends through which the changing needs of business are anticipated and special helps are created.

In the foreign field, this Bureau, through its analytical and informational services, is the major governmental source of data on economic trends and developments abroad, particularly as they affect American business, and on exchange, tariff, and trade controls and other foreign regulations of special concern to United States exporters and importers. It follows trends in the market situation in foreign countries and in the flow of international trade and keeps the public apprised of resource development abroad and foreign investment trends and opportunities.

Office of International Trade. As its name suggests, the Office of International Trade is mainly interested in foreign commerce. In carrying out its responsibilities, it

. . . promotes the expansion and balanced growth of international trade; cooperates with other nations in the solving of trade and exchange problems through international organizations, conferences, and otherwise; seeks to reduce obstacles and restrictions abroad affecting international trade and to stabilize international economic relations; and participates with other governmental agencies in the formulation of American foreign economic policies.[4]

The Office furnishes a wide range of statistical and analytical foreign-trade information vital to the government in carrying out the defense program and to the business community in the conduct of international trade and business abroad. It maintains current information on the business standing or facilities of more than 300,000 foreign firms and individuals engaged in international trade, and prepares trade lists, classified by commodity and country, covering foreign suppliers, importers and dealers, and service organizations and professional groups. It brings specific trade opportunities to the attention of United States exporters and importers, supplies useful information on trade problems and procedures, and helps in resolving trade disagreements between United States and foreign businessmen.

Through the exercise of export-control authority, the Office regulates the flow of United States commodities to foreign countries so as to

[4] *United States Government Organization Manual, 1951–52,* p. 267.

assure the equitable distribution of the supplies which can be spared and to serve national-security and foreign-policy objectives.

The Office maintains liaison with the Foreign Service of the United States, being especially interested in the coverage and frequency of reports requested of the Foreign Service, and conducts training courses for Foreign Service personnel.

In addition, the Office takes a responsible part in the development of regulations governing operations in United States foreign-trade zones; coordinates the Point Four program in so far as responsibility of the Department of Commerce is involved; and administers the British Token Import program, under which some 200 products are imported into the United Kingdom up to a stated percentage by value of the exporter's prewar shipments, and the China Trade Act.

The principal publications of the Office are *Foreign Commerce Weekly, Foreign Commerce Yearbook*, reports in *Business Information Service,* and *Comprehensive Export Schedule* with its supplements, *Current Export Bulletins.* These publications are described in some detail in Chapter 19.

The Office of International Trade includes the following major operational units: Office of the Director; Offices of the Assistant Director for Economic Affairs, Assistant Director for Export Supply, Assistant Director for Foreign Development, Assistant Director for Foreign Requirements and Claimancy, and Assistant Director for Intelligence and Services; American Republics Division; British Commonwealth Division; European Division; Far Eastern Division; Near East and African Division; International Economic Analysis Division; Foreign Service Operations Division; Insurance Staff; Transportation Communications and Utilities Division; Travel Division; and Export Supply Divisions for agricultural products, chemicals, finished products, materials, petroleum, and producers' equipment, as well as an Export Control Investigation staff, Operations Division, Projects and Technical Data Division, and Strategic Controls Division.

Other Offices of the Bureau. These other offices of the Bureau of Foreign and Domestic Commerce are described here to the extent that their work touches on foreign trade. The Office of International Trade was discussed in more detail because it is the organizational unit which, perhaps more than any other agency in the executive branch, is *the* government to the average exporter and importer in the conduct of his business.

The Office of Business Economics plays an important role in the foreign field, in that it prepares the annual balance-of-international-payments estimates. Also, it is currently (1952) conducting a census of

American direct investments in foreign countries. This census will provide potential private investors with up to date information regarding
existing American investments abroad—their geographic and industrial
distribution, their value, the amount of capital being currently invested,
and the amount of income received. The services of this Office in the
domestic field are widely known to the public through its monthly publication, *Survey of Current Business.*

The Office of Industry and Commerce is normally the main agency
through which Department of Commerce services in the fields of domestic commodity, distribution, small business, and area development
are made available to business. Its work, especially until late 1950, has
affected United States foreign trade in many ways. At that time, however, a major part of the Office was transferred for an indefinite period
to the newly created National Production Authority. The impact of the
National Production Authority on foreign commerce is principally
through its administration of priorities and allocations.

The Office of Field Service is directly interested in foreign commerce.
The field offices are the principal media for disseminating information
issued by the Bureau of Foreign and Domestic Commerce and for furnishing assistance to businessmen, on a local basis, on all matters relating
to export and import trade.

UNITED STATES DEPARTMENT OF AGRICULTURE

The many activities and interests of the Department of Agriculture in
foreign commerce compel a restriction of attention in this text to the
more direct ones. This excludes regulatory and inspection processes required on the importation of certain products. Instead, we shall deal
with functions of the Department as an "active" participant in foreign
commerce. This action is the responsibility of the Commodity Credit
Corporation and the Production and Marketing Administration.

Commodity Credit Corporation. The Commodity Credit Corporation
acts, among other capacities, as procurement agency for agricultural
commodities desired by other government agencies, foreign governments,
and domestic, foreign, or international rehabilitation agencies. It also
acts as an agent in other special programs relating to both export and
import operations. Specifically, it is authorized to "export or cause to be
exported, or aid in the development of foreign markets for agricultural
commodities." In carrying out its functions, the corporation is charged
with using to the maximum extent practicable the "usual and customary
channels, facilities and arrangements of trade and commerce."

Part of this Corporation's activity is purchasing commodities abroad, such as sugar, rice, copra, beef, vegetable oils, long-staple cotton, and wool. Procurement activities have declined somewhat since 1947, the total foreign purchases appearing below:

1951	$ 63,000,000
1950	31,000,000
1949	121,000,000
1948	242,000,000
1947	382,000,000

The Corporation also participates for the United States government in the International Wheat Agreement. Subsidies paid under this Agreement amounted to $178,200,000 in 1951.

Production and Marketing Administration. The Production and Marketing Administration played a part in the exportation of considerable quantities of the following commodities in the fiscal year 1949:

Wheat and wheat products	Meat
Other grains	Cotton
Fats and oils	Flaxseed
Dairy products	Tobacco
Hemp and flax fiber	Seeds

These "export" programs may be by government operation or through subsidized commercial sales. The latter show export payments for the fiscal year 1949 of $245,000 to exporters of pears, $182,000 to exporters of raisins, $25,000 for prunes, $2,600,000 for tobacco, $780,000 for citrus fruits and juices, and $2,000 for cotton. The subsidy on cotton exports was $2,044,000 for the fiscal year 1948 on the export of 945,000 bales. The number of bales so covered in the fiscal year 1947 was 1,750,000; in 1946, 2,200,000.

The export programs provide for benefit payments to United States exporters of a specified percentage of the sales price f.a.s. United States ports. This subsidy was 20 to 25 per cent for citrus fruits and juices for the fiscal-year-1949 program, and 33⅓ per cent for tobacco. Even higher subsidies are offered at times. For the 1950 program, as an example, the subsidy was up to 50 per cent on apples and pears, but not more than $1.25 per bushel, to encourage exports of these fruits to countries or dependencies approved by the Department of Agriculture. The cost to the government on the pear program was over $100,000; on apples, over $2,400,000.

An indication of the extent of this foreign-trade activity may be seen in Table 35, which appeared in the report of the Production and Marketing Administration for the fiscal year 1949.

The high proportion of total exports accounted for by the Production and Marketing Administration renders this agency of prime significance in the field of agricultural exports.

Table 35. Exports of Selected Agricultural Commodities, Fiscal Year 1949

Total exports		Exports of grain and grain products purchased or acquired under price-support program of Production and Marketing Administration	
Commodity	Quantity, bushels	Commodity	Quantity
Corn and corn products	93,500,000	Corn................	68,363,000 bu.
Oats and oatmeal......	24,100,000	Oats................	7,081,000 bu.
Barley and malt.......	27,400,000	Barley..............	24,188,000 bu.
Grain sorghums........	34,500,000	Grain sorghums.......	27,354,000 bu.
Rye.................	5,400,000	Rye.................	5,346,449 bu.
Wheat and wheat prod-		Rye flour............	4,430,000 lb.
ucts...............	501,000,000	Wheat...............	356,436,000 bu.
		Wheat flour, white....	1,682,347,000 lb.
		Wheat flour, graham...	149,837,000 lb.
		Macaroni............	399,920 lb.

THE CUSTOMS SERVICE

Administration of the Customs Service is the responsibility of the Secretary of the Treasury. He has, under legal authority and subject to certain exceptions and conditions, delegated to the Commissioner of Customs all the rights, privileges, powers, and duties vested in him which pertain to imports and exports of merchandise.

Bureau of Customs. Under this order of the Secretary of the Treasury, the Commissioner of Customs administers the Bureau of Customs, which directs the functioning of the Customs Service through 46 customs-collection districts, 7 comptroller districts, 12 customs-agency districts, 3 customs-patrol districts, and 9 customs laboratories.

Principal functions of the Customs Service are to

. . . enter and clear vessels; supervise the discharge of cargo; ascertain the quantities of imported merchandise, appraise and classify such merchandise, and assess and collect the duties thereon; permit the warehousing of imported merchandise; enforce customs and other laws by patrolling the international borders and inspecting international traffic by vessel, highway, railway and air; review protests against the payment of duties; determine and certify for payment the amount of drawback due upon the exportation of articles manufactured from duty-paid or tax-paid materials or articles; prevent the smuggling of contraband merchandise (including narcotics) and the introduction of prohibited articles; prevent and detect undervaluations and frauds on the customs revenue; apprehend violators of the customs laws; enforce the anti-dumping act; and perform certain duties under the Foreign Trade Zones Act.[5]

Ports of Entry. In a country as large as the United States, facilities could not be expected to be maintained in every town or city for official entry of merchandise. Accordingly, ports of entry have been designated at which a customs officer is assigned with authority to accept entries of merchandise, to collect duties, and to enforce the various provisions of the customs and navigation laws. Each port of entry is assigned to a customs district for administrative purposes, some customs districts consisting of only one port, others of a headquarters port and as many as 21 additional ports of entry.

Customs territory of the United States (including Alaska, Hawaii, and Puerto Rico) was divided into 45 customs-collection districts as of 1950,[6] and the number of ports of entry was about 300. Many of these ports are quite small, located along the Canadian and Mexican borders or well inland. Not all customs districts are of equal importance, volumewise; New York is the leader, by far, in most measurements. The race for second place is among New Orleans, Philadelphia, Baltimore, San Francisco, Houston, and perhaps others, depending on whether the measurement used is imports, exports, or both or dollars, tonnage, or both.

Customs officers are classified according to functions, the principal designations being collector of customs, comptroller of customs, customs appraiser, and customs agent.

Collectors of Customs. The collector is the chief of each district and is authorized to cause "inspection, examination and search . . . of persons, baggage or merchandise" if such action is deemed necessary or appropriate for enforcement of the customs and navigation laws. Under Sec. 488 of the Tariff Act of 1930, he is specifically charged with causing entered merchandise to be appraised. Accordingly, he takes custody of merchandise upon its arrival and is not permitted to deliver such merchandise from customs custody except under bond or upon formal entry. He is authorized to employ deputy collectors or assistants. Collectors of customs are appointed by the President, by and with the advice and consent of the Senate.

Comptrollers of Customs. Responsibility of the comptroller is the examination of collectors' accounts of receipts and disbursements of funds and receipts and disposition of merchandise, and certification of them to the Secretary of the Treasury for transmission to the General Accounting Office. Comptrollers of customs verify all assessments of duties and

---

[5] *Custom House Guide* (New York, Import Publications, Inc., 1948), p. 26.

[6] Another customs-collection district, not included in these 45, has jurisdiction over the Virgin Islands.

allowances of drawbacks made by collectors of customs in connection
with the liquidation thereof.

For accomplishing this duty, customs districts are assigned to comptrollers of customs, each of whom has jurisdiction over more than one
district. Assignment as of 1950 was as follows:

Office of Comptroller	Customs Districts Assigned
Boston..............	Maine and New Hampshire, Vermont, Massachusetts, Rhode Island
New York..........	Connecticut, St. Lawrence, Rochester, Buffalo, New York, Puerto Rico, Virgin Islands
Philadelphia........	Philadelphia, Pittsburgh, Michigan, Indiana, Ohio, Kentucky, Tennessee
Baltimore..........	Maryland, Virginia, North Carolina, South Carolina, Georgia, Florida
New Orleans........	Mobile, New Orleans, Sabine, Galveston, Laredo, El Paso, Arizona
San Francisco......	San Diego, Los Angeles, San Francisco, Oregon, Washington, Alaska, Hawaii
Chicago............	Montana and Idaho, Dakota, Minnesota, Duluth and Superior, Wisconsin, Chicago, St. Louis, Colorado

Comptrollers of customs are appointed by the President by and with
the advice and consent of the Senate.

Appraising Officers. The appraiser is charged by Sec. 500 of the Tariff
Act of 1930 with the following duties:

To appraise the merchandise in the unit of quantity in which the merchandise
is usually bought and sold by ascertaining or estimating the value thereof
by all reasonable ways and means in his power, any statement of cost or cost
of production in any invoice, affidavit, declaration, or other document to the
contrary notwithstanding;

To ascertain the number of yards, parcels, or quantities of the merchandise
ordered or designated for examination;

To ascertain whether the merchandise has been truly and correctly invoiced;

To describe the merchandise in order that the collector may determine the
dutiable classification thereof; and

To report his decisions to the collector.

In the performance of these responsibilities, he may employ assistant
appraisers and examiners who "examine and inspect the merchandise
and report the value and such other facts as the appraiser may require
in his appraisement or report."

Appraising officers at the various ports of entry, and their appraisal
functions, are under administrative control of the supervisor of appraisers. He, in turn, is under general supervision of the Commissioner
of Customs. Appraisers are appointed from the civil-service register.

Customs Agents. The office of customs agent is the principal designation in the Customs Agency Service. There are, as mentioned earlier, 12

customs-agency districts. This office is the investigating arm of the Customs Service and is employed generally in the prevention and detection of frauds on the customs revenue.[7] Customs agents are appointed from the civil-service register.

Mechanism for Protests and Appeals. In order to provide importers, producers, and collectors of customs with recourse to higher authority, customs laws have established procedures for protests and appeals against rulings of administrative employees and appeals against court decisions. Recourse is first to the United States Customs Court, rulings of which may be appealed to the United States Court of Customs and Patent Appeals. Rulings of the latter may be appealed on certain grounds before the United States Supreme Court.

In mentioning this mechanism, one must distinguish between "protest" and "appeal." Sections 514 and 516 of the Tariff Act of 1930 provide that a *protest* on the part of an importer, consignee, or his agent may be filed against decisions of a collector of customs, and that a *protest* may be filed by a manufacturer, producer, or wholesaler against classification of, or rate of duty assessed upon, merchandise. The first type must be filed with the collector of customs, who must either modify his ruling to the satisfaction of the protestor or submit it for decision to the United States Customs Court. Protest by a manufacturer, producer, or wholesaler (one who did not import the merchandise) must first be filed with the Secretary of the Treasury, whose subsequent actions may bring the matter before the United States Customs Court.

An *appeal,* on the other hand, is filed by a collector of customs against the decision of an appraiser; it is filed with the United States Customs Court. An *appeal* may also be filed by an importer or producer or by a collector of customs against decisions of the United States Customs Court. This latter appeal must be filed with the United States Court of Customs and Patent Appeals.

UNITED STATES TARIFF COMMISSION

The United States Tariff Commission was first established in 1916; its present (1952) authority and functions are prescribed by the Tariff Act of 1930, as amended.

Basically a fact-finding body, the Commission is charged with certain investigatory responsibilities, such as:

1. Investigating the administration and fiscal and industrial effects of the customs laws of the country, the relation between the rates of duty on raw materials and finished or partly finished products, all questions relative to the arrangement of schedules and classification of

[7] *Custom House Guide,* p. 582.

articles in the several schedules of the customs law, and, in general, the operation of customs laws, including their relation to the federal revenues and their effect upon the industries and labor of the country.

2. Investigating differences in the costs of production of any domestic article and of any like or similar foreign article (this feature, linked with the "flexible" provisions of the Tariff Act of 1930, has been substantially nullified by a provision of the Reciprocal Trade Agreements Act, which excludes articles covered by reciprocal trade agreements from flexible tariff arrangements).

3. Investigating alleged violations of the Unfair Trade Practices section of the Tariff Act of 1930, as a means of assisting the President in making decisions with respect thereto.

4. Ascertaining and at all times being informed as to whether discriminations against the commerce of the United States exist, and, if discriminations are disclosed, bringing the matter to the attention of the President, together with recommendations.

Responsibility Modified by Reciprocal Trade Agreements Act. Functional responsibility of the Tariff Commission has been modified somewhat by developments of the Reciprocal Trade Agreements program. Under the enabling legislation, the President, before concluding an agreement with any foreign government, is charged with seeking information and advice with respect to the proposed agreement from, among others, the Tariff Commission. This is accomplished through the Interdepartmental Committee on Trade Agreements, on which the Tariff Commission is represented.[8] The same membership comprises the Committee for Reciprocity Information, which holds public hearings prior to negotiations in order to assist the trade-agreements committee in recommending to the President a list of concessions to be sought and offered. In this connection, the Tariff Commission provides factual data relative to production, trade, and consumption of imported articles on which the possibility of concessions is being considered and facts on probable effects of granting concessions and on the competitive factors involved. Similar responsibility with regard to exported goods rests with the Department of Commerce.

Under the 1951 extension of the Act, the Tariff Commission was charged with determining "peril points" for each commodity on which it is proposed to offer reduced rates of duty. These are points below which reductions in duty are considered harmful to the industry facing competition from imported goods. Hence, even though the Act permits re-

---

[8] Other members represent the Departments of State, Treasury, Defense, Interior, Agriculture, Commerce, and Labor, and, during its life, the Mutual Security Agency. The State Department representative is chairman.

ductions in duty up to 50 per cent of those in effect on Jan. 1, 1945 (see Chapter 19), the peril points, as determined by the Tariff Commission, may call for a reduction of no more than 25 or 10 per cent or, perhaps, none at all. If the President grants concessions beyond the determined peril points, he must explain to Congress the reasons for his having exceeded the recommendations of the Tariff Commission.

Commission Responsible for "Escape-clause" Investigations. Another function of the Tariff Commission in connection with the Reciprocal Trade Agreements program pertains to the "escape clause," which is now a part of each agreement entered by the United States. By this clause, the Tariff Commission may on its own motion, by request of the President, or upon application of an interested party[9] investigate to determine whether increased imports of an article, *as a result of trade-agreement concession,* are causing or threatening to cause serious injury to domestic producers.

Also in the capacity of a fact-finding body, the Tariff Commission is the agency to be used by the President in conducting investigations ordered by him to determine whether imported articles are rendering or tending to render ineffective or materially interfering with the agricultural price-support operations.

Personnel Obtained through Appointment or Examination. Membership on the Commission is by appointment of the President, by and with the advice and consent of the Senate. There are six members, appointed for terms of six years each, at a salary of $15,000 per year. During tenure, no Commissioner may actively engage in any other business, vocation, or employment. A secretary of the Commission, a clerk for each Commissioner, and special experts may be appointed without civil-service listing. All other employees are appointed from the civil-service eligible list.

A number of excellent studies have been published by the Tariff Commission, notable among which are the War Change in Industry Series, representing changes in specific industries, and an alphabetical compilation of United States import duties, as modified by reciprocal trade agreements.[10]

THE EXPORT-IMPORT BANK

The Export-Import Bank of Washington is an independent agent of the United States, created for the purpose of rendering "aid in financing and to facilitate exports and imports and the exchange of commodities

[9] If the commission decides that good and sufficient reason exists for conducting such an investigation.

[10] *United States Import Duties*, 1948 or 1950.

between the United States or any of its Territories or insular possessions and any foreign country or the agencies or nationals thereof."[11]

In order to carry out its purposes, the bank is

. . . authorized and empowered to do a general banking business except that of circulation; to receive deposits; to purchase, discount, rediscount, sell, and negotiate, with or without its endorsement and guaranty, and to guarantee notes, drafts, checks, bills of exchange, acceptances, including bankers' acceptances, cable transfers, and other evidences of indebtedness; . . . to accept bills and drafts drawn upon it; to issue letters of credit; to purchase and sell coin, bullion, and exchange; to borrow and to lend money . . . [12]

As presently constituted, the bank functions under the Export-Import Bank Act of 1945, as amended. This Act is an amendment of earlier legislation dating back to February, 1934, when an Export-Import Bank was created to finance anticipated export trade with the Soviet Union following diplomatic recognition in November, 1933. However, these anticipated transactions never materialized. A second Export-Import Bank was organized in March, 1934, to finance trade with nations other than the Soviet Union, especially Cuba. In 1936, the first and second Export-Import Banks were merged, at which time the second bank was liquidated. In 1947, the bank's District of Columbia corporate charter was dissolved, and it was reincorporated under federal charter.

The bank has a capital stock of $1,000,000,000, subscribed by the United States, and is authorized to borrow from the Secretary of the Treasury an amount not to exceed at any one time two and one-half times its authorized capital stock. While there is no limitation on the amount that can be loaned to any one borrower, the bank is prohibited from having outstanding at any one time loans and guarantees in excess of three and one-half times its authorized capital stock, or $3,500,000,000.

Types of Credit Operations. The bank's financing of exports is of two general types:

1. Direct credits to United States exporters, or participation in such credits. If without recourse to the exporter, the bank usually requires the guarantee of a foreign bank or government.
2. A line of credit in favor of a foreign government, bank, or firm, available during a stipulated period of time for facilitating the purchase in the United States of specific materials, equipment, and services.

Small and medium-sized exporters and importers are also financed by direct loans, being extended credit lines if they are experienced and of good repute but are hampered by lack of capital in obtaining adequate accommodation from private sources.

[11] Export-Import Bank Act of 1945, 59 Stat. 526 (1945), as amended by Pub. L. 89, 80th Cong.
[12] *Ibid.*

Another classification of credit operations is as follows:

General export-trade credits: These cover the export of raw materials, capital goods, services, agricultural equipment, and other purchases from the United States.

Commodity-export credits: Raw cotton and tobacco are the commodities whose financing falls under this heading. As an example, allocations are made to a foreign country (government or bank) and cotton shippers designate commercial banks in the United States to handle documents and negotiate drafts under commitments issued by the Export-Import Bank.

Small exporter-importer credits: These are revolving credit lines in amounts sometimes less than $5,000; $1,000,000 has been set aside for this purpose.

Other credits: In this group would fall emergency-reconstruction credits, lend-lease-termination credits, development credits, and credits under the Foreign Assistance Act of 1948.

Basic Principles of Lending Operations. Following passage of the Export-Import Bank Act of 1945, the bank published a *General Policy Statement*, revised in 1947 as a result of amendment to the Act, in which the following principles of lending operations are listed:[13]

The bank makes only loans and guarantees which serve to promote the export and import trade of the United States.

The bank generally makes loans for specific purposes, and disbursements are made only upon receipt of satisfactory evidence that purposes of the loan have been carried out.

The bank makes only loans which offer reasonable assurance of repayment.

The bank extends credit only to finance purchases of materials and equipment produced or manufactured in the United States and the technical services of American firms and individuals, as distinguished from outlays for goods, labor, and services in the borrowing country or purchases in third countries.

The bank does not compete with private capital, but rather supplements and encourages it. It confines its dealings to certain risks which private banks are not in a position to assume. It has indicated its preference for receiving applications for loans from private firms and individuals through commercial banks to make certain that private credit is not available. Furthermore, it holds itself ready to sell paper which it has acquired and undertakes in advance to purchase from commercial

---

[13] These principles do not necessarily apply to the bank's operations under the Foreign Assistance Act of 1948, which are carried on the books of the bank independently of operations under the Export-Import Bank Act of 1945.

banks notes arising out of specific transactions financed in the first instance by the commercial banks.

Bank Prohibited from Certain Activities. Either by law or by its general policies, the bank is prohibited from:

Extending credits when private credit is available in adequate amounts on reasonable terms

Purchasing stock in any corporation

Making lump-sum advances for use as borrowers see fit

Financing trade between the United States and its territories or insular possessions

Financing expenditures other than for United States goods and services, except in unusual cases

Assuming responsibility for issuance by the United States government of priorities, allocations, or licenses pertaining to commodities being financed

Selecting suppliers of materials and equipment or engineering or other technical firms or individuals whose services are sought by foreign borrowers in connection with projects financed by the bank

Bank Has Special Functions under Foreign-assistance Legislation. By provision of the Foreign Assistance Act of 1948, when the ECA Administrator[14] determines that foreign assistance is desirable on credit terms, he allocates funds for the purpose to the Export-Import Bank. The bank is authorized to make and administer the credits on terms specified by the ECA Administrator, who shall have consulted on the proposal with the National Advisory Council. As of June 30, 1950, the bank had paid out $964,000,000 on these credits to 14 countries.

·The bank also issues, as agent for and upon terms specified by the ECA Administrator, the transfer guarantees extended on certain foreign investments and transactions under the Foreign Assistance Act of 1948, as amended. It also receives ECA[15] funds for this purpose. Up to June 30, 1950, these guarantees totaled $22,800,000, involving 23 separate guarantees.

Lending Operations Summarized. From its inception in 1934 until June 30, 1950, the bank had granted authorized credits amounting to a little under $4,800,000,000, exclusive of credits under the Foreign Assistance Act of 1948. Giving effect to expirations and cancellations of authorized credits, the cumulative amount disbursed as loans was $3,150,-000,000. Credit authorizations outstanding (loans and undisbursed authorizations) as of June 30, 1950, were $2,786,000,000.

[14] Succeeded, 1951, by Director of Mutual Security.
[15] Succeeded, 1951, by Mutual Security Agency.

Lending operations, some of which are apparently similar to those of the International Bank for Reconstruction and Development (see Chapter 22), are coordinated as to policy with this institution through the National Advisory Council (see Chapter 21).

FOREIGN CONSULAR OFFICES

The functions of our Foreign Service have already been covered, but a survey of the institutional structure through which foreign commerce is conducted would omit an important segment if it did not include the consular offices of other countries.

These offices perform various functions and services, most of which are required by regulations covering shipments to the respective countries. Certification of invoices, preparation of certificates of origin, stamping of bills of lading, and compliance with national import-control regulations all mean that foreign consular offices in the United States play an important role in the processing of exports. They further serve in the picture as a source of information or reference regarding individual firms in their respective countries and laws or regulations which are of importance both to exporters and to importers. In addition, their issuance of visa permits for travel in their respective countries render them of significance in this phase of foreign commerce.

Consulates Are Maintained in Many United States Cities. Foreign consulates were located in cities shown in the following list, in the United States in 1950, with representation in several others not included.

City	Number of Consulates	City	Number of Consulates
Baltimore	27	Mobile	17
Boston	34	New Orleans	39
Chicago	44	New York	66
Detroit	13	Norfolk	14
Galveston	19	Philadelphia	33
Houston	24	Portland, Ore	18
Jacksonville	13	San Francisco	40
Kansas City	11	Savannah	8
Los Angeles	39	Seattle	22
Miami	24	St. Louis	19
Minneapolis	11	Tampa	17

SOURCE: *International Trade Reporter*, Vol. 65, No. 351, 1950.

PORTS

Among the most active institutions in foreign commerce are the seaports, each striving to build up its own traffic in order that the various services operating in the port may have a better opportunity to sell their wares.

Most port organizations are officially public agencies acting as co-ordinators of private service facilities and at times as participants in the provision of certain services. For example, water frontage is sometimes owned and operated by private interests. At other times or places, the frontage may be publicly owned and either publicly or privately operated; privately operated frontage may be under lease.

Port Agencies Perform Varied Functions. Among the activities of ports as a functional institution are:

1. Promotion of commerce or traffic. Several ports maintain "salesmen" in interior points from which traffic may be drawn.
2. Supervision or operation of certain facilities, such as wharves, foreign-trade zones, etc.
3. Coordination of interest and expression on legislative matters pertaining to the welfare of one or more of the service functions.
4. Entertainment of prospective patrons whose interest, actual or potential, may pertain to several functional services.
5. Economic development of the area from which traffic may be drawn. This is done largely by aiding prospective businesses in finding suitable sites and in obtaining necessary economic or physical data to permit sound decisions. This work may be in conjunction with chambers of commerce, state departments of commerce and industry, and quasi-public and private organizations of one type or another.
6. Public relations. Through statistical data and analyses and such features as picture service and port publications, the advantages offered by individual ports are brought constantly to the attention of users, either shippers or travelers.

Other institutions, public and private, could be listed as participating in some substantial degree in foreign commerce, but those shown are sufficient to indicate the varied types of activity which go to make up those occupations generally considered to be in the field of foreign commerce.

Employment opportunities must be sought out in one of these specific functional institutions or activities, and it should be evident that port cities have no monopoly on opportunities or employment in foreign commerce. The several functions discussed in the last three chapters indicate the existence of a large and active foreign-trade fraternity in many sections of the United States.

REVIEW QUESTIONS

1. What is the National Advisory Council?
2. What is the function of the Assistant Secretary of State for Economic Affairs?

3. What is the Foreign Service of the United States? Distinguish between the political and the commercial activities of Foreign Service personnel.

4. Describe the organization and functions of the Office of International Trade.

5. What does the Commodity Credit Corporation have to do with foreign commerce? Has the Department of Agriculture any interest or influence in foreign commerce other than through the Commodity Credit Corporation? Explain.

6. Describe the organization and functions of the Customs Service.

7. Describe, step by step, the mechanism for protests and appeals under customs procedure.

8. What are the functions of the United States Tariff Commission?

9. What is the responsibility of the Tariff Commission in connection with reciprocal-trade agreements?

10. What types of credit operations are undertaken by the Export-Import Bank?

11. What types of activities are prohibited to the Export-Import Bank by law or by established policy?

12. What is the responsibility of the Export-Import Bank in connection with our foreign-aid activities.

CHAPTER 8

Financial Practice I

RISKS FACING SELLER AND BUYER

In any business transaction, domestic or foreign, certain risks are taken by both the seller and the buyer. Ordinarily, at least in domestic commerce, one is inclined to look on these risks as the worry primarily of the seller, whose principal concern is whether he will be paid. In foreign business, however, several considerations other than the risk of nonpayment enter the picture.

A number of specific risks are involved in foreign commerce and are usually reducible to such generalizations as (1) the buyer's willingness and financial ability to pay, (2) the seller's willingness and ability to perform under the sales contract, (3) exchange-rate fluctuations, (4) the buyer's legal ability to pay, which is determined by his country's laws on transfer of funds internationally, and (5) physical hazards to the merchandise. These risks may in turn be classed as *moral, financial,* and *physical,* and the last could even be considered part of the moral and financial risk. In fact, they all touch on one another to some extent, and all must be weighed in arriving at decisions involving extension of credit. However, the foregoing risks do not cover the risk of price changes, which must be borne by the owner of the product in question. Nor do they include the risk of lack of clarity as to the point at which expenses related to movement of goods internationally cease being for account of the seller and become for account of the buyer. This chapter and the next deal with all these problems except the risk of price changes of merchandise.

Moral Risks. Fundamentally, the moral risk is whether the buyer and seller will be willing to perform under terms of the contract if adverse circumstances develop.

Many unfavorable happenings, often impossible to anticipate, may occur between the time an order is placed and the time the merchandise is received or its accompanying financial obligation matures. One of these is a change in the financial position of the buyer, but this is not necessarily a prerequisite of the buyer's delaying or refusing payment. Another is a change (which may be unfavorable to either buyer or seller) in the price of the merchandise. This may be a real problem to both the seller and the buyer; the seller may find that the buyer is unwilling to accept the merchandise at the agreed price, using a number of evasive tactics to avoid doing so, while the buyer may find himself faced with a substantial purchase in the face of falling prices and may be impelled to try evasive action in the hope that the seller will adjust his price or even recall the shipment. On the other hand, in the face of a rapid rise in prices, the seller may at times attempt to delay shipment, to reduce quality, or otherwise to avoid the technical loss on the shipment. It is not suggested that these tactics are widely practiced, but they are quite possible and at times constitute a risk of considerable size. However, through careful credit practice and experience, such risks can be minimized.

Indicative of the importance of moral responsibility, as far as the exporter's interest is concerned, is the risk that merchandise may perish or otherwise deteriorate physically during the time the buyer is delaying acceptance of the merchandise on any of several technicalities. From the buyer's point of view, also, the moral risk is very real because the condition of merchandise, its arrival in time for seasonal processing or sale, its arrival in good and undamaged condition and in quality and quantity consonant with the order are all chances taken by him when placing his order. They become much more important with increases in distance and time, because of the impossibility of replacing from alternate sources at a late date.

Financial Risks. These risks rest on the ability of the buyer to pay, assuming his willingness, on the possibility of exchange-rate fluctuation between the time of placing the order and the time of payment, and on the possibility of governmental interference which might preclude transfers of funds internationally. Again, through careful credit practice, these risks may be anticipated and minimized. Depending on the currency in which quoted, the risk could bear on either seller or buyer. From the seller's point of view, all the specific risks combine into one *credit risk*, which means financial loss if all does not go well.

Physical Risks. Merchandise is subject to damage of internal and external origin. In the case of perishables, recognition must be taken of this possibility in arranging for financing. Externally, the risk of physical damage may be transferred by insurance, which becomes a vital part of the financial understanding. At every moment, someone must carry the risk—exporter, importer, or carrier. Accordingly, the prudent man will insure.

Arrangements Fix Responsibility on Seller or Buyer. These basic risks have given rise to a number of commonly used pricing quotations, documents, and financing arrangements, intended to clarify and fix on either the seller or the buyer the specific risks mentioned and to provide some assurance to each that performance of the other party is under way or has been accomplished. From the purely selfish point of view, the shifting of risks to others is what is sought, but, as in the case of the incidence of taxation, no one will bear the burden if he is not compelled to do so through being unable to shift it to anyone else. Accordingly, determination of where risks will rest, by contract, is a matter of negotiation.

REVISED AMERICAN FOREIGN TRADE DEFINITIONS—1941

In response to the need for clearer understanding of the responsibility for costs accumulated up to the point at which seller's responsibility ends and buyer's responsibility begins, as well as the particular obligations of each up to and beyond that point, a series of formal definitions has been prepared. These are Revised American Foreign Trade Definitions—1941.[1]

Six principal terms of this type are included:

1. EX (POINT OF ORIGIN). This might be ex factory, ex mine, ex warehouse, etc. Under this term, the price quoted applies only at the point of origin, and the seller agrees to place the goods at the disposal of the buyer at the agreed place on the date or within the period fixed.

2. F.O.B. (FREE ON BOARD). On board may be on an inland carrier, on a vessel, or at an inland point in the country of importation. Provision may be made for freight being prepaid or allowed. The seller must pay all charges up to the point named, including costs and charges pertaining to documents.

3. F.A.S. (FREE ALONG SIDE). A widely used term, it calls for the seller to pay the cost (and include it in the selling price) of delivering the merchandise along side an overseas vessel, within reach of its loading tackle.

4. C. & F. (COST AND FREIGHT). Under this term, the seller's price must include the cost of transportation to the named point of destination.

5. C.I.F. (COST, INSURANCE, AND FREIGHT). In addition to the transportation costs, as under c. & f., the seller must also include the cost of marine insurance in his quotation.

6. EX DOCK (NAMED PORT OF IMPORTATION). Under this term, seller

---

[1] Adopted in 1941 by a joint committee representing the Chamber of Commerce of the United States, the National Council of American Importers, Inc., and the National Foreign Trade Council, Inc.

quotes a price including the cost of goods and all additional costs necessary to place the goods on the dock at the named port of importation, duty, if any, paid. This term is used principally in United States import trade and is not recommended for quotations for export.

Responsibilities Listed for Seller and Buyer. Each of these terms includes a statement of what the seller must do and what the buyer must do. In addition, suggested points of caution are listed for most of the standard terms. As an example of the former, the following is the listing of responsibilities under a c.i.f. quotation:

Seller must
(1) provide and pay for transportation to named point of destination;
(2) pay export taxes, or other fees or charges, if any, levied because of exportation;
(3) provide and pay for marine insurance;
(4) provide war risk insurance as obtainable in seller's market at time of shipment at buyer's expense, unless seller has agreed that buyer provide for war risk coverage (it is desirable that the goods be insured against both marine and war risk with the same underwriter, so that there can be no difficulty arising from the determination of the cause of the loss);
(5) obtain and dispatch promptly to buyer, or his agent, clean bill of lading to named point of destination, and also insurance policy or negotiable insurance certificate;
(6) where received-for-shipment ocean bill of lading may be tendered, be responsible for any loss or damage, or both, until the goods have been delivered into the custody of the ocean carrier;
(7) where on-board bill of lading is required, be responsible for any loss or damage, or both, until the goods have been delivered on board the vessel;
(8) provide at buyer's request and expense, certificates of origin, consular invoices, or any other documents issued in the country of origin, or of shipment, or both, which the buyer may require for importation of goods into country of destination and, where necessary for their passage in transit through another country.

Buyer must
(1) accept the documents when presented;
(2) receive the goods upon arrival, handle and pay for all subsequent movement of the goods, including taking delivery from vessel in accordance with bill of lading clauses and terms; pay all costs of landing, including any duties, taxes, and other expenses at named point of destination;
(3) pay for war risk insurance provided by seller;
(4) be responsible for loss of or damage to goods, or both, from time and place at which seller's obligations under (6) or (7) above have ceased;
(5) pay the cost of certificates of origin, consular invoices, or any other documents issued in the country of origin, or of shipment, or both, which may be required for importation of the goods into the country of destination and, where necessary, for their passage in transit through another country.

The foregoing specifications provide a clear basis for understanding as to the costs to be included up to a certain point, at which point the seller's job has been done and subsequent responsibility rests on the buyer. However, while these definitions have been adopted and are in extensive use in sales contracts, customs of the trade in some lines are not necessarily the same as these definitions. Accordingly, it may be advisable at times to spell out certain details as, for example, the cost of consular fees in c.i.f. quotations, and the designation and cost of special risk insurance. Another point of variance may be found in the problem of arranging for certain documents at the buyer's "request." At some ports and for some products, the shipper understands, as a custom of the trade, that he must see to it that a consular invoice is provided even without specific request of the buyer. In fact, he may not be able to make the shipment without the consular invoice.

DOCUMENTS

The foregoing definitions do not cover such matters as packaging instructions, delivery date, time of payment, conditions under which documents of title may be obtained by the buyer, and currency in which payment is to be made. The first two, packaging instructions and delivery date, may be considered part of the order proper, and the third and fourth are generally incorporated in what may be referred to as terms of payment, credit terms, or export-sales terms. Precaution may be taken in the terms of payment to assure compliance with delivery date, especially if the documents are to be passed through a bank for negotiation or collection.

Within the wide range between payment (in full or in part) at time of order and payment sometime after receipt of shipment by the buyer, a number of customary terms are found. These may include no formal credit instrument, the use of drafts by the seller on the buyer, or the use of letters of credit whereby bank financing is employed. These credit terms are discussed later in the chapter, but at this point a few definitions applicable to them must be understood along with a description of some of the documents used.

Some of the documents listed below are widely used; others are called for only under special conditions. For purposes of discussion, they are grouped as drafts, bills of lading, and other documents.

Drafts. Drafts may be classified as follows:

Sight: Payable on presentation to the drawee (usually buyer).[2]
Time: Payable a specified number of days after sight (presentation for

---

[2] Some authors consider sight drafts to include those payable a designated number of days after sight [Frank Henius, *Dictionary of Foreign Trade* (New York, Prentice-Hall, Inc., 1947), p. 279] or after presentation and acceptance by the buyer

acceptance) or after the date on which drawn by the seller, regardless of the date on which presented for acceptance.

Clean: Either a sight or time draft without shipping documents attached. The documents would be sent direct to the buyer, who could, with them, obtain the merchandise without first paying or accepting the draft.

Documentary: Either a sight or time draft to which is attached the documents which enable the drawee to obtain the merchandise. Ordinarily sent through a bank, accompanying instructions indicate whether the documents are to be released to the drawee upon payment or acceptance.

Bills of Lading. Bills of lading are of two main types:

Straight: Drawn in favor of the consignee and deliverable only to him. This type is not negotiable, and some difficulty is found in using the straight bill of lading when financing by means of bank letters of credit or with assistance of bank credit of other types.

Order: Drawn in favor of a consignee, who may receive the goods or endorse the bill of lading over to another party who may receive the goods. This type of bill of lading is negotiable and conveys title to the merchandise, but in some countries the consignee may be able to obtain the merchandise without the bill of lading. Another form of order bill of lading is identified as "order notify." This type is used when the name of the party who is to be notified of arrival is not then known; it will be forwarded for insertion during the course of shipment of the merchandise.

The bill of lading serves three purposes. It conveys title to the merchandise, it is a receipt for the goods signed by the common carrier, and it defines the terms of the contract between shipper and carrier. Customs laws ordinarily require presentation of a bill of lading by the importer or his agent and in some countries (Venezuela and Bolivia, for example) the respective laws prescribe special regulations regarding use of the order bill of lading. In some countries, order bills are not recognized, while in others, there seems to be inadequate protection against delivery of merchandise without presentation of documents.[3] As an alternative, to permit the exporter's retaining control in this situation, the merchandise may be consigned to a foreign bank with its previous consent, with a draft on the buyer forwarded to the bank for collection. Upon payment, the buyer obtains the merchandise. Or an established forwarder might provide similar service through his agent.

---

[11] J. Rodríguez Sánchez, *Foreign Credits and Collections* (New York, Prentice-Hall, Inc., 1947), p. 242].

[3] *Exporters' Encyclopedia, 1948* (New York, Thomas Ashwell and Co., 1947), pp. 1717–1718.

A feature of bills of lading which bears mention is the distinction between bills "received for shipment" and bills "on board." The former may be issued upon receipt at shipside by a steamship company and something may occur to prevent lading on a certain vessel, thus delaying receipt by the importer. The latter type is thus sometimes specified when the importer particularly desires shipment by a certain route or vessel.

Another feature of some interest is the "through" export bill of lading. This type is executed inland and serves on both the railroad, for transportation to port, and the steamship line. Through bills are not in wide use, being available principally for shipments to the Far East. They seem to reduce the trouble and expense in making out different sets for the two carriers. But the close coordination required between inland- and ocean-carrier schedules and the processing of documents at the port make use of a through bill inadvisable at times. Loss of or damage to part of a shipment while inland or errors in documents may call for delay of the entire shipment at port unless a new bill of lading is made out for the ocean carrier. An underlying obstacle may be the allocation of rates between carriers. Complications also arise if special documents are required.

Other Documents. Other documents frequently called for are the *insurance policy* or *insurance certificate,* inasmuch as the problems presented in overseas shipment call for clear understanding as to responsibilities in case of damage or loss. *Commercial invoices* are evidence of value in transactions and lend support both to banks, for financing purposes, and to governments, for tariff and statistical purposes. They are often required by the law of the importer's country, and it may be specified that these invoices be certified by the consul of the importing country. In this case, they become *certified invoices,* or *consular invoices.*

In addition, other documents may have to be provided, such as the *shipper's export declaration,* required by United States law, and *export licenses* (when required) or *import clearances* or *authorizations* (when required).

Perhaps less commonly used, in general, are such documents as the *inspection certificate,* which may be required by law, as in the case of the United States Grain Standards Act, or by the importer; the *certificate of weight,* which the importer may require; and the *certificate of origin,* required by some governments as the basis for application of certain customs duties.

TERMS OF PAYMENT

Factors Affecting Terms of Payment

Terms of payment may be of as many types as the individual sellers and buyers find suitable for the thousands of commercial transactions having to be financed. They have, however, been reduced to a few practical classifications.

It is frequently stated that, in the selection of terms, customs of the trade are of great significance. This is to be expected, but one must look behind the scenes to ascertain which factors determine customs of the trade, for the "trade" is nothing but the sum total of individual sellers and buyers. The exporter will consider what other opportunities may be found offering greater advantage to him; the importer, on the other hand, will expect treatment as favorable as the most liberal of several suppliers may offer, other things being equal. Within this broad limitation, several specific factors will weigh in the case. Some pertain to the individual circumstances of the exporter or importer, some to the nature of the article, and some of the physical or institutional facilities or obstacles.

Individual Circumstances of Seller and Buyer Dominant. As to the individual circumstances of the exporter or importer, such factors as size, financial strength, credit standing, and market situation bear heavily. A small buyer may be in a weaker bargaining position than a large seller; the financial condition of the seller may not permit him to extend liberal credit accommodation, while the credit standing of the buyer may compel him to buy from hand to mouth, in small quantities and without being able to ask effectively for liberal credit accommodations. Further, the seller may at the moment be heavily burdened with inventory and may be compelled to adopt an easier price or credit policy to dispose of it, while the buyer may be in rather urgent need of certain merchandise and not in position to shop around, delay, or otherwise bargain for more favorable terms. In other words, the intensity of individual demand and the adequacy of individual supply in any situation play an important part in determining the trade pattern.

Then there is the subtle situation arising from the question of whether the seller seeks out the buyer *and tries to sell him* or whether the buyer seeks out the seller. The implication here is that the one courted may be in the better bargaining position.

Nature of Product Is Significant. The nature of the article, itself, also influences the terms under which possession is surrendered. If the article is a staple, with a wide and rather constant market, the problem is different from that presented in the case of specialties, with limited or seasonal markets. Many products are made to order, and these, of course, call for different financing arrangements than would the manufacturing and distribution of standard products. The element of perishability is a significant one, as in the case of fresh fruit and vegetables. However, even packaged products are often perishable, and this characteristic must be considered in the exporter's willingness to release the merchandise without payment or the importer's willingness to pay in advance of receipt of the merchandise. Another factor entering the picture is the marketing or processing time faced by the importer, which may in turn be influenced by the use to which the product goes—consumer or industrial.

Physical and Geographic Factors Play a Part. Coupled with these factors pertaining to the traders and the product are such physical or institutional factors as distance, which means time, including transportation schedules of various types, and the facilities for caring for the merchandise and for handling the documents and financial arrangements—in effect, for collecting payment. This is also affected by the availability of credit information and by the nature of laws under which creditor-debtor relationships may have to be settled by court action.

Legal Limitations, Control, and Protective Features Have a Bearing. In making financial arrangements, certain other underlying considerations affect the terms selected. Among these are (1) legal limits on time of payment, (2) control over merchandise pending payment, (3) desire for evidence of debt, (4) the use of third parties in the financing process, and (5) certain protective features.

In point of *time,* one of the provisions of the Federal Reserve Act has bearing on the structure of terms. While longer terms are often used in the sale of items such as heavy equipment and machinery, the Federal Reserve Act sets six months as the outside figure for many transactions. Sec. 13 of the Federal Reserve Act provides that: "Any member bank may accept drafts or bills of exchange drawn upon it having not more than six months' sight to run, excusive of days of grace." This limitation, carrying through to the point of eligibility for purchase by or rediscount with the Federal Reserve banks, sets a pattern within which financing by means of bank acceptances must fit. *Control* over the merchandise by the exporter may be surrendered at once or it may be retained until payment is made by the importer. Contrariwise, the importer may request the merchandise without payment, or he may be compelled to wait for possession of the merchandise until he has made payment and at times even beyond payment. While *evidence of debt* does not increase the debtor's responsibility, it may be desired at times, either to aid the seller in his own financing or for its psychological effect on the debtor. Thus, the financial terms may provide for no credit instrument, as in the case of a sale on open account, or for notes, trade, or bank acceptances. Whether *third parties* will be brought into the picture will depend in part on whether credit instruments are employed. In the case of a sale on open account, because the seller and buyer know each other so well and credit standing justifies the arrangement, or in the case of a shipment on consignment, the entire transaction, including surrender of the bill of lading, may be handled between the seller and the buyer.

On the other hand, it is undoubtedly much more common to bring in third parties, mainly banks, at some stage in the transaction.

The exporter may find it advantageous to employ the services of a bank in maintaining control over documents of title to merchandise, and at times several banks may be brought into the picture because of the network of bank correspondent relationships and the location or banking connections of either the exporter or the importer. With regard to other protective services, these may be desired by either the exporter or the importer. This feature is accomplished by the use of documents which evidence specified characteristics or measurements. A prime example is the use of inspection certificates, which assure the buyer that some independent person has looked over the shipment and found it to conform to specifications or classification as to qualify, quantity, or accuracy.

CREDIT TERMS

To accommodate these several factors and restrictions, a range of credit terms in common use has evolved. In the order of increasing protection to the seller, they may be listed as follows:

Consignment
Open, or current account
Sight draft, clean
Time draft, documents against acceptance
Time or sight draft, documents against payment
Bank letter of credit
Cash with order, or against export documents

This is only a rough listing, as modification of one or another of these may alter their order, and at times the question of retaining control over the merchandise may have as much significance to the seller as the time of payment. One may well question, for instance, the suggestion that consignment offers the least protection to the seller, for the use of a consignment arrangement would properly be used only where the credit standing of the consignee is such as to warrant the risk of nonpayment, when payment becomes due, a risk of little probability. Detailed operational data pertaining to credit terms or arrangements constitute the major part of the next chapter.

Wide Variety of Terms in Use. There are no "typical" credit terms for all foreign trade. For any seller, terms may vary among (1) products in the same or different markets, (2) buyers, in the same or different markets, and (3) the same buyer at different times.

The wide variety of terms in use was brought out in a survey conducted by *Exporters' Digest* during August and September, 1951. The

entire tabulation, published in the issue of November, 1951, covers eight
commodity classifications and 71 countries or trading areas. Table 36,
extracted from the tabulation, is for three of these eight commodity
classifications and for 14 selected countries.

Table 36. Credit Terms in Use, 1951[a]
(Percentage of firms reporting)

Country	Hardware[b]				General merchandise[c]				Heavy machinery[d]			
	A	B	C	D	A	B	C	D	A	B	C	D
Cuba...............	5	34	28[e]	33[f]	7	36	18[e]	39[e]	35	45	5	15
Dominican Republic...	12	63	19[g]	6	8	68	10[e]	14[h]	54	38	..	8
Argentina............	78	12	5[g]	5	86	9	2	3	83	17		
Brazil...............	25	67	5[g]	3	36	56	6	2	38	56	6	
Chile...............	36	55	3[g]	6	45	44	6[f]	5[g]	46	40	7	7
Venezuela...........	8	46	22[e]	24[f]	14	55	18[f]	13[d]	53	37	5	5
Belgium.............	42	38	5[e]	15	47	40	3[g]	10[g]	60	25	..	15
France..............	84	8	..	8	82	10	..	8	64	18	..	18
United Kingdom......	40	5	..	55	33	33	9	25	45	37	..	18
Iraq................	95	5	..	..	83	15	..	2	100			
Turkey..............	86	14	..	..	88	10	..	2	86	7	..	7
Union of South Africa..	35	50	..	15	46	38	6	10	38	38	..	24
Australia...........	42	20	8	30	59	33	4	4	66	34		
Panama.............	10	65	10[e]	15	10	57	14[e]	19	38	38	..	24

[a] Code: A—letter of credit, cash; B—sight draft, documents/payment; C—time
draft; D—open account.

[b] Hardware and allied lines: includes paints, building materials, tools, home appliances, hardware, housewares, kitchenware.

[c] General merchandise: consumer lines; dry goods; notions; men's, women's, and
children's wear; shoes; hats; etc.

[d] Heavy machinery and capital goods.

[e] 30–90 days.

[f] 30–120 days.

[g] 30–60 days.

[h] 30–180 days.

The variety of terms employed is due to the several factors described
above, to the economic condition of the buyer's country, to government
regulations, or to anything else which affects the buyer's ability to pay
and the seller's ability to wait for payment. Within each product group,
also, a wide variation is found in each country, depending on local or
regional economic conditions.

Information on changes in foreign credit conditions is of prime value
to financial officers interested in exports. Altered conditions may develop
from changes in the economic health or foreign exchange position of the
buyer's country or from changes in the buyer's own standing. As an
aid to those interested in export credits to Latin America, the Foreign

Credit Interchange Bureau of the National Association of Credit Men surveys its members as to their current practice in relation to past periods and publishes the results as shown in the following table.

Survey of Terms Granted during Last Half of 1951
as Compared with 1950 Terms
(In percentage of replies received)

Country	No change	More liberal	Less liberal
Argentina	95	2	3
Bolivia	92	4	4
Brazil	92	4	4
British possessions	94	3	3
Chile	88	3	9
Colombia	81	13	6
Costa Rica	77	21	2
Cuba	94	2	4
Dominican Republic	95	2	3
Ecuador	90	5	5
French possessions	94	3	3
Guatemala	85	6	9
Haiti	95	1	4
Honduras	93	4	3
Mexico	95	1	4
Netherlands possessions	96	2	2
Nicaragua	90	8	2
Panama	94	2	4
Paraguay	84	4	12
Peru	90	7	3
Puerto Rico	91	4	5
El Salvador	91	3	6
Uruguay	87	3	10
Venezuela	90	4	6

SOURCE: *Weekly Bulletin* 1620, Feb. 15, 1952, p. 8.

The export credit officer, noting these changes arising from other credit practitioners, may thus be in better position to determine a safe policy. Of course, changes reported may be in lines of merchandise different from the one in which his company is interested. But, if the change were made because of developments regarding the buyer's *country*, all lines would probably be affected in some way.

SOURCES OF CREDIT INFORMATION

The need for sound evaluation of credit information is probably more pressing in foreign than in domestic business, because of the longer time factor, the distance, different legal systems, and the lack of opportunity for buyer and seller to know each other personally. Credit information is needed by both seller and buyer. The seller's interest in the buyer's ability and willingness to pay is the same as in domestic business. But the buyer is also vitally interested in knowing something about the seller's reputation and his ability to deliver the merchandise on time and in proper order. Failure to receive inventory, especially when replacement may take several weeks and even months, could be close to disastrous for some importers.

The principal sources of foreign credit information are generally the same as in domestic credits. First of all is the importer, himself. While there is no reason to say that what the buyer reports about himself is apt to be misleading, it is only natural that what he says will be slanted in his own favor. He would probably name only references who he considers would give him a favorable report. Then there are the exporter's own files, if he has already had experience with the importer, and other suppliers known to the exporter. If the exporter belonged to the National Association of Credit Men, he would probably use the Foreign Credit Interchange Bureau of that organization, which would bring out the experience of several creditors (without necessarily identifying any of them) with the importer; this is a far greater coverage than the average exporter could hope to attain by himself. Credit reports may also be had from organizations such as Dun and Bradstreet, Inc., and the American Foreign Credit Underwriters Corporation. The World Trade Directory Reports of the U.S. Department of Commerce also provide detailed information on a single company. When possible, newspapers and magazines may be scanned for information bearing on the individuals or companies concerned. One of the chief sources of credit information is the banking system. A major bank in the United States will probably already have in its files credit data on many foreign firms; if not, it is a routine matter for it to communicate with its correspondent or another bank in the region of the person being investigated. If desired by cable, the report can be so requested, the charges, of course, being for account of the inquirer. Aiding in this arrangement is the practice of many companies abroad of listing on their letterheads the name of a bank to which inquiries may be addressed for credit information. Finally, a very important source of information is the exporter's agent in the country of the importer. Obtaining credit information is an important function of an agent, and, as stated before, if the agent goes so far as to guarantee the credit to the exporter, he becomes known as a "del credere" agent.

REVIEW QUESTIONS

1. Distinguish among the moral, physical, and financial risks facing the seller and buyer in foreign commerce.

2. What are Revised American Foreign Trade Definitions—1941?

3. What are the responsibilities of the seller and the buyer under a c.i.f. quotation?

4. If you were selling abroad, what quotation would you probably prefer, f.a.s. or c.i.f.? Why?

5. Describe the following:

sight draft	commercial invoice
time draft	certified or consular invoice
clean draft	inspection certificate
documentary draft	certificate of weight
straight bill of lading	certificate of origin
order bill of lading	shipper's export declaration
through export bill of lading	export license

6. List the factors affecting terms of payment. Which do you consider the most important? Why?

7. Explain the significance of legal limitations, control, and protective features as they relate to terms of payment.

8. Why is a wide variety of credit terms in use?

9. With regard to credit terms, what may the student, exporter, or importer find in *Exporters' Digest*? What special feature with regard to credit terms is offered by the Foreign Credit Interchange Bureau of the National Association of Credit Men?

10. List five sources of credit information for export sales.

CHAPTER 9

Financial Practice II

METHODS OF FINANCING

Consignment and Cash with Order

Because of the relatively small volume of foreign trade financed under arrangements whereby the importer deposits cash with order, little time need be spent on this method except to point out its suitability for goods manufactured to unique specification and its acceptance by the buyer only when his credit standing is very poor or when a sellers' market exists and alternate sources of supply are not available.

Foreign commerce in consigned merchandise has been quite usual in connection with the movement of raw materials or colonial products to central international markets. At the time of shipment, the purchaser may be unknown; in fact, the goods may not have been sold. They are thus consigned to a representative of the shipper, with instructions for their sale. They remain the property of the consignor until sold; the proceeds of the sale, less certain fees and a brokerage, are remitted to the foreign shipper.[1] Typical of commodities which have been handled on a consignment basis in the past are those which are sold at European auctions such as furs, cacao beans, wool, tobacco, and spices. The imposition of exchange controls, under which exporters are required to turn over to their governments foreign exchange derived from exports, and governmental action to influence the direction of export trade, interfere with the free working of markets of this type; in the postwar period, consignments will probably play a less important part than they have in the past. Some cases are reported for the use of consignments by United States exporters of finished goods, but the volume is not believed great. A difference in detail may be noted here, in that the consignment may provide for the goods to be turned over to the importer (buyer) while ownership is retained by the exporter (seller). Laws of the various countries must be

[1] George B. Roorbach, *Import Purchasing* (New York, McGraw-Hill Book Company, Inc., 1927), p. 50.

studied in each case to determine the extent of protection offered a consignor, since the question of title for the purchaser, and agency relationship between exporter and importer, may influence the advisability of shipping on consignment.

When this arrangement is used, however, the need is evident for a highly satisfactory credit standing of the importer as well as a personal acquaintanceship between the exporter and the importer. If the importer, on the other hand, finds it necessary to deposit all or part cash with his order, it is readily seen that he must make more than ordinarily certain that the seller is honest and capable and will perform according to contract. All indications point to the conclusion that the large majority of foreign trade is financed either on open account or, more importantly, by means of drafts and bank letters of credit.

Open, or Current, Account

The existence of a document of credit, such as a draft or note, does not make an obligation any greater on the part of the debtor. The principal advantages are that there is provable evidence of debt (where a draft is accepted), the amount is definitely understood, as are the time, method, and place of payment. Since the credit instrument is primarily of benefit to the seller, lack of such an instrument leaves the inference that the seller may be in a less favorable position. Whether this is so is an arguable point. Aside from the more definite clarity and certainty of the obligation, the principal benefit the exporter derives from credit instruments is that he can use them more easily in financing his operations. Some facilities exist for the discount and sale of accounts receivable, domestically, but it would be quite a difficult task to find financing accommodations resting on the pledge of accounts receivable for foreign debtors. However, because of their own financial strength or ability to finance otherwise than by the sale or discount of credit instruments arising from foreign sales, some exporters are in position to finance foreign sales on open or current account. Again, the credit standing of the buyer must be highly satisfactory for this arrangement, inasmuch as the documents are sent direct to the buyer or consignee. He is entrusted with the merchandise before payment. Payment may be specified as due by return mail after receipt of shipping papers, or under agreed terms (ten days, thirty days, month end, etc.). Remittances are normally expected to be in the form of bank drafts, wherein the importer buys from a bank in his country its draft on a bank, sometimes in a specified city such as New York or New Orleans, in the exporter's country, or by international money order. Remittances by currency appear subject to the risk of loss without recourse by the importer, unless the currency shipment has been insured.

Drafts

A draft is an order to pay, drawn (in the trade) on the importer unless someone else is specified. The draft embodies the usual qualities of a negotiable instrument. As indicated in the preceding chapter, drafts are commonly classified as to tenor and documentary attachments. If the draft specifies payment at a time other than on first presentation, the drawee is expected to *accept* the draft, signifying his agreement with the amount, manner, time, and place of payment; the document then is known as an acceptance, and the acceptor is looked on to be ready and willing to pay the obligation at maturity. These instruments facilitate financing by the exporter, for he is then in better position to pledge, discount, or sell the acceptance and receive his own funds without delay but at the cost of negotiating fees and interest charges. A further advantage, to both the exporter and importer, is to be found through use of documentary drafts. The exporter has assurance that the bank through which presented for payment or acceptance will not release the documents to the importer until the importer either pays or accepts, whichever is specified. This retention of ownership eases the position of the exporter. A documentary draft offers the importer real advantages, in that the documents are evidence that certain provisions of the order have been complied with. For example, the bill of lading proves that shipment was made by the exporter as specified and indicates whether the merchandise was in apparent good condition when received by the common carrier. The insurance policy or certificate shows the type of coverage and for whose account. The commercial invoice and consular invoice describe the merchandise and cover prices and other charges on which an understanding had to be reached when the order was placed. And the certificate of inspection, if one is specified, is evidence of the quality or condition of the merchandise. Certain other documents may be required which, if not available, would subject the importer to expense or penalty when attempting to pass the merchandise through customs.

Collection of Foreign Drafts. Inasmuch as drafts commonly are used in conjunction with documents of title, such documents being released on payment or acceptance of the draft, the problem of collecting foreign drafts is of interest to every exporter. As suggested above, a satisfactory arrangement is to collect these drafts through banks, the bank of the drawer forwarding the instrument for collection through its correspondent serving the area of the buyer or drawee.

Instructions to the bank are based on selling terms, in part, and detailed advice is given the bank as to what to do under certain possible developments. Figure 5 illustrates an instruction form which the drawer turns over to his bank with the draft. In it, the draft is described, and the attached documents, if any, are listed. At the same time, and based on

F122

THE BANK OF NEW YORK
FOREIGN DEPARTMENT
48 WALL STREET. NEW YORK 15. N. Y.

————— May 1 ——— 19 52

Dear Sirs:

We enclose for collection the undermentioned draft with documents enumerated. Please follow instructions marked "X"

NUMBER	DRAWN ON	TENOR	AMOUNT	B/L	Inv.	Cons. Inv.	Ins. Ctf.	Ctf. Orig	VARIOUS
				\multicolumn{6}{c} DOCUMENTS ATTACHED				
506	Electric Appliances Ltda.,Cali	sight	$852.37	3	2	1		2	

Forward draft and/or documents [ ] Ordinary Mail [X] Air Mail

[ ] Present on arrival of merchandise

[ ] Deliver documents on acceptance ,

[X] Deliver documents on payment

[ ] Protest for non-acceptance

[ ] Protest for non-payment

[X] Do not protest

ADVISE BY ~~CABLE~~ AIR MAIL
[ ] Non-acceptance
[X] Non-payment
[ ] Payment

[ ] Payable at collecting bank's selling rate for checks on New York on date of payment

[ ] Payable at collecting bank's selling rate for cable transfers on New York on date of payment, remitting proceeds by cable.

[X] Payable at collecting bank's selling rate for Air Mail checks on New York, on date of payment, remitting proceeds by Air Mail.

[ ] Remit proceeds by cable, difference between check and cable funds and cable expenses for our account.

[ ] Remit proceeds by Air Mail, difference between ordinary check and Air Mail funds and Air Mail expenses for our account.

[ ] Interest to be collected at——————% from date of issue until approximate arrival of cover in New York

[ ] Allow drawee interest at——————% per annum for anticipated payment

[ ] Interest to be collected at——————% per annum for any delay in payment

All charges are { [X] Drawer
for account { [ ] Drawee

[ ] Waive charges if refused by Drawee

[ ] Do not waive charges if refused by Drawee.

[ ] In case of need, refer to

——————— Colombian Agency ——————
Name

——————200 Avenida Bolivar,Cali, Colombia——
Address

Who is authorized

[ ] Only to obtain honoring of draft as drawn

[ ] To give instructions which may be followed in every respect

[ ] Special instructions——————

It is understood and agreed that, having exercised due care in the selection of any correspondent to whom the above mentioned item may be sent for collection you shall not be responsible for any act, omission, default suspension, insolvency or bankruptcy of any such correspondent or its sub-agent, or for any delay in remittance, loss in exchange or loss of said items or their proceeds during transmission or in any course of collection.

Very truly yours,

—————(signed)—————

· Marc Export Company
Authorized Signatu equired

Fɪɢ. 5. Instructions to bank for collecting foreign draft. (*Courtesy of Bank of New York.*)

prior arrangements made with the bank, the drawer indicates whether he wishes immediate credit or credit or remittance when paid. The bank is instructed to release the documents against either payment or acceptance (to be specified), what to do regarding discount if paid before maturity, whether to protest, when to present, and so on. The drawer's bank passes the same instructions along to its correspondent.

Some protection is offered in that documents conveying title will or may be held until payment or acceptance. Upon payment, the bank in the drawee's country either remits to the United States bank, for account of the exporter, or credits the account of the United States bank on its own books or with some other bank designated by the United States bank, which can then sell drafts against the account.

From the point of view of lapsed time between shipment of merchandise and receipt of payment, even the draft payable on presentation may call for several weeks to intervene. The Federal Reserve Bank of New York compiles a monthly survey of Latin-American collections in which reporting banks indicate the number of items paid promptly, up to thirty days slow, from thirty-one to sixty, sixty-one to ninety, and over ninety days slow. The time elapsed in "prompt" payment is of interest here, for in a recent report of *prompt* payments, which means payment of demand collections, the schedule below was employed.

Argentina	2 months	Honduras	1 month
Bolivia	2 months	Mexico	1 month
Brazil	6 weeks	Nicaragua	6 weeks
Chile	2 months	Panama	1 month
Colombia	7 weeks	Paraguay	2½ months
Cuba	3 weeks	Uruguay	2 months
Dominican Republic	1 month	Venezuela	6 weeks
Ecuador	6 weeks	British Guiana	6 weeks
El Salvador	1 month	Dutch Guiana	5 weeks
Guatemala	6 weeks	French Guiana	5 weeks
Haiti	1 month	Other West Indies	6 weeks

The significance of having to consider drafts as being paid promptly if within three weeks to over two months has particular bearing in connection with internal financing problems of the exporter. It should be observed, however, that these are in the nature of average figures. Between some points, and with some drawees, collection is very much faster than the schedule indicates.

Extent of Financing by Drafts and Acceptances. It is not known exactly to what extent foreign trade is financed by trade drafts or trade acceptances and, even if it were, the method of financing changes with conditions. Evidence indicates that this is perhaps the method used in arranging payment for the greatest volume of trade. A study of export financing in 1938, made by the Federal Reserve Board in 1945, showed that about half of the financing of export shipments provided by banks was in the form of purchase or discount of, or advances against, drafts drawn on foreign buyers or banks.[2]

Another interesting statistic in this connection is the total of bank

[2] *Hearings before a Subcommittee on Banking and Currency on Participation by Small Business in Foreign Exports on S. 414,* U.S. Senate, 80th Cong., 1st Sess. (1947).

acccptances outstanding, as reported in the *Federal Reserve Bulletin,* when adjusted to an annual estimate by assuming an average life of ninety days and relating the result to reported export and import volumes. The computation suggests that in the year 1946–1947 something less than 2 per cent of exports of merchandise and 15 per cent of imports was financed by bank acceptances, but considerably higher percentages appear for the 1930s and late 1920s. It should be noted though, that this figure is of *acceptances,* and that sight credits by banks, under letters of credit, are not included. Accordingly, the proportion of foreign trade financed by means of bank letters of credit (both sight and time arrangements) would be substantially larger than the percentages indicated for acceptances alone.

Letters of Credit

These instruments are letter forms issued by a bank authorizing the beneficiary to draw on it or on some other bank with which arrangements have been made and signifying the bank's commitment to honor drafts if drawn under conditions stipulated in the letter of credit. In effect, letters of credit amount to "undertakings by banks to pay against shipping documents, or documents of title, provided certain terms are complied with."[3] Letters of credit may cover exports or imports, or goods stored in or moving between foreign countries. Drafts drawn under letters of credit may be sight or time, in the latter case becoming bank acceptances.

Terms to be complied with are those specified by the party requesting the bank to open the letter of credit. They must, of course, be agreeable to both the seller and the buyer. It is primarily the seller's uncertainty as to the buyer's ability or unwillingness to pay that compels him to ask the buyer to arrange this type of bank credit. In doing so, this phase of the credit risk is practically eliminated. But the credit must be one the seller can live with, for he then runs the risk of performing as specified before expiration of the credit. In addition, the seller may desire this type of credit as it makes his own financing arrangements easier.

Advantages to Both Importer and Exporter. There are other advantages, to both seller and buyer, in the use of bank letters of credit. For the seller, if the draft is to be in a foreign currency, the high standing of a reputable bank as drawee makes it easier for him to dispose of it. And, as in the case of collecting drafts through banks, the seller obtains protection by reserving documents of title in his effective possession until the draft has been accepted by a bank satisfactory to him. In this connection, there is an added advantage, in that before negotiating the

[3] A. M. Strong, *Financing Export Shipments* (Chicago, American National Bank and Trust Company, 1946), p. 5.

draft the bank will give the documents a careful checking to assure that all specified conditions have been complied with.

Although a letter of credit is an expense, the buyer will also find advantages in using this type of financing. It is a source of funds to him, just as a direct loan from a bank would be, and the total cost may be less than that on a direct loan. Other benefits also accrue. In the first place, with the credit risk reduced or practically eliminated, the buyer is in position to obtain more favorable price consideration. Since the bank makes a check of documents against specifications, the buyer's interest is protected—if the seller fails to conform to the points specified in the letter of credit, the buyer is under no obligation. Thus, sellers' malpractices or mistakes are screened as a protection to the buyer. These malpractices and mistakes may relate to such aspects as time of shipment, quality of goods, quantity of goods, packing, insurance, and marking. However, none of the seller's or buyer's responsibility is placed on the bank's shoulders. The bank pays off on documents only, as explained later.

Federal Reserve Act Limits Bank Acceptances. The Federal Reserve Act (Sec. 13) specifies that any member bank may accept drafts or bills of exchange under certain conditions. Regulation C of the Board of Governors of the Federal Reserve System reads, in part, as follows:[4]

Any member bank may accept drafts or bills of exchange drawn upon it which grow out of any of the following transactions. . . .

The importation or exportation of goods, that is, the shipment of goods between the United States and any foreign country, or between the United States and any of its dependencies or insular possessions, or between dependencies or insular possessions and foreign countries, or between foreign countries. . . .

The storage in the United States or in any foreign country of readily marketable staples, provided that the draft or bill of exchange is secured at the time of acceptance by a warehouse receipt or other such document conveying or securing title covering such readily marketable staples.

As these provisions pertain to acceptances only and not to the issuance of letters of credit, many of which undertake bank liability to pay on sight, it must be observed that they are, in the words of Ward and Harfield,[5] a restriction and not a grant. Accordingly, the right of a member bank to issue letters of credit stems from general banking powers and not from the Federal Reserve Act. By way of restriction, several

---

[4] Pursuant to Regulations A and B, Federal Reserve banks may neither discount nor purchase bills arising out of the storage of readily marketable staples unless the acceptor remains secured throughout the life of the bill.

[5] Wilbert Ward and Henry Harfield, *Bank Credits and Acceptances* (New York, The Ronald Press Company, 1948), p. 91.

points should be noted as of direct interest to the importer or exporter. As to *maturity*, member banks are not permitted to accept drafts unless at the date of acceptance the draft has not more than six months to run, exclusive of days of grace. A *limitation on acceptances for one person,* company, or corporation is provided by restricting such credits outstanding at any one time to 10 per cent of the bank's paid-up and unimpaired capital stock and surplus, unless the bank is protected by attached documents or some other actual security growing out of the same transactions as the acceptance. In addition to the limitation on credits for any one person, the Federal Reserve regulation also specifies a *limitation on the aggregate amount* of acceptances outstanding for any one bank. This is 50 per cent of its paid-up and unimpaired capital stock and surplus, unless permission is granted to individual banks by the Federal Reserve to increase the aggregate to 100 per cent of capital stock and surplus.

Types of Letters of Credit. Classification of letters of credit may be according to tenor, purpose, revocability, and responsibility of the negotiating bank. Under tenor, the credit will be referred to as *sight* or *time*, depending on whether it provides for drafts to be drawn payable on sight or after a period of time. Only in the latter case does a bank acceptance arise, for the sight credit would call for immediate payment, not acceptance, by the bank on which it is drawn. The second classification, purpose, pertains to the nature of the underlying transaction. As has already been mentioned, this may be for *foreign transactions, export, import,* or *storage*. Banks may also accept drafts drawn for the creation of dollar exchange.

Credits May Be Revocable or Irrevocable. A letter of credit may be *revocable* or it may be *irrevocable*. The former reserves to the issuing bank the right to revoke the credit at any time before negotiation, without prior notice to the beneficiary. Accordingly, use of this type is restricted to circumstances wherein the exporter and importer have some other satisfactory basis for proceeding with the business at hand. The irrevocable credit is a firm commitment by the issuing bank for the period specified in the letter of credit. During its life, it cannot be canceled or modified to the detriment of the beneficiary without agreement on the part of all parties concerned. This gives the exporter greater protection, as the importer cannot decide to cancel, reduce, or modify the order to the disadvantage of the exporter, who looks to the bank to pay or accept the draft drawn under terms of the credit regardless of the bank's relationship to the importer.

Important Difference between Confirmed and Unconfirmed Credits. Another significant classification of letters of credit is that between *unconfirmed* and *confirmed*. The former refers to a credit opened by a

THE BANK OF NEW YORK

48 WALL STREET, NEW YORK 15, N.Y.

FOREIGN DEPARTMENT

OUR ADVICE NO. 10000

May 2, 1952

MENTION THIS ADVICE NUMBER AND DATE ON ALL DRAFTS AND COMMUNICATIONS

Sterling Export Company
Dallas, Texas

DEAR SIRS:
     WE ARE INSTRUCTED BY   Bank of Bombay, Bombay, India

IN THEIR   cable   OF May 1, 1952   TO ADVISE YOU THAT THEY HAVE OPENED THEIR IRREVOCABLE LETTER OF CREDIT NO. 500   FOR A SUM OR SUMS NOT EXCEEDING A TOTAL OF   One Hundred Twenty-Seven Thousand Dollars ($127,000.00) U.S. Currency

FOR ACCOUNT OF   India Cotton Co., Bombay
AVAILABLE BY YOUR DRAFTS ON US AT   sight
ACCOMPANIED BY
Signed commercial invoice

Copy of Export Declaration certified by U.S. Customs that the cotton was grown in the U.S.A.

Full set "on board" ocean bills of lading drawn to "order" and blank endorsed marked: "Freight Prepaid" dated not later than May 31, 1952

Evidencing shipment of 625 bales Raw Cotton from the United States Gulf Ports to Bombay cost and freight. Partial shipments permitted. Transshipments not permitted

We have been informed that the insurance will be covered by buyer

     ALL DRAFTS, WITH DOCUMENTS AS SPECIFIED, MUST BE PRESENTED AT THIS OFFICE NOT LATER THAN   June 15, 1952

     EXCEPT SO FAR AS OTHERWISE EXPRESSLY STATED, THIS CREDIT IS SUBJECT TO THE UNIFORM CUSTOMS AND PRACTICE FOR COMMERCIAL DOCUMENTARY CREDITS FIXED BY THE THIRTEENTH CONGRESS OF THE INTERNATIONAL CHAMBER OF COMMERCE; FOR THE DEFINITIONS OF CERTAIN EXPORT QUOTATIONS REFERENCE IS MADE TO THE GENERAL DESCRIPTIONS OF THOSE TERMS INCLUDED IN THE "REVISED AMERICAN FOREIGN TRADE DEFINITIONS—1941".

     THE ABOVE MENTIONED CORRESPONDENT ENGAGES WITH YOU THAT ALL DRAFTS DRAWN UNDER AND IN COMPLIANCE WITH THE TERMS OF THIS ADVICE WILL BE DULY HONORED ON PRESENTATION.

     WE HEREBY CONFIRM THE ABOVE CREDIT AND UNDERTAKE THAT ALL DRAFTS DRAWN AND PRESENTED AS ABOVE SPECIFIED WILL BE DULY HONORED BY US.

YOURS VERY TRULY.

AUTHORIZED SIGNATURE

FIG. 6. Form of confirmed letter of credit. (*Courtesy of Bank of New York.*)

foreign bank in favor of an exporter with notification being given the exporter by a bank in his own country, but without that bank's assuming obligation or responsibility. It will clarify the discussion if we assume the exporter to be in the United States.

Advice to the exporter (by the United States bank) that such a credit has been opened is usually accompanied by a clause reading more or less as follows: "This advice conveys no engagement on our part and is simply for your guidance in preparing and presenting drafts and documents." It may be of interest to note that even though the exporter is authorized to draw the draft on the bank in the United States, the bank assumes no formal responsibility to pay or accept the draft. So long as the credit remains in force, the draft will be honored.

The confirmed letter of credit is shown in Fig. 6, the last sentence of which reads: "We hereby confirm the above credit and undertake that all drafts drawn and presented as above specified will be duly honored by us." It should be observed that only irrevocable credits are confirmed, and that the designations "confirmed" and "unconfirmed" pertain solely to credits opened by other banks. They are not issued by the bank notifying the exporter of their existence. An irrevocable letter-of-credit form is shown in Fig. 7. As may be seen from the forms shown, provision is made for the specification of certain documents to be attached to the draft. When documents are specified, which is by far the common practice, the drafts are referred to as *documentary;* when no documents are required to be attached, the draft drawn under the letter of credit is referred to as *clean.* Another distinction which may be made is that between *mail* and *cable* credits; this refers to the form in which the credits are communicated by the issuing bank. The advice may go direct to the beneficiary, but ordinarily it will move through correspondent-bank channels.

Letter-of-credit Procedure

Letters of credit covering exports are initiated by the foreign buyer. He arranges with his bank either to open a letter of credit in favor of the exporter (which may or may not be confirmed by a bank in the United States) or to have a bank in the United States open the letter of credit, with his bank assuring the bank in the United States against loss. These expenses are borne by the buyer, who must satisfy his bank as to his credit-worthiness and who may obtain these accommodations on either a secured or an unsecured basis, depending on his credit standing and on the banking laws of his country. Of course, what is an "export" credit to the exporter is an "import" credit to the importer.

Import letters of credit are commonly preceded by establishment of a line of credit between the importer and his bank. Bringing this line of credit into operation calls for a sequence of actions and documents. These are as follows:

Application for letter of credit
Letter of credit agreement
Issuance of letter of credit
Processing of draft or acceptance

Releasing of goods to the importer
Reimbursement of bank by the importer
Honoring of acceptance by bank

1. APPLICATION FOR LETTER OF CREDIT. The initial step in having a letter of credit opened is, after arrangements have been made for credit accommodation, the execution of an *application for letter of credit.* The application is usually on forms supplied by the bank (see Fig. 8) and

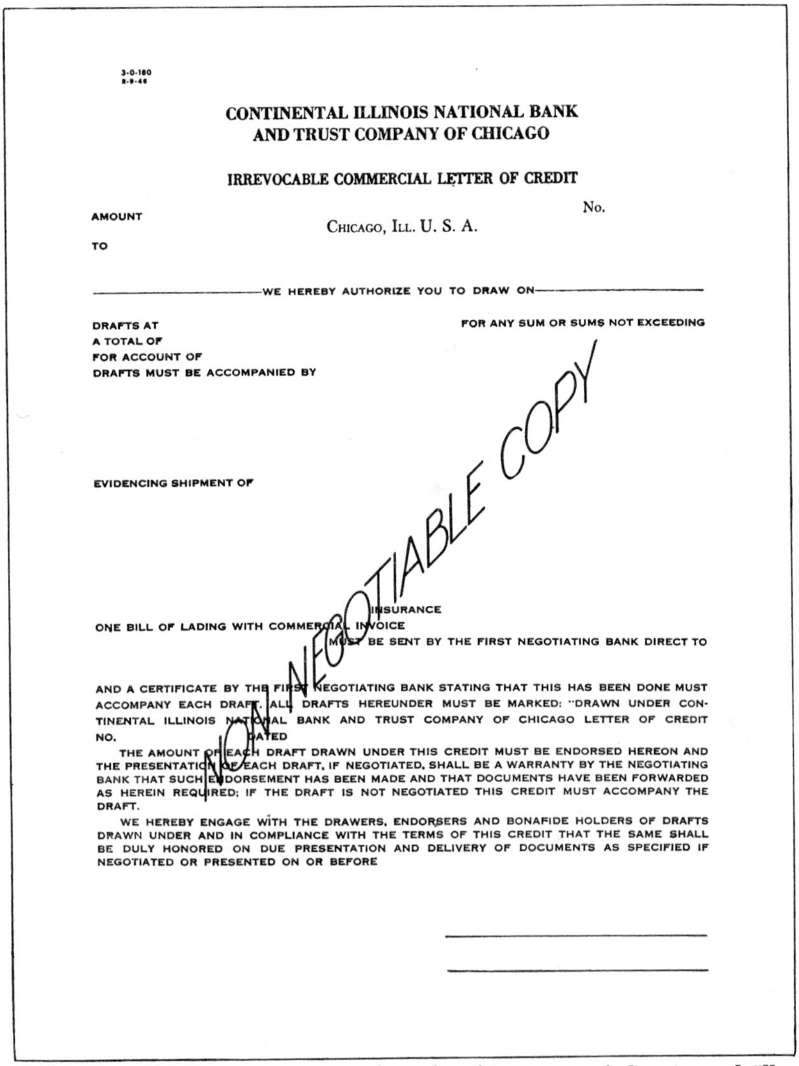

3-0-180
8-9-46

CONTINENTAL ILLINOIS NATIONAL BANK
AND TRUST COMPANY OF CHICAGO

IRREVOCABLE COMMERCIAL LETTER OF CREDIT

No.

AMOUNT

CHICAGO, ILL. U. S. A.

TO

WE HEREBY AUTHORIZE YOU TO DRAW ON

DRAFTS AT
FOR ANY SUM OR SUMS NOT EXCEEDING
A TOTAL OF
FOR ACCOUNT OF
DRAFTS MUST BE ACCOMPANIED BY

EVIDENCING SHIPMENT OF

INSURANCE
ONE BILL OF LADING WITH COMMERCIAL INVOICE
MUST BE SENT BY THE FIRST NEGOTIATING BANK DIRECT TO

AND A CERTIFICATE BY THE FIRST NEGOTIATING BANK STATING THAT THIS HAS BEEN DONE MUST ACCOMPANY EACH DRAFT. ALL DRAFTS HEREUNDER MUST BE MARKED: "DRAWN UNDER CONTINENTAL ILLINOIS NATIONAL BANK AND TRUST COMPANY OF CHICAGO LETTER OF CREDIT NO. DATED

THE AMOUNT OF EACH DRAFT DRAWN UNDER THIS CREDIT MUST BE ENDORSED HEREON AND THE PRESENTATION OF EACH DRAFT, IF NEGOTIATED, SHALL BE A WARRANTY BY THE NEGOTIATING BANK THAT SUCH ENDORSEMENT HAS BEEN MADE AND THAT DOCUMENTS HAVE BEEN FORWARDED AS HEREIN REQUIRED; IF THE DRAFT IS NOT NEGOTIATED THIS CREDIT MUST ACCOMPANY THE DRAFT.

WE HEREBY ENGAGE WITH THE DRAWERS, ENDORSERS AND BONAFIDE HOLDERS OF DRAFTS DRAWN UNDER AND IN COMPLIANCE WITH THE TERMS OF THIS CREDIT THAT THE SAME SHALL BE DULY HONORED ON DUE PRESENTATION AND DELIVERY OF DOCUMENTS AS SPECIFIED IF NEGOTIATED OR PRESENTED ON OR BEFORE

NON NEGOTIABLE COPY

FIG. 7. Form of irrevocable letter of credit. (*Courtesy of Continental Illinois National Bank and Trust Company of Chicago.*)

covers all the detailed instructions which the customer wishes his bank to incorporate into the letter of credit. Besides the name of the beneficiary, amount, and maturity date, instructions may be given pertaining to the merchandise, the documents to be attached to drafts drawn against it, insurance coverage, and bills of lading. It is essential that these instructions to the bank be complete, precise, and workable; modification

X117-A Rev.

New Orleans, La.____________19___

WHITNEY NATIONAL BANK OF NEW ORLEANS
Foreign Banking Department
NEW ORLEANS, LA.

This Letter of Credit to be opened by:
( ) Regular Mail
( ) Air Mail
( ) Cable

Please issue for our account an irrevocable letter of credit on____________

____

in favor of____________

not exceeding in the aggregate____________
(Amount of This Letter of Credit)

available by drafts at____________
(Tenor of Drafts)

for______% of invoice cost of____________

____
(Merchandise to Be Shipped—Give Only Quantity and Commodity, Not Details of Commodity)

to be shipped to____________
(Destination)

for account of____________
(Purchaser in Whose Name This Credit Is Being Issued)

The drafts must be negotiated on/or prior to____________

and bills of lading dated at____________

on/or prior to____________

Drafts are to be accompanied by the following documents evidencing shipment as above:

( ) Insurance certificate or policy
( ) Consular invoice
( ) Complete set of ocean bills of lading to the order of the Whitney National Bank
( ) Complete set of On Board ocean bills of lading to the order of the Whitney National Bank
( ) Commercial invoice____________
( ) ____________
( ) ____________
( ) ____________
( ) ____________

The description of the merchandise given above is in strict accordance with our wishes and is to govern you in dealing with drafts and documents under this letter of credit.

To assist you in keeping proper margin against this credit, but not to be incorporated therein, we beg to advise that the merchandise to move under it is more accurately described as follows:

____

YOURS VERY TRULY,

____

FIG. 8. Application for letter of credit. (*Courtesy of Whitney National Bank of New Orleans.*)

may be expensive if it is possible. It may be advisable to discuss these instructions with the bank, which issues the letter of credit in strict accord with instructions contained in the application. Hence, thoroughness and care in making application for a letter of credit are necessary in order to render issuance easier and to avoid having to revoke or amend for error or inadequacy at a later date.

2. LETTER-OF-CREDIT AGREEMENT. When the application for the letter of credit has been executed, the next instrument called for is the *letter-of-credit agreement,* which is, in effect, the "note" signed by the party requesting the bank to open the credit, or the contract between the two. It is sometimes attached to or printed on the reverse side of one of the copies of the letter of credit. In this agreement, the party requesting the credit signifies his intention of placing the bank in funds to pay the draft or acceptances when due, and when necessary gives to the bank a specific claim and lien on the goods covered by it (through means of an order bill of lading or a trust receipt) or on the proceeds of the sale of these goods. Figure 9 shows a letter-of-credit agreement. It may be seen, also, that the agreement relieves the bank of responsibility in connection with the existence, quantity, quality, condition, and delivery of goods purported to be covered by the documents or for the genuineness of the documents. This stems from the fact that the bank rarely sees the physical goods—activities are by means of documents issued by supposedly reputable parties.

3. ISSUANCE OF LETTER OF CREDIT. Upon issuance of the letter of credit and its receipt by the beneficiary (exporter), the beneficiary has some assurance of coverage in the manner specified in the credit. He prepares or obtains the documents specified, draws his draft, and presents the draft and documents to the negotiating bank. The draft and documents are then forwarded by the negotiating bank to the issuing bank, unless the draft is drawn on the negotiating bank, for payment or acceptance. At this stage, a major test arises; depending on the bank's decision that the documents are all in order and that the terms have been complied with, it will either honor or reject the draft. How careful a check on documents is a bank expected to make? Article 9 of *Uniform Customs and Practice for Commercial Documentary Credits*[6] reads: "Banks must examine all documents and papers with care so as to ascertain that on their face they appear to be in order." Lack of conformity to specifications of the letter of credit may be agreeable to the exporter and importer and may be so indicated in the sales contract, but, before the bank can honor the draft, it must be released of responsibility for deviating from the terms of the credit. On the other hand, conformance with terms

---

[6] International Chamber of Commerce, 1951.

F. X. 26

....19......

THE NATIONAL BANK OF COMMERCE
IN NEW ORLEANS

Gentlemen:

Having received from you the Letter of Credit, of which a true copy is on the other side, ...hereby agree to its terms, and in consideration thereof, ...bind ....to furnish you, not later than..............days before the maturity of the acceptances under it, with first-class approved Bankers' Demand Bills of Exchange, for the same amount, payable in......................and bearing our endorsement, or to pay the equivalent thereof in cash at the current rate of exchange for first-class demand Bankers' Bills.

And..............hereby give you a specific claim and lien on all goods and the proceeds thereof for which you or your correspondents may come under any engagements, under said Credit, on all policies of insurance on such goods, and on all Bills of Lading given therefor, with full power and authority to take possession and dispose of the same at discretion, and to charge all expenses, including commissions, for sale and guarantee. .... further agree to give you any additional security that you may require.

It is understood that neither you nor your Correspondent is to warrant or be responsible for the existence, quantity, quality, condition or delivery of goods purporting to be shipped and covered by the documents presented by the party in whose favor the credit is opened, nor for the genuineness of such documents.

It is understood that on all payments made by..................to you in.. the..shall be calculated at the current rate of Exchange in ....for Bankers' Bills on......................................, existing at the time of settlement.

Any credits which may be granted shall be considered under this agreement, and on the basis thereof with such variations, if any, as may be arranged.

The Marine Insurance to be done by....................in..................................satisfactory to you.

Your charge for commission under such Credit shall be....................per cent. for such parts as shall be used.

Merchandise imported under this Credit to be paid for, or approved security lodged with you before surrender of the Documents.

All securities which shall be received by you hereunder may be held and applied by you, also to secure all other indebtedness of liability existing, or which may hereafter arise from us to you.

Any goods imported under this or any other Credit issued by you for our account, or their proceeds, whether the draft against same shall have been paid or not, or whether the goods shall have been delivered to us or not, may be held by you as general collateral security for our account with you, upon the terms and conditions herein contained.

This obligation is to continue in force and to be applicable to all transactions, notwithstanding any change in the composition of the firm or firms, parties to this contract, or in the user of this Credit, whether such change shall arise from the accession of one or more new partners, or from the death or secession of any partner or partners.

FIG. 9. Form of letter-of-credit agreement. (*Courtesy of National Bank of Commerce in New Orleans.*)

of the credit, even though contrary to terms of the sales contract, justifies the bank's honoring the draft. According to *Uniform Customs* as well as when stipulated in the letter-of-credit agreement, banks "assume no liability or responsibility for the form, sufficiency, correctness, genuineness, falsification or legal effect of any documents or papers, or for the description, quantity, weight, quality, condition, packing, delivery or value of goods represented thereby"[7]

Under these interpretations, a bank is expected to see that the documents evidence that the goods have been turned over to a common carrier, but not that they were actually shipped, unless so prescribed. The amount of the invoice must conform to the amount provided for in the credit, but the bank is not expected to check all detailed extensions to ascertain that all charges are mathematically and contractually correct. Thus, while the bank is to be relied on to make a careful check, it cannot be expected to act as a substitute for the exporter's or importer's own clerical force. It would, of course, be expected to assure that the draft and shipment were within the time specified in the letter of credit, that the amount of the invoice was within the provisions of the underlying credit, that all documents requested had been provided and appeared to be in order, that insurance had been provided as specified, that any special charges for which arrangement was made in the letter of credit had been satisfactorily covered, that the bill of lading read "on board" if so required, and that the description, marks, and numbers of the merchandise packages were as specified and were consistent as among the various documents. Some goods, by their nature, do not allow the delivery of the exact amount indicated, due to evaporation, loss, spoilage, and so on. Definite prices or quantities may not be determinable in advance. Accordingly, the terms "about," "circa," or similar designations may be used to permit accomplishment of the transaction. According to *Uniform Customs,* these terms allow a difference not to exceed 10 per cent in the amount of the credit, quantity, or unit price of the goods. For some products, such as oil in barrels, ore in bulk, and chemicals in bulk or in cylinders, a difference of 3 per cent is allowed even if the terms of the credit call for a fixed weight or measurement.

4. PROCESSING OF DRAFT OR ACCEPTANCE. If examination discloses that all provisions of the letter of credit have been complied with, the bank must either pay or accept the draft, depending on its tenor. If it is paid, notice is sent to the person who had the letter of credit opened in order that he may at once repay the bank. If it is accepted, the newly made bank acceptance will be disposed of in accordance with instructions of the owner (drawer or holder in due course).

A difference to be noted at this point pertains to the question of whether the draft is drawn on a bank in the exporter's country, in his own currency, or whether it is drawn on a foreign bank, probably in a foreign currency. If the former, the exporter obtains funds without delay or liability. If it is a sight draft, payment can be effected at once; if an

[7] *Ibid.,* Art. 11.

acccptance is to be created, the exporter comes into possession of a claim on a bank in his country, payable at some future date. But he will have no difficulty in realizing cash immediately, for such obligations of first-class (or prime) banks always have a ready market at a very favorable discount rate. The risk is so little, relatively, that the acceptances move at a very slight discount. The exporter really has three choices in the matter. He may hold the acceptance until maturity, thus avoiding the discount expense; he may discount the acceptance with the accepting bank; or he may discount the instrument in the open market. Determination of choice will depend on a number of considerations, probably the most important being his banking connections, the rate of discount, and the exporter's need for funds at the moment.

If the draft is drawn on a foreign bank, and is in a foreign currency, other considerations enter the picture. First of all is the additional time elapsed between drawing of the draft and its payment, even when payable at sight. If payable after sight or presentation, in which case it would become an acceptance, this time period would be extended. The exporter's need for funds, probably more acute over an extended period, might make it necessary for him to discount the acceptance, whose rate would now take into consideration its more distant maturity. Also, if in a foreign currency, the discount rate would take into account the prevailing indication of future values of the currency in question. And if held until maturity, the exporter would be running the risk of an unfavorable turn in exchange rates unless he covered his exchange position by hedging.

The importer faces an exchange problem if the draft he is contracting to cover is to be drawn in a currency other than his own. Proceeding conservatively, he would cover his exchange position by purchasing a forward contract, thus assuring himself of the cost of the exchange to be needed at the future date.

5. RELEASING OF GOODS TO THE IMPORTER. After paying or accepting the draft drawn under its letter of credit, the bank retains the documents required in the credit and has effective control over the merchandise, assuming an order bill of lading to have been used. The party requesting the letter of credit desires the goods for processing or sale, the proceeds of which may be needed for his repayment of the bank. How, then, can he obtain the merchandise, especially when the bank desires to remain secured with title? The possibility of his paying the bank in cash has been ruled out of consideration. But there could be partial releases by the bank, at the time the importer sells the merchandise and either places the bank in funds or turns over an account receivable (or good evidence of sale). This method, too, has many limitations. There has

FORM 1

Form adopted by the
New Orleans Clearing House Association

10-51—50M.

APPLICATION AND TRUST RECEIPT

New Orleans, La.,_____, 195__

The Hibernia National Bank in New Orleans
_____

I
We hereby make application to withdraw, on the terms and conditions of the subjoined TRUST RECEIPT, the documents (hereinafter referred to as the "withdrawn documents"), hereinafter described, which withdrawn documents and the property represented thereby are pledged to you

me \ my

to secure advances made to us on our obligations, dated_____ L/C #_____, in the amount of $_____, for one or both of the following purposes:

First, for shipment and/or sale of the property represented by said withdrawn documents;

Second, for substituting and/or changing said withdrawn documents for warehouse receipts or other documents representing and describing the identical property

The documents to be withdrawn are:

Commercial Invoice, Consular Invoice, Bill of Lading, S/S
_____
_____
_____
_____
_____
_____
_____
_____

DESCRIPTION OF COLLATERAL PLEDGED — MARKS, NUMBERS AND

Signature...

TRUST RECEIPT

New Orleans, La.,_____, 195__

Received in trust from__The Hibernia National Bank in New Orleans__
the withdrawn documents described in the foregoing application, held by said Bank as collateral pledged to secure advances made to the undersigned, and, in consideration thereof, the undersigned hereby expressly agree/agrees to pay over to said Bank, or its assigns, on demand, the proceeds of the sale of the property described in and/or represented by said documents, or any part thereof, or should the amount of said proceeds exceed the entire indebtedness to said Bank, in principal and interest, the undersigned expressly agree/agrees to pay over to said Bank, or its assigns, on demand, a proportion thereof equal to the full amount of said entire indebtedness, in principal and interest.

It is stipulated that the payments herein contemplated shall be specifically applied against the identical advances secured by the withdrawn documents and the property represented thereby.

In the event that the undersigned withdraw/withdraws said withdrawn documents for the purpose of substituting and/or changing them for warehouse receipts or other documents, representing and describing the identical property pledged, it is expressly agreed that said new documents shall be delivered to said Bank, or its assigns, within one (1) day from the receipt thereof by the undersigned.

In either or both of the above cases, it is expressly agreed that the delivery of the withdrawn documents is being temporarily made to the undersigned for convenience only, without novation of the original debt, or giving the undersigned any title to the withdrawn documents or the property represented thereby, and the undersigned is/are given possession thereof solely as trustee/trustees for said Bank, and as such to receive the avails thereof or the documents therefor for account of said Bank.

It is further stipulated that the undersigned shall not, under any circumstances whatsoever, use, sell or repledge the withdrawn documents and/or the property represented thereby, or any part thereof, withdrawn under the terms of this TRUST RECEIPT, for any other purpose than that of paying the indebtedness for the security of which the said withdrawn documents are pledged to said Bank.

(Any violation of the terms and conditions of this TRUST RECEIPT is made a felony by Section 201 of Title 14 of the Louisiana Revised Statutes of 1950, printed in full on the back hereof.)

Signature_____

Fig. 10. Form of application, and trust-receipt agreement. (*Courtesy of Hibernia National Bank in New Orleans.*)

been developed for use in these instances a *trust receipt,* which is a document signed by the importer in which he acknowledges receipt of the merchandise *belonging to the bank,* such merchandise to be held in trust for the bank in which title rests. The document gives the importer the right to display, process, or sell the merchandise, but he at the same time agrees either to return the merchandise to the bank or to hold in trust

FORM X124

WHITNEY NATIONAL BANK
OF NEW ORLEANS
FOREIGN BANKING DEPARTMENT

NEW ORLEANS, LA. ____________

____

____

____

DEAR SIRS:

Please note that under our Commercial Letter of Credit No. ________ *which we issued on* ________ *for your account in favor of* ____________

____

we have accepted the draft of the beneficiaries

For $ ________

Due in ________

And due here ________

Yours respectfully,

WHITNEY NATIONAL BANK
of New Orleans
Foreign Banking Department

____
Vice-Pres.—Manager

FIG. 11. Notice to debtor of acceptance creation and maturity date. (*Courtesy of Whitney National Bank of New Orleans.*)

or immediately turn over to the bank any proceeds of such sale, including accounts or notes receivable. A uniform trust-receipt law has been adopted in 16 states.[8] Figure 10 illustrates the trust-receipt agreement.

6. REIMBURSEMENT OF BANK BY IMPORTER AND HONORING OF ACCEPTANCE. Upon acceptance by the bank of the draft drawn under its letter of credit, the bank may never know who holds the acceptance until its maturity. What it does know is that it has a definite obligation (which

[8] Morris S. Rosenthal, *Techniques of International Trade* (New York, McGraw-Hill Book Company, Inc., 1950), p. 370. States having adopted the uniform law are New York, California, Connecticut, Illinois, Indiana, Maryland, Massachusetts, Minnesota, Nevada, New Hampshire, New Jersey, Oregon, Pennsylvania, Tennessee, Virginia, and Washington.

appears as a liability on the bank statement) to meet on a definite date. Whether the person requesting the bank to open the letter of credit goes bankrupt or defaults on his agreement with the bank or otherwise fails to repay the bank before maturity of the acceptance is the bank's own credit risk. The acceptance must be honored by the bank regardless of whether the importer ever pays. Since, however, the letter of credit was issued only after satisfactory credit arrangements had been made by the importer with his bank, which presumes satisfactory credit standing to justify the risk, the normal procedure is for the bank to notify the importer in time for him to place the bank in funds on the day before maturity of the acceptance. Figure 11 is a form notice used for this purpose.

Miscellaneous Financing Methods

Authority to Pay and Authority to Purchase. Modifications of the letter of credit are found here, the authority to pay being somewhat similar to a revocable letter of credit. The principal differences between the authority to purchase and the letter of credit are that, under the former, authority stems from the buyer and not the bank, the draft is drawn on the buyer and not on a bank, and the drawer is subject to recourse. This means that bank protection against the credit risk of the buyer is not offered and that the authority is merely an arrangement to negotiate and help the seller obtain his funds earlier. Ward and Harfield point out that "the practical effect of an authority to purchase is simply to make available to his suppliers a buyer's line of credit with his own bank for the discount of foreign bills."[9]

The authority to pay also stems from the buyer, but stipulates that drafts are to be drawn at sight on the branch or correspondent of the buyer's bank in the seller's country. When drafts are so drawn and paid, the seller is no longer liable as drawer, the negotiating bank in his country looking for reimbursement from the buyer's bank.

Financing by Factors. Participation by factors in financing foreign commerce appears to have been a development of some proportion following the Second World War.[10] A factor is a combination mercantile and banking house, performing such financial services as assuming credit risks and discounting drafts and other receivables. While well known in the textile trades, domestically, the activity of factors in other fields is less recognized. Ordinarily, factoring functions pertain to the financial operations alone, but Sánchez finds some advantage in having the exporter's shipping function transferred to the factor.[11]

[9] *Op. cit.,* p. 10.
[10] E. E. Pratt, *Foreign Trade Handbook* (Chicago and London, The Dartnell Corporation, 1949), p. 539.
[J. Rodríguez Sánchez, *Foreign Credits and Collections* (New York, Prentice-Hall, Inc., 1947), p. 313.

Back-to-back Letters of Credit. At times, an exporter may not be in a position to acquire the merchandise to be covered by documents without financial aid. He may have obtained an order from abroad but, in order to obtain payment, the terms call for documents to be surrendered at time of payment. For situations such as this, the back-to-back credit has been devised, through which an exporter applies for a bank letter of credit to be opened in favor of the exporter's supplier. On the strength of this, the supplier releases the merchandise to the exporter who can then procure necessary documents to obtain payment under the basic credit. Terms of the back-to-back letter of credit may generally be said to coincide with those of the basic. But the arrangement may be complicated by such factors as the exporter's desire to conceal his profit margins, his unwillingness to reveal to his supplier the name of the foreign buyer, and f.o.b. quotations (to the exporter) as against c.i.f. quotations (to the foreign buyer). The exporter, when shipment is ready, is paid on the basic credit; he receives the basic amount less the sum needed for settlement of the back-to-back credit. Other than for margin required of the exporter, this difference should amount roughly to gross profit on the transaction.

Revolving Letters of Credit. In international trade in some commodities, several shipments are made over a long period of time, in amounts relatively uncertain at the time negotiations to purchase are made. Credit accommodation may be had which takes care of these several shipments but which limits the amount that may be outstanding on the credit as of any one time. For example, a line of acceptance may be set up not to exceed $100,000 at any one time. Drafts may be drawn for several times the amount of this line over the period of a season or a year, but only as credits which exceed $100,000 are paid back may new drafts be drawn. Then, when the need has been fulfilled, the entire line will be liquidated. Provision for forewarning of the beneficiary before the credit is cut off may be advisable.

Financing through the Export-Import Bank. Individual importers and exporters are one type of borrower accommodated by the Export-Import Bank of Washington. The aid may be direct or, as preferred by the Export-Import Bank, through the exporter's or importer's own commercial bank. In fact, the Export-Import Bank suggests that the application for credit be forwarded to it through a commercial bank, which will then present the case for consideration. The Export-Import Bank may make the entire loan if commercial-bank accommodation cannot satisfactorily be found; the commercial bank may make the loan, with a guarantee to it by the Export-Import Bank; or the arrangement may be one of joint participation between the Export-Import Bank and a commercial bank. Accommodation through this facility may be found useful in cases involving lengthy credits (member banks being limited to accepting with a maturity not to exceed six months) or for risks otherwise unacceptable to commercial banks.

CREDIT INSURANCE

In brief, credit insurance is an arrangement to shift to someone other than the seller certain risks to be found in selling on credit. These risks may be economic or political. The former include the buyer's default because of either inability or unwillingness to pay. Any number of excuses may be offered as to the reason for nonpayment, but all of an economic nature can be reduced to the debtor's own unwillingness or inability. On the political side, the buyer's government may not permit him to make payment abroad, although he is both willing and able to do so in his own currency. Through blocking the convertibility of exchange, the government makes it impossible for the individual to execute his obligation to the satisfaction of the creditor and at times, in order to prevent legal recourse, rules that the buyer has executed his obligation by the process of depositing with the central bank or other government agency sufficient funds in his (buyer's) currency to cover the obligation payable in a foreign currency. Then these blocked funds are converted by government direction as circumstances permit.

Attempts to avoid some of these risks are made by terms of sale, but often the liberality encouraged by competition induces a seller to enter into a sales contract without the protection he desires. He is then faced with the problem of carrying the risk or attempting to pass it along to someone else. It was stated in the preceding chapter that a del credere agent may offer the desired protection, but this is only against a certain type of risk—economic. Where other protection is not to be had, the seller may seek to cover his position with a credit-insurance policy. Insurance against credit losses on foreign sales may be offered either by commercial (private) or by government organizations.

United States Experience. United States experience in export credit insurance appears to date from 1919, when the American Manufacturers Foreign Credit Insurance Exchange was set up.[12] This organization ceased to function in the early 1930s. In 1934, the Export Credit Indemnity Exchange began to operate under direction of the American Foreign Credit Underwriters Corporation, but in 1940 insurance of export credit risks was suspended. Under the arrangement, members were indemnified up to 75 per cent of their credit losses under specified conditions, one being that the individual shipments be first approved by the

[12] Philip McDonald, *Practical Exporting* (New York, The Ronald Press Company, 1949), p. 272.

American Foreign Credit Underwriters Corporation. The latter corporation now (1952) functions as an active credit-rating organization and publishes the *Market Guide for Latin America,* containing credit data on over 80,000 names; the *Market Guide for the Philippines;* and the *Exporters' Digest,* a leading trade journal.

Export-Import Bank Proposed as Insurer. On the governmental side, the United States offers no credit insurance in the complete sense. The Export-Import Bank of Washington offers direct advances to exporters (and importers) under certain conditions and also provides guarantees to exporters or their banks against certain foreign commitments. To this extent, it may be said that some sort of protection is available. However, a bill known as the Export Insurance Act was introduced in Congress in 1946, 1947, and 1949, but had not yet passed by the end of 1952. This bill would increase the regular capital stock of the Export-Import Bank by an "insurance capital stock" of $100,000,000 and would set up a Foreign Trade Insurance Division in the bank with authority to insure export credits up to a total outstanding at any one time of $500,000,000. Insurance would be available up to 90 per cent of the contract price if nonpayment was due to any reason other than foreign-government imposition of exchange restrictions, and up to 100 per cent in case nonpayment was due to such action. There has been widespread opposition to the bill, as well as some favorable reaction, but the more conservative interests appear to feel that "insurance" by government against the ordinary risks of business is a cloak to cover subsidization. Further, they feel that if the exporter is not satisfied that he can carry the account or run the risk, he should look elsewhere for sales, ask the importer to pay in advance, or arrange a bank letter of credit. Objection is also found in the fact that exports stimulated by government insurance to overcome foreign competition *increase the export-trade surplus;* this is already a continuing problem of major proportions in foreign commercial policy. On the other hand, proponents argue that many businesses, especially small ones, are not in a position to carry long-term credits, nor can they be independent and demanding that buyers provide bank letters of credit since competitive exporters from this and other countries might not be doing so.

Whether government should provide facilities for protection against ordinary business risks is questionable, inasmuch as the problem touches on the point of competitive strength, ability, and efficiency. However, with the introduction of political risks, more clamor may be heard for the government to protect exporters selling on credit against such a risk as nonconvertibility of exchange brought about by foreign-government imposition of exchange restrictions. It will probably be felt that more justification exists for this kind of blanket protection than for intervention in individual creditor debtor relationships. Of course, if the United States government assumes the risks and thereby precludes pressure from importers in other countries for their governments to put their own houses in order, it will simply delay any corrective action other governments might feel impelled to take. As was already indicated, some United States government action has been taken in this regard by the arrangement whereby the Economic Cooperation Administration set up a special guarantee fund to assure convertibility of exchange to Americans on investments and sales of certain products such as books and periodicals in European-aid countries. This provision is that, within specified limits, a guarantee will be given that net receipts in foreign currencies from the sale of informational media in the ECA countries can be converted into U.S. dollars.[13]

Other Governments Active. Other governments have been more active in export credit insurance than has that of the United States. The proposed Export Insurance Act is patterned on the British (1926) and Canadian (1944) systems. At hearings on the proposed bill, it was brought out that the following countries have or had some variety of government-operated export credit insurance plan:

Australia	Finland	The Netherlands
Austria	France	Norway
Belgium	Germany	Poland
Canada	Great Britain	Spain
Czechoslovakia	Italy	Sweden
Denmark	Latvia	

One could take a "tough" attitude with the foreign buyers and demand confirmed letters of credit on export sales. Obviously, this would tend to make exports more difficult in the light of more lenient, and perhaps subsidized, credit facilities offered by sellers in other countries, to say nothing of easier terms offered by other sellers in the United States able to do so on their own. Where the lure of government guarantee also enters is in connection with sales abroad of goods commonly financed on long-term credit, such as machinery. Member banks are prohibited from accepting drafts with a maturity in excess of six months, and loans and discounts are restricted as to maturity if eligibility for rediscount with the Federal Reserve is desired. Yet sellers in the United States find it advantageous and perhaps necessary to sell abroad on longer terms because the foreign buyers claim they can receive more lenient terms from, say, some European sources. It is felt by some that if government guarantees could be had, banks might be more willing to

[13] The 1950 renewal of the Act extended coverage to include expropriation and limited total insurance coverage to $200,000,000. ECA was succeeded, 1951, by MSA.

handle the paper with a longer maturity, as the government guarantee would in the first place tend to reduce the possibility of criticism by bank examiners and in the second place take care of the credit risk itself. The former point could be met by a relaxation of restrictions on maturity for Federal Reserve credit availability, if that were to be considered desirable. British and Continental bankers are not under the same restraint as are their counterparts in the United States in the matter of accepting and offering bills to the market.[14]

However, such relaxation would not mean a wide break in actual practice, for the accepting bank becomes a debtor, and it does not incur a debt simply because the paper can float around the market easily. It still looks to the underlying transactions for soundness, in the belief that economic health is more important than economic expansion.

REVIEW QUESTIONS

1. What types of instruction are given a bank in the collection of foreign drafts?

2. What is the significance of "prompt" payment in the tabulation of Latin-American collections reported by the Federal Reserve Bank of New York?

3. What is a letter of credit? What advantages does it offer the exporter? The importer?

4. What limitation on bank acceptances is found in the Federal Reserve Act?

5. Why must great care be exercised in executing an application for a letter of credit?

6. What are *Uniform Customs and Practice for Commercial Documentary Credits?*

7. What is the responsibility of a bank in the examination of documents provided or called for under letters of credit?

8. Describe the workings of a back-to-back letter of credit. Why may it probably be issued for an amount different from that of the basic credit?

9. What is the proposed export credit insurance scheme whereby the Export-Import Bank would be authorized to insure foreign credits?

10. Evaluate the desirability of a system of export credit insurance offered by an agency such as the Export-Import Bank.

[14] Ward and Harfield, *op. cit.*, p. 99.

CHAPTER 10

Marketing Practice

In addition to selecting the most advantageous organizational arrangement and channels for conducting his business, the seller is faced with a number of other continuing problems which may be designated as in the field of marketing. These include pricing, study of foreign markets, promotion, and advertising. They constitute the subject matter of this chapter.

PRICE QUOTATIONS

A price quotation on any overseas merchandise transaction must take into consideration a number of factors found in domestic business but a greater number which are peculiar to foreign business. In both, there are problems regarding terms and conditions of sale and credit terms. In both, the question of when title passes is of high importance.

Quotation of Importance to Both Buyer and Seller. The quotation, including price and all attendant details, is of prime importance to both the seller and the buyer. Accordingly, it is necessary that there be as clear a meeting of minds as possible. The seller must know what his net return will be; the buyer must know what his total cost will be. The buyer will wish to assure, also, that necessary precautions are taken on such matters as packaging, time of shipment (to assure time of receipt), and certainty as to grade, quality, or condition. In each case, he may specify the packaging desired, the routing or vessel on which shipment is to be transported or the date by which shipment must be made, and the nature of inspection desired to indicate grade, quality, or condition.

The following list of factors includes most of the arrangements and costs which enter the picture somewhere along the line between the warehouse of the shipper and the warehouse of the buyer. It includes, also, the important features of currency of payment, since buyer and seller are in different countries, and of special credit considerations which have a bearing on price.

FACTORS BEARING ON PRICE QUOTATIONS OR ON FINAL
COSTS TO THE BUYER

A. Terms and conditions of sale
  1. Delivery date
  2. Warranties
  3. Place of delivery and responsibility for subsequent arrangements and costs
  4. Price-adjustment provisions
  5. Export-license requirements
  6. Import-preference rating
B. Extra costs involved (either because of movement overseas or because of specifications of buyer)
  1. Packing and tests
  2. Marking
  3. Ocean freight
  4. Marine insurance
  5. Expense of documents
    a. Inspection certificates
    b. Consular invoices
    c. Export or import clearance
  6. Import duties and other taxes
  7. Storage
  8. Port charges
  9. Coordination of shipment
    a. Goods
    b. Documents
    c. Shipping space
C. Currency of payment
D. Credit arrangements
  1. Time of payment may be longer than in domestic sale
  2. Less chance for seller and buyer to know each other
  3. Less complete credit information
  4. Probably less frequent transactions
  5. Retention of title by seller until payment or acceptance of liability by buyer

The problem presented by the impact of these several factors, then, may be better understood if the quotation is looked on as embracing the exporter's selling price and specifying clearly the point at which seller's responsibility ends and buyer's responsibility begins for costs and charges incurred in preparation for shipment and moving the merchandise from seller to buyer. The complete quotation should specify, also, the time of payment and of transfer of possession, the type of credit arrangement or instrument, and the currency in which payment is to be made.

PRICING PRACTICES

Foreign and Domestic Pricing Compared

The wide use of subsidies and of antidumping and countervailing duties (see Chapters 17, 18, and 19) suggests a widespread practice of selling abroad at less than the domestic price. Certain agricultural interests in the United States claim that industry follows a two-price policy, one for domestic and one for foreign business, and that such a program—under government supervision and aid—may be the answer to, for example, the cotton grower's complaint of selling in world markets but having to buy in a protected domestic market. In fact, the commodity-export program of the Department of Agriculture, whereby a subsidy is paid commercial exporters of specified products, is nothing but selling abroad commercially at a lower price than in the home markets. Even government sales of "surplus" products abroad at less than local open-market prices represent selling abroad at lower prices.

Special Processing or Adaptation May Be Required. Some sales abroad call for special adaptation or processing and special marking and packing. Right-hand drives on automobiles, for instance, different typewriter keyboards, and foreign-language labels all call for more than the usual processing required for domestic markets. Additional costs may thereby be incurred, and it would seem that these sales should call for higher prices on foreign sales, not lower. Furthermore, sale abroad, even of out-of-style items, would appear to call for prices higher than can be realized domestically, otherwise the goods would not be shipped abroad. In addition, the longer credit period on foreign as compared with domestic sales would appear to call for a higher price to the foreigner.

Allocation of Costs an Important Factor. However, an analysis of costs might reveal several reasons for different prices between domestic and foreign sales.* Chief of these is selling expense which can be definitely allocated to one or the other. For example, the salaries of the export manager and his staff should not be charged as a cost in pricing for domestic sales, nor should the domestic-sales manager's costs be attributed to foreign sales. Advertising in domestic, as against foreign, publications should be similarly allocated between the two. Travel, delivery, and service expenses allocable to domestic sales have no place in the cost of foreign sales, and vice versa.

Study Shows Many Foreign Sales at Prices Lower than Domestic. This fact of selling abroad at lower and also at higher prices than domestically is brought out in a study made for the Temporary National Economic Committee in 1940. This study was based on 76 case histories

* For stimulating discussions on this problem, see articles by Derek Brooks, appearing occasionally in *Exporters' Digest.*

covering over 125 products. Such classes of products were covered as foods, textiles and products, machinery and transportation equipment, paper and allied products, metal products, and glass, stone, and clay products.

As shown in Table 37, export prices were higher than domestic in 9

Table 37. Case Study of Export Pricing Policy

Name of case	Total number of cases	Export-price variation by markets	Separate profit statements computed for export sales	Exports more profitable than domestic sales	No consistent difference in profitability	Exports less profitable	Management not sure which is more profitable
Group I. Export prices higher than domestic......	9	5	8	9			
1. Export monopoly........................	2	2	2	2			
2. No standard export price; accept export business only when price is equal to or above domestic price.........................	3	3	1	3			
3. List prices for export higher than domestic prices..	4	0	4	4			
Group II. Export prices equal to domestic prices...	21	0	10	2	13	2	4
1. Market price plus distribution costs for all types of customers......................	4	0	4		4		
2. Factory price plus distribution costs for all customers...............................	1	0	1		1		
3. One price policy for all customers...........	16	0	5	2	8	2	4
Group III. Export prices lower than domestic prices	46	45	32	6	4	31	5
1. Standard export price same as domestic, but concessions given in some markets...........	8	8	3	3	..	1	4
2. Export business with different type of customers than domestic, but concession given in some markets......................	7	7	6	1	1	4	1
3. Standard export prices lower than domestic prices for some commodities...............	6	5	4	1	1	4	
4. Domestic- and export-sales departments establish prices independently on basis of factory costs plus distribution costs; some concessions in export....................	15	15	15	1	2	12	
5. All foreign sales made by company affiliates; concessions in some markets...............	1	1	1	..	..	1	
6. All foreign sales made at lower than domestic prices.......................................	6	6	3	..	..	6	
7. Export agents and commission houses........	3	3	.	..	..	3	
Total...............................	76	50	50	17	17	33	9

SOURCE: *Export Prices and Export Cartels*, TNEC Monograph 6, 1940, p. 31.

cases, equal to domestic in 21 cases, and lower than domestic in 40 cases.[1] This may be rationalized somewhat by the consideration that Groups I and II included (1) items which were peculiarly American and for which there was no serious foreign competition, (2) a few internationally traded commodities, and (3) branded consumer goods. A characteristic of items in Group III was the experience of much greater foreign competition.

Export sales were reported as more profitable than domestic sales in 17 cases and as less profitable in 33 cases. In 17 cases, there was no consistent difference in profitability; in 9, the management was not certain as to which was the more profitable. In the 17 cases in which export sales were more profitable than domestic, 9 showed export prices higher than domestic, 2 used the same prices, and 6 priced export sales lower than domestic. In the 33 cases reporting less profitability in export sales, 31 showed export prices lower than domestic, 2 stated that prices were the same, and in none were export prices higher. In those instances in which export prices were either higher or lower than (but not the same as) domestic prices, the general practice seems to have been to vary prices by markets, depending on necessity.

The principal reason given for selling abroad at the same prices as domestically is that the local price is too well known to permit a different one for sales abroad. Foreign buyers visiting salesrooms would be aware of differentials unfavorable to them, and it was felt that this would cause complications.

Reasons Listed for Selling Abroad at Lower Price. Several reasons were offered in explanation of selling abroad at lower prices than domestically. Among these were the following:

1. It would not pay to break the domestic price. Selling the lower priced exports in domestic markets would mean less profit for the entire output.
2. Some export sales could be made at domestic prices, but a much larger increase could be experienced at lower prices.
3. Domestic demand is inelastic, and the market is absorbing about as much as practically possible, even at lower prices.
4. No foreign sales are possible at domestic prices.
5. Foreign sales, even at lower prices, may cover variable costs, absorbing part of fixed charges.
6. Increased volume normally lowers the average manufacturing costs. But in some cases (increasing cost per unit) export business increased manufacturing costs.

[1] Text explanation of the study shows that these practices were not always uniform in each case, *i.e.*, most sales might be at lower than domestic prices, but some, by the same company, could be at the same level or higher than domestic.

7. Export sales were made, even at a loss, in order to maintain employment and avoid labor turnover and training expense.
8. Some sales were made at low price in order to sell other items at full domestic price or more.

In summary, it appears that, as might be expected, the practice of pricing for export shows some flexibility. This is borne out by the fact that a company may sell some products at less than domestic price, while others are sold at the same or higher price. Also, the indicated export-price variation by markets, in 50 of the 55 cases in which domestic and export prices differ, would seem to be called for the realization that no one is willing to sell in any market at a lower price than in another if it can be avoided, whether these markets are domestic or in one or more foreign countries.

Dollars or Foreign Currencies?

Of particular importance in foreign commerce is the question of whether the quotation is to call for payment in the currency of the seller or of the buyer. Each should prefer to operate only within his own, normally, for to contract to pay or to receive payment in another currency than his own is to run the risk of changes in exchange rates which will affect either costs (for the buyer) or income (for the seller).

In some currencies and, one might say, in somewhat normal times, facilities may be found for averting this risk through the practice of hedging in the foreign-exchange futures market (see Chapter 14).

If this is not practicable, debtors may protect themselves by buying the foreign exchange today and holding it until needed (although this means tying up funds which could either be invested or used to pay off the invoice at an earlier date, thereby obtaining either a discount or a more favorable price), but sellers would have a more difficult time of determining definitely today what they will receive in dollars for the foreign exchange they are to acquire in the future.

Danger of Blocked Accounts. Under exchange-control schemes, another problem is posed in that a seller in the United States will have less desire for a foreign currency since it is not fully disposable. If the amount of inconvertible balances (inability to use them to buy dollars in the respective countries) mounts up, quite a long wait may have to be endured by creditors before realization of dollars for sales made. This was the case in Brazil and in Argentina in 1950, and part of the $125,000,000 Export-Import Bank loan to Argentina in 1950 was for the purpose of paying off blocked accounts. The large sum of blocked sterling balances in London banks following the war has been in the process of settlement for several years.

These same exchange-control schemes may dictate the currency quotation for United States imports—dollars would be preferred, if not legally specified. The requirement that exporters in other countries turn over to their governments (or central banks) foreign exchange they derive from exports is a *de facto* requirement that quotations must be in dollars, in the case of sales to the United States. At least one country, Pakistan, specifically requires that quotations be in dollars for sales to the United States. In other countries, when sellers are compelled to turn over dollars to cover their exports, the best way to obtain them is to quote in dollars, which is what the United States importer would normally prefer unless he desired to speculate in exchanges.

Quotation May Be in Currency of Third Country. The international standing of a strong currency like the dollar, and the pound sterling at times in the past, coupled with a weaker currency and perhaps the lack of international banking facilities in some countries, results in a large volume of trade being quoted in a currency which is not that of the seller or of the buyer. For instance, sales may be made from Sweden to Venezuela, the transaction being quoted in U.S. dollars or in pounds sterling.

How extensive this practice may be is, of course, unknown. The London *Economist,* however, estimated that in 1948 about 36 per cent of world trade in goods was conducted in terms of pounds sterling. It further estimated that over 50 per cent of international trade in securities and services was financed in terms of pounds sterling.[2]

FOREIGN-MARKET SURVEYS

Knowledge of the foreign commerce of the United States and the world is of interest and value in arriving at an understanding of the relative importance of countries and of products comprising the world's international commerce.

But for economic intelligence to be of practical applicability to the various functional institutions engaged in foreign commerce, more detailed information must be compiled and studied in relation to the specific problems of the company or individual. This chapter, accordingly, deals with foreign-market surveys—or market analyses—principally from the point of view of the exporter. Not only exporters, however, find good use for these surveys; they are helpful to importers and to the several services, such as banks, forwarders, steamship companies, and packaging firms or engineers. The type and detail of information desired by each will depend on the problem at hand.

[2] Mar. 8, 1950, p. 607

Purpose of Surveys

Perhaps the best way to place the subject in perspective is to consider why anyone would go to the trouble and expense of making or having a survey made. Costs range from a few dollars to thousands of dollars. How can this expense be justified?

It should be evident at the outset that market surveys or analyses are not an end in themselves but a means to an end—the sale of goods and services, now or later.

Several Objectives May Be Desired. The interest of the exporter in market analysis has been aptly summarized as follows:[3]

a. to avoid losses and difficulties *now*
b. to successfully enter a new market
c. to increase sales in an old market
d. to recapture former markets lost during the war
e. to maintain his position in an established market in the face of new competitive factors
f. for purposes of good will and public relations

Mr. Becker's tabulation implies serious consideration as to the *purpose* of a survey. If a company is considering entry into a new market (country), the first problem might be to decide which one. A brief survey might suffice here, based on the simple knowledge that other United States exporters are or are not in specific markets or that, for his product, some countries provide much better markets volumewise than do others.

As a matter of fact, before an exporter spends any great effort or sum of money on promotional and organizational matters within a particular country, he should first satisfy himself that there are no great obstacles to his proposed course. For instance, a preliminary survey would disclose whether there is significant domestic production as competition in a foreign market. This may be quite formidable if there is a tariff or quota barrier. Also, it may be that import licenses are needed for the entry of merchandise into a foreign market or that exchange controls make importing difficult. This and other restrictions may amount to a practical prohibition of his merchandise and may render unwise any detailed analysis or survey.

If the exporter's problem is to increase sales in an old market, a more detailed and specific analysis will have to be made, pertaining not only to the country or sales territory but also to existing distribution channels.

Surveying May Be a Continuous Engagement. In the matter of avoiding losses and difficulties *now*, the implication is clear that surveying or

[3] Edmund F. Becker, "Market Analysis," released by Office of International Trade U.S. Department of Commerce, January, 1948.

studying markets is somewhat of a continuous engagement, but the type
or detail of survey will naturally vary. Not only will current analysis pertain to one's own present and past records; the position of an exporter
relative to his competition is significant.

The survey can be made to determine whether the most advantageous
distribution method is being employed. Or it may be made to determine
the advisability of establishing a branch office or plant abroad. While
thus applicable to one already in the export field, it is also a tool to be
used by one deciding whether to enter export trade or not and, if so,
in what country or countries.

While differing from the analysis of a market for a specific product or
group of products, other surveys may be made for a variety of purposes,
such as inquiring into the effectiveness of advertising, ascertaining
features of consumer acceptance in problems of color, packaging, and
size, and determining the scope of the market for services either abroad
or to those conducting the trade. For example, the decision to originate
banking and insurance services, or transportation, both water and air,
calls for a survey of the market potential. Steamship lines and airlines,
banks, and freight forwarders are interested in foreign-market surveys
in general because their services cover a wide variety of products. The
general indication of market potential is then to be reduced to specific
company problems by those interested in the specific aspects.

In a recent determination of the type of economic survey which
should be made and published by a promotional institution, considerable
discussion developed in arriving at a satisfactory solution. Exporters and
importers seemed to prefer specific commodity analyses; steamship lines
and freight forwarders preferred the more general type, giving more
weight to geographic, physical, and transportation features. The solution
was, of course, two distinct types of surveys.

Methods of Making Surveys

Also depending on the purpose of the survey is the method to be used
in making it. If the survey is to be general, whether brief or extensive,
published statistical and other data should suffice. If it is to be specific
or concrete, it will probably be necessary not only to use the primary
data already available but also to employ mail-questionnaire or personal-
survey techniques. For certain purposes, only one or both of the latter
can be used.

In making foreign-market surveys, practically all roads lead to the
U.S. Department of Commerce, which, through its own domestic offices
and the Foreign Service of the United States, is by far the principal collector of primary statistical and economic data. Not only is it preeminent
in the collection of statistics, but economic intelligence in every corner

of the world is collected and interpreted by Foreign Service representatives. Some of its publications, such as *International Reference Service*,[4] are the backbone of certain phases of foreign-market surveys.

Content of Surveys

Since there may be as much or as little detail in a foreign market survey as is dictated by its end purpose, it is not possible to say that all surveys should contain any specific detail. Depending on whether it is made to determine the immediate or the potential market, different approaches will have to be used. Fundamentally, however, basic elements are numbers of buyers or consumers, standards of living, buying habits, ability to buy, competition for the available funds, and influence of such factors as climate on necessities and modes of living.

For a particular product, the data desired will vary with the item itself—whether a consumer or an industrial product, a staple or a branded product, a luxury available to relatively few or a mass-market item. Thus the coverage needed by an exporter of raw materials would be quite different from that needed by an exporter of finished goods. Another factor is the manner in which sales are now made—whether through a resident agent or a foreign sales office and the type of contract outstanding.

Many details of economic and statistical importance can be included, such as:

1. Past record of United States exports to the country concerned.
2. Imports into the country under survey, from all sources.
3. Domestic production in the country under survey.
4. Data on consumption, including location of potential users. Location is important from the point of view of ocean transport, ports of call, and inland transportation facilities.

High on the list, also, is the prime importance of government regulations dealing with restrictions on imports and on exports.

If general characteristics of the market are the features desired, certain other data would be sought.

General Structural Characteristics of Foreign Markets. Among several points which may be considered in describing the general structure of a foreign country as one market are physical, human, and economic features, such as:

Population and characteristics thereof:
Age groups, races, birth and death rates, rural and urban density, occupational structure

[4] More recently, *Business Information Service.*

Literacy and communications data:
  Newspapers, telephones, radio sets and stations, educational facilities
    and educational level of population
Income:
  National and per capita, especially by income groups
Customs:
  Religious, racial, and social
Geographic features
Transportation facilities, external and inland:
  Ports, rail, motor, water, and air
Power facilities
Industrial structure
Agricultural and mineral resources and development
Government, especially its economic activity
Tax system, with special reference to foreign sellers
Financial structure and facilities
Facilities for marketing products of interest to the exporter such as
  established wholesale and retail channels
Climate, by seasons
Foreign trade
    Each of the foregoing items provides the basis for a detailed in-
vestigation, and any one or several may have a decisive bearing on the
problem the solution of which called for the survey.

Regional Foreign Markets

One of the very beneficial postwar developments in foreign trade is
the increasing realization that a country is not a market, that within any
country are several marketing areas each of which is more or less distinct
and even independent. This holds true, most obviously, in the case of
large countries, the prime example being the United States.

Some European Countries Apply Regional Concept to United States.
Belated recognition of this fact, combined with an urgent demand for
U.S. dollars from abroad, has resulted in the establishment in several
United States cities of selling offices representing foreign producers or
groups of producers. Belgium, Great Britain, the Netherlands, Norway,
and several other European countries have made specific efforts to tap
markets in the United States other than New York. One agent for a
country this large is insufficient for intensive development in the important markets of, say, New York, Chicago, St. Louis, Texas, Louisiana,
and the West coast, unless that agent has numerous branch offices.
Accordingly, the United States has been arbitrarily divided into marketing regions by some foreign sellers on the same basis as is done by many
domestic manufacturers. The foreign promotional or selling agency is

sometimes attached to a consulate, as commercial adviser to agent, or to that particular country's chamber of commerce in the United States.

From the point of view of United States exports, the comparable development would be either appointment of a distributor in, say, Paris for all of France, or in Paris for one region, Bordeaux for another, and Marseille for a third. The arrangement must of necessity conform to normal marketing channels in the country whose markets are sought. In this connection, *International Reference Service* of the U.S. Department of Commerce encompasses a series of marketing-area studies for some countries. The Venezuela report, for instance, divides that country into three principal marketing areas, the Maracaibo, the Caracas, and the Ciudad Bolívar. Each area is described in considerable detail.

Naturally, market surveys of this type will call for detailed analysis of some features not stressed in others. What the regional concept of markets calls for is the exporter's looking on his broad foreign market in the same way as a domestic sales manager does. The larger area must be "zoned," and assurance must be had that even the secondary centers of importance are properly manned in order to provide adequate market coverage. For only out of good coverage comes large-scale distribution, which means volume and a larger base from which to draw profit.

Summary

Summarizing, it may be stated that a great volume of statistical and economic data is available for use in making foreign-market surveys, the principal amount being developed by the U.S. Department of Commerce and the Foreign Service of the United States. Data from foreign sources are quite often sparse and out of date. The author recalls an incident in late 1948 in which a foreign-government consulate in the United States was asked for a list of exporters of a certain product for which a demand had been discovered in the United States. A mimeographed list of names was received, which might have been satisfactory except that in the lower left-hand corner the date of compilation was shown—1940. Many of these could have gone out of business, perhaps died, or been guilty of unpatriotic or antisympathetic activities during the war, and many new ones might have come into the picture in the eight years intervening. The list was not usable. Information is also available from a number of private sources, some of which are mentioned later in this chapter.

In view of the great supply and wide variety of data on foreign countries, the problem of market surveys, after determining the need in the light of objectives, is substantially a matter of reference to reliable sources of information and the use of sound judgment in selecting and interpreting applicable material.

PRIVATE PROMOTIONAL EFFORTS

Along with extensive governmental efforts to promote foreign commerce (described in Chapter 19), many private organizations take an active part in the same direction. Many are national in outlook, but the more active, promotionally, are local and regional organizations. Accordingly, their efforts should be expected to be in the direction of promoting more trade for their particular areas of interest.

In its publication titled *United States Associations in World Trade and Affairs*,[5] the U.S. Department of Commerce lists 900 active groups in 190 cities as having special interest in foreign trade, international affairs, and world peace. This is a staggering number, but it may be recalled that the efforts of some must necessarily be an attempt to get a bigger slice of the pie for their own supporters—competition among cities, regions, and ports. However, all serve to bring foreign commerce more clearly into the public view. Not all are interested in foreign commerce (about 200 are primarily cultural or interested in world peace or other affairs), and of those interested, many are trade associations having perhaps a minor interest in the foreign as compared with the domestic business of their memberships. Some 190 of these are chiefly interested in export, 80 chiefly in import, and 430 in both export and import business. It is estimated that about 640 (except for a few regional) are national in scope, 60 are state-wide, and 200 are local organizations.

Several of the organizations active in the field are described below. Their order of listing is not intended to indicate relative importance, influence, or effectiveness.

National Foreign Trade Council, Inc. This association was formed in 1914, and its purposes are reported as being to study with unprejudiced minds the position of the United States in world trade with the object of contributing to the establishment of sound commercial policies. In its 1948 publication *American Agencies Interested in International Affairs,* the Council on Foreign Relations, of New York, reports activities of the National Foreign Trade Council to be:

Analyzes legislative proposals affecting foreign trade interests and, when occasion arises, is represented at hearings or by filing of briefs or other appropriate action, cooperates with government departments, sponsors National Foreign Trade Conference, whose Final Declarations have had a recognized influence, analyzes governmental and commercial developments in foreign countries to determine effects on foreign business, provides investigations, surveys and trade information for members, carries on nation-wide education program to inform and create a sound public opinion on international trade problems.

[5] 1947.

Membership is nationwide and is composed of firms in the export and import trades; manufacturers; owners of industrial enterprises and other business properties located abroad; banks; insurance companies; ocean-, railroad-, and air-transportation companies; communications companies; agricultural interests; and others types of American enterprises doing business with or within foreign countries.

National Council of American Importers, Inc. Founded in 1921, this organization is a nonprofit commercial body representing the general import trade. Membership is national in scope and consists of importers, banks, customhouse brokers, steamship lines, and others serving the import trade. The Council studies and makes official representation on broader problems affecting the import activities of the United States. Its *Current Information Bulletin,* issued two or three times monthly, contains brief summaries of official developments affecting imported commodities and selected items of general interest to American importers. Among its other publications is *The American Importer,* issued bimonthly, which contains current discussions and articles, and a tabulation and brief summary of recent official decisions of the Court of Customs and Patent Appeals, the United States Customs Court, and the Treasury, all of which affect actual conditions under which importers must work.

In addition, it publishes a *Members' Service Bulletin,* containing up-to-date information and analysis of some particular development as it affects importers, such as the proposed International Trade Organization, and a *Special Information Bulletin,* containing detailed information about imported commodities.

Chamber of Commerce of the United States (Foreign Commerce Department). This important organization conducts studies in current problems affecting foreign trade, expresses organizational views, and issues a number of publications intended to provide economic intelligence of a type which can be used by a prospective trader. Among its prominent publications are *Our 100 Leading Imports, The United States in the World Economy, 1949,* and *An Introduction to Doing Import and Export Business.* It is a prime mover in the annual World Trade Week, and its relationship with the chambers of commerce all over the United States makes it an influential body. In addition, it includes among its membership a number of American chambers of commerce abroad, which are active in promoting trade between the United States and the respective countries in which they are located.

International House, New Orleans. This organization was founded in 1945 and is dedicated to "world trade, peace, and understanding." It is unique in that it represents a coordinated effort on the part of many functional elements engaged in world trade. It is a businessmen's club, with dining and bar facilities, and among its attractive features is the availability of offices and secretarial assistance to foreign businessmen who may require such accommodation for a few days. International House maintains a fine reference library, and its members and non-members (within its facilities) may obtain reference and even research assistance on their trade problems. Its publicity department has served to make both various sections of the United States and many foreign areas more aware of the importance of the entire United States as several markets. Perhaps the outstanding feature of the organization is the active promotional work undertaken by the World Trade Development Department. This office maintains a file of inquiries and offers; on receipt of either, the process of matching prospective buyers and sellers immediately begins. They are put in touch with each other and sometimes introduced. A number of traders now active in business were encouraged and aided in their early steps by this department. No credit information is given, and International House assumes no responsibility for the moral or financial standing of the individuals whose names are exchanged. The activity of this organization is not entirely business, however. Cultural relations are also encouraged, and conference rooms are available for meetings and for visits by foreign students and others interested in this phase of international relations.

Export Managers' Clubs. In many cities of the United States, export managers' clubs have been organized as a medium for exchanging views, for maintaining a vehicle which can make fast and official representation in matters of interest to the export fraternity, and for encouraging and sponsoring wider education of their cities or areas in foreign-commerce matters. Annual conferences are sponsored by several of these clubs, among the better known ones being those sponsored by the Export Managers' Club of New York; the Chicago World Trade Conference, sponsored by the Chicago Export Managers' Club; and the annual Mississippi Valley World Trade Conference, one of the principal sponsors being the Export Managers' Club of New Orleans. In several cities, interest is not solely limited to the export side of foreign commerce, and organizations performing similar functions may be titled Export-Import Club, as in Fort Worth, Texas; the Foreign Trade Club of Cincinnati; the Foreign Trade Club of Kansas City; and the Foreign Traders Association of Philadelphia.

Foreign-trade Bureaus, Chambers of Commerce. In many cities of the United States there is sufficient foreign-trade activity to justify the existence and operation of a foreign-trade bureau of the local chamber of commerce. This type of activity also provides a good means to marshal the indirect interests in foreign-trade problems, for hardly any city can fail to recognize its interest in foreign commerce to some extent. About

100 chambers of commerce maintain foreign-trade bureaus and, aside from the principal port and inland cities, these bureaus are also maintained in smaller inland cities such as Cedar Rapids, Iowa; Elkhart, Indiana; Fort Smith, Arkansas; Mishawaka, Indiana; and Wichita Falls, Texas. These organizations sponsor or cooperate in the sponsorship of functions pertaining to foreign commerce. They may issue periodic bulletins or reports on foreign-commerce matters, or advertise the foreign-trade interest of their respective areas through lists of exporters and importers. Some publish lists of world-trade opportunities and otherwise serve to promote more trade or trade opportunities.

National Association of Credit Men. Mainly through its Foreign Credit Interchange Bureau, the National Association of Credit Men performs an outstanding function in paving the way or pointing up obstacles for the trader. Several services are offered, all of which serve to enhance the economic intelligence of the recipient and thereby enable him better to engage in his foreign commercial activities. Ledger experience, weekly bulletins reporting current changes in credit, collection, or exchange conditions in foreign countries, round-table conferences, and consultation service are all features which smooth the road of the trader.

Dun and Bradstreet, Inc. This private organization sells credit information and service, both on the domestic and on the foreign side. Comparable to its domestic reference book is the *Latin America Sales Index.* Detailed reports on individual names practically anywhere in the world are available, as the company operates 67 foreign offices and maintains correspondent relationships where offices are not located. In addition, and by way of promotional work, the company issues a considerable amount of published information, including a monthly bulletin titled *International Markets* and an occasional special study, such as its *Geo-economic Survey of Latin America. International Markets* contains factual articles of interest to foreign traders, statistical studies, and other data providing credit and foreign-commerce intelligence.

Periodicals. An exhaustive listing of magazines, newspapers, or other periodicals could be made, indicating those whose activities in whole or in part contribute to the promotion of foreign commerce. By feature articles, analyses, and current-information reports and through other activities, the work of these publications must be ranked high as private promotional efforts. By no means an exhaustive list, but as an indication of a few of the more prominent publications in the field, one may refer to *Exporters' Digest, Export Trade and Shipper, International Trader, American Import and Export Bulletin, American Exporter,* and *McGraw-Hill Digest.*

Two of the outstanding reference works (issued annually) are *Exporters' Encyclopedia* and *Custom House Guide.* The former is published by Thomas Ashwell and Co., Inc., New York, and covers topics of particular interest to exporters. A feature is a review by country, showing consular regulations, ports and trade centers, shipping routes, communications facilities, exchange restrictions, data on customs, tariffs, and packing, and miscellaneous information. The latter publication is issued by Import Publications, Inc., New York. It covers the United States Customs Tariff and its administration, the Internal Revenue Code as affecting imports, and shipping and commerce regulations. Data are given on United States ports, as the special field of interest is imports. The publisher of *Custom House Guide* also publishes the *American Import and Export Bulletin.*

House Salesmen. In addition to the coordinated or group efforts to promote trade on the part of private agencies, there must also be included as private promotional effort the several programs conducted by single companies in the same direction. These may be conducted by banks or trading companies, but the most usual have been on the part of ports, steamship lines, and railroads.

Railroads. One of the outstanding efforts of this type is that done by the Illinois Central Railroad. Shortly after the end of the war, it sent two of its abler representatives on an extended tour of South America to make a commercial survey of that continent. One was the foreign traffic agent in Chicago; the other was the general agent in Havana. The purpose was twofold: "to tell South America about the tremendous industrial and agricultural importance of the middle west and Mississippi valley of the United States; and to ascertain on-the-spot information for the Middle West and Mississippi Valley respecting their future trade possibilities with South America."

After the tour, the results were made available in a brochure titled *A Commercial Survey of South America.* The brochure is a statement as to organization of the tour, observations made, explanation of the area of particular interest to the railroad, and conclusions to specific objectives sought by the team. An interesting chart is included which lists the commodities expected to be imported from the United States into South America, by country and by volume (heavy movement, medium-heavy movement, light movement, or no movement of consequence expected), and a sister chart lists commodities expected to be exported to the United States, from the same countries and according to the same general volume indications. The railroad made available these pamphlets for distribution throughout the wide area in which it has an interest and in South America, and it made available to several cities in the vicinity the services of its travelers for lectures and explanations of their findings. This stimulation of interest on the part of traders, banks, and other services attending an export or import was an example of trade promotion of very practical application. Naturally, the railroad was serving its own interest, but it was doing so in a manner which served to build up the area it serves.

Banks. Among the principal promotional efforts by banks are advertising and regular or special bulletins conveying information of a type to be of interest to and applicability by a trader, forwarder, or other auxiliary service. Some banks issue monthly reviews, such as the National City Bank, Guaranty Trust Company, and Irving Trust Company of New York; the First National Bank of Boston; and the Continental Illinois National Bank and Trust Company and the American National Bank of Chicago. Other less widely known banks also make this economic intelligence available, and it serves to promote at least an interest in more world trade.

Ports. The major ports of the country have representatives located in the interior of the United States for the purpose of meeting with prospective customers and making available data of interest and value to the prospective trader, bank, or forwarder. Interest is, of course, in the direction of promoting trade via their respective ports, but the activities of inland representatives of ports like Boston, New York, Baltimore, and New Orleans must be considered as promotional of trade in general.

Shipping Companies. Through advertising and solicitation, shipping lines are among the active trade promoters. Advertisements in national and foreign magazines and solicitation both in the United States and abroad serve to increase interest in trade, although the effort of the individual companies is primarily in the hope that their individual companies will stand to gain.

Many more instances than those listed could be found as evidence of widespread activity in promoting world trade, but it will suffice to list only these few as an indication that serious, coordinated, and organized efforts are made to encourage and promote trade at the same time that obstacles are placed in the way of certain types of trade. Again the thought may be mentioned as to the possible gain to the nation from a policy of consistency.

ADVERTISING

An increasing awareness of the benefits of good public relations has resulted in considerable interest in advertising and its related undertakings. In seeking good will, the foreign trader is not concerned with his direct customers alone. His business success can be influenced as well by his standing in the eyes of local government officials and by the attention his interests receive from banking, shipping, and other service connections. Consider, for example, the good or ill will which may hinge on the allocation of shipping space if that should become necessary, or on special attention a steamship line or airline may give to an important visitor. Regardless of the implications, one may be sure that not all business is done on a basis of first come, first served.

Primarily, of course, the customer is the number-one man, so the job of good public relations here is to influence favorably the trader's overseas counterpart. In accomplishing this, formal advertising stands in a preferred position, but along with this goes hospitality to foreign visitors, such as providing desk space, interpreters, and entertainment where advisable.

Several Media May Be Used. On the advertising side, several media are available and selection of the proper one or more may have an important bearing on returns from expenditures. Some companies effectively use printed house organs, with occasional feature stories of important visitors, interesting articles on shipments, sources, or markets, and current news items of interest to the trade. If a member of the firm writes an article or speaks on radio or to some representative group, reprints may serve a good purpose in bringing about a closer understanding.

By way of formal advertising, the following are in extensive use:

1. Newspapers: These are probably more carefully read than in the United States, occasionally passing from hand to hand.
2. Magazines: Some authorities feel that foreign magazines lack the influential position which they occupy in the United States.
3. Billboards and signs: These are considered effective.
4. Radio: Owing to limitations or taxes on the ownership of receiving sets, and the resultant relatively small number of sets, radio is not considered an effective advertising medium for many products. In some countries, advertising is prohibited or strictly limited; in others, it may be so widely used as to be overdone, with a resulting loss of impact.
5. Catalogues: Highly effective in some lines, useless in others. Authorities recommend adequate illustrations and simple, clear, descriptive language.
6. United States trade papers: Widely and effectively used in some lines. Examples are *Exporters' Digest, American Exporter, The American Automobile* (overseas edition), *El Automovil Americano, Pharmacy International, El Farmaceutico, Ingenieria Internacional Industria,* and *Ingenieria Internacional Construccion.*

Quite widely used, also, are films and demonstrations, with samples.

Export-advertising Budgets. A recent survey by Francis L. Bohannon, of the Graduate School of Business Administration, New York University, sponsored and issued (December, 1950) by *American Exporter*, offers interesting data on export-advertising budgets and practices. Among the results were:

1. Fifty-three per cent of companies reporting showed advertising expenditures to be less than 2 per cent of export sales; 19 per cent reported advertising expenditures of more than 5 per cent of export sales.
2. Seventy-four per cent of the companies spent the entire advertising amount direct; 5 per cent passed along the entire appropriation to the foreign representative.
3. Sixty-two per cent of the companies placed their entire foreign advertising in the United States, 33 per cent placed some in the foreign markets, and 5 per cent placed all in the foreign markets.
4. Fifty-two per cent placed their advertising with domestic companies having no foreign branches; 8 per cent with United States agencies having foreign branches; 12 per cent with specialized export advertising agencies; and 27 per cent directly.
5. Some companies used more than one medium, and the following types of advertising were employed:

United States export-trade, business, or industrial magazines	88%
Direct mail	27
Foreign popular consumer magazines	15
Newspapers	15
United States popular magazines with foreign editions	12
Point of purchase	9
Radio	8
Other	12

Another survey, made in 1951 for the fourth consecutive year by *Export Trade and Shipper*, discloses wide differences in the selection of advertising media by industries. The type of product has a great deal to do with this, but, within each industry group, there were wide variations among individual companies. The 1951 survey shows percentage allocations of advertising budgets to the respective medium types as indicated in the table on page 212.

In a text of this sort, treatment of a subject as big as advertising must be sketchy. Detailed coverage may be found in, for example, Pratt's *Foreign Trade Handbook, The Sales Executives' Handbook,* and *Advertising Handbook*. Organizations such as McGraw-Hill International Corporation and J. Walter Thompson Advertising Agency offer specialized facilities in the field of export advertising. The names or references used here are, of course, not all-inclusive, and their use is not intended to indicate superiority over those not named.

Industry	United States export publications		Foreign publications	Radio and television
	Trade	Consumer		
Agricultural machinery.............	15.5	3.5	81.0	
Automotive......................	46.5	25.3	26.4	1.8
Clothing and textiles..............	0.5	11.1	77.9	10.5
Foods and beverages..............	22.9	9.3	41.9	25.9
Hardware and office equipment.....	11.1	27.0	44.8	6.7
Heavy machinery.................	42.3	23.4	33.9	0.4
Household appliances.............	5.8	29.1	65.1	
Pharmaceuticals..................	5.9	7.7	63.2	23.2

SOURCE: *Export Trade and Shipper*, Jan. 21, 1952, pp. 11–13.

REVIEW QUESTIONS

1. Why is the price quotation in foreign commerce of interest to both seller and buyer?

2. How does it happen that even with the expense of special processing or adaptation of exported goods, a company can afford to sell abroad at a lower price than domestically?

3. What are some of the reasons offered for selling abroad at a lower price than selling domestically?

4. How is it possible for a company to sell goods abroad at a lower price than domestically, yet find its export business more profitable than its domestic?

5. What should a foreign-market survey include?

6. Explain the concept of regional foreign markets. How does this coincide with domestic marketing practice?

7. Identify and describe the functions or activities of (*a*) National Foreign Trade Council, Inc., (*b*) National Council of American Importers, Inc., and (*c*) Foreign Commerce Department, Chamber of Commerce of the United States.

8. What are the problems faced in administering the export advertising budget with regard to (*a*) media and (*b*) control over content of advertising and selection of channels?

PART THREE

Economic Aspects

CHAPTER 11

Economic Basis of Foreign Commerce

Foreign commerce may be conducted between individuals, companies, or governments located one mile or thousands of miles apart; each of these may be a trading unit or entity engaged in the international movement of goods, services, or investments.

The main purpose of this chapter is to inquire into the fundamental theories of foreign commerce and to examine some of the broader factors that influence the volume and direction of international trade. What should evolve from this study is an understanding of the basis of all trade, of the gains from trade, and of the problems and costs involved in national attempts at self-sufficiency. Stated in another way, the student will want to satisfy himself as to the economic feasibility of foreign commerce and its benefits and disadvantages.

The fact that accomplishing the trade may be prohibited or less strongly discouraged will be considered at length in later chapters. But with an understanding of these economic fundamentals, it will be possible to interpret more fully or to eliminate by logic many of the local or spur-of-the-moment objections to such commerce.

Basic Long-run Economic Factors

All significant economic literature on international commerce is built up on one or both of two explanations of such commerce; they, in turn, rest on one basic economic phenomenon—individual and geographic specialization as reflected in the international division of labor. One of these explanations is the concept of interregional cost differentials; the other is the concept of comparative cost advantages. We shall discuss these later.

Perhaps it is advisable to mention here that principal discussion of the subject rests on the assumption of relatively free enterprise, which means that the foreign commerce in which we deal is one in which the main role of governments is the creation or permission of conditions under which a trader may (or may not) find an opportunity to buy and/or sell profitably. Similarly, an investor may or may not find an opportunity to place his funds to advantage in one country or another. In other words, the government would "condition" the business atmosphere to encourage, or at least not to restrict unnecessarily, commerce carried on by private decision and under private direction.

It would be unrealistic to assume these conditions to be uniform or even present in any wide degree, for the trend in political economy has been definitely away from expanding trade opportunities to be used or refused by the individual. An outstanding illustration of this trend is the widely publicized view that a nation cannot afford to allow its internal economy to be influenced in any substantial degree by the results of its citizens' foreign commercial activities. This means that citizens' individual decisions, in their own individual interests as seen by them, must be subordinated to some economic plan of one sort or another. It is also a way of saying that socialistic planning cannot stop with domestic economies or at national borders; it must take on international flavor.

Significance of International Division of Labor. Neither population nor natural resources nor man's abilities nor productivity are distributed uniformly over the globe. The result is specialization—individually and geographically. This specialization has greatly increased productive capacity, and it is rather difficult to deny the potentialities and advantages of further specialization. However, the more specialized people become, the more dependent and the less self-reliant or self-supporting they are. The possibility of further expertness and specialization depends on the possibility of exchanging the additional production as well as on the acquisition of the skill and technical knowledge to accomplish it.

All trade, whether domestic or foreign, whether between individuals and/or companies and/or governments, is essentially an exchange of goods and services. The ultimate gain is not money, but economic utility. All voluntary trade results in an advantage to both the buyer and the seller, but not necessarily in equal degree. If it failed to result in advantage to either, there would be no trade; the voluntary action of the trader would compel him to the decision not to enter an unfavorable transaction. This is not to imply that a financial loss may not be experienced by one of the traders; but if there is to be one, it resolves itself into the comparison of a known loss now with an unknown and perhaps larger loss later, or perhaps a loss on one transaction in order to avoid difficulty and possible legal complications on others. Moreover, the increased production, encouraged because of the possibility of exchanging, means that some, if not all, parties involved are better off and none is worse off.

Accordingly, on three main counts, the benefits derived from foreign commerce and based on the international division of labor are manifest.

These are that (1) trade encourages specialization, thus increasing productivity, (2) trade results in increased economic utility, and (3) trade results in advantages to both buyer and seller. The entire concept assumes a *tendency* for the benefits of technical progress to be spread over the producing and trading community, although not equally or necessarily to the entire world—say, both developed and underdeveloped areas—until and unless all areas become producers or traders.

Now, what has this to do with commerce between nations? Why not look for this trade within a country, rather than between countries? Certainly this is done, but the size of the respective countries and the abundance or scarcity of factors involved in production relative to population and standards of living determine any one country's ability to produce competitively all that it needs. Competitive production internationally must take into account cost differentials, which appear as between plants situated side by side, in the same locality, in the same country, or in different countries.

Various Factors Give Rise to Cost Differentials. Since the economic possibility of foreign commerce depends so fundamentally on differences in price, arising from differences in costs of the factors of production in different geographic regions, it is advisable to survey the circumstances which give rise to these cost advantages and disadvantages. The survey must take into account cost differentials arising from natural (physical), economic, and social causes. "Production" encompasses the distribution process as well as manufacturing or mining, for the goods and services must reach the same market to be competitive. Stated another way, comparative prices must take into account place utility as well as form utility.

Compilation of a complete list of factors of cost could be very extensive and practically unlimited, but among the more important differences are:

Of a natural (physical) order: Climate, soil characteristics, mineral resources, and topography.

Of an economic and social order: Population density and characteristics, literacy, social status of labor, social status of capital, extent of development of management skills and techniques, degree of industrial development, degree of capital accumulation, development of communication and transportation facilities, types of business and legal organizations permitted, existence or absence of monopoly or near-monopoly and other forms of imperfect competition, tax burden, stability of government, and the need for large-scale units of production (accumulations of factors of production) to attain the benefits of technical progress and, in some cases, mass production.

Not only the existence of these singular differentials is involved. Their *proportionate* scarcity and application and the *skill* with which they are coordinated and managed all affect the final unit cost and its selling price.

How Cost Differences Influence Commerce. Differences in costs of production, based on the abundance or scarcity of the several factors of production in nations and in regions, on their proportionate employment, or on the skill and effectiveness of their application, cause international price differences. Out of these, trade arises, for the multitude of buyers is constantly in search of the lowest price, and the less numerous sellers are constantly in search of the widest, or most remunerative, markets.

This is where the concept of interregional trade explains the basis of trade between two men in the same locality, in different sections of the same country, and in different countries. In this view, international trade is fundamentally not different from domestic trade; both are *interregional*. Special emphasis can be given to international commerce only when national sovereignty gives rise to economic or social institutions which in themselves either affect cost directly or prevent the entry into the competitive field of factors of production or of goods and services, themselves.

From the foregoing, it is evident that the motive for trade—that which stimulates trade—is either *gain* to the individual(s) concerned or *governmental development* of the national economy or of some segment of it. As to private gain, the motive is identical with that of domestic trade, where profit opportunities also arise from differences between costs of production (relative efficiency of producers) and selling prices. In a competitive economy, this takes place with the producers and merchants experiencing various degrees of profit—some just breaking even and others actually suffering losses.

Conditions of Absolute, Equal, and Comparative Advantage. Of the theories developed to explain and analyze the economics of foreign commerce, probably none is better known than that of the classical school, which develops the concepts of absolute, equal, and comparative advantages in the production of various items. The degree of advantage pertains to one *product* as compared with another. Ricardo is credited as being the originator of the view, but Taussig[1] offers perhaps the outstanding presentation of the idea. Under a condition of *absolute advantage,* country A would be producing article Z more efficiently (cheaply) than could country B; country B would be producing article Y more efficiently than could country A. Therefore, trade could profitably occur between the two countries and should result in country A's concentrating on the production of article Z and country B's concentrating on the pro-

[1] F. W. Taussig, *International Trade* (New York, The Macmillan Company, 1927).

duction of article Y, with their respective supplies of the other article being obtained through mutual trade.

A condition of *equal advantage* would be said to exist if country A could produce both articles Z and Y more efficiently (cheaply) and with the same advantage of efficiency in each, than could country B. Under this condition, trade would not be possible unless B could pay A with the proceeds of the production of some other article, or some service, or, perhaps, gold or a loan on the part of someone able to provide a currency acceptable to the producers of country A.

But the principal idea is that of *comparative advantage,* in which country A can again produce both articles Z and Y more efficiently than can country B; however, the difference in advantage which country A enjoys over country B in the production of one article, say article Z, is greater than the difference which country A enjoys over country B in the production of the other (article Y). Accordingly, country A should find it to advantage to concentrate on the production of article Z and buy its requirements of article Y from country B, as in that way country A will be making best use of its productive capacities. Country B, by concentrating on the production of article Y, in which it has the least comparative disadvantage, and buying its requirements of article Z from country A, would also be making the most efficient use of its productive capacities.

Ordinarily, the law of comparative costs is stated in terms of units of labor cost; but its workings can be as well illustrated in terms of monetary units. Certain assumptions must be made in discussing the point, three of which are of prime importance. The first is that domestic competition will already have lowered costs as far as they can go in each country, as determined by alternative production and employment possibilities. Hence, the chances of further arbitrary cuts in costs are remote because, in preference to accepting lower remuneration, the factors of production—taking advantage of their mobility—will look to their alternative opportunities for employment. The second is that foreign-exchange rates are rather firm and will not change materially. The third is that each country can produce sufficiently more than its own needs to satisfy those of its trading partners. These assumptions emphasize the point that the principle is intended to describe a competitive position under a given set of conditions.

The basis of the entire concept of comparative costs is that one man may be both a better salesman *and* a better carpenter than another. He has two competitive advantages over the second man and, for this example, we shall assume that his greater advantage lies in his salesmanship. It can, accordingly, be to his financial advantage to concentrate on selling and to hire the carpenter. The concept may also be applied to

regions or nations—to groups of men—and to various economic undertakings calling for the accumulation and managing of factors of production, even though the negotiations may not be so direct between the two
producers.

Suppose that in reaching competitive markets in the United States and
Canada, farmers in each country can alternatively produce wheat and
corn. Their costs are such that the same given acreage, labor, and other
factor costs yield amounts of the two commodities as below. Canada can

Country	Wheat, bushels	Corn, bushels
United States.............	1.0	1.2
Canada.................	1.1	1.4

produce both commodities at less cost than the United States can and
so seems able to buy more cheaply at home than by importing; it would
therefore appear that there would be no opportunity for trade in these
items between the two countries. This appearance is strengthened if the
comparative costs shown above are reduced to dollars and cents per
bushel. If we assume, as a basis for illustration, that the price of corn in
Canada is $1.75 per bushel, then the other proportionate prices, based on
different productivity for equal effort, are as shown below. However,
application of the principle of comparative costs discloses opportunities

Country	Wheat	Corn
United States...........	$2.45	$2.04
Canada...............	2.228	1.75

for mutual advantage through trading.

This comparative ratio of costs means that the United States producer
must be able to sell his wheat at 20 per cent more than his corn to produce the financial yield obtainable from growing corn.[2] However, foreign
corn is available at an even lower price than domestic. Hence, if we use
as our starting price the assumed availability of corn from Canada at,
say, $1.75 per bushel, and match it with comparative costs in the United
States, it can be seen that the United States can advantageously exchange
wheat for corn in a ratio of 1 bushel of wheat for 1.2 bushels of corn as
long as the price of wheat is no lower than $2.10. At that price or better
for wheat, enough money can be obtained to buy corn at $1.75.[3]

[2] $2.45 × 1.0 = $2.04 × 1.2.
[3] $2.10 × 1.0 = $1.75 × 1.2.

Canadians, on the other hand, would have to obtain $2.228 or more for wheat to justify growing it instead of corn. They can produce $14/11$, or 1.273, bushels of corn for each bushel of wheat, and the corn can be sold at $1.75. Multiplying these items, we get $1.273 \times \$1.75$, or $2.228.

Now, our supposition was that farmers in each country could produce more than their own country's needs, *i.e.*, enough for the second country as well. We have seen that the United States can afford to produce wheat to sell at $2.10 if it can buy corn at $1.75. Therefore, it will be to the interest of the United States to produce wheat and exchange it for Canadian corn, of which it can get 16⅔ per cent more than of United States corn; it will be to Canada's advantage to produce corn, wherein it has a production advantage of 27 per cent over wheat, and exchange it for United States wheat, even though it can produce wheat more cheaply than can the United States. This comparative advantage in *producing and trading* is the basis on which trade between the two countries rests in this instance.

Assuming that the same farmers and the same ground can grow either crop, in which case they have mobility of use, or employment, the United States farmers will be driven to producing wheat, since Canadian corn undersells theirs; Canadian farmers will be induced, in their own self-interest, to plant corn. In corn, it is obvious, the Canadian comparative advantage is greater; in wheat, the United States comparative disadvantage ($1/10$ instead of $1/6$) is least.

The upper limits of price are the costs to produce in each country rather than buy abroad. Consequently, the end result is that corn sells for between $1.75 and $2.04 in the respective markets, and wheat sells for between $2.10 and $2.228. Both countries are better off than if they produced their own and did not trade.

Production and Trade Are by Competing Enterprises. When one speaks of country A doing this or Country B doing that, it should always be borne in mind that it is one or several men in the respective countries who actually act as entrepreneurs and take advantage of the business opportunity afforded by the existence of these circumstances. One must also constantly bear in mind a point which merits repetition—that even though a country may be said to enjoy an advantage over another in the production of a certain article, each country's productive capacity will normally consist of several competing productive units, not all of which will be equally efficient; indeed, it is quite possible that the most efficient company in any given country may be more efficient than the least efficient company in almost any second country. This also suggests consideration of the size and proximity of the producer and consumer countries, which will have a bearing on theoretical generalizations.

Furthermore, these relative advantages are not necessarily static; they may increase or decrease as conditions affecting costs and prices in the competitive countries vary. For instance, the development of communication, power, and transportation facilities has a definite effect on relative costs of production which, in the final analysis, must be measured in the market where goods are sold against competition. Some other varying elements of cost are the technical skill of labor, which may constantly improve, but probably at an unequal speed in different countries; social legislation in such areas as minimum wages and maximum hours; and what the more socialistic-minded economists call the "positive" monetary and fiscal policies they would recommend to maintain full employment or to combat depressions.

Despite many qualifications and limitations, it is obvious that, from differences in costs of production, whether they are due to managerial efficiency, to conditions imposed by nature or legislation, or to technological progress at uneven rates, opportunity arises for profitable, hence economically feasible, business.

Short-run Economic Factors

While basic cost differentials provide the most fundamental and long-range economic justification for foreign commerce, current volumes and directions of trade, especially in merchandise, are influenced by other economic phenomena. These pertain to transitory circumstances which affect relative prices and which may be looked on as short-run economic factors. Examples are, as described below, fluctuations in exchange rates, changes in prices arising from economic conditions and employment levels, and the adequacy and cost of services such as transportation, communications, banking, and insurance. Volumes and directions are also influenced by political factors, which will be discussed later in this chapter.

Investments and Other Transactions Influence Trade in Goods. "Trade follows the dollar" is a frequently made statement. If we start with the assumption that more attractive investment possibilities are to be found abroad than in the home country, and that foreign investment is permitted, *i.e.*, that the country of the investor and the country of the "debtor" do not prohibit investment, it will follow that once an investment is made, a chain of international transactions is started. The original investment, the interest or dividends, and the repayment or repatriation of the investment all result practically in the movement of goods or services between two or more countries over several years. Thus, investment makes trade in goods or services possible and they, in turn, make investment possible. There are also rather significant effects on prices and employment, which in turn affect the foreign commerce of both the lending and the borrowing nation.

Other transactions or facilities which influence trade in merchandise, either through the foreign-exchange markets or in a direct manner, are transportation, banking, and similar services. Their international sales or purchases as a service affect the foreign-exchange market, and their rates or prices are an element in determining total costs in a single market.

Exchange Rates and Prices Play Dominant Role. The result of cost differentials is price differences, but the latter may also arise through fluctuations in exchange rates, as well as through the action of individual entrepreneurs. Thus the importer and the exporter are directly concerned with foreign-exchange rates, which determine the final price to each in his own currency.

It may be considered theoretically possible, although hardly probable, that exchange rates between and/or internal prices within any two countries would be in such a state of equilibrium that there would be no advantage to a trader's buying in one country and selling in the other. Whatever could be bought in one country would also be obtainable in the other, at substantially the same price and in adequate volume. As suggested, this situation is definitely not a probable one, and as long as cost differentials remain, there will be the opportunity for a merchant to buy in one country—the one in which he can buy at the most favorable price—and sell in another—the one in which he can obtain the most favorable price.

For all practical purposes, changes in exchange rates or changes in internal prices underlie a very large part of world trade; they are probably a very important element in the trade of goods moving between countries as a result of comparative advantages prevailing at one time or another. It would seem that goods moving between countries *because they are not practically producible in sufficient quantities in the consuming country* would move regardless of changes in exchange rates or prices unless the change were too great or sudden. The commodities intended in this reference are those such as coffee, sugar, petroleum, tin, wheat, bananas, and rubber. Some countries, because of their small size or because of the nature of their natural resources, simply cannot produce some of these items, which are, to a considerable extent, necessities. The question of substitutes must always be weighed in reducing such a general statement to a specific case.

National Factors

National boundaries give rise both to the need for foreign commerce and to efforts to avoid it. Without them, the commerce would not be foreign. Despite the basic advantages of expanded markets, policies adopted by every nation have been in the direction of blocking international commerce in some respect or other. Let us look into some of the characteristics of nations bearing heavily on the mobility either of goods and services or of the factors of production which provide the goods and services.

It has been seen that trading regions, in so far as "natural" cost differentials are concerned, may be intranational or international. They do not correspond to political boundaries. However, political bases of cost differentials may be delineated by national boundaries. Nevertheless, we shall see that commerce must cross international boundaries. Foreign commerce is unavoidable.

No Nation Is Self-sufficient. The truest statement which can be made in this connection is that no nation in the world is completely self-sufficient in worldly resources. Therefore, a certain minimum of foreign commerce is necessary from the point of view either of military security or of living standards. It is with the volume over and above this that we must concern ourselves.

First of all, one must accept the proposition that a higher standard of living is universally desired. By this is meant a higher material standard. A perennial element of unsatisfied demand compels one to conclude that a higher standard of living is desired by most individuals; on a country-by-country basis, it points up the concept of the haves and the have nots. Secondly, the premise is made of an enlightened populace, in which knowledge of the existence of higher living standards elsewhere may be had and in which the will of the people may be heard and obeyed.

Pressure of Population an Important Factor. It has been stated that differences in costs of production exist in part because of the uneven distribution of resources and population over the world. Man continually struggles to overcome this inequality, sometimes because of dire need and sometimes because of convenience. This uneven distribution of resources among nations and of opportunities among people is reflected in part by a few simple observations. First of these is the pressure of population on land. Results of recent estimates of the population per square mile in several countries appear in the table on page 225.

It is practically impossible for the available land in a country like Belgium or the Netherlands to produce enough to support the population. In this respect, small, densely populated countries may be compared roughly with a concentrated metropolitan area within a larger country. It is almost inconceivable that the area surrounding New York City, for example, could produce enough to support New York's metropolitan population all year round.

This feature of annual "replaceable" production is not the only factor. Of equal and perhaps greater importance is the uneven availability of nonreplacable resources, such as the various minerals. The drive or the

Country	1950
Netherlands	777
Belgium	718*
Japan	586
United Kingdom	539
Italy	399
United States	50
Mexico	33
U.S.S.R.	22†
Brazil	15
Argentina	16
Canada	4
Australia	3

*1949.
†1946.
SOURCE: *The Economic Almanac, 1951–52*, (New York, National Industrial Conference Board, Inc., 1951), pp. 18, 19.

urge to acquire minerals not produced in a particular nation is exceptionally intense; sometimes the motive may be peaceful living needs, while at other times it may be national security. Millions of people over the globe do not have, and are not vigorously pressing for, some of the comforts or evidences of civilization not available to them. But this by no means enables anyone to pass lightly over the intense pressure for raw materials available only in countries other than their own, either for immediate consumption or for industrial processing.

The Meaning of "Surplus" Production. Another aspect of regional and national geographic limitations is that which is commonly referred to as "surplus" production. One may well ask whether a country ever has surplus production of goods so long as any individual in that country has not acquired his basic wants. This leads to a mention of the differing types of demand for particular products. Brazil can produce more coffee than Brazilians can drink, no matter how low the price may go; even if coffee were given away, the probability is that Brazilians could never consume all the coffee their country can produce. The same holds for Cuba and its sugar, Venezuela and its petroleum, Australia and its wool, and Honduras and its bananas. However, when the notion of surplus production is applied to many other products, it must be considered in the light of the producers' desire not to break the market price in the preferred market. This would hold in the case of several manufactured goods whose mass-production output is probably greater than can be absorbed locally without disruptive effect on the price structure, if at all. The determining factor would be the degree of elasticity of demand for the respective items; the home market may absorb more at a lower price but not enough to offset price reductions. Here, the idea is that foreign markets are a necessity for modern nations, as they offer a wider potential market than can be found solely in the country of the producer. Thus foreign commerce is more than merely economically feasible; it is necessary.

What Are the Alternatives? Reverting again to regional and national geographic limitations, we might ask what the alternatives may be in the circumstances outlined, assuming that man and goods belong together. They seem to be (1) migration, (2) trade, (3) doing without, or (4) conquest.

Immigration and migration restrictions effectively limit the first point. The desire for a higher standard of living and the knowledge that such standards may be attainable seem to nullify the third point over any length of time. There are many who would say that military conquest is often made necessary because it is the only way in which certain economic desires can be attained.

Thus, on the basis of economics, it would appear that every step taken should be in the direction of encouraging wider markets and thus more world trade. But the history of the world is one of continuing efforts to modify, control, or reduce the volume, direction, or flow of trade.

Politico-economic Factors

In the foregoing discussion, the assumption was made that relatively free enterprise does prevail, leaving the type, direction, and volume of foreign commerce to the judgment of the world market—the aggregate of millions of individuals interested in and thousands of traders engaged in foreign commerce. In a world in which the elements of production and the natural resources are unevenly scattered, over which nations have become superimposed, it can hardly be otherwise under free enterprise than that nations will produce and trade in accordance with their ability to do so on the most profitable basis.

Governmental Agreements Interfere with Free Markets. Under pressure of economic conditions prevailing at the time, however, and sometimes as a result of politico-economic philosophies, many governments have attempted to overcome free market influences on the volume and direction of multilateral trade by entering into bilateral agreements with others whereby two countries agree to exchange (or to make it possible for the exchange to be accomplished) certain products to mutual benefit. Thus, while the basis of trade is economic in that the goods are produced more advantageously in one of the countries than in the other, the actual transaction depends on political necessity rather than on the most economic and profitable impetus, which would be the case if buyers were able to purchase in any of two or more markets rather than being restricted to the one with which the agreement is entered. Examples of governmental agreements that interfere with the free working of international markets are foreign-exchange clearing and compensatory agreements, bulk-purchasing agreements, and a variety of rules and regulations based on foreign commercial policy. It will be evident that political arrangements of this nature normally result in higher prices to consumers, hence a lower standard of living. But in some cases, as those involving governmental agreements in rubber and tin in 1951, the market price of these commodities was probably kept below the level that would have prevailed in an uncontrolled market.

Many governmental agreements, as well as unilateral controls, are required for security purposes in the postwar tension. These security considerations naturally call for a deviation from the less restricted system that may be expected to prevail more widely in times of peace. Economic warfare is thus obviously a very powerful short-run factor in the volume and direction of world trade.

Uneconomic Employment May Be Preferred to Economic Unemployment. It may also be argued that during the continual adjustments which must be expected under a free multilateral concept, the distress and unemployment necessary to correct disequilibrium arising from world-wide competition are so unpalatable as to call for every step being taken to avoid these corrections. Even uneconomic employment is to be preferred to economic unemployment, in this view, although it means the production of goods at home at higher cost than available abroad, and even though it means buying in the dearer of two markets. Observation might also be made that of the two bargaining countries the one in more desperate circumstances might make a greater sacrifice in order to obtain needed goods abroad, but whether this would result in more favorable prices to the better situated of the two countries is doubtful. No government will agree to sell its goods abroad for a lower price to one country than to another if it can do better by selling to the third and converting exchange received for purchases in the rest of the world. Quite obviously, some of these arrangements are worked out for other than strictly economic reasons.

Another aspect of the politico-economic trade is the recent tendency toward increased government control over the economy, both domestic and in foreign commerce. It is estimated that "nationalized" activities account for about 95 per cent of the foreign trade of Eastern Europe (Albania, Bulgaria, Czechoslovakia, Hungary, Poland, Romania, and Yugoslavia).[4] This assumption of economic activity or control by government, and its removal from private hands, must of necessity involve political as well as, and sometimes more than, economic considerations in the type, direction, and volume of foreign commerce.

[4] Kathleen B. Rivet, "Nationalization of Foreign Trade in Eastern Europe," *Foreign Commerce Weekly*, May 8, 1950, p. 4.

The Free- vs. the Restricted-trade Controversy

In many texts on economic and foreign commerce, a common practice is to inject some comment on the advantages of free, as contrasted with restricted, foreign commerce.

When considered objectively, it is practically impossible to argue down the principle of free trade; through specialization because of some relative advantage, it means lower prices and higher living standards to the consumer and maximum international economic opportunity. But assuming a condition of objectivity is not practical. Implementation of any theory through legislative action must always bring the issue face to face with the existing state of society. Unfortunately, the state of society in many instances is filled with objectively untenable institutions and relative positions. Each such institution or relative position represents one person or many who object to being dislodged. Sometimes these many people represent a strong political bloc; at other times they may not, but the economic cost of readjustment is a tolerable obstacle to putting a long-run theory into short-run practice. Then there is the question of nationalistic security and pride; it may well be argued that the cost of not permitting the optimum of free multilateral trade is less than would be the cost of permitting it and exposing the national safety to avoidable risks,[5] or less than would be the cost of making the necessary internal economic adjustments which could be forced by unrestricted competition from abroad.

Fear of Cheap Foreign Labor vs. Fear of Efficiency. Perhaps the most influential popular argument used by proponents of protectionism is the appeal to fear through the specter of competition from "cheap" foreign labor. In some lines, this fear is undoubtedly well founded, for low-priced labor (assuming approximately comparable productivity) is as much a contribution to relative advantage in the cost of production as is the availability of raw materials or any of the other factors making up total cost. In particular economic activities, labor cost is a very high percentage of competitive costs of production. The implication is that the standard of living of the American worker would be lowered by having to meet such competition. The most tenable view would seem to be that, while some would be seriously hurt to some extent and even thrown out of employment as producers, more would be benefited as consumers through lowered prices all around. Lowered costs are, after all, the very heart of efficiency and technological improvement. Low wages of a few cents per day abroad should not be compared as equal competitively to higher wages in this country running into dollars per day. The basic

[5] Not only the lack of productive physical facilities, but also the lack of skilled labor which could be converted into production of military material in event of emergency.

point is unit cost—not pay per hour or per day. It is the combination of pay and productivity which counts, and the observation can well be made that many people abroad are more afraid of the productivity of American labor than we are of the low wages paid many foreign workers. Most importers can cite numerous instances in which the foreign exporter is unable to consummate sales in the United States because foreign costs are too high relative to costs in the United States, even though the labor abroad may be paid only a few cents per day. The record speaks for itself in the fact that in some of our domestic industries in which wage rates per hour or day are highest, we are actually exporters, able to compete with anyone in the world.

Other Popular Arguments for Restrictions. Another popular argument used in favor of trade restrictions is that by reserving the home market to domestic producers, domestic employment will be increased and money will be kept at home. Within limits, some domestic employment *may* be so increased, *but at a higher production cost per unit.* By the same process, some domestic employment may be *reduced,* if export markets are lost by a stoppage of imports. The suggestion of keeping money at home may be dismissed with the observation that money itself is not wealth. The measure of wealth is what the money can buy.

Free Multilateral Trade Offers Widespread Benefits. A most powerful argument in favor of multilateral trade is that the benefits from free multilateral trade are available to all and are based on the assumption of the right of individual entrepreneurs to deal in the most advantageous market at any particular time. Over the long run, the benefits are those available through an optimum of specialization based on some relative advantage. The favorable features are basically economic and not political, although political liberty must rest on a certain degree of economic self-reliance and independence. There are those, of course, who feel that economic stability is the keystone of popular happiness, but this goal of economic stability, to be achieved by governmentally planned and sometimes directed economic activity, must be weighed against the freedom of the individual to decide what he wishes to produce, sell, or buy, and where and when he wishes to do so.

Conclusions

Many items of value are produced only, or at least at less cost, in places distant from and in countries different from that of the consumer. The combination of differing population pressures (as well as different characteristics of skills among nationalities or races) and of differing availability of the natural resources of the world result in a widely differing *productivity* of the many thousands of items of value entering trade. Examples of the effect of these forces are as follows.

WHEAT. About five countries produce wheat in significant exportable quantities. These are Argentina, Australia, Canada, the United States, and Russia. Wheat is produced and consumed in practically every country. About 10 per cent of wheat production enters world trade.

RICE. Rice is another commodity produced and consumed over the world. Principal exporting countries are India, Burma, French Indochina, and Thailand, but China is the principal producing country. The major importing countries are about the same as those exporting. About 6 per cent of world production was exported in immediate prewar years, but in the postwar period this seems to have fallen to about 2 per cent of total world production.[6]

WOOL. Australia, Argentina, New Zealand, and the United States rank as the leading producers of wool. Principal exporters are Australia, New Zealand, Argentina, and South Africa, and the most important importing countries are the United Kingdom, France, Germany, Belgium, Japan, and the United States. About two-thirds of world production enters world trade.

TOBACCO. World production is largely dominated by the United States, China, and India, although several other countries are important sources. A little over 20 per cent of total world production of unmanufactured tobacco enters international trade. This portion moves principally to the United Kingdom, Germany, the United States, the Netherlands, France, Belgium, and China.

COTTON. This is another important item, with about half of total production entering world trade. Principal producing countries are the United States, India, Russia, and Brazil. Importing countries are principally the United Kingdom, Japan, France, Germany, Italy, and Belgium.

COFFEE. This is a good example of a commodity whose production is dominated by one country—Brazil, whose production is about two-thirds of the world total. Other large producers are Colombia and Venezuela, Guatemala, Mexico, and Haiti. About half of total world consumption is accounted for by the United States, other major importers being France, Germany, the United Kingdom, and the Netherlands.

TEA. Over half of world production of tea is exported; if data for China are excluded, about 80 per cent of total production is consumed in countries other than the producer. Production is primarily in China, India, Ceylon, Netherlands East Indies, and Japan. Principal importing countries are the United Kingdom, Argentina, Uruguay, the United States, and Australia.

The list of items whose production is so relatively concentrated could be expanded very much more, but this is not necessary if we merely

[6] *World Economic Report, 1948,* United Nations, 1949, p. 209.

consider the areas of production and areas of consumption of products such as leather, furs, rubber, vegetable oils and oilseeds, copper, tin, and petroleum. Nor should we overlook the concentration in production and exporting of manufactured goods. Detailed statistics comparable to those for commodities are not available for the wide variety of manufactured goods, but the point may be made by referring to the concentration of production of automobiles in the United States, Canada, Great Britain, and a few European countries; the production for export of textiles by Japan, Great Britain, the Netherlands, France, and Italy, and of machinery by the United States, Great Britain, Belgium, Germany, Italy, and a few other countries.

In the long run, the *desirability* of foreign commerce is based on its affording the opportunity for wider markets which in turn render possible more specialization. This, in turn, means lower costs and lower prices—the greatest gain to the greatest number. Its *feasibility* rests on the existence of differences in costs among people, regions, and countries. These differences in costs arise from the ease or difficulty of acquiring and employing the various factors of production. Its *necessity* devolves from the fact that unequal geographic distribution of nature's gifts, and the concentration or sparsity of population in relation to these productive facilities, makes it necessary for some system to exist which will serve to bring men and goods together peaceably. Moreover, foreign commerce is practically unavoidable in a measure far above the minimum dictated by the requirements of military needs and the simple necessities of life.

In reality, though, current volumes of foreign commerce are influenced by many factors other than those arising from purely long-run economic foundations. High in influence is a variety of short-run economic factors which give rise to trade opportunities for either selling or buying. Some of these are temporary in nature and are, in fact, adjustments to the long-run economic factors. Equally influential are political factors whereby governmental policies are pursued to limit or overcome the pressures arising from purely economic considerations. Typical of the latter are government actions to influence the volume and direction of trade, these being rendered necessary if government is to pursue a policy of controlling the economy and of undertaking what are called "positive" measures to create full employment.

The extent of government interference in the workings of free international markets, normally for political purposes, points up the controversy between those who favor freer multilateral trade and those who find more advantage in restricted bilateral trade. There are many valid positions which may be held temporarily between the two extremes of maximum free trade and socialism or communism as an economic system. However, surrender of the widespread benefits of freer markets, which means losing opportunities for greater production at less cost and inviting limitation of political liberty, is the price to be paid for government-directed or -influenced activity aimed at the objective of economic stability.

Obstacles to Multilateralism. Overcoming the most formidable obstacles to multilateralism in trade calls for political and economic policies along the following lines: (1) nationalistic aspirations must be rendered of secondary importance; (2) economic "control" and "power" by some central authority must not be adopted or must be zealously minimized; and (3) the cost involved in *adjustments in employment and in established channels and positions* must be made logically acceptable. One should not be optimistic that such a broad change in practical economic philosophy may soon occur; probably every one of us, if we were individuals directly affected, would find it very easy to comprehend the impact on ourselves of foreign competition. We would tend to overlook the benefits to others of their being able to buy in the cheapest market— an advantage which redounds to all.

REVIEW QUESTIONS

1. Why has international specialization—individually and geographically— developed?

2. Explain the statement that all voluntary trade results in an advantage to both the buyer and the seller.

3. Discuss or evaluate the proposition that through trade the benefits of technological progress tend to be spread over the producing and trading community, although not equally, nor necessarily to the entire world. Why not equally, and why not to the entire world, both the developed and undeveloped areas?

4. List several factors which give rise to cost differentials.

5. By what economic process or processes do cost differentials influence commerce?

6. Evaluate the validity of the statement that international trade is fundamentally not different from domestic; both are *interregional.*

7. Explain the condition of comparative advantage. To what extent does the working of this condition affect the volume and direction of world trade?

8. What does the fact of production and trade's being by competing enterprises have to do with acceptance and application of the principle of comparative advantage?

9. Explain how investments and travel influence trade in goods.

10. What is the meaning of "surplus" production? Under what conditions might production which is "surplus" today not be "surplus" tomorrow?

11. What are the alternatives to commerce among nations? Why?

12. Discuss the economic, political, and social implications in the statement that uneconomic employment may be preferred to economic unemployment.

13. List several popular arguments for a policy of restriction in foreign commerce. Which of these do you consider the most valid, and why?

14. In what way can it be said that free multilateral trade offers widespread benefits as compared with restrictions?

15. Outline the pros and cons to the claims that foreign commerce is (*a*) desirable, (*b*) economically feasible, (*c*) economically, politically, and socially necessary.

16. What would have to be done to bring about multilateralism in world commerce, *i.e.*, what are the present obstacles to multilateralism? Is there any hope of multilateralism being accomplished in the reasonably near future?

CHAPTER 12

Foreign Commerce and National Economies

The preceding chapter dealt with foreign commerce rather abstractly, the broad theories not being focused on any particular nation. In this chapter, the view will be more closely related to conditions of, or circumstances faced by, single countries. Of course, no single country need be used as a model or experimental subject, and it may well be that the several points mentioned do not all apply to any one country, or they may apply in varying degree. The chapter is organized into the following sections: (1) Benefits and Disadvantages from Imports, (2) Benefits and Disadvantages from Exports, (3) Foreign Commerce and National Income, (4) Foreign Commerce and Employment, and (5) Foreign Commerce and Natural Resources.

BENEFITS AND DISADVANTAGES FROM IMPORTS

Merchandise

Imports Raise Standard of Living. The principal benefit to be derived from imports of merchandise is very likely the fact that it enables a higher standard of living to be enjoyed by the public. Imports bring in goods not producible in the home country or, if produced at all, not available domestically in sufficient quantity, of comparable quality, or at competitive cost. Our standard of living would indeed be quite different from what it is if we had to do without or with much smaller quantities of sugar, coffee, bananas, spices, cocoa, wools, and certain types of tobacco, cotton, and various food products. It would also be quite seriously affected if our supply of many mineral resources were to disappear and a smaller quantity or less satisfactory substitutes were to be available only at higher cost. Imports also mean a wider variety of choices and types and, very importantly, they mean lower prices for domestic as well as foreign merchandise if there is a possibility of importing similar merchandise or an acceptable substitute from abroad.

Quite often, also, imports are the only means of obtaining many manufactured goods whose patents, processes, and production may be concentrated in one or a few companies or countries.

A second very important consideration is the fact that imports help pay for exports; they enable recipients of dollars spent for foreign merchandise to buy United States exports, both of merchandise and of services, and to buy United States investments.

Another significant benefit from importing foreign merchandise is that it avoids or deters the exhaustion of domestic raw materials; this has special applicability to resources of the nonreplaceable type. The question of whether the United States ought to impose a higher duty or an import quota on foreign petroleum products must certainly make ample allowance for the fact that our own petroleum reserves are exhaustible and, in the space of one generation, lack of an adequate conservation program may prove distastefully costly.

Imports May Also Mean Temporary Disadvantages. It would be a mistake, however, to overlook the list of disadvantages which may be arrayed on the question of merchandise imports. Many supporters can be found for these arguments, which bear on such matters as military considerations, employment, entrepreneurial competition, and economic stability or instability. As to the first, it may be stated that dependence on foreign sources for raw materials or, more likely, finished goods, makes a nation more vulnerable in a prolonged war. This is undoubtedly true, as the experience of Japan, especially, shows. But few, if any nations are self-sufficient, and the point may be countered by the observation that while one country may depend on others as a *source* of merchandise, others depend on the first as a *market* for their sales.

Imports May Force Dislocation and Unemployment. As indicated in the preceding paragraph, perhaps the most appealing objection to imports (or to particular imports) is that they may mean dislocation and unemployment, even of a temporary type, pending reabsorption into the economy of the displaced resources. Unemployment, even for a few days, is a bitter pill for many with families to support and obligations to meet. Further, some economists may wish to state that the loss to the nation through unemployment (or underemployment) of the factors of production may be greater than the benefit to be derived from allowing the forces of competition to make their effects felt through adjustments resolved by the common denominator of price. It could also very probably be that the impact of imported merchandise would appear at a time when employment possibilities would be scarce, so that the reabsorption of displaced labor might be a relatively long drawn out process. Accordingly, during a more than insignificant portion of a generation's working life, the political and social appeal to abolish unemployment, even if it means what might otherwise have been noneconomic employment, is quite strong.

A counterpart of the unemployment of labor is the possibility of unemployment of management skills, loss of capital, or temporary unemployment of an enterpreneurial combination of factors of production. Imports mean wider competition for the producer, and competition is something many people wish to avoid. For it means security only through effort. It is not at all necessary to confine this view to international commerce; witness the number of efforts made by some business leaders to gain advantages through reduction or elimination of competition, even locally.

Imports May Interfere with Controlled Economy and "Full-employment" Aims. Finally, on a point which has drawn much popular observation in the past twenty-five years, it is sometimes stated that dependence on foreign sources, even in peacetime, makes a nation more vulnerable to economic fluctuations generated from foreign countries. If the nation attempts a policy of controlled economic stability, it may find that its welfare is greatly affected by the policies of its suppliers, especially when the supplier is a large, strong country and the purchaser is a small, relatively weak one. As will be seen later, the argument appears to have more direct application in the consideration of disadvantages to exporting. Moreover, a nation's own economic policies must be drawn up in the light of the ever possible conflict between national "full-employment" measures and foreign purchases which are necessary if it is to enjoy the benefits of international specialization. The newness of this concept of governmental responsibility in the field of employment does not permit a record of experience indicating its effect on foreign commerce, except perhaps in the case of Russia and a few other countries which have all but throttled not only foreign commerce but individual liberty as well.

Services

When it comes to purchasing services from abroad, the principal advantage is that the services, like merchandise, may not be available in the home country or, if they are, they may be too expensive. Services are often highly specialized and require unique training; they often call for world-wide experience or connections, and the purchasing country may not have these in sufficient amount. As with merchandise, purchase of services from abroad enables the seller to obtain dollars with which to buy our goods, services, or investments, but purchasing foreign insurance, banking, or shipping services for instance, means that domestic facilities for these services are compelled to meet foreign competition.

Chief among the disadvantages is probably the fact that purchase of foreign services, especially shipping, renders the purchasing country somewhat dependent on others in case of military need and tends to preclude the existence of a skilled or experienced labor and organization which in time of need might be very desirable.

Investments

Weighing the advantages and disadvantages of foreign investments seems to lead to occasional cloudiness in the concept of the question. This is because the reader may look on the investment paper, the capital goods, or the funds as representing the foreign investment. Actually, the importer of a foreign investment "brings in" a piece of paper representing evidence of foreign debt or of ownership in some physical facility in another country; for it, his country may record the exportation of capital goods, although settlement may be accomplished through bank balances and the foreign-exchange markets. The construction of a branch plant in Canada or Mexico would accordingly result in an "importation" of a foreign investment by United States interests; it would represent technically an export of foreign investments on the part of Canada or Mexico.

What, then, may be said to be advantages arising from imports of foreign investments? First of all is the obvious—better investment opportunities may be found abroad than in the home country. What constitutes "better" may fall under several headings, relating to such features as earnings, taxes, and safety of funds or of savings (relative political stability).

Investments May Develop New Sources of Supply. A second consideration is that the investment may provide a new source of supply from abroad which, to a nation's economy, may be quite desirable in that it means lower prices and/or a larger supply of goods or services. New supplies of food and raw material are of much importance to a country without adequate domestic supplies, such as some of the smaller countries of Northern Europe which depend on exports of processed goods or services to bring in desired food and raw materials.

A third point is that importing the foreign investment makes more possible the exportation of capital goods, services, and technically and professionally trained manpower.

Investments May Be Best Access to Foreign Markets. Quite important, especially from the individual company point of view, is that importation of a foreign investment such as establishment of a branch plant abroad may facilitate sales. By producing abroad, it may be possible to get inside the tariff or quota 'wall, thereby overcoming foreign obstacles to goods produced in the home country of the "investor." Foreign buyers' resistance to "foreign" goods may be overcome by meeting their preference for "domestically produced" merchandise. As an example, *Business*

Week[1] reports that White Motor Company, as a result of difficulties in obtaining import licenses for the sale of trucks into Mexico, entered into a licensing agreement whereby parts will be shipped into Mexico for assembly and sale, inasmuch as no restrictions are put on the sale of trucks assembled in Mexico. Ford Motor Company and General Motors also have set up assembly plants in Mexico. While technically not classifiable as a *foreign* investment, an expansion in textile manufacturing in Puerto Rico was also reported, with the investments by continental United States interests. Production possibilities appeared extremely attractive there because of low wages, plentiful labor, and tax exemptions, plus the fact that textiles could be sent to the United States from Puerto Rico without the payment of duty. Not only do the foreign investments make it easier to circumvent obstacles to imports into the country in which the plant may be located, but more advantageous production possibilities might make it easier to break into other foreign markets, especially if the other markets have less restrictions on imports from countries not requiring payment in U.S. dollars.

Finally, it is not at all unusual to hear that foreign investments may be the answer to the postwar dollar shortage, the implication being that private or government loans or investments abroad will serve as the means by which foreign countries may continue to buy our exports in substantial volume.

Foreign Investors Face Extra Risks. There are, as might be expected, numerous disadvantages or *special risks* which the importer of a foreign investment must face. First of all is the possibility of expropriation, whereby the investor may stand to lose if the price paid for his property is inadequate to compensate for his expenditures or for what he considers to be present values. Then, the foreign investor may find it a disadvantage to lose the benefits of political jurisdiction; actually, there may be times when a different political jurisdiction is what he seeks. A very important disadvantage is the risk the investor must run of the possible imposition of additional or new exchange controls which make it difficult for him to receive service or to repatriate his foreign investment. He also faces the possibility of double taxation, although this burden is being eliminated through treaties between governments. But punitive taxation is possibly a formidable feature discouraging such investment. A good example of this is a tax law or rate which applies only to businesses falling in certain categories, such as size, when it happens that the only such businesses in the country in question are foreign owned. Labor requirements and joint-ownership provisions favoring nationals of the country in which the investment is placed are also to be classed as disadvantages or special risks.

[1] Feb. 11, 1950, p. 108.

Investments Have Stabilizing but Sometimes Disruptive Effects on Foreign Commerce. From a broader point of view, a principal disadvantage (of investments) may arise from the fact that international transactions in and the servicing of securities have an effect on the balance of payments and on exchange rates similar to the movement of merchandise. Many foreign investments are of the "direct" type, which means they are rather fixed physically. On these, service charges are a relatively fixed element in international balances, both to the importing and to the exporting country. However, uneven volumes of international capital movements, sparked by any cause whatever, could disrupt otherwise relative equilibrium. Transactions in outstanding securities are also subject to greater volatility than are transactions in merchandise. This is because of the usually smaller volume, in which case a given dollar change means a greater percentage variation, and because of the variety of causes which might bring about movements of capital in erratic directions and volumes for reasons quite unrelated to the normal movement of goods. In the United States, using 1949 as a base, the index of exports and imports of goods and securities in 1950 and 1951 was as indicated in the table below. The subject of capital transfers is discussed in some detail in Chapters 3 and 15.

Item	Exports		Imports	
	1950	1951	1950	1951
Merchandise..........	86	125	132	165
Securities.............	233	197	181	292

Furthermore, to a country as a whole, investments abroad mean the placing of funds and energy outside the country when they might beneficially be used at home. Some evidence of this is suggested by Salter, who observes that in Great Britain, in the years preceding the big depression, there was a tendency to lend abroad on too big a scale for the diminishing surplus on her international account. On the matter of lending more than the balance of payments would seem to warrant, he comments:[2] "Great Britain continued to lend abroad through the institutions built up during the period when she had by far the biggest surplus on international account available for foreign lending; and to guide her action by much the same rules and criteria." One may wonder whether the foreign lending may have been a contributing factor to, or may have resulted from, the neglect of Britain's plant and equipment.

[2] Sir Arthur Salter, *Recovery—The Second Effort* (New York, Appleton-Century-Crofts, Inc., 1936), p. 113.

Travel

Several advantages may be named for the "importation" of travel. In the first place, the travel account is an important one in the economies of several countries, and purchases made in this manner serve to aid in the export of merchandise and services. Travel "imports" also serve a good purpose when entered for business reasons, and their contribution to personal enjoyment and education is beyond measure. It may also be stated that travel serves as a factor in peace, through better knowledge and understanding among the peoples of the world.

There are no strong disadvantages to travel imports. Perhaps the fact that funds for travel may mean fewer funds for what government authorities consider to be more essential to the national welfare is a potent argument. Another is perhaps the disadvantage through possible contamination by foreign ideologies and by the immediate realization that in some countries individuals are more free than in others to express their views about their government or its officials. However, this may be as much of an advantage to the traveler as it is a disadvantage to the dictator.

BENEFITS AND DISADVANTAGES FROM EXPORTS

Merchandise

Exports Lead to Increased Employment and at Times, Lower Costs. High on the list of benefits from exports is that they mean additional markets which are not so available in the home country. Satisfaction of the demand in these markets means additional or sustained employment, with consequent effect on individual incomes. Exports may also permit the realization of lower costs through mass production, resulting in lower prices for that portion of production sold domestically. This holds, of course, only in decreasing-cost-per-unit industries. Furthermore, through widened international markets, producers are better able to specialize in or concentrate on the production of items that they can turn out best, thus increasing their productivity. Finally, exports may be said to pay for imports in that through them we are able to obtain necessary foreign exchange to purchase goods which are best, or perhaps only, available from abroad.

Dependence on Foreign Markets Sometimes Leads to Disadvantages. In the face of the benefits to employment from exports, one must search hard to find a comparably strong argument opposing export trade. One of the sounder ones is the possibility of exhaustion of nonreplaceable resources; this assumes that the goods would not be consumed in the home market, even at lower prices. A second important disadvantage is that dependence on foreign markets may render the exporting country susceptible to economic fluctuations occurring in the importing countries; this would hold especially in the case in which one large country is the principal market for a very substantial part of the export trade of a smaller one. Examples would be that of the United States as the importer and the "banana" republics as the exporters. Of course, the difficulty arises as much from the lack of diversification of production in the exporting country as it does from the relationship mentioned. Parallel to this is the dependence on markets which may be lost during a war, as was the case with several South American countries during the war when some of their European markets were blockaded.

Services

In general, it may be stated that one of the principal advantages of exports of services is that they permit the purchase of foreign goods or services which are not available domestically, especially when the production of exportable merchandise may not be sufficient to cover requirements of these foreign needs. Another advantage is that world-wide markets for services permit a wider specialization, with a resulting higher degree of skill or expertness. Skills may be valuable in case of military emergency, and it might be mentioned, also, that the availability of the services may make possible or easier the development of foreign markets for merchandise exports and investment imports. Then, being the provider of services, through which international commerce is transacted, the exporting country, may be expected to wield more influence on other countries through control of communications, transportation, and banking. Disadvantages to the exportation of services would seem to be few and far between, except that some dislocation might arise from the loss of foreign markets through developments peculiar to the particular foreign market, including such matters as taxes, political upheavals, restrictions on the purchase of foreign services, or the imposition of exchange controls.

Investments

Foreign Investment Permits Development beyond a Nation's Own Savings. Reference has already been made to possible cloudiness in the concept of imports and exports of foreign investments. At this time, the export of a foreign investment will be looked on as (1) the counterentry of an importation of capital goods or technical skills or funds or (2) the actual selling of outstanding securities, either domestic or foreign. With regard to the former, possibly most of the advantages are to be realized. First of all, economic development of the country is released from the limitation imposed by savings or capital accumulation in the country receiving the capital goods. History is full of instances in which a borrowing country was able to develop its resources through the importation of foreign capital goods, such importation being offset by the exportation of an investment. Secondly, as a result of the exportation of an investment of this type, technical abilities may be brought into a country as the corresponding import; thus technical knowledge or direction may be acquired in this manner, which serves to speed up the economic diversification or industrialization of a country.

Foreign Capital Means Incomplete Political Jurisdiction. There are, however, several serious disadvantages to a country's exportation of its obligations or equity investments. First of these is the fear that the country may be placing itself under the domination of foreign investors or capitalists, who have their own personal interests in prime position. Secondly, the existence of large foreign-owned investments in its country may serve to tie the hands of the local government because of incomplete political jurisdiction (control over the property but not the person). Action taken by a government in this position could set off a wave of selling by foreigners who are not under personal political jurisdiction or domination, which could be very embarrassing to the government. Thus, balanced international transactions might be more easily upset through capital transactions. At the same time, and as mentioned before, servicing the foreign debt may become a heavy burden at times; in the case of some countries, such as Canada and Iran, the payment of interest and dividends constitutes a substantial proportion of "purchases" from abroad. These must, of course, be paid for by the exportation of merchandise or services which might otherwise have been available for home consumption.

Travel

The principal advantage to exporting travel (entertaining visitors from foreign countries) is probably to be found in the fact that tourist expenditures are an important source of foreign funds to many countries. These were mentioned in some detail in Chapter 2. But aside from the income to be derived from selling services and goods to travelers from abroad is the benefit to be derived from intellectual and business contact with people from other countries. Too often, instances are reported of travelers offending their host countries, but it is more likely the case that worthwhile bond of respect and understanding is developed from such in- and ex-cursions. On the side of disadvantages to exporting travel is the possibility that ostentatious, or even simple and accidental, evidences of differences in economic position may be the source of friction and ill feeling between foreigners and the source of dissatisfaction with domestic conditions by those who compare. For instance, the reservation in the last few years of food or clothing specialties for the tourist dollar must have left only a feeling of frustration or envy in the minds of holders of domestic currencies to whom these goods were not available.

FOREIGN COMMERCE AND NATIONAL INCOME

Leaving the view of foreign commerce as a market for buying and selling goods or services, or a market for foreign funds or investments, we now turn to somewhat broader aspects of the position which foreign commerce holds with regard to national economies. The first of these relates to national income.

Foreign Commerce Not Clearly Reported in National-income Estimates. In some economic literature, percentage comparisons have been made between merchandise import and export volumes and national income and gross national product. These are probably based on a liberal interpretation of the meaning of these two over-all estimates. But exports and imports are not clearly reported as such in national-income and -product estimates. The difference between the two on current account, less the net outflow of gifts, is calculated as *net foreign investment,* and this net figure is incorporated into the summary estimate.

The Significance of Exports. One method of determining national income incorporates wage and salary disbursements to factors of production supplied by residents of the United States for which, presumably, goods and services were received. Hence goods and services produced and exported having been received, although subsequently sent abroad, some idea of their relative importance in the national economic picture may appear to be indicated. Actually, the fact of their being exported has no bearing, for the measure used in their cost of production. So no matter how much exports increase or decrease, they do not affect the *national-income account* except as they cause an increase or decrease in production, whose costs comprise the measure of national income. It could be said that favorable export opportunities stimulate the employment of the economic factors in production, and in this way exports could contribute to a higher national income by encouraging the undertaking of their costs of production.

The gross-national-product estimate, on the other hand, is intended to reflect the market value of the output of goods and services produced by the nation's economy, before deduction of depreciation charges and other allowances for business and institutional consumption of durable capital goods. Its computation calls for including purchases of United States exports by foreigners and excluding purchases of foreign production by United States producers and consumers. The difference between the two, as stated above, is incorporated on a net basis into the summary estimate. Hence exports if or since they provide a demand and thereby encourage production, influence the national-product account. However, the same could be said of domestic demand; the "sales" are included, wherever made. But if failure to sell abroad would result in failure to produce, it would have to be said that decreased exports could be the cause of a reduction in national product and also in national income.

The Significance of Imports. Imports being sold, but not produced, in the United States, their value must be deducted from gross sales estimated in the United States, to which exports are added in order to arrive at sales value of United States–produced goods and services (gross national product).

If imports are high, their sale will enhance the gross sales figure (by which gross national product is measured, after appropriate adjustments), but deduction of the value of imports from gross sales will accordingly eliminate the immediate influence of imports from gross national product. On the other hand, if imports are low, their sale will initially increase gross sales by this smaller amount (of imports), which must be deducted in the statistical process of computing gross national product. Thus *imports, as such,* affect neither national income nor national product; income is ordinarily not paid to domestic factors for their production,[3] and they are not the product of the United States.

However, the level and types of production, out of which national product and income arise, may be significantly affected by the availability of imported goods. Moreover, but indirectly, imports provide foreigners with the means to buy our exports; this, as has been indicated, *can* have a direct bearing on national production and income.

Another shortcoming in relating foreign commerce to national income, at least in the United States, is that the geographic basis differs for the two tabulations. The territory for which balances of payment are calculated includes, in addition to continental United States, our territories and possessions. National-income and -product estimates are calculated for continental United States only.[4] Even with this indicated lack of exact comparability and lack of direct causal relationship, Table 38 may be of some help.

It would appear from Table 38 that neither imports nor exports of merchandise are a very significant percentage of national economic activity in the United States, and there can hardly be said to be

[3] Income accruing to United States–owned factors of production employed in other countries, whether the goods produced were sold here or abroad, would affect the national-income totals. It is the ownership of the factors, not the importing of the goods, which determines inclusion in national-income data.

[4] Adjustments are made for geographical coverage as regards "net foreign investment;" this account, however, includes goods, services, and unilateral transfers.

Table 38. Ratio of United States Imports to National Income, and of Exports to Gross National Product, 1919–1950

Year	Imports as % of national income	Exports as % of gross national product
1919	6.1	11.0
1920	7.1	9.4
1921	4.2	6.2
1922	5.1	5.2
1923	5.3	4.8
1924	5.0	5.4
1925	5.6	5.3
1926	5.4	4.9
1927	5.2	5.1
1928	5.0	5.2
1929	5.0	5.1
1930	4.1	4.3
1931	3.6	3.3
1932	3.2	2.9
1933	3.7	3.1
1934	3.4	3.5
1935	3.6	3.3
1936	3.6	3.1
1937	4.1	3.8
1938	2.9	3.8
1939	3.1	3.7
1940	3.1	4.1
1941	3.1	4.3
1942	2.0	5.8
1943	2.0	7.8
1944	2.1	8.1
1945	2.2	5.7
1946	2.7	6.0
1947	2.8	6.9
1948	3.5	5.1
1949	3.2	4.8
1950	3.9	3.8

any consistency or trend in the array of figures. Accordingly, some more meaningful measure must be developed to indicate the significance of foreign commerce to a national economy. But even with this shortcoming in the figures, it is interesting to note that imports amount to a much higher percentage of national income in some other countries than in the United States (see Table 22). During the period 1922 to 1939, imports of 11 countries combined[5] were computed to be between 12 and 24 per cent of their combined national income, with the proportion running as high as 40 per cent in several instances and over 50 per cent for three years in the case of Denmark. The comparable figures for the United States during the same period ranged from 2.9 to 5.6 per cent.

FOREIGN COMMERCE AND EMPLOYMENT

Reference is often made to the necessity of maintaining our export volume in order to maintain a high level of employment in the United States; we are also told of the necessity of maintaining a high level of industrial activity and national income because, it is reasoned, only in that way will our imports remain high or expand.[6]

To calculate even an approximation of our own dependence on foreign markets for domestic employment is very difficult. This is primarily because of the lack of comparable statistical data by series. For example, employment, physical production, sales, exports, value added by manufacture, and many other statistical series are arranged and maintained in nonidentical groupings. Then, even where it is possible to find similar coverage, there is no way of ascertaining definitely the exact amount of employment provided by the exported items. Several estimates are to be found, though, suggesting the importance of export markets to employment. One reports that in 1939, 15 per cent of the employees in the motor-vehicle, industrial-heating, and equipment industries were working directly or indirectly on export goods. Similar figures for other industries are nonferrous metals and products, 23 per cent; chemicals, 16 per cent; rubber, 15 per cent; transportation, 15 per cent; business and consumer services, 11 per cent; and food, tobacco, and kindred products, 12 per cent.[7]

Another over-all estimate, perhaps as good as any, is that afforded by Table 39.

The figures in the table average, very roughly, around 10 per cent.

[5] The countries concerned are the United Kingdom, France, Germany, Norway, the Netherlands, Sweden, Denmark, Canada, Australia, New Zealand, and Japan. See *The United States in the World Economy*, U.S. Department of Commerce, Economic Series 23, 1943, pp. 63–71.

[6] See C. B. Hoover, *International Trade and Domestic Employment* (New York, McGraw-Hill Book Company, Inc., 1945), pp. 13–14; and J. Hans Adler, "United States Import Demand During the Inter-war Period," *The American Economic Review*, Vol. 35, No. 3, pp. 418–419.

[7] Edward A. O'Neal, "The Farmer's Stake in Foreign Trade," *Report of the Thirty-fourth National Foreign Trade Convention*, National Foreign Trade Council, Inc., New York, 1948, p. 161.

Table 39. Ratio of Exports to Production,*
Selected Years, 1919–1950
(Dollar figures in millions)

Year	Total production	Merchandise exports	% of exports to production
1919	$ 47,515	$ 7,750	16.3
1921	33,875	4,379	12.9
1923	44,767	4,091	9.1
1925	47,192	4,819	10.2
1927	47,505	4,759	10.0
1929	52,786	5,159	9.8
1931	32,025	2,378	7.4
1933	25,245	1,647	6.5
1935	33,059	2,243	6.8
1937	43,534	3,279	7.6
1939	41,376	3,123	7.6
1941	65,050	5,020	7.7
1943	110,708	12,841	11.6
1945	103,774	10,310	9.9
1947	129,900	15,173	11.7
1948	139,680	12,532	9.0
1949	129,131	11,936	9.2
1950	147,224	10,142	6.9

* Production includes agricultural products, manufactures, mining, and freight receipts.

SOURCE: 1919–1947: *Statistical Abstract of the United States*, U.S. Bureau of the Census, 1948, p. 901; 1948–1950: *The Economic Almanac, 1951–52* (New York, National Industrial Conference Board, Inc., 1951), p. 532.

If 10 per cent is applied to the employed civilian labor force of 55,843,000 as of December, 1950, it appears that approximately 5,500,000 jobs are so indentifiable. But if we relate the 10 per cent to reported employment in agriculture (7,138,000), manufacturing (14,110,000), mining (971,000), and transportation and public utilities (4,252,000), the export-related employment is a little over 2,600,000. This latter figure omits those employed in trade, finance, construction, service, and government activities, of whom many would be active in foreign trade in merchandise or services. Professor Paul V. Horn has wisely stated:[8] "It is probably just as important not to exaggerate the significance of exports to national welfare as it is not to underestimate their value."

[8] Paul V. Horn, *International Trade—Principles and Practices* (New York, Prentice-Hall, Inc., 1945), p. 28.

Over-all Figure Not so Indicative as Detailed Study The over all per centages just referred to may be misleading if left without reference to the wide difference in the proportions exported of the many items produced. Table 40 suggests the importance of these differences for selected products; the influence on employment may be more correctly seen if we consider that, for each product, the indicated percentage of exports is also an indication of employment dependency on foreign markets.[9]

Table 40. Exports as Percentage of Production
(Selected products)

Product	1929	1939	1948	1949
Lard	34.5	13:6	11.7	23.7
Milk, condensed, evaporated, and dried	4.8	1.3	12.8	12.7
Wheat	15.4	11.6	35.0	39.0
Leaf tobacco	46.0	37.2	20.8	25.6
Cotton, raw	56.3	28.6	17.0	32.6
Turpentine	*	39.2	14.4	24.7
Cotton cloth and duck	7.5	4.4	9.3	9.9
Lubricating oil	31.1	33.6	25.0	25.0
Paraffin wax	50.7	50.1	28.3	30.8
Iron- and steel-mill products	5.7	7.2	6.8	8.3
Tin plate and terneplate	14.0	13.6	15.5	15.1
Copper	27.3	32.4	10.6	12.6
Electrical machinery and apparatus	5.5	5.9	5.4	5.3
Machine tools	13.2	44.5	25.1	32.2
Agricultural machinery and tractors	31.4	24.0	26.9	*
Passenger cars	9.8	5.7	6.0	3.0
Motor trucks and coaches	36.7	21.3	14.6	11.2
Carbon black	25.1	38.8	24.8	24.8
Paint, varnish, lacquer, and filler	3.2	2.2	2.9	2.8
Zinc	3.3	2.8	9.4	8.2

* Not available.
SOURCE: *Foreign Commerce Weekly,* Apr. 24, 1950, pp. 42–43.

Even the striking figures included in Table 40 are not sufficiently indicative, though. They do not include employees engaged in trading or transporting the merchandise or those engaged in providing various services to the producers of exported good—the grocers, barbers, physicians, dentists, lawyers, service-station operators, etc. The importance of these servicing elements may be seen by comparing the number of people employed in manufacturing, agriculture, and mining (22,219,000, as of December, 1950) with either the total employed civilian labor force (55,843,000) or the total population.

[9] A much more complete table, from which these figures were extracted, may be found in *Foreign Commerce Weekly,* Apr. 24, 1950, pp. 42–43. The study is titled "What Export Markets Mean to United States Producers."

Table 41. Dependence of Nonagricultural Employment on Exports

Employment	Employees in nonagricultural establishments (000 omitted)						% of total dependent on exports	
	1939		First half of 1947				1939	First half of 1947
	Total	Dependent on exports	Total	Total	Directly	Indirectly		
All groups	30,288	944	41,963	2,364	1,189	1,175	3.1	5.6
Food, tobacco, and kindred products	1,258	29	1,610	59	50	9	2.3	3.7
Iron mines, steel works, and rolling mills	483	53	665	131	67	64	10.9	19.7
Iron and steel products	600	38	1,054	113	53	60	6.3	10.7
Electrical machinery	425	30	909	105	91	14	7.2	11.5
Machinery, except electrical	777	92	1,570	246	221	25	11.9	15.7
Motor vehicles	466	44	955	133	125	8	9.3	13.9
Transportation equipment, except motor vehicles	241	26	636	61	58	3	10.7	9.6
Nonferrous metals and their products	267	38	423	61	23	38	14.4	14.5
Nonmetallic minerals and their products	439	21	610	47	30	17	4.7	7.7
Petroleum production and refining	295	32	382	34	19	15	11.0	8.8
Coal mining and manufactured solid fuel	504	39	505	94	59	35	7.7	18.5
Manufactured gas and electric power	432	13	458	22	.....	22	3.0	4.7
Chemicals	445	38	753	84	56	28	8.5	11.2
Lumber and furniture	850	35	1,203	75	37	38	4.2	6.2
Wood pulp, paper, printing, and publishing	893	29	1,165	65	27	38	3.2	5.6
Textiles and apparel	2,129	55	2,569	242	188	54	2.6	9.4
Leather and leather products	383	10	396	19	17	2	2.7	4.9
Rubber	150	12	286	42	23	19	7.7	14.7
All other manufacturing	432	20	695	61	48	13	4.5	8.8
Construction	1,150	.....	1,605					
Transportation	1,984	133	2,699	266	.....	266	6.7	9.8
Trade	6,614	114	8,439	295	.....	295	1.7	3.5
Business and professional services	5,215	44	7,088	109	.....	109	0.8	1.5
Government (federal, state, and local)	3,857	1	5,289	2	.....	2	*	*

* Less than ⅒ of 1 per cent.
SOURCE: *Monthly Labor Review*, U.S. Department of Labor, December, 1947, p. 676. Reprinted with permission of Commissioner of Labor Statistics.

What appears to be the most thorough estimate on this point was made by the Bureau of Labor Statistics in 1947, and appears in Table 41. This tabulation is based on a study of interindustry relations made in 1939 and brought up to the first half of 1947. Those reported as being indirectly dependent on exports for their employment are those engaged in the production and transportation of the raw materials, components, and services purchased by other industries for incorporation in goods for export. No allowance is made for secondary or "induced" effects, such as on the services or merchandise sold to those 2,364,000 reported as being dependent on exports for employment. Nor is any figure included for agricultural dependency on exports, of which cotton is probably the most outstanding example, nor for the manufacturing of agricultural equipment or motor vehicles whose domestic market depends in part on the exportation of agricultural products. Accordingly, while the computation is probably the most thorough made on the question of the importance of exports to manufacturing employment, it is probably quite short of the actual figure which would be developed if agricultural exports, manufacturing employment depending on agricultural exports, and transportation and services depending on these, to say nothing of imports, were all included.

FOREIGN COMMERCE AND NATURAL RESOURCES

Another fundamental indication of any country's dependence on foreign commerce, especially in time of military emergency, is to be found in the unequal distribution throughout the world of the economic factors of production. It is here that imports come into their utmost prominence and importance, because of their vital role in military production. Figure 12 developed by the Industrial College of the Armed Forces, shows at a glance how dependent certain parts of the world are on other parts for what might be termed basic materials.

In so far as reliance on foreign supplies is concerned, the chart highlights a wide variance among countries and, within countries, among products. It illustrates clearly the great dependency of Great Britain on foreign materials, although within the British Empire the picture is not so discouraging.

Another striking feature of the chart is the indication that, while the United States was not self-sufficient in 23 materials in 1938, a peacetime year, a lack of self-sufficiency was shown for only 21 materials in 1944, a year of peak wartime demand. This points up the necessity of understanding how self-sufficiency is measured. The basis used for developing the chart of a state's self-sufficiency was the ratio of domestic production to domestic consumption over the selected time period.

The Question of Self-sufficiency

For some purposes, it is quite valid to suggest that to the extent to which we import any quantity of any item, the nation is not self-sufficient; thus we would be self-sufficient only in those items consumed which were produced entirely by domestic sources. What this view would overlook, though, are practical considerations of price, quality, variety, and perhaps seasonal supply or demand. However, it properly emphasizes the very important element of *time,* based on military urgency.

Domestic Production May Be Expansible at Higher Prices. In industries or economic activities composed of several competing producers, there will always be the marginal producer; this concept also extends to quality. Many, in fact, most, of the thousands of items imported into the United States are produced in some degree domestically; in many cases, production through submarginal sources could be increased—but at an uneconomic cost. Thus it is that, at a given price, foreign costs can be covered, but the costs of some (the submarginal) domestic producers cannot economically be met. For that reason, it is cheaper to import than to pay the higher price required to cover costs of the less efficient domestic producer. Under this condition, if foreign costs increased, or if the foreign source of supply were to be cut off through military operations, it would not necessarily mean that we would have to do without. Theoretically, there would seem to be an expansibility to domestic production which is practically unmeasurable. However, during the Second World War, attempt was made to bring into domestic production a number of critical metals. Among these were marginal and low-grade ores of manganese, chromite, nickel, and other scarce materials. These measures made no material contribution, primarily because the requirements for a quick supply of equipment, manpower, and electric power could not be met under the conditions of wartime shortages in these items.

Quality, Variety, and Season Also Affect Imports. Closely related to the question of price is that of quality. But, as in all other items under a price economy, the quality of any given lot of a product is reflected in terms of the common denominator, money. Quality also embraces variety, and this is an especially important point in considering self-sufficiency. For example, cotton, wool, and certain ores and metals which must be mixed or alloyed for most desirable results call for a variety of characteristics. Thus it is that we export cotton, but we also import cotton. We export rice, yet import rice. We export wool, yet import wool. It will be seen, then, that merely the act of importing an item is not an entirely accurate basis for declaring that we are or are not self-sufficient in the item. Two other points also bear on the consideration. One is that exports

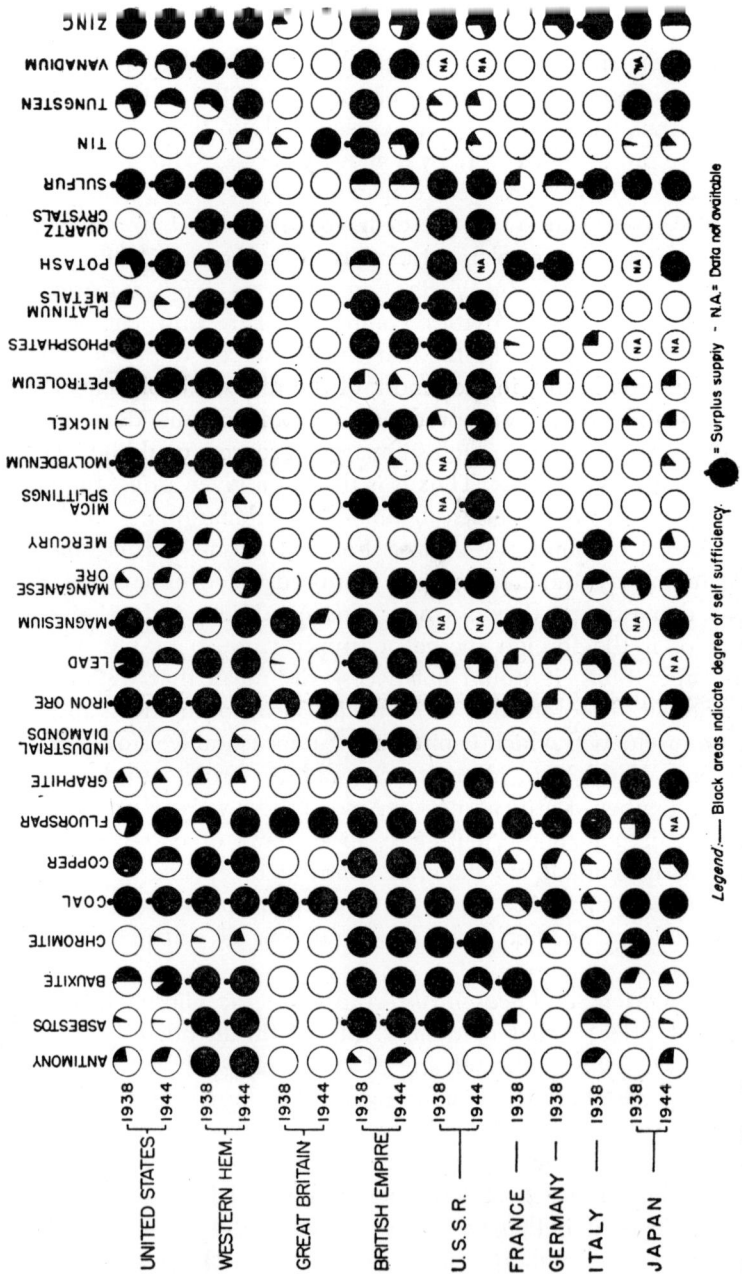

FIG. 12a. Self-sufficiency in mineral raw materials. (*Reproduced, with special permission, from Raw Materials in War and Peace, West Point, N.Y., Department of Social Sciences, United States Military Academy, 1947, pp. 137, 139, 141.*)

SELF-SUFFICIENCY IN MISCELLANEOUS RAW MATERIALS

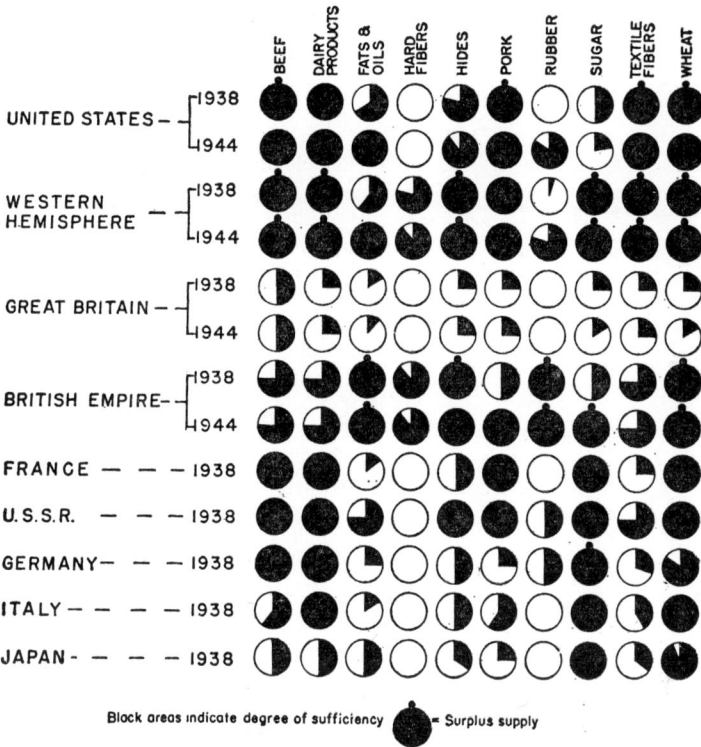

FIG. 12b. Self-sufficiency in miscellaneous raw materials. (*Rreproduced, with special permission, from Raw Materials in War and Peace, West Point, N.Y., Department of Social Sciences, United States Military Academy, 1947, pp. 137, 139, 141.*)

and imports of some items are seasonal, and at one time of the year we may export certain fruits and vegetables while at other times they will be imported. Substitution is another aspect which must be considered. If, for example, certain grades of wool or metals are not readily available, some less desirable but still useful grades may be used, or other items may be substituted.

Supply of Some Resources Is Quite Limited. The discussion would omit an aspect of great interest and importance if it failed to cover the possibility of exhaustion of nonreplaceable minerals. Quite often estimates are made, for certain minerals, of the number of years of domestic supply remaining visible in this country. Among these are coal, petroleum, and lead. Table 42 shows a recent estimate of the number of years of visible supply of several selected minerals.

Table 42. Estimated "Commercial" Reserves of Selected Minerals
in the United States, 1944*

Commodity	Number of Years' Reserves	Commodity	Number of Years' Reserves
Magnesium................	Unlimited	Gold....................	19
Nitrates..................	Unlimited	Copper..................	19
Salt.....................	Unlimited	Petroleum...............	15
Bituminous coal and lignite..	4,386	Silver...................	13
Phosphate rock............	600	Cadmium................	11
Helium...................	235	Lead....................	10
Anthracite................	187	Vanadium...............	8
Molybdenum..............	157	Manganese...............	4
Rutile....................	124	Platinum metals..........	3
Potash...................	99	Antimony................	3
Iron ore.................	76	Mercury.................	2
Ilmenite.................	73	Tungsten................	2
Arsenic..................	73	Tantalum................	1
Natural gas..............	55	Chromite................	1
Cobalt...................	53	Mica (strategic)..........	Negligible
Sulphur..................	39	Asbestos (long fiber)......	Negligible
Bismuth....	36	Graphite (flake)..........	Negligible
Fluorspar................	33	Nickel..................	Negligible
Bauxite..................	23	Tin.....................	Negligible
Zinc.....................	20	Industrial diamonds.......	Negligible
		Quartz crystal...........	Negligible

* In known deposits, compared with 1935–1944 annual rate of consumption.
SOURCE: *Mineral Resources of the United States*, written by the staffs of the Bureau of Mines and Geological Survey (Washington, Public Affairs Press, 1948), p. 8.

Stock-piling

The thesis developed thus far is not intended to minimize the importance of our dependency on foreign sources, but merely to emphasize the practical difficulty of asserting that we are or are not self-sufficient in a particular item or group of items. Considerations are mainly economic, but there are very pressing military considerations as well. These involve an anlaysis of the rate of flow of desired items from abroad, the possibility of their increased production in this country within a specified time limit, the possibility of interference with their overseas transportation, and the possibility of substitutes or alternative sources of supply.

Munitions Board Directs Stock-piling Program. Realizing the importance of having under practical availability in case of war adequate supplies of several items of significance to industry and to the military establishment, a government program of stock-piling of selected items was inaugurated in 1939. The Secretary of War, the Secretary of the Navy, and the Secretary of the Interior were charged to act jointly through the agency of the Army and Navy Munitions Board (now Munitions Board of the National Military Establishment) to determine which materials are strategic and critical and to determine the quality and quantities of each which are to be purchased within the amount of funds appropriated. The 1950 program was based on the Strategic and Critical Materials Stockpiling Act of 1946,[10] as modified by the National Security Act of 1947, the Economic Cooperation Acts of 1948 and 1949, the 1949 revision of the charter of the Commodity Credit Corporation, and the Federal Property and Administrative Services Act of 1949. Under these, the original program has been materially expanded.

REVIEW QUESTIONS

1. Evaluate critically the statement that imports raise standards of living.
2. Evaluate critically the statement that imports may force dislocation and unemployment.
3. How is it possible for imports to interefere with national full-employment aims?
4. On what basis can it be said that imports of investments may be the best access to foreign markets?
5. How can investments have a stabilizing, yet at times a disruptive, effect on foreign commerce?
6. List the advantages to the "export" of new foreign investments.
7. How do imports of merchandise affect national income in so far as (a) economic assimilation of the imported merchandise is concerned and (b) the act of importing is concerned?
8. How do exports of merchandise affect national income and gross national product in so far as (a) the physical goods are concerned and (b) the act of exporting is concerned?
9. What conclusions may be drawn from the fact that imports are a larger or smaller percentage of national income of various countries?
10. Write a one-page statement describing the significance of foreign commerce to employment.
11. Evaluate the statement that the degree of a nation's self-sufficiency in a particular product may be indicated by the percentage of its consumption of that product which is imported.
12. What is the stock-piling program?

[10] A clause of which specified that purchases shall be subject to provisions of the "Buy American" Act of 1933.

CHAPTER 13

Analysis of Balances of Payments

The first thing to be comprehended in studying the balance of payments is composition of the several segments and their detailed as well as their over-all interrelationship. The individual segments were described in Chapter 2. This chapter deals with their fitting into the broad picture of the international sector of the nation's economy.

All types of international transactions act and react on one another because each is influenced by a common factor—foreign exchange.[1] Our sales of merchandise abroad call for payment, immediate or eventual, in U.S. dollars, since that is the currency in which the exporter has incurred his costs. So do our sales of freight and shipping services; so do our "sales" of the use of the United States capital invested abroad; and so do foreigners' demands for our food, goods, or services if they happen to be traveling in the United States. Thus they all withdraw their means of payment from the same common pool—the foreign-exchange market.

The purpose of this chapter is to inquire into the uses to which balances of payments may be put and into their interpretation and analysis as a source of beneficial data. It will be recalled that the usual balance-of-payments presentation consists of five major segments:

Goods and services
Unilateral transfers
Long-term capital
Gold and short-term capital
Errors and omissions

Basically, all these are included in any presentation used, the arrangement being dictated by the purposes for which the data are intended.

The U.S. Department of Commerce's reports, while the forms are

---

[1] Some recorded transactions do not fall into this pattern, as, for instance, the export of capital goods in the making of a direct foreign investment instead of the "export" of funds which may be used to buy the capital goods abroad. In time, of course, capital goods so exported for direct investments influence the foreign-exchange market when earnings therefrom are remitted.

occasionally changed, are designed to show as detailed data as practicable on movement of goods across the borders and on other international transactions of commercial significance. Until fairly recently, there has been no segregation as to, or emphasis on, governmental participation. The International Monetary Fund format is just as detailed, and an additional arrangement has been adopted to emphasize that portion called "compensatory official financing." This has been done inasmuch as many countries, members of the Fund, exercise direct control over gold, banking, and capital movements.

Objectives of and Limitations to Analysis

Balances of payments provide the best available indication of how one country's claims against others, and their claims against it, arose. Using the United States as an example, these claims generally represent the accumulation of foreign currencies or of foreign exchange during the period covered, and the demand for foreign currencies on the part of persons initially concerned with U.S. dollars but with payments made or to be made abroad. Allowing for inherent limitations, as described in Chapter 2, they show whether a country's international transactions in goods, services, and capital movements are offsetting themselves in total, or whether they result in a surplus or deficit, made up by other segments of the total.

However, since the day-to-day effects of these transactions on prices of foreign exchange may long since have occurred, and in any case do not appear in the summary, the practical use of such a tabulation is only for analysis and study on a broad base, either by country or by the total of international transactions during previous periods of time.

Two types of information may be derived from the study of balances of payments, one informative and the other operative. The former is for the purpose of ascertaining, if possible, what may be expected to happen, in order that targets may be set up and that something may be done to bring actual experience into conformity with predetermined limitations. Another principal interest in balance-of-payments analysis stems from operations of the International Monetary Fund, three of its main areas of applicability pertaining to (1) use of the fund's resources, (2) continuance of exchange controls, and (3) exchange-rate adjustments.

Obtaining information for operative purposes leads to the question of who can do anything as a result of the analysis, or who can do something deliberately to influence the balance of payments. By way of economic background, some banks or large companies doing business with foreign markets or having investments in foreign countries will be interested in such data. However, they can normally do little or nothing to influence the balance of payment, nor is there any motive for doing so. For governments and monetary authorities, though, the same cannot be said. Depending on the economic system under which each country functions, some governments have made it their responsibility—actually, the voters may in effect have charged their governments with this responsibility—to "do something" about the balance of payments. This means either preventing the balance of payments from getting out of line or bringing about adjustments in foreign commerce to effect and maintain a desired "equilibrium." Consideration of controls over foreign economic relations calls for an understanding of the mechanism of adjustment and of the means by which equilibrium in international prices is attained and maintained. This may seem a bit removed from balanceof-payments analysis but, actually, economic analysis must go behind the figures of the balance-of-payments statement. What one must study in order to understand the changes that have taken place is the significance of underlying considerations.

It should be recalled at this time, also, that data contained in the summary reports are not all of a cumulative nature. Very important segments are of the inventory type, with the difference between beginning and ending totals reported as net activity for the period under consideration. At the same time, the reports can only point up, as an example, short-term capital movements, without explaining the impelling forces behind them. Among many other causes may be settlements of trade obligations, service, or travel transactions, the building up or repatriation of foreign bank balances, the search for high earnings on short-term capital, or the search for relative safety of wealth. Any or all of these may long since have occurred by the time the inventory figure is available to indicate that there was an increase or a decrease in short-term balances between reporting dates.

Relationship of Selected Accounts

If a double-entry system of bookkeeping were followed, it would be a simple matter to tie together many of the figures appearing in the usual balance of payments. But since this is not done, the relationship must be reasoned out, even though basic data thereon may be collected from different sources.

Merchandise and Short-term Capital. In view of the predominant importance of merchandise in most balances of payments, it will serve as a good illustration of the interdependence of certain accounts in the total tabulation. Merchandise is ordinarily sold and exported in such a way that the final payment does not occur on the exact date of export. Even when sold on a sight-draft basis, the normal collection time for drafts payable at sight may run from six to ten weeks, sometimes more. Not all exports are financed by means of drafts, of course; some are effected by means of open account, but not in great volume. Accordingly, the export of merchandise ordinarily gives rise to a draft of some type— a credit instrument—which will be outstanding and unpaid for some time after the actual physical export has taken place. Thus, an export of $10,000 in merchandise, which is valued at the port of exportation and does not include ocean freight and marine insurance, gives rise to a credit instrument which may appear in "short-term investments outstanding." However, the credit instrument may include both ocean freight and marine insurance, depending on the quotation used (see Chapter 8). The shorter the reporting period, the more likely it is that the draft will have been unpaid by reporting date. On the other hand, if the .draft originated in and was paid within the period covered by the balance of payments, the amount would not necessarily appear as a short-term capital movement; such a capital movement *could* occur, if the receipts were left on deposit in a foreign bank after payment or if used to buy short-term securities or other investments. It could, however, and most likely would have been used to pay for imports of goods and services of some type, or perhaps to pay for a long-term investment, or even for the purchase of gold abroad and its shipment into the United States. There is no possible way to track down these amounts, which are so numerous and which represent many thousands of crosscurrents.[2]

The picture is not so clear with regard to *imports* of merchandise, although the procedure is substantially the same. However, drafts held by foreigners for collection in the United States are not incorporated into the inventory of short-term investments made in the United States by foreigners. After satisfaction of the import obligation, it could be, for instance, that the account of a foreign bank was credited in the United States through payment by a domestic importer for account of a foreign exporter. The foreign exporter would then have been paid in his own currency by his bank. The result of this would be a net change in the amount of balances held for foreign account by the banks of this country, with a resulting change in short-term investments in the United States by foreigners. Or the same result could have occurred had the account of the foreign exporter been credited in a bank in the United States.

Investments and Merchandise Exports and Imports. Another important tabular interrelationship is that of long-term investments and merchandise. As was pointed out in Chapter 2, the balance of payments does not and cannot tell whether merchandise exported was paid for or will

[2] As a reflection of operational influences, a decrease in the short-term account, arising from a smaller volume of collections outstanding, could be the result of (*a*) same volume at lower prices, (*b*) same volume and shorter credit terms, (*c*) smaller volume of exports just prior to "inventory" date, or (*d*) smaller volume of collections being handled through banks (more liberal credit terms, as from draft basis to open account).

ever be paid for. It reports exports, and not financing, although the
evidence would suggest most exports to be on a *quid pro quo* basis. However, let us assume that a company in the United States makes arrangements with an individual or company abroad to ship a sawmill and to
set it up in operation in the foreign country. The reports would show an
export of merchandise and, from a different source entirely, an increase
in foreign investments made by United States interests. Naturally, not all
foreign investments mean the payment abroad of dollars; many are made
by the process of shipping machinery and equipment, and the interrelationship is thus between exports of merchandise, on current account,
and a long-term investment, in the capital segment of the balance of
payments. The same arrangement could hold in reverse in the case of
imports, and it could be that production of merchandise abroad, by virtue
of the foreign investment, would be the basis of imports for sale in the
country in which the investment originated, this to provide earnings for
the payment of interest or dividends.

Investments, Interest and Dividends, and Merchandise. In this connection, another close relationship is found over a period of time between
the accounts representing long-term and short-term investments, investment income (or interest and dividends), and merchandise and services.
In order to illustrate the relationship, let us have the original investment an import, or the making of a new foreign investment by Americans.
Soon after such an investment is made, assuming it to have been carefully
planned, the contract will call for its servicing by the payment of interest
or dividends. This receipt of interest or dividends, now, will represent an
export—an export of the use of American capital. It represents a return
on the original investment, which was an import. Thus the making of an
investment sets in motion a chain of counterentries in balances of payments over the life of the investment.

More than this, the servicing of the investment, recorded as an export,
can be accomplished only if the foreign "debtor" economy can earn
acceptable funds with which to pay for our export of the use of American
capital. This can be done, in the course of time, only by its or another
country's sale of something in the American market, *i.e.*, merchandise or
services which we would import. Thus the *import* of (the making of) a
foreign investment calls for the periodic *export* of the use of our capital—
whenever interest or dividends are received in payment. But in order
for the foreigners to have the funds with which to pay for our export,
it becomes necessary for us to *import* something from them and pay
for it.

If the investment is for productive purposes, the foreign "debtor"
economy is better able to earn the funds with which to pay for our export

of the use of our capital; if and when the foreign investment is repaid or repatriated, the same procedure must hold, but on a bigger scale. This interrelationship is further discussed in Chapter 15.

Balance and Equilibrium

Before discussing problems of equilibrium and adjustment, it is appropriate to recall that analysis is made difficult by the dearth of data. For many countries, annual balances of payments may be had. For very few, the figures are made available quarterly. In those countries exercising exchange control, a substantial amount of unpublished data is certainly available, and probably in much greater detail as to the causes of or reasons for the movements of funds.

There are, unfortunately, no ratios, ideals, or averages which mean anything, for each country's balance of payments is a case in itself, and will reflect or be influenced by the nature of the economy and its stage of economic development. It takes many years for a nation to change from the underdeveloped to the developed state. Of course, those which are basically agricultural may never become industrialized, and vice versa. Competitive growth of many nations in foreign commerce being irregular, establishment of a trend for analytical purposes is practically impossible.

Furthermore, the payment period is often longer in foreign trade than in domestic. Before one may conclude that any disequilibrium exists in, say, quarterly balances of payments, account should be taken of the fact that a good part of merchandise exports in any three-month period is likely not to have been paid in the same reporting period. What may thus appear to be an increase in short-term investments may really be only the backwash of credit instruments resulting from the normal credit and collection process of a prior exporting period.

Published balances of payments becoming available, at the most, quarterly, and appearing several months after the facts reported, it would seem in order to question whether they can be used as a basis for determining that there is or is not a condition of equilibrium. Since changes in gold or monetary reserves resulting from lack of balance in foreign commerce may long since have taken place, and possibly with some counterequilibrating movements developing therefrom, it is questionable whether any analysis of the published balances of payments is very usable practically. If intended to serve as a basis for doing something to remedy a condition of disequilibrium, action taken would have to be decided on and put into force some time before the summary tabulations become available to the public. On the other hand, if action were taken by governmental or monetary authorities, based on other "operating" data, analysis of the final balance of payments for any period could serve mainly to substantiate or prove erroneous decisions taken on the basis of less complete data.

For this operating procedure to have taken place, the government would have to have stepped into the international economic picture, and the ultimate in this, even without turning the economy into one of socialism, would be that the government would look on foreign-commerce earnings and requirements as part of a budget, to be expanded or contracted under various policies, depending on nationalistic aspirations. Budget receipts would then be parceled out to individuals or businesses according to the "program" into which such transactions must fit.

Balancing the "Balance" of Payments. By definition and construction, the balance of payments must always balance. However, it is not, as some writers suggest, a system of double-entry bookkeeping, as the same underlying documents are not used for counterentries.

Reference to Chapter 2 will serve to recall that exports of goods are tabulated from shippers' export declarations, with no counterentry (or double entry) for the payment of offsetting imports. The figure for goods imported is derived from an accumulation of data appearing in the customs entries; short-term capital movements, shown net, are the result of an inventory report filed by banks and some other reporting institutions. Balance, or the arithmetic equalizing of the two sides of the periodic report, is brought about by an item called Errors and Omissions which automatically brings the total of the two sides to the same figure. The error or omission may be on either the credit or the debit side.

Internally, and on a continuing basis, balance is brought about by a multitude of buyers and sellers who find a particular foreign market or any specific foreign item more or less attractive from time to time depending on relative prices. Included in this are gold and capital movements, which arise *in part* from the lack of balance between purchases and sales of goods and services and which thereby serve to "balance" the total picture.

Balance and Disequilibrium May Be Coexistent. Although the summary of international transactions is aggregated into a tabulation whose two sides are substantially equal, this act of balancing is not necessarily good or bad in itself. In total, it tells nothing; and meaning or benefit to be derived must come from detailed analysis of the principal components.

This is the same as saying that although the total may be in balance, there may be a considerable lack of balance—a disequilibrium—in some of the more important segments of the total. Hence, balance and disequilibrium may be present at the same time, in the same manner as in a corporate balance sheet, which is necessarily in balance but detailed

Table 43. Balances of Payment for Selected Countries

Item	(A) United States, 1949 (in millions of dollars)			(B) Norway, 1949 (in millions of Norwegian kroner)			(C) Iran, 1949–1950 (in millions of rials)		
	Credit (export)	Debit (import)	Net credit	Credit (export)	Debit (import)	Net credit	Credit (export)	Debit (import)	Net credit
Merchandise	$12,298	$ 7,105	$5,193	2,184	3,933	—1,749	16,633	9,266	7,367
Nonmonetary gold (net)	.....	26	— 26	.....	1	— 1	.....	44	— 44
Foreign travel	363	688	— 325	79	139	— 60	29	128	— 99
Transportation	1,289	768	521	1,966	1,344	622	7	7	.....
Insurance	103	149	— 46	217	246	— 29	.....	.....	.....
Investment income	1,818	472	1,346	19	83	— 64	23	8,944	—8,921
Government, not included elsewhere	307	681	— 374	8	25	— 17	44	303	— 259
Miscellaneous	270	58	212	149	141	8	.....	26	— 26
Total goods and services	$16,448	$ 9,947	$ 6,501	4,622	5,912	—1,290	16,736	18,718	—1,982
Donations	302	6,029	— 5,727	730	78	652	123	32	91
Total current transactions	$16,750	$15,976	$ 774	5,352	5,990	— 638	16,859	18,750	—1,891
	Assets	Liabilities	Net assets	Assets	Liabilities	Net assets	Assets	Liabilities	Net assets
Net movements increasing or decreasing (−):									
Private:									
Long-term capital	$1,265	$286	$ 979	— 103	47	— 150	.....	.....	.....
Short-term capital	24	— 37	61	— 44	11	— 33	.....	.....	.....
Official and banking institutions:									
Long-term capital	500	— 17	517	— 10	89	— 99	— 742	96	— 838
Short-term capital	15	— 4	11	— 73	184	— 257	—1,096	— 219	877
Monetary gold	— 164	.....	164	— 1	.....	— 1	.....	.....	.....
Total capital and monetary gold	$1,938	$228	$1,710	— 231	309	— 540	—1,838	— 123	—1,715
Net errors and omissions	.....	.....	$ 936	.....	.....	98	.....	.....	176

SOURCE: *Balance of Payments Yearbook, 1949–50,* International Monetary Fund, 1951.

analysis of which is undertaken to disclose fundamental strengths and weaknesses.

Evidence of balance and disequilibrium in coexistence is illustrated in Table 43, which shows in column A (United States) a country with a heavy excess of exports of goods, but with part of them given away and with part of them represented by or offset by long-term investments (which may be either, and which are both, in this instance, private and governmental). In column B (Norway), on the other hand, imports of goods and services exceed exports; the difference is made up by donations from abroad and by a net increase in short- and long-term capital invested in it. Column C (Iran) shows the summary for a nation with a big excess of exports over imports of goods and with its biggest single import being the *use* of foreign capital, represented by interest and dividend payments.

Evidence of Disequilibrium. Wide attention has been given the problem of this determination, especially since the International Monetary Fund used the term "fundamental disequilibrium," in its articles of agreement, without defining its exact meaning. Several definitions of the concept may be found, and a basic consideration in all—in so far as balance-of-payments items may be expected to yield the answer—involves a decision as to what components of the balance of payments should be included. For example, capital transfers between countries may be included or excluded, depending on whether they are private or governmental, or, if the former, depending on whether they are under government control. Also, the question will arise as to whether the balance of payments in foreign commerce should be controlled with the objective of having equilibrium only on an over-all basis, or whether transactions should be expected to balance on a geographic (country or regional) basis or even on a country basis.

One might suggest that the balance of payments, on an over-all basis, is in a state of approximate equilibrium when the commercial transactions (including investments) between any country and the rest of the world are such as not to cause a large, sustained change in its gold holdings and monetary reserves.[3] This change in gold and monetary reserves should be traceable to international transactions, in order to eliminate changes due to internal production. To determine that the change is sustained rather than erratic, one would have to analyze the underlying transactions to ascertain just what major changes in trade and

---

[3] If, however, economic indicators other than the balance of payments are relied on in determining evidence of disequilibrium, such a simple definition cannot suffice. For example, Great Britain in 1925 has been held up as a classic case of a country in "fundamental disequilibrium" despite balance in the international accounts. But unemployment, low wages, and subnormal profits were rampant throughout the economy.

investment patterns had taken place to bring about the demand for exchange which brought about the changes in reserves. Of course, this presupposes a fixed rate to begin with, and considerable leeway for individuals to decide, in their own best interests, the volume and direction of world commerce. What is apparent, also, is that an equilibrium rate of exchange, which must exist if the balance of payments is to be in equilibrium, cannot be said to exist in the true sense if a government is to insist on exchange control or if there are governmental transfers of funds to make up for any deficiency or irregularity in private transactions. The *test* of equilibrium or lack of equilibrium must be made in a free market. A balance, without equilibrium, may be forced in a restricted market by governmental authority. Such authority would go so far as to dictate the volume and direction of foreign commerce and the types of transactions permitted or encouraged.

Adjustments in Balances of Payments

Adjustment implies a reaction to disturbance of a previous norm or equilibrium. In the international economy, adjustments may be small in volume and short term or they may be large scale and long term.

The Market Reconciles Leveling of International Values. The problem of adjustments in balances of payments is, at the heart, one of market reconciliation of international values, as reflected in prices; balances of payments are only evidence of the balance or lack of balance which may have developed.

The sum total of international transactions is kept in balance by constant adjustments in the international markets which render a given commodity, service, or investment an advisable or inadvisable import or export. Among the factors which bear on and which result from relative international prices at any one time are:

1. Prices themselves
2. Exchange rates
3. Levels of income (and employment)
4. Changes in gold-reserve holdings (movements of gold and reserves)
5. The volume and direction of capital movements

Naturally, international price relationships are significant only when considered in conjunction with international prices in several markets and with domestic prices of the same goods as well as with international and domestic substitutes or alternative choices. Nonetheless, the movement of goods and services internationally both causes and is caused by changes in prices and in exchange rates, levels of income, gold and reserve holdings, and capital movements. The last two make their influence felt primarily through changes in exchange rates, although they may influence production volumes.

The Role of Gold and Monetary Reserves. In economic theory, the well-known price-specie-flow mechanism held the interest of students for several decades. But since the mid-1930s, interest in employment and income have focused attention on the relationship of foreign commerce to both employment and national income (see Chapter 12). In brief, the price-specie-flow mechanism is that international values are linked by cost and price, subject to transportation costs and restrictions on imports and exports, and that price levels are influenced by money and credit volumes. Hence, an inflow of gold or other monetary reserves, resulting from an international disparity of prices, would tend to increase the level of prices in the country receiving the reserves and to lower them in the country losing them, thus reversing and "adjusting" the movement of goods and/or services. This would happen, of course, if there were no offsetting changes in the turnover of money and credit and in the volume of business transactions.

For the specie (or other reserves) to have moved from one country to another, the demand for exchange of one relative to the other must have been so strong that it became cheaper to buy the specie and ship it than to pay the higher price for the exchange. Thus, prices or investment opportunities in, say, country A (the country losing specie) must have been higher or less attractive than comparable prices or investment opportunities in country B (the country into which the specie flows). How, then, does adjustment come about?

Either (or both) prices or investment opportunities must become less relatively attractive in B or they must become more relatively attractive in A. Considering prices alone, they must come down in country A, go up in country B, or do both.

Deflation Is the Unpopular Feature. It is the adjustment in country A which causes the main trouble here, for price declines are less popular and more generally inconvenient to organized groups than are price increases. All sorts of arguments will be brought forward to avoid or postpone the deflation in prices, for deflation means, at least temporarily, reduced production, unemployment, smaller national income, increased number of bankruptcies, and any other element of retrenchment to bring oneself back into a competitive position.

Among the principal arguments is that the deflation may affect all economic activity, not only that sector immediately concerned with foreign commerce. It is also argued that the lowered income levels will result in lowered imports, thus causing economic hardship in third countries and giving rise to what is called "exporting unemployment." Accordingly, domestic instability, which arose through the international movement of goods, services, and investments, themselves coming about in response to cost-price differentials, is not to be allowed to correct itself through reconciliation with contemporary market conditions.

One need not look far to see that these price differentials reflect the working of cost differentials, put into operation by the more or less free business entrepreneurship of free men. How, then, can these "harmful" developments be avoided, if we are not willing to pay the price for making the mistakes?

Obviously, the only answer is (1) not to permit, or at least to restrict, business judgment in its opportunity to introduce into the market the fruits of low-cost competition or (2) to doctor up the patient who runs afoul of low-cost competition with economic medicine that will keep him in funds and not make it necessary for him to become economically immobilized. To accomplish the first, entrepreneurial decision must be removed from the individual and taken over by a government bureaucrat, who is supposed to be more capable of wise economic decisions and judgment than is the individual businessman, motivated by self-interest. The ultimate, if this is followed, is, of course, socialization of the economy. There is not much of a middle ground. Accomplishment of the second is wound up in the web of "compensatory" financing with its effect through the "foreign-trade multiplier." These will be explained later in the chapter, but suffice it to say here that efficiency in attaining the objective would call for preventive as well as curative economic medicine; if the latter, timely and adequate but not excessive medication would have to be administered upon a prompt and correct diagnosis.

Influence of Seasonal and Cyclical Factors. In Chapter 4, the importance of several items in the world-trade pattern was shown. Many of these items, especially agricultural, are of a seasonal nature. It might be expected that seasonal patterns in balances of payments and in exchange-rate movements should be found. For example, cotton exports from the United States to England are characterized by a seasonal variation. Some years ago, in a freer exchange market than has prevailed for some time, it was felt that pressure on the dollar by holders of pounds sterling could be expected in the fall. Similar variations in big-volume trade in other commodities and in various directions were a factor of considerable influence, as were demands for services and travel during the summer months.

However, a survey of exchange rates, which should be expected to show the pull of financing of goods and services, discloses no pattern, seasonal or cyclical, which can be traced to these factors. Several reasons may be found for this. First, commerce moving between any two countries is not necessarily financed through either of the two trading countries' currencies. Most of today's world trade is in terms of U.S.

dollars and pounds sterling, and prior to the two big wars, sterling was
the leading currency used in foreign commerce. A second reason is that
countermovements of investments, especially short term, are, in effect,
balancing factors which keep exchange rates from swinging too far
seasonally. Illustration of this is acceptance of drafts by commercial
banks for the purpose of creating dollar exchange. Thus, seasonal or
short-term variations in commerce in goods and services may be offset
by short-term capital movements which, while made in response to interest rates, actually serve to equilibrate the balance of payments in its
effect on foreign exchange. Another is that the sum total of international
transactions is so complex and is affected by so many diverse factors,
some seasonal and others erratic, that when pressure on exchange rates
develops, a new set of price relationships results, bringing corrective elements into play.

Is There a Cycle—Debtor to Creditor? It is felt by some that a nation
goes through stages in international economic development, beginning
as a debtor and finally becoming a creditor. Horn,[4] for example, lists the
following successive stages: borrowing, interest paying, principal repaying, lending or investment, interest receiving, and finally, although sometimes postponed indefinitely, principal receiving. Samuelson suggests four
principal periods which, of course, require decades to evolve. Referring to
the experience of the United States, Samuelson's categories are[5] (1) a
young and growing debtor nation (from the Revolution to just after
the Civil War), (2) a mature debtor nation (from about 1873 to the
First World War), (3) a new creditor nation (from the First World War
to date), and (4) a mature creditor nation (a stage which the United
States has not yet reached).

While there is no specific break between the periods, the sequence
is logical. But when we consider the composition of a country's net
foreign-investment position, we find that it may be at one and the same
time a net creditor or net debtor to various other countries or regions,
being a creditor and debtor in some degree to both. It may also be a net
creditor on long-term account and a net debtor on short-term account at
the same time. In the face of large-scale capital movements, either long
or short term, its position may alternate from year to year.[6]

The orderly sequence of developments suggested above is also subject
to interference by major catastrophes, such as war. The record of countries such as France, Belgium, and the Netherlands shows in the modern
world that positions as creditor or debtor are not constant. Further, the

[4] Paul V. Horn, *International Trade—Principles and Practices*, 3d ed. (New York,
Prentice-Hall, Inc., 1951), pp. 356–360.

[5] Paul A. Samuelson, *Economics: An Introductory Analysis*, 2d ed. (New York,
McGraw-Hill Book Co., Inc., 1951), pp. 661–662.

[6] See Chap. 15, especially the reference to hot money.

activity of governments is likely to interrupt or materially change this sequence.

As far as a private "borrower" is concerned, it really makes no difference to whom the obligations are payable, so long as they are payable in the currency used by or easily available to him. He must produce in order to pay. To a nation as a whole, payment of interest or dividends abroad calls for the export of goods or services, but if the debt is owed locally instead of abroad, such goods or services would have to be produced and disposed of locally. One might say, then, that until savings and capital are accumulated *and put to use in the same country,* those desiring funds will seek them abroad. This contributes to being a debtor nation. As funds are accumulated and investment opportunities are not found locally, the owners of the fund will seek to find investment—or safety—opportunities abroad. This contributes to being a creditor nation. Ceasing to be a debtor nation does not necessarily mean repaying foreign "obligations" or replacing them with domestic. This could be so, as in the case of the Argentine government's buying up its railroads from the British in 1947, but the more usual development would seem to be the acquisition of assets abroad sufficient to offset in volume the foreign "investments" owned in the former "debtor" country.

Special Terms Encountered in Analysis

Terms of Trade. Among the broad economic phenomena which bear on detailed, internal self-adjustment in the balance of payments through market processes is the price level of a country's exports as compared to the price level of its imports. This relationship is designated "terms of trade," and the figure is developed by dividing an index number for export prices by an index number for import prices. The volume of trade is not involved in the measurement directly, although, in derivation of the index, volume would have to be evaluated to arrive at appropriate weights for each item. When export prices rise relative to import prices, the trend may be said to be favorable, since a larger volume of imports can be had for a given volume of exports. This is tantamount to saying that you get more for what you sell and pay less for what you buy. However, it could in reality be unfavorable if the result of higher prices for exports was less export volume.

Changes in terms of trade may occur whether prices of both exports and imports rise or fall or whether they move in opposite directions. Since changes in terms of trade occur because of changes in prices, certain factors influence the relationship. Among these are the relative position of the country in question in total world trade of commodities making up the index, and changes in exchange rates, but the primary factor is the make-up of each country's export or import trade. If, for example, a

country is primarily a producer of raw materials, and another's international sales are of industrial products, then the movement of prices of
raw materials as compared with industrial goods would have a deciding
effect on the terms of trade of each. In the period 1949, 1950, and early
1951, for example, the Federal Reserve Bank of New York concluded
that terms of trade in selected industrialized countries (United States,
England, France, Belgium, etc.) were generally downward, while terms
of trade improved very markedly for several of the primary-producing
countries such as Australia, Cuba, Malaya, Ceylon, and Turkey. Much of
this was undoubtedly due to international activities related to the Korean
campaign and to military preparedness under the North Atlantic Treaty
Organization.

   Compensatory Official Financing. In postwar economic literature, a
term which has come into wide use is "compensatory official financing."
It has been adopted by the International Monetary Fund and is defined
as "financing undertaken by the monetary authorities to provide exchange
to cover a surplus or deficit in the rest of the balance of payments."[7] What
lends added importance to the concept is the widespread retention of
control by government over foreign commerce, as well as over domestic.
In fact, the concept is built around the fact that international movements
of gold and monetary reserves are almost universally controlled by governments. Accordingly, it may be reasoned, it is government that permits
or deliberately plans or executes changes in gold and reserves and many
capital transfers; such changes and transfers by or through government
largely constitute the extent of "compensatory official financing."

   As indicated before, the International Monetary Fund has adopted
use of a "financing form" to point up compensatory financing activities
of respective countries. Included in the compensatory-official-financing
section of the report forms for several countries is a variety of loans,
grants, and other transactions designated as follows:

U. S. Stabilization Fund Loan
Settlement of "Coffee Realization Loan"
Changes in short-term assets
Changes in short-term liabilities
Use of International Monetary Fund resources
Changes in monetary gold
Gifts
Grants extended
Loans extended
Loans received
Payments and clearing agreements

   [7] *Balance of Payments Yearbook, 1938, 1946, 1947,* p. 5.

Noncontractual debt retirement

Nationalization of foreign investments

For some countries, only three or four of these categories may be used; for others, the subdivisions may be more than 10.

In the words of the Fund, what is significant about compensatory financing is that it "reflects pressures on the monetary authorities arising out of a balance of payments within which authorities are attempting to maintain orderly exchange conditions."[8] Actually, the pressure is on exchange rates, which in turn bear on gold and foreign-exchange assets of a country. In those countries which employ exchange control and thereby prohibit private holdings of gold or foreign exchange, almost all such transactions are by or through the government and the *net difference* between acquisitions and surrender of foreign exchange thus becomes part of the *official* financing undertaken to *compensate* for lack of balance between other segments of the balance of payments. Lack of balance, on the other hand, may be due in part to restrictions on commerce. In those countries which permit private transactions in gold or short-term capital items, that part carried out by the government with the objective of maintaining orderly exchange conditions is reported as "compensatory."

Distinction is made, also, between what is termed "special" official financing and "compensatory" official financing, although the difference is at times difficult to draw. In some cases, government loans may not represent compensatory financing; an example would be an Export-Import Bank loan to finance some development project abroad. The reasoning behind this is that the purpose of the loan was one of development and not one of equalizing the foreign-trade totals during the reporting period. In the same category would be United States aid to Mexico in the campaign to eradicate hoof-and-mouth disease in Mexico. Contractual obligations, such as payment of interest by governments on their borrowings abroad, or the repayment of principal, would also be classed as special and not compensatory financing. In short, compensatory financing is intended to offset a surplus or deficit in a balance of payments; payment of interest or repayment of principal may have to be carried out irrespective of whether there is a surplus or a deficit. Accordingly, such a financial transaction by government may increase a balance-of-payments deficit rather than help "finance" it.

It should be noted, furthermore, the compensatory official financing is intended to bring about a balance because the rest of the international transactions do not offset each other. But it does not, nor is it apparently intended to, bring about a correction in international prices, which are

[8] *Ibid.*

usually the very basis for the look of balance in international commercial transactions. This aspect is discussed further in Chapter 15.

In its *Balance of Payments Yearbook, 1938, 1946, 1947*, the Fund points out that when a government engages in compensatory official financing it does not necessarily mean that a disequilibrium exists in its balance of payments. On the other hand, absence of compensatory official financing is not an indication of a condition of equilibrium. In the first case, the condition calling for compensatory financing may be temporary and not one of fundamental disequilibrium, or the "official" financing may simply reflect the net change in the controlled exchange fund; in the latter, there may be a state of balance at the moment with a strong prospect of disequilibrium just ahead and with compensatory financing then contemplated. Or the tendency to a disequilibrium may be held in check by direct controls. Hence a state of equilibrium must, in the words of the Fund, "revolve around prospects rather than a static cross-section of the past."[9] *Official* financing, as a gross amount, may take place whether the balance of payments is in a state of equilibrium or not; it derives from exchange control and governmental commercial activities. The official financing becomes *compensatory* when other transactions, either free or regulated, and represented in other segments of the balance-of-payments statement, do not offset each other during the time period covered. To be noted, accordingly, is that both debit and credit accounts are included in the official-financing section, when one is incorporated into a balance-of-payments presentation. Part of this reflects governmental commercial activity, but it is the *net* remainder which *compensates* for the *surplus* or *deficit* shown in the other sections of the tabulation.

The Foreign-trade Multiplier. Among the fruits of Keynesian economic plantings is a widely used term, the "multiplier." The concept of the multiplier is that as a given original sum of money, say $100, passes from hand to hand, each recipient tends to save part of it and to pass the remainder along by spending; it thus permeates the economic system in steadily diminishing increments. Within a given period of time, the amounts passed along, when cumulated, provide a number which is accepted as indicating the extent to which the original expenditure has been multiplied. Hence, if in a year the cumulated figure is $250, the multiplier is said to be 2½, or two and a half times the original (new) expenditure. Accordingly, if an acceptable multiplier can be determined or estimated, an approximation may be made of the amount of *new* funds that would have to find its way into the income stream of a country in order to bring about a predetermined increase in the national income.

Additional exports are one of the sources of new monetary receipts

[9] *Ibid.*

from which the multiplier effect can be expected to start functioning. In the over-all view, however, expenditures for imports are one of the "leakages" faced by the analyst. While use of the multiplier concept is best suited to national-income analysis, it will be helpful, for our purpose, to inquire into the impact of the "muliplied" income on the economy in more specific terms. There will be an *application* of part, if not all, of the multiplied income to the economy, with resultant effect on prices, employment, or both. Thus the income aspects and the price aspects are linked by somewhat of an extension of the price-specie-flow mechanism.

In so far as foreign commerce is concerned, the multiplier principle may be related to (1) an *increase* of a country's exports (of goods and services) merely because incomes were paid out for their production; the question of payment to the seller in pounds, francs, or other currency than dollars does not enter here; and (2) an *increase* in its borrowing from abroad, which is the exportation of a credit instrument, provided, in this case, that the borrowing country received something usable as domestic money or monetary reserves, which actually entered the income stream. In either case, the "seller," and therefore the economy, receives a new or expanded supply of funds with which the multiplier principle begins to function. In due time, then, incomes in the exporting country are increased by more than the original supply of new funds, the amount of increase depending on the size of the multiplier.

Furthermore, there is statistical correlation between the level of national income and a country's imports, so the increase in incomes as just described can have a two-fold effect on a country's balance of payments. One is an increase in imports due to the propensity to import more at higher levels of income. The second, if the result of increased incomes is increased prices, is to make the country a more expensive place in which to buy, thus making exporting more difficult and rendering imports more attractive for the two reasons of higher prices internally and higher national income with a broader base of demand.

Now, what of the other country or countries to which the exports were made or from which the funds were borrowed? The manner in which payment was to be made for the importation of goods or services was set aside as not directly relevant; the multiplier effect in the exporting country was based on incomes paid out as costs of production, and not on the introduction of money from abroad. Nevertheless, introduction of new funds from abroad can serve as such a base. It was stated that for the investment to have a multiplier effect in the borrowing country, there would have to be made available to it something usable as money or monetary reserves. The country would have to *receive funds.*

Payments for either goods, services, or investments by the importing (and lending) country would have a depressive effect on that country as long as such payment resulted in a reduction in the amount of its money or monetary reserves. It would have to *lose funds.*[10]

From the viewpoint of national income, and regardless of the technicality, if the income derived from exports has a multiplied effect upward in the exporting country, it should follow that the payment for imports has a shrinking, or depressive, effect on the national-income level of the importing country. The pressure on prices in the importing country would thus be downward due to the "loss" to foreign countries of funds whose circulation, had they been retained, would have contributed to multiplied income in it. However, lowered prices in the importing country would then tend to make domestic purchases more advantageous as compared with imports, and would make of that country a less desirable sales market for some foreign exporters and a more desirable source market for some foreign importers.

In this way, the foreign-trade multiplier is an extension of the mechanism for adjusting the various balances of international payments, along with movements of gold or monetary reserves, changes in exchange rates, and the movement of capital between countries.

REVIEW QUESTIONS

1. Who may find analysis of a nation's balance of payments of practical use?

2. How would the following developments influence the short-term capital account?

   a. Slower collections with same volume of exports at about same prices
   b. Same volume and price but shorter credit terms.
   c. Smaller volume of collections being handled through banks
   d. Higher prices for exports with same volume and collection period
   e. Blocking or freezing of bank accounts abroad

3. What is the relationship between foreign investments and merchandise imports and exports?

4. Who balances the balance of payments? How?

5. Explain how balance and disequilibrium in balances of payments may be coexistent.

6. When does a balance of payments reflect a state of equilibrium?

7. What is the central problem of adjustment in balances of payments?

8. Explain the statement that the movement of goods and services inter-

---

[10] From a balance-of-payments standpoint, the recorded net "borrowing" could reflect a disinvestment abroad by a country's nationals; a new loan could be obtained from abroad by the borrowing country without disturbing the lending country's monetary base, if it meant merely the transfer of the lending country's foreign investments from a third country to the one now becoming the "borrower." In the latter case, the depressive effect would fall on the country from which the investment was transferred rather than on the country whose nationals made the transfer.

nationally causes and is caused by changes in prices and in exchange rates, levels of income, gold or reserve holdings, and capital movements.

9. What is the role of gold and/or monetary reserves in foreign commerce?

10. Why is deflation, as a price and cost corrective, an unpopular economic phenomenon?

11. Is there a cycle—debtor to creditor?

12. Explain the meaning and significance of terms of trade.

13. What is compensatory official financing? How does it differ from special official financing?

14. What is the foreign-trade multiplier? Does it operate on funds lost to other countries as well as on funds gained from other countries?

CHAPTER 14

Foreign Exchange

By definition, "foreign exchange" is a term used when referring to the currencies or moneys of other countries in terms of any single one. To the person with United States funds, the pound, franc, and peso are foreign exchange. To the British, the dollar, franc, and peso are foreign exchange. The term "foreign exchange" is also commonly used in referring to some instruments used in international commerce, such as bills of exchange and bank drafts. They are called pieces of foreign exchange.

In form, foreign exchange may be currency, either paper or metallic, which people carry around in their pockets. But by far the greater amount is in the form of drafts drawn by sellers on buyers, by creditors on debtors, by banks on other banks (including checks) or by sellers or creditors on banks. Thus, instruments may be for immediate or delayed payment and conversion of the currency specified. This point is discussed more fully in the section titled The Foreign-exchange Market.

Source of Foreign Exchange

All types of foreign exchange arise from the settlement of multitudinous transactions recorded in the Summary of International Transactions (Chapter 2) and probably a sizable sum from transactions not accurately recorded. But all the transactions summarized do not necessarily result in a supply of or demand for foreign exchange during the period covered. Currency comes mainly from travelers, although probably some is smuggled between countries. Drafts arise mainly from sellers of goods and services and from creditors. Bank transfers, including cable transfers, arise from any number of sources, such as gifts, donations, investments, and trade in goods and in services. Foreign-exchange instruments also arise from the repatriation of funds, investments, or other assets held in other countries.

THE FOREIGN-EXCHANGE MARKET

Since quotations and payments on United States import and export transactions may be in U.S. dollars or any foreign exchange, and since

276

commerce between other countries may be quoted and settled in their own or foreign currencies, including U.S. dollars, it is evident that many sellers come into possession of foreign exchange which they do not intend to use as money, and many buyers come into the need for foreign exchange which they do not possess. This supply of and demand for foreign exchange provides the essentials of a market or, more accurately, several markets in foreign exchange.

No Formal, Centralized, Organized Market. Markets are to be found in cable or mail transfers and in futures, in point of time of delivery. But with regard to facilities, there is no formal, central, organized market except in those countries in which owners are compelled to sell and users are obliged to buy from a designated authority. Even in these countries, other markets may be permitted to function for specified transactions or may exist as black markets.

The principal market facilities for foreign exchange consist of the commercial banks, supplemented by central banks and foreign-exchange brokers and dealers. Not all commercial banks are to be included, of course, but many of the larger ones maintain balances in one or more foreign countries or operate branches abroad. Balances are built up by the purchase of drafts or claims payable abroad and are reduced by the sale of such funds to purchasers or debtors in need of them. Thus it is that foreign exchange is looked on as a commodity, or inventory, to be accumulated and bid up in price, if demand so suggests, or to be reduced in individual holdings and driven down in price when alternative uses for dollars or lessened demand for any one or all types of foreign exchange appear to be the order of the day.

Commercial Banks Serve as Market Place. Through acting as a collection mechanism for drafts drawn on foreign buyers, banks engaged in foreign activities are constantly coming into possession of foreign bills and other claims. They thus act as a market place in which originators or owners of such draft or claims may dispose of them for U.S. dollars and in which those with U.S. dollars who need foreign exchange may acquire it. The commercial market for foreign exchange may then be said to consist of the elements listed below.

Sellers of Exchange	Buyers of Exchange
Exporters	Importers
Travelers (currency or checks)	Travelers
Dealers in or sellers of foreign securities	Buyers of foreign securities
Shipping companies	Buyers of foreign services
Insurance companies	Other banks
Other banks	

Other principal participants in the foreign-exchange market are brokers and dealers, travel bureaus or agencies, and central banks. The first play an important function by serving principally as middlemen between banks and between banks and large foreign-exchange interests. In the United States, these function almost only in New York City and serve the desirable function of spreading the impact of demand and supply factors by drawing on several sources (banks) for any unusual demand and finding several buyers for any large supply. The travel bureaus or agencies deal principally in currency and traveler's checks.

Central Banks Play Very Important Role. Most countries have established central banks and charged them with certain responsibilities, common ones being to act as a depository for reserves of the commercial banks and to have final jurisdiction over currency and credit volumes in the respective countries. Among these are the Bank of England, Banque de France, Bank of Canada, Banco do Brasil, Banca Central de Argentina, and, in the United States, the Federal Reserve System. In carrying out responsibilities pertaining to currency and credit conditions, such banks are particularly interested in movement of foreign exchange, because it may mean the accumulation of or loss of legally constituted reserves. Accordingly, some central banks are active in the purchase and sale of foreign exchange, the action being influenced by the effect desired on the domestic economy. Fundamental interest centers around influencing or maintaining the *rate of exchange.* Commercial banks, on the other hand, while not unmindful of changes in exchange rates, can go about their business at any rate, although gains or losses may be experienced on positions taken. Thus, the central banks may be said to be interested in the sufficiency of volume and the stability of rates of foreign exchange, while commercial banks may be said to be more directly interested in the financing and transfer functions of the foreign-exchange market.

Federal Reserve banks are permitted to maintain balances abroad and to act as depository for their foreign correspondents or agencies. In order to be able to carry out open-market operations, Sec. 14 of the Federal Reserve Act authorizes Federal Reserve banks, under rules and regulations prescribed by the Board of Governors, to:

(a) . . . purchase and sell in the open market, at home or abroad, either from or to domestic or foreign banks, . . . cable transfers and bankers' acceptances and bills of exchange of the kinds and maturities . . . eligible for rediscount;

(b) . . . buy and sell . . . (through foreign correspondents or agencies) . . . bills of exchange (or acceptances) arising out of actual commercial transactions which have not more than ninety days to run;

(c) . . . purchase from member banks and to sell, . . . bills of exchange arising out of commercial transactions. . . .

They may also be active in the foreign-exchange market through discounting of acceptances meeting standards of eligibility.

Daily Prices Set by Interplay of Banks and Traders. Since there is no organized market in the United States with posted quotations, and since each individual bank faces the daily problem of building up or not building up its foreign holdings by purchases or of deliberately reducing its holdings by sales, it follows that the price any bank is willing to pay for, say, British pounds will be influenced not only by general market conditions but by the bank's own specific condition on that date. Its determination that the foreign-exchange market is strong or weak, or that some exchanges are "stronger" than others or more desirable to the bank, makes the price a matter of determination at a particular moment. For instance, the market for any one currency may have opened rather strong one morning; if, later in the day, word came of rioting or of some governmental pronouncement or other event that would tend to render that currency *less desirable for any purpose, including investment and travel,* the effect would be a softening in the price. Accordingly, buyers and sellers may at times find it to advantage to go to different banks to find the most favorable rate at a particular time.

Types of Foreign-exchange Transactions

It was mentioned earlier that there could be found markets for cable or mail transfers or futures contracts. A few words about these are necessary before other aspects of foreign exchange are discussed.

Cable transfers are those effected by means of cable notification, with the ownership of foreign funds changing hands with the least possible delay. In the case of a sale by a bank on cable transfer, the bank obtains dollars and loses foreign funds at the same time.

Mail transfers are effected by the drawing of checks. The comparable illustration of a sale by a bank or mail transfer means that the bank is paid today in U.S. dollars for its check drawn in pounds, francs, etc., but it is several days before the check arrives *by mail* to reduce the bank's account abroad. Accordingly, the bank has the use of dollars obtained from the sale of the mail transfer, and it also retains use of its funds abroad until the check arrives by mail and is presented for payment. This double use of funds makes it possible for banks to offer mail transfers for sale at a slightly lower rate than cable transfers (aside from the cost of the cable). In purchasing mail transfers, on the other hand, the bank has less dollars at once and does not obtain usable funds abroad until the bill or check arrives and is credited to its account. Naturally, at any given time, the bank could *buy* and *sell* mail transfers and equalize the time required by transportation. However, it is a factor to be considered in the setting of rates, although its influence is somewhat lessened through use of air mail and in times of low interest rates.

Futures contracts in foreign exchange are agreements calling for purchase or delivery of specified amounts of exchange. Unlike futures contracts on organized commodity exchanges, margins are not formally required, although banks will be cautious in selecting individuals or firms with whom contracts are so made. The balance in an account with a bank serves as margin and, since the forward contract is in the nature of a credit transaction, banks will normally enter into them only with customers of satisfactory credit standing. Payment is made at the time of delivery and not at the time the contract is entered.

A clearer understanding of foreign-exchange futures may be had if the sale or discounting of a ninety-day draft today is compared with the sale of a forward contract to be delivered in, say, ninety days. Under the first, the seller offers a draft, drawn on a specific name and endorsed by the seller. The seller obtains cash at once, and the bank surrenders cash. To be considered in the transaction are:

1. Rate of discount, compared with other means of borrowing
2. Indicated premium or discount on the exchange for ninety days
3. Possibility of exchange-rate fluctuation, such risk being avoided by transferring it to the bank
4. Risk that the drawee or acceptor may not pay

In the case of a forward contract, it is not vital that an underlying draft be involved. Instead, the transaction is a contract to deliver to the bank (protected possibly by margin or satisfactory credit standing) a specified amount of foreign exchange in a specified month. The seller does not obtain cash immediately; instead, his funds for margin may be tied up. Nor, obviously, does the bank pay. Of particular consideration are the following factors:

1. Where the seller will get the exchange. He may be selling short, or he may be covering an open account or draft transaction involving goods, securities, or services.
2. In what market the seller prefers to be (this involves the elements of safety and interest income).
3. The possibility of exchange-rate fluctuation—whether the seller desires to bear the risk or whether he desires to transfer it by selling a forward contract, thereby pinning down the price he is to realize.

Relationship between Spot and Forward Prices

A study of foreign exchange calls for an analysis of the relationship between spot and forward rates. The principal questions are (1) whether spot prices determine the forward price or whether forward prices determine spot and (2) whether forward prices indicate that spot prices at that distant date will be the same as today's price of the forward.

As to the first, a forward purchase contract is merely a contract to accept at some specified time in the future a "commodity" which *could* be bought today and held until that time. A sale contract is one in which the agreement is to deliver at a future date—future rather than present because either the "commodity" is not now in the possession of the seller or, if it is, it is employed for some specified time.

Future Prices May Be at Premium or Discount over Spot. At times, the future price is at a premium over spot; at other times, it stands at a discount. This variation is determined by a number of factors such as the following:

1. The need of the buyer and seller. This is influenced by (and influences) the volume of commercial transactions requiring settlement.
2. Interest rates in the two countries. This influences the movement of short-term capital, when it is free to move and to be repatriated.
3. The future outlook for factors comprising demand and supply and, very significantly, stability or safety. The latter influence an investor's desire to leave funds in one country in preference to another, again assuming freedom to make a choice.

Subject to limiting influences such as gold movements or government intervention, future prices will not rise above spot by more than the cost of interest, for it would be possible for a purchaser to buy spot (paying for it at once) and hold it until the future date. It will not fall to a heavy discount from spot, because if the indication is that the exchange will be worth less in the future than at present, owners of spot will not hold in the face of a declining market and buyers will not offer to pay higher prices for spot unless it is to be used at once in settlement of contracts. Accordingly, the price of spot will follow the price of the future down, except as immediate demand to fulfill contracts keeps the price up.[1] On the other hand, the future price is not necessarily an indication of what the spot price will be at that time. The daily events influencing exchange rates are such that no one can predict accurately what prices will be in the future, but the certainty of settling on the

[1] As suggested before, the decline in price of spot exchange would be subject to limiting influences, such as gold movements or government intervention. Validity of the general statement rests on the assumption that the foreign exchange in question is convertible at the owner's option. If this condition holds, it follows that the foreign exchange (as a "commodity") would be rather readily disposable at whatever the changing market price might be. The conclusion would not be valid if the holder of foreign exchange, say, blocked currencies, could not liquidate his holdings freely because of government restrictions.

price and avoiding the risk of unfavorable exchange movements are benefits of the forward market.

Hedging. Through existence of a futures market, it is possible to settle at once the price at which exchange to be acquired can be sold, and the price at which exchange to be required can be purchased. The principal need for this determination arises from credit transactions, with the sellers receiving payment sometime in the future and the buyers obligating themselves to pay in the future. But another important need for hedging arises from interest-arbitrage operations.

VOLUME AND PRICE FLUCTUATIONS IN FOREIGN EXCHANGE

Foreign exchange is bought for the same reason that people desire domestic funds—to be used to buy or pay for something in the market in which that particular exchange is the money of account. This simple and general statement touches on several most fundamental questions: Why is one currency worth a certain amount in terms of another? What determines the value of exchanges? How do they get out of line? How are they brought back into line? Is it advisable or desirable to have rates held in line by some government action? Before we look into some of these questions, it may be stated that the price of foreign exchange is determined by and also affects the price of goods, services, and investments comprising the total of foreign commerce.

Parity of Exchanges

Commonly found in writings on the subject of foreign exchange are the terms "mint par of exchange," "purchasing-power parity of exchange," and "equilibrium rate of exchange." Discussion of these follows in the next few pages.

Mint Par. Mint par of exchange is the legally established ratio between exchanges, based on the commodity content of the respective currencies. When two currencies are on gold, the amount of gold in each determines the ratio between them because, if the market should attempt to change this ratio, individuals would buy and sell gold instead of drafts or checks and the strained market rates would find no takers. These are the well-known gold-points, at which it becomes more advantageous to buy and ship gold than to buy exchange at a high price and more advantageous to convert the exchange into gold and import the gold than to sell the exchange at a low price.

Although this mechanism may sound extremely simple, its coming into play—the movement of gold—is expected to set into motion a series of consequential potential actions. This is sometimes referred to as the "automatic functioning of the gold standard," whereby gold movements (gold being legal reserve) increase or decrease the amount of monetary and banking reserves, with some resultant effect on credit and prices. However, the factors which brought the market ratio of exchanges to the point where gold movements become advisable are the problems to be solved. We go back to the question of how exchange rates get out of line and how they are brought back into line.

Conditions May Preclude Automatic Corrections of Gold Movements. The supposed automatic correction of gold movements under the pure-gold standard may be obstructed by a number of conditions, among which are:

1. Currency and credit may not be expanded to the limit in the gold-exporting and -importing countries. Hence a gain or loss of gold reserves may not force a contraction of credit in one and encourage an expansion in the other.
2. Productive factors in either or both countries may not be fully employed, with the result that expanded currency and credit may bring about increased production but with little change in prices.
3. Different percentage reserves in the two countries affect the rate or degree of contraction or expansion.
4. The sum transferred may be of little or much importance to the respective countries, depending on size of the country as well as percentage of reserve. A movement of $10,000,000 in gold would be proportionately less important to the United States than to Guatemala or Norway. Also, the movement of $1 in gold could have a potential expansion or contraction influence of $5 on a required reserve of 20 per cent and $4 in a country with a reserve requirement of 25 per cent.
5. Action taken by individual countries may deliberately offset the increase or decrease in gold reserves. Among these may be changes in the percentage of required reserve or in the volume of reserve bank credit outstanding. The United States gold-sterilization program of the mid-1930s was deliberate action taken to prevent gold imports from exercising full potential effect on bank reserves.
6. Pressure on the exchanges may be the result of something other than maladjustment of prices, so corrective action through prices may be uncalled for. In fact, price structures may not have to be rectified at all. This point emphasizes strongly the fact that demand for exchange arises not only from the desire to buy *goods* at favorable prices.

Most of the foregoing points accept the premise of a close relationship between the volume of currency and credit and all prices. The principal difficulty here is that it is impossible to predict which types of prices will be affected by an increase in currency and credit and to what extent—whether commodities, real estate, or securities. Furthermore, the commodities affected, and not all are affected equally by any means, may or may not be internationally traded items. Opening this side of the question leads to the second common explanation of the rate of exchange.

Purchasing-power Parity. Purchasing-power parity of exchange suggests that exchanges are worth a certain amount in terms of each other because of the amount of goods (or goods and services) each commands. Hence, when prices in one country tend to rise it should be possible for its residents to buy from abroad more cheaply (increasing imports) and advisable for foreigners to reduce purchases in it (decreasing exports). An attempt to establish a mint par of exchange on this basis, or to explain changes in rates—rates moving out of line—by this relationship is practically doomed to failure. If such were possible, the setting of rates, or currency values, by government should be easy, and they should never have to be adjusted. Or if they did happen to get out of line, realigning them would be a much simpler problem than it actually is. Consider, for example, the problem of deciding to set the value of the pound sterling at $2.80. Why not $2.85 or $2.75?

One reason for the difficulty is the inadequacy of an index for measuring price changes. Specifically, the difficulties are somewhat as follows:

1. Selection of items to be included. A product may be of much greater significance to the economy of one country than to another. This relative importance, and weighting, may in itself call for change from time to time. Further, the prospect of solving this relationship between any one country and several others is dimmed materially when one contemplates the parallel relationships among the several currencies. These are usually referred to as cross rates.
2. Items of considerable significance in some countries may not be widely traded in internationally. Further, they may be exported from one and imported into another, or exported from both; perhaps exported to each other because of variations in quality. Consequently, price changes may have no immediate or traceable effect on imports or exports between any two countries.
3. Prices of some commodities may move up while others move down by a corresponding amount. The result could be substantial variations in individual prices, but no or small change in the index.

Impossible to Predict Interactions. That price changes do have considerable effect on the ratio of exchanges is, of course, undeniable. But the effect is unpredictable. Similarly, the effect of changes in exchange rates on prices is unpredictable. Probably the most important reason why the purchasing-power concept is inadequate, though, is that money is usable for many things besides goods. It bears repetition that the supply of and demand for foreign exchange are as much influenced by transactions in services and investments as in goods. Over and above this, the question of political uncertainty enters. When a nation is approaching economic or political disturbance, it ceases to be a haven for capital. Other countries are relatively more desirable because of safety from confiscation, taxes, and other fears.

To attempt, therefore, to ascribe exchange values to any measurable purchasing-power parity is to overlook these several invisible factors which bear equally on exchange demand and supply and probably with greater volatility. Determination of what should be mint par or, in the absence of mint parity, "official" rates of central banks must accordingly be based on some market indication, which may even be the black market. That is the way in which men acting rather freely indicate their evaluation of commodities, including foreign exchange. No government has yet been able to dictate to the public for any length of time the value which each man himself must place on anything.

An Equilibrium Rate. It has been suggested, in recent economic literature, that the value of foreign exchange is based on some equilibrium rate, into and out of which must be converted, as a common denominator, free men's evaluations of a multitude of goods, services, and investments, as well as political safety—in fact, anything for which money can be used.

As to the question of how exchange rates get out of line, it must be concluded that someone or many decide, for whatever reasons, that:

1. They desire more goods from a certain country than holders of that country's currency desire from theirs. This is probably due to price or quality differentials and adequate and dependable productivity. These changes in desire arise from business and technological progress by one or several producers in a country and take place constantly between competing producers in the same country. Rectifying of unit costs or of production and quality control are the logical answers to bring rates back into line if the disparity had this origin.
2. They desire more services from a certain country than holders of that country's funds desire from theirs. Again, the correction leads to cost and dependability of the service.
3. Investment opportunities are more attractive in one country than in another for reasons of income or safety. The income aspects are affected by earnings or taxes, and the relative attractiveness of one country over another is also influenced by relative safety of principal or ability to convert earnings or repatriate principal into the currency

desired by the investor. When war, economic dislocation, or uneconomic political pronouncements and actions occur, a "flight of
capital may result, with those able to do so transferring their property
to what seems to them a safer haven. The corrective action needed
here is perhaps the most unpalatable to certain governments. They
find themselves restricted in action which they consider good for
domestic affairs or palatable politically. Thus an issue is made of the
selfishness and cold-bloodedness of the foreign investor, who may be
accused of having no interest in the social welfare of the country in
which investment was made. Doubtless, there have been many instances of international exploitation and, while not absolving the
guilty ones, the same accusation must be leveled in purely domestic
spheres.

As far as the rate of earnings is concerned, such factors as productivity and taxes of all types enter the picture. But over and above these is
the fear of political action which, for popular appeal and support, points
to less opportunity and safety for capital and perhaps a greater share in
the distribution of income to labor. The fact that these actions take place
nationally, in differing degrees and at different times, provides the possibility of comparing relative opportunities among countries such as
Canada, the United States, England, France, Germany, Italy, Brazil, and
Argentina. Of course, once a direct investment is made and a factory
or other facility is installed, the possibility of a flight of capital is greatly
reduced.

In summary, then, the corrective action needed to offset the pressures
forcing rates out of line on this account are the adoption and maintenance of policies which are attractive to owners of funds or other
capital assets. There are alternative opportunities, including repatriation
and sitting tight on wealth until the atmosphere clears. As long as this
holds, it must be conceded that the price a country, or its private borrowers, must pay for capital must be as high as that offered by others
who are at the same time bidding for the use of the limited capital.

The Fixed- and Fluctuating-rate Controversy

Especially in postwar writings, the proposal is found that fixed exchange rates are on the way out and that a country cannot afford to have
its entire economy hinge on the maintenance of a fixed exchange rate.[2]
Accordingly, changes in the values of currency, practically always a
devaluation, would be looked on with less disdain than in the past. They
might even bear the aura of respectability because, by gentlemen's agree-

---

[2] Alvin H. Hansen, *America's Role in the World Economy* (New York, W. W. Norton & Company, 1945), pp. 50, 62.

ment, some prior discussion on the subject had been held between governments. To explore the problem in detail would exceed the objectives of this text, but it cannot be ignored or passed by too lightly, because of the far-reaching impact.

Problem Substantially Same as in Domestic Monetary Standards. Fixed exchange rates, which mean an established metallic content (basis of mint par of exchange) or a stated value to be maintained by official purchases and sales of exchange, are no more or less than the creation on an international basis of a sound currency. The problem is substantially the same as in adoption of a domestic monetary standard.

Sound money calls for certain characteristics in order adequately to perform its recognized functions. Some of these functions, like measure of value and medium of exchange, are of greatest importance in doing today's business. Others, like providing a standard of deferred payment and a store of value, are of special significance with regard to saving and capital formation.[3] These latter two are the link between past, present, and future. Money, domestic or international, may be considered a parallel or trapeze bar, around which all sorts of economic gymnastics take place by a multitude of performers. Included in this would be immediate, short-range, and long-range plans and investments.

While barter transactions could overcome to some extent the uncertainty in value or shortage of foreign exchange, any transactions involving time would be faced with a serious obstacle if the quality of national currencies were to be compromised by a less serious effort to adhere to past values and to bring costs and prices into line with some competitive determination of individual values.

On the other hand, opponents of fixed exchange rates, and of the implications therefrom through convertibility, claim that it is unsound and undesirable to compel a nation to adjust its costs and prices downward to meet competition. Deflation is not the answer or the corrective action, in their view; it must not be allowed, presumably because of its effect on the national income. As an aside, it may be pointed out that this so-called "expansionist" approach to the problem is distinctly inflationary.

Closely related to the problem of a fixed rate of exchange is the need for financing trade in a situation of uneven ratios of exports to imports for each country in its trade with each other country. When the people of one country specialize in the production of some item and exchange some of this production for that under specialization in several other countries, the result is that the excess of exports and imports between countries is not in the same proportion for each. Thus the ratio of imports

[3] These are functions as described in Foster and Rodgers, *Money and Banking*, 3d ed. (New York, Prentice-Hall, Inc., 1947), pp. 10–14.

of merchandise to exports of merchandise is not the same for any given country in its transactions with every other country with which trade is undertaken. In fact, although a country may experience an over-all excess of exports, it may just as easily experience an excess of imports in its dealings with one or more of the several countries of the world. *It is this unevenness in trading relations which gives rise to the necessity for multilateral trade and exchange*—an unevenness which arises from differences in productivity due to natural forces, size and the like, and from variations in desire for a particular product.

THE EUROPEAN PAYMENTS UNION

A most interesting illustration of the difficulties encountered in being unable to convert exchange at a fixed rate is offered by the experience of several European countries in the postwar period. Following the breakdown of European financial systems during the war and the scramble for position and trade during the immediate period of reconstruction, little progress was made toward convertibility of exchange. By 1947, European countries with export surpluses in their trade with other European countries had become increasingly reluctant to sell to the countries which continued to import excessively; attempts at bilateral balancing of commerce, country by country, resulted in a maze of quotas and of bilateral trade and clearing agreements.

It was in the face of these obstacles to trade that the European Recovery Program (Marshall Plan) was undertaken by the United States and interested European countries, comprising the Organization for European Economic Cooperation (OEEC). Through gifts or loans by the United States, reconstruction and reorganization on a scheduled basis were put under way. This section is concerned with only one aspect of this broad program—that of restoring convertibility of exchanges. But convertibility takes for granted, because it requires it, relative freedom in the movement of goods, services, and investments.

The first intra-European payments plan was adopted in October, 1948. Its central feature was that ECA would allot "conditional" dollars to countries with expected export surpluses in their trade with other members of OEEC. The condition was that the creditor country would, in turn, extend equivalent grants or "drawing rights" to their intra-European debtors. Thus, if Belgium expected net exports of $1,000,000 to the Netherlands, and the Belgians did not wish to receive guilders or Dutch obligations, dollar aid requested by Belgium from ECA would be made available on *condition* that it set up a grant or drawing right in the amount of $1,000,000, in terms of Belgian francs, for the Dutch to use in paying for imports from Belgium. These drawing rights were expected to be used only in the country setting them up and only by the country receiving them, but some provision was made for transfer of the rights under stipulated conditions.

In practice, the transferability proved unworkable, due largely to the conditions, which required that the debtor prove that despite every reasonable effort he had been unable to use his drawing rights on the original creditor.

A compromise was reached in July, 1949, upon adoption of the second intra-European payments plan, which provided that 25 per cent of the drawing rights could be unconditionally transferred by the debtor to any other country in the OEEC, and that within this limitation transfers would be automatically accompanied by equivalent transfers of conditional aid. This feature made it possible for the recipients of drawing rights, themselves paid for in dollars to the country granting them, to shop around and buy in the most advantageous market; conversely, it encouraged creditor countries to continue being so, in order to obtain the dollar grants, and to strive for efficiency, in order to meet competition within the OEEC and retain the benefits of the dollar grants. Special provisions were made with respect to Belgium, as its sales within Europe were expected to exceed by far its purchases in the same area.

Recovery and the freeing of a good part of intra-European trade from import quotas laid the groundwork for the European Payments Union (EPU) as successor to the two earlier payments plans. These earlier plans had endeavored to bring into being some measure of convertibility of European currencies but, with drawing rights having to be spent principally in the country granting them, the limits to convertibility were substantial.

Union Functions as Clearinghouse. The EPU, itself, functions in somewhat the same manner as does a clearinghouse for central banks. At first bimonthly, and later monthly, the central banks of the respective countries have advised the Bank for International Settlements of balances on their books for account of other EPU-member central banks. Balances are then offset and cleared, the resulting debits or credits becoming liabilities to or claims on the EPU. The manner of settlement is determined by the extent of the debit or credit in relation to quotas previously agreed on. Settlement must be either by extension of credit as between the respective creditor and debtor nations or through movements of gold between EPU and the respective creditor or debtor country. The schedule for settlement of members' credit and debit balances with EPU is as shown in the table below. Quotas were established on the basis of each member's total payments and receipts on current account with other members, in 1949, and the quotas and settlements are in terms of "EPU units," which are units of account calculated, on a gold basis, to be equal to the U.S. dollar.

Under the plan, a member may spend its current earnings from an-

Borrowing Rights and Lending Obligations

% of quota	Debtors		Creditors	
	Use of credit	Gold payments	Use of credit	Gold receipts
1st 20	20	. .	20	
2d 20	16	4	10	10
3d 20	12	8	10	10
4th 20	8	12	10	10
5th 20	4	16	10	10
Total...100	60	40	60	40

other member in any country belonging to the Union, thereby expanding the feature of convertibility for intra-European trade. Moreover, the arrangement pertains to currency areas, which reach into colonial trade as well. In view of the importance of sterling as an international currency, and fears that convertibility might result in a loss of gold or dollars by Great Britain via the settlement process, an arrangement was made whereby ECA guaranteed to underwrite any British dollar losses resulting from the use of sterling resources by other EPU members. Special provisions were also made to take into account the unusual positions of Belgium, normally a large-scale creditor, and Switzerland, also a creditor and one which had taken only a limited part in previous schemes.

Plan Induces Correction of Basic Trouble. Looked on as a major accomplishment is the fact that the Union uses credits and gold payments (to and from members) rather than United States grants in the initial financing of surplus or deficit balances between members. This throws added inducement on members to correct the causes of lack of balance. However, United States aid is still a very important part of the plan. First of all, there is the agreement by ECA to underwrite British gold or dollar losses; secondly, ECA provided a $350,000,000 working-capital fund to cover any difference between gold payments due from EPU to creditor countries and the gold payments due to EPU from debtors.[4]

Provision Not Made for Convertibility into Dollars. The EPU does not provide for convertibility of earnings in European currencies into U.S. dollars except as the working-capital fund and the special guarantee to the British may make dollars available. Nor does it lift exchange controls from the picture. It did, though, contribute to a substantial reduction in trade barriers within the EPU area, it being estimated that the proportion of nongovernmental imports that members were required to admit free of quotas had been increased to 75 per cent of the 1948 trade,

[4] The London *Economist*, July 15, 1950, p. 131.

with certain exceptions.[5] However, in early 1952, reimposition of quotas began to appear in several countries.

ARBITRAGE

A practice which can be followed in foreign-exchange markets when governments do not employ exchange-control schemes is that of arbitrage. The term means the operation by which a person simultaneously buys and sells the same commodity, the purchase and sale being in different markets and being induced by a price differential in the different markets. Most commonly, two markets are involved, but three or more could be employed. It may be completely in cable transfers, or it may involve a time element for the purpose of allowing interest earnings to mature. The former may be called "exchange arbitrage," the latter "interest arbitrage."

Exchange Arbitrage. Exchange arbitrage depends on free convertibility of exchange and lightning-fast transactions. As suggested above, arbitrage is possible when prices of the same article differ in different markets. For instance, the value of the pound sterling may be $2.79 in New York, while the dollar-pound ratio in London is $2.80. At the same time, the French franc-pound ratio may differ between London and Paris, and the franc-dollar ratio may not be the same in Paris as in New York. Assume the following rates for purposes of illustration:

In New York: The pound sterling is about $2.79; the French franc is 350 to the dollar.
In London: Dollars are 7s. 1½d. (approximately $2.80 per pound); francs are 980 to the pound.
In Paris: Dollars are worth 360 francs; pounds sterling are worth 950 francs.

In this situation of extremely wide price differentials, it would be possible to clear a gain by some of the following methods (omitting the cost of commissions and cables, although cables must be used):

1. Buy pounds in New York at $2.79.
   Buy dollars (with the pounds) in London at price equivalent to $2.80.
2. Buy francs in New York at 350 to the dollar.
   Buy pounds in Paris at the rate of 950 francs to the pound.
   Buy dollars in London at the rate of $2.80.
3. Buy pounds in New York at $2.79.
   Buy francs in London at 980 per pound.
   Buy dollars in Paris at 360 francs, or sell francs in New York at 350 francs per dollar.

[5] *Monthly Review*, Federal Reserve Bank of New York, September, 1951, p. 129.

Start and Finish in Same Currency. It will be noted that in each case we start with dollars and finish with dollars. Also, transactions may be concluded on a buy, buy, buy basis. This is because in dealing in any money center, the money of account is basic and all others become, in effect, commodities, although there are cases in which the money of one country is widely accepted and used in business in others. However, no one buys dollars in New York; to obtain dollars, if he holds foreign exchange, he sells the exchange in New York or buys dollars in the market in which his exchange is the money of account. Similarly, no one with dollars buys pounds in London or francs in Paris. To obtain these, he sells dollars in London (and thereby obtains pounds) or sells dollars in Paris and is paid in francs.

Gold Arbitrage. Quite similar to exchange arbitrage, in that it depends on free convertibility of exchange and lightning-fast transactions, is gold arbitrage. An additional requisite is rather free exportation and importation of gold and either (or both) open trading in it as a commodity or a price fixed by one or both governments.

To illustrate the principles, fictitious quotations will be used which offer wide differentials. Let us assume that gold is available in New York at $35 per ounce and that shipping charges to London are, say, $0.25 per ounce. This would make the landed cost in London US$35.25. Now let us suppose the following two situations existing at one time or another, and the opportunity for financial gain in each will be evident:

1. The market price for gold in London is strong, and sterling in New York is moving around $2.82. The gold could be sold in London for, say, £12 15s., and the sterling so derived could be sold in New York for $35.955, leaving a gain of 70.5 cents per ounce of gold, minus commissions and cable expenses.

2. The market price for gold in London is not strong, say £12 10s., and the price of the dollar in London is strong, say 8s. By selling dollars in London, the seller could obtain £40 for US$100. Using the sterling to buy gold, he could obtain 3.2 ounces of gold (£40 ÷ £12½), ship the gold to New York, and sell it at $35 per ounce. He would thus realize $112, minus commissions, cables, and shipping charges, and without taking into account the Treasury's buying margin.

Throughout, and since the Second World War, it has not been possible to conduct private arbitrage in gold due to restrictions on its exportation and importation, uncertainty as to its price, and controls over uses of foreign exchange.

Interest Arbitrage. Interest arbitrage is the process of investing in a foreign-money market and protecting at the same time the principal and the interest income in foreign money by covering the exchange position with a futures contract. The operation involves both differences in interest income and a spread between spot and forward exchange rates, as illustrated in the following examples:

1. Assume prime short-term rates to be around 1 per cent in New York and 1¼ per cent in London. Assume the price of the pound sterling in New York to be $2.80 for spot and $2.805 for ninety-day futures. Is there a possibility for a short-term investor with, say, $112,000 in New York to earn more than the 1-per-cent rate indicated for New York and to do so with a high degree of safety? Study of the situation shows the following possibilities, omitting commissions and cable expenses:

   a. If invested in New York, $112,000 invested at 1 per cent would earn $280 in ninety days.
   b. If invested in London, $112,000 would bring £40,000 at $2.80 per pound. Invested for ninety days at 1¼ per cent, the earnings would be £125, so the investor would end up with £40,125. But he started with dollars and must finish with the same currency. He does this by hedging his contracted position at the time it is entered, through selling a forward contract to deliver pounds when his investment matures. Using the assumed figures, he would have contracted to sell £40,125 at $2.805 and realized $112,550.63.

2. Assuming the same interest rates, but with the ninety-day sterling future price at a slight discount, say at $2.795, the investor would have been able to realize only $112,149.38 (£40,075 at $2.795), thus making it inadvisable to accept the higher interest return in London. The higher interest earning would be offset by the discount on the forward exchange.

Conceivably a situation could hold, also, in which interest rates in New York were higher than in London, but in which it would be advisable for the investor to accept the lower interest return in London if the premium on forward sterling were sufficient to offset the difference in interest income.

Interest arbitrage is possible only when individuals are free to move funds without restriction (or even the threat of restriction) from one money center to another. This condition has not held for many years, and whether free convertibility of exchange will occur for some years following the Second World War is uncertain. Other essentials which must be present to permit this operation are a satisfactory forward market, which means the existence of a sizable volume of commerce in the exchanges involved, buttressed by a speculative interest to round out the futures market. Finally, the small spread between interest earnings and between spot and forward exchange quotations makes it necessary to employ very large sums of money in this type of short-term investment, which practically precludes participation by individuals and small banks or businesses.

REVIEW QUESTIONS

1. What is the source of foreign exchange?
2. Where is the foreign-exchange market in the United States? Of what is it composed?
3. How does the interest of central banks differ from that of commercial banks in the foreign-exchange market?
4. In what way are Federal Reserve banks interested or active in the foreign-exchange market?
5. How is the daily price of foreign exchange set?
6. If there is a difference between the prices of cable and of mail transfers, for which would you have to pay a higher price as purchaser? Why?
7. Do spot prices of foreign exchange determine the future price, or is the forward price based on the spot quotation?
8. Why is it that future prices may at times be at a premium over spot and at other times be at a discount from spot?
9. How far above spot can future prices rise? What is the basis for this limit or link?
10. What is meant by "mint par" of exchanges? How does it come about?
11. List the conditions which may preclude automatic corrections of gold movements internationally. Can anything be done about this, or may it be desirable to do something about it?
12. What is the significance of purchasing-power parity?
13. *a.* How do foreign-exchange rates get out of line?
    b. How may they be brought back into line?
14. Discuss the merits of a fixed as compared with a fluctuating exchange rate.
15. What was the European Payments Union expected to accomplish?
16. Assume the value of the pound sterling to be $2.805 in New York and the value of the French franc to be 360 to the dollar. In London, the dollar-pound ratio is about $2.80; francs are 1,000 to the pound. In Paris, dollars are worth 370 francs and pounds sterling are worth 990 francs. Calculate a gain through arbitrage operations.
17. Assume prime short-term rates to be around 2 per cent in London and 1¾ per cent in New York. Assume the price of the pound sterling to be at $2.80 in both New York and London and ninety-day sterling futures to be at $2.79. Is there a possibility for a short-term investor with dollars to earn more in London than in New York? Is there a possibility for a short-term investor with pounds sterling to earn more in New York than in London?

CHAPTER 15

Foreign Investments

Next to international trade in merchandise, no aspect of foreign commerce captures the imagination and draws the attention of the public more than that of foreign investments. This is possibly because of the popular impression that foreign investments may be a solution to off-setting the "dollar gap." It is reasoned that the excess of exports over imports of goods must be narrowed and that the price of reduced export volumes is unpleasant to contemplate. Foreign investments are also the subject of popular consideration because of the vast amount of publicity attending such institutions or operations as the International Bank for Reconstruction and Development, the Export-Import Bank, the United States government loan to Great Britain, and the Point Four concept.

Of What Do Investments Consist? Since the principal difference between foreign and domestic investments is their location with respect to ownership, it may be said that all types of property ownership or claims should be included in the concept. But broad concept and measurement are two different things. Accordingly, in order to understand what is included in the figure purporting to represent the volume or movement of foreign investments, one must look into the manner of reporting. In describing methodology and sources of data used in collecting statistics on private account, the Department of Commerce reports as sources at least the following:

1. Direct reports to the Department of Commerce by leading companies
2. Reports to the Securities and Exchange Commission
3. Corporate income-tax returns
4. Reports by banks, brokers, and dealers to Federal Reserve banks
5. Underwriters and financial services

In addition, public transactions are reported by the appropriate government agency.

Study of the report forms shows that data collected include stocks, bonds, buildings, land, bank balances, commercial paper and acceptances outstanding, and drafts in process of collection. Thus, both debt and equities are summarized in determining whether a nation is a "creditor." Both long- and short-term investments are included, the distinction being that the former have a maturity in excess of one year. Included, also, are branch plants, but such assets as personal property, including homes, jewelry, and the like, are excluded because there is no satisfactory basis for collecting reports on such holdings. Excluded, also, are such assets as property of educational, religious, and charitable institutions and property held for governmental use such as embassies and military installations.[1]

Investments May Be Publicly or Privately Made. Investors may be either private or public. Ordinarily, United States data do not include First World War credits by the government (they having been, in effect, written off), but they do include Second World War and postwar credits by the government. The large investments by the government in the International Monetary Fund and the International Bank for Reconstruction and Development are looked on as "foreign" investments.

Distinction between Direct and Portfolio Investments. The purpose of the investment, in so far as control is concerned, is at times of significance with regard to long-term private investments. A classification of "direct" or "portfolio" is, accordingly, generally accepted. This means that the former is primarily for purpose of control over operations; it represents, in effect, branch operation abroad by domestic concerns. For statistical measurement, the Department of Commerce considers an investment to fall into the "direct" category if domestic interests (or foreign, in the case of an investment in the United States) own as much as 25 per cent or more of outstanding voting stock.[2] Portfolio investments consist of the holdings of miscellaneous foreign securities, including dollar bonds, which do not involve any controlling interest on the part of the American investor.[3]

Definition of a Creditor Nation. The usually accepted definition of a creditor nation is one whose citizens or government own more assets abroad than are owned in it by foreigners. The definition is simple and easy, but rather hard when it comes to measurement. This is seen by reference to the several items making up the total of investments, considering not only the difficulty of collecting accurate data on changes made but also the difficult problem presented by changes in valuation of outstanding assets. Should the statistic used be market value, if there

---

[1] Robert L. Sammons, "International Investment Position of the United States," *Foreign Commerce Weekly,* Jan. 27, 1945, p. 5.

[2] *The Balance of International Payments of the United States,* 1946–48, U.S. Department of Commerce, 1950, p. 134.

[3] *Ibid.*

is a market? Should it be book value? What difference does it make which value is used? This leads to a second definition of a creditor nation—one whose citizens or government receive more in interest and dividends from abroad than is paid in interest and dividends to foreigners. This definition is doubtless the one of more continuing significance because the impact of interest and dividend payments is a continuing proposition. However, under this criterion, as pointed out by Lewis,[4] "a country with a large excess of investments would still be rated with the debtor group if, for the time being, a considerable part of its foreign holdings were yielding little or no return." It would seem that next to the impact of interest and dividend payments, the feature of greatest significance would be the possibility of sudden or large-scale capital movements. Analysis of a country's position with regard to this risk would have to involve not the total of foreign investments, but its composition—what proportion is short term and what proportion, either short or long term, is likely to move out (or in) because of various international developments. A third definition is somewhat the reciprocal of the other two plus any new investment. This concept would define a creditor nation as one which, during any particular year or other period of time, experienced an outflow of funds and a corresponding importation of foreign investments.

The foregoing discussion suggests that it is not the definition used which is most important. It is the significance of an anticipated happening which will or may occur and for which governments must prepare, or else deny to their citizens the right to take advantage of such developments.

Why Foreign Investments Are Made

Referring now to individual investments, it is possible to narrow down the motives out of which foreign investment springs. First of these is the desire on the part of individuals for greater safety or greater income. Then there is the element of speculation and arbitrage operations. Industrially, the impelling forces seem to be, and this pertains to direct investments, (1) to develop or protect a source of raw materials (rubber, copper, oil), (2) to get into a country or an area under its tariff or other protective wall (textiles, automobiles), and (3) intensive cultivation of a foreign market, which can best be done by such an arrangement.

Foreign investments also being made by governments, it is well to recognize that the motives here are principally political or military. Economic considerations would appear to be more in the nature of a means to an end, the end being political or military security.

[4] Cleona Lewis, *The United States and Foreign Investment Problems* (Washington, Brookings Institution, 1948), p. 12.

How Foreign Investments Are Made

Portfolio investments, made without view to control, represent the type of investment in which payment is made in dollars or in which foreign exchange is purchased in the market for the purpose of buying the foreign asset. Public sale of securities of foreign governments, utilities, or industrials would fall into this category. So would purchases on foreign exchanges by Americans. An increase in the amount of notes or drafts held for collection by banks would similarly result in an increase in foreign investments, as would larger bank balances held abroad.

Direct investments, on the other hand, may arise or increase in several ways:

1. Original investments may be made in the form of funds or capital goods being exported, and perhaps in the form of technical services rendered.
2. Advances may be made to existing businesses for operating or expansion purposes (these may be short or long term).
3. Revaluation, either of book or of market value, may occur.

Short-term private foreign investments, consisting in large part of bank balances, commercial paper, short-term government obligations, and drafts and acceptances outstanding will be affected largely by ordinary commercial transactions in goods and services. This is because part of these "investments" represents the commercial settlement of business transactions. The blocking of bank balances or slowing down of remittances due to operation of exchange controls also contributes significantly to the amount of short-term foreign investments outstanding. Interest arbitrage, when permitted, affects the volume of short-term foreign holdings (commercial paper, acceptances, or government obligations).

The discussion on how the volume of foreign investments appears or increases must leave the thought in mind that they can just as easily disappear from the records. This may be brought about in several ways which are the reverse of operations mentioned above. A few specific additional ones may be mentioned, though. These are nationalization, whereby foreign governments may take over partial or full control of certain industries,[5] with resulting "liquidation" of the foreign investment upon payment by the foreign government; expropriation, whereby the liquidation is accomplished sometimes without full reimbursement; destruction, as in war or calamity; revaluation, for any other reason; and, as a countertransaction to the purchase, an outright, voluntary sale.

[5] In 1945–1947, American companies disposed of certain foreign public-utility holdings direct to the Spanish, Argentine, and Chinese governments. *The Balance of International Payments of the United States, 1946–48*, p. 142.

The net foreign-investment position might show an increase either because of an increase in United States investments abroad or because of a decrease in foreign holdings in the United States; it would show a decrease, even in the face of an increase in United States foreign holdings, if foreign holdings in the United States showed a greater decrease.

Impact on Foreign Exchange

Analysis of this point also calls for a breakdown of the investment operations. In the case of an original investment, or an expansion of existing investment, the impact depends on the manner in which accomplished. To the extent that the investment is brought about by the export of machinery or other capital goods, the effect on foreign exchange is nil. If accomplished by the purchase of foreign exchange or the payment of dollars to sellers in a third country from which the capital goods may have been obtained, the effect is an increase in the supply of dollars and a reduction in the supply of such foreign funds on the foreign-exchange markets.

Probably of much more importance is the effect of capital movements on foreign-exchange markets. These rather sudden, sometimes large-scale, and not necessarily commercially inspired demands on the foreign-exchange markets play havoc at times. This holds particularly for portfolio long-term and for short-term investments. It does not apply so much to direct investments, although it is possible to liquidate these. But the flight of capital pertains particularly to investments other than those classifiable as direct.

Influence of "Hot-money" Transfers. Chapter 13 dealt with the evolution of a nation from debtor status to creditor. The subject has bearing here, also, since a country's international investment position, which determines its status as debtor or creditor, is directly affected by *all* capital movements across its borders, regardless of the reasons therefor. Capital movements may represent the flow of funds for investment income (both short and long term) or for other purposes. The latter are commonly termed "hot money," or the flight of capital; the short-term markets— short-term at least mechanically—are the usual instrument for their execution.

Motives for the transfer may be political or economic in origin as, for example, rumors of impending exchange fluctuations, drastic changes in the political scene, war scares, peace scares, inflation scares, and continued major losses in a particular country's holdings of gold and foreign exchange, suggesting either an unwillingness or an inability to permit the economy to make necessary adjustments in costs and prices. Naturally, these movements may be unsettling to both the country losing the funds (sometimes gold) and the country gaining them, for how long they will remain where placed is unknown. Building up a monetary and credit structure on highly erratic reserves, or having to contract one proportionately, may be very disturbing to the economy as a whole. The impact on foreign exchange is, of course, most direct and inexorable.[6]

To what extent, and how quickly, hot-money transfers are made, *assuming that they are permitted,* depends on the financial positions of individuals and on the impelling motive. The individuals must be in a financially liquid position, and the possibility of their transferring funds internationally makes it necessary for the respective monetary authorities to maintain their economies in a more flexible rather than a more rigid position.

Impact of Interest and Dividends Is Continuous. The continuous impact of interest and dividend requirements is probably the biggest annual influence of all, because of its volume and recurrence by contract. It was shown earlier that in 1948 and 1949 the net demand for dollars for this purpose was about $1,000,000,000 per year, and there is ample evidence that this net demand will increase materially as foreign investments continue to expand.

Not only do these investments and their servicing and movements influence the foreign-exchange markets, but they are in turn influenced by foreign-exchange fluctuations. Changes in rates of exchange may be the deciding factor in arbitrage operations, for instance, or the most important influence in inducing an investor to place his funds in one country or another. When the contract for interest must be met, the debtor (or creditor at times) may be seriously affected by then current exchange rates. To use an old illustration which is sometimes heard of even today, the Citizens' Bank of Louisiana, founded in New Orleans in 1833, raised part of its funds by the sale of bonds guaranteed by the state and payable in dollars, pounds sterling, or guilders. The currency selected was at the buyer's option at the time of purchase, as it was necessary to obtain funds from New York and the East, from London, and from Amsterdam. Interest was similarly payable in any of the selected currencies. The bonds ran from fourteen to fifty years, and the risks assumed could have placed the bank and the state in an unfavorable position many times during its indebtedness.

Rates of Return

One should probably expect that, other things being equal, the added elements of uncertainty, distance, and all other differences between

---

[6] Professor Marsh states, as an illustration, that a flight of short-term funds from London in 1930–1931 was the immediate cause that forced Great Britain to suspend gold payments. Donald Bailey Marsh, *World Trade and Investment* (New York, Harcourt, Brace and Company, Inc., 1951), p. 45.

foreign and domestic situs would result in noticeably higher returns on foreign than on domestic investment. In contrast to this is the point that if returns in one nation or area are noticeably higher than in others, there should be that much less reason for foreigners to invest in those areas offering less return. This should tend toward an extreme situation of capital moving in large amounts from areas of relatively less to areas of relatively more return, and eventually evening out the return. Discussion thus far, however, should have given the understanding that investments are domiciled in one place or another for many reasons other than return alone. Even within a country, the rate of return varies among industries, and within industries it varies from being a profit to being a loss. At the same time, the irregularity of earnings in any enterprise renders comparisons of qualified value.

Within recognized limitations, the postwar spread between foreign and domestic earnings is worth noting. For the years 1946 through 1950, the comparison was as indicated in the following tabulation.

Earnings	1946	1947	1948	1949	1950
Rates of return on United States direct investments abroad*	10.7	14.3	16.6	13.8	14.9
Rates of return on leading domestic corporations†	9.5	12.3	14.0	11.0	13.4

* Data provided by Office of Business Economics, U.S. Department of Commerce.
† Net income after taxes, related to net worth. Data compiled by National City Bank of New York and published in its *Monthly Letter on Economic Conditions*, April, 1948; April, 1949; April, 1951; and April, 1952.

Qualifying the data are the following points: (1) Basic data are less exact for the foreign than for the domestic figures; (2) direct-investment data are before United States income taxes, while domestic data are after taxes; (3) data for domestic corporations include foreign operations; and (4) domestic data are only for leading corporations, while foreign data are less selective. Furthermore, from the point of view of an individual investor, the occasional wide swings in the market value of listed securities is a factor rendering difficult a comparison of rates of return. He would buy on market price—not book value as determined by net worth.

Return Varies with Activity and Geographic Location. Also to be noted is the wide range of returns among types of activity and among geographic locations. For the years 1946 through 1948, this is shown in Table 44. While petroleum investments would appear to have been the most profitable over-all, this activity was not the most profitable in several areas. And there is not sufficient uniformity to single out any area as having been more fruitful than any other, percentagewise, although

Table 44. Ratio of Earnings to Equity of United States Direct Investments, 1946–1948

(By industry and area)

Area	Total	Man-ufac-tur-ing	Dis-tribu-tion	Agri-cul-ture	Min-ing and smelt-ing	Pe-tro-leum	Pub-lic util-ities	Mis-cella-neous
1946 Total.............	10.9	11.9	13.8	14.3	7.5	17.1	3.7	7.0
Canada...............	9.7	12.9	14.8	2.3	7.7	6.4	4.1	6.3
American republics......	13.2	16.3	22.5	17.5	9.8	20.8	3.6	23.3
OEEC countries........	7.4	10.2	9.2	....	0.8	3.1	....	2.9
OEEC dependencies.....	14.2	1.7	6.9	0.5	3.0	27.0	....	5.6
Other Europe..........	1.3	1.7	0.5	....	....	1.7	3.0	4.2
Rest of world..........	19.2	9.4	20.6	....	20.3	29.4	3.7	15.8
1947 Total.............	13.7	14.8	11.9	16.3	10.0	23.9	4.0	8.2
Canada...............	12.5	17.2	13.4	11.5	10.3	9.1	4.8	6.8
American republics......	16.0	19.4	20.4	19.2	13.4	25.2	3.8	20.3
OEEC countries........	8.4	11.2	8.0	....	0.3	5.2	....	4.9
OEEC dependencies.....	23.5	11.4	....	2.2	12.8	40.4	....	9.7
Other Europe..........	0.9	1.2	2.0	....	....	1.3	1.0	0.4
Rest of world..........	24.4	12.2	14.9	....	....	40.3	4.0	22.6
1948 Total.............	15.6	17.6	14.7	11.9	10.6	26.8	2.4	8.5
Canada...............	14.0	20.2	24.5	....	6.7	9.8	4.0	7.4
American republics......	17.4	19.8	23.0	14.4	18.4	28.4	1.6	16.6
OEEC countries........	10.2	14.4	5.1	....	1.7	8.5	....	5.4
OEEC dependencies.....	20.0	16.2	24.4	0.4	5.8	28.3	....	1.3
Other Europe..........	1.3	1.6	3.7	....	....	0.8	3.8	0.4
Rest of world..........	29.1	17.7	12.2	....	30.6	43.6	4.6	17.5

SOURCE: *The Balance of International Payments of the United States,1946–48*, U.S. Department of Commerce, 1950, pp. 93–96.

OEEC countries, OEEC dependencies, and other European countries appear to have been in general not such profitable areas in many industries as were other areas shown.

The Record

Despite the wide attention given the problem of foreign investments in the postwar period, especially with a view to encouraging new investments, the record of many countries or their subjects is not such as to invite confidence. Defaults and repudiations may be charged to international borrowers of most countries, such defaults being as to either

principal or interest. Some United States borrowers are in this group.
The record shows, further, that some governments have bought up de-
faulted obligations at the time they claimed to have been short of ex-
change with which to pay interest on such obligations. On this point, the
Chairman of the Executive Committee, Foreign Bondholders Protective
Council, Inc., stated in the 1939 *Annual Report:*[7]

. . . while governments allege they are unable to find either funds or dollar
exchange to pay the interest and sinking fund on their bonds, nevertheless,
such governments (many, and indeed most of them) have been able to find
both funds and dollar exchange to buy up in our markets their own bonds
at the very low prices at which the bonds are selling due to their own wilful
default. . . .

Excellent studies of foreign obligations outstanding in the United
States have been made by the Institute of International Finance of New
York University, which states that $3,922,492,000 of publicly offered
foreign bonds were outstanding on Dec. 31, 1950. The Institute's *Bulletin* 172 (June 18, 1951) reports that of 32 foreign countries with public
or private dollar bonds outstanding at the end of 1950, interest was in
default on some obligations of borrowers in 26 of them. Principal was in
default on some issues of 19, and only 5 were not in default either as to
interest, principal, or sinking-fund requirements on some one or more
issues.

Large Amounts of Foreign Dollar Bonds in Default. Table 45, also

Table 45. Status of Publicly Offered Foreign Dollar Bonds
(In per cent, at year end)

Year	Debt service paid in full	In default as to	
		Interest	Sinking fund or principal
1945	50.8	46.8	2.4
1946	50.0	47.6	2.4
1947	51.8	46.6	1.6
1948	54.5	43.8	1.7
1949	57.5	40.7	1.8
1950	65.2	33.0	1.8

SOURCE: *Bulletins* 150 (June 30, 1947); 156 (June 21, 1948); 167 (June 12, 1950);
172 (June 18, 1951).

from the Institute of International Finance, shows that close to half of
the publicly offered foreign dollar bonds were in some degree of default
in the early postwar period. No single geographic area or type of bor-

[7] Cited in Lewis, *op. cit.,* p. 144.

rower was especially responsible for these defaults; they were general. For example, 25.2 per cent of Latin-American bonds and 75.6 per cent of European bonds outstanding were in default as to interest. As to type of borrower, 35.6 per cent of foreign national government dollar bonds was in default as to interest; 14.7 per cent of bonds of states, provinces, and departments was in similar straits, as were 33.9 per cent of municipals and 37.4 per cent of foreign corporation bonds.[8]

It is only proper to mention that, although most defaults go back to the early 1930s and some even beyond, several of the countries involved were ravaged by war or have fallen under internal revolution, and there is little hope of their obligations being honored in the foreseeable future.

The Marketing of Foreign Securities in the United States

During the period 1919 to 1930, more than $8,000,000,000 of foreign securities were placed in this country for new capital, about one-third of which subsequently went into default.[9] This experience was possibly a strong influence in the fact that in the period 1946 to 1948, only three countries (Canada, Norway, and the Netherlands) and the International Bank for Reconstruction and Development sold dollar bonds to private investors in the United States. These issues amounted to $413,000,000; of these, the International Bank accounted for $244,500,000 and Canada for $150,000,000, the latter being for the purpose of repaying an Export-Import Bank loan.[10]

Many of these securities were offered publicly through investment houses, but a good part of the borrowing was placed on the market privately by negotiation direct with the purchaser. Other means by which foreign securities may reach American investors is by their being listed on an exchange in the United States, with international transactions taking place through it, or by an American investor making the purchase through a foreign securities exchange. For the week ended Oct. 14, 1950, for example, transactions took place on the New York Stock Exchange involving 91 issues of foreign bonds. These reflected as wide a variation in price as is found on domestic issues. Government of Belgium 7s of 1955 moved at 110, Peruvian 7s of 1959 (in default) were at 30, and Kreuger and Toll 5s of 1959, also in default, were moving at practically a complete loss—87.5 cents per $100 bond. The transactions could, of course, have taken place domestically, that is, not involving an international transfer.

In the way of corporate stocks, some American concerns, such as International Telephone and Telegraph Company, operate primarily in

---

[8] *Bulletin* 172, Institute of International Finance, pp. 28–29.
[9] *The Balance of International Payments of the United States, 1946–48*, p. 139·
[10] *Ibid.*, pp. 264–265.

foreign countries, while others are less fully in foreign operations. However, stocks or corporations organized under the laws of foreign countries
are also listed on the New York Stock Exchange or the New York Curb
Exchange. In late 1950, the listing of foreign securities (both bonds and
stocks) was as indicated in the tabulation below.

Foreign securities	Number on New York Stock Exchange	Number on New York Curb Exchange
Common-stock issues.............	18	91
Preferred-stock issues.............	3	10
Corporate-bond issues.............	41	28*
Foreign-government (including sub-divisions) issues................	182	17*

* Nineteen of these were German issues on which dealings had been suspended.
SOURCE: Data through courtesy of New York Stock Exchange.

The marketing process pertains, of course, only to the "portfolio" group
of investments, as the direct type are ordinarily branch or subsidiary
operations, with ownership held by the parent for long periods. An activity such as International Telephone and Telegraph would be a direct
investment, as far as the corporation is concerned, and the corporation
would have received the larger part of its funds by the issuance of
securities domestically.

The Responsibility of a Creditor Nation

Two points of view must be considered in weighing this problem—the
nation as a whole and the individual investors involved. In raising the
question, it is because of evidence that the credit mechanism may at
times offer to the borrower an overly easy means of going into debt.
Competition among investment houses for foreign issues, for example,
has been given as one reason why some foreign borrowers have gone
into debt extravagantly.

More Goods or Services Must Be Bought Abroad. From the national
point of view, being a creditor nation means that foreign debtors' requirements result in a net demand for its currency with which to pay
interest and dividends; developing into a creditor nation means that the
demand for its currency relative to debtors' demands for foreign currency
is increasing. Fitting this development into the picture of total international transactions means that *something additional* must be bought from
abroad in order to make dollars, in our case, available for the obligation.
This may call for a reexamination of policy with regard to imports of
merchandise or to purchases of other services. Simply making additional

foreign investments is far from the answer for this merely postpones and aggravates a fundamental lack of balance.

Productivity and Capacity to Pay Are Essential Considerations. The first consideration of any creditor, assuming that he is satisfied as to the borrower's character, must be to assure himself that the borrower has capacity to pay. Internationally, it means satisfaction that the loan or investment is put to productive use and that the earnings therefrom may be converted into the currency of the creditor.

Take, for example, the construction of a power plant or a transportation facility in a foreign country. That development could provide power to reach every resident at the lowest price in the world; the lights could burn and the radios could play all day and all night. Or the transportation system could offer movement at such low rates that every citizen could travel from one end of the country to the other many times a year. Yet these, in themselves, would not yield one cent of foreign exchange, even for the payment of interest or dividends, let alone amortization or repayment of principal. "Productivity" alone, we must understand, is not enough; what is called for is *productivity of something exportable.*

But even production of something exportable is not enough in itself. "Exportable" must mean not only something a country can afford to have leave its borders—a sort of surplus production. It also contemplates that there must be a recipient. Some country must do the importing—the creditor country—either direct or indirect.

It must be said, then, that the prime responsibility of a creditor nation is to be willing to be paid in goods or services which the debtor nations produce or in foreign exchange which they can obtain for what they produce. This sounds simple enough, but the individuals who receive the funds from abroad are not the same as those whose markets and jobs are affected by competition of foreign producers seeking entry into domestic markets.

From the viewpoint of the individual creditor, the productivity of the loan probably stands first. He must see to it that the loan is sound economically and will be used for productive purposes. It must not be used, for example, for building statues or zoos or parks. He is, of course, concerned with the capacity to transfer, as an added risk to foreign investment, but the underlying credit problems are the same as in domestic investments.

Debtor Has Basic Responsibilities. This is not to suggest that the borrower or debtor individual, company, or country has no responsibility in the matter. It, too, is or should be as much concerned over the possibility of repayment *under unfavorable conditions* as should the creditor. However, for many years, the retirement of public obligations has not been looked upon in the same light in some countries as it has been in the

United States. The concept of "obligations" in perpetuity has been apparently readily accepted by some countries, and it may be that the tremendous United States public debt, whose liquidation would involve several generations of citizens, may bring about a similar view on our part as to public debt.

There is apparently no satisfactory manner in which a nation may prevent individuals or businesses in it from going too much into foreign indebtedness or into unsound undertakings without lifting from them their free right of contract. In those countries practicing exchange control, it may be made difficult or impossible for the "borrower" to obtain foreign exchange to satisfy foreign obligations; in other cases, somewhat less drastic, the nation may legislate that a certain part of the capital stock of corporations must be reserved for domestic interests, or it may prohibit foreign ownership of dominant interest in certain lines of economic activity.

International Investment Position of the United States

Since earliest days, and for over a century, the United States has been a debtor nation to the rest of the world. The development of transportation, banks, industry, and even agriculture has been aided for generations by the use of foreign capital in amounts over and above available savings. Governments, both federal and state, have also enjoyed the privilege of operating on funds borrowed from abroad.

United States a Debtor Nation until First World War. It is generally agreed that the United States was a debtor nation until the First World War, when large loans by the government plus big volumes of exports for war purposes brought the world as a whole into debtor status with us. Of course, many individual and public debtors in the United States remained in "debt" to foreigners and still are. And prior to this time, many United States interests had begun to acquire foreign investments. Excluding war debts, the international investment position for selected years has been estimated as below.[11]

Year	Net Status
1919	$3,700,000,000 creditor
1930	8,800,000,000 creditor
1933	9,500,000,000 creditor
1939	340,000,000 debtor

[11] *The United States in the World Economy,* U.S. Department of Commerce Economic Series 28, 1943, p. 123, and *International Transactions of the United States during the War, 1940–45,* U.S. Department of Commerce Economic Series 65, 1948, p. 110. Evidence of the caution with which these figures must be read is shown by a revision of the 1939 figure from $1,800,000,000 creditor, reported in the first reference cited. Also, a different estimate for 1939 was made by a leading writer in the field. Lewis, *op. cit.,* p. 26, estimates our net position to have been about on balance, neither net creditor nor net debtor.

It may be noted that our creditor status fell considerably between 1930 and 1939, even though our net exports of merchandise for the period were reported at over $3,000,000,000. Chief among the causes of this change were the following estimated volumes of transactions:

United States long-term capital abroad decreased by $907,000,000.
Foreign long-term capital in the United States increased by $1,121,-000,000.
United States short-term capital abroad decreased net $858,000,000.
Foreign short-term capital in the United States increased net $3,037,000,000.

These net changes account for about $6,000,000,000 of the reduction. The remainder may be explained as due to, among other things, variations in market value or other factors, including the possibility of error and omission.

This great shift in investment position was brought about chiefly by the movement of capital from Europe, which was being threatened with war, into the United States. Not only did United States investments abroad, long and short term, decrease substantially, but foreign investments in the United States, particularly short term, increased sufficiently to account for the major portion of the change. It may clarify the change to recall that the process of a foreigner building up bank deposits or buying stocks or bonds in the United States makes us a debtor and thereby reduces our "net" creditor position, and the process of our liquidating bank deposits or investments abroad reduces our status as a creditor.

War and Postwar Changes. Defaults by foreign debtors, the great economic depression, flight of capital to the United States, and the Johnson Act of 1934 all served to make the decade of the 1930s one in which United States investments abroad decreased and were not replaced by new undertakings, and one in which United States holdings belonging to foreigners increased substantially. The decade of the 1940s was entered with the United States a net debtor by about $340,000,000. By the end of 1945, the position had changed to a debtor status of about $550,000,000, as shown in Table 46. During this time, both United States investments abroad and foreign investments in the United States increased, but our increased investments abroad were mainly of the long-term type, while increased foreign investments in the United States were principally of a short-term nature. Thus, the international investment position did not change materially up to 1945.

Beginning in 1946, however, international reconstruction and private opportunities pent up during the war, plus a new emphasis on the role of foreign investment as the savior of foreign export markets, all contributed to a relatively sudden and great expansion of United States investments abroad, both private and public.

Table 46. International Investment Position of the United States, 1939–1951
(Year-end data in millions of dollars)

Year	Net long term	Net short term	Net position
1939	+$ 2,575	−$2,915	−$ 340
1940	+ 3,140	− 4,400	− 1,260
1941	+ 4,760	− 4,070	+ 690
1942	+ 5,240	− 4,205	+ 1,035
1943	+ 5,425	− 5,400	+ 25
1944	+ 5,410	− 5,685	− 275
1945	+ 6,821	− 7,369	− 548
1946	+ 11,222	− 6,699	+ 4,523
1947	+ 19,314	− 6,714	+ 12,600
1948	+ 21,935	− 7,317	+ 14,618
1949	+ 22,729	− 7,553	+ 15,176
1950	+ 22,869	− 8,324	+ 14,545
1951	+ 24,200	− 9,300	+ 14,900

SOURCE: 1939–1944: *International Transactions of the United States during the War, 1940–45,* U.S. Department of Commerce Series 65, 1948, p. 110; 1945–1948: *The Balance of International Payments of the United States, 1946–48,* U.S. Department of Commerce, 1950, p. 162; 1949: *Foreign Commerce Weekly,* Apr. 2, 1951; 1950–1951: *Foreign Commerce Weekly,* Apr. 21, 1952.

Greatest Change Occurred in Government Investments. During the postwar period, the greatest change in these transactions occurred in United States government foreign investments. From foreign holdings of about $80,000 at the end of 1940,[12] the United States government expanded its credits abroad until they were about $13,800,000,000 at the end of 1951. Since foreigners held about $5,400,000,000 of United States obligations in 1951, the net government position was about $8,400,000,000. This compares with a net debtor position of $230,000,000 in 1940, at which time foreigners held obligations of the United States government in the amount of $310,000,000.

No Uniform Investment Position by Area. As in all other types of international transactions, there is no uniform distribution by country or area in so far as foreign investment position is concerned. This holds both for our investments abroad and for the foreign ownership of holdings in the United States. Table 47 shows our investment position by area, in detail as between long- and short-term, and private and public interests.

[12] Excluding war debts of the First World War.

Table 47. International Investment Position of United States, by Area, End of 1950

(In millions of dollars)

Item	Total	Canada	American republics	OEEC countries	OEEC dependencies	Other Europe	Other foreign countries	International institutions
United States investments abroad:								
Private..............	$21,018	$7,298	$6,073	$ 4,220	$605	$ 663	$1,932	$ 22
Long-term.........	19,377	7,048	5,514	3,682	588	601	1,717	22
Direct............	13,550	3,850	5,065	2,272	561	349	1,453	
Foreign dollar bonds.....	1,702	1,113	159	71		17	115	22
Other.............	4,125	2,085	290	1,339	27	235	149	
Short-term.........	1,641	250	559	538	17	62	215	
Deposits..........	598	145	70	277	6	36	64	
Other.............	1,043	105	489	261	11	26	151	
United States government......	13,676	11	455	8,515	75	478	713	3,421
Long-term..........	13,364	9	445	8,286	73	477	645	3,421
Short-term.........	312	2	10	229	2	1	68	
Total.........	$34,694	$7,309	$6,528	$12,735	$680	$1,141	$2,645	$3,655
Foreign investments in United States:								
Private............	$14,959	$2,123	$2,475	$ 7,999	$398	$ 219	$1,570	$ 175
Long-term..........	8,457	1,696	803	5,333	197	125	300	3
Direct............	3,293	876	141	2,158	18	25	75	
Corporate stocks.....	3,190	608	392	1,966	75	20	129	3
Other.............	1,974	212	270	1,209	104	80	96	
Short-term........	6,502	427	1,672	2,666	201	94	1,270	172
Deposits..........	5,831	393	1,549	2,303	131	72	1,255	128
Other.............	671	34	123	363	70	22	15	44
United States government obligations..	5,190	1,055	150	895	81	20	381	1,836
Long-term........	1,415	511	86	443	37	17	36	285
Short-term*.......	3,775	544	64	452	44	3	345	1,551
Total........	$20,149	$3,178	$2,625	$ 8,894	$479	$ 239	$1,951	$2,011
Net debtor (−) or creditor (+).....	+$14,545	+$4,131	+$3,903	+$ 3,841	+$201	+$ 902	+$ 694	+$1,645
Private account......	+ 6,059	+ 5,175	+ 3,598	− 3,779	+ 207	+ 444	+ 362	+ 52
United States government account....	+ 8,486	+ 1,044	+ 305	+ 7,620	− 6	+ 458	+ 332	+$1,593
Long-term.........	+ 22,869	+ 4,850	+ 5,070	+ 6,192	+ 427	+ 936	+ 2,026	+ 3,368
Short-term.......	− 8,324	− 719	− 1,167	− 2,351	− 226	− 34	− 1,332	− 1,723

* Includes estimated $772,000,000 of U.S. currency and coin held abroad, not distributed by area.

Source: U.S. Department of Commerce.

United States a Net Creditor to All Regions in 1950. Perhaps the most striking feature of our international investment position in 1950 was the fact that the United States was a net creditor to all the regions shown. However, while we were a net creditor to all areas on long-term account, the position was reversed in all areas on short-term account. This may be said to reflect the heavy United States direct investments abroad and the *relative* confidence which foreigners and their governments have in the United States as compared with our own short-term holdings in other countries. Unsettled political and economic conditions and the impact of exchange controls and other governmental measures are the primary cause of this condition.

United States a Debtor on Private Account to Europe. Of significance, also, is the fact of our being a net debtor on *private* account to Western European countries, which is not out of order, although this "indebtedness" was reduced from $4,303,000,000 in 1945 to $3,779,000,000 in 1950. This change of about $525,000,000 was brought about by increases in our long-term investments in Europe of a little over $610,000,000, increases of about $190,000,000 in our short-term claims on OEEC countries, an increase of about $125,000,000 in their holdings of long-term investments in the United States, and an increase of about $150,000,000 in their short-term claims on us.

The fact that the United States is a net *debtor* on government account to Canada and Canadian interests is a tribute to Canada's ability to stand on its own feet without government loans from the United States. In fact, private United States long-term investments in Canada increased by over $1,800,000,000 between 1945 and 1950. In strong contrast to this is the United States government position with respect to OEEC countries, most of which were, it is only fair to say, physically damaged by the war.

Principal Creditor and Debtor Nations of the World

Just as the uneven distribution of resources, population, and skills has resulted in the development of multilateral trade, with producers concentrating in those fields in which they seem to feel that they have an advantage over competition, the uneven trade and personal incomes and human characteristics have resulted in a varying degree of capital accumulation. From this have come different degrees and rates of economic development.

Those countries whose citizens have been more energetic and at times favored with more or a better distribution of resources, have been able to experience greater incomes, greater savings, and greater capital formation. From the individual whose savings have enabled him to become a capitalist of sorts, the concept of owning more than is owed may be projected onto a national and an international basis. The result is that some countries are called creditor nations. There must be a debtor, of course, for every creditor.

This section reviews the international investment position of several of the important nations with the intent of determining which countries have been traditionally creditor and which traditionally debtor.

Basic Statistics Not Very Satisfactory. Preceding pages in this chapter should have left an impression of doubt as to the exactness of data pertaining to our international investment position. Yet on this point, the United States stands out as the country with probably the most complete published information. But the lack of uniformity in information for each country leaves much to be desired in the matter of accurate data regarding foreign investments.

Perhaps the difficulty may be best illustrated by comparing the foreign investment position to a balance sheet of a corporation, showing condition as of one date. The Balance of Payments, or Summary of International Transactions, would represent the operating, or profit-and-loss statement. Reliability of the data then depends on the thoroughness and accuracy of the original inventory and on the completeness and accuracy of reported transactions during the years that follow. The term "reported" is used advisedly in preference to "recorded," for there is no formal recording of the several international transactions, and nothing at all in the nature of a double-entry set of books. The best we have, then, is an estimate.

It has already been shown that the United Nations is just beginning to accumulate relatively uniform data on balances of payments by countries. Until this can be done, the reliance to be placed on estimates of foreign investment position must be well guarded. Even after the acquisition of uniform data, the possibility of adjustments of one type or another, not the result of reported transactions, must be acknowledged.

It may be that, based on inventories of foreign investment holdings by the nationals of countries at war, and the continuing imposition of exchange controls which either prohibit or limit severely further transactions in securities, the investment picture by country is more reliable than we may be led to believe. At any rate, it is the only thing available and the best use must be made of it.

The Historical Development. World economic development since the discovery of America, the rise and fall of several European nations as dominant in the world, the period of colonization, the industrial revolution, and other modern great developments left Great Britain, France, the Netherlands, Belgium, and, to some extent, other European countries as the principal creditor nations by about 1900. At the outbreak of the First World War, Great Britain was the leading creditor country of the world and continued to hold that position in 1938.[13] It is estimated that its net long-term position was probably about $21,000,000,000, and the net short-term position about $3,700,000,000 debtor, leaving a net creditor position of about $17,000,000,000.

1938 and 1947 Positions Compared. In her thorough study, *The United States and Foreign Investment Problems,* Dr. Cleona Lewis has developed what is called an International Investment Map of the World, 1938.[14] This feature shows that of more than 65 countries enjoying relative political independence, only 10 were in the creditor class on long-term account. Further, only 5 had net investments of $1,000,000,000 or more. Her data show that over 63 per cent of the world total of foreign investments was held by 6 creditor nations of Western Europe—Belgium, France, the Netherlands, Sweden, Switzerland, and the United Kingdom. The other major creditor nation at that time was the United States, and creditors by rather small balances were Japan, Portugal, and Italy.[15]

As would be expected, the development of their colonial possessions accounted for a large part of the investments held by nationals of the countries named. And Japan and Italy are credited with being creditor countries as a result of their invasions of nearby areas.

The general long-term investment positions of the countries listed as creditors by Dr. Lewis appear in the accompanying table. The lack of

Country	Investments (000,000,000 omitted)	Obligations (000,000,000 omitted)	Net investments (000,000,000 omitted)
United Kingdom............	$22.9	$2+	$21+
United States.............	11.5	7.0	4.5
Netherlands..............	4.8	0.5	4.3
France..................	3.9	0.6	3.3
Switzerland..............	1.6	0.2	1.4
Belgium.................	1.3	0.4	0.9
Japan...................	1.2	0.5	0.7
Sweden..................	0.4		
Portugal.................	0.4		
Italy....................	0.4		

SOURCE: Cleona Lewis, *The United States and Foreign Investment Problems* (Washington, Brookings Institution, 1948), p. 49.

figures in the second and third columns for the last three countries listed is due to inadequate information.

[13] Lewis, *op. cit.,* p. 40.
[14] *Ibid.,* p. 37.
[15] *Ibid.,* p. 40.

Of the principal debtor countries, only 11 were debtor by as much as $1,000,000,000 in 1938, as shown on the following tabulation of indebtedness for these countries.

Country	Obligations (000,000,000 omitted)	Investments (000,000,000 omitted)	Net obligations (000,000,000 omitted)
Canada	$6.6	$1.9	$4.7
Australia	3.7	0.3	3.4
Argentina	3.2	0.04	3.2
India	2.8		
China	2.6	0.8	1.8
Germany	2.7	0.7	2.0
Netherlands East Indies	2.4		
Brazil	2.0		
Mexico	1.8	0.02	1.8
South Africa and Rhodesia	1.4		
Chile	1.3	0.02	1.3

SOURCE: Cleona Lewis, *The United States and Foreign Investment Problems* (Washington, Brookings Institution, 1948), p. 50.

In several of these countries, the per capita income is quite high, higher, in fact, than in some of the "creditor" countries listed.

It was estimated that by 1947, owing to the impact of war, political changes, nationalizing of certain industries, and other factors associated with war expenditures, the international investment position of several countries had changed substantially.

Outstanding Changes Experienced by Great Britain. Perhaps the outstanding shift has been that experienced by Great Britain. It was estimated by Dr. Lewis that, as of December, 1947, Great Britain had shifted from a creditor to a debtor status.[16] This great change was brought about by the following principal factors:

1. Sale of some overseas investments by the British
2. Repurchase of some of their securities from the British by countries such as Canada, South Africa, and Argentina (this is the same as a sale by the British, but the impelling motive is different)
3. The freezing of sterling balances belonging to other countries
4. Reduction of British balances by other countries
5. Large loans by the United States government to the British government

The Netherlands and Belgium were still reported to be in creditor status as of December, 1947, as were Switzerland, Sweden, and Portugal.

[16]*Ibid.,* p. 62.

France's position was rather undecided, by a narrow margin in either case, and Germany, Japan, and Italy will have lost large parts of their foreign holdings and will no doubt fall into the debtor class.

Of the debtor nations in 1938, several improved their international investment position by 1947; Argentina is estimated to have changed into creditor status in the interim. More recent authentic figures, however, are not available.

The Point Four Program as It Affects Foreign Investments

Characteristic of much of the economic writings since the Second World War is the so-called "expansionist" approach to economic problems. It is either inherent or implicit in many of the policies adopted by governments. Part of this view has to do with the economic and optimum use of resources—human and material. This is to be found in hearings on bills introduced into Congress for the purpose of implementing the broad concept now identified as Point Four, in which was brought out the high priority given the maintenance of a high level of employment and production. Part of the same is found in such utterances as the following: "It is no longer possible to rely entirely upon the vigorous expansive power of private enterprise and investment."[17] What is called for by this approach is working the economy under forced draft, on the assumption that social ambitions of the welfare state cannot adequately be accomplished if the impetus to economic activity is left to private enterprise.

Origin of Point Four. This line of thought was advanced in the inaugural address of President Truman in January, 1949, when he said:

> We must embark on a bold new program for making the benefits of our scientific advances and our industrial progress available for the improvement and growth of underdeveloped areas . . . we should make available to peace-loving peoples the benefits of our store of technical knowledge in order to help them realize their aspirations for a better life. And, in cooperation with other nations, we should foster capital investment in areas needing development. Our aim should be to help the free peoples of the world, through their own efforts, to produce more food, more clothing, more materials for housing, and more mechanical power to lighten their burdens.

The meaning of these lines will be better understood if beside them are placed three other points which the President suggested as major courses of action that we should follow in our international affairs. These were (1) continued support of the United Nations and its related agencies, (2) continuance of our foreign-aid program for reconstruction and re-

[17] J. B. Condliffe, *Point Four: Economic Development* (report summarizing papers prepared by graduate students in seminar on economic development, conducted by Teaching Institute of Economics, University of California), Foreign Policy Association, Headline Series 79, New York, January-February, 1950.

covery, and (3) the strengthening of freedom-loving nations against the dangers of aggression.

The Point Four concept, thus, proposed two broad aspects leading toward economic development and expansion of the world. These were the interchange among nations of technical knowledge and skill and the fostering of capital investment. It is the latter which concerns us now.

In support of this fostering of capital investment abroad, a bill was introduced into the 81st Congress (H.R. 5594; S. 2197) to amend the Export-Import Bank Act by adding to its powers the power "to guarantee United States private capital invested in productive enterprises abroad which contribute to economic development in foreign countries against risks peculiar to such investment." This is a power and responsibility distinct from that of credit insurance, as discussed in a preceding chapter, and would amend the fundamental purpose of the Export-Import Bank. The bill was designed to implement the Point Four proposal and to induce American enterprise to come to the support of foreign policy.

In hearings on these bills, it was stated by Secretary of the Treasury Snyder that principal obstacles to foreign investment could be traced to four difficulties:[18]

1. The antiforeign sentiment generated by the regrettable experience of some countries with investments from abroad
2. The growth of ideologies favoring state ownership and control of industry
3. The existence of political instability and extreme nationalism
4. The prevalence of exchange controls stemming from economic difficulties

In a more succinct expression, Winthrop Aldrich, Chairman of the President's Advisory Committee on Foreign Financial Problems, stated that the two great obstacles were fear of the transfer problem and fear of expropriation.[19]

Guarantee Provisions Would Cover "Political" Risks. In view of these obstacles as outlined, the bill was drawn up to cover three points: (1) inability to convert earnings in foreign exchange into dollars, (2) expropriation without adequate compensation, and (3) physical destruction by war.

The program would be frankly experimental, as there has been practically no experience with programs of this kind. It was pointed out by Secretary of the Treasury Snyder that at that time (1949) it was impossible to determine precisely the type of risks which should be covered,

---

[18] "Foreign Investment Guaranties," *Hearings before the Committee on Banking and Currency on S. 2197,* U.S. Senate, 81st Cong., 1st Sess. (1949), p. 3.
[19] *Ibid.,* p. 30.

the effectiveness of such a guarantee in stimulating foreign investment, and the possibility of loss to the United States.[20]

In connection with the latter, if such a guarantee scheme were to be adopted the risks avoided by individual investors would have to be assumed by someone else—in this case the United States government and eventually the public, except as any losses could be covered or avoided by a reserve fund set up from fees to be charged those whose investments are insured; by success of the government in recapturing from foreign governments any "losses" assumed under the guarantee scheme; and by prearrangement between the United States government and others on a bilateral basis in matters relating to rights and remedies of individual investors placing funds in the foreign countries and being covered by the United States guarantee scheme.

The idea of bilateral treaties between the United States government and others in the matter of foreign investments is closely related to the fundamental principle of reciprocal national treatment, described in Chapter 19. The State Department has been active in negotiating a number of treaties to bring about a basic understanding with the governments of countries needing foreign investment as to treatment which will be accorded foreign capital by these respective countries. These treaties provide that (1) property of investors will not be expropriated without prompt and adequate compensation; (2) investors will be given a reasonable opportunity to remit earnings and withdraw their capital; (3) investors will have reasonable freedom to manage, operate, and control their enterprises; and (4) they will enjoy security in the protection of their persons and property, and nondiscriminatory treatment in the conduct of their business affairs.[21]

Assuming, now, that private investors could be induced to place a number of new investments abroad and that any of the operative clauses would place the burden of loss on the government, an interesting question develops as to whether the United States government should resort to force to collect on the default. On this point, the House Committee on Banking and Currency queried the Under Secretary of State, James E. Webb, who submitted the following statement:[22]

I should like to add that a United States Government guaranty of American investments abroad should operate to reinforce our policy. If, through events in another country, American investors should be deprived of their property, they would be reimbursed by the Export-Import Bank and would not, there-

---

[20] *Ibid.,* p. 5.

[21] *Ibid.,* p. 17.

[22] "Export-Import Bank Loan Guaranty Authority," *Hearings before the Committee on Banking and Currency on H. R. 5594,* U.S. House of Representatives 81st Cong., 1st Sess. (1949), p. 57.

fore, be under pressure to urge the United States Government to take drastic action in order to preserve their property rights. The United States Government, on the other hand, would then have a financial claim against the foreign government which could be settled in accordance with the contemplated intergovernmental agreement for handling such cases, or could be subject to arbitration or decision of the International Court of Justice. Such a claim would have the same general status as other claims which often arise between governments. Certainly, it would defeat the very purpose of the Point IV program and would violate our international commitments if we intervened in the affairs of another nation in order to protect guaranteed investments, and we have no intention whatever of doing so.

There is always the possibility that agreements made with one government may be terminated by its successor, and the line of questioning which elicited the statement above had to do with the possibility that United States authorities might be attempting to keep friendly governments in power, thus, in effect, guaranteeing the stability of existing governments.

Objections to Proposed Program. Some of the objections to the proposed guarantee scheme have to do with policy, others with technical difficulties. Among the former are fears that such a program would entrench governments more completely in economic life in that it would funnel more activity through government hands. There is also the fear that fairly successful businesses in the United States may find their competition in foreign markets underwritten by their own government; this could happen, for instance, to a company which was selling in a foreign market through an agent or through some other arrangement because it concluded that all factors pointed to that as the best way of doing its business. Its competition, a domestic concern, might take advantage of government insurance of some of its risks and thereby be in a position to undersell the already "established" company.

Some people will feel that if foreign governments do not wish our capital sufficiently to make it attractive to private investors, we should keep out; all they need do, for instance, is make it sufficiently attractive to induce *one* substantial investor to run the risk. And the investor could be a national of that country, with foreign holdings, who could hire the engineering and managerial services of United States technicians if that is what is desired by the foreign country. The same line of thought would conclude that if the proposition is not good enough to justify the risk by private investors, the investment should not be made. A government guarantee would remove some element of this risk. Along this line, the fear may be expressed, with some justification, that such a program would merely invite exploitation of inexperienced and credulous American investors by foreign traders and their governments and by American promoters.

Technical as well as policy difficulties would arise, for instance, if it became necessary to decide between two applicants for insurance.[23] In one case, they may be asking for insurance to cover a venture in the same country. Or it may be that two applicants would seek government insurance for ventures in different countries—one in a country with political advantages, the other in a country of doubtful political relationship. These two companies might compete in the home market or in each other's foreign domiciles, or in third-country foreign markets. Which should be favored, and why?

What Are the Underdeveloped Areas? One of the principal troubles with catchy generalities is the difficulty of becoming specific about them. No one knows clearly, for instance, what an underdeveloped area is. There is no real measure by which an area may be said to be under- or quarter- or half-developed; one wonders whether there may be any over-developed areas. In hearings on the bills just described, it was decided not to press for the naming of countries or areas which are considered underdeveloped for fear of causing ill feeling on the part of those so designated. Without doubt, some colonial areas would have to be called underdeveloped, as would some countries. But when does a country move over from the underdeveloped to the developed side? Is it to be measured by literacy, wealth, per capita income, distribution of income, land ownership, the right to vote?

Economic opportunities, as we know them, are built on the production or distribution of goods—products or services—and not on areas. The difference in rates of return in different industries in the same area, and at different times, is evidence of the difficulty in classifying an *area* as underdeveloped. Within the United States, there are many areas which are below average. Should they be called underdeveloped? Is it the responsibility of government to prod entrepreneurs into economic development? As long as all goes well, there will be no complaint, but when a few bad years appear, where does it lead?

[23] If the guarantee covered "political" risks only, this might not be a problem; competitors could be equally covered. But it would seem overly trusting to expect that the scheme would not call for some appraisal of the economic *and political* soundness or desirability of one investment over another. The guarantee fund would be limited in amount and, since there is a practical limit on the ability of any country to earn foreign exchange, some measure would have to be developed as a basis for denying the guarantee to any applicant. Perhaps this could be found in the wording of the proposed bill, which reads, in part, " . . . capital invested in productive enterprises abroad which contributes to economic development in foreign countries . . . . ." But, then, what is *economic* development?

A final point in this connection is that the program as proposed pertains only to *new* investment, not to existing foreign risks. If a company domiciled in the United States has a branch plant in a foreign country and the risks named are not covered, would it not have a logical claim against the government if competition were set up abroad under government guarantee which resulted in lowering its rate of return? Of course, one may say that the first company, too, had the chance to expand its plant or build a new one, but many considerations may have led to a decision against such a move, none of which was particularly based on government guarantee. One wonders, also, whether such a program could not lead to foreign governments agreeing to giving franchises only to American companies "clearing" their foreign investment with the United States government.

What Can the Foreign Countries Do? This discussion should ask the question of whether these underdeveloped areas wish to be developed. Naturally, one may always answer in the affirmative with the proviso that certain conditions hold. But who wishes to be developed? The average resident or citizen? The entrepreneur? The government? Why are they not willing to make investment opportunities sufficiently attractive on their own? It must be remembered that the person with funds to invest has his choice of employment of those funds. Moreover, it should be obvious that the borrower is competing with other borrowers, both domestic and foreign, for the use of accumulated capital.

The Venezuelan government, as an example, is alert to this situation, as shown by its Washington embassy's monthly publication, *Venezuela Up-to-Date.* The December, 1950, issue summarizes a report titled "Why Your Investments Are Sound in Venezuela." The report lists a number of specific factors as contributing to a "favorable Venezuelan investment climate," among which are absence of discrimination, availability and transfer of dollars, cooperation of local capital, existence of a fair tax system, and government assistance and protection.

One cannot ignore the need for political stability and governmental efficiency as prime requisites for safety of capital. Along with these in the way of economic development, go such matters as technical training, power and transportation facilities, health, and medical advancement. It may be that the process of more equitable distribution (by our standards) of land and natural resources and greater personal freedom and individual opportunity, as guaranteed by the Constitution of the United States, are basic requisites. In these latter instances, technical and ideological assistance may be called for before investment opportunities may be found fruitful. In any case, the investment must be found fruitful to the investor who, as stated before, looks on such opportunities objectively, comparing them with opportunities in other fields and in other countries. It gets close to the question of whether a man has the moral and political right to invest a million dollars in speedboats when people around him as well as in other countries would like to see that million dollars invested in making more bread and clothing.

REVIEW QUESTIONS

1. Of what do foreign investments consist?
2. What is a creditor nation?
3. Why are investments made abroad rather than domestically?
4. What is the mechanism by which foreign investments are made?
5. May a nation show a decrease in its net foreign investment position even though its own foreign investments have increased? Explain.
6. What is the impact of hot-money transfers on balances of payment?
7. Are foreign investments more profitable than domestic?
8. What may be said to be the politico-economic responsibility of a creditor nation?
9. Describe the international investment position of the United States.
10. What have been the greatest changes in our international investment position since 1945?
11. List the principal creditor and the principal debtor nations of the world.
12. What is the relationship of the Point Four program to foreign investments?
13. Evaluate the guarantee provisions proposed as a stimulus to foreign investments.
14. What can foreign countries do by way of stimulating foreign investments in them?

PART FOUR

Policies

CHAPTER 16

Restrictions on Imports I

In most economic literature over the years, the traditional barrier to world trade has been the import tariff, but developments following the First World War—its wake of shattered economies, wrecked currencies, and dislocation of major trading channels—have resulted in a series of other restrictions which have practically rendered the tariff of secondary importance. The tariff was designed to block trade between individuals. Many of the more recent restrictions are of the type required to carry on the nationalistic or socialistic economic plans of the respective governments. Accordingly, the tariff, compared to such restrictions as quotas and exchange controls, was considered too slow to accomplish the desired ends.

A discussion of restrictions on imports should specify early in its course that, aside from tariffs and other governmental restrictions, there have been and are private restrictions which function through cartels or producer arrangements. But most of those to be considered are governmental in origin and, in several cases, in operation. It is impossible to say which type of restriction is most harmful to the idea of free trade or to the concept of relatively free enterprise in foreign commerce. Accordingly, no attempt is made to arrange these restrictions in order of importance or even of chronological appearance on the international scene.

CUSTOMS DUTIES

Probably the most universal restriction is and has been the tax or duty imposed on merchandise when it enters the national boundary. This tax, commonly called "tariff," dates from antiquity, and is an institution in practically every country in the world. Writings in economics over the past two centuries have dealt in substantial part with discussions of the tariff problem. The discussions have touched many angles, such as the free- vs. the restricted-trade controversy, the place of the tariff in the

325

public-finance picture (tariff for revenue or for protection), and the economic effects of the tariff, both on the importing and on the exporting country. For ease of discussion, the subject will be classified as follows: (1) purpose, (2) time of imposition, (3) basis of application, (4) type of tariff system, and (5) special and additional import duties.

Purpose

From the point of view of primary policy, tariffs may be imposed either for revenue or for protection, as to primary policy. Of course, a tariff for revenue is bound to protect domestic businesses to some extent as a secondary effect, while a tariff for protection is bound to yield some revenue unless the rate of duty is so high as to prohibit importation. But there is a large area in which the tariff may be used for revenue while not, at the same time, providing overly uneconomic protection to domestic businesses. In the past, it has sometimes been argued that a protective tariff is needed for the benefit of "infant" industries; the difficulty is that the infants never seem to grow up, and they soon become so-called "vested interests."

Time of Imposition

Tariffs may be imposed at the time an item enters the country, at the time it is entered by the importer for consumption, on the occasion of its transit through a country, or, as will be seen in a following chapter, at the time of exportation or reexportation. Obviously, the import tariff most generally applies at the time the merchandise enters the country, the physical entry and the entry for consumption being almost simultaneous.

Basis of Application

In putting a tariff system into effect, some measurement must be established, and this will be either a physical unit, value, or a combination of the two. To accommodate the basis of application, three well-recognized types of duty are used—the specific, the ad valorem, and the compound.

Specific Duty Simple to Administer, but Affords Inconsistent Protection. *Specific* duties are those levied on a product according to some physical measurement, such as pound or gallon. Typical is the duty applicable against copper (per pound), hyacinth bulbs (per thousand), gasoline (per gallon), and lumber (per board foot). A perplexing problem, and a constant source of questioning between the importer and the customs appraiser, is the monetary value of an imported product. The specific type of duty does not pose this continuing problem except as to the decision involving classification of the import. Accordingly, it affords the opportunity for a simple and easily administered tariff-collection system, since little judgment is involved in the processing of imports beyond the classification. But the specific duty does not provide the continuous protection against foreign competition demanded by some domestic producers. True, in a period of falling prices, the proportionate burden of the tariff increases, but in an upward price movement, the protection offered by the specific duty decreases with each increase in value of the imported product. Also, the specific duty is not adaptable to all products. Would a duty of $1 or $10 or $100 be feasible to apply to every piece or, say, ton of machinery? Clearly not. Thus the need arises for employment of the two other types of duty.

Ad Valorem Duty More Logical for Some Products. When duties are levied on the basis of value of the item, they are called *ad valorem*. The prescribed legal basis for valuation is described in Chapter 2. These duties must be employed in many cases simply because it is not practicable to apply a specific duty. We could not, for instance, satisfactorily adopt a specific rate applicable to jewelry, machinery, books, or furs. As a protective device, also, the ad valorem basis offers more continuous cushioning against foreign goods than would a specific rate in a period of rising prices.

Compound Duty Required under Certain Conditions. The third type of duty in this category is the *compound* duty. As its name suggests, it consists in part of a specific duty plus a percentage rate based on value. It is used effectively where the processed or manufactured article imported and subject to duty is made from a raw material which is also subject to duty. An example of this application would be that of the duty on raw wool and woolen cloth, the latter being subject to the compound rate, or on wheat and wheat flour. The compound duty is also used in cases in which the physical measurement is easy to accomplish, or simple to administer, but in which varying values of the products make it necessary to compensate for price differentials. Illustrations of this are sardines packed in oil, men's leather gloves, wines, cigars, shoes, and optical glass lenses.

Classification and Valuation Are the Basic Problems. Administratively, relative uncertainty as to classification and uncertainty as to valuation present a most difficult problem. *Classification* is the determination of exactly what a product is, and of what type, in order that the applicable tariff rate may be determined accurately. The customs appraiser is concerned lest he allow the entry of merchandise at less than proper duty; this could work to the disadvantage of the government, from the viewpoint of collection of revenue, to the detriment of the protected domestic industry, from the viewpoint of total cost of the imported product, and to the injury of other importers in the appraiser's own and other customs districts by the workings of competition through total costs. The importer is most definitely concerned from the viewpoint of total cost, which determines his ability to compete with other importers or with domestic producers, and from the viewpoint of his possible prior commitments based on the expectation of a certain duty being applicable. Thus an ever present problem facing the importer is classification and valuation of his merchandise, especially when an ad valorem rate applies, for this uncertainty means that his final costs may be unknown for several months.[1]

An example of the impact of classification is found in a recent case in which an importer brought in miniature replicas of Chinese smoothing irons with copper bowls and enameled handles. He entered them as copper household utensils, dutiable at a 20 per cent ad valorem rate. Customs authorities, however, classified the articles as smokers' articles, bearing a duty of 30 per cent ad valorem.

It could happen, also, that an importer, by an erroneous estimate of duty, might enter the merchandise at a higher value than that determined by customs authorities. Under such circumstances, it might appear proper that a refund be made to the importer. However, Sec. 503 of the Tariff Act of 1930 specifies that the basis for assessment of ad valorem duties is to be the entered (by the importer) or the final appraised (by the collector of customs) value, *whichever is higher.*[2]

Type of Tariff System

The tariff system of any country must specify more than merely the basis for applying a rate of duty against a product. Also to be included is the important consideration of whether the same rate applies to all countries or whether a different set of rates is to be prescribed, to apply to different countries depending on a number of circumstances. In the case of only one rate applying to a product, regardless of the country of origin of the import, the designation of *single-column* tariff is used. In cases in which different rates are applicable, depending on the country of origin, the designation of *multiple-column* tariff is used. Application of the proper rate to the different countries under a multiple-tariff system is determined by and in reality constitutes preferences given one or more countries over others.[3]

[1] In November, 1950, a ruling was issued by the Treasury Department providing for advance information by customs authorities as to classification and valuation. Such advance ruling would be binding on customs.

[2] The proposed customs-simplification act of 1950 would amend the Tariff Act of 1930 to extend relief beyond provisions which recognize clerical errors only. The amendment would make allowance for mistakes of fact or any other inadvertence not amounting to an error in the construction of a law.

[3] An unusual application may be found in the case of Guatemala, which in May,

Closely related to this classification is another by which tariff rates may be described as being of general or individual applicability. A tariff of *general* applicability is the same for all countries to which it applies, while the *conventional* tariff is one which is subject to modification or adjustment by agreement between interested countries. In other words, (the tariff rate generally established may be reduced through negotiation and presumably on a value-received basis. A further distinctive limitation is that the area within which rates may be adjusted by negotiation is commonly well defined as consisting of a *maximum* and a *minimum* figure. Between these two, adjustments may be made.

It may be said that the United States has generally followed the policy of using a single-column tariff, without discrimination among countries. But under the Reciprocal Trade Agreements Act, this has been modified somewhat through negotiations or conventions with several other countries. Under the Act, its unconditional most-favored-nation clause makes concessions available to all countries except those discriminating against the United States. Withholding of concessions was applied for a considerable time during the 1930s against Germany and for a short time against Australia. Under the 1951 extension of the Trade Agreements Act, the President is specifically directed to withhold concessions from the Union of Soviet Socialist Republics or any Communist-dominated area. Further, the Reciprocal Trade Agreements Act specifies the limits within which concessions may be made, and this provides the maximum and minimum rates within which effective rates must rest.

SPECIAL AND ADDITIONAL IMPORT DUTIES

In addition to the foregoing broad framework of tariff systems, some special types of import duties also enter the picture. These are for the purpose of offsetting undesirable action on the part of other countries, such as dumping and the use of subsidies. However, the application of these special rates is a matter of permissive judgment on the part of the President or the Secretary of the Treasury. The Tariff Commission or the Treasury Department is charged with investigating certain conditions to determine whether the situation is such as to call for imposition of the extra duty.

1950, began to apply 100 per cent ad valorem duties to imports from Chile, China, the Dominican Republic, Japan, and Spain. Basis for this action was a decree which permits this high duty against imports of countries with which Guatemala has a trade deficit of more than 75 per cent. Such deficits existed with many other countries, but existing commercial agreements precluded application of the increased duty. *El Imparcial, News Survey,* June 16, 1950, cited in *International Financial News Survey,* International Monetary Fund, June 16, 1950, p. 387.

Antidumping Duties

"Dumping" is the term used to identify the practice of some exporters of selling abroad at less than the comparable price in the home market; the offsetting special rate which may be invoked is called the antidumping duty. Except in unusual circumstances, no one would sell abroad at any price if he could obtain a higher price in his home market; unless importation at this considerably lower price were distinctly harmful to producers in the importing country, there should be no objection to being able to buy at lower prices from abroad. It may be, however, that this practice of dumping goods abroad is for the purpose of driving out domestic competition in the importing country (which would be impractical), of injuring other foreign competition in the importing country, or of temporarily stimulating sales abroad either to gain much-needed exchange or to attain some other goal of a country whose foreign trade is under rather centralized control, either public or private. Of course, lowering the price in the home market of the producer—which means selling at home and abroad at the same price—would eliminate the complaint of dumping, as such.

The antidumping duty (Antidumping Act of 1921) is imposed if the Secretary of the Treasury finds after due investigation that imported merchandise of that class or kind is being sold or is likely to be sold in the United States or elsewhere at less than its fair value and that by reason of the importation of such merchandise a domestic industry is being or is likely to be injured or is prevented from being established. Special dumping duty is assessable on all importations of merchandise, whether dutiable or free; for purposes of application, merchandise is considered to be sold at less than its fair value if the purchase price or exporter's sales price of such merchandise is less than its foreign-market value (or in the absence of such value, than the cost of production). In recent years, antidumping duties have been enforced against wool knitted berets from France, incandescent bulbs and lamps from Japan, woven-wire fencing and netting from Germany, rubber-soled, fabric-topped footwear from Japan, glass frostings from Germany, veneer chair seats from Canada, and ribbon flycatchers from Belgium, Germany, Japan, and the United Kingdom. In December, 1949, the Treasury Department (Treasury Decision 52370) revoked the findings on most of these products, and in late 1950, the only item subject to antidumping duty was wool knitted berets imported from France.

Countervailing Duties

In some instances, exportation of certain products has been stimulated through a subsidy or other direct or indirect aid offered by the government of the producing country. This permits the individual sellers to quote lower commercial prices, with their governments making up what would otherwise be a loss on the transaction. To offset this type of operation, the countervailing duty has been devised. It is applicable only against dutiable goods and in an amount equal to the bounty or grant received by the manufacturer or exporter (Sec. 303, Tariff Act of 1930). Countervailing-duty orders were outstanding against specified products from about eight countries in late 1950, among these being cheese from Canada, sugar from the United Kingdom, wine from Australia, the sugar content of certain articles from Australia, meat products (indirect shipments) from the Netherlands, milk products (indirect shipments) from the Netherlands, silk and silk articles from Italy, shelled almonds from Spain, and butter from Australia, Denmark (indirect shipments), and Lithuania.

The use of multiple exchange rates by several countries, whereby a different price is paid the exporter for foreign exchange derived from the sale of different products, may be looked on as somewhat of a relative subsidy for the exportation of the more favored products. This has been a problem for both customs officials and importers but, since the differential is basically not between the domestic and the export price, the problem has generally been resolved by determination of the rate of exchange to be used for conversion purposes.[4] However, a customs-simplification bill, passed by the House of Representatives in 1951, included a clause to make mandatory the application of countervailing duty when a foreign country uses multiple exchange rates for the purpose of offering a bonus to its exporters.

Antidiscrimination Duties

New or additional duties may be imposed on articles "wholly or in part the growth or product of, or imported in a vessel of, any foreign country"[5] if that country is found to be discriminating in any manner against the commerce of the United States. These duties may not exceed 50 per cent ad valorem or its equivalent, but none had been imposed up to 1950.[6]

Another type of duty to combat discrimination by foreign countries, amounting to 10 per cent ad valorem in addition to ordinary duties, is provided for by the Tariff Act of 1913[7] if the merchandise (1) is imported in a foreign vessel or (2) is produced in a noncontiguous country

[4] In 1931, 1932, and 1933, France imposed "compensation surtaxes" to offset the indirect subsidy arising from certain currency depreciations.

[5] Sec. 338, Tariff Act of 1930.

[6] *United States Import Duties* (*1950*), U.S. Tariff Commission, 1950, p. 171.

[7] 19 U. S. C. 128.

and imported from a contiguous country. The duty which may be imposed only on specific instructions from the Commissioner of Customs, is
not applicable if treaty, convention, or act of Congress makes exception
or if the merchandise is imported from contiguous territory in the course
of strictly retail trade. Provision for this duty was specifically excepted
from repeal in the Tariff Act of 1930, but no instructions for its imposition
had been issued up to 1952.

SPECIAL TAXES APPLICABLE TO IMPORTS

A number of taxes other than basic and special customs duties apply
to imported goods. Some of them are collected at the time of importation,
by the collector of customs, and others are collected at specified times
by the collector of internal revenue. While both are excises, the levies are
designated as import and processing taxes.

The purpose of or basis for most of these special taxes is generally
to compensate for imposition of a similar tax on the processing or sale of
domestically produced articles with which such imported goods compete
directly or indirectly. Thus, while applicable to imports, they do not
necessarily single out imports as compared with competing domestic
production. However, some apply to imports and not to domestic production, as shown below.

Import Taxes

What seems to be a subtle protective tariff is to be found in the
designation "import tax," which is levied in addition to other tariffs imposed on the importation but not on the domestic production of certain
materials. Under various sections of the Internal Revenue Code,
taxes are imposed on the following articles imported into the United
States unless treaty provisions prescribe otherwise: certain whale and
fish oils, tallow, certain inedible animal fats, oils, and greases, certain
vegetable oils and seeds, petroleum, fuel oil, coal, certain kinds of
lumber, copper and certain articles containing copper,[8] and sugar and
sugar products. These taxes are levied, assessed, collected, and paid in
the same manner as a duty imposed by the Tariff Act of 1930, and the
economic effect is the same as that of the usual customs duty. Moreover,
they are reducible through reciprocal trade agreements. Not appearing
in the Tariff Act of 1930 or its amendments, this tax is somewhat concealed in the revenue acts and thus does not get special attention or
publicity.[9]

[8] Application of the import tax on copper or certain articles containing copper (except copper sulphate) was temporarily suspended by Congress in April, 1947.
[9] Professor Pratt looks on excise taxes, both processing and import, as instruments
of protection, which could easily become an abuse under an administration com-

Processing Taxes

In addition to the customs duty applicable, processing taxes are imposed on the first domestic processing of a number of fats and oils, such as coconut oil, palm oil,[10] palm-kernel oil, or fatty acids or salts derived therefrom. These are not taxes imposed on or in connection with the importation of the articles, but they apply principally to imported commodities.[11] Collection of the tax is accomplished by the Bureau of Internal Revenue.

MARKS-OF-ORIGIN REGULATIONS

Many foreign traders feel that what might appear to be minor regulatory measures or precautions are an even greater obstacle to the international movement of goods than is the tariff rate. One of these pertains to marks of origin.

Marks-of-origin regulations in the United States devolve mainly from the Tariff Act of 1930, Sec. 304 of which reads, in part:

. . . every article of foreign origin (or its container . . .) imported into the United States shall be marked in a conspicuous place as legibly, indelibly, and permanently as the nature of the article (or container) will permit in such manner as to indicate to an ultimate purchaser in the United States the English name of the country of origin of the article. . . .

Under certain conditions, an additional duty of 10 per cent ad valorem may be levied for failure to mark the merchandise in accordance with regulations. Exceptions are authorized if the Secretary of the Treasury finds such marking to be impracticable, and special marking is prescribed for certain articles, such as cutlery and thermos bottles. In the case of penknives, for instance, each article when imported is to have the name of the maker or purchaser and beneath this the name of the country of origin "die sunk conspicuously and indelibly on . . . at least one or, if practicable, each and every blade thereof." Thermos bottles or jugs must have the name of the maker or purchaser and beneath this the name of the country of origin "legibly, indelibly and conspicuously etched with acid on the glass part, and die stamped on the jacket or casing or metal or other material, in a place that shall not be covered there-

---

mitted to the policy of protection. E. E. Pratt, *Foreign Trade Handbook* (Chicago and London, The Dartnell Corporation, 1949), p. 1046.

[10] The tax does not apply if the first use of the palm oil is in the manufacture of iron or steel products, tinplate, or terne plate, or any subsequent use of palm oil residue resulting from the manufacture of iron or steel products, tin plate, or terne plate.

[11] *United States Import Duties (1948)*, U.S. Tariff Commission, 1950, p. 348.

after." Also, each label, wrapper, box, or carton in which they are packed must, *when imported*, show the name of the maker or purchaser and beneath this the name of the country of origin.

Markings Are Required by Many Countries. Most foreign countries have varying types of similar regulation, as reported in the publication *Foreign Marks of Origin Regulations,* issued by the U.S. Department of Commerce.[12] A few selected requirements are:

1. The United Kingdom requires that articles of china or translucent pottery be stamped, printed, embossed, or impressed on each article indelibly. Also, hair combs are to have the name of the country of origin die stamped or impressed on each comb.
2. Canada requires that thermometers be marked as to country of origin by printing, die stamping, or blind embossing on each article. Safety razor blades are to be etched or die stamped on each blade.
3. Australia requires that the marking on cotton towels and toweling be indelible and removable only by soap and hot water or be on fabric labels stitched by machine on all four sides of the label.
4. Denmark requires that the name of the country of origin be shown on each separate pencil, piece of chalk, or crayon. Perhaps the most amusing requirement (also required by France) is that eggs be marked both on the individual eggs and on the packages to show the name of the country of origin. On the individual eggs, the marks must be applied in letters not less than two millimeters high. One is tempted to wonder whether the marking "Laid in U.S.A." might be acceptable.
5. France requires that, whenever a name, a picture, the national colors, emblems, or coats of arms or such national, regional, or local signs are used which might lead the observer to infer that the goods were made in France, a corrective marking be used, giving the name of the country of origin in full, as well as marking the goods as specifically import. For products originating in the United States, the corrective marking would be either *"Importe des États-Unis d'Amérique"* or *"Fabrique aux États-Unis d'Amérique."* Among the many specific requirements are that scented soap be marked in the composition of each cake and on the wrapper and box, reeds of clarinets and saxophones be marked by stamping with a die or by engraving at the base of the reed perpendicularly to the axis, and neckties be marked in gilt letters by means of a hot stamp. Sewing on is not allowed.

Marks of Origin Serve Little Valid Economic Purpose. The justification for requiring marks of origin on goods offered for public sale can serve no *economic* purpose; if such a purpose were to be served, distinguishing

---

[12] Economic Series 62, 1947.

marks would be attached somewhere along the production or distribution line without compulsion. Of course, there is a well-recognized sales appeal—an element of "distinction"—attaching to many types of imported merchandise. But there is an element of the public in whose eyes the origin of goods may be made to constitute the basis for a potential boycott in the market, and there are producers or merchants who feel that an indication that the product is of foreign origin may serve to dissuade the consumer from purchasing it in preference to an item made domestically, with local labor. However, a more important and probably much more restrictive effect of these regulations is that they increase the cost of the foreign goods compared with the domestic. Not only must the imported goods pay customs duty, but they must in many cases bear specific individual marking as being of foreign origin. This is simply another operation in production or a supplemental expense after the goods come off the production line.

Requirements Mean Added Expense and Restriction on Merchants. Recalling the few specific marks-of-origin regulations mentioned above, one may easily picture the added expense involved in complying with the regulations. At the manufacturer's level, for instance, when the goods are passed through the production line it is very often not known just where they will be sold. Unless made to specific advance foreign order, with the design or color specified by the foreign buyer or usable primarily abroad, the same product should be salable domestically or abroad. If sold abroad, it should be salable in one or several foreign countries. But in order for the goods to be acceptable abroad, they must be marked in the prescribed manner. If this could be done while the goods were going through the process of production, it would be a simple matter. But to unpack, mark specifically according to country of destination, and repack is an operation whose expense is a strong deterrent to considering foreign markets for any uncertain portion of production—uncertain as to time or volume. A good example of this is cutlery or shoes. The specific restriction out of which most trouble arises, then, is the requirement of being marked in the language of the importing country or being marked in a different manner for different countries. In effect, the geographic market for the product is limited if the product is marked at the time of manufacture.

A considerable volume of foreign commerce in manufactured goods is carried on by merchants who rely on some manufacturer to provide the goods for which he seeks a market. If he buys in the domestic market and has to put the goods through a special run in order to affix the required markings, not only is he placed in the position of having to bear added expense which may prohibit the transaction from taking place, but he is placed at a disadvantage in competing with the manufacturer of a substitute product who may be able to cover his costs in one less operation affecting each item. If the marking is done by hand, there is not only the element of added expense but also the possibility of breakage, in the case of fragile items. It appears fairly evident that, however one may attempt to justify such regulations, they constitute a formidable and in some cases a paralyzing expense and restriction on foreign commerce. One may well ask how the consumer benefits by these regulations in any country.

Difference between Certificates of Origin and Marks of Origin. Distinction must be drawn between the *certificate of origin* and the *mark of origin.* The former is a statement indicating that the imported product originated in a particular country and because of such origin a different rate of duty may apply. In the case of the United States, for example, merchandise sought to be admitted free of duty from Guam, Wake Island, Midway Islands, Kingman Reef, American Samoa, and the Virgin Islands must be covered by a certificate of origin showing such merchandise to be the growth or product of those islands or actual importations into those islands. These islands are American territory but not within the customs territory of the United States. Also, in the case of Cuban goods, which enter the United States at a preferential rate of duty, there must be filed in connection with the entry a declaration that the articles are of Cuban growth, produce, or manufacture.

Contrast this with the mark-of-origin regulation, which calls not for a certificate indicating where a total shipment originated, in order to determine whether the shipment may be entitled to full or partial exemption from duty, but for detailed marking on each item imported. These identifying marks do not subject the articles to any higher or lower rate of duty, and the indication as to country is not for the benefit of customs authorities but for the difficult-to-avoid observation of the consumer. Almost everyone must have seen glassware or cutlery on display, with each piece individually bearing a notation that it was made in some country other than the one in which displayed. Practically by default, the notation "Made in U.S.A." or the lack of any specific mark of origin is looked on by some as implying that the product has some special qualities not possessed by its competitive offering which is marked "Made in France" or "Made in England."

THE TARIFF ACT OF 1930

The foregoing comprise in large part the restrictions imposed on imports into the United States by the Tariff Act of 1930, as amended. This is the basic customs law of the United States. While it incorporates several of the restrictions discussed in the next chapter, description of the law at this juncture will place it in context with discussion of its major provisions.

The Act's original rates of duty, many of which have now been reduced, and its administrative features are of interest to practically all importers, especially those who bring in dutiable products. As mentioned before, a proposed customs simplification bill was introduced in Congress in 1950. It reached the floor of the House of Representatives and was approved by that body in October, 1951. However, it had not reached the Senate by the time Congress adjourned. The bill was aimed at administrative features or procedures and not at rates of duty; the latter, except for items being added to or removed from the free list, are directly affected by the Reciprocal Trade Agreements Act.

The Tariff Act of 1930 is written under four main titles.

Title I. Dutiable List. This title lists items which are dutiable in any manner under the Act, subdividing them into 15 schedules:

1. Chemicals, oils, and paints
2. Earths, earthenware, and glassware
3. Metals and manufactures of metals
4. Wood and wood manufactures
5. Sugar, molasses, and manufactures thereof
6. Tobacco and tobacco manufactures
7. Agricultural products and provisions
8. Spirits, wines, and other beverages
9. Cotton manufactures
10. Flax, hemp, jute, and manufactures thereof
11. Wool and wool manufactures
12. Silk manufactures
13. Manufactures of rayon or other synthetic textiles
14. Papers and books
15. Sundries

These 15 schedules are further subdivided into paragraphs, with allowance made for 100 paragraphs under each schedule except Schedule 1, which can expand to 200 paragraphs. Until 1948, paragraphs in use numbered 517, but many pertain to several articles or groups. The number of paragraphs is not indicative, therefore, of the number of items subject to duty. Except for about five or six paragraphs of an explanatory nature, each paragraph used sets the rate of duty applicable to articles covered by it.

Title II. Free List. As suggested by its title, this list includes articles which are specifically exempt from duty. It is provided in Par. 1559 of Title I that any imported article not enumerated in the Act which is similar, in material, quality, texture, or use to which it may be applied,

to any article enumerated in the Act as chargeable with duty shall be
subject to the same rate of duty which is levied on the enumerated article
which it most resembles in any of the particulars mentioned. If two or
more rates of duty are thus applicable, it shall be subject to duty at the
highest of such rates.

Title II comprised 215 paragraphs as of 1948, most of which have
been bound on the free list under individual reciprocal trade agreements
or under the General Agreement on Tariffs and Trade.

Title III. Special Provisions. This important section deals not with
rates of duty but with such matters as prohibited importations, marks of
origin, marking of containers, countervailing duties, bonded warehouses,
drawbacks and refunds, the United States Tariff Commission, and the
Reciprocal Trade Agreements Act.

The title is divided into sections, not all in sequence. Part I, dealing
with miscellaneous provisions, includes 21 sections, numbered from 301
through 321. Part II, dealing with the United States Tariff Commission,
includes 12 sections, numbered 330 through 341. The Reciprocal Trade
Agreements Act is Section 350 of Part II.

Title IV. Administrative Provisions. This very far-reaching title is
divided into six parts and covers generally procedural matters incorporated into law. These are:

Part I. Definitions: This is the part defining, among other things, the
value to be used in assessment of duties.

Part II. Report, entry, and unloading of vessels and vehicles: This portion
of the Act prescribes the requirement of a manifest, specifying its form
and content. In 37 sections, the obligations and regulations pertaining
to vessels and vehicles are listed.

Part III. Ascertainment, collection, and recovery of duties: Possibly no
part of the customs laws is of greater interest to importers than this,
which prescribes details on such matters as invoices, entry of merchandise, appraisement and classification, examination of merchandise,
appeals or protests pertaining to appraisement or classification, the
United States Customs Court, and conversion of foreign currencies.
Forty-eight sections are included in Part III.

Part IV. Transportation in bond and warehousing of merchandise:
Various types of entry of merchandise, for other than immediate consumption, are covered in this part, as well as the law on bonding of
warehouses and carriers. The subject matter is dealt with in 15 sections.

Part V. Enforcement provisions: Among matters dealt with in the 43
sections of this part are boarding and examination of vessels, smuggling,
fraud, bribery, seizure, award of compensation to informers, and the
like.

Part VI. Miscellaneous provisions: A principal section of this part pertains to customhouse brokers, tenure of judges of the United States Court of Customs and Patent Appeals, repeals of superseded laws or resolutions, and separability of provisions (saving clause of remainder of Act if some part is found to be invalid).

While the proposed customs-simplification act of 1950 was directed primarily at Titles III and IV of the Tariff Act of 1930, it also included provision for the repeal of special marking requirements specified in Title I of the basic Act.

Customs Regulations of the United States

Of perhaps equal interest with basic law in a consideration of the customs and tariff administration are the Customs Regulations of the United States, published by the Secretary of the Treasury. It is his responsibility, as chief enforcement officer, to prescribe such rules and regulations as may be necessary to carry out provisions of the Act (and duties under applicable navigation laws).

Under Customs Regulations (edition of 1943), these rules and regulations are divided into 26 parts, listed as follows:

1. Customs districts and ports
2. Measurements of vessels
3. Documentation of vessels
4. Vessels in foreign and domestic trades
5. Customs regulations with contiguous foreign territory
6. Air-commerce regulations
7. Customs regulations with insular possessions and Guantánamo Bay Naval Station
8. Liability for duties; entry of imported merchandise
9. Importations by mail
10. Articles conditionally free or subject to a reduced rate
11. Packing and stamping; marking; trade-marks and trade names; copyrights
12. Special classes of merchandise
13. Sugars, sirups, and molasses; petroleum products; wool and hair
14. Appraisement
15. Relief from duties on merchandise lost, stolen, destroyed, injured, abandoned, or short shipped
16. Liquidation of duties
17. Protests and reappraisements
18. Transportation in bond and merchandise in transit
19. Customs warehouses and control of merchandise therein
20. Disposition of unclaimed and abandoned merchandise

21. Cartage and lighterage
22. Drawback
23. Enforcement of customs and navigation laws
24. Customs financial and accounting procedure
25. Customs bonds
26. Disclosure of information

Those portions of special interest to the student of foreign commerce seeking more of an over-all picture than specific detail are perhaps those pertaining to customs districts and ports (Part I), entry of merchandise (Part 8), packing, marking, etc. (Part 11), special classes of merchandise (Part 12), appraisement (Part 14), liquidation of duties (Part 16), and protests and reappraisements (Part 17).

REVIEW QUESTIONS

1. Why does a specific duty afford inconsistent protection?
2. What makes a compound duty desirable under certain conditions?
3. Explain the significance of classification and valuation in so far as customs duties are concerned.
4. How may an antidumping duty be defended when imports are valued for customs purposes as they are required to be by the Tariff Act of 1930? Reference to Chapter 2 may be of assistance in considering this question.
5. Discuss the advisability of making mandatory the application of countervailing duties when a foreign country uses multiple exchange rates for the purpose of offering a bonus to its exporters.
6. Describe briefly the economic significance and economic impact of marks-of-origin regulations on the volume and direction of world trade.
7. Distinguish between certificate of origin and mark of origin. What purpose does each serve?
8. Describe briefly the structure of the Tariff Act of 1930.
9. What are Customs Regulations of the United States? How are they related to the Tariff Act of 1930?

CHAPTER 17

Restrictions on Imports II

In addition to the broader restrictions described in the preceding chapter, a number of other devices limiting, blocking, or controlling import volumes and directions are in wide use. In so far as the United States is concerned, several have been incorporated into customs law or are under administration of the Customs Service.

For convenience in study, these have been grouped according to their main effect, whether on price, quantity, quality, or preparation of imports. The classification leaves some overlapping, to be sure, and the types listed in this chapter are not the only ones to be found. But they do seem to represent the principal restrictions other than those described in Chapter 16.

"BUY AMERICAN" LEGISLATION

Some federal legislation, and procurement legislation in several states, requires that preference in public procurement be given domestic materials. This federal policy appears to have originated in the 1930s as a means of stimulating business and alleviating unemployment.

The following specific restrictions on foreign purchases may be noted:

1. The "Buy American" Act of 1933, which reads, in part:

> . . . unless the head of the department or independent establishment concerned shall determine it to be inconsistent with the public interest, or the cost to be unreasonable, only such manufactured articles, materials and supplies as have been mined or produced in the United States, and only such manufactured articles, materials and supplies as have been manufactured in the United States substantially all from articles, materials, or supplies mined, produced or manufactured, as the case may be, in the United States, shall be acquired for public use. This section shall not apply with respect to articles, materials or supplies for use outside the United States. . . .

341

Every contract for the construction, alteration, or repair of any public building or public work in the United States growing out of an appropria-tion heretofore made or hereafter to be made shall contain a provision that in the performance of the work the contractor, subcontractors, material men, or suppliers, shall use only such unmanufactured . . . and only such manufactured articles, materials and supplies as have been manufactured in the United States substantially all from articles, materials or supplies mined, produced or manufactured, as the case may be, in the United States. . . .

Certain exceptions are permitted but, in order further to clarify its intent, Congress declared on Oct. 29, 1949, that the original law was intended to require the purchase of articles produced in the United States in sufficient and reasonably available commercial quantities and of a satisfactory quality, subject to the two principal limitations of being contrary to public interest or unreasonably more expensive than goods purchasable abroad.

2. Public Law 434 (Eighty-first Congress), the Appropriations Act for the National Military Establishment for the Fiscal Year ending June 30, 1950. This law contained the proviso that

. . . no part of this appropriation . . . shall be available for the procure-ment of any article of food or clothing not grown or produced in the United States or its possessions, except to the extent that the Secretary of the Army shall determine a satisfactory quality and sufficient quantity . . . cannot be procured . . . at United States market prices without unduly increasing future United States market prices. . . .

Certain exceptions are listed, but the discretion is narrower than under the "Buy American" Act. This provision is especially significant since the National Military Establishment buys the larger part of commodities purchased for use by the federal government.

3. The Strategic and Critical Materials Stockpiling Act of 1946, which requires that purchases of strategic and critical materials be made in accordance with provisions of the "Buy American" Act of 1933. In signing this Act, the President pointed out that this requirement would materially increase the cost of the proposed stock piles and would tend to defeat the conservation and strategic objectives of the bill. He also brought out that these restrictions were in conflict with then current foreign economic policy. Further, he expressed regret that the Act would be used as a device to give domestic interests an advantage over foreign producers of strategic materials greater than that pro-vided by the tariff laws.

4. The Merchant Marine Act of 1936, which provides that, so far as practicable, only materials of the growth, production, or manufacture of the United States shall be used in ship construction under a con-

struction-differential subsidy. The same prohibition applies in the
case of an operating-differential subsidy "whenever practicable."
5. Federal housing legislation. Use of funds made available for carrying
out the work of the United States Housing Administration is subject
to restrictions under the "Buy American" Act. Thus, every contract
of the Public Housing Administration with local housing authorities
must contain the restrictive provision. This effectively limits the use
of foreign lumber, brick, glass, and other building materials over and
above any tariff restrictions.

"Buy American" legislation is thus a substantial obstacle to federal
procurement of foreign materials, or goods manufactured from foreign
materials unless (1) these materials are not available in the United States
in satisfactory quality, quantity, or time; (2) the price of corresponding
domestic materials, or products made from them, is "unreasonable," and
(3) procurement of domestic materials is inconsistent with public interest.

In an extensive discussion of the principle, *Report of ECA–Commerce
Mission* states that as far as could be readily ascertained, no agency has
undertaken any significant volume of procurement from foreign sources,
on the ground that it would be inconsistent with public interest to purchase domestically.

Uniform Policy Adopted on "Unreasonableness" of Cost. With regard
to the unreasonableness of cost, the general policy adopted is that on
purchases exceeding $100, domestic goods must cost 25 per cent more
than the comparable foreign product, exclusive of duty, in order to be
unreasonably higher; in the case of smaller purchases, the differential
rises to 100 per cent. This is an agreement entered in 1934 by the agencies
and departments of the federal government in order to provide a uniform
procurement policy. What this means is that on a purchase of articles
for, say, $100,000, when such articles are subject to a duty of 20 per
cent ad valorem, the cost of domestic articles would be unreasonable
only if priced at $145,000 ($100,000 basic, plus $20,000 duty, plus $25,000
differential).

Whether relaxation of these restrictions would result in a significant
over-all increase in imports in debatable. There is the usual red-tape
formality in public procurement, the already established channels, and
the fact that procurement is often accomplished in small lots in different
parts of the country. Import merchants, however, would find an additional market in which to attempt disposal of their goods. Aside from
changes in circumstances affecting the public interest, suggestions have
been made that the uniform policy could be amended without undue
harm by setting the degree of "unreasonable" differential at 10 per cent,
but in any event not to exceed $5,000 on any single procurement.

State restrictions do not seem to be so prohibitive as is the national requirement.

QUANTITATIVE LIMITATIONS

Quotas

One of the relatively modern, but very widely used and direct obstacles to imports is the quota system. There are, in reality, two types of quotas. One, the *tariff quota,* admits a certain volume or any quantity within a specified season under one schedule of customs duties, with additional volumes or with quantities imported outside of the specified season being subjected to higher rates of duty. The other, the *import* quota, places a definite limit on the total quantity of an article which may be imported within a specified period of time or from a particular country. None beyond the stated amount may be brought in, with or without the payment of duties.

The United States has invoked the use of tariff quotas in several instances. One is the importation of whole milk and cream. Under the General Agreement on Tariffs and Trade, the tariff quota on whole milk, either fresh or sour, was set at 3 million gallons per year; the limit on cream, either fresh or sour, was set at 1.5 million gallons per year. Butter is another product on which the United States has established a tariff quota, it being 50 million pounds on imports entered during the period Nov. 1 of any year to Mar. 31 of the following year. Tariff quotas have also been set for several other items, such as shelled walnuts, Irish potatoes, cattle, and fresh or frozen fish fillets. The quota on potatoes was tied to domestic production in that if domestic production fell below a specified figure (350 million bushels), the quota could be increased. The quota on fish was tied to domestic consumption; it was the greater of 15 million pounds per year or 15 per cent of the "average aggregate apparent annual consumption" in the three preceding years. Actually, a tariff quota, if so designed, can make possible a liberalization rather than a diminution of trade. This would occur, for example, if a tariff quota were involved in order to render more acceptable to domestic interests a reduction in the rate of duty.

Import quotas were apparently first used by France, in 1931, based on a law passed in 1910, and they have since been adopted by many countries. In France, quota limitations had been set on over 1,100 articles by July, 1932, or one out of every seven on the tariff list. By 1934, there were quota limitations on about 3,000 items. As could have been expected, the plan resulted in many retaliatory measures, and it is interesting to note that France subsequently indicated its intent to abolish the official use of import quotas for protective purposes, although it felt compelled to maintain control over imports, on a selective basis, for some time because of a critical shortage of foreign exchange.[1]

Import Quotas Are Powerful Agents for Restrictive Policy. It is obvious that a quota system is a very powerful weapon in negotiating international commercial agreements. It may be used for bargaining, for controlling the type of import, for protecting the supply of foreign exchange, for favoring certain industries, for dictating the source (country) of imports, and, of course, for purposes of reprisal. As compared with the usual tariff system, no matter how high the rate, a quota scheme imposes a much more dampening effect on foreign commerce. A tariff system does not say you cannot import if you pay the duty and the price is satisfactory; under an import quota, however, once the limit has been reached, price makes no difference. Even though the price is made ridiculously low, there is to be no more trade above a certain volume, so the system provides an effective block on the working of the forces of supply and demand. It is hardly surprising that a wide introduction of quotas has been a substantial factor leading to a number of bilateral agreements whereby both countries attempt to improve their positions by exchanging within or above the portions of the quotas they themselves have established.

Agricultural Price Stabilization Act Authorizes Quotas on Imports. It was mentioned earlier that the United States has employed tariff quotas on several products. Import quotas have also been employed in some instances, and there has been established a legal framework for the employment of import quotas to a still greater extent. Under the Agricultural Act of 1948,[2] the President is authorized, after appropriate investigation by the Tariff Commission, to impose *quantitative limitations* on any article or articles which may be imported for consumption if such importation tends to render ineffective or materially interferes with the agricultural price-support program. The same law prescribes that the President is limited in imposing this quantitative restriction to a reduction of not more than 50 per cent of the total quantity which was entered or withdrawn for consumption during a representative period as determined by the President. It is to be noted that the President may employ either an increased ad valorem duty or an import quota in limiting imports for this purpose.

Among items on which the United States has established import quotas are sugar, wheat, wheat flour, certain petroleum products, and certain

[1] Prior to the Geneva Conference, out of which evolved the General Agreement on Tariffs and Trade, France formulated a new tariff on an ad valorem basis, without quotas for protective purposes. *Analysis of General Agreement on Tariffs and Trade,* U.S. Department of State Publication 2983, 1947, p. 79.

[2] Pub. L. 897, 80th Cong.

types of cotton. In the sugar quota arrangement, domestic and Cuban growers were given the major part of the United States market, the Philippine Republic was given about half as much as Cuba, and the small remainder was allotted to other countries. In 1941, the United States agreed to an import quota on coffee, under the Inter-American Coffee Agreement, but this was an emergency measure and the Agreement expired in September, 1948. Under the pressure of war, the United States also participated in arrangements whereby quotas were established on the importation of a number of products under allocation by the International Emergency Food Council. These were mainly fats, oils, and edible food products. International allocation and the resultant quotas for many of these articles have been eliminated since the end of the war. But through agreements sponsored by the International Materials Conference, postwar quotas on either imports or exports may be expected. The Defense Production Act of 1950, as amended, also provided for imposition of quotas; under it, imports of cheese and casein were placed on a quota basis in late 1951.

The number of countries using import quotas is very large, and the obstacle is so general and throttling in its effect that the proposed International Trade Organization devoted a section to quantitative restrictions and exchange controls.

Import Licenses

A natural consequence of the adoption of a quota system by a country is the use of import licenses as a means of parceling out to interested importers the limited amount available under the quota. As a general rule, it would appear that import licenses should not be necessary, if the quota is about as large as the usual import volume. This seems to have been the case under the Inter-American Coffee Agreement, for which the United States did not impose any licensing arrangement to assure that imports remained within established quotas. Instead, and probably because of the special circumstances surrounding this Agreement, the mechanism employed was certification by United States consuls of invoices in the exporting countries. Before such certification, the individual exporter was required to produce to the certifying officer an official document showing that the coffee was within the producing country's quota for exportation to the United States. But if the amount set as the quota is less than the amount which would be brought in without the quota, the problem of rationing presents itself. If left on the basis of first come, first served, there can be expected a rush to buy—and, as well, a rush to sell—in order to get in under the limitation. Either of these might have a strong effect on immediate prices. There is also the possibility that larger firms might be in a position to monopolize the trade to the detriment of smaller importers. In addition, it is not an uncommon practice, when a rationing arrangement is imposed, for the prospective buyer to put in a request for more than he needs, in the expectation that if his requisition is reduced in amount he may end up with approximately the quantity desired. Hence, licensing for imports is a natural consequence as it could well mean a more orderly—because controlled—conduct of business.

Fair Basis Needed for Issuing Licenses. The basic practical problem which develops from the adoption of import-licensing schemes is the determination of a fair basis for issuing such licenses. A common base has been historical experience, which means that importers would be permitted to bring in about the same proportion of total imports as they did in a representative period prior to introduction of the licensing arrangement. Here, the question is the selection of a fair period of time for measuring historical experience. Should it be one year or several years? If only one year, should it be the most recent year, a typical year, or a typical period? It could be that the period selected was one of extreme activity or inactivity for the individual importer.

Another practical difficulty in the application of historical experience is that it tends to freeze trade into a pattern difficult to break. For example, what is to be done in the case of a new importer desiring to enter the field, or what provision may be made for different rates in growth of the various importers? Complaint may be made that the small importer is forcibly kept small, even though he may be willing and able to do better, and that several years of this hindrance may occur at a crucial time in his business career.

From the point of view of government administration, import licenses also provide an effective means of selecting import sources by the process of denying licenses to importers desiring to bring merchandise in from a country whose trade may not be particularly desired at that time. Enke and Salera report that through licensing textile imports, Australia was able in 1935 to exclude Japanese textiles in order to restore the market to British suppliers. This was accomplished by the process of denying a license for imports from Japan.[3]

Program Calls for Additional Planning and Scheduling. From the point of view both of business operation and of government administration, functioning under a system of import licenses means perhaps more planning than would otherwise be necessary. Applications for import licenses may have to be drawn up on a monthly or quarterly basis, and drawn up sufficiently far in advance to permit the administrative office to determine from the sum total of applications how much of a license

[3] Stephen Enke and Virgil Salera, *International Economics* (New York, Prentice-Hall, Inc., 1947), p. 309.

may be granted to each importer, either monthly, quarterly, or annually For each item so covered, a "program" must be adopted for administrative operational purposes. In cases in which import licenses must come in for a general application, the opportunistic purchases, because of favorable spot conditions in some markets of the world, may have to be missed.

It was mentioned earlier in this connection that the importers' big problem regarding import licenses is that in which the volume to be imported is less than what might be expected under unrestricted conditions. The situation also develops, occasionally, wherein the available supply is larger than "normal" imports would absorb, and governments are led to another device for restricting imports. This is an intergovernmental commodity arrangement, a device which has expanded materially in recent years.

Intergovernmental Commodity-control Agreements

Objective of Arrangements Described. These intergovernmental arrangements are described by the International Labour Office as a device aimed at "the expansion, by appropriate international and domestic measures, of production, employment, and the exchange and consumption of goods." In accomplishing their objectives, the schemes cover some, if not all, of the following important problems: producers' control, export- and/or import-volume control, prices, and reserve stocks (and surpluses). Their effect on foreign commerce is such as to render them potentially dominant, and a rather substantial percentage of the value of world-traded commodities is the subject of national and international governmental control schemes.

For many years, raw materials have been the subject of international conferences between interested governments, and the acceptance of inter-governmental commodity-control schemes has developed substantially during the years since the depression. Occasionally these have involved only producing countries but, at other times, both producing and consuming countries have been parties to the agreement.

In its review of intergovernmental commodity-control agreements, the International Labour Office points out that the majority of the inter-governmental schemes have grown out of earlier producer schemes, most of which were unsuccessful and some of which, like the Chadbourne sugar scheme and the Stevenson rubber scheme, have been severely criticized as contrary to public interest.[4] The International Labour Office is interested in this problem because of the social consequences of price fluctuations.

---

[4] *Intergovernmental Commodity Control Agreements,* International Labour Office, Montreal, 1943, pp. xvi–xvii.

Require High Degree of Governmental Economic Planning and Control. Intergovernmental commodity arrangements require a high degree of governmental economic planning and control, inasmuch as they must necessarily restrict freedom of action on the part of individual producers if they are to succeed. Accordingly, any student of foreign commerce ought to reexamine, and ponder over, the economic basis of world trade. In theory, the cornerstone is pointed out to be specialization in production by individual entrepreneurs, with buyers seeking goods in the most advantageous market and sellers seeking the most advantageous market for them. On the other hand, governmental commodity-control schemes serve to deter the functioning of free enterprise in foreign commerce, but they are put into effect because some other greater good to a larger number is assumed to outweigh the curtailment of freedom of the individual. Some detail as to their operations will be found in Chapter 20.

Exchange Controls

It is difficult, if not impossible, to mention a restriction on imports more complete, far reaching, and immediate in effect than the system known as foreign-exchange control. Under it, the exporter is obliged to sell all or a large part of the foreign exchange he obtains to his central bank or the agency designated by his government for the purpose; the importer is obliged to buy all or a large part of the foreign exchange needed to pay for his purchases from the same agency. This presumes, and in effect almost requires, that exports will be quoted in terms of the desired foreign currency and that imports will call for payment in some currency other than that of the country employing the exchange-control scheme.

Economy Is Severed from International Price System. Such a control by government, or its agency, covers, or can cover, all items in the field of international transactions. There are varying degrees, of course, in application of this system. For some purposes, a "free" market may be permitted, but only when its operation does not interfere with the major effort to dictate how foreign exchange owned by or accruing to a country's nationals may be used. Tariffs, quotas, import licenses, and intergovernmental commodity-control arrangements cover trade in goods; exchange control says, in effect, "You may spend money for this, but not for that." The original earner of the foreign exchange is not permitted to spend all or even a large part for travel, services, or investment abroad, although some modifications in various systems were observable in 1949 and 1950. (Holland and France, for example, permitted the exporter to retain a modest portion of his foreign earnings for advertising or trade promotion.) The purchaser of the foreign exchange from the central bank or agency is permitted to obtain the exchange only if the purpose for which it is intended is looked on by the government as essential to its program. What such a system does effectively is to sever a country's economy from the price system of the world, at least for a time; the length of time it remains severed will vary with circumstances. One country may be in position to go for many years under such a scheme, while another may be compelled by the force of circumstances, or the bargaining power of its neighbors, to modify the program.

Price of Exchange Is Set by Government. Basically, the price at which foreign exchange can be bought and sold is set by government direction and not by the continuous interplay of the many forces of supply and demand. This may be considered to be advisable in order to prevent unusually wide swings in the price of exchange which is not tied to some sort of anchor which limits such fluctuations. The control must be quite strict, once the daily indication of value in the eyes of the public is denied.

In many cases, multiple rates have been set for the purchase or sale of identical exchange, depending on the manner in which earned and the use to which it will be put. By manner in which earned, one means the type of product or type of transaction out of which the exchange arose. In some cases, although there may be be more than one price at which foreign exchange moves, some "free" transactions may be allowed on a limited basis to cover such items as travel or interest and dividends on investments owned by foreigners.

May Accomplish Several Objectives. It is apparent from the foregoing that there are several types of exchange controls, and the objectives may vary in some degrees. These objectives are, and there may be others:

1. To maintain the exchange rate and avoid a flight of capital
2. To direct channels of foreign commerce, in and out, by country and by item
3. As a source of revenue, some gain being derived from the spread between buying and selling prices
4. To stimulate or discourage the production of different goods

Origin Is Fairly Recent. The current wave of exchange-control popularity dates back to the interwar period and more properly to the early 1930s, when the idea was quickly adopted by a number of European countries and many others all over the world. While most countries adopted this direct control, the United States followed the policy of using a stabilization fund to maintain exchange rates and to restrain somewhat the effect of uncertainty in the minds of the public over governmental manipulations of the gold content of the dollar. It is easy to see that, in order to remain in power, and a plausible defense could be found to rationalize such action as a means of avoiding economic difficulty for their respective countries, many governments felt unable to avoid taking the step. For if the government in power refused to do so, it might well be succeeded by another which would follow a different line of economic reason.

Widespread Use Due to International Economic Breakdown. As to the cause of the growth of exchange-control schemes, it is impossible to pin any one thing down as specific. It was part of an international financial breakdown, with more than usual gains or losses of gold or other internationally desired assets—in general, a disruption in the means of making international payments, with an increasing number of currencies becoming less and less desirable and acceptable for doing business. The vague term "balance-of-payments difficulties," which is widely accepted as suitable grounds for any imposition or extension of government controls, does not seem to offer any hope that these systems will be abolished for many years. They can only be abolished if governments are willing to subject themselves as well as private business transactions to a common denominator—the market price. Single, small countries may clarify their local situations, as did Peru in early 1950, in removing many government controls and returning to a system of private enterprise.

Out of 88 countries and areas reviewed in January, 1951, by the Department of Commerce, all but 13 were employing an exchange-control scheme. The tabulation is published from time to time in *Foreign Commerce Weekly.*[5]

Multiple Rates Mean Classification of Goods and Services. Typically, the mechanism of operation of the multiple-exchange-rate system is that items are placed in certain categories, depending on their essentiality as determined by the economic authority charged with the decision. It is not a question of what the individual citizen deems more desirable, essential, or profitable to him at a particular time; government decides that national welfare requires abrogation of the right of free choice by the individual. Those items deemed more essential, hence more to be desired as imports, may be purchased and paid for with exchange bought at the most favorable or encouraging price. Luxuries and nonessentials may have to be paid for with exchange bought at a higher or even the highest stated price. As an example, in early 1950, imports into Paraguay from the United States were paid for at four rates (selling prices of U.S. dollars in terms of Paraguayan guaranies), depending on their importance to the Paraguayan economy. Dollars to cover items in Category I could be bought at 3.121 guaranies apiece. For imports in Category II, the price was 5.0817 guaranies per dollar, and for those in Category III, the importer had to pay 6.3862 guaranies per dollar. Imports in Category

[5] See, in this instance, the issue of Feb. 12, 1951.

IV, travel abroad and family remittance, called for payment of 8.8573 guaranies per dollar.[6] The percentage differential was obviously quite substantial and an effective restriction on certain types of imports. At about the same time, the Peruvian sol was quoted at 15.38 U.S. cents for the official sol (which had to be used for some imports), while the free sol was only 5.58 cents.

Reports were heard that one means of evading these controls, on the import side, was to have the official invoice executed at a higher price than the actual. The importer might then obtain exchange from the central bank or other agency and send it to the exporter who would charge the actual price and credit the account of the foreign importer with the difference. Such measures not only avoid, they *evade*, exchange restrictions, and they involve official declarations which are deliberately false. Naturally, acts of this sort are to be condemned, yet such is often the depth of patriotism when it is felt that the demands of government are unsound or unfair.

Milling and Mixing Restrictions

Another somewhat concealed obstacle or restriction to importing is the requirement in some countries that in the manufacture or processing of certain products a specified proportion of domestically produced raw materials or products will be used. Brazil has for some time required that in the grinding of flour a certain percentage of the content must be locally produced manioc, which means that no more than the reciprocal percentage of total content can be imported wheat. The importation of wheat and other grains has been lessened by this device in several European countries, while in Argentina, some importers of fuel have been compelled to buy a specified amount of domestic corn for fuel from the Argentine Grain Board.[7] In Venezuela, in 1950, an importer of butter had to buy one unit of the domestic product for every two units imported, powdered milk could be imported duty free, provided importers purchased a certain amount of nationally manufactured product.[8] This obviously serves the purpose not only of restricting imports but of making a market for certain domestic products as well.

While the General Agreement of Tariffs and Trade reserves to the United States the right to impose a duty on the importation of crude rubber, the method adopted as a protection of the domestic synthetic industry was the specification that a certain minimum percentage of the

[6] *La Tribuna*, Asuncion, Paraguay, quoted in *International Financial News Survey*, International Monetary Fund, May 26, 1950.

[7] Asher Isaacs, *International Trade—Tariff and Commercial Politics* (Chicago, Richard D. Irwin, Inc., 1948), pp. 645–646.

[8] "How Imports into Venezuela Are Regulated," *Venezuela Up-to-Date*, Venezuelan Embassy, Washington, October, 1950.

rubber content of manufactured articles, like tires and tubes, must consist of synthetic rubber. The Rubber Act of 1948 made mandatory the minimum use of about 220,000 tons of synthetic rubber, but some opposition appeared in ensuing years on the grounds that purchases of crude rubber from abroad would serve to ease the shortage of dollars in foreign countries, which was a spectacular phenomenon of postwar years.

Embargoes

Foreign merchandise may be denied entry into the United States in a number of circumstances other than the foregoing. Probably the best known of these prohibitions is that against importations of cattle, sheep, swine, and fresh, chilled, or frozen meats from countries in which rinderpest or foot-and-mouth disease exists. The Secretary of Agriculture determines those areas of the world to which the embargo applies; this exclusion has been an issue for years between Argentina and the United States. Applying to several countries as conditions require, the embargo was made applicable in early 1952 to meat imports from Canada.

Also prohibited is all merchandise made wholly or in part by convict and/or forced labor and/or indentured labor under penal sanctions of a foreign country, except in those cases in which domestic production is not in sufficient quantity to meet the consumptive demands of the United States.

Prohibitions also apply against the importation of books, other literature, and pictures advocating treason or insurrection against the United States; against obscene literature, lottery tickets, goods protected by trade-marks or trade names belonging to United States citizens (unless authorized by the owner of the trade-mark or name), certain seeds, certain wild animals and birds, material under false United States copyright, and a variety of other products specified in the Tariff Act of 1930 and Customs Regulations of the United States.

Embargoes against importations also stem from temporary legislation, such as the Defense Production Act of 1950. This Act was amended in late 1951 (the Andresen amendment) to provide for restriction of imports of certain products if their importation would (1) impair or reduce domestic production, (2) interfere with orderly domestic storing or marketing, or (3) result in any unnecessary burden or expenditure under any government price-support program. Under this authority, the Department of Agriculture promptly announced an embargo against commercial importations for domestic consumption of peanuts, peanut oil, butter, butter oil, and nonfat dried-milk solids. Considerable opposition to the amendment was voiced, after its passage, on the grounds of its being unnecessary and inconsistent with United States efforts toward broader multilateral trade.

Under Sec. 337 of the Tariff Act of 1930, merchandise made the subject of unfair methods of competition and unfair acts in their importation may be denied entry by Presidential direction. The Presidential decision must be based, though, on an investigation conducted by the Tariff Commission to determine whether the effect or tendency is to destroy or substantially injure an industry, efficiently and economically operated, in the United States.

The Tariff Act of 1930 (Sec. 338) also provides that entry of merchandise from a foreign country may be denied if the foreign country persists in discriminating against the commerce of the United States, directly or indirectly. This is the extreme development following imposition of an antidiscrimination duty.

QUALITATIVE LIMITATIONS

Import Requirements of the Pure Food and Drug Laws

Many complaints have been registered by importers because of application of the food and drug laws. At times the complaint is heard that these laws are such a restriction on imports that trading cannot be carried on, or that foreign exporters find the laws obnoxious and that compliance with them is not worth the cost. It is advisable that the facts of such a general complaint be understood, and also that appreciation be had that the food and drug laws are not aimed at foreign goods alone.

The Federal Food, Drug, and Cosmetic Act of 1938 is the basic law under which this restriction operates. It provides for supervision of traffic in food, drugs, and cosmetics in order to safeguard public health. No distinction is made between domestic and foreign goods in its application, and its purpose obviously is to serve as a protection to the general public.

In many countries, such regulations are not in force, or, if they are, they differ from those of the United States. For example, in many countries, some coloring matter, which is not permitted to be used on food in the United States, may be used in the manufacture of candies. And while goods may be stored seasonally in a warehouse abroad or may have to take a long journey, the possibility of decay or of contamination with filth from rats and vermin is present. Conditions under which food products must be manufactured in order to permit the food to pass requirements of the food and drug laws are such that a deliberate effort must be made to prevent any filth from entering. Either because less care is taken or because it may not be required in some places, a substantial amount of food products and drugs is denied entry into the United States. At the same time, misbranding or mislabeling, wherein the food or drugs may be said to contain components not actually found on inspection or, if so, in lesser or greater amount than indicated on the label, or where the drugs may, on the label, lay claim to certain curative or remedial qualities which tests prove untrue, provide another cause for denial or admission to certain products.

Many Imports Denied Entry. The annual reports of the Food and Drug Administration for 1949, 1950, and 1951 list the following number of import shipments as having been denied entry in the fiscal years shown.

Import shipment	1948	1949	1950	1951
Foods.	5,254	4,082	4,936	3,851
Vitamins and foods for special dietary use.	54	38	101	42
Drugs and devices.	4,164	1,902	2,249	1,385
Cosmetics and colors.	573	350	88	66
Caustic poisons and miscellaneous.	3			
Total.	10,048	6,372	7,374	5,344

Overall, about 32 per cent of import inspections were refused entry in 1948, 17 per cent in 1949, 16 per cent in 1950, and 14 per cent in 1951. As an indication of the dual application of this supervision, domestic as well as import, only 9.2 per cent of enforcement time was devoted to import inspections in 1951.

Pamphlet Aids Foreign Exporters. If merchandise is brought in and is dirty, or otherwise cannot pass the food and drug inspection, it may at times be cleaned, relabeled, or otherwise processed to comply with regulations. However, this reworking is not a legal right of the importer; it is a privilege which may be given him under administrative regulations of the administrator. There may be times when the food and drug inspector judges the goods to be so far beyond the possibility of effective reworking that he denies to the importer the right to clean, sort, or treat the product and orders its destruction. The question then resolves itself into a struggle between the exporter abroad and the importer in the United States to determine who stands the loss, with the possibility of contamination while in shipment having entered the case. Recognizing the need for foreign shippers to be more aware of these regulations, the Food and Drug Administration issued a pamphlet, in 1947, titled *Import Requirements of the United States Food, Drug and Cosmetic Act.*[9] Copies were sent to our consuls over the world and made available to importers for distribution to their suppliers, in order that exporters abroad would know what the regulations called for and could take steps, accordingly, to render the goods able to pass inspection. It should be repeated that the

[9] Miscellaneous Publication 2, Food and Drug Administration, 1947.

same regulations apply to domestic and to foreign goods; it is not the purpose of the law to create a block against imports. Standards are set by consideration of what is safe for public consumption and the degree of purity or cleanliness which can be attained in the processes of production. They are not arbitrary or discriminatory regulations.

Packing, Marking, and Labeling Regulations

Closely related to the problem of marks of origin on individual imported products is the varied requirement one finds in the matter of packing, marking, or labeling either the immediate container or the complete package. A rather complete set of instructions on the subject may be found in *International Reference Service,* issued by the U.S. Department of Commerce for individual countries in the series titled *Preparing shipments to*_____. Marking in metric measure may be required and, as in the case of Venezuela, the importation may be dutiable on its gross weight, which includes cases and packing. In Venezuela, cases and packing are appraised in the same customs classification as their contents unless they consist of materials specified in the customs tariff in a higher class than the contents, in which case they are dutiable separately and must be invoiced separately. In many countries, regulations have been issued pertaining to the number of sides on which each package must be marked, the height of the letters to be used, and the method of application (stencil or by hand). Use of any marking other than that specified in the respective regulations may be prohibited; this appears to apply particularly to advertising on the exterior of packages.

In the matter of labeling, some laws specify that the name of the agent in the importing country be shown or that the merchandise be described in a certain manner. Regulations of the Department of Agriculture and the Food and Drug Administration in the United States prescribe, in some cases, that each separate container shall show specific marking as to use or detailed analytic content.

OTHER OBSTACLES

Reservation of Items for State Trading

The foregoing discussion of restrictions on imports pertained to those which apply to all imports, regardless of who brings them in. Throughout this text, the point is drawn from time to time to private as against state trading. It is necessary, therefore, to mention at this point a restriction against *private* trading in imports. This may be accomplished by reserving certain items for state trading—in effect, prohibiting private trade in such merchandise. Examples of this are offered by Argentina, whose Argentine Institute for the Promotion of Trade (IAPI) conducts foreign trade in selected items unless permitted to individuals, and Mexico, whose CEIMSA (government trading agency) functions in the same capacity but on a somewhat modified basis. Monopolies are also used by some governments in products such as tobacco, salt, matches, and alcoholic beverages. The extreme in state trading is Soviet Russia, in which the individual has no free function in foreign commerce. Temporary use is made of this type of restriction as evidenced by United States prohibitions in 1951 against private importations of tin and rubber. These had to do with stock-piling operations, and the restrictions against private imports of rubber were terminated in early 1952.

Restrictions on Imports Other than Merchandise

Foreign commerce, as we know, consists of substantially more than trade in merchandise, and the volume of transactions in these other items (sometimes called "invisible" items) is often as great as or even greater than the total of transactions in goods. Since *one* of the reasons for erecting restrictions on the importation of merchandise is the shortage of foreign exchange, and since the same drain on foreign exchange arises from other transactions, it is only to be expected that some restrictions, direct or incidental, will have developed with respect to these other items.

One of these is the restriction pertaining to the purchase of freight and shipping services. Those countries attempting to build up and support a merchant marine may find it to advantage to use this type of indirect aid which at the same time reduces the demand for foreign exchange with which to pay for foreign services.[10] The move to compel the use of local insurance services, such as has been attempted by Argentina[11] and Chile, is also one which reduces the demand for foreign exchange, although the services may cost the user more in his local currency. Another effective restriction is that foreign exchange will not be made available for travel abroad except under approved and/or very restricted conditions. Instances are known in which highly respected visitors from abroad, although quite wealthy at home, have almost out of necessity had to be the "guest" of some friend while in the United States. People traveling to the United States from England, for instance, have been permitted

[10] In 1950, Ecuador allowed a 50-per-cent reduction in consular fees on goods moved to Ecuador in vessels under that nation's flag or on ships operated by Flota Mercante Grancolombiana. It was estimated that this would amount to about 3½ per cent of the value of the merchandise. A. J. Pasch, cited in *The New York Times*, July 30, 1950, Sec. V, p. 9, Col. 1. In the United States, under act of Oct. 3, 1913 (38 Stat. 196), it was provided that a discount of 5 per cent was allowable on all duties if the goods were imported in a vessel registered under laws of the United States· This legislation was not permitted to abrogate, impair, or affect any treaties. The law was repealed in 1922.

[11] Insurance on imports into Argentina is required to be placed with Argentine companies where the risk of transit is for account of the buyer.

to take with them only a limited amount of British currency, and from Holland only a relatively small amount in guilders. One reason for this is to prevent too much of their national currency from escaping abroad and forming the nucleus of a large-scale black market; the other, most naturally, is that with exchange rationed as to imports of merchandise, no more freedom can be allowed for travel abroad (which may not be considered to be so essential as merchandise) or for the purchase abroad, while traveling, of merchandise which cannot regularly be imported.

Long- and Short-term Capital Movements Restricted. A similar restriction has developed in the matter of "importing" investments. In many cases, the available short-term foreign capital must be turned over to the government, its central bank, or other agency, for use according to the decisions of public authorities. In other words, the citizen or resident of one country may not be allowed to build up a balance of short-term credits abroad for some immediate or future use. This restriction on the building up of short-term balances may also result in a restriction on long-term investments, if they are considered to be not so essential to the immediate welfare of the country imposing the control as the importation of merchandise.

In the case of the United States, which employs no such general restriction on the use to which individuals may choose to put their funds, restricted imports of foreign investments may be the result of regulations of foreign governments themselves in the matter of investment in the respective countries.

The Johnson Act, 1934. A significant change in policy regarding foreign investments occurred in the United States in the interwar period. Let us revert to 1934, when an act was passed by Congress (the Johnson Act) which prohibited the sale in the American private-capital market of securities of other governments which were in default on outstanding obligations held by the United States government. The restriction was not made to apply to loans by a "public corporation created by or pursuant to special authorization of Congress, or a corporation in which the government of the United States has or exercises a controlling interest." This was a most direct and abrupt restriction on capital export by a country some of whose citizens were in a position to lend abroad. Effectiveness of the law was practically set aside when it was amended in 1945 to exempt from its provisions the governments which were members of the International Monetary Fund and the International Bank for Reconstruction and Development.

Double Taxation Is Also a Deterrent. A law such as the Johnson Act is not the only restriction on the movement of capital to which the lending country is a part. Another is the impact of double taxation. For example, if income from foreign investments is taxed at 20 per cent in the country in which earned, and at 20 per cent on the remainder in the country in which the owner is domiciled or under whose laws he is taxable, the result is a total tax of 36 per cent on the original income. Several conventions have been held to eliminate double taxation, and this obstacle appears to be undergoing a gradual correction.

Private Restrictions: Cartels

All the foregoing restrictions on imports of merchandise are government dictated and operated, although they bear equally well on both private and public trade. There is another restriction on imports to be noted, which is private in origin and operation. It is the arrangement commonly known as the cartel, through which producers agree among themselves on matters of price, production, exports, or markets. The arrangement which most severely limits or restricts imports is one whereby "competing" producers (cartel members) agree to an allocation of markets. For example, if a producer located in country A and a producer located in country B agree to recognize their respective countries as each other's back yards, so to speak, they may agree not to ship their product into each other's country, each of which thereby becomes a closed market regardless of whether or not there is a tariff. Even if the tariff were to be completely abolished, this agreement not to export would be a very strict obstacle to imports, for they are the necessary counterpart of each other. It may be argued that the reason why producers enter such agreements is to avail themselves of each other's patent rights or that the patent rights will be made available only under such arrangement. Whatever it is, the effect is that such an agreement, with or without government sanction, is a restriction on the amount or type of imports which enter the respective countries.

In late 1951, the United States proposed international action on cartels by the Economic and Social Council of the United Nations. As a result of the proposal, a resolution was adopted, establishing an *ad hoc* Committee on Restrictive Business Practices.[12] The Committee was instructed to submit proposals, not later than March, 1953, on methods to be adopted by international agreement aimed at preventing, "on the part of private or public commercial enterprises, business practices affecting international trade which restrain competition, limit access to markets, or foster monopolistic control, whenever such practices have harmful effects on the expansion of production or trade, on the economic development of underdeveloped areas, or on standards of living." In making the proposal, the United States delegate pointed out that since the beginning of 1946 the United States had found it necessary to institute legal pro-

[12] With members from Belgium, Canada, France, India, Mexico, Pakistan, Sweden, United Kingdom, United States, and Uruguay.

ceedings against 29 different business arrangements restrictive of international trade, in each of which both American enterprises and enterprises from other countries participated.[13]

REVIEW QUESTIONS

1. What is the background of "Buy American" legislation? How does it influence United States imports?

2. What is the uniform policy adopted on "unreasonableness" of cost under
"Buy American" legislation? Is a uniform policy desirable?

3. Distinguish between tariff quota and import quota.

4. What basic legislation of the United States underlies our employment of
import quotas?

5. What fundamental risk to free enterprise and economic opportunity is to
be found in a system of import licensing?

6. Do intergovernmental commodity-control agreements encourage or discourage free enterprise and economic opportunity? What bearing have they
on national full-employment policies?

7. Explain the statement that, through a system of exchange controls, a
nation's economy is severed from the international price system.

8. What objectives may be attained or made easier of accomplishment by a
system of foreign-exchange control?

9. Describe briefly the extent to which embargoes against importations are
used or may legally be used in the United States.

10. Are import requirements of the pure food and drug laws a discriminatory restriction in favor of United States producers?

11. Cite an example or two of restrictions on imports of (a) freight and shipping services, (b) travel, (c) long-term capital, and (d) short-term capital.

12. How may cartels restrict a nation's imports, even though there may be no
customs duty or import tax on foreign goods?

13. What important step has the United States taken, through the United
Nations, in the direction of reducing restrictive business practices by cartels?

[13] *Department of State Bulletin*, Oct. 8, 1951, pp. 590–596.

CHAPTER 18

Restrictions on Exports

In a world suffering from shortage of sound foreign exchange and in general from an international hunger for more goods, it might seem inconsistent that obstacles to export trade are so prevalent on the part of some countries most severely in need of hard-currency goods. It should be observed, however, that some of these obstacles are not intended primarily to discourage or restrict exports as such; this effect may be secondary or incidental. Many restrictions, it will be seen, are employed to accomplish directional control of exports for the very purpose of channeling sales into areas whose currencies (or goods) are highly desired.

Several Objectives Sought. Actions taken which serve or tend to restrict exports may be said to be for the following main purposes:

1. Revenue
2. To assure standard or quality
3. To reserve to the home market all or a significant portion of items in short supply
4. To permit more centralized direction of items in short supply
5. To prevent goods of strategic importance from reaching the hands of unfriendly powers
6. To permit control over *surpluses* through controlling exports, production, and/or price

Several types of restrictions have evolved; each may differ in some degree among countries employing it. Naturally, to invoke, or enter, such policies, the exporting country must feel that its product or products are very necessary to others, and production must be relatively localized among only a few countries.

As with imports, restrictions may be public or private in origin, but they generally affect private trade. There seems, moreover, to be an increasing tendency to remove from private hands the unrestricted exportation of certain items.

REVENUE-PRODUCING, OR QUALITATIVE, RESTRICTIONS

Export Tariffs

Historically, the traditional obstacle to export trade, as well as to imports, has been the tariff. Probably no government would impose an export tariff if its effect were to be to reduce substantially its export trade. Hence it is evident that the primary purpose of the export tariff must be something else. This may be revenue or it may be some form of discrimination. Export taxes are a fairly easy tax to collect and, for revenue purposes, may be as feasible, since they have the same effect, as any other type of tax falling on the producer or exporter. This point is sometimes overlooked. A tariff is no more of a burden on the exporter than any other form of tax on him. As with all other taxes, its incidence is on the exporter unless it can be shifted, but this may be impossible, unless it applies also to the exporter's competitors, because no subsequent purchaser will pay the resultant higher price if it can be avoided.

Many Countries Impose Export Duties. While this is by no means a complete list, the following countries all use or have used export tariffs:

Afghanistan: On most items and running as high as 35 per cent ad valorem
Brazil: On coffee
Ceylon: On copra, coconut oil, and fresh and dessicated coconut
Colombia: On hides, livestock, bananas, coffee, gums, and others
Dominican Republic: On tobacco, lumber, cacao beans, and coffee
Ecuador: On current manufactures of silver
France: On scrap iron
Honduras: On wood, bananas, and other agricultural products
Iceland: On salt herring, other fish products, and all agriculural products
India: On tea, cotton, textiles, pepper, jute, and carpets
Indonesia: A general export duty of 20 per cent, with numerous exceptions reducing the rates to as low as 3 per cent
Iraq: On dates, gold, horses, and licorice root
Mexico: A surtax on all exports, even when there is no export duty; export duty on pineapples, bananas, and coffee
Morocco: On olives and iron ore
Panama: On bananas
Peru: On certain lumber, copper, silver, and lead
Portugal: On coarse wool
Sierra Leone: On palm kernels, kola nuts, and ginger

Purpose Varies among Countries. The variety of objectives of an export tariff may be seen from a few illustrations. British Malaya imposed an export tariff on tin exported outside of the British Empire; this was a form of empire preference and really a discrimination against nonempire areas. Haiti realized 83 per cent of its total governmental revenue from customs (import and export) in 1936–1937, 79 per cent in 1940–1941, 68 per cent in 1942–1943, and 74 per cent in 1945–1946. Uruguay used an export tax on some goods to discourage exports if the goods were in short supply locally. The Belgian Congo employed three types of export duties:

1. Intended for revenue only. This was a flat percentage on each commodity, usually 6 per cent.
2. Customs surtax, for revenue. This was imposed to enable the government to capture some rainfall profits.
3. Selective tax, to support the governmental institute for agricultural experimentation.

Under the second and third types, the tax was an actual amount rather than a percentage of value. It varied according to the world market price of the commodity and was subject to change every three months if the world price changed by at least 10 per cent.[1] Cuba, in December, 1948, imposed taxes on import and export documents, revenue from which was to support in part a retirement and pension fund for customhouse brokers. Nicaragua imposed an export tax on coffee to finance the building of highways and an additional export tax, if the price of coffee rose exorbitantly, to build up reserves of the Banco Nacional.

Use in United States Prohibited. Export duties are not employed by the United States; the subject is dealt with specifically in two articles of the Constitution. Article I, Sec. X, Par. 2, reads:

> No state shall, without the consent of the Congress, lay any impost or duties on imports or exports, except what may be absolutely necessary for executing its inspection laws; and the net produce of all duties and imposts, laid by any state on imports or exports, shall be for the use of the Treasury of the United States; and all such laws shall be subject to the revision and control of the Congress.

In *Merritt v. Welch* (104 U.S. 694, 700, 26), this clause has been interpreted to mean that Congress alone has the authority to levy such duties. Art. I, Sec. IX, Par. 5 of the Constitution reads: "No tax or duty shall be laid on articles exported from any state." Hence, since Congress alone has the authority to levy such (export) duties, and since the Constitution prohibits a tax or duty on articles exported from any state, the policy to be followed by the United States is clear.

Further, in *Fairbanks v. U.S.* (181 U.S. 283, 289), a tax on a foreign bill of lading was declared void because it is, in effect, a tax on exports.

---

[1] *International Reference Service,* U.S. Department of Commerce, Vol. 59, August, 1948.

However, a general tax, laid on all property alike, and not levied on goods in the course of exportation or because of their intended exporta- tion, is not within the Constitutional prohibition, although the goods may happen to be exported afterward (*Turpin v. Burgess*, 117 U.S. 504, 507).

Restrictions of Pure Food and Drug Laws

In the preceding chapter, it was stated that some importers complain of the food and drug laws as an obstacle to imports. It is interesting to note that a comparable complaint is registered by some exporters, with the charge that necessity to comply with United States regulations in these matters would be an effective obstacle to some export business. In reporting Senate subcommittee hearings on legislation intended to ban exportation of adulterated or misbranded food and drugs,[2] the *New York Journal of Commerce*[3] stated that spokesmen for the Grocery Manu- facturers of America, the National Canners Association, and the California Dried Fruit Export Association assailed the proposed bill (H.R. 562) re- quiring exported products to meet Food and Drug standards now apply- ing to domestic trade.

The counterproposal of the interested groups would "permit the ex- port of any food or drug fit for human consumption and not injurious to health if it is prepared and labeled in a form and manner sanctioned by official action or local custom usage in the foreign country to which it is destined." The Food and Drug Administration favors amending the law, especially Sec. 801, to require that exports meet domestic standards, except when these conflict with the law of a foreign country. In that case they must meet foreign law or requirements.

Views Depend on Position of Viewer. As of this writing, in early 1952, outcome of the controversy is unknown. One may speculate, though, on the effect on international good feeling when our laws permit United States firms to export products which cannot be sold to United States citizens because the products do not meet the standards of cleanliness or purity prescribed for home consumption. On the other hand, United States producers may solidly argue that foreign manufacturers are en- abled under their laws to operate under conditions which may not be as costly as those imposed by United States regulations for domestic products. Accordingly, competition is made more difficult.

In any case, an enforcement problem prevails if goods ostensibly marked for export and not meeting standards for distribution in the United States "accidentally" reach domestic distribution channels.

---

[2] Under the Food, Drug, and Cosmetic Act, exporters of foods, drugs, and cos- metics cannot be charged with adulteration or misbranding if the product meets specifications of foreign buyers and is labeled to show that it is intended for export.

[3] Aug. 9, 1949.

Inspection procedures are imposed by some other countries to provide assurance that the product exported meets grade or class standards. These serve as a general benefit to the export trade of the country in its selling abroad by grade designation and are supposed to encourage reliance on the part of the foreign importer as to the uniformity or quality of the commodity. Most coffee countries, for example, require inspection of the coffee as to grade; incidentally, a double purpose is served, in that inspection affords the government a more definite basis for checking on reported receipts for exchange-control administration.

In the United States, the Grain Standards Act requires inspection and certification every time a shipment, interstate or foreign, is made of wheat, corn, oats, rye, barley, flaxseed, or other specified grains.[4] While classed as restrictive, the main purpose of the Act is not to reduce exports. The poorer qualities may be blocked from being exported if minimum standards are not met, but the objective is to assure reliance on designated grades or quality.

QUANTITATIVE RESTRICTIONS

Export Quotas

Quotas are established under certain conditions which limit, regardless of price, the quantity of exports in total or to any particular country or area. The action may be unilateral or by agreement.

When an item is in relatively short supply, as in the case of burlap shortly after the Second World War, or when a monopoly position or something close to it prevails, a quota scheme may be used to divert exports away from countries whose foreign exchange is not especially desired at the time, or for political reasons. Examples of the application of export quotas for whatever reason are:

Angola: On peanuts
Argentina: On pink garlic
El Salvador: On vegetable oils and sesame seeds
India: On raw hides and raw sheepskins (for exportation to hard-currency
     areas only), pepper, and manganese ore

In addition, the international allocation of and resultant quotas for many products, such as fats and oils, cereals and cocoa, were accomplished through the International Emergency Food Council during and immediately following the Second World War.

Many items were placed under export control, with quotas established, by the United States because they were in relatively short supply, but with record postwar production in practically all fields, both here and

[4] 2, F.C.A., Title 7, Par. 76.

abroad, this danger of export drain had practically disappeared in early 1952. Coupled with this, also, were lack of acceptable currency in many foreign hands for purchases in the United States and a very significant shift in the purpose of export control as far as the United States was concerned. An export quota on cotton, its major export commodity, was instituted by the United States in October, 1950, in view of a short crop and dwindling supplies.

Export Licenses

The system of licensing exports serves both to control and to restrict exports. As a counterpart to the quota scheme, a licensing system can serve to allocate goods in short supply. But in many countries employing close control over foreign commerce, export licenses are required as a means of assuring more complete control, which can refer either to volume or to direction, and which also serves to render even more binding the restrictions prescribed on foreign exchange. It means, also, where such may be the objective, that the hand of the government is strengthened in the daily conduct of business, thus limiting in a corresponding degree the right of the individual.

United States Experience, 1940–1951. The United States experience has been as follows. On July 2, 1940, the office of Administrator of Export Control was established. It was charged with deciding which exports were to be licensed and with administering the program which then served (1) to prevent an excessive drain of scarce commodities, (2) to retain for domestic use those materials deemed essential to national defense and to the welfare of our civilian economy, and (3) later to help prevent our goods from reaching actual and potential enemies. The number of commodity classifications under control of this type was about 3,000 in 1944, and was reduced from about 800 on V-J Day to about 350 by the end of 1947. But in March, 1948, when export control became predominantly an instrument of national security, approximately 2,300 groups were under control. Continuous review of the relative strategic importance of each classification enabled the freeing of many from control so that in August, 1949, the commodity classifications on the Positive List[5] numbered 1,004. Further deletions were made, and in March, 1950, the Positive List contained 697 commodity classifications.[6] But in view of expansion of demands on the economy due to rearmament incident to and following the Korean engagement, the Positive List underwent a significant change. The number of Census Schedule B

[5] A prescribed list of commodities requiring a validated export license from the Department of Commerce. This list is subdivided (1951) to exempt from license requirements certain commodities if destination is in the Western Hemisphere.
[6] *Foreign Commerce Weekly,* Mar. 27, 1950, p. 4.

export classifications on it had increased to 737 by September, 1950; to 775 by December, 1950; and to 916 by June 30, 1951.[7]

The continuation of export control in 1948 as a security measure and an instrument of national foreign policy placed an emphasis other than commercial on the export licensing program. Over the following two years, commodity coverage was limited to highly strategic commodities and, after the beginning of hostilities in Korea, substantially increased geographic coverage was widely expanded. Export licensing technique in the United States in 1951 was a matter of both commodity-supply status and geographic destination. As of August, 1951, commodities in the "RO" designation required an export license for shipment to any destination except Canada,[8] and those under control to "R" destinations required a license to all destinations except those in the Western Hemisphere. Of the 916 commodity classifications on the Positive List in June, 1951, 685 were in the "RO" group and 337 were in the "R" group.

The impact of controls is illustrated by the following tabulation of percentages of controlled to total exports. The figures reflect the increased

Quarter	1948	1949	1950	1951
1st	25.9	42.5	17.6	31.7
2d	42.3	41.7	17.3	32.6
3d	41.4	31.2	20.0	33.1
4th	41.1	21.7	29.2	27.9

percentage of exports made subject to security control in March, 1948; the selective removal of commodities in 1949 and early 1950, which brought the number on the list to its lowest level; the expansion of the group "R" area in March, 1950, to include all destinations except the Western Hemisphere; and the addition of short-supply items to the Positive List during later 1950.

For a complete coverage of the subject, the student is referred to the annual *Comprehensive Export Schedules,* and supplementary *Current Export Bulletins,* issued by the U.S. Department of Commerce.

Intergovernmental Commodity-control Agreements

As was mentioned in the preceding chapter, intergovernmental commodity agreements involve either exporting countries alone or both exporting and importing countries. The restriction on exports arises from

[7] Fourteenth, fifteenth, and sixteenth quarterly reports required of the Secretary of Commerce by the Export Control Act of 1949, as amended.

[8] Canada, itself, has an export-control system, but compliance authorities of the United States may revoke a United States exporter's license if it is found that he shipped merchandise into Canada with prior knowledge that it would be reexported.

agreement concerning the amount to be exported and the countries to which the exports are to move. Actually, a restriction on exports to one country may mean increased exports to another, so it is not to be inferred that all intergovernmental agreements mean a reduction in total exports of the product. What may be sought is governmental control over directional flow of the trade to effect planned social distribution of items in short supply or to accomplish any one of several political or economic aims.

The Problem of Surpluses. The concept of intergovernmental commodity agreements is substantially encouraged by the social implications of what are called "burdensome" surpluses. Agreements may evolve from efforts to control home production and/or prices or from the rationalization of "more orderly marketing." In this respect, agreement on export quotas is an integral part of governmental schemes to control prices. These involve bilateral or multilateral agreements setting quotas and, sometimes, production; they mean negotiation with foreign governments or private foreign interests before the quota is established.

The fundamental point involved, in so far as the student of foreign commerce is concerned, is whether such agreements are good economics, for they vitally affect the freedom of enterprise on the part of world traders as well as on the part of producers. But since these agreements have been adopted, and there is in force an Interim Coordinating Committee for International Commodity Arrangements, the student should inform himself well on their organization and operation. For the present, it will suffice to indicate that these agreements are an obstacle to total exports or to freedom of action on the part of the individual trader, as well as to imports, whatever their purpose may be. By way of consideration of their over-all effect on the volume and direction of trade, it should also be mentioned that under bilateral or multilateral quotas, provision can better be made to have exports spread evenly over the quota period, if desirable. Licensing by the exporting country tends to eliminate difficulties associated with appeals and pressures from importers in the quota country.

Several Agreements Now in Force. Examples of governmental restrictions on the free flow of exports, as to either volume or direction, are the Inter-American Coffee Agreement, now discontinued (see Chapter 20), the International Wheat Agreement (which became operative on July 1, 1949, as far as the United States is concerned) and allocations under the Food and Agriculture Organization of the United Nations. While not all-inclusive, the list of items affected to some extent, and at some time or other in recent years, includes beef, coffee, cotton, petroleum, rice, rubber, sugar, tea, timber, tin, wheat, and wool. It is interesting to note that all of these items except timber are included in the list of 26 of the more important foodstuffs and raw materials entering world trade as tabulated by the League of Nations.[9] This list shows exports of these 26 items to have been about 31 per cent of total world exports in 1938; the list affected by intergovernmental agreements of some type totals about 63 per cent of the value of the 26 leading items and about 20 per cent of total world exports. Caution should be exercised in pondering the significance of the figure, inasmuch as many countries may not be or have been parties to the arrangements concerning specific items; indeed, as for the United States, we were party to the agreement on coffee and wheat, but neither of these was in effect in 1938. Interest of the United States in other arrangments in early 1950 was restricted to participation in the study groups which will be described in Chapter 20.

Exchange Controls

Concurrent with the restriction which exchange control imposes on volume and directional flow of imports is its similar effect on exports. Under the scheme, the exporter is required to turn over to his government, central bank, or other designated agency all or part of the foreign exchange he acquires. It is bought by his government at a price determined by it. In those countries in which the exporter is permitted to retain part of the exchange he acquires, he may be allowed to do so in order to use that part for promotional work; in other cases, he may be permitted to dispose of it in the free market. In some cases, there are several prices or buying rates for the same foreign exchange, depending on the basic transactions out of which the exchange was derived. This system is known as multiple exchange rates.

The Argentine Multiple-rate System. In Argentina, for instance, the following rates, in pesos per U.S. dollar, prevailed in October, 1949:[10]

FOR EXPORTS

Basic: 3.3582, applied to beef, mutton, wheat, corn, barley, rye, and oilseeds

Preferential A: 4.8321, applied to wool, hides, vegetable oils, oil cakes, tallow, meat extracts, and certain prepared meats

---

[9] *The Network of World Trade*, League of Nations, 1942, p. 30.

[10] *Foreign Commerce Weekly.* Oct. 17, 1949, p. 10, and *International Financial Statistics*, July, 1950, p. 146.

In August, 1950, the Argentine peso was devalued and a free exchange market was permitted for specified exports not readily marketable abroad, nonessential imports, and specified financial transactions. Under the new system, transactions for the majority of exports and imports will be at the two fixed rates of 5 and 7.5 pesos per dollar. *The Journal of Commerce* and *The Wall Street Journal,* cited in *International Financial News Survey,* International Monetary Fund, Sept. 1, 1950. See also *International Financial Statistics,* October, 1950, p. 137.

Preferential B: 5.7286, applied to combed wool, cheese, butter, casein, powdered milk, quebracho extract, cattle hair, pulses, pork, eggs, and shark-liver oil

Special: 7.1964, applied to casings, gelatin, stearin, ground bones, leather, salted meats, fresh fruits, tung oil, tungsten, and mica

Free: 8.98, financial remittances

Preferential and special export rates were also reported to apply to various manufactured products.

FOR IMPORTS

Preferential A: 3.7313, applied to coal, coke, petroleum, and petroleum by-products

Preferential B: 5.3714, applied to drugs and various raw materials and articles of popular consumption

Basic: 6.0857, applied to essential imports not granted exchange at preferential rates

Auction: 13.6188, applied to other permitted imports.

The rate in the free market, controlled by the Central Bank, was about 9 pesos on Oct. 3. This rate applied to nontrade transactions, including authorized remittances on account of foreign capital.

Obviously, the possibility of stimulating or discouraging the exportation of individual items is very great. Classification of items into the group more favored or less favored will be either promotional or restrictive, since the exporter will receive more or fewer pesos for the same number of U.S. dollars, depending on what product he exported from Argentina. Suppose the exporter were to sell merchandise to a United States importer for, say, U.S.$10,000. He can receive for his U.S. dollars the basic rate of 3.3582 pesos per dollar if the goods exported happen to be oilseeds. But he can receive the special rate of 7.1964 pesos per U.S. dollar if the merchandise exported is a shipment of tung oil. To acquire the same number of pesos, in which his costs are incurred, the exporter would have to quote a very much higher price (for the supposedly similarly valued merchandise in Argentina) to the buyer of oilseeds in the United States than he would have to quote to the buyer of tung oil. Thus, exports of goods the government desires to discourage, or finds it unnecessary to encourage, will be possible only at a lower or less favorable realization to the exporter. Conversely, he will be able to quote a lower price in terms of foreign exchange if he is dealing in one of the more favored items.

Effect Same as Special Tax on Producers and Exporters. The effect of this type of exchange control is the same as a special tax on one group of producers and exporters. The differential in price may be due to the importance of the exported item to the economy of the exporting country by way of jobs involved or drain on resources, to the need or desire to stimulate export trade in particular items, or to difficulty encountered abroad in selling the respective items. It may also serve as an indirect subsidy to the exporter of processed or manufactured goods as compared with the exporter of raw materials (example, hides at 4.8321 and leather at 7.1964). The directional flow of export trade can also be influenced by the offer of a relatively more attractive price for foreign exchange of one country than for that of another, even though the exportation of identical goods provided both types of exchange. At least one country, Pakistan, instituted the requirement that all exports to the United States be paid for in dollars, with the proceeds returned to proper authorities.

Discussion of the various ways in which exchange control may influence trade, or the other goals which may be achieved through employment of the scheme, should not be understood as an endorsement of the idea. The goals may be desirable, in the eyes of some, but the means are quite questionable or undesirable if one sides with freedom of enterprise and against statism. It would be very difficult, indeed, to propose here that the end justifies the means.

Embargoes

Many prohibitions had to be imposed on export trade for security reasons during the war. But in times other than war, embargoes may also be applied because of the desire to have raw materials processed in the home country, in order to conserve nonreplaceable resources or perhaps in order to protect a favored position by making it more difficult for competition to develop. Success of such a policy may depend on the extent of monopoly which the country prohibiting the export may enjoy. Among the products facing some degree of embargo are:

Mahogany or mahogany logs from certain Central American countries: This is a good example of the use of an embargo for different objectives. In May, 1946, Cuba prohibited the exportation of mahogany or mahogany cuttings for a period of five years, in order to preserve its dwindling supplies. (It is estimated that it takes from 40 to 60 years for a mahogany tree to grow to mature size.) Guatemala, on the other hand, placed an embrago on the exportation of mahogany logs, but not on the exportation of mahogany sawn lumber.

Live lobsters and clams from Mexico: Only boiled lobsters and shucked clams may be exported, under a government resolution published in June, 1948. This measure was taken to protect the fish-packing industry.

Raw alligator skins from Peru: By a decree of December, 1948, this prohibition was adopted to promote and protect the industrialization of Peruvian domestic raw materials. Exports of tanned skins and finished skin products are permitted.

Natural gas from Alberta, Canada: In the summer of 1949, the provincial government prohibited natural-gas exports from Alberta to other Canadian provinces or to the United States, at least until the government could be satisfied that sufficient reserves are available, through conservation and proration practices, to meet domestic and industrial requirements.

Tobacco seeds from the United States: Neither tobacco seeds nor live tobacco plants may be exported from the United States or its possessions without written permission of the Secretary of Agriculture. This permit is to be granted only after presentation of satisfactory proof that the seeds or plants are to be used for experimental purposes only.

From the foregoing, it is evident that embargoes are not one of the most encompassing restrictions, but use for any of several purposes is found in many countries.

OTHER RESTRICTIONS

Reservation of Items for State Trading

Just as the importation of some items is reserved for trading by the state or its designated agency, the exportation of others is similarly in vogue. The oustanding examples are possibly the U.S.S.R., which maintains strict control over all trading, and the Argentine Institute for the Promotion of Trade, which has the power to reserve to itself the trading in any item, leaving the remaining items for trade by individuals. The United States government's activity in reserving to itself certain exportations of grain; Peru's establishment of a monopoly over the production and sale of coca; and the establishment of over 20 monopoly foreign-trading companies in Czechoslovakia following its entry into the Soviet orbit may be listed as only a few of the many illustrations of this restriction on exports by private traders. Some of these, of course, are temporary, while others are permanent; some pertain to only one or a selected few products, while others go across the board.

RESTRICTIONS ON EXPORTS OTHER THAN MERCHANDISE

Since the end of the Second World War, and with growing recognition of the interdependence of all the factors comprising world trade, probably more attention has been given the movement of capital than at any time in the past. In view of the apparent inability of several countries to acquire sufficient sound currency to continue large purchases from the United States, and the general dislike on the part of many United States interests of seeing exports and imports brought into closer balance by reducing exports to the level of imports, a relatively "painless" remedy has become popular. That remedy is the hope that the export surplus will be offset by purchases of foreign investments (actually an import, but commonly referred to as the exportation of capital). Whether this proposal is to be considered feasible or not, restrictions are to be found, as in the case of many other international economic dealings. Some restrictions are imposed, perhaps inadvertently or incidentally, by the country able to provide the capital. But most restrictions are attributable to the foreign countries which would appear to be ripe for development and thus fit subjects for capital investments.

Restrictions on Investments by Foreigners. There is a natural fear on the part of many smaller governments of domination by foreign creditors and of exploitation by financial interests in other countries. In this respect, most of these countries have adopted laws or regulations which prescribe that a certain percentage of ownership in a business enterprise must be reserved to citizens of the country in which the business is located. Such is the case in Mexico, Brazil, and many other countries. Another regulation which can serve to restrict foreign investment imports is the prescription that a high percentage of the jobs must be filled by citizens of the country in which the business is located, or that no position in a business domiciled in that country may be held by a foreigner if it can be filled by a citizen of the country in question. Furthermore, governments may reserve to themselves the development of certain lines of activity, such as transportation or public utilities. This, of course, makes it impossible for a foreign country to import the investment. In the same direction, limitations on the amount of dividends which may be drawn out, taxation, or social laws may also serve to deter foreign investment which, to the creditor, is an import.

Fear for Safety of Capital Is Powerful Factor. Aside from laws to guard excessive influence by foreign investors, a fear for the safety of capital is a powerful deterrent (although at times a stimulus) to capital movements. Such are the possibility of the expropriation of capital, the imposition of a restriction on the transfer or convertibility of earnings from foreign investments, and the uncertainty of political developments in several countries of the world. Proposals have been suggested, as described in Chapters 15 and 19, to reduce these obstacles to the category of insurable risks.

Restrictions Apply on Transfers of Currency. In addition to restrictions on the movement of capital funds, another prevalent obstruction pertains

DICHIARAZIONE DI DIVISE E TITOLI ESTERI
DECLARATION DE DEVISES ET DE TITRES ETRANGERS
FOREIGN EXCHANGE DECLARATION

DA PRESENTARE ALLA DOGANA ITALIANA
A PRESENTER A LA DOUANE ITALIENNE
TO BE SURRENDERED TO THE ITALIAN CUSTOMS OFFICER

Io sottoscritto (Nome e Cognome)
Je Soussignè (Nom et prénoms)
I the undersigned (Surname and name) ....

Indirizzo completo
Adresse complète
Full postal address ....

Nazionalità   Passaporto N.
Nationalité .... Passeport N.
Nationality   Passport N. ....

Dichiaro di importare in Italia i valori e i capitali qui appresso indicati.
Déclare importer en Italie les valeurs et devises indiquées ci-après.
Declare that I import into Italy the undermentioned foreign exchange.

BIGLIETTI BILLETS NOTES	AMMONTARE IN CIFRE MONTANT EN CHIFFRES AMOUNT IN FIGURES	AMMONTARE IN LETTERE MONTANT EN LETTRES AMOUNT IN LETTERS
Lire Italiane Lires Italiennes Italian Lire		
Dollari Dollars U. S. A. U. S. A. dollars		
Sterline Livres Anglaises Pounds Sterling		
Fiorini Olandesi Florins Hollandais Dutch Florins		
Franchi Belgi Francs Belges Belgian Francs		
Franchi Svizzeri Francs Suisses Swiss Francs		
Altre divise Autres devises Other foreign currency		
Chèques de voyage Travellers' cheques		
Assegni Circolari Chèques		
Lettere di credito Lettres de crédit Letters of credit		
Titoli di Stato Titres d' Etat Government Securities		
Oro (MONETE) Or (Monnaie) Gold (coins)		

DATA DATE	FIRMA SIGNATURE	VISTO DELLA DOGANA (VISE DE LA DOUANE)

9243-61083

Fig. 13. Copy of foreign-exchange report for foreign visitors. (*Courtesy of Pan American Airways.*)

to the movement of currency. Several European countries have imposed limitations on the amount of currency which can be taken out of the country by travelers; the reason for this limitation is to prevent the growth of a market abroad in currency which is controlled at home. For the same reason, limitations hold on the amount of currency which a traveler may bring into a country—the currency of the country being entered, and sometimes of others. Figure 13 is a reproduction of the form which was required to be filled out by travelers entering Italy in 1950 and to be surrendered to customs when leaving. On the reverse side are instructions for selling imported foreign currency only to banks and authorized money changers and a space for entering transactions in exchange by the traveler in question.

PRIVATE RESTRICTIONS ON EXPORTS

Cartels

The several impediments to exports arising from governmental action might appear to leave little open in the way of further types of restrictions. Yet a very direct obstacle appears through private rather than governmental arrangement. Specifically, the restriction is by means of a cartel agreement. International cartels have at times been entered and maintained so secretly, as far as the public is concerned, that the upheaval caused by a war brings out investigations and studies which reveal the extent and effect of our own participation. Typical are two excellent studies by Stocking and Watkins, who estimate that about 47.4 per cent of agricultural products, 86.9 per cent of mineral products, and 42.7 per cent of manufactured products sold in the United States in 1939 were to some extent the subjects of cartelization at some time during the 1930s. Items included in these computations were those having both a direct and an indirect, if substantial, effect on the United States market.[11]

Types of Cartel Organization. Cartels may be classified into three types: the association, the patent-licensing agreement, and the combine.[12]

The association may seek by mutual agreement to settle such competitive problems as price, production, exports, and/or geographic division of markets. The combine, evidenced by common ownership or management, is perhaps the least widely used and the least far-reaching. Patent-licensing arrangements are based on the legal consideration that most countries grant monopolistic rights to the patent owner and that these are recognized to a large extent internationally. Thus, in order to be able to use the patents owned by foreign companies, there may have to be an agreement or specification as to the conditions under which they can be used, pertaining to prices, production, markets, and the like. The patent-licensing agreement appears to be most widely used

[11] George W. Stocking and M. W. Watkins, *Cartels or Competition* (New York, The Twentieth Century Fund, Inc., 1948), p. 93.

[12] E. E. Pratt, *Foreign Trade Handbook* (Chicago and London, The Dartnell Corporation, 1949), pp. 1106–1107; Stephen Enke and Virgil Salera, *International Economics* (New York, Prentice-Hall, Inc., 1947), pp. 390–392.

in highly technical industries such as the chemical, the electrical, and the petroleum.

Whatever may be the legal basis or rationalization on which the cartel is based, the functions or objectives may be several:

1. They may serve to fix prices.
2. They may limit or apportion production.
3. They may limit or apportion markets.
4. They may allocate markets.
5. They may require selling through a special cartel agency.
6. They may call for a redistribution of profits according to an adopted formula.

Abandon Free Working of Cost-price Differentials. By price-fixing agreements, the international movement of goods in response to the struggle for markets based on cost and price differentials is estopped. This affects both imports and exports. An example is found in the case of tungsten.[13] Limiting or apportioning exports on the part of each producer is the most direct restriction on exports, for the producers simply agree not to export more, regardless of sensitive changes in the market. Naturally, the limitation or apportionment of exports will also be felt by the importing country. Allocation of markets serves as a regulator of the directional flow of exports and as a very potential limitation on both exports and imports. For example, in several agreements between foreign cartels and United States producers or export associations, the United States market was respected as the reserved territory for domestic producers, while United States producers agreed not to export to certain areas abroad.[14] Thus, by producers agreeing not to export to these delineated areas, the possibility of importing by merchants in these areas was effectively precluded. Among products involved in such agreements were magnesium, alkali, plastics, paints and varnishes, and fertilizers. Agreements such as these do not necessarily limit exports of the respective companies (countries) which are parties to the agreement, provided they are to the specified or permitted areas. But it is clear that imports into the delineated areas are deliberately restricted and even more reduced when the market is reserved for domestic producers. Pratt, in his *Foreign Trade Handbook,* discusses the effect of cartels on international trade and reasons that they have cut down to some extent the volume and value of products entering world trade. He suggests the possibility, also, that more orderly processes and greater attention to

[13] C. D. Edwards, *Economic and Political Aspects of International Cartels,* Monograph 1, Subcommittee on War Mobilization of the Committee on Military Affairs, U.S. Senate, 1944.

[14] George W. Stocking and M. W. Watkins, *Cartels in Action* (New York, The Twentieth Century Fund, Inc., 1946), pp. 336, 433–435, 451.

the promotional aspects of the business may actually increase the total volume of business over a period of years.[15]

Export Associations

Export associations are not new to the American scene. They have been made legal through the Webb-Pomerene Act, which was passed in 1918. This law permits American firms to combine among themselves, or with foreign companies, in matters affecting export trade, provided there is no restraint of domestic trade or restraint of the export trade of any domestic competitor. They are allowed, for instance, to agree on prices; they are allowed to allocate markets and to agree not to compete with each other in the designated areas. Both of these agreements could not stand legally if practiced on United States markets, but it has been pointed out that "intent of the Webb law notwithstanding, there is ample evidence to indicate that American firms have combined with foreign firms in connection with purely domestic as well as export business."[16] The possibility of restricted exports *by agreement* is clear, although this may not have been or may not be the foremost reason for forming an export association.

REVIEW QUESTIONS

1. What are the objectives of restrictions on exports?
2. On what basis may it be said that use of export tariffs is prohibited in the United States?
3. Are provisions of the pure food and drug laws a restriction on exports?
4. Describe the United States experience with export licenses, and the export-control system as of 1951.
5. What is the Positive List?
6. How may intergovernmental commodity-control agreements serve to be a restriction on export opportunities?
7. Explain how a system of multiple exchange rates operates as a restriction on exports.
8. List a few cases in which countries have imposed embargoes on exports.
9. If foreign investments are so roundly proclaimed as desirable, and one means of attaining international economic development, why do some foreign countries impose restrictions against them?
10. In what way may cartels be said to abandon the free working of cost-price differentials? Is this economically desirable?
11. How may cartels and export associations be said to be a restriction on exports?

[15] Pratt, *op. cit.*, p. 1111.
[16] Enke and Salera, *op. cit.*, p. 390.

CHAPTER 19

Promotion of Foreign Commerce

In foreign commerce, as in other economic activities representing the individual decisions of thousands of entrepreneurs, or in governmental actions where government represents many varied interests, there will be found at one and the same time certain inconsistencies in policy or in action. In some respects, we take action or follow policies designed to reduce our foreign commerce, particularly imports, either in specific items or apparently overall. In other respects, we take action or follow policies designed to stimulate or promote our foreign commerce. At times, the over-all emphasis differs; as of the time of this writing (1952), emphasis is definitely in the direction of promoting the expansion of our foreign commerce, especially imports. The much-publicized world dollar shortage, the reconstruction of Europe, and the development of the underdeveloped areas of the world all point toward an increase in our total foreign commerce. Further, the "expansionist" approach to world trade seems high in the policy of our government, as evidenced by official statements appearing at the time of adoption of our adherence to a number of international economic arrangements. Accordingly, promotion of foreign commerce must be studied because the several efforts in that direction play as prominent a part as do the various restrictions.

Promotion May Be of Private or of Governmental Trade. At the outset, the question may be asked whether promotion of foreign commerce means the promotion of more commerce by government (more participation in international trading) or the promotion of more trade on the part of private traders. Since United States foreign-trading activities are primarily under private operation, it must be evident that action to promote commerce should be directed toward creating an atmosphere in which private traders may find more opportunity to conduct their affairs. After all, no government or organization can create additional trade for individual importers and exporters carrying their own risks. It can only strive for improved circumstances or conditions under which an entrepreneur can find opportunities. It is, then, with a view to activities aimed primarily at promoting more trade by individuals that this chapter is organized.

Importer and Exporter Are the Principals. The numerous promotional activities may be better understood by looking on the traders—the importer and the exporter—as the two principals. They may be compared, to use a rough illustration, to boxers in a ring, supporting a retinue of service functions. These functions are, among others, banks, transportation companies, freight forwarders, customhouse brokers, insurance people, and ports. Many of these private service functions would continue to derive some employment, even if state trading were to expand or if governmental purchasing missions were to become even more general than now. But the mutual interdependence of the principals and their service elements functioning in any locality rests not only on the volume of commerce, but on the routing as well. This explains the fact that trade promotional activities are both public and private, national, regional, and local, and are the effort of an organization of several companies or associations or of a single company.

GOVERNMENTAL ACTIVITIES: TRADE POLICY

For purposes of this chapter, governmental activities, at least in the United States, may be looked on as policy setting in general, as being educational, or as being of a financial nature. In the field of trade policy, at least the following deserve special mention: (1) The principle of reciprocal national treatment, (2) the unconditional most-favored-nation principle, (3) the Reciprocal Trade Agreements program, and (4) treaties of friendship, commerce, and navigation. These will be discussed in this order.

Principle of Reciprocal National Treatment

All countries do not accord the same treatment to their nationals; in some, the citizen is more or less free than in others. The idea of reciprocal national treatment rests on the desire of a country to protect its own citizens from discrimination when under jurisdiction of other countries. Officially, the principle is incorporated in the so-called "establishment provisions" of our treaties of friendship, commerce, and navigation. These provisions are rules governing the treatment to be accorded persons, property, and interests of the nationals of one country who establish themselves in other countries. The United States follows the policy of according to citizens of other countries the same treatment before law as is accorded citizens of the United States; it demands, in exchange, that in other lands citizens of the United States receive equal treatment with nationals of the respective countries. Maintenance of this principle naturally serves as an element promoting, or at least not discouraging, private international commerce.

Unconditional Most-favored-nation Principle

In the making of commercial treaties, authorities of one country may be impelled to grant special concessions to a second for any of several reasons. Not being available to third countries, these concessions become doubly important competitively. Most-favored-nation clauses, which serve to extend to the commercial interests of one country treatment or consideration at least as favorable as that extended to any other, are of two types, *conditional* and *unconditional*. Under the conditional type, for example, country A extends to country B the same privileges or concessions which it extends to country C, provided that country B also extends to country A the same concessions received from C. This could, of course, work out among any number of countries, as long as any other or others were not equally favored. What this amounts to is relatively narrow negotiating in order to obtain limited concessions practically on a purchase basis. A point to note in this connection is that benefits received by A from C may be of special significance because of the importance of C as a market for A's product; B may not be such a desirable or important market. Furthermore, the competition experienced by A from both C and B will be based on size, volume, and other factors. Accordingly, for the same products, B may actually be a much greater competitive threat to A than is C. On this basis, the *equivalence* of concessions is doubtful, and perhaps these "same privileges or concessions" relating to specified products may not be the same at all when applied to different pairs of countries.

The unconditional type, which is that now followed by the United States,[1] provides that any reductions in trade barriers, even those resulting from bilateral agreements, are to become available to all countries which are not themselves discriminating against the grantor country.[2] Although they are called unconditional,[3] there actually is a condition, which is that the other country party to the agreement must also extend

[1] Since 1923. See Lawrence W. Towle, *International Trade and Commmercial Policy* (New York and London, Harper & Brothers, 1947), p. 383.

[2] Here, by "unconditional" is meant not having to render specific benefits to a second country in exchange or payment for specific benefits received from it.

[3] This feature is covered by the following excerpt from the Reciprocal Trade Agreements Act: "The proclaimed duties . . . shall apply to articles the growth, produce or manufacture of all foreign countries, whether imported directly or indirectly: Provided that the President may suspend the application to articles . . . of any country because of its discriminatory treatment of American commerce. . . ."

to the United States, in this instance, the same concessions extended by the other country to third countries.[4]

The unconditional type more effectively broadens the reductions in trade barriers and contributes to a wider availability of goods internationally with less restrictions. By the process of selective reductions in tariff rates, on a product basis and in negotiations with principal suppliers of these products, the modification of customs duties is put on a more scientific basis. Also, since these reductions are withheld from countries which themselves discriminate against the commercial interests of the United States, domestic producers are offered good protection. The end result of international adherence to the principle of unconditional most-favored-nation clauses will be the abolition of any most favored nation. All will be treated equally.

The Reciprocal Trade Agreements Program

On June 12, 1934, the Tariff Act of 1930 was amended by the signing of the Reciprocal Tariff bill (better known as the Reciprocal Trade Agreements Act), under which the President was given authority to enter into foreign trade agreements with foreign governments or instrumentalities thereof. This authority was definitely circumscribed to a reduction or an increase not to exceed 50 per cent of the duty in effect at the time of signing. By renewal of the Act in 1945, the basis for limitation in reduction or increase was set at Jan. 1, 1945. Thus, the maximum change in the tariff rate permissible is 75 per cent of the rate in effect at the time of original signing—50 per cent up to Jan. 1, 1945, and, if the maximum reduction had been made by that date, 50 per cent of the remainder after Jan. 1, 1945. If the maximum change had not been adopted by Jan. 1, 1945, the total permissible change from the 1934 rate would be correspondingly reduced.

Under this law, no item may be moved from the free to the dutiable list, or vice versa, and specific denial of authority to cancel or reduce, in any manner, any of the indebtedness of any foreign country to the United States is incorporated in the bill.

The intent of *reciprocal* reductions in barriers to trade is indicated by the opening sentence of the amendment, which reads, in part:[5] "for the purpose of expanding foreign markets for the products of the United States . . . so that foreign markets will be made available to those branches of American production which require and are capable of developing such outlets by affording corresponding market opportunities

[4] Some limited exceptions are to be found, arising from previously existing agreements or treaties, such as the British Empire preference scheme and the preference granted Cuba by the United States.

[5] Sec. 350 of the Tariff Act of 1930.

for foreign products in the United States. . . ." What constitutes a satisfactory reciprocal concession for the purpose is left to the President, who conducts these negotiations through the Department of State. Concessions received from other countries may range from reductions in tariffs to binding of duties at existing levels, or from an increase in established quotas to assurance of nondiscrimination in the application of quotas or exchange-control schemes.

As indicated above, the principle of unconditional most-favored-nation treatment is adopted in the Act. Further, no agreement is to be concluded without reasonable public notice of the intention to negotiate such an agreement having been given. In practice, such notices specify the countries with which negotiations are proposed and the list of items on which it is proposed to offer concessions by the United States.

Reciprocal Trade Agreements Procedure. The mechanism by which these arrangements are made (1951) are set out in Executive Order 10082, titled "Prescribing Procedures for the Administration of the Reciprocal Trade Agreements Program." The 1951 extension of the Trade Agreements Act, which imposed on the Tariff Commission the determination of "peril points" on proposed concessions in advance of negotiations, may alter somewhat the detailed procedure outlined in Executive Order 10082. Until March, 1952, however, the order had not been amended.

Under this order, an Interdepartmental Committee on Trade Agreements is provided for. It consists of persons appointed by the Secretaries of State, Treasury, Agriculture, Commerce, Defense, Labor, and Interior, the Administrator for Economic Cooperation, and a commissioner of the Tariff Commission. The Committee submits to the President for his approval a list of articles on which it is proposed to offer concessions through negotiation. Upon approval, the list is made public. Then the Committee for Reciprocity Information, consisting of the same persons, but with the representative of the Tariff Commission as chairman, announces to the public the opportunity to present written or oral testimony concerning the proposed concessions.

After due consideration of this public testimony, the Interdepartmental Committee on Trade Agreements recommends to the President concessions to be sought and offered. Actual negotiations are conducted by government representatives, the proceedings being closed to the public.

"Escape Clause" a Part of Agreements. However, from this point on, interests of individuals or the public are still very much in the picture. Each agreement concluded or renewed since 1942 includes a comprehensive "escape clause," under which any concession granted may be withdrawn if imports traceable to the concession injure or threaten to injure seriously any domestic industry.

As of August, 1952, investigations involving 21 products had been instituted by the Tariff Commission as a result of applications under escape-clause procedure. Four applications had been denied and dismissed by the Commission, 5 had resulted in recommendations to the President that concessions be withdrawn, hearings had been completed or were in process on 10, and the investigations had not reached the stage of hearings on the remaining 2. Of the 5 recommendations made to the President, 3 resulted in proclamations by him, withdrawing the concessions. One of these was on hatters' fur, another was on dried figs, and the third was on certain types of women's fur-felt hats and hat bodies. In this last case, the reduction had been made in a concession to the United Kingdom, but it resulted in greatly increased imports from Czechoslovakia.

Two recommendations to the President that concessions be withdrawn were rejected by him. The first was on garlic; the second, apparently destined to be a classic decision, was on watches, watch movements, parts, and cases. Both were on split decisions by the Tariff Commission, and in acting on the latter the President emphasized several major considerations leading to his conclusion not to adopt the majority recommendations. One was that the fundamental purpose of reciprocal trade agreements is to expand exports and imports. He reasoned that if we should erect new barriers against the importation of Swiss watches, we would at the same time necessitate the erection of additional barriers abroad against our export markets. Secondly, he rejected as a dangerous precedent acceptance of the "share doctrine" employed by the Tariff Commission as the determinant of serious injury. This referred to the Commission's findings that, while domestic watch production had itself increased materially, the expansion did not keep pace with expansion of imports, "so that the industry today enjoys a smaller share of the larger market." On this point, the President felt that there could be no serious injury to the industry, traceable to tariff reductions, if it failed to gain something it had never had. A third major aspect was that by invoking the escape clause and withdrawing concessions, thereby increasing our rates of duty, "we would be striking a heavy blow at our whole effort to increase international trade and permit friendly nations to earn their own dollars and pay their own way in the world."[6] It should be borne in mind that the Tariff Commission's recommendations were by law factual and rather narrow in scope; the Commission is not charged with considering the international implications which may arise from withdrawal of a concession.

[6] Letter from President Truman to Chairmen of Senate Finance Committee and House Ways and Means Committee, published in *The New York Times,* Aug. 15, 1952, p. 8.

Under the program, individual reciprocal trade agreements were concluded with 29 countries. Most of these have been superseded by, and additional agreements have been made through, three multilateral agreements. The first was concluded at Geneva, in 1947, and is known as the General Agreement on Tariffs and Trade. It is commonly referred to as GATT. The second such agreement was made at Annecy, France, in 1949; in effect, it extended GATT by bringing into it 10 additional countries and, by the process of specific negotiations with these 10 countries, extending the list of items on which negotiations had been conducted. The third was undertaken at Torquay, England, concluded in April, 1951, during which time 6 additional countries acceded to GATT. At the Annecy meeting, negotiations were conducted between GATT members and the 10 new countries and among the 10 new countries themselves. But at the Torquay conference, several of the GATT members renegotiated agreements with each other as well as entering new ones with the new members.

Countries with which individual agreements had been entered and which have not acceded to GATT are Argentina, Colombia, Costa Rica, Ecuador, El Salvador, Guatemala, Honduras, Iceland, Iran, Mexico, Paraguay, Peru, Switzerland, and Venezuela. Our agreement with Colombia was discontinued in 1949, and that with Mexico was terminated in 1950.

The General Agreement on Tariffs and Trade. GATT deserves particular attention for two reasons other than the trade-barrier negotiations between the United States and a number of other countries. First of these is that the meeting was the first multination attempt to reduce trade barriers on a reciprocal basis. Negotiations were carried on simultaneously between 106 pairs of countries, with the United States being a party to 15 of the negotiations.[7] Under terms of the Agreement, concessions granted in any of the negotiations inure to the benefit of all countries signatory to the Agreement. Thus, the United States received benefits not only from the 15 negotiations in which it participated directly but also from the 91 other negotiations carried out by other countries.

The second reason for special significance is that GATT went beyond merely negotiating the reduction of trade barriers by incorporating a number of "general provisions" having to do with policy and the long-range conduct of trade. Part I of the general provisions "incorporates the most-favored-nation clause in its unconditional and unlimited form."[8]

[7] *Participation of the United States Government in International Conferences, July 1, 1946–June 30, 1947,* U.S.Department of State Publication 3031, 1948, p. 206.
[8] *Analysis of the General Agreement on Tariffs and Trade,* U.S. Department of State Publication 2983, 1947, p. 195.

Part II deals with the use of barriers to trade other than tariffs. It specifies the principle of reciprocal national treatment on internal taxes and regulations, lays down rules confining the use of antidumping and countervailing duties, sets out a definition of "actual" value for customs purposes, establishes a principle to be followed in connection with importing and exporting formalities, and provides for the liberalization of marks-of-origin regulations. Considerable attention is also given the problem of quantitative restrictions and exchange controls. The articles of agreement represent something in the nature of a *de facto* policy among the contracting governments regarding the use of quotas and of a set of rules governing their employment as a means of adjusting balance-of-payments difficulties. In addition, the use of exchange controls is similarly restricted as a matter of policy. Other problems covered in this part have to do with subsidies and programs for economic development, the general rule being to keep other contracting parties fully informed.

Part III deals with procedural matters, modification of schedules, relation of the agreement to the proposed International Trade Organization, amendments, and withdrawals.

Under the protocol of provisional application, the United States and a few other key countries undertook "to apply provisionally on and after January 1, 1948, (a) Parts I and III of the Agreement and (b) Part II of the Agreement to the fullest extent not inconsistent with existing legislation."[9] At the Torquay conference, a code of standard practices, based on a proposal by the United States delegation, was recommended for general adoption by signatory governments. The conference proposed that the code be used in the application of import- and export-licensing systems, exchange controls, and like measures.[10]

It was indicated in December, 1950, that even more importance would be attached to GATT in view of the decision not to resubmit a request to Congress for legislation permitting United States participation in the proposed International Trade Organization. In its stead, legislation would be requested to permit more complete official adherence to the policies and principles outlined in GATT (especially Part II).[11] These principles are, in substantial part, the same as those embodied in the proposed International Trade Organization charter.

[9] *Ibid.*, p. 206.

[10] See Henry Chalmers, "Standards for Operating Trade Controls Approved at the Torquay Conference," *Foreign Commerce Weekly,* Jan. 15, 1951, p. 3.

[11] Such legislation had not been forthcoming by early 1952. Sec. 10 of the Trade Agreements Extension Act of 1951 reads: "The enactment of this Act shall not be construed to determine or indicate the approval or disapproval by the Congress of the Executive Agreement known as the General Agreement on Tariffs and Trade."

The list of countries involved in each agreement was as follows:[12]

Countries party to the General Agreement on Tariffs and Trade:
Australia
Belgium-Netherlands-Luxembourg
Brazil
Burma
Canada
Ceylon
Chile
China
Cuba
Czechoslovakia
France
India and Pakistan
New Zealand
Norway
Southern Rhodesia
Syro-Lebanese Customs Union
Union of South Africa
United Kingdom
Newfoundland
United States

Additional countries party to the Annecy Agreement:
Denmark
Dominican Republic
Finland
Greece
Haiti
Italy
Liberia
Nicaragua
Sweden
Uruguay

Additional countries party to the Torquay Agreement:
Austria
Western Germany
Korea
Peru
Philippine Republic
Turkey

China withdrew from GATT on May 5, 1950, after due notice by the Nationalist government of China to the United Nations. Indonesia became a member in 1950, and Syria and Lebanon withdrew in 1951. A few other members of GATT did not participate in the Annecy and Torquay conferences.

Treaties of Friendship, Commerce, and Navigation

Bringing of principles such as those described earlier in this chapter into formal adoption by countries is accomplished through governmental treaties.

Historically, the undertaking of commercial treaties as a matter of United States policy dates from the Continental Congress. A Treaty of Amity and Commerce with France was entered in 1778; since that time, about 130 treaties have been negotiated by the United States. Not all of these have covered the same points, as the matters to be in-

[12] Uruguay had not signed the Annecy provisional protocol by October, 1952. Up to the same date, the Torquay protocol had not been signed by Brazil, Nicaragua, Korea, the Philippine Republic, and Uruguay.

corporated have been determined largely by circumstances of the times. In the early years of our country, it was not a matter of urgency to press for formal agreements respecting the rights of persons and property in several foreign countries. But in recent years, this has become of much more importance, especially in view of the postwar position of the United States as both producer and investor.

An extensive program was undertaken at the close of the Second World War for the negotiation of bilateral treaties incorporating principles deemed desirable by United States interests. The instrument used in these agreements is the treaty of friendship, commerce, and navigation.[13] Further impetus to the program evolved from increased emphasis on economic development and from the imposition and retention of restrictions on commerce (aimed largely at the dollar area, principally the United States) on the part of many countries.

General objectives of commercial treaties are manifold, but they hinge largely on matters of developing an assurance to United States business interests against discrimination or unfair treatment in their commercial interests in foreign countries. This deals, for example, with such problems as the right to establish new foreign investments, the question of assurances of fair treatment in control over the enterprise, taxation, and application of exchange controls. Importantly, also, they incorporate provisions dealing with basic personal rights—more, perhaps, than would be accruing under a treaty of reciprocal national treatment.

Specific Rights Sought by Agreement. With such increased interest in economic development of various parts of the world, the government has been pressing for assurances from other governments on such matters as the following:[14]

1. Substantial rights approximating national treatment with respect to the establishment, control, and management of business enterprises in the foreign country concerned
2. National treatment for the enterprise in matters such as taxation which directly affect its operations
3. An unqualified right of prompt and just compensation in the event of expropriation of property
4. The right to withdraw from the foreign country in reasonable amounts earnings, funds for capital transfers, and other funds
5. The right to engage the services of expert technicians and other specialized employees, regardless of nationality

[13] Vernon G. Setser, "Treaties to Aid American Business Abroad," *Foreign Commerce Weekly*, Sept. 11, 1950, p. 3.

[14] *Commercial Treaties and U.S. Economic Foreign Policy*, U.S. Department of State, May, 1950.

The need for current emphasis of this nature is obvious when some of the conditions adverse to investment are considered. Among these are the following:[15]

1. National treatment: Many foreign countries are reluctant to grant the same treatment to foreigners for a wide variety of economic activities as they grant to their nationals. They fear undue economic penetration should foreign enterprises be placed on an equal footing with local enterprises.

2. Screening: For many reasons, and in varying degrees, applications to undertake commercial activity in foreign countries are "screened" by authorities of those countries. They may thus permit the entry, establishment, and operation of only those business enterprises which are deemed beneficial. They may wish to retain to their nationals the ownership and operation of certain segments of the economy or they may wish to screen not only the initial investment but its operations and any subsequent expansion as well.

3. Convertibility: As a means of perfecting their control over foreign-exchange dealings, many countries prohibit or make special provision for the conversion of earnings into foreign exchange for the benefit of their foreign owners. This may apply to certain categories of earnings, certain amounts, within certain time limits, or it may apply as well to amortization and repatriation of foreign investment.

4. Expropriation: For many years, this has been a sore spot among countries, involving governments at times. The basic question is not whether the foreign government has or has not the right to expropriate property within its borders. No one could argue well that it does not have. The main question is the amount to be paid for such property, in the case of nationalization, the promptness in doing so, and the obligation to pay foreigners and local owners on an equal and fair basis.

As of late 1950, commercial treaties in force numbered 28, but the provisions of some were of little value. Some had been in existence for over 100 years,[16] and their scope reflects economic problems prevailing at the time. Changing conditions may call for amendments to outstanding treaties, and one of the purposes of the postwar program is to bring obsolete treaties up to date and to bring together in one comprehensive agreement treaty matters now represented by a number of minor agreements.

[15] *Ibid.*, pp. 6–7.

[16] The commercial treaty with the United Kingdom was signed in 1815 and that with Denmark in 1826. Except for the treaty with Uruguay, the most recent commercial treaty with a South American country is that concluded with Paraguay in 1859. *Ibid.*, p. 7.

Four postwar bilateral treaties had been signed by late 1950,[17] and proposals for about 20 additional ones were under various stages of consideration.[18] This treaty structure has great bearing on the general right of United States commercial interests to conduct business and hold investments or other property abroad.

Other Governmental Trade Policies

In addition to the foregoing examples, the participation of government in many international commercial agreements, most of which are for the purpose of creating a more favorable or more predictable atmosphere for commercial interests, is further indication of its promotional efforts in foreign commerce. An example of this is a number of tax treaties through which governments attempt to iron out the impact of double taxation on their citizens with foreign interests.

Our laws also allow creation of special business formations offering one advantage or another. Webb-Pomerene export associations are exempt from application of certain antitrust legislation. Businesses which can qualify as Western Hemisphere trade corporation may, under specified conditions, obtain exemption from corporate surtaxes or from excess-profits taxes and may obtain tax credits for payments of taxes to foreign countries. China trade corporations may also obtain certain tax benefits under stipulated conditions.

Foreign-trade Zones

Another promotional effort of considerable significance is legislation in the United States permitting foreign-trade (free) zones, which allow the importer to store or process his merchandise without payment of duty until entered for consumption. The basic United States law authorizing establishment of foreign-trade zones dates from 1934. For over ten years, the only zone in operation was New York. This was followed by Zone 2, in New Orleans, in 1947. By 1950, six zones were active—the two mentioned and one each in San Francisco, Los Angeles, Seattle, and San Antonio.

Foreign-trade zones have existed for many years in some European countries, especially those in which transshipment is an important activity. Not only is there the advantage of avoiding payment of duties while the merchandise is in the zone, but such merchandise is not subject to quota restrictions or the expense of bonds, it may be cleaned or inspected prior to entry, thus precluding payment of duties on damaged or unsalable merchandise, and it may be mixed, cleaned, sorted, processed, or otherwise made ready for more immediate sale before entering and

---

[17] With China, Italy, Ireland, and Uruguay. The last two had not yet been ratified.
[18] Setser, *op. cit.,* p. 3.

paying duty. In effect, goods stored in a foreign-trade zone retain their foreign status as far as customs duties are concerned and may bo re-exported without entry and payment of duties. They are of course subject to warehousing charges, as a foreign-trade zone is simply a warehouse with special privileges.

From 1934 until 1950, a point of misunderstanding arose in the matter of defining "manufacturing." Under the basic law, manufacturing was prohibited. Processing was permitted, but if the operation was called manufacturing, it could not take place. Typical of the activities under-taken were the aging of tobacco, the cleaning of food products, relabel-ing or repacking, and the placing of watch movements in cases. In 1950, the law was liberally amended to abolish the prohibition against manu-facturing or exhibiting goods in foreign-trade zones and to simplify a number of legal aspects which will tend to enlarge the scope of zone operations. In addition to granting the new manufacturing and exhibit-ing privileges, the amendment clarified jurisdiction of certain federal agencies, forms and procedures were simplified on the basis of the new law, certain clarifying definitions were adopted, certain time limitations were removed, and provision was made for allowance, in assessing duties and taxes, for recoverable and unrecoverable waste.[19]

Administration of the law is handled by the Foreign Trade Zones Board of the Department of Commerce.

GOVERNMENTAL ACTIVITIES: EDUCATIONAL

The principal manner in which economic intelligence collected by government employees and pertaining to foreign commerce is made available to the public as educational material is through a large number of publications. Other media are attendance by government representa-tives at meetings pertaining to foreign-commerce matters, the holding of conferences for interested people, and press releases which appear in the public press. It is in connection with the first of these that the promotional aspect appears, because through these detailed publications opportunities are made known and conditions are publicized in order that the interested businessman may be better informed as to the pos-sibility of originating or concluding satisfactory business dealings. Among the specific publications of an educational nature are the following.[20]

[19] See "Foreign-trade Zones Prepared to Meet New Trade Conditions," by Alfred B. Carr, and "New Business Created by Use of Foreign-trade Zone Privileges," by F. Preston Forbes, both articles appearing in *Foreign Commerce Weekly*, Nov. 12, 1951.

[20] In 1951, publication of several of these was suspended, but much of the basic information was made available through the *Business Information Service* of the De-partment of Commerce, and through reproduced, but unprinted, Foreign Service

International Reference Service. This is a series of publications by the U.S. Department of Commerce pertaining to foreign commerce in general or to areas. The series consists of the following:

SUMMARY OF CURRENT ECONOMIC INFORMATION SERIES. This series, by country, is a concise report on basic economic factors in the country in question. The series covers such topics as geography, climate, population, agricultural and industrial production, transportation, communication, currency, banking, weights and measures, the foreign-trade and tariff structure, and trade practices. For exporters or salesmen considering new territory, and even for those now operating in other areas, this type of intelligence is of high value.

ANNUAL ECONOMIC REVIEW SERIES. This particular series covers an annual economic review. It deals with developments during the period and supplements the *Summary of Current Economic Information* series mentioned above. Topics covered include agriculture (sometimes by principal products), labor, cost of living and prices, transportation, fuel and power, finance, and foreign trade. For keeping up with such broad developments, this series is quite helpful to the exporter, the importer, and the service elements interested in the foreign country, such as steamship lines, forwarders, and banks.

PREPARING SHIPMENTS SERIES. Owing to the fact that expense, delay, and much trouble can be encountered abroad if exports have not been shipped in exact accordance with specifications laid down by the laws or regulations of the foreign countries, this type of information is very helpful to the exporter, the forwarder, and the banker. The series deals with documentation, consular, and customs requirements of the country in question. The topics covered are import-license requirements, specifications as to commercial invoices, consular invoice requirements, certificates of proofs of origin, bills of lading, sanitary certificates, and other special documents. Also covered will probably be such points as consular fees, labeling, packing and marking of goods, shipments by air or by mail, samples, entries, fines and penalties, and appeals and claims.

LIVING AND OFFICE-OPERATING COST SERIES. This series is maintained for a number of countries and offers information of special interest to those contemplating moving abroad and particularly to those companies with, or contemplating the establishment of, offices or plants abroad. A typical study covers such topics as health conditions, housing and household expenses, medical facilities and supplies, transportation, communication, recreation, taxation, churches and social services, and several others bearing on the general subject.

---

reports, available for consultation in the Office of International Trade in Washington and in regional and certain other field offices of the Department of Commerce.

ESTABLISHING A BUSINESS SERIES. This series is one of importance to the company or individual in the United States contemplating the opening of a branch office or factory abroad. The legal considerations are often quite different from those in the United States, and the reports cover such points as corporate organization, including the rights of foreigners in corporations, forms of business organization common to the country concerned, procedure for organizing a business, government aid to industry, government regulation and participation, commercial policy and agreements, foreign-trade and -exchange controls, taxation of the several types (of which there are likely to be many), the labor force (population, composition, literacy and education, standard of living, wages), labor legislation (labor contracts, hours of work and compulsory rest periods, wages and salaries, profit sharing and reserve and retirement funds, if any), social security, and a short statement as to principal economic activities of the country.

MARKETING AREAS SERIES. Again by country, this series presents area studies to indicate their general economic potential, which may serve as a guide to the exporter, the importer, the banker, or other service element in foreign commerce. Among the detailed topics covered will usually be the topography and climate, data on important fields of production such as agriculture, mining, industry, forest products, foreign trade, transportation, and, for particular areas, perhaps data on population, advertising media, standard of living and purchasing power, commercial advertising, law, holidays, and valuable statistics.

FOREIGN COMMERCE YEARBOOK SERIES. This series offers data on the foreign trade of particular countries, both with the United States and with the rest of the world. Information included is similar to that shown in *Foreign Commerce Yearbook*.

UNITED STATES FOREIGN TRADE WITH _____. A rather detailed analysis is provided in these studies regarding the nature and volume of our trade with selected countries or areas, such as Latin America or European Recovery Program countries.

MISCELLANEOUS SERIES (SEMIANNUAL). This series includes such features as a tabulation of controls exercised by the respective countries. Included in one basic report (March, 1947) are, for each country, the date of imposition of exchange control, exchange-control authority, control over incoming exchange, control over payments abroad, and exchange rates. Other studies in this series cover such subjects as international trade during a specified period or an index to *International Reference Service*.

World Trade in Commodities. Contrasted with *International Reference Service*, which is principally by geographic organization, this series of reports is on a commodity basis, although some topics are restricted geographically. This series was formerly known as *Industrial Reference Service,* but the present designation was adopted in 1947. The 1949 series was published in 21 parts, according to commodity grouping. These parts are listed below, with a few titles to indicate the extent of their coverage.

Transport, Communications and Utilities: Review of South American Railroads in 1947; Communications in Colombia; Sweden's Electric Power Supply; The Pan American Highway.

Chemicals: Latin American Markets for United States Insecticides; Developments in the Swiss Chemical Industry in 1946 and 1947; Coal Tar Dyes in Belgium.

Drugs and Toiletries: Argentina and Venezuela as Sources of Crude Drugs and Essential Oils; Oils of Lemon, Bergamot, Grapefruit and Lime.

Motion Pictures and Equipment: This series discusses the motion-picture industry in individual countries and includes United States Foreign Trade in Photographic Goods and Digests of International Developments in Motion Pictures.

Electrical Appliances and Radio: Radio Apparatus in Chile and Lebanon, and Incandescent Lamps in Iraq; Incandescent and Fluorescent Lamps, and Domestic Sewing Machines in the Union of South Africa.

Feeds and Related Agricultural Products: The Pepper Industry in the Netherlands East Indies; the Market for Confectionery in Specified Latin American Countries; Cuba's Tobacco Industry; United States Foreign Trade in Dairy Products.

Lumber and Allied Products: China's Timber Imports and Quotas; The Veneer and Plywood Industry in Brazil.

Pulp and Paper: The industry in selected countries, or developments within the industry, is covered in this section.

Leather and Products: Footwear and Leather Manufactures; Hides and Skins.

Houseware and Furniture: Venetian Blinds and Venetian Blind Hardware in Australia and India; Paint Brushes in Canada and Costa Rica; Glassware in France.

Office Equipment and Supplies: This section deals with such matters as the production and marketing of typewriters, duplicating machines, and office equipment in selected countries.

Personal Durables: Toys in Sweden; Handicraft in Brazil; The Diamond Industry in Belgium.

Plumbing, Heating and Hardware: Mechanics and Craftsmen's Tools in Chile; Razor Blades in Mexico, Colombia, Argentina and Chile.

Rubber and Products: Chicle and Allied Gums—Sources and Markets; International Rubber Developments.

Scientific and Professional Goods: Dental Equipment and Supplies in Brazil; Swiss Trade in X-Ray Apparatus and Tubes.

Special Products: The Swedish Match Industry; Book Publishing in Argentina and Other Countries; the Cement Industry in Uruguay.

Textiles and Products: Belgian Congo Fibers; Wool Carpets and Rugs in the United Kingdom; Jute and Jute Manufactures in World Trade.

Machinery: Industrial, Electrical and Agricultural: Norwegian Standards for Electrical Equipment; Tractors in Argentina and Paraguay; Commercial Refrigerating and Air-conditioning Machinery in Panama and Guatemala.

Motive Products: The Spanish Motor Vehicle Industry; Automotive Market Conditions in Denmark; Motorboats, Marine Engines, Marine Accessories, Equipment and Hardware in Ecuador and Peru. Included, also, are reports on aeronautical topics, such as Aircraft Industry in Belgium and Notes on the British Aircraft Industry. Aeronautical equipment was formerly designated as a separate part of the series.

Metals and Minerals: Manganese Ore; Argentina's Iron and Steel Imports; Mineral Developments in Peru.

Petroleum and Coal: Coal in Europe; South America—A Profitable Market for United States Coal and Coke.

It is evident from the foregoing that *World Trade in Commodities* covers a wide variety of sales information in goods and services produced, used, and sold throughout the world. It also provides information on import sources; the Department of Commerce points out that in the 1949 volume approximately 100 reports discuss areas where numerous commodity import or manufacturing opportunities exist. The 1949 volume comprised about 600 publications in the 21 parts listed above and, in addition, 139 supplements on topics such as Indirect Sales of Australian Wool in the United States, Television in Canada, and Suggested Comparability Guide for United States and Latin American Hides. The 1949 index included listings for 200 commodities, 36 major industries, 10 utilities and services, and 7 foreign commercial standards and regulations. Geographically, references were made to 125 countries and 6 major areas.

In November, 1950, the Department of Commerce announced discontinuance of this series as such, indicating that an attempt would be made to provide similar data to business through other media.

Foreign Commerce Weekly. This is the weekly publication of the U.S. Department of Commerce (Office of International Trade) to which the subscription price (1952) is $3.50 per year to domestic subscribers and $4.50 to foreign. As a matter of general organization, each issue contains one or two feature articles, such as "World Trade Review," "International Transactions of the United States [during a specified period]," and "The Dollar Value in United States Import Statistics." Two of its principal sections are titled News by Countries and News by Commodities. About 25 countries are ordinarily covered in the former, the content being based largely on data received from our Foreign Service and serving to bring the reader fairly up to date on economic conditions, tariff, trade, and exchange controls. In the commodities section, 20 to 25 commodities are usually covered, with data being largely country or regional reports on the products under consideration. Other regular features are announcements or articles pertaining to reciprocal trade agreements; transport and communications; trade fairs and exhibitions; selected European, Latin American, and other exchange rates; United States government actions affecting foreign trade; and business opportunities (world-trade leads). In addition, a good volume of statistics is provided. The value of this type of economic intelligence is quite obvious; the activity can well be considered as an outstanding example of world-trade promotion.

World Trade News. This report, issued without charge, is published by the field offices of the Department of Commerce. It contains news items of special local interest or applicability and data pertaining to foreign countries or products somewhat in advance of the monthly publication *Foreign Commerce Weekly* and the special studies in *World Trade in Commodities,* in *International Reference Service,* or in *Business Information Service.* The publication appears weekly.

World Trade Lists. One of the most immediately beneficial and promotional efforts of the U.S. Department of Commerce is the compilation and issuance of World Trade Lists. These are lists of the names of manufacturers, importers and dealers, exporters, or merchants for each country on which data are available. Names and addresses are given, as well as an indication of the type of product or products in which interested. In the case of merchants, sales territories are sometimes shown. These lists are available at $1 per list per country. For example, a list of importers and dealers of hardware in Australia would cost $1; a similar list for Mexico would cost $1. Obviously, listing of the names does not constitute an endorsement as to the financial or moral standing of the concerns. That is a matter for the prospective exporter or importer to verify for himself. Nor can the Department of Commerce assure that the list includes every firm or individual engaged in the indicated activity. Keeping trade lists up to date is a very difficult task and many times may not be worth the cost. However, in those cases in which an American firm wishes to establish foreign sales representation and there is no satisfactory trade list, assistance is available on application. The application form contains extensive details which is necessary to permit the appropriate Foreign Service installation to select the most promising representation, and to avoid the nomination of prospective foreign sales agents who are already handling competitive lines. Figure 14 is an illustration from one of the World Trade Lists.

World Trade Directory Reports. While World Trade Lists include several names of possible interest to the user of the list, consideration

U N I T E D   S T A T E S   D E P A R T M E N T   O F   C O M M E R C E

CHARLES SAWYER, SECRETARY
OFFICE OF INTERNATIONAL TRADE
Thomas C. Blaisdell, Jr., Director
WASHINGTON 25

This trade list has been compiled for the Department of Commerce by American Foreign Service Officers abroad under the direction of the Secretary of State. While every effort has been made to include in trade lists only firms of good repute, no reasponsibility can be assumed in connection with any of the persons or firms listed herein, nor for any transactions had with such persons or firms.

This list is NOT FOR PUBLICATION

NOVEMBER 1948   PRICE: $1.00

ELECTRICAL SUPPLIES AND EQUIPMENT –
IMPORTERS AND DEALERS – NORWAY

Stars indicate relative size of firm in its community: *Small; **Medium; ***Large. No stars, no information as to size.

WHOLESALERS

BERGEN

*Bergens Elektriske Aktieselskap, 7 Torvalmenning. Importers, wholesalers, retailers, handling household electrical equipment and appliances, industrial electrical equipment, electrical wiring equipment, fixtures, radios, electrical barber shop and beauty parlor equipment. Sales territory: Western Norway.

*Sigbjørn Birkeland, 3 Valckendorffsgate. Handles household electrical equipment and appliances. Sales territory: Bergen and district.

**Ole Bjerke, 2 Chr. Michelsensgate. Also retailers, handling all kinds of household, ships', industrial and wiring equipment and appliances, fixtures and radios. Sales territory: Western Norway.

*Bohuset Wessen A/S, 27 Kong Oscarsgate. Also retailers and agents handling household electrical equipment and appliances, fixtures and radios. Sales territory: Bergen and district.

***Elektromagasinet A/S, 14 Strandgaten. Also retailers, handling all kinds of household, ships', industrial and wiring equipment and appliances, fixtures and radios. Sales territory: Western Norway.

*Mark Iversen, Elektrisk Engros, 5 Skostredet. Handles household electrical equipment and appliances. Sales territory: Bergen and district.

FIG. 14. Illustration from World Trade List. (*U.S. Department of Commerce.*)

will eventually narrow down to one or very few. As an aid in promoting trade opportunities, the Department of Commerce also offers a service through which detailed information on an individual or company abroad can be obtained. It issues World Trade Directory Reports, which are in the nature of credit reports although no evidence is apparent that credit checking is done with the list of trade references (some of whom are very likely to be in some other country than that of the subject). Figure 15 is a reproduction of a World Trade Directory Report, filled out with a fictitious name and address.

Foreign Commerce and Navigation of the United States. This is the annual publication giving extensive statistical information on our foreign trade by commodity and country. The publication also includes various summary tables of interest and data covering several years for comparative purposes. One of the principal difficulties to the current use of this publication is the fact that it must necessarily be several months late in appearance because of the tedious work involved in its thousands of statistical cumulations and compilations.

Various Monthly Foreign-trade Reports. Since annual releases are often too infrequent and too late to be of immediate application to the problems at hand in foreign commerce, the Department of Commerce issues a series of monthly or quarterly reports which eventually are incorporated into *Foreign Commerce and Navigation of the United States.* This list is subject to change, depending on developments which may make one of the reports of more or less interest or which may call for a new one, or depending on budgetary limitations. Among the reports being offered in 1950 were a Monthly Summary of Foreign Commerce of the United States; Imports, by Commodity and Country of Origin; Imports, by Country of Origin and Subgroup; Exports, by Commodity and Country of Destination; Exports by Country of Destination and by Subgroup; Trade by Customs Districts; Water-borne Foreign Trade; Vessel Entrances and Clearances; and Trade in Gold and Silver. About six of these reports must be paid for; the others are free.

Foreign Commerce Yearbook. For many years, the Department of Commerce published an annual book covering the principal economic statistics of foreign countries. The last report covering prewar data was published in mid-1942 and covered statistics for 1938 and, where available, for 1939. Publication was suspended during the war, which rendered impossible and practically meaningless data which would have appeared in several subsequent annual issues. Publication was resumed in 1950, covering the year 1948.

Other Publications. On the educational side of world-trade promotion, the Department of Commerce is not the only active government department. The Department of Agriculture (Office of Foreign Agricultural Relations) publishes a monthly bulletin titled *Foreign Agriculture.* It deals not only with agricultural production abroad but also with world trade in agricultural products. The State Department has been very active in recent years with publications pertaining to reciprocal trade agreements, the General Agreement on Tariffs and Trade, and the proposed International Trade Organization. Much of the material issued by

FIG. 15. Form of World Trade Directory Report. (*U.S. Department of Commerce.*)

the State Department is explanatory in nature and is obviously uncritical. The United States Tariff Commission publishes interesting studies on our trade in certain commodities, and its *War Change in Industry* series is recommended as being economic intelligence of considerable value. Another outstanding piece of promotional assistance has been rendered by the Food and Drug Administration, through its brochure, *Import Requirements of the Pure Food and Drug Act.* This brochure was pub-

-2-

WTD Report dated April 19, 1952 - Gonzalez & Smith, S. A., Montevideo, Uruguay.

Item 3 - Importers, wholesalers, retailers and manufacturers' representatives
handling hardware, tools, automotive parts, industrial machinery
and tools, radios and refrigerators, leather goods, upholstery
materials, sport goods, etc.

This concern was established in 1888 under the name of Rincon Gonzalez and
reorganized in 1895 as Gonzalez Hermanos & Smith, until 1917 when it adopted
the name of Gonzalez & Smith, S. A. Finally, it was incorporated in
November 1945.

The firm's sales territory covers the entire country which is attended
through sub-agents appointed in the most important towns and districts, and
four travelling and one city salesman. Adequate advertising is effected by
the press, radio, posters, etc., and the firm can correspond in English.

Offices, warehouse, sales and show-rooms are located in a modernized three
story building with a total floor space of 30,000 square feet and large
display windows, in the busiest business section of the city.

The firm enjoys an excellent reputation, being considered both energetic and
competent.

The subject firm is interested in establishing further commercial connections
with United States concerns to act as importers and distributors on a free or
exclusive basis.

Item 15 - Exclusive distributors for:

E. I. Du Pont de Nemours & Co., Inc., Wilmington, Delaware - paints and
    "Duco-Cupont" materials.
General Motors Overseas Operations, New York, N. Y. - for the following lines:
    Delco Remy - automotive starting, lighting and ignition, etc.
    "A-C" - pumps, gasoline filters, etc.
    Lovejoy - Automotive parts.
    Delco Brake - Spare parts for automotive brakes.
    Guide Lamp - Lamps and automotive spare parts.
    Harrison - Radiators for automotive vehicles.
    New Departure - Ball bearings for automotive vehicles & agricultural machinery.
    "A.T.B." -   ditto
    Huatt   -   ditto
The Electric Auto Lite Co., Toledo, Ohio - Automotive starting, lighting and
                                 ignition.
Johns-Manville International Corp., New York, N. Y. - Automotive parts.
McQuay Morris Mfg. Co., St. Louis, Mo. - Automotive vehicles & tractors spare parts.
McCord Corp., Detroit 11, Michigan - Motor joints, etc.
Van Norman Co., Springfield 7, Mass. - Machinery for workshops, etc.
Sunnen Products Co., St. Louis, Mo. - Machinery for workshops, etc.

                                                    (cont'd)

FIG. 15. (*Continued.*)

lished in order to assist importers in the United States by making it
possible for them to inform suppliers abroad of the legal requirements
pertaining to food, drugs, and cosmetics.

Also, the Economic Cooperation Administration was exceptionally active in stimulating more United States—European trade. It published a
list of ECA-financed importers in the Marshall Plan countries and also a
directory of United States exporters interested in participating in the

ECA program. Both publications were expected to be of particular aid to the small exporter.

It is not the author's intent to include all possible publications of a promotional nature or of promotional assistance. A sufficient number has been mentioned, though, to indicate that very extensive efforts have been and are being made to promote trade at the very time that many obstacles are being created or are permitted to exist. Think of the possible results of a consistent policy!

GOVERNMENTAL ACTIVITIES: FINANCIAL

Many activities of a financial nature may be listed as evidence of governmental effort to promote world trade, but only a few will be shown. One of the first is the provision for a market for bank acceptances, which arise largely through foreign trade. Prime acceptances carry a most favorable rate. This is due in part to the possibility of immediate conversion into cash by disposal of the eligible acceptances to the Federal Reserve banks.

Credit Insurance. Credit insurance is another manner in which some governments have aided in the promotion of their country's foreign trade. In the United States there has been some agitation for foreign credit insurance, especially of long-term credits, as a means of more effective competition with some European countries in, for instance, the South American markets. Apparently the majority of foreign traders oppose the idea.

Credit insurance is of two types—against actual loss because of inability or refusal of the buyer to pay and against inconvertibility of funds, assuming the buyer to be willing and able to pay. Opposition has been principally to the former, it being felt that ordinary credit risks are best borne by the seller, who is free to arrange for some other private economic function to assume the risk. But in recent years, and because of the almost world-wide adoption of exchange-control schemes, many sellers have felt that their inability to convert funds which a foreign buyer is willing and able to pay (in his own currency) but for which he is not permitted exchange by his government is a matter for our government to handle. This view will doubtless be strengthened by increased governmental discussion and agreement on international financial matters. So far, however, the United States government has taken no widespread action on the subject. The ECA[21] set aside a sum to guarantee convertibility of exchange arising from certain types of transactions with European buyers or from certain approved foreign investments (see Chapter 9).

[21] Succeeded, Dec. 31, 1951, by Mutual Security Agency.

Examples of ECA-insured "Credits." Transactions covered by the guarantee are, for example, the sale of books and periodicals of a nature consistent with national interests of the United States. Among the investments covered by industrial guarantee contracts are:

1. Expansion of a British subsidiary owned by a New Jersey electrical-equipment company
2. Expansion and tooling of a French sewing-machine company affiliated with a New York manufacturer
3. Establishment of a carbon-black plant in England by a Massachusetts corporation
4. Establishment of a company in the Netherlands to manufacture Venetian-blind material, the Dutch company being wholly owned by an American corporation with offices in New York and California.

Industrial guarantee contracts may also cover intangible investments of industrial patents, processes, and techniques. The first of these was concluded in May, 1951, by contract between the Export-Import Bank, as agent for ECA, and the Gardner-Denver Company of Quincy, Ill. The contract assures the company of convertibility of specified foreign royalty earnings into U.S. dollars.

Export-Import Bank and International Organizations. Another effort by the government which serves to promote trade was establishment of the Export-Import Bank. Sec. 2(a) of the Export-Import Bank Act of 1945 authorizes the bank to

. . . make loans, to discount, rediscount or guarantee notes, drafts, bills of exchange, and other evidences of debt, or participate in the same, for the purpose of aiding the financing and facilitating of exports and imports and the exchange of commodities between the United States or any of its territories or insular possessions and any foreign country or the agencies or nationals thereof.

And, of course, our participation in the International Monetary Fund and the International Bank for Reconstruction and Development is evidence of effort to create conditions under which trade can more efficiently be carried out.

Easing of Investment Regulations. From time to time, governments take action to make investment opportunities more, sometimes less, attractive. Typical of the former are laws in Israel, Turkey, and India in 1950 which covered such features as exemption from certain local taxes and from customs duties of authorized machinery and equipment, and assurance of freedom to withdraw earnings and to be able to convert the earnings into other currencies without penalty. Rendering the investment less attractive would, of course, be in the nature of a restrictive rather than a promotional effort.

Foreign Investment Guarantees. On the part of countries attempting to stimulate the "importation" of foreign investments, *i.e.,* the making of loans or investments abroad, it may be found that individuals able to provide the funds choose not to do so for any of several reasons. Chief among these are fears of:

1. Inability to convert earnings in foreign currencies into their own
2. Expropriation, with delay and perhaps loss in final settlement
3. Physical destruction in case of war
4. Discriminatory taxation

To overcome these fears, proposals are made from time to time for the government to establish a guarantee fund to underwrite such risks. As an example, a bill was introduced into the 81st Congress (S. 2197) which would authorize the Export-Import Bank to guarantee United States private capital against the risks outlined above which are peculiar to foreign investment. Hearings on the bill produced divided opinion, both as to the principle involved and as to whether, if the idea were adopted, the Export-Import Bank would be the proper agency to undertake the function. As has already been said, the Economic Cooperation Administration set aside a sum ($300,000,000) for the purpose of underwriting certain credit and investment risks in connection with the European Recovery Plan. Up to Dec. 31, 1951, total guarantees amounted to $45,200,000.

Other Governments Also Active. Other countries have at times been even more active in promotion of trade, especially export. Seventeen countries have or have had export credit guarantee schemes. Government sponsored displays and advertisements, the Portuguese export promotion fund, and numerous export subsidy programs testify to the energy sometimes exerted by governments in this direction. A type of investment guarantee was reported in April, 1950, in a commercial agreement signed by Italy and Brazil. Under the terms, private Italian firms are to establish plants in Brazil for producing such items as cellulose, synthetic ammonia, and aluminum. The agreement provides for free repatriation, with exchange guarantee, of interest and amortization of Italian capital, up to 20 per cent per annum of the total invested capital.

INTERNATIONAL TRADE FAIRS

One of the oldest promotional efforts in foreign trade is the international trade fair. Such fairs have been held in Europe for many years, and today, an international fair is scheduled in almost every Western European country. The first such fair in the United States was held in Chicago in 1950.

These fairs are usually held once or twice a year, and some of them maintain permanent buildings of considerable size, with permanent staffs to attend to the sale of space, advertising, organization, etc. Fairs usually run for a week or two, and the arrangement includes displays of a wide variety of products, in product or country sections, with salesmen and other personnel stationed at the displays to take orders or discuss business negotiations with visiting buyers.

For example, at the Royal Netherlands Industries Fair in Utrecht, in 1949, a building or a section was arranged with displays of 20-odd groups of products (and services), of such a diverse nature as office supplies, musical instruments, boots and shoes, hospital goods, electrical products, and banking and insurance. In addition, a building was set aside for "official" country sections, those displaying at the time being Belgium, Czechoslovakia, France, Italy, Luxembourg, Poland, Switzerland, and Yugoslavia. Some products from these same countries as well as from the United States and other countries were displayed in the "product" sections, usually by the Dutch representatives.

Whether the idea of international fairs will become popular in the United States is problematical, but the U.S. Department of Commerce has actively encouraged the development to the extent of setting up a fairs and exhibitions branch in its organizational structure. There is first the question of normal marketing practices, which have not evolved in a manner calling for general industrial fairs; there are, instead, annual shows (sometimes called fairs) for products such as furniture, office equipment, and foods. Another aspect is that a common language makes possible the high development of large-scale advertising by publication or radio in the United States. This is not possible in Europe, where the use of several languages in an area smaller than the United States materially reduces the opportunity for similar large-scale market approaches.

Indicative of the general significance of trade fairs is the occasional listing of fairs and exhibitions in *Foreign Commerce Weekly*. The issue of Oct. 1, 1951, for example, lists 84 dates for fairs, mainly international, in the space of a year. Several of these are specialized and not the broader type of trade or industry fair. But the objective of all is the same, and fairs play a very important role in the promotion of foreign commerce.

REVIEW QUESTIONS

1. Explain the significance to foreign commerce of the principle of reciprocal national treatment.

2. What is the unconditional most-favored-nation clause? Is it truly unconditional? If not, what are its conditions?

3. What is the relationship between the unconditional most-favored-nation clause and reciprocal trade agreements?

4. What is the Reciprocal Trade Agreements Act? How does it differ from the mechanism formerly employed in the setting of tariff rates?

5. What is a satisfactory reciprocal concession, under the Act?

6. How is the interest of the domestic producer protected in the making of a reciprocal trade agreement?

7. After a reciprocal trade agreement has been made, what provision has been made for the protection of the domestic producer? Is this provision adequate?

8. What is the General Agreement on Tariffs and Trade? How is it related to the reciprocal trade agreements program?

9. To what extent has the United States participated in GATT? Is there any relationship between GATT and the proposed International Trade Organization?

10. What are treaties of friendship, commerce, and navigation? Of what significance are they to foreign commerce?

11. What are foreign-trade zones? How do they serve to promote foreign commerce?

12. What are some of the government's educational activities directed toward promoting foreign commerce?

13. What is *International Reference Service?*

14. What is the content of a typical issue of *Foreign Commerce Weekly?*

15. What is a World Trade List? What is a World Trade Directory Report?

16. Evaluate the desirability of credit insurance as a means of promoting foreign commerce.

17. What are the chief fears of the foreign investor that underlie the pressure for foreign-investment guarantees? May there be other, perhaps hidden, motives in the proposal to offer foreign-investment guarantees?

18. Would international trade fairs in the United States probably be as effective as they are in Europe? Why or why not?

PART FIVE

Intergovernmental Organizations and Agreements

CHAPTER 20

International Commodity Arrangements

International commodity arrangements may be defined as agreements or undertakings between private producers (with or without government sanction) or between governments, having to do with production, exporting, importing, pricing, or other marketing practices relating to a commodity. When of a private nature, they may bear the designation of "cartel," although cartels are usually agreements between manufacturers. When publicly undertaken, they are commonly referred to as "intergovernmental" commodity arrangements or intergovernmental commodity-control agreements. The term "arrangement" is looked on as being somewhat broader in scope, including the preliminary activities leading up to the technically defined "commodity-control agreement."

National and international regulatory schemes of several types have generally developed from the accumulation of large stocks, which could not be disposed of at economic levels because of declines in price. The social consequences of price fluctuations, in turn, became the basis for governmental and intergovernmental interest.

The International Labour Office reports that by the time of the London Monetary Conference, in 1933, "intergovernmental commodity control schemes had come to be regarded as a form of international industrial agreement clearly distinct from, and in many respects preferable to, producers' cartel agreements, especially as a means of regulating the production and marketing of foodstuffs and raw materials."[1]

Wide postwar interest in intergovernmental arrangements stems from activities directed toward expanding international trade by a number of devices and from social objectives given prominence in declarations of the United Nations Charter.

Objectives Vary. If these arrangements (agreements) are private in establishment and operation, they are generally producers' agreements the objective of which is to eliminate or control competition, divide markets, and raise (or at least prevent the fall of) prices. The last should be

[1] *Intergovernmental Commodity Control Agreements* (Montreal, International Labour Office, 1943), p. xx.

obvious, because competitors rarely get together to agree to cut prices; when they do get together along these lines, it is for the purpose of agreeing not to cut prices or not to compete with each other in certain areas or agreeing to restrict production or exports.

These are, in effect, monopolistic practices expected to result in higher prices and profits per unit of sales than would otherwise be realized. Accordingly, in order to achieve this objective, cartels must succeed in restricting sales to a smaller quantity than would have prevailed in the absence of an agreement.[2]

If the agreements are governmental in nature and operation, the objectives are often described in such terms as "minimizing price fluctuations," "establishing more orderly marketing conditions," "contributing to the expansion rather than the restriction of employment and trade," and "establishing a more orderly adjustment of supply and demand." Both private and governmental agreements may tend toward monopolistic positions and practices; in fact, some of the past intergovernmental agreements have been restrictive in effect.

The principal difference between the two (private and governmental) is in social objectives, it being felt that private agreements (often with government sanction) are designated mainly to restrict competition with a primary view to greater profit for the producer members. Governmental agreements, on the other hand, can be and are more concerned with both sides of the market; increased or stable profit for producing is not the only objective.

Private agreements have been found to result in undesirable developments such as:[3]

1. Delaying or prohibiting the introduction of new techniques
2. Protecting inefficient producers
3. Blocking full utilization of efficient plants
4. Reducing the volume of trade
5. Tending ultimately to lower the standard of living

Postwar Concept Stresses Expansion. The postwar concept of intergovernmental arrangements, on the other hand, is held out to be constantly alert to the need for expanding production, trade, and employment, and constantly fighting the restrictive practices of producer cartels.

[2] Robert P. Terrill, "Restrictive Business Practices," *American Trade Proposals,* U.S. Department of State Publication 2551, 1946, p. 7.

[3] *The International Trade Organization—Key to Expanding World Trade and Employment,* U.S. Department of State Publication 3882, June, 1950. Excellent discussions on this general subject are found in George W. Stocking and Myron W. Watkins, *Cartels or Competition* (New York, Twentieth Century Fund, Inc., 1948); Edward S. Mason, *Controlling World Trade* (New York, McGraw-Hill Book Company, Ind., 1946); and Corwin Edwards, *Economic and Political Aspects of International Cartels,* Senate Committee Print, 78th Cong., 2d Sess., 1944.

In general, this is accomplished by having representation on controlling bodies of both producer and consumer governments, which was not formerly the case. As expressed in the *Department of State Bulletin:*[4]

. . . such cooperation will provide an atmosphere during which an orderly shift of resources may occur without accompanying disorderly markets and which will make it unnecessary for individual countries to take unilateral action which would tend to shift the burden of their problem to other countries through the imposition of quotas or embargoes.

To obtain a better perspective of this changed concept of intergovernmental arrangements, we must consider two background developments. One is that during the interwar period there was a substantial spread of economic nationalism, followed by imposition of tariffs, quotas, and support prices to encourage home production. Intergovernmental agreements evolved in some cases, but the significant fact was that former suppliers (exporters) to the newly protected markets found their markets cut off or greatly reduced, and their production could not be or was not reduced fast enough to avoid what are called "burdensome surpluses," with resulting low prices and unemployment.

From this point, the developing line of politico-socio-economic policy is about as follows:[5]

Because commodities in which serious problems are likely to occur are important, in many cases, to the economic life of particular countries, producers' distress is likely to create depressed conditions throughout the entire Nation. The consequent reduction in purchasing power results in curtailment of demand for the products of other nations which in turn contributes to a general decline in levels of employment and production. In order to prevent individual commodity situations from menacing the general program for the maintenance of high levels of employment and income, a program is necessary for dealing with them.

Employment and Income Levels Are Part of Policy. In its *Proposals for Expansion of World Trade and Employment,*[6] the United States government suggested a way in which concerted action and policy in international trade could work to the general benefit of all countries. Part of this was elimination of many trade barriers—private and governmental. This would be intended to make possible wider exchange of goods and services. However, in some cases, it would not serve another objective, which is the maintenance of a high level of employment and income. This shortcoming is expressed in the following statement that "the fact that tariffs are low will not by itself prevent a decline in income

[4] William T. Phillips, "The American Trade Proposals: Intergovernmental Commodity Arrangements," *Department of State Bulletin,* March 31, 1946, p. 510.

[5] *Ibid.*

[6] U.S. Department of State Publication 2411, November, 1945.

and demand which communicates itself from country to country through international markets."[7]

Interest in "positive" steps to maintain high levels of employment and income is based on a solution to two points, listed as contributing to keeping down the volume of world trade:[8]

1. Fear of disorder in the markets for certain primary commodities
2. Irregularity, and the fear of irregularity, in production and employment

It may be said, then, that the United States government's concept of intergovernmental commodity arrangements is based substantially on the following considerations: (1) Some commodities are of major interest to the economies of certain countries; (2) international trade in certain primary commodities does not follow the pattern of trade in, say, manufactured goods; the demand is relatively inelastic[9] and "production adjustments cannot be effected by the free play of market forces as rapidly as the circumstances require"; (3) "burdensome surpluses" are accompanied by widespread distress to small producers because a "substantial reduction in price leads neither to a significant increase in consumption or to a significant decrease in production";[10] and (4) national measures to relieve hardship caused by low income and unemployment often result in action bearing on other countries—to use a popular term, in exporting their unemployment to other countries.

Entrepreneurial Decision Involved. The policies of intergovernmental commodity arrangements, in the postwar view, are proposed to overcome some of the economic risks and social discomforts and as well to overcome the restrictive policies of private producers' cartels. The economic philosophy is toward an economy of plenty and away from an economy of scarcity. However, little publicity seems to be given the fact that, while a "burdensome surplus" may arise from the vagaries of nature, it may be due just as much to the fact that some individuals, *or even one,* were free to decide that they wanted to produce or plant something in a certain place and at a certain time. Naturally, someone must make this entrepreneurial decision, and if it is to be a government bureau it will mean regimentation, more or less, of various sectors of the economy and loss of economic freedom on the part of individuals. One

[7] "Employment and Economic Activity," *Preliminary Proposals for an International Trade Organization,* U.S. Department of State Publication 2756, 1947.

[8] *Proposals for Expansion of World Trade and Employment.*

[9] Inelastic in terms of price. Demand may be and would be said to be elastic in relation to income levels, but these two views of elasticity are like two sides of a coin. In price-elasticity estimates, income must remain rather constant; in income elasticity, income changes and price remains rather constant.

[10] *Proposals for Expansion of World Trade and Employment,* p. 21.

can only observe that political freedom cannot long prevail where there is not economic freedom, and that political freedom imposes continuous responsibility on the free person to assume certain risks, one of which is that the actions of other free persons—not designed maliciously—must be condoned. Of course, this is not to suggest that such political freedom may disappear overnight; it may last a generation or two, but ever increasing economic regimentation can lead nowhere but to political regimentation.

TYPES OF INTERNATIONAL COMMODITY ARRANGEMENTS

As suggested earlier, commodity arrangements may take the form of producer agreements (cartels) or of intergovernmental arrangements. The former operate principally in items whose production is relatively concentrated by company or country, as in certain manufactured goods. As described in Chapter 18, producers agree, through cartel arrangements, (1) to fix prices, (2) to limit or apportion production, (3) to limit or apportion markets, or (4) to allocate markets. The policy of all these is obviously restrictive.

A proposal has been made to require registration with the government of all such international restrictive business practices in which United States companies participate. Until 1951, however, this proposal had not been enacted into law. A significant objection appears to be that if registration is required only in the United States, it may work to the disadvantage of American members as compared with members from other countries whose governments are not so opposed to the idea of cartels as is the United States.

Distinction between Commodity Arrangement and Trade Agreement. Intergovernmental commodity arrangements are of several types. An essential characteristic is that they must be multilateral in composition and each must pertain to a specific commodity. They are not to be understood to be the same as bilateral agreements pertaining to the purchase or exchange of one or several commodities. Nor do they include such bilateral and multilateral undertakings as our reciprocal trade agreements, which cover rates of duty and other restrictions on trade in a wide variety of commodities and manufactured goods.

Definitions and Procedures Standardized. Certain definitions with regard to intergovernmental commodity arrangements, coming to the scene in succesive order, appear to have become fairly standardized. They conform to and are, in effect, the operating procedure for the "surplus-adjustment" approach discussed above; they are found in the international economic structure contemplated by the proposed International Trade Organization. In addition, they fall within the so-called "expansionist" approach, which looks on intergovernmental agreements as a suitable vehicle for "the expansion of the production of a primary commodity where this can be accomplished *with advantage to consumers and producers* [italics added] including, in appropriate cases, the distribution of basic foods at special prices."[11]

These successive undertakings are as follows:[12]

1. *Study group:* This organization is composed of the representatives of countries which consider themselves substantially interested in the production or consumption of, or trade in, a particular commodity. It investigates all these aspects and reports to the participating governments.

2. *Commodity conference:* After the difficulties have been studied by the study group, a commodity conference is called to consider appropriate "measures" to meet the special difficulties of the particular commodity. A new commodity-control agreement can be entered into only through such a conference.

3. *Commodity-control agreement:* This term denotes an agreement which either through the regulation of production or through the quantitative control of exports or imports reduces or prevents an increase in the production of, or international trade in, a primary commodity, or which regulates prices.[13]

4. *Commodity council:* This is the body responsible for the administration of a commodity-control agreement.

While both in the proposed International Trade Organization and in United Nations specialized agencies such control schemes are accepted as a matter of fact, albeit at times with moderation, the number of agreements[14] actually made has affected directly only a limited number of products. Some of these are beef, coffee, rubber, sugar, tea, timber, tin, and wheat.

[11] *Review of International Commodity Problems, 1948,* United Nations, 1948, p. 5.
[12] *Ibid.,* pp. 6–7.
[13] Not all of these conform to the definition of an intergovernmental commodity-control agreement as used in the proposed ITO charter, of which Art. 58, Par. 2, reads:

"Subject to the provisions of paragraph 5 of this Article, a commodity control agreement is an intergovernmental agreement which involves:

(a) the regulation of production or the quantitative control of exports or imports of a primary commodity and which has the purpose or might have the effect of reducing, or preventing an increase in, the production of, or trade in, that commodity; or

(b) the regulation of prices."

[14] Study groups and commodity conferences can be participated in rather freely, as they do not obligate the government. But commodity-control agreements represent a commitment on the part of governments and accordingly require ratification.

Principal Patterns of Intergovernmental Commodity Agreements. In a comparative discussion of the subject,[15] Davis classifies intergovernmental commodity agreements into three main patterns: *commodity control, buffer stock,* and *surplus adjustment.* These relate mainly to long-range, continuing problems. But in addition, allocation of shortages in emergency situations may develop. This was the case in 1951, when the International Materials Conference was established to provide a basis for international cooperation in the allocation of scarce raw materials. In military emergency or economic "warfare," also, allocation of manufactured goods may become necessary. This was demonstrated in the United States in the postwar period.

There is no one standard type of commodity agreement, and various types may be expected to be retained or adopted because of circumstances peculiar to the commodities concerned. However, the United Nations takes the view that intergovernmental commodity arrangements should be subject to some degree to supervision to assure conformance to specified principles and requirements designed to compel remedial rather than restrictive features (the latter would be permitted only when in the public interest). Accordingly, the Economic and Social Council of the United Nations, in March, 1947, established an Interim Coordinating Committee for International Commodity Arrangements. This interim committee may eventually be succeeded by a standing committee of some agency of the United Nations.

The main features of the three types of intergovernmental commodity agreements will be outlined below.

Commodity-control Agreements

Prewar experience is found in this type for such products as tea, tin, rubber, sugar, and wheat. It was the declared object of regulatory schemes operated by some governments or under their auspices "to reduce stocks to a normal level, to maintain them at that level, and to maintain a fair and equitable price for reasonably efficient producers."[16]

Accordingly, dealing with such problems as liquidation of excessive stocks and raising of prices, these control agreements endeavored to attain their goals mainly through regulation of exports and production. While some moderate success may be claimed for liquidation of stocks at one time or another, not much can be said for success in the matter of price fluctuations. Davis states.[17] "None of these ICAs (tea, tin, rubber) made any significant contribution toward readjustment of excessive

---

[15] Joseph S. Davis, *International Commodity Agreements: Hope, Illusion or Menace?* (New York, The Committee on International Economic Policy, 1947), p. 14.

[16] *Intergovernmental Commodity Control Agreements,* p. xx.

[17] Davis, *op. cit.,* p. 16.

producing capacity, regularity of production, or selective expansion by low-cost producers."

Newer Concept Calls for Producer and Consumer Representation. The newer pattern described earlier in this chapter, with social as well as purely economic goals, calls for consumer as well as producer participation. It may have to call for regulation of production or export and for control over imports, reserve stocks, and prices.

Commenting on these devices, Davis states:[18]

These proposed ICAs, like their prewar prototypes, would undertake to exercise essentially monopolistic restraints on production and trade, with governmental blessing, designed to protect producers and profits . . . What is clearly implied may fairly be called thoroughgoing regimentation of production and international trade, and more or less substantial regulation of stocks and prices, by governmental action, national and international. It would mean official cartelization of primary foodstuffs and materials, with assigned quotas reached by bargaining, instead of permitting quality and price competition to determine the flow of commodities. It would necessarily entail far more extensive governmental controls, and more governmental buying, selling, and holding, than have been common in peacetime except in totalitarian countries, or than democratic governments have shown themselves competent to conduct to advantage, at least in times of peace. . . .

Buffer-stock Schemes

Considerable interest in this type of intergovernmental agreement was fostered by discussion of the subject at the United Nations Conference on Food and Agriculture at Hot Springs, Va., in 1943. The conference preceded by about two years the Food and Agriculture Organization of the United Nations, which came into being in Quebec, in 1945.

World Food Board Proposed. At a special meeting of the Food and Agriculture Organization in the spring of 1946, steps were taken to work out a long-term plan for international cooperation on food and agricultural problems. One of the results of this was a recommendation made to the agency by its director general, in September, 1946, for a World Food Board, as one way to accomplish the general objectives of "assuring ample food supplies with a reserve against catastrophe, of stabilizing prices to assure fair rewards to producers, and of helping underdeveloped countries to produce more food and other goods so that they might have greater buying power and more adequate diets."[19]

This proposal, made at a conference in Copenhagen, was to create an internationally managed and internationally financed body which would buy and sell exportable surpluses at agreed minimum and maximum

[18] *Ibid.*, pp. 22, 23.

[19] *Food and Agriculture Organization of the United Nations*, U.S. Department of State Publication 2826, 1947.

prices, thus providing a buffer stock against fluctuations in price and supply. The conference, while accepting the objective of the proposal, did not recommend establishment of a World Food Board, but set the proposal aside for further study. At a later meeting, the proposal was passed by, it being the recommendation to develop "international commodity arrangements, applying in each case to a specific commodity situation in which widespread unemployment or burdensome surplus had developed or was expected to develop."[20]

Along the same line, the League of Nations Delegation on Economic Depressions, in its 1945 report, endorsed a buffer-stock scheme as an antidepression measure. It recommended that such a program be amply financed to guard against its breakdown and that the proposed agency acquire ample supplies to assure against exhaustion of stocks. High priority is thus given to consideration of fluctuations in price, for these are often followed by national governmental measures which may be conflicting and in any case may be harmful to the economies of several nations.

Numerous Technical Difficulties Appear. In critically observing this proposal, Davis finds a number of technical questions to be solved in such matters as finance, timing, commodities to be included, and determination of basic price ranges. He then notes that "what we call simply wheat, coffee, tea, wool, or cotton is not a homogeneous commodity but a complex of commodities differing greatly in value."[21]

Concluding his analysis, he finds a disposition to regard normal price fluctuations as excessive and a disposition on the part of producers not to be satisfied with "equilibrium prices"; they strive, by political means, for higher prices. A potentially great obstacle is also noted in determining the size of the buffer stock (which must be viewed in relation to price ranges), especially when national policies involving domestic price maintenance prevail.[22]

There seems to be little possibility that such a scheme will be adopted, but implications of the proposal stagger the imagination.

Surplus-adjustment Patterns

While not differing from commodity-control agreements in method of operation, this pattern considers such control agreements as somewhat undesirable in principle and to be used as the exception rather than the rule.

An agreement would be adopted only as a temporary scheme, only

[20] *United States Report on the Food and Agriculture Organization,* U.S. Department of State Publication 3560, November, 1948.

[21] Davis, *op. cit.,* p. 32.

[22] *Ibid.,* pp. 32–33.

after considerable discussion by producer and consumer governments, and would be used only during the time needed to effect "the necessary processes of readjustment."[23]

Commodity arrangements by governments are considered justified because unilateral action by governments to cope with local situations has brought intervention in the production and distribution process. This intervention has led in the past to "economic warfare and the restriction and distortion of world trade."[24]

Government Arrangements May Play Important Role. There is wide belief that intergovernmental commodity arrangements may play a significant part for many years in effecting a balance between supply and demand, replacing market price as the allocator of factors of production. This view is clearly found in recommendations of the Second Inter-American Conference on Agriculture, held in Mexico City in July, 1942. One of the resolutions adopted cited as models the World Sugar Agreement of 1937, the Inter-American Coffee Agreement, and the Washington Wheat Agreement of 1942. The Conference then recommended endorsement of the approach to surplus-commodity problems, whenever applicable, through international agreements which:[25]

1. Provide for adjustment of production or market supply in the individual exporting countries.
2. Assure individual exporting countries of fair shares of the available market at prices reasonably renumerative to efficient producers, giving appropriate consideration to the historical position of the producing and exporting countries
3. Assure importing countries of adequate supplies at prices fair to consumers

This is quite a big order, and the Conference also urged that the solution be approached through international collaboration not only among producing and consuming countries of the Western Hemisphere but among producing and consuming countries of the entire world.

As indicated before, this approach to the problem is that favored by the United States government, as expressed in its *Proposals For Expansion of World Trade and Employment,* which served as the working base for a proposed International Trade Organization.

Unfavorable Developments Must Be Guarded Against. While this last pattern may seem the most desirable (or least undesirable) of the three, some characteristic developments must always be guarded against. One is that, once set up, a temporary arrangement tends to become permanent. It does not take long for interests to become vested, for either those

[23] *Preliminary Proposals for an International Trade Organization,* p. 16.
[24] *Ibid.*
[25] Cited in *International Commodity Control Agreements,* pp. 145–146.

"benefited" or personnel working for the government. Another is that if the "correction" means taking out of production the less efficient producers and acres, they must be kept out of production by compulsion, and some other employment must be found for them. They are factors of production and they can hardly be expected to remain idle. But before that problem is faced, someone must determine who the most and least efficient producers are, *on a world-wide basis*. One can easily see that the degree of mechanization, of personal and managerial skill, of general industry, of national and specific price levels, and of alternative employment opportunities and a host of other factors would present administrative problems of an economic and political nature more delicate and greater in scope than any yet devised. The result could be a freezing of economic positions and levels by not releasing private initiative to expand or improve in efficiency. Think of the political appeal which could be made to a farmer, say, who is told that he cannot plant something because another farmer in some other part of the world is considered more efficient than he or less able to do something else, or because another government has made a stronger case than his own for a share of the planned production of the world!

UNITED STATES GOVERNMENT PARTICIPATION

Directly and indirectly, the United States government has undertaken an increasing participation in intergovernmental commodity arrangements.

Through membership in the Food and Agriculture Organization, the World Health Organization, and the Internatinoal Labour Office, all specialized agencies of the United Nations, the United States participates in intergovernmental discussions and activities affecting numerous commodities. These are not all considered as formal, advanced intergovernmental commodity agreements. Also on a broad scale, the United States participates in the Interim Coordinating Committee for International Commodity Arrangements.

With regard to specific commodity arrangements, the United States was a participant in the following in 1951.

International Cotton Advisory Committee

Formed in 1939, this Committee is a medium for assembling and analyzing data on world cotton production, consumption, stocks, and prices. Meetings are held approximately annually, at which time the world cotton situation is reviewed, as well as cotton conditions in each of the member states. Members numbered 26 in 1949. In 1945, a study group was appointed to prepare a report "to include definite proposals for international collaboration looking toward a reduction in cotton surpluses through the regulation of one or more of the following: exports, export prices, and production, and also through expansion of cotton consumption."[26] Until 1952, a program had not been agreed on.

Rubber Study Group

This Group was initially begun in 1944, after informal discussions among the Netherlands, the United Kingdom, and the United States. The Group is advisory only, and since organization its membership has been expanded by offering representation to all countries substantially interested in the production of, consumption of, or trade in rubber. As of April, 1951, about 18 countries had become members.

The Group has as its purpose the promotion of international cooperation concerning international trade in rubber. It is authorized to "make such studies of the world rubber position as it sees fit, to consider measures designed to expand world consumption of rubber, to consider how best to deal with any difficulties which may exist or may be expected to arise, and to submit reports and recommendations on the subject to participating governments."[27]

International Sugar Council

The International Sugar Council was established in 1937 pursuant to the International Sugar Agreement of the same year. The Agreement, itself, evolved from recommendations of the World Monetary and Economic Conference of 1933.

The Council administers the Agreement, which is "designed to establish and maintain an orderly relationship between the supply and demand for sugar in the world market at prices which will be equitable both to producers and consumers."

The United States is permanently represented on the executive committee of the Council as an *importing* nation. Participation by the United States was made official through ratification of the Agreement, but prior to the Agreement's coming into force, the Sugar Act of 1937 (50 Stat. 903) provided for cooperation in the international regulation of the production and marketing of sugar. The Departments of State and Agriculture are primarily concerned with formulation of United States policy in the Council and with participation in meetings.

Combined Tin Committee

Formed in 1945 to carry on the work previously performed by the Combined Raw Materials Board (liquidated in 1945), this Committee

[26] *Intergovernmental Organizations in Which the United States Participates, 1949,* U.S. Department of State Publication 3655, 1950, pp. 65–67.

[27] *Ibid.,* p. 77.

is composed of governments of the major tin-producing and tin-consuming countries. Its purpose is principally to recommend allocation of supplies. The United States participates under executive authority for participation in international conferences. Agencies chiefly concerned with the work of the Committee are the Departments of State and Commerce and the Reconstruction Finance Corporation.

International Tin Study Group

This Group held its first meeting in London, in April, 1947. It is composed of representatives of governments principally interested in production or consumption of tin. Basic purpose of the group is to "maintain a continuous intergovernmental review of the world supply and demand situation, both present and prospective, with respect to tin in all its forms." An International Tin Conference was in session in Geneva, in late 1950, to discuss the advisability of forming an intergovernmental control agreement on the commodity, but agreement could not be reached. The Conference was adjourned with a closing statement that the various measures proposed differed so greatly that further examination by governments was needed.[28] The United States participation is under executive authority for participation in international conferences.[29]

International Wheat Council (and International Wheat Agreement)

Succeeding an International Wheat Advisory Committee, which had been established in London, in 1933, to administer a wheat agreement, of which the United States was a signer, an International Wheat Council was established in 1942 by the governments of Argentina, Australia, Canada, the United Kingdom, and the United States. This Council was set up to administer a new agreement undertaken at that time.

Following the war, sessions gave more serious consideration to a form of agreement which would provide maximum and minimum wheat prices. A proposal of this type was made by United States representatives in November, 1945, but agreement was not reached at the Council sessions in 1946. However, in January, 1947, the Council found sufficient agreement to support an International Wheat Conference in London, in March and April of 1947. This Conference was intended to revise the 1942 Agreement, and a draft agreement evolved which incorporated the principle of undertaking a multilateral long-term contract among interested governments. Agreement could not be reached, however, on the range of prices and the duration of the proposed agreement.

[28] *The New York Times*, Nov. 22, 1950.
[29] *International Organizations in Which the United States Participates, 1949*, pp. 65–67.

In 1948, a new draft agreement was drawn for a five-year pact within an established price range. It was the first multilateral agreement of its kind in history,[30] but the draft agreement failed of acceptance by enough governments to bring it into force.[31] At the 1949 conference, another agreement was negotiated and submitted for acceptance by the governments of 41 countries, to be effected by July 1, 1949. It was accepted by that date, and provided for a new International Wheat Council, composed of countries which ratified the Agreement.[32]

The Agreement's stated objectives were "to assure supplies of wheat to importing countries and markets for wheat to exporting countries at equitable and stable prices."[33]

Under terms of the Agreement, exporting countries—Australia, Canada, France, Uruguay, and the United States—guaranteed to sell 456,283,389 bushels annually to the signatory importing countries, of which there were 37 and which in turn agreed to buy this quantity at the minimum and maximum prices as shown in the following tabulation.

Crop year (August–July)	Minimum	Maximum
1949–1950	$1.50	$1.80
1950–1951	1.40	1.80
1951–1952	1.30	1.80
1952–1953	1.20	1.80

SOURCE: *Participation of the United States Government in International Conferences, July 1, 1948–June 30, 1949,* U.S. Department of State Publication 3853, 1950, p. 129.

Wheat flour could be substituted for wheat if agreed between the governments of the buying and selling countries, and governments were permitted to carry out their obligations either by private trade or by government institutions.

Two substantial producing countries, Argentina and U.S.S.R., are not members of this Agreement, although Argentina was a member of its predecessor. It was reported by *The New York Times* of Aug. 6, 1950, that Wheat Agreement sales for its first year fell far below original goals. The United States was to have markets for 235,800,000 bushels and actually sold only 156,000,000. Shortage of dollars abroad was offered as a principal cause of the pact's failure. What this means, of

[30] *Participation of the United States Government in International Conferences, July 1, 1947–June 30, 1948,* U.S. Department of State Publication 3443, 1949, p. 147.

[31] *International Organizations in Which the United States Participates, 1949,* p. 68.

[32] Exporting countries covering 80 per cent of quantities guaranteed for export, and importing countries covering 70 per cent of quantities guaranteed for import.

[33] *International Organizations in Which the United States Participates, 1949,* p. 69.

course, is that the governments concerned felt that available dollars should be used for other purposes than complying with the Agreement.

International Wool Study Group

Pursuant to the London Wool Conference of 1946, the International Wool Study Group was established initially to face the problem of a large increase in world stocks. Membership is of governments of countries substantially interested in the production of, consumption of, or trade in wool.

The Group makes continuous studies of the world wool position, and its activities are of primary significance to the Departments of State, Agriculture, and Commerce.

The United States participates under executive authority for participation in international conferences.

Inter-American Coffee Board (Defunct)

In 1940, after loss of some European markets by Latin-American producers, an Inter-American Coffee Agreement was entered into by the United States and 14 Latin-American countries. This Agreement fixed export quotas to the United States market for those producing countries in order to provide for the equitable marketing of coffee. It also established the Inter-American Coffee Board, which functioned until September, 1948, when the Agreement expired. The Agreement specified that participating governments were to maintain, in so far as possible, the normal and usual operation of the coffee trade. In addition to the export quotas for the producing countries, it required the United States to limit imports for consumption to these quotas. However, it never became necessary for the United States to impose an import licensing system, as policing was accomplished by the exporting countries.

The Inter-American Economic and Social Council of the Organization of American States created a Special Commission on Coffee for the purpose of continuing the consultative aspects of inter-American coffee matters.

International Materials Conference

In early 1951, several countries became interested in establishing new international machinery for dealing with the problem of a growing shortage of many essential materials. Prime movers in the effort were the governments of France, the United Kingdom, and the United States. These governments were later joined by Australia, Brazil, Canada, India, Italy, the Organization of American States, and the Organization for European Economic Cooperation.

The new institution is the International Materials Conference, which functions through a Central Group, composed of the 10 members listed above, and through a series of separate international commodity committees. The task of these committees is "to review the supply position for essential materials which are in short supply, or in danger of becoming so, and to recommend measures for increasing the production and insuring the effective distribution and use of such materials."[34] Neither the Central Group nor the committees have any charter or by-laws, and the respective committees are independent. They have no powers except to make recommendations, and these are made directly to the governments concerned and not to the Central Group.

Committees are established as circumstances warrant; as of early 1952, seven committees had been formed, with membership distributed as shown on page 423.

These committees are organized along lines similar to the study groups described above, and make arrangements to safeguard the interests of nonmembers. While some governments belong to both, there are no formal relationships between the committees and the study groups; in general, membership in the commodity committees is more limited than that in the study groups.

Typical of the workings of the committees is the development of a schedule of allocations of crude sulphur for the fourth quarter of 1951. After making a survey of world requirements and supply, the committee recommended allocations, import quotas, and export quotas for 30 countries and a few other areas. Allocations took into account stocks on hand, production, and needs. The difference between supply and demand was represented by import or export quotas.

For the fourth quarter of 1951, allocations were recommended, in addition to those for sulphur, for tungsten, molybdenum, copper, zinc, nickel, and cobalt, and an emergency allocation of newsprint was also undertaken. Beyond allocation, however, the committees have made some recommendations for increasing production, conservation, and end-use controls of many of the materials. The Tungsten-Molybdenum Committee recommended a price range on tungsten during part of 1951 and, for the same commodity, it presented a plan for long-term contractual arrangements for securing increased production.

Reports as of late 1951 indicated a general willingness of member and nonmember governments to comply with the allocations made for the third quarter of 1951. The recommendation on the price of tungsten was set by agreement of all but one of the participating governments.

United States Procedure for Handling Recommendations. In the United States, acceptance of recommendations made by committees of the International Materials Conference is normally accomplished by the

[34] *Department of State Bulletin,* Mar. 5, 1951, p 383.

Participation in International Materials Conference

Countries and organizations	Central group	Commodity committees						
		Copper–zinc-lead	Sulphur	Cotton–cotton linters	Tungsten–molybdenum	Manganese–nickel-cobalt	Wool	Pulp-paper
Argentina							X	
Austria	X	X	X					X
Australia		X	X	X	X	X	X	X
Belgium						X	X	
Bolivia	X							X
Brazil	X	X	X	X	X	X		X
Canada	X	X	X	X	X	X		X
Chile								
Cuba								
France	X	X	X	X	X	X	X	X
Federal Republic of Germany		X	X	X	X	X	X	X
India	X	X	X	X		X	X	
Italy		X	X	X	X	X	X	X
Japan			X					X
Mexico					X			
Netherlands				X				
New Zealand								
Norway		X	X	X		X	X	X
Peru		X	X		X			
Portugal					X			
Spain					X			
Sweden			X		X			X
Switzerland								
Turkey			X	X				
Union of South Africa	X	X	X	X	X	X	X	X
United Kingdom	X	X	X	X	X	X	X	X
United States	X	X	X	X	X	X	X	X
Uruguay							X	
Organization of American States	X							
Organization for European Economic Cooperation	X							

Defense Production Administrator. He acts on behalf of the Director of Defense Mobilization, whose authority is derived from the Defense Production Act. The essential parts of the recommendations, regarding limits on imports, levels of consumption, and export availabilities, must frequently be implemented by a number of agencies in accordance with their several responsibilities. Appropriate agencies are consulted by the Defense Production Administrator before recommendations are accepted, and they also have an opportunity periodically to review developments within the International Materials Conference, through a system of interagency committees which advise the United States delegate on each committee.

REVIEW QUESTIONS

1. What are the objectives of intergovernmental commodity arrangements?

2. Describe the difference between an international trade agreement and an intergovernmental commodity agreement.

3. Identify (*a*) study group, (*b*) commodity conference, (*c*) commodity-control agreement, and (*d*) commodity council.

4. Evaluate the desirability of buffer-stock schemes from the view of politics, economics, and social welfare.

5. What technical difficulties present themselves with regard to buffer-stock schemes?

6. To what extent has the United States government participated in intergovernmental commodity arrangements?

7. Describe the functioning of the International Wheat Agreement. Is it a desirable undertaking as far as the United States is concerned? As far as United States farmers are concerned?

8. What is the International Materials Conference? How significant is it or can it be in foreign commerce?

CHAPTER 21

International Monetary Fund

The International Monetary Fund is a specialized agency of the United Nations, designed to promote, and aid in the realization of, international monetary cooperation. Organizationally, it consists of member countries which, through its Articles of Agreement, subscribe to certain principles in international monetary relationships and transactions. Physically, it consists of a pool of gold and currencies of the member nations, which may be used for purposes and under conditions specified in the Articles of Agreement.

The idea of an international fund of some sort evolved during the war and was sponsored independently, at first, by the governments of Great Britain and the United States. After substantial unilateral consideration had been given the idea,[1] representatives of these two governments and later of several others began to work jointly on the proposal, as it would have to be an intergovernmental undertaking.

There developed a British and a United States proposal, the differences between which were initially ironed out in informal conferences among experts of these two and a few other countries. In the spring of 1943, the plans were made public, and in June an informal conference of 19 governments was held in Washington at which a number of proposals and memoranda were discussed.[2]

As evolved, the International Monetary Fund seems to be largely a compromise of United States and British plans, modified mainly by Canadian, Chinese, Ecuadorian, and French proposals and suggestions.[3] Between the United States and British plans there were similarities but at the same time important differences. Both provided for stabilization of exchange rates as a main objective; both provided for an inter-

---

[1] In the United States, this was accomplished through a "cabinet committee," consisting of representatives of the Treasury Department, the Departments of Commerce and State, the Board of Governors of the Federal Reserve System, and the Board of Economic Warfare.

[2] John Parke Young, "Developing Plans for an International Monetary Fund and a World Bank," *Department of State Bulletin*, Nov. 13, 1950, p. 781.

[3] *Ibid.*, p. 781.

national currency unit defined in terms of gold. Both provided for quotas based on economic importance, the quotas to determine voting rights and drawing privileges.

Among the fundamental differences were the British view, that the Fund should operate on an overdraft principle with "creditor" countries agreeing to accept balances of "debtor" countries on the books of a proposed clearing union, and the United States plan, which called for a contributory fund subscribed by members. A second difference was the British desire for an exchange rate that could be more flexible than as contemplated by the United States. Thirdly, a fundamental difference arose over the conditions under which the Fund's resources would be available to members. The British took the position that a member should have automatic access to the Fund's resources up to the amount of its quota. Its argument was that a government would have to rely on unhampered access to the Fund in order to formulate certain policies. The United States, on the other hand, felt that the Fund should have the right to disapprove a member's request if the use proposed for the funds received was not in keeping with the Fund's objectives. Other points of disagreement had to do with provisions for an international currency—a monetized unit (British) or an accounting unit (United States)—and with requirements regarding repurchase by a member of its currency held by the Fund.

Agreement was finally reached, and in April, 1944, a Joint Statement by Experts on the Establishment of an International Monetary Fund was made public.[4] This statement contained the fundamentals of a plan finally resolved by 44 nations at Bretton Woods, N.H., in the summer of 1944. The result of the Bretton Woods Conference was a proposed International Monetary Fund and International Bank for Reconstruction and Development, Articles of Agreement of which were signed by representatives of 30 countries in December, 1945, when the two institutions were brought into formal existence.

Relation to Other International Organizations

Cooperative arrangements with other international organizations were provided for in the Fund's Articles of Agreement and, aside from its relationship to the International Bank for Reconstruction and Development, origin of which paralleled that of the Fund, prompt action was taken to make the Fund a specialized agency of the United Nations.

Close liaison is maintained with several organizations through attendance at each other's meetings. Indicative of the Fund's relationships in this manner is the following extract from the *Annual Report, 1950*.[5]

[4] *Ibid.*, p. 784.
[5] P. 81.

Fund representatives have participated in meetings of the United Nations General Assembly, the Economic and Social Council, the Economic Commission for Europe, the Economic Commission for Latin America, the Economic Commission for Asia and the Far East, the Economic and Employment Commission, several United Nations Sub-Commissions, and the Administrative Committee on Coordination and its subordinate bodies. The Fund was represented at the Fifth Session of the Food and Agriculture Organization, the Annual General Meeting of the Bank for International Settlements, the Second Congress of the Inter-American Statistical Institute, the Second Meeting of Central Bank Experts of the American Republics, and a number of other international meetings.

In addition, close working arrangements have been entered between the Fund and GATT and between the Fund and OEEC. The former call for consultations in matters of balance-of-payments restrictions, and for Fund determination of what constitutes "a 'serious decline' in a country's monetary reserves, a 'very low level' of monetary reserves, or a 'reasonable rate of increase' in monetary reserves."[6] These are basic criteria incorporated in GATT for permitting a member to adopt import restrictions as a means of influencing the volume or direction of its foreign trade. Arrangements with OEEC is mainly concerned with establishment of payments arrangements compatible with the Fund's purposes. Specifically, the Fund is closely interested in the functioning of the EPU.

Purposes and Objectives

The extensive relationships with other international organizations, just described, are evidence that the Fund was not designed to function in isolation but "was conceived as one of several instrumentalities through which the nations of the world would seek to attain certain broad purposes which they held in common."[7] Carrying out this general concept, the Fund is expected to assist in creating "such an economic environment that the collaborating countries would normally not need to pursue restrictive policies in their economic relations, once the transitional period of post-war adjustments has been terminated."[8]

By the Articles of Agreement, the Fund is charged with assisting "in the establishment of a multilateral system of payments in respect of current transactions between members and in the elimination of foreign exchange restrictions which hamper the growth of world trade."[9]

[6] *Analysis of the General Agreement on Tariffs and Trade,* U.S. Department of State Publication 2983, 1947, p. 201.

[7] *Annual Report· 1947,* International Monetary Fund, p. 1.

[8] *First Annual Report on Exchange Restrictions,* International Monetary Fund, 1950, pp. 20–21.

[9] Art. I(iv).

In the light of agreement on these broad purposes, the Articles of Agreement thus constitute a formal repudiation of restrictionism as a normal instrument of international economic policy.[10] More concisely, and organizationally, the Fund's purposes and objectives may be said to be:

1. Establishment of a permanent organization for consultation as a means of promoting monetary cooperation
2. Promotion of exchange stability as a means of facilitating the expansion of world trade
3. Maintenance of orderly exchange arrangements
4. Avoidance of competitive exchange depreciation
5. Elimination of multiple currency practices
6. Progressive removal of exchange controls which hamper the growth of world trade

Operationally, the Fund, as a pool of currencies and gold, is designed to "give temporary assistance in financing balance of payments deficits *on current account for monetary stabilization operations* [italics added]." This is an official interpretation by the executive directors of the Fund, made on Sept. 26, 1946, at the request of the governor for the United States.

So far, principal attention would apparently be paid to preventing restrictive foreign-exchange policies by members because of the disruptive effects on other countries. However, another line of economic thought, usually described as the positive expansionist approach to economic programs, is found in Art. I of the Agreement and in official publications, which describe additional Fund purposes or objectives, as follows:

1. Aiding members in "maintaining arrangements that promote the *balanced expansion* [italics added] of international trade and investment and in this way contribute to the maintenance of high levels of employment and real income."[11]
2. Relieving the "strain on the payments position of its members . . . while corrective measures are instituted by the national authorities."[12]
3. Extending members, in accordance with the Agreement, "financial assistance to help them overcome temporary disequilibria in their international payments without . . . being obliged to adopt policies detrimental to their own welfare or that of other nations."[13] This point refers to lower costs brought about through lower wages, if necessary, in

[10] *First Annual Report on Exchange Restrictions*, p. 20.

[11] *Report of Executive Directors, and Summary Proceedings of First Annual Meeting of the Board of Governors*, International Monetary Fund, 1946, p. 25.

[12] *Annual Report, 1949*, International Monetary Fund, p. 42.

[13] *Annual Report 1947*, International Monetary Fund, p. 1.

lieu of increased efficiency—the much-feared deflationary adjustment process. It also refers to unilateral surprise and competitive devaluations.

A transitional period of about three years was anticipated following establishment of the Fund, at the end of which the Fund was charged with reporting on restrictions still in force at that time. The first report was issued in March, 1950, accompanied by the comment that progress in establishment of a multilateral system of payments had not been so marked as had been hoped initially. The 1951 and 1952 reports stated that some restrictions had been abolished but that changed conditions had prevented some removal and had brought about increased restrictions in several countries.

Concept of Exchange Stability. Since the Fund has as one of its purposes the promotion of exchange stability and the avoidance of competitive depreciation, it is significant to question the concept of exchange stability. Does it mean, as has apparently been feared by many countries, that "membership in the Fund might impose upon national authorities control by an organization which would make a fetish of exchange stability and would regard any changes from the agreed par value (outside the 10 per cent limit on the total of all changes—for which Fund approval is not necessary) as highly abnormal and to be sanctioned only reluctantly and in the most unusual circumstances"?[14]

The Fund's views on this question, as expressed in its *Annual Report, 1948,* are that stability and rigidity are different concepts. To it, exchange rates must be in touch with "economic realities" and adjustment of rates may be "an essential element in the measures necessary to enable a country to pay for the goods and services it needs from abroad without undue pressure upon its international reserves."[15] Furthermore, stability implies that adjustments be made in an orderly manner and that competitive exchange depreciation be avoided.

As viewed by the National Advisory Council, exchange stability implies that the market prices of foreign exchange do not fluctuate except within a narrow range.[16] The Fund Agreement calls for a par value for each member's currency, in terms of gold or U.S. dollars, and provides that minimum or maximum rates of exchange between currencies may not differ by more than 1 per cent above or below the par value in case of spot transactions. For other transactions, a larger margin may be established.[17]

[14] *Annual Report, 1948,* International Monetary Fund, p. 21.

[15] *Ibid.*

[16] Special Report of National Advisory Council, 1948, published in *Federal Reserve Bulletin,* July, 1948, p. 800.

[17] Art. IV, Sec. 3.

Origin of Fund's Resources

Under the Articles of Agreement, each member of the Fund subscribes to a quota based on economic importance. Receipts from these contributions constitute the original resources of the Fund.

The total of the quotas of countries represented at Bretton Woods was $8,800,000,000, of which the United States quota was. $2,750,000,000.[18] But by June 30, 1947, following ratification of the Agreement and establishment of par values, total *subscriptions* to the Fund amounted to $6,535,000,000. Through increases or reductions in quotas, accession of additional members, and withdrawals (one: Poland), the subscribed quotas were as follows in succeeding years.

Apr. 30, 1948	$7,976,000,000
Apr. 30, 1949	8,034,000,000
Apr. 30, 1950	7,921,500,000
Apr. 30, 1951	8,036,500,000

Members and their quotas as of Apr. 30, 1951, are shown in Table 48.

Payment of the subscriptions was called for partly in gold and partly in gold or U.S. dollars, but mainly in local currencies of the subscribing members. The Agreement calls for payment in gold of 25 per cent of a member's quota or 10 per cent of the member's net official holdings of gold and U.S. dollars, whichever is smaller. In addition, members are required to pay $\frac{1}{100}$ of 1 per cent of their quotas in gold or U.S. dollars to provide a fund for meeting administrative expenses, most of which will be incurred in the United States, where the Fund is domiciled. As of Apr. 30, 1951, the Fund had received subscription resources as follows:

$\frac{1}{100}$ of 1% paid in U.S. dollars	$ 759,650.00
Paid in gold	1,469,565,955.48
Paid in members' currencies	5,659,629,912.75
Subscriptions receivable	906,544,481.77
Total quotas	$8,036,500,000.00

Relationship to Monetary Reserves. The amount of monetary reserves held by a member country is of primary meaning, in its Fund membership, in connection with repurchase obligations.

But an even more important connection between Fund membership and monetary reserves is found in the fact that membership permits the acquisition of foreign exchange which would otherwise not be available unless a country's reserve or gold position were pressed hard. Thus without reducing its reserves or gold (except as required under repurchase obligations), a member may come into possession of foreign exchange not earned commercially.

[18] Quotas are subject to change by Fund decision. The U.S.S.R. quota agreed to at Bretton Woods was $1,200,000,000, but that nation did not subscribe to membership.

Table 48. International Monetary Fund, Membership and Quotas*
(Quotas in millions of U.S. dollars)

Country	Quota	Country	Quota
Australia	$200	India	$ 400
Austria	50	Iran	35
Belgium	225	Iraq	8
Bolivia	10	Italy	180
Brazil	150	Lebanon	4.5
Canada	300	Luxembourg	10
Ceylon	15	Mexico	90
Chile	50	Netherlands	275
China	550	Nicaragua	2
Colombia	50	Norway	50
Costa Rica	5	Pakistan	100
Cuba	50	Panama	0.5
Czechoslovakia	125	Paraguay	3.5
Denmark	68	Peru	25
Dominican Republic	5	Philippine Republic	15
Ecuador	5	Syria	6.5
Egypt	60	Thailand	12.5
El Salvador	2.5	Turkey	43
Ethiopia	6	Union of South Africa	100
Finland	38	United Kingdom	1,300
France	525	United States	2,750
Greece	40	Uruguay	15
Guatemala	5	Venezuela	15
Honduras	0.5	Yugoslavia	60
Iceland	1	Total	$8,036.5

* As of April 30, 1951.
SOURCE: *Annual Report, 1951,* International Monetary Fund, pp. 100–103.

While the circumstances which lead any government to seek foreign exchange from the Fund is low demand for its own currency relative to its citizens' demands for foreign currencies, acquisition of the foreign currencies does not serve to reconcile the price differentials (of all things involved) which are reflected in the market value of its exchange relative to others. Because of this, the corrective adjustment in costs and prices which could be promptly compelled by the loss of monetary reserves is delayed, possibly in the hope of being avoided. This is the opposite of the gold-sterilization program followed by the United States in the middle 1930s, undertaken to offset a gain in monetary reserves. Whatever will happen to bring the exchange rates back into line will then have to be (1) progressive, but orderly, devaluation, (2) the imposition or extension of trade or exchange restrictions, or (3) the vague "suitable corrective measures" to be "instituted by the national authorities."

During discussions of the proposed Fund, Australia, New Zealand,

and the United Kingdom were among the countries expressing fear that certain Fund provisions might be inconsistent with a domestic policy of full employment and other social objectives.[19] On this score, the Articles of Agreement contain a provision that the Fund "shall not object to a proposed change [in rates] because of the domestic, social or political policies of the member. . . . "[20] Accordingly, it would appear that adjustment of exchange disequilibria may not come about primarily by numerous adjustments in individual positions to meet competition, but instead by a progressive devaluation of national currencies which will only serve to render more rigid the positions of the factors of production in any one country.

Manner of Operation

In exercising its functions, the International Monetary Fund operates both by consultation and statements of policy and by transactions in foreign exchange and gold.

Consultations and Policy Statements. As to consultations, this may be said to be a continuous undertaking with regard to the condition of each country, as the Fund attempts to keep itself well informed at all times in order to be able to respond quickly to the requests of members for dealings in currencies. In fact, the consultative mechanism is of great importance as, through it, plans or programs of individual member countries can be evaluated and informally encouraged or discouraged as they evolve. This is necessary in arriving at a conclusion that members' requests for the Fund's resources are in line with purposes of the organization.

Probably the outstanding evidence of consultative benefits was the series of orderly devaluations in September, 1949. The background leading to this concerted devaluation was that in December, 1946, a statement of initial par values for member countries was issued by the Fund. This was the basis for initial Fund operations and, in order to permit prompt functioning of the Fund as a going organization, parities proposed by the members themselves were accepted. It was recognized at the time that some later adjustment would have to be made after the respective countries had had more time to analyze postwar developments and positions. Accordingly, after considerable discussion within the Fund, new par values (in terms of gold and the U.S. dollar) were agreed on by the Fund as an organization. This was, as stated before, in September, 1949, and was accomplished with prior knowledge by Fund-member governments, whose views on the proposed extent of devaluation could be given due weight. There was thus avoided a piece-

[19] Young, *op. cit.*, p. 787.
[20] Art. IV, Sec. 5(f).

meal devaluation, with each country taking unilateral action as a surprise to other countries.

Statements of policy have been made regarding use of the Fund's resources, maintenance of established par values of currencies, and international sales of gold at premium prices. When gold is so sold, it means that gold is being bought for hoarding, perhaps in anticipation of a devaluation, and is not available as monetary reserve. In fact, the sale of gold at premium prices amounts to a devaluation as such. The effect of these policy statements is to bind members to comply with the stated policy.

Transactions in Exchange and Gold. As stated before, the physical Fund is a pool of currencies and gold, subscribed by and available for use by members under certain conditions. Currency operations are limited in general by the Articles of Agreement to "transactions for the purpose of supplying a member, on the initiative of such member, with the currency of another member in exchange for gold or for the currency of the member desiring to make the purchase."[21]

The member desiring to purchase another's currency must represent to the Fund that such currency is needed for making payments which are consistent with provisions of the Articles of Agreement, the member must not have been declared ineligible to use the Fund's resources, and the Fund's holdings of the currency desired must not have been declared "scarce" by the Fund. Quantitative limitations are that the proposed purchase must not increase, during the year preceding it, the Fund's acquisition of the buying member's currency by more than 25 per cent of that member's quota, nor the Fund's total holdings of such currency to more than 200 per cent of that member's quota. Thus it would take at least four years for a member, through its own transactions with the Fund and excluding any repurchase requirements, to exhaust its access to the Fund's resources.[22]

In principle, the sum total of the Fund's resources will not change materially, except as operations result in profits or losses or as members enter or resign. But the composition of the Fund's resources will change by the process of any member's buying the currency of another and paying for such currency with its own or with gold, by the process of repurchasing its currency with a convertible currency or with gold, or by the process of selling its currency to the Fund for gold.[23] Mechanics of the transactions in exchange are illustrated in Fig. 16.

[21] Art. V, Sec. 2.

[22] Art. V, Sec. 3. The 25-per-cent limitation applies only to Fund acquisitions in excess of 75 per cent of a member's quota if holdings had been below 75 per cent.

[23] Art. VII, Sec. 2(ii) provides that the Fund may require a member to sell its currency for gold (in effect, the Fund selling gold) to replenish the Fund's holdings of that member's (scarce) currency.

In Phase I, the Fund's resources consist originally of, say, 21 units—10 units of currency A, the equivalent (in terms of currency A) of 6 units of currency B, and 5 units of currency C. In Phase II, let it be assumed that both country B and country C bought from the Fund 1 unit each of currency A, paying for it in their own currencies. The result of these transactions will be that the Fund's holdings of currency A will have been reduced from 10 to 8 units, by its sale of 2 units, 1 each to countries B and C. Its holdings of the currencies of B and C will have been increased from 6 and 5 units, respectively, to 7 and 6 units, respectively. Thus, the Fund's total holdings remain unchanged at 21 units, but the composition of currencies A, B, and C has been altered. Eventually, it is the plan, countries B and C will repurchase their own currencies over and above their quotas, and the Fund will be back in its original position, or country A may buy currencies of countries B and C from the Fund, thus reducing the Fund's excess holdings of these

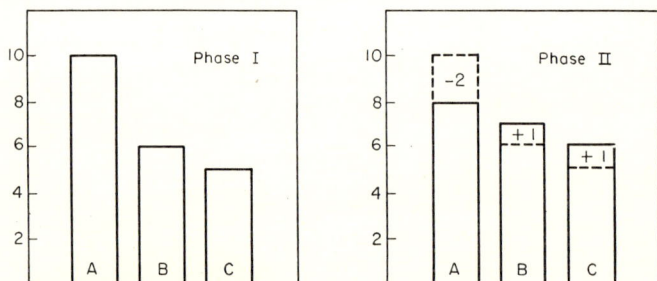

Fig. 16. Illustration of mechanics of Fund transactions in exchange.

currencies and making it unnecessary for any repurchase operations to take place between the Fund and countries B and C.

The Fund's transactions in gold should be much less frequent and much smaller in volume than those in exchange. Gold depositories of the Fund have been established in New York, London, Shanghai, Paris, and Bombay, at which points transactions in gold may be effected. However, since the Fund can sell gold only to replenish its holdings of currency, and must anticipate expenses in moving it, the price it can pay for gold in New York, in dollars, is less than a member country could obtain by direct sale to the United States Treasury.[24]

Repurchase Arrangements. When a member government purchases another's currency and pays for it with its own (payment could also be made in gold), it undertakes somewhat of an obligation to repurchase its own currency at the end of the Fund's financial year. This may be done either with a convertible currency or with gold.

Terms of the obligation are hedged with references to monetary re-

[24] Art. V, Sec. 7(c) and Sched. B, Articles of Agreement.

serves of the member and to Fund quotas. Repurchases are not required if:

1. The member's monetary reserves as of the end of the fiscal year are below its quota (in the Fund) or to the extent that repurchase would reduce those monetary reserves to an amount less than the member's quota
2. The Fund's holdings of the currency of a member are less than 75 per cent of the member's quota, or to the extent that repurchase would result in the Fund's holdings of the repurchasing member's currency being reduced below 75 per cent of the member's quota
3. The Fund's holdings of any currency required to be used in repurchase (a convertible currency) are in excess of 75 per cent of the quota of the member concerned, or to the extent that repurchases would bring about this condition

Nevertheless, whether to provide income or in order to encourage members to repurchase their own currencies when not excused by the foregoing conditions, the Fund imposes a service charge for the use of its resources. The charge is at an increasing annual rate until a maximum is reached under the original schedule. At that point, the member involved and the Fund must consult on means to reduce the Fund's holdings of the member's currency. If agreement cannot be reached, the Fund can fix any charge which it deems appropriate.

Until late 1951, repurchases were rather slow in taking place, so the Fund's schedule of charges was accelerated to bring higher rates into effect at an earlier date. The schedule for 1952 appears below.

Sequence of charges	If Fund's holdings exceed member's quota by	
	Less than 25%	More than 25%
Period for which no charge...............	6 months	none
Annual rate 1st 6 months.................	0	1 to 2%, depending on Fund's holdings
Annual rate 2d 6 months.................	1%	½% higher than first six months
Semiannual increase in rate.............	½%	½%
Point at which member and Fund must consult on means to reduce Fund's holdings........	3½%	3½%
Point at which Fund can assess higher rate....	over 4%	over 4%
Maximum annual rate..................	5%	5%

A member is permitted to substitute with the Fund non-interest-bearing, nonnegotiable notes payable at par value on demand for the Fund's holdings of its currency in excess of the amount required by the Fund for operations.[25] This amounts, practically, from 74 to 99 per cent of a member's quota (excluding the $\frac{1}{100}$ of 1 per cent payable in gold or dollars).[26] On this basis, the Fund's principal assets on Apr. 30, 1951, consisted of the following:

Gold.....................................	$1,495,042,780.46
Currencies.............................	714,679,738.45
Securities (as described above)..........	4,914,122,949.49
Subscriptions receivable...............	906,544,481.77

These special securities are considered to be currency by the members in determining repurchase obligations. However, as far as the United States is concerned, they are not listed as currency issued by the Treasury, on which a reserve must be maintained. Accordingly, if legal reserves are not maintained by members against these demand obligations due the Fund, and the members may have for domestic use their total reserves, foreign exchange may be obtained not only without a diminution of their unencumbered reserves but without a diminution of their money.

Operations to 1951

Consultations and Policy Statements. Through both missions and consultations between executive directors and representatives of member governments, the Fund's activities as a consultative body have been influential in keeping member governments' monetary policies in line with the Fund's basic objectives. Consultations have involved both Fund review and approval of specific measures and general advice on a wide range of matters affecting the restrictive policies of member countries.

Articles of Agreement of the Fund provide for members to maintain a fixed rate of exchange. Yet, exceptional circumstances have arisen whereby members had to abandon their agreed par value and where they were unable to determine a new one. In such cases, the Fund has considered the circumstances and, if the member's case was "persuasive," has acceded to the member's temporary suspension without deciding whether any action under the Articles of Agreement would be necessary or desirable. As expressed in the *Annual Report, 1951*, the Fund's economic and financial judgment "must be tempered by recognition of its responsibilities in the wider field of international relations." As of mid-1951, three Fund members—Canada, France, and Peru—had decided

---

[25] Art. III, Sec. 5.

[26] Gold to be paid in is the smaller of 25 per cent of a member's quota or 10 per cent of its net official holdings of gold and U.S. dollars. The remainder of the quota (except for the $\frac{1}{100}$ of 1 per cent payable in gold or dollars to cover administrative expenses) is payable in local currency. However, Rules and Regulations E–2 of the Fund limit this substitution of these special notes to *currency subscriptions* in excess of 1 per cent of a member's quota.

temporarily not to maintain exchange rates in accordance with par values agreed with the Fund.

Only once, apparently, has a member acted openly in conflict with the Fund's views. This was in 1948, when France modified its exchange system and provided for devaluation of the franc, at which time it set up a fluctuating rate on U.S. dollars and some other currencies but not on all. Since this was considered by the Fund as discriminatory to some members and as inconsistent with its objectives, it could not concur in the proposal. Nevertheless, France decided to proceed with the change.

Aside from the general devaluations of 1949, several changes have taken place in the par values of currencies or in exchange arrangements by individual member countries. These have, however, been after consultation and agreement with the Fund, even though original or new par values have not been established in some cases. Countries in which such changes occurred between 1947 and April, 1951, were Ecuador, Italy, Chile, Colombia, French Somaliland, France, Peru, Paraguay, and Canada.

The principal policy statements, which themselves involved consultations, pertained to transactions in gold at premium prices, multiple currency practices, gold subsidies, and the unenforceability of exchange contracts which were in violation of a member country's exchange-control regulations, provided the regulations were approved by the Fund. The policy questions on gold prices have been in the nature of a running battle with gold producers.

The Fund has as a stated objective, and has consistently reminded members of the need for, the removal of exchange restrictions on current transactions. This point is discussed later in the chapter. However, it is appropriate to mention here, as part of the consultative program, that under the Articles of Agreement, member countries still retaining certain restrictions five years after the Fund began operations were to consult with the Fund as to their further retention. As of this terminal date (March, 1952), and in the face of strong postwar tendencies toward bilateralism and restrictionism, the Fund was confronted with evaluating the needs and problems of individual members, the effects of their actions on the international community, and the effects of the maintenance of restrictions on the Fund's aims as set forth in the Articles of Agreement.

Transactions in Exchange: Sales and Repurchases. Although several countries have been informally advised that the Fund "did not regard it as desirable for them to use the Fund's resources under prevailing circumstances,"[27] and have accordingly not made formal requests for

[27] Special Report of National Advisory Council, 1948, published in *Federal Reserve Bulletin,* July, 1948, p. 807.

exchange, transactions have been carried out with many members. On this point, the National Advisory Council, in its 1950 report, states that United States policy with respect to the Fund has been one of trying to avoid the extreme of "acquiescing in the virtually automatic use of the Fund's resources to meet any type of current deficit, while also, on the other hand, avoiding the extreme of insisting upon such rigid standards as would practically have suspended the Fund's currency operations until greater progress had been made toward general convertibility, particularly sterling." Continuing, the report states:[28]

Thus, in the first period of the Fund's operations the Council concurred in some Fund drawings, principally by European countries, in the hope that financial stability might be more rapidly attained thereby. As it became apparent that Fund drawings would merely be one additional source of dollars in a situation of fundamental disequilibrium which would not be remedied within a few years, the Council has favored a policy of conservation of the Fund's resources to the future date at which their use might be more efficacious in bringing about the realization of the Fund's basic objective as stated in the Articles of Agreement.

From the time operations began, in 1947, to Apr. 30, 1951, the Fund sold foreign exchange to 19 of the 49 members. Currencies sold, though, were only three—Belgian francs ($11,400,000), British pounds ($34,-000,000) and U.S. dollars ($766,000,000). Repurchases were effected by 6 of these countries—Belgium, Costa Rica, Egypt, Ethiopia, Union of South Africa and Nicaragua.[29] The result of these operations was that the Fund's holdings of U.S. dollars were reduced materially, while its holdings of currencies of several other countries were in excess of the respective quotas.

Transactions in Gold. As indicated above, part of each member's subscription is payable in gold, and when a member purchases currency of another and pays with its own, it may use gold to repurchase its currency in excess of quota. Furthermore, the Fund may, if it rules that a member's currency is scarce, require the member to sell its currency to the Fund for gold.

Between the beginning of operations, in 1947, and Apr. 30, 1951, the Fund also carried on several transactions involving gold. Currency sold against gold (gold purchased by the Fund) amounted to $6,200,000, and the Fund received gold in the amount of $10,400,000 through repurchasing operations of members.

---

[28] Published in *Federal Reserve Bulletin*, June, 1950, p. 669.

[29] *Annual Report, 1951*, International Monetary Fund, p. 87.   Other repurchase obligations had been computed and agreed to, and Chile had effected a repurchase, in June, 1951.

Internal Organization

The Fund is directed by a board of governors, and operations have been delegated to a board of executive directors, no less than 12 in number, some appointed and some elected.

Each of the five members with the largest quotas appoints an executive director (and an alternate), and remaining members elect the other (nine, as of 1951) executive directors and their alternates.[30] The executive directors, in turn, select a managing director who is the principal administrator of the Fund.

As of April, 1951, the 456 staff members were organized into six departments and three offices. These were:

European and North American Department
Latin American, Middle Eastern and Far Eastern Department
Exchange Restrictions Department
Legal Department
Research Department
Treasurer's Department
Office of Administration
Office of Public Relations
Office of the Secretary

United States Participation

United States participation in the International Monetary Fund is by authority of the Bretton Woods Agreements Act, approved by the President in July, 1945. Its quota in the Fund is, as stated before, $2,750,000,000. This quota was 29.96 per cent of the total as of Apr. 30, 1951; the United States is by far the largest subscriber. The United Kingdom was next, with a quota of 14.31 per cent of the total; China was third, with 6.21 per cent; France was fourth, with 5.94 per cent; and India was fifth, with 4.59 per cent. As one of the five largest members, the United States appoints an executive director.

Payment of the United States subscription to the International Monetary Fund was completed in February, 1947, and the subscription is held as an international investment by the government.[31]

The National Advisory Council

The Bretton Woods Agreements Act also set up the National Advisory Council, which is charged with coordinating the policies and opera-

[30] A certain number are elected by members other than the American Republics, but not entitled to appoint directors, and a certain number are elected by American Republics not entitled to appoint directors.

[31] See Table 47, "International Investment Position of United States," p. 310.

tions of the representatives of the United States on the International
Monetary Fund and the International Bank for Reconstruction and Development, the Export-Import Bank of Washington, and all other agencies of the Government "to the extent that they make or participate in
the making of foreign loans or engage in foreign financial, exchange or
monetary transactions."

The National Advisory Council is composed of the Secretaries of the
Treasury, State, and Commerce, the Chairman of the Board of Governors of the Federal Reserve System, the Chairman of the Board of Directors of the Export-Import Bank, and, during the life of his office,
the Mutual Security Administrator.

The Council is required to submit a biennial report to the President
and to Congress on the operations and policies of the International
Monetary Fund and the International Bank for Reconstruction and Development. These reports are to cover:

The extent to which the Fund and the Bank have achieved the purposes for
which they were established; the extent to which the operations and policies
of the Fund and the Bank have adhered to, or departed from, the general
policy directives formulated by the Council, and the Council's recommendations in connection therewith; the extent to which the operations and policies
of the Fund and the Bank have been coordinated, and the Council's recommendations in connection therewith; recommendations on whether the resources of the Fund and the Bank should be increased or decreased; recommendations as to how the Fund and the Bank may be made more effective;
recommendations on any other necessary or desirable changes in the Articles
of Agreement of the Fund and of the Bank or in this Act; and an over-all appraisal of the extent to which the operations and policies of the Fund and
the Bank have served, and in the future may be expected to serve, the interests of the United States and the world in promoting sound international
economic cooperation and furthering world security.

Conditions Precedent to Fund's Success

This powerful organization—the International Monetary Fund—conceived in good faith and dedicated to high purposes, would seem to merit
only public approval and confidence. However, some features call for
words of caution and doubt.

The Articles of Agreement were predicated on the assumption of a
relatively short period of adjustment following the war and the assumption that countries of the world would rapidly remove exchange restrictions and take necessary steps to render their currencies convertible.
Furthermore, it was assumed that exchange markets would be dominated
by private exchange transactions, which means that private enterprise
would be free to conduct such international dealings as seemed advantageous at the time—not forced and not widely restricted. In that

cause, the Fund would be called on for action to meet *temporary* deficits in balances of payments.

Failure to realize these assumptions is voiced by the National Advisory Council in its May, 1950, report, in which it is stated that "all except five countries have availed themselves of the right to retain exchange restrictions and a number of countries have intensified restrictions. It cannot so far be said that the total movement has been large in the general direction of unrestricted convertibility of currencies."

Of course, one could not have foreseen the increasing threat of war; the U.S.S.R. and China both participated in the Bretton Woods discussions, and China actually became one of the large-quota members of the Fund.

However, the Fund's success must rest on the working of certain economic principles. Its calling for a multilateral convertibility of exchange means calling for conditions under which multilateral trade can flourish. Among these conditions, as listed by the Fund in its *Annual Report, 1950*, are:[32]

1. Restoration of productive capacity
2. A well-balanced flow of international trade
3. Appropriate relationships among cost-price structures of the main trading nations
4. Freedom from undue inflationary or deflationary pressures
5. An active international capital market
6. Adequate monetary reserves
7. Modification of rigidities characteristic of many economies

Some of these conditions, notably the second, third, and fifth, *cannot be brought about by government action* without regimenting enterprise; they must be allowed to come about, themselves, by the business activities of millions of people, each adjusting his own position to the circumstances faced. This is because price, as an allocator of the factors of production, has a subjective origin (in the minds of both buyer and seller) as well as an objective level.

Governmental interference with the price mechanism is called for by one of the Fund's principal objectives—providing foreign exchange *temporarily*, thus affording member governments the opportunity to do something by way of correcting their balance-of-payments disequilibria without resorting to measures "destructive of national or international prosperity." Since the Fund's resources are also available for use as a contribution to the maintenance of high levels of employment and income, this can only mean that downward adjustments in costs and prices—deflation—will be delayed or not allowed to take place in the

[32] Pp. 55–56.

hope that something else may happen to enable the country affected to export more rather than import less.

The "export" most commonly in the foreground is an investment of some sort. But on this point a conflict arises. Among the conditions under which convertibility of exchange can function is "an active international capital market." No individual will ordinarily place his funds, or funds of others entrusted to his administration, in a foreign country threatening to impose restrictions on capital movements, if he can find less risk elsewhere.

But the Fund's Articles of Agreement point to the "establishment of a multilateral system of payments *in respect of current transactions* [italics added] between members." Capital transfers are not classed as current transactions[33] and, in fact, "control of capital movements is permitted to Fund members at all times."[34] This being the case, an important segment of the total supply of and demand for exchange is excluded from the field of unrestricted multilateral payments, but it is considered a necessary condition for success of the idea of multilateral convertibility.

The basic difficulty here is that as long as a person is free to choose between spending and saving, and between spending for consumer goods or services and for an investment, and between an investment in his own and in any of several countries, he will not save or place his funds where he is not reasonably certain of being able to recover them.

Foreign investments, *including capital transfers* (original investment or repatriation), are as essential to "current transactions" as are any other international transactions. All provide and demand foreign exchange in some degree; all are reducible to the same common denominator.

Accordingly, one must be doubtful of the Fund's ultimate success in achieving a multilateral system in respect of current transactions unless it is at the expense of stifling foreign investments undertaken by private enterprise, without government guarantee, and thus stifling the capitalistic development of the world's productive resources.

REVIEW QUESTIONS

1. What is the relation of the International Monetary Fund to the United Nations? To the International Bank for Reconstruction and Development?
2. Explain briefly the purposes and objectives of the Fund.
3. What is the concept of exchange stability as adopted by the Fund?
4. Where does the Fund obtain its resources?
5. Describe the relation of the Fund to a country's monetary reserves.

[33] Art. XIX (i).
[34] *Annual Report, 1947*, International Monetary Fund, p. 33.

6. Consultations and policy statements are an important function of the Fund. What is the basis for the strength of these, such that they bear weight with the members?

7. When does a member which obtains foreign exchange from the Fund, and pays for it in its own currency, have to repurchase its currency?

8. How important is the United States in the Fund, *i.e.*, what is the amount of our subscription and what proportion of the Fund's total does this represent?

9. Explain the difficulty faced in rendering freely convertible exchange on current transactions, yet retaining to nations the tacit approval of control over capital transactions.

CHAPTER 22

International Bank for Reconstruction and Development

As was indicated in the preceding chapter, the Bretton Woods Agreement provided for two organizations, the International Monetary Fund and the International Bank for Reconstruction and Development. Although of the same parentage, and brought into being at the same time, these two institutions are separate and distinct legal entities, with different functions.

Both are specialized agencies of the United Nations in well-delineated fields of responsibility, yet the success or failure of one will to a large degree influence the success or failure of the other. Expanded international investment activity, as contemplated by the International Bank for Reconstruction and Development, calls for monetary stability of the type necessary to induce private investors to risk their limited funds in one country in preference to another. At the same time, the conditions of monetary stability contemplated by the International Monetary Fund call for a rather free flow of foreign investments as a means of contributing to, among other things, conditions under which monetary stability can be *attained and maintained.*

A principal obstacle to this otherwise well-oiled effort is that it provides for a flow of investment only one way—funds from the rich investor to the poor "borrowing" country. The option of disposing of such an investment to a national of the country in which the investment is made, at any time the investor sees fit, and in such a way that he can convert the proceeds into another currency, is apparently considered an unnecessary luxury for the investor. Thus, control over capital movements, the volume and direction of which initially are encouraged, promoted, and stimulated by the International Bank, is reserved to the respective countries by the International Monetary Fund.

Relation to Other International Organizations

Aside from this very close kinship to the International Monetary Fund, the International Bank participates in and collaborates with a number of

444

other international organizations. Chief of these is the United Nations, especially the Economic and Social Council. In this connection, the following clause from the agreement between the United Nations and the Bank is of interest, in that it definitely recognizes the legal and functional independence of the Bank:[1]

The United Nations recognizes that the action to be taken by the Bank on any loan is a matter to be determined by the independent exercise of the Bank's own judgment in accordance with the Bank's Articles of Agreement. The United Nations recognizes, therefore, that it would be sound policy to refrain from making recommendations to the Bank with respect to particular loans or with respect to terms or conditions of financing by the Bank. The Bank recognizes that the United Nations and its organs may appropriately make recommendations with respect to the technical aspects of reconstruction or development plans, programs or projects.

In the year ending June 30, 1950, the Bank was represented at meetings of the United Nations General Assembly, the Economic and Social Council of the United Nations, the International Monetary Fund, the Food and Agriculture Organization, the International Labour Organisation, the Organization of American States, the Bank for International Settlements, and other organizations. Similarly, observers from these organizations attended certain meetings of the Bank's governors.

Purposes and Objectives

In brief, the purposes of the Bank, as prescribed in its Articles of Agreement, are:

1. To assist in the reconstruction and development of members by facilitating the investment of capital for productive purposes. . . .
2. To promote private foreign investment by means of guarantees or participations in loans and other investments made by private investors; and when private capital is not available on reasonable terms, to supplement private investment by providing, on suitable conditions, finance for productive purposes out of its own capital, funds raised by it and its other resources.
3. To promote the long-range balanced growth of international trade and the maintenance of equilibrium in balances of payments by encouraging international investment for the development of the productive resources of members, thereby assisting in raising productivity, the standard of living and conditions of labor in their territories.
4. To arrange the loans made or guaranteed by it in relation to international loans through other channels so that the more useful and urgent projects, large and small alike, will be dealt with first.
5. To conduct its operations with due regard to the effect of international investment on business conditions in the territories of members. . . .

[1] *Summary Proceedings, Second Annual Meeting of the Board of Governors,* International Bank for Reconstruction and Development, October, 1947, pp. 25–26.

Based on activities of the first five years of operation, two features of these stated purposes require close and careful attention. The first is emphasis on development, by which is meant productivity. The second is the arrangement of projects in an order of priority.

The first is forcefully brought out in the annual report for 1947, which reads, in part:[2]

The Bank's task is to help raise the level of the world's production as greatly and as rapidly as it can. It cannot accomplish this task simply by examining the need of individual countries for external assistance for their reconstruction or development. Rather, the Bank must emphasize the financing of those projects or programs, be they for reconstruction or development, which promise the greatest increase in productive output in the shortest possible time.

Of course, as reconstruction was accomplished, it was only to be expected that the Bank would be devoting its major attention to its other titular purpose, development. This brings up the second of the features calling for close study. One of the purposes listed, the fourth, calls for an order of priority. For how else can it be determined which projects, whether large or small, are "the more useful and urgent" and to be "dealt with first"?

Concept of "Development" Clarified. As more attention was paid the developmental phases of its activities, especially with regard to carrying out its assigned responsibility of dealing first with the more useful and urgent of the projects for which financing was being sought, the Bank's annual reports reflect some of the fundamental line of thinking which such a program entails.

The 1948 report,[3] for example, points out that "to raise the income level of the underdeveloped countries requires an expansion of their production, primarily through technological development and increased capital investment." The urgency of such programs is greater than ever "because, as a result of modern means of communication, their peoples are becoming increasingly aware of the contrast between their status and that of the peoples of the more economically advanced nations."

The same report states:[4]

Again, there is lacking in many countries any well-formulated concept of the over-all lines along which sound development is most likely to make progress. In the absence of such a general pattern of development, it is difficult to estimate the relative importance and urgency of different undertakings, their ability to function economically, and the need for power, transportation and other basic facilities to support them.

[2] P. 8.
[3] Pp. 14–15.
[4] P. 16.

Along the same line, the Bank observes that "one of the most essential tasks facing the less developed countries is to take more effective measures to channel their limited domestic savings into the most productive investment projects."[5] Specifically, better organization of their capital markets and financial institutions is mentioned as one measure which might be taken. But if one were to indulge in a less traditional economic philosophy, the extent to which a government could go in accomplishing such an objective is frightening—a thorough regimentation of productive institutions in which investment opportunities would have to be cleared through some government functionary to ascertain that the "limited domestic savings" are applied to the "most productive investment projects." The function of market price, as an allocator of the factors of production in the field of new investments or expansion of facilities, would be substantially debarred.

However, the Bank is charged with dealing first with the more useful and urgent projects. Its practice, accordingly, is to look on a loan application as only one phase of a country's economic development. The other phases must be known and, in effect, rated as to importance. This view was well expressed by the president of the Bank, in an address at the fifth annual meeting of the Board of Governors in September, 1950, when he said:

A first essential seems to me to be the formulation of a properly balanced development program, calling for investment expenditures which are within the capacity of the country concerned, including its capacity to borrow abroad, and for the allocation of those expenditures among different types of projects in accordance with an appropriate pattern of priorities.

In interpreting these official comments, it must be remembered that the Bank's interest is in part concerned with projects which may not be attractive to private capital or, if they are, perhaps not at the moment.

In view of its stated purposes, the Bank functions in two ways, lending (either its funds or its name) and consulting. In fact, the latter appears at times to be about as important as the former, as the Bank can "provide impartial advice on questions of priorities and on means for better mobilization of local resources."

Source of Funds

Although the Bank has an authorized capital of $10,000,000,000,[6] and capital subscribed by member governments was over $8,400,000,000 in 1951, payments on these subscriptions will probably not provide the major part of funds available to the Bank for lending.

[5] *Fifth Annual Report, 1949–1950,* International Bank for Reconstruction and Development, p. 10.

[6] May be increased by a three-fourths majority of voting power.

The Articles of Agreement contemplated the institution as one to stimulate private investment. Accordingly, only part of the Bank's subscribed capital, 20 per cent, is ever to be available for lending. The remainder is only subject to call to meet bank obligations incurred through borrowing or through guarantees given private investors. Lendable funds of the Bank, then, will arise from (1) capital subscriptions, (2) borrowing, through the sale of bonds, or selling loans either with or without Bank guarantee, and (3) earnings. As indicated, the Bank may function without immediate need for large volumes of funds, by the process of guaranteeing investments meeting specifications.

Capital Stock. The Bank's capital stock is divided into 100,000 shares, having a par value of $100,000 each, and available for subscription only by members. The 50[7] members and their subscriptions as of Dec. 31, 1951, are shown in Table 49. Three additional countries, Haiti, Liberia, and the U.S.S.R., were assigned quotas in the Articles of Agreement, but up to the end of 1951 had not subscribed to their shares in the Bank.

Capital subscriptions are divided into two parts: (1) 20 per cent, of which one-tenth (2 per cent) is payable in gold or U.S. dollars, and the remainder (18 per cent) is payable in the currency of the member; and (2) 80 per cent, callable only to meet Bank obligations, and payable in gold, U.S. dollars, or the currency required to discharge obligations of the Bank arising from the purpose for which the call was made.

When local currencies are not needed by the Bank, members may substitute nonnegotiable, non-interest-bearing demand notes for currency portions of their subscription requirements under (1) above or for meeting amortization payments on loans made with such currencies.

Bonds and Sale of Loans or Other Securities. Potentially the largest source of lendable funds for the Bank is the sale of its bonds in different countries whose currencies are needed. The Bank is authorized to borrow such funds (by selling its bonds) only with the approval of the member country in whose markets the funds are raised, and then only if the government agrees that the funds will be convertible, *i.e.,* that the proceeds may be exchanged for the currency of any other member without restriction. Similarly, the Bank may raise funds by selling loans or other securities in which it may have invested, but approval of the member in whose territory the dealings take place is required. These sales may be with or without Bank guarantee.

Legal restrictions on the type of investments which may be made by banks, insurance companies, and trustees have presented obstacles to distribution of the Bank's bonds, but these difficulties are being corrected, as will be shown later.

---

[7] Sweden became the fiftieth member in August, 1951, and Burma became the fifty-first in January, 1952.

Earnings. On direct loans made with borrowed funds and on guarantees, the Bank is required to charge a commission to the borrower. This commission must be set aside as a *special reserve,* to be kept available for meeting obligations of the Bank arising from defaults of borrowers, by means of either direct loan or guarantee.

Additional reserves and a surplus account may be built up at the discretion of the Board of Governors of the Bank. Assets represented by these additional reserves and the surplus account may be used in lending operations; accordingly, these amounts may be looked on as lendable funds.

Use of Funds

Resources of the Bank are available to members through two principal operations—making or participating in direct loans and guaranteeing loans. In the first, the Bank actually expends funds; in the second, it lends its name to strengthen the credit of the borrower. The Bank is also authorized to buy and sell securities deemed a proper investment for the Bank's special reserve, which is described later in this chapter.

The Bank's ability to lend its funds and its name is restricted in several ways. Some portion of the subscribed capital cannot be used at all for lending; other parts can be used only with the subscribing member's approval, and then perhaps only for certain approved purposes.

Limitations are also found as to the borrower. The Articles of Agreement provide that when the member in whose territory the project to be financed is located is not itself the borrower, "the member or the central bank or some comparable agency of the member which is acceptable to the Bank" must fully guarantee the principal, interest, and other charges on the loan.

The sum total of the Bank's credit power outstanding at any one time, whether in the form of guarantees, participation in loans, or direct loans, is not to exceed the unimpaired subscribed capital, reserves, and surplus of the Bank.

With regard to the Bank's lending policy, criticism has appeared from time to time to the effect that it refuses to take risks and is guided too much, in its lending policy, by commercial considerations. In fact, inability on the part of some governments to tap the Bank's fund of resources for projects which they would like to undertake, but on whose economic soundness the Bank is not satisfied, has led to complaints that the Bank is not doing what should be done for them. This position is supported by groups such as the International Development Advisory Board, which reported to the President in March, 1951, that there are many development projects of economic and social importance which cannot be financed on a regular loan basis.

Remedies suggested usually involve the establishment of a supple-

Table 49. International Bank for Reconstruction and Development: Statement of Subscriptions to Capital Stock and Voting Power* (Dec. 31, 1951)

Member	Subscriptions		Amounts paid in			Subject to call to meet obligations of bank	Number of votes
	Shares	Amount	U.S. dollars	In currency of member other than U.S. dollars	Noninterest-bearing, non-negotiable demand notes		
Australia	2,000	$ 200,000,000	$ 4,000,000	$ 360,368	$ 35,639,632	$ 160,000,000	2,250
Austria	500	50,000,000	1,000,000	90,000	8,910,000	40,000,000	750
Belgium	2,250	225,000,000	4,500,000	2,344,422	38,155,578	180,000,000	2,500
Bolivia	70	7,000,000	140,000	12,600	1,247,400	5,600,000	320
Brazil	1,050	105,000,000	2,100,000	18,900,000	. . . .	84,000,000	1,300
Canada	3,250	325,000,000	6,500,000	16,675,909	41,824,091	260,000,000	3,500
Ceylon	150	15,000,000	300,000	2,700,000	. . . .	12,000,000	400
Chile	350	35,000,000	700,000	6,300,000	. . . .	28,000,000	600
China	6,000	600,000,000	9,030,000†	1,080,000	106,920,000	480,000,000	6,250
Colombia	350	35,000,000	700,000	6,300,000	. . . .	28,000,000	600
Costa Rica	20	2,000,000	40,000	360,000	. . . .	1,600,000	270
Cuba	350	35,000,000	700,000	63,000	6,237,000	28,000,000	600
Czechoslovakia	1,250	125,000,000	1,875,000†	225,000	22,275,000	100,000,000	1,500
Denmark	680	68,000,000	1,360,000	520,539	11,719,461	54,400,000	930
Dominican Republic	20	2,000,000	40,000	3,600	356,400	1,600,000	270
Ecuador	32	3,200,000	64,000	576,000	. . . .	2,560,000	282
Egypt	533	53,300,000	1,066,000	95,940	9,498,060	42,640,000	783
El Salvador	10	1,000,000	20,000	180,000	. . . .	800,000	260
Ethiopia	30	3,000,000	60,000	540,000	. . . .	2,400,000	280
Finland	380	38,000,000	760,000	6,840,000	. . . .	30,400,000	630
France	5,250	525,000,000	10,500,000	2,909,611	91,590,389	420,000,000	5,500

Greece	250	25,000,000	500,000	4,500,000	. . . . . .	20,000,000	500	
Guatemala	20	2,000,000	40,000	360,000	. . . . . .	1,600,000	270	
Honduras	10	1,000,000	20,000	3,600	176,400	800,000	260	
Iceland	10	1,000,000	20,000	180,000	. . . . . .	800,000	260	
India	4,000	400,000,000	8,000,000	721,800	71,278,200	320,000,000	4,250	
Iran	336	33,600,000	672,000	60,480	5,987,520	26,880,000	586	
Iraq	60	6,000,000	120,000	20,880	1,059,120	4,800,000	310	
Italy	1,800	180,000,000	3,600,000	32,400,000	. . . . . .	144,000,000	2,050	
Lebanon	45	4,500,000	90,000	810,000	. . . . . .	3,600,000	295	
Luxembourg	100	10,000,000	200,000	18,000	1,782,000	8,000,000	350	
Mexico	650	65,000,000	1,300,000	11,700,000	. . . . . .	52,000,000	900	
Netherlands	2,750	275,000,000	5,500,000	552,631	48,947,369	220,000,000	3,000	
Nicaragua	8	800,000	16,000	144,000	. . . . . .	640,000	258	
Norway	500	50,000,000	1,000,000	174,000	8,826,000	40,000,000	750	
Pakistan	1,000	100,000,000	2,000,000	180,008	17,819,992	80,000,000	1,250	
Panama	2	200,000	4,000	36,000	. . . . . .	160,000	252	
Paraguay	14	1,400,000	28,000	252,000	. . . . . .	1,120,000	264	
Peru	175	17,500,000	350,000	31,500	3,118,500	14,000,000	425	
Philippines	150	15,000,000	300,000	1,200,000	1,500,000	12,000,000	400	
Sweden	1,000	100,000,000	2,000,000	18,000,000	. . . . . .	80,000,000	1,250	
Syria	65	6,500,000	130,000	11,700	1,158,300	5,200,000	315	
Thailand	125	12,500,000	250,000	22,500	2,227,500	10,000,000	375	
Turkey	430	43,000,000	860,000	77,400	7,662,600	34,400,000	680	
Union of South Africa	1,000	100,000,000	2,000,000	180,000	17,820,000	80,000,000	1,250	
United Kingdom	13,000	1,300,000,000	26,000,000	4,050,000	229,950,000	1,040,000,000	13,250	
United States	31,750	3,175,000,000	635,000,000	. . . . . .	. . . . . .	2,540,000,000	32,000	
Uruguay	105	10,500,000	210,000	1,890,000	. . . . . .	8,400,000	355	
Venezuela	105	10,500,000	210,000	1,365,000	525,000	8,400,000	355	
Yugoslavia	400	40,000,000	800,000	7,200,000	. . . . . .	32,000,000	650	
Total	84,385	$8,438,500,000	$736,675,000†	$153,218,488	$794,211,512	$6,750,800,000	96,885	

* Expressed in U.S. currency.

† China and Czechoslovakia owed, respectively, $2,970,000 and $625,000 payable in gold or U.S. dollars.

montary lending authority, as there has been general endorsement of the Bank's original aims and purposes. Illustrative of remedial proposals are:

1. A resolution passed at the Ninth International Conference of American States, at Bogotá, in 1948, recommended a special study to consider the possibility and advisability of establishing an Inter-American Bank or an Inter-American Development Corporation or both. This bank and/or development corporation could then pay more attention to the development of Latin America than can or does the International Bank for Reconstruction and Development.
2. Recommendations by the International Development Advisory Board[8] for establishment, under management of the Bank, of an International Development Authority and an International Finance Corporation, both of which would provide funds on a basis not now open to the Bank. Moreover, another study group[9] reported that the volume of loans made by the International Bank for Reconstruction and Development and the Export-Import Bank, in the fiscal year 1950, was not adequate to meet the basic requirements for development abroad. It suggested as a combined aim for United States government loans a *net* outflow—net of repayments—of from $600,000,000 to $800,000,000 annually. Half of this, was the conclusion, should be by the International Bank. The same group recommended expansion of the Export-Import Bank's lending authority from $3,500,000,000 to $5,000,-000,000.

Under the Articles of Agreement, the International Bank is charged with several specific considerations in so far as lending policy is concerned:

1. Facilitating investment for productive purposes
2. Promoting *private* foreign investment and, when private capital is not available on reasonable terms, supplementing private investment out of its own resources
3. Promoting long-range balanced growth of international trade and the maintenance of equilibrium in balances of payment.

Economic development is of course the fundamental aim, but the Bank's officials must satisfy themselves as to the probability of repayment. This means an element of conservatism in recognizing the possibility of bad as well as good times. From a banking point of view, the underlying considerations must be commercial rather than political or

[8] *Partners in Progress,* Report to the President by the International Development Advisory Board, March, 1951, pp. 72, 84.

[9] *Report to the President on Foreign Economic Policies (Gray Report),* Nov. 10, 1950.

social. One may argue that "commercial" loans are nearly always available if economic conditions and rate warrant the risk to the lender. This is probably true, but it is also implicit in the Articles of Agreement that the Bank was not intended as a device for pumping its funds out just for the sake of putting its resources to use all at once. The study and planning of development projects all require an extensive amount of time, and the *Report to the President on Foreign Economic Policies* concluded that lack of "reasonable prospects for payment of interest out of the receiving country's future foreign exchange earnings on current account, and [lack of] soundly planned purposes for spending the money" have been the main restrictions on public investment, rather than limitations of resources available to the lending agencies.

Indicative of the accelerated loan activity *for development purposes* after initial organization and after allowing time for economic surveys to be made on which a lending program could be based were the following facts:[10]

In 1948, 2 loans were made, totaling $16,000,000.
In 1949, 3 loans were made, totaling $109,000,000.
In 1950, 8 loans were made, totaling $134,000,000.
In 1951, 21 loans were made, totaling $300,000,000.

It would not appear therefore, that commercial considerations render impossible a lively lending activity on the part of the Bank. One should also bear in mind the fact, as is shown later, that many members had not as yet made their currencies usable for loans by the Bank. Of the principal amounts outstanding on Sept. 30, 1951, about 97 per cent was in U.S. dollars; this was about 32 per cent of the total United States subscription and was well over the amounts paid in in U.S. dollars. The dollars other than those paid in were obtained by the sale of Bank bonds in the United States.

Some of the proposed supplementary "lending" authorities would be devised to provide funds for capital stock and for outright grants. The proposals, while recognizing the need for integration of foreign investment activities by the government, nevertheless recommended in effect a multiple tapping of the United States Treasury for foreign economic development. Accordingly, the question of unifying rather than multiplying public investment activities might profitably bear study.

Limitations on Use of Currency Paid In. By far the larger part of members' paid-in subscriptions consists of their own currencies.[11] But the currencies so paid in can be loaned out only with the approval in

---

[10] *Summary Proceedings, Sixth Annual Meeting of the Board of Governors,* International Bank for Reconstruction and Development, Nov. 30, 1951, p. 5.

[11] 18 per cent of subscribed capital.

each case of the member whose currency is involved."¹ Why, one may ask, are there such restrictions? The answer is that most members employ an exchange-control scheme, and to permit the holder of some of its money (the Bank or its borrowers) to convert such exchange freely not only would present administrative difficulties but would interfere with success of the scheme. Secondly, the government concerned may feel that it does not desire certain exports to leave the country. A freely convertible currency, in the hands of a holder in due course, could interfere with a government's export-control program.

Even when loans made with these currencies are repaid, the funds received may be released only with the approval, in each case, of the members whose currencies are involved.

Limitations as to Borrowers. The Bank deals with member governments only through their treasuries, central banks, stabilization funds, or other similar fiscal agencies. However, in buying or selling securities it has issued, guaranteed, or otherwise invested in, the Bank is permitted to "deal with any person, partnership, association, corporation or other legal entity in the territories of any member." It will lend or guarantee loans only to member governments or on the guarantee of member governments. Except in special circumstances, loans are made only for the purpose of specific projects of reconstruction or development. Accordingly, the Bank's loans should be well supported.

While imposing no conditions that proceeds of a loan shall be spent in any particular country, the Bank sees to it that proceeds are used only for the purposes for which the loan was granted. But since the loan must be in a specified currency or currencies, there is apt to be a *de facto* tying in the expenditures of proceeds in certain countries. A loan of U.S. dollars could be spent in France, for example. But in such a case it would probably be sounder to make the loan in francs if it is known just where the purchases will be made at the time the loan is arranged.

Unlike the International Monetary Fund, in which members have something akin to drawing rights based on the amount of their quotas, there is no set amount which members are entitled to borrow from the Bank. This situation encouraged several countries to press for large quotas in the Fund but to desire their subscriptions in the Bank to be as small as possible.[13]

Nor is there a statutory limit as to the amount which a member may borrow. As of June 30, 1951, several countries had borrowed more than their subscriptions. These are listed in the tabulation below.

[12] Up to the point at which the Bank's subscribed capital has been entirely called, at which time these currencies may be used without restriction in meeting the Bank's liabilities arising out of its borrowing or lending operations.

[13] John Parke Young, "Developing Plans for an International Monetary Fund and a World Bank," *Department of State Bulletin,* Nov. 13, 1950, p. 786.

Country	Subscriptions	Loans
El Salvador..........	$ 1,000,000	$12,545,000
Ethiopia............	3,000,000	8,500,000
Iceland.............	1,000,000	3,458,000
Iraq...............	6,000,000	12,800,000
Luxembourg........	10,000,000	12,000,000
Nicaragua..........	800,000	5,250,000
Paraguay...........	1,400,000	5,000,000
Thailand...........	12,500,000	25,400,000
Uruguay...........	10,500,000	33,000,000

Conceivably, one borrower would seem legally able to avail itself of the majority of the Bank's resources. In practice, this would never be, for two reasons. First, each loan (or guarantee) request must be passed on by the executive directors of the Bank. Overborrowing, as far as a single government is concerned, would not be permitted by prudent operating policies.[14] By the same token, a concentration of loans in any one underdeveloped country would be avoided. But if such a concentration of borrowing by one country should get by the Bank's operating officers, it would come up against the possibility of being vetoed by member countries whose funds would be desired by the borrower.[15] A minimum of 2 and a maximum of 20 per cent of a member's subscription is available for lending without the member's approval. All amounts over 20 per cent of a member's subscription, whether in the form of loans or of guarantees, are available for use "only with the approval of the member in whose markets the funds are raised and the member in whose currency the loan is denominated."[16]

Except for statutory commissions to be charged borrowers, the Bank decides the terms and conditions of interest and amortization payments, maturity, and dates of payment of each loan. Interest rates, including commissions, on loans made to Dec. 31, 1951, have ranged from 3 to 4½ per cent, with most rates being 4 per cent or more.

Operations to 1951

Details of operations, just described in principle, may be subdivided into five main categories: loans and guarantees, borrowings, consultations, availability of currencies for operating purposes, and income.

[14] The Bank is charged with acting prudently in the interests both of the particular member in whose territories the project is located and of the members as a whole.

[15] This might be difficult for some governments to do, as it would mean the denial of exports with payment assured by the Bank.

[16] Art. IV, Sec. 1(b).

Loans and Guarantees The general qualification that loans may be made for purposes of reconstruction or economic development covers a wide range of detailed purposes, such as electric power development, flood-control projects, and agricultural or industrial development. Loans as of June 30, 1951, classified as to purpose, are listed below.

For postwar reconstruction............	$ 497,000,000
For development purposes:	
Electric power.....................	271,000,000
Transportation.....................	119,000,000
Communications...................	30,000,000
Agriculture and forestry.............	92,000,000
Industry..........................	67,000,000
Development banks................	21,000,000
Total for development............	$ 600,000,000
Total........................	$1,097,000,000

Fifty-seven loans, on projects in 24 member countries, had been made up to Dec. 31, 1951. The total loaned out was $1,231,783,000. Repayments, refundings, and cancellations amounted to a little over $27,000,-000. There was outstanding, sold partly with and partly without Bank guarantee, $33,442,380 of obligations of its borrowers.

Total disbursements made on the Bank's loans amounted to the equivalent of $770,809,831. Expenditures had been mainly in the United States. Principal outstanding on loans disbursed, repayable in currencies other than U.S. dollars, was (dollar equivalent) as below.

Canadian dollars............	$13,785,038
Swiss francs................	7,417,584
Belgian francs..............	2,070,002
Pounds sterling.............	2,781,589
French francs...............	1,016,370
Italian lire.................	99,140
Danish kroner..............	216,182
Norwegian kroner...........	39,648

Borrowings. In its early years of operation, the Bank's raising of funds in member countries served mainly to season its obligations for investment by private interests.

The first public offering of bonds was in the United States, as was the first issue of bonds sold by competitive bidding to underwriters. Other sales of Bank bonds were made in Great Britain and Switzerland. It may be noted that Switzerland is not a member of the Bank and is therefore not eligible for a loan. But Swiss francs are desired by some borrowers, for making purchases either in Switzerland or in other countries in which Swiss francs are acceptable. As of Dec. 31, 1951, the Bank had outstanding $400,000,000 in bonds payable in U.S. dollars and the equivalent of

$22,222,222 payable in Swiss francs and $14,000,000 payable in pounds sterling.

Considerable uncertainty has prevailed in regard to the right of institutional investors in some countries to buy the Bank's bonds. In the United States, banking law had to be amended to permit national banks and state member banks of the Federal Reserve System to deal in and underwrite obligations issued by the Bank. In addition, many state laws or administrative regulations had to be modified to permit investment in the Bank's obligations on the part of savings banks and life insurance companies. As of June 30, 1949, the Bank's securities were, or were soon to be, legally authorized investments as follow:[17]

For all national banks and for commercial banks in 45 states and the District of Columbia

For savings banks in 29 of the 36 states having such institutions and in the District of Columbia

For insurance companies in 36 states

For trust funds in 33 states and the District of Columbia

During the year ending June 30, 1950, the investment position of the Bank's obligations was improved in Chile, Cuba, Italy, Mexico, the Netherlands, the Philippine Republic, and some states in the United States.[18] Other countries have been urged to clarify the investment status of the Bank's bonds in their respective domains.

Consultations. Through informal discussion with the Bank's executive directors and through technical missions, when requested by members, the Bank has been active in aiding members in the analysis and establishment of development programs as well as in operational problems. Missions have engaged in estimating the possibilities of loans, reviewing specific projects, and conducting actual loan negotiations. In addition, they have helped member governments or potential borrowers in defining priorities among projects, made suggested modifications in technical plans, and offered proposals as to administrative, organizational, or financial aspects of a project. Technical assistance, unrelated to any immediate request for financing, is an important phase of the Bank operations.

Availability of Currencies for Operating Purposes. Since the major part, by far, of a member's subscription is usable only with approval of the member, the Bank has on several occasions urged a liberalization of the use of currencies (or their equivalent holdings in nonnegotiable,

[17] *Fourth Annual Report, 1948–1949,* International Bank for Reconstruction and Development, 1949, p. 37.

[18] *Summary Proceedings, Fifth Annual Meeting of the Board of Governors,* International Bank for Reconstruction and Development, November, 1950, p. 23.

non-interest-bearing demand notes) received by it for the 18 per cent portion of capital subscriptions.

Up to June 30, 1947, the Bank had received permission to use the 18-per-cent portion of its capital subscription from the United States, alone, and it had received permission to lend Belgian francs up to the equivalent of US$2,000,000. Subsequently, several other countries consented to the use of some or all of this portion of their subscriptions. As of June 30, 1951, the Bank had received permission from the United States, Ecuador, El Salvador, and Honduras to use the entire 18 per cent without further approval of the member concerned, and from Belgium, Canada, Denmark, France, Guatemala, Italy, Mexico, Paraguay, and the United Kingdom to use a specified portion of the 18 per cent without further approval.[19]

In addition, the following countries had agreed, subject to further consultation in each particular case, to the use of all or part of their 18-per-cent currency for loans:[20]

Colombia	Netherlands
Costa Rica	Norway
Denmark	Pakistan
Finland	Peru
France	Philippines
Greece	South Africa
Iceland	Syria
India	Thailand
Italy	United Kingdom
Lebanon	Yugoslavia

Income. Total net income of the Bank for its entire period of operations up to Dec. 31, 1951, amounted to a little more than $50,000,000, exclusive of statutory commissions held in the special reserve in the amount of $23,684,660. The net income of the Bank has been allocated to a general reserve against losses on loans and guarantees made by the Bank, and, until policy is changed by official action, the Bank is committed to allocating future net income to this general reserve. The Bank statement for Dec. 31, 1951, showed no surplus account.

Internal Organization

As mentioned earlier, the Bank is under general supervision of a board of governors, some appointed and some elected. Active operations are conducted by a board of executive directors, and administration of the Bank is the responsibility of the president, vice-president, and other principal officers.

[19] *Sixth Annual Report, 1950–1951*, p. 42.
[20] *Ibid.*

The 424 staff members as of June 30, 1951, were organized into the following operating departments:

Loan Department
Research Department
Marketing Department
Administration Department
Public Relations Department
Office of the General Counsel
Office of the Secretary
Office of the Treasurer

United States Participation

Membership in the Bank by the United States government was provided for in the Bretton Woods Agreement Act, approved by the President in July, 1945. The Articles of Agreement were signed on Dec. 27, 1945, thus bringing the Bank into formal existence.

The United States subscription is for 31,750 shares, representing, at par, $3,175,000,000. The United States has paid in, in dollars, both the 2-per-cent and 18-per-cent portions of its subscription; this amounts to $635,000,000, all of which is subject to use at the Bank's discretion and most of which has been loaned out. As of Dec. 31, 1951, the Bank held no nonnegotiable, non-interest-bearing demand notes of the United States government.

United States dollars have also been available to the Bank by the sale of its bonds in the United States, and the government is subject to a call for the remaining 80 per cent of its subscription, or $2,540,000,000. This can be called, as was already mentioned, only to meet obligations arising out of loans, guarantees, or borrowings. It is significant to note that, on the occasion of a call for funds, the failure of any member to meet the call does not excuse other members from their liabilities under their capital subscriptions.

Benefits to United States. Several segments of the United States economy stand to benefit by operations of the Bank, but the general welfare to be experienced through international economic cooperation should probably be mentioned first.

Exporters, mainly of capital goods, and perhaps later on of consumer goods, will find the opportunity of increased foreign markets as a result of bank loans or guarantees. Importers should find increased access to foreign supplies as a result of better transportation, power, communications, and industrial or agricultural development abroad. In fact, to the extent that loans are made in dollars and must be so serviced and repaid, the pressure for earning dollars by foreign debtors to the Bank should offer attractive import possibilities as well as present a challenge to import policy.

United States investors and other investors in dollar securities may find the Bank's bonds desirable investments to hold; tax features of the bonds render them attractive to certain non-United States investors when compared with returns on other dollar investments of similar type and quality.

Coordination with Other Governmental Foreign Lending. As with the International Monetary Fund, United States participation in the Bank is under general supervision of the National Advisory Council. Coordination is particularly necessary between the lending policies of the Export-Import Bank (in which the United States government is the only stockholder) and the International Bank for Reconstruction and Development, in which the United States owns only part of the capital stock. Both may make loans for reconstruction and development, but the former must adhere to its purpose of financing and facilitating exports of the United States.

This coordination is accomplished by consultation on the part of the United States executive director in the International Bank with the National Advisory Council and by consultation between officials of the two banks. Such coordination makes possible the reference of requests to one bank or the other, depending on their characteristics.

REVIEW QUESTIONS

1. What are the purposes and objectives of the International Bank for Reconstruction and Development?

2. If you had to choose between the Bank and the Fund, which would you retain as the institution likely to do more good and to have the greater chance of success? Why?

3. Evaluate the Bank's concept of "economic development."

4. Where does the Bank obtain its funds for lending?

5. Why have there been limitations on the lending of currency paid in to the bank?

6. Is the Bank's lending policy too strict? Could it be liberalized? How?

7. Who may borrow from the Bank? Are there any limitations placed on borrowers? Explain.

8. Describe briefly the lending operations of the Bank during the first five years of its existence.

9. Why did the Bank initially have some difficulty in marketing its bonds?

10. How important is United States participation in the Bank, and how does participation benefit the United States?

CHAPTER 23

Other International Organizations with Economic Influence[1]

The public institutions and organizations described in the last three chapters and in Chapter 7 are those of major significance in the field of foreign commerce. However, a number of others must be brought into the picture to round out a more complete view of the institutional structure in which foreign commerce must be conducted. Since this aspect is only a part, and in some respects an incidental part, of the functions of these other organizations or agreements, this chapter will merely outline their activities regarding the subject matter of the text. It will serve again to focus attention on the interdependence of all phases of foreign commerce, including merchandise, travel, services, and investments.

Some of these organizations are world-wide in scope, while others are regional; some pertain to agriculture in general, others to specific commodities; some find their major interest in finance and trade, while others are more fundamentally concerned with social problems; and some are concerned with services such as transportation and communications.

The order of presentation in this chapter is not a suggestion as to their importance to the subject of this study. Instead, they are arranged in four groups. Those affiliated with the United Nations are listed first. International agreements not a part of the United Nations are next. Those organizations closely related to the Organization of American States are third, and the last few are organizations of regional jurisdiction. Activities of several of these are coordinated in some degree by attendance or observation at meetings and by action of the respective participating governments.

[1] Most of the material used in this chapter was obtained from *International Organizations in Which the United States Participates, 1949*, U.S. Department of State Publication 3655, 1950, and *Participation of the United States Government in International Conferences* (by fiscal years beginning July 1, 1945), U.S. Department of State Publications 2817 (FY 1946), 3031 (FY 1947), 3443 (FY 1948), and 3853 (FY 1949).

ORGANIZATIONS AFFILIATED WITH THE UNITED NATIONS

Food and Agriculture Organization

In view of the great importance of agricultural products in foreign commerce, the objectives and functioning of the Food and Agriculture Organization should be understood by the student and the practitioner of foreign commerce.

The Food and Agriculture Organization evolved from the United Nations Conference on Food and Agriculture, held at Hot Springs, Va., in May, 1943. It was formally established in Quebec, Canada, in October, 1945, and became the first of the specialized agencies of the United Nations. Forty countries became members of the Organization at Quebec and, as of late 1949, membership numbered 58 nations. The United States government, especially the Department of Agriculture, took a prominent lead in establishing the Organization.

Purposes and Objectives. Broad objectives, social and economic in nature and far-reaching in impact, have been adopted by the Organization. Its chief aims are the following:[2]

To help nations raise the standard of living
To improve nutrition of the peoples of all countries
To increase the efficiency of farming, forestry, and fisheries
To better the condition of rural people
Through these means, to widen the opportunity of all people for productive work

These are based on agreements, at the initial conference at Hot Springs, that two-thirds of the world's people are undernourished, that their health could be vastly improved if they were able to get enough of the right kind of food, that farmers of the world could produce enough if they used the best agricultural methods, and that full-time work for all could be provided by increased production and efficient distribution.[3]

However, it is in the attainment of these objectives that the Organization has its principal significance to foreign commerce. At the first annual conference after its founding in 1945, a commission was set up to "develop concrete recommendations for an inter-governmental program for preventing both shortages and surpluses of food and other agricultural products."[4] Thus, "the conference recognized the riddle of want

[2] *FAO—What It Is, What It Does, How It Works,* Food and Agriculture Organization of the United Nations, May, 1949.

[3] *Ibid.*

[4] *Participation of the United States Government in International Conferences,* July 1, 1946–June 30, 1947, p. 70.

amid plenty as one of the world's gravest long-range problems and *recorded its conviction that the riddle could be solved only through positive international action* [italics added]."[5]

The Commission was also charged with considering the proposed World Food Board[6] and any other proposals for international machinery for reaching two objectives:

Developing and organizing production, distribution, and utilization of basic foods to provide diets on a health standard for the people of all countries

Stabilizing agricultural prices at levels fair to producers and consumers alike

Manner of Operation. The Organization is governed by a Conference in which each member nation has one vote. The Conference meets annually but, between sessions, its responsibilities are undertaken by the Council of the Food and Agriculture Organization, composed of representatives of 18 member nations. This group meets at least twice a year. Continuity of administration is accomplished through a director general, from headquarters in Rome. The organization functions in three areas of activity:

It gathers basic statistics on food and agriculture, forestry, and fisheries.

It offers technical assistance to member governments regarding production and distribution of foods, fibers, and timber.

It promotes action by member governments and international organizations by making definite recommendations for concerted action and assisting nations in agreeing on programs and carrying them out.

Significance in Foreign Commerce. Impact on foreign commerce arises through the Organization's interest in problems of production, distribution, and price. It is officially and actively supporting the "commodity-agreement" approach to specific stabilization problems.[7] It also attempts to coordinate and integrate national "programs" concerned with agricultural and food products, and emphasizes development of national programs for improving nutrition.

As a result, international production and trade in a number of important commodities may be increased through expanded technical knowledge but, depending on where the increased production occurs relative to consumption, international movement of such production may be curtailed or governmentally controlled as to volume and direction. For example, to the extent that new areas are brought into production of cot-

[5] *Ibid.*
[6] See pp. 414–415.
[7] See Chap. 20.

rrin, wheat, corn, etc., imports by those new producing areas may be reduced or eliminated, and former exporting countries may lose their markets. The corollary of such a development will have to be "internationally coordinated national programs" to assure that individuals in the former producing and exporting countries will not upset the applecart, so to speak, and continue producing to such an extent as to break prices significantly or interfere with the international plan.

Moreover, "coordinated national programs" must concern themselves with exports and imports as well as with domestic production and prices and must accept as a normal expectancy the imposition and perhaps continuance of export and import licensing schemes by government. These may be regular or irregular in occurrence and extent, and will make more difficult the exporter's opportunity to seek out the most favorable market pricewise and the importer's opportunity to seek out the cheapest market at any given time. At the same time, established foreign-commerce connections of long standing may have to be broken temporarily or permanently because they do not or no longer fit into the international plan. Effect of these developments will have a bearing not only on the exporter or importer, whether producer, merchant, or manufacturer, but also on the banks, transportation companies, and other services catering to trade in the affected geographic areas.

International Labour Organisation

At first glance, one may wonder what possible connection there may be between foreign commerce and an international organization concerned with labor. The relationship arises from the fact that labor is a cost of production and as such is an important influence in cost differentials among producers located in different countries. It has already been shown that cost differentials are basically the reason why goods may be bought in one place and transported to another at a price to compete with similar goods or substitutes which may be produced at the second location.

The International Labour Organisation is the oldest of the specialized agencies of the United Nations; it antedates the United Nations, as it was founded in 1919 at the time of drawing up terms of peace following the First World War. In January, 1950, the International Labour Organisation had 60 members. The United States did not become a member until 1934, although United States citizens were very active in its formation.

While its purposes may appear to be rather removed from foreign commerce—fostering international action to improve labor conditions, to raise living standards, and to promote economic and social stability—the possible impact of these on competitive costs is not difficult to see. Their effect may be the same as that of features of "equalization of cost of production" in import tariffs. For if they result in increased foreign unit costs of production, the effect on price to an importer in the United States is the same as that caused by a higher tariff. But the objectives are different, the International Labour Organisation being basically an instrument of social justice.

The International Labour Organisation consists of representatives of government, labor, and industry, and these are organized into the International Labour Conference, which usually meets once a year. Its executive council is called the Governing Body, which meets about four times a year. The International Labour Office provides the permanent secretariat in Geneva.

Conventions, if Ratified, Involve Legislation. Under the constitution, the member countries are required to bring *conventions* adopted by the Conference to the attention of national authorities for possible ratification. If the convention is ratified, the member country obligates itself to bring its laws in line with the convention. From its origin until 1950, the International Labour Organisation had adopted 98 conventions and had made 87 official recommendations to governments. The United States had ratified six up to April, 1951, but two of these six had not entered into force since they had not been ratified by the required number of other countries.

In 1945, the Organisation began to establish a number of industrial committees to deal with problems peculiar to the respective industries. As of early 1950, industrial committees had been established for coal mining, textiles, construction, iron and steel production, the metal trades, inland transport, petroleum production and refining, chemicals, and plantation labor.

The possible effect on comparative costs[8] of improved and somewhat equalized labor conditions, to which no one can object, may be indicated by the following subjects of conventions adopted by the Organisation and forwarded to member governments for possible ratification:

1. An eight-hour day and a forty-hour week
2. Holidays with pay
3. Improved working conditions on board ship
4. Freedom of association and bargaining rights
5. Sickness and old-age insurance

---

[8] The term "possible effect" is used advisedly, for improved working conditions need not necessarily increase unit costs; they may actually result in lower unit costs owing to increased output.

By the same token, conventions may deal with certain prohibitions, as.

1. Forced labor
2. Night work for women
3. Employment of women in underground mines
4. Employment of children under 15
5. The use of white lead in painting

It may be recalled that products made with labor under conditions of slavery or forced indenture are usually prohibited entry into the United States. But as yet there is no prohibition against imports of goods made or transported under labor conditions contrary to those incorporated in the International Labour Organisation conventions.

Economic and Social Council of the United Nations

This organization has responsibilities in international economic matters, as its designation indicates. It works through a number of functional commissions, such as the Economic and Employment Commission and the Transport and Communications Commission, through three regional commissions, and through several "specialized" agencies, among which were, as of 1950:

International Labour Organisation
United Nations Educational, Scientific and Cultural Organization
Food and Agriculture Organization
International Monetary Fund
International Bank for Reconstruction and Development
International Civil Aviation Organization
World Health Organization
International Refugee Organization
International Telecommunications Union
Universal Postal Union

Additional organizations may be designated as "specialized agencies of the United Nations" from time to time. The more important of these specialized agencies, in so far as foreign commerce is concerned, have already been discussed. A few others deserve special attention because of their effect on international economic conditions under which foreign-commerce opportunities may be discovered, cultivated, and consummated. These are the World Health Organization, the International Civil Aviation Organization, and the Provisional Maritime Consultative Council.

The World Health Organization

The objective of this specialized agency of the United Nations is "to raise the health level of all peoples." The World Health Organization was established in 1948, and the extent of its interest may be inferred by its definition of health as a "state of complete physical, mental, and social well-being and not merely the absence of disease or infirmity."[9]

Working in close coordination with the Food and Agriculture Organization of the United Nations, the World Health Organization, up to 1950, had concerned itself largely with biological standardization, unification of pharmacopoeias,[10] organization of public-health services, and campaigns against epidemics and communicable diseases. It has also been given authority to "develop regulations concerning standards with respect to safety, purity, and potency of biological, pharmaceutical and similar products, as well as concerning the advertising and labeling of such products moving in international commerce." Since the Organization is so new, little had been done along the latter line of responsibilities up to early 1952.

International Civil Aviation Organization

Also a specialized agency of the United Nations, the International Civil Aviation Organization is interested in fostering development of international air transportation. It establishes standards for international air navigation and provides financial and technical aid for the maintenance of some air-navigation and air-transport facilities.

To some countries, and in some fields of foreign commerce, air transportation is and will become a very important international business factor. This is of direct interest to the services and travel accounts in foreign commerce and of substantial interest in the movement of merchandise. In this regard, the International Civil Aviation Organization deals with such matters as communications systems and air-navigation aids, rules of the air and air-traffic control, licensing of personnel and registration of aircraft, customs and immigration procedures, and collection and exchange of meteorological information.

Provisional Maritime Consultative Council

This is a temporary organization serving until conclusion of a proposed Intergovernmental Maritime Consultative Organization,[11] which is scheduled to become a specialized agency of the United Nations upon its activation. The purposes of the organization are to "provide machinery

[9]*WHO—What It Is, What It Does, How It Works*, World Health Organization, May, 1950.

[10] Books providing sets of formulas for making up medicines of uniform strengths.

[11] This organization will not be activated until 21 nations are party to the convention, of which 7 shall have a tonnage of not less than 1,000,000 gross tons. As of early April, 1951, the United States, the United Kingdom, Ireland, Canada, Greece, and the Netherlands had deposited their acceptance of IMCO with the United Nations.

for cooperation among governments in regulatory and technical matters affecting shipping engaged in international trade; to encourage the adoption of the highest practicable safety standards in matters affecting shipping; and to encourage the removal of discriminatory and restrictive actions by governments." The organization will also consider matters concerning unfair restrictive practices by shipping concerns, but those which are suitable for settlement through the normal processes of international shipping business are not within the scope of the Council. Indications are that rate differentials designed to tie shippers to conference lines and to discourage or prohibit use of nonconference facilities for any part of their business which could be handled by the particular steamship conference will be looked on as a matter capable of settlement "through the normal processes of international shipping business."

In view of the importance of the merchant marine in the military and economic considerations of several countries, this organization will probably serve a very important function.

INSTITUTIONS NOT OFFICIALLY PART OF THE UNITED NATIONS

International Union for the Protection of Industrial Property

This body was formally established in 1883. Its general object is the international protection of industrial property rights, which include "patents, utility models, industrial designs and models, trade-marks, commercial names and indications of origin, or appellations of origin." It is of significance in foreign commerce, not only in connection with the movement of merchandise among nations, but also in connection with manufacturing arrangements under license among persons in different countries, and with establishment of branch plants in foreign countries.

The basic agreement among members of the Union is the principle of reciprocal national treatment, which means that nationals of any member enjoy, in the territories of other members, the same rights and advantages as are granted to nationals of those members. The agreement also covers special problems such as right of priority, abolition of forfeiture for importation of patented articles, and restriction of the obligation to work the patent.

International Union of Official Travel Organizations

In earlier chapters, the importance of travel in the foreign-commerce picture of several countries was explained. The United States government (Department of Commerce) became affiliated with this International Union in 1949. Members numbered about 40, at that time, and consisted of national official travel organizations or the government bodies designated to represent travel interests.

The organization is dedicated to promoting the free flow of visitors among member countries by developing with respective governments uniformity and simplicity of travel procedures. More specifically, it aims at a reduction of barriers to international travel; the simplification and standardization of the documentary, registration, and inspection requirements and procedures for persons and their personal effects, funds, and means of transport; and the reduction or elimination of fees, charges, and other special costs incidental to travel. Working toward the same objectives as this organization, but on a regional basis, is the Inter-American Travel Congress, the fourth meeting of which was held in Lima, Peru, in 1951.

ORGANIZATION OF AMERICAN STATES

The Organization of American States was officially established at the ninth International Conference of American States at Bogotá, Colombia, in 1948. Its functions and purposes of application to foreign commerce are "to seek the solution of . . . economic problems that may arise among them; and to promote, by cooperative action, their economic, social, and cultural development."

Specialized agencies are also designated by this Organization, such as the Inter-American Economic and Social Council, originally created in 1945, for the purpose of promoting the "economic and social welfare of the American nations through effective utilization of their natural resources, the development of their agriculture and industry, and the raising of the standard of living of their peoples."[12]

The permanent secretariat of the Organization of American States is the Pan American Union, in which there is a Department of Economic and Social Affairs.

Inter-American Institute of Agricultural Sciences

Created in 1940, this Institute was designed to "encourage and advance the development of agricultural services in the American republics through research, training, and extension activities in the theory and practice of agriculture and other related arts and sciences." Its field headquarters are at Turrialba, Costa Rica, on a 2,500-acre tract of land donated by the government of Costa Rica.

Inter-American Statistical Institute

Lack of dependable statistics is a significant deterrent to foreign commerce. To aid in overcoming this deficiency, the Inter-American Statis-

---

[12] *International Organizations in Which the United States Participates, 1949,* February, 1950, p. 24.

tical Institute was created in 1940 by Western Hemisphere members of the International Statistical Institute. The Institute's purposes are, among others, to encourage methods for improving the comparability of economic and social statistics among the nations of the Western Hemisphere and to stimulate improved methodology in the collection, tabulation, analysis, and publication of both official and unofficial statistics.

REGIONAL ORGANIZATIONS

Caribbean Commission

The Caribbean Commission, composed of the governments of the United States, the United Kingdom, France, and the Netherlands, was established in 1946 and entered into force in 1948. It is concerned with economic and social conditions of the *non-self*-governing territories of the member governments in the Caribbean area, as they are not members of the Organization of American States.

The Commission's function is to "study, formulate, and recommend measures, programs, and policies with respect to social and economic problems designed to contribute to the well-being of the peoples of the area. . . . " It accomplishes these objectives largely through cooperative research and consultations among the governments and people concerned on matters of common interest.

South Pacific Commission

This is a regional commission similar to the Caribbean Commission, but concerned with *non-self*-governing territories of the South Pacific region. Member governments are Australia, France, the Netherlands, the United Kingdom, and the United States. The Commission acts as a consultative and advisory body to the participating governments in matters affecting the economic and social development of the territories within its jurisdiction.

Organization for European Economic Cooperation

While immediately concerned with ensuring success of the European Recovery Program at the time of its founding in 1948, the long-range objective of this Organization is a sound European economy. This calls for economic cooperation of European countries of a type most difficult of accomplishment over a long term. In the postwar period, when cooperation was necessary for and strongly encouraged by United States financial aid, this Organization established over-all European production, import, and export targets, based on national estimates, and was designed to press for reduction of intra-European trade and financial barriers and to coordinate foreign purchasing powers of its members. Of course, success of the Organization calls for strong national economic control by respective governments; a very big question is its ability to effectuate reductions in economic barriers to trade, with enterprisers free to take advantage of the opportunities so opened, without effectuating a reduction in political barriers.

Central Commission for Navigation of the Rhine

Dating from 1815, but modified several times in the interim, this Commission has as its purpose to ensure that the navigation of the Rhine river and its mouths shall be free to vessels and nationals of all nations for the commercial transportation of merchandise and persons. United States interest in this Commission dates from 1945, and its significance to several elements of United States foreign commerce is self-evident.

REVIEW QUESTIONS

1. How does the Food and Agriculture Organization have a bearing on foreign commerce?
2. Describe the purpose of the Economic and Social Council of the United Nations.
3. Describe the establishment and objectives of the Organization of American States, in so far as foreign commerce is concerned.
4. Has the Organization for European Economic Cooperation any significance in foreign commerce?

CHAPTER 24

The Idea of an International Trade Organization

Fundamentally, foreign commerce is not very different from domestic commerce. Both are based on specialization in production and trade, arising from differing opportunities and/or cost differentials, and both are but a composite of a number of individuals so engaged. Thus, foreign commerce may be described as interregional trade, cutting across national boundaries, no different theoretically from that between Pennsylvania and Missouri, but more complex in practice owing to assumptions with respect to national best interest. Moreover, as shown in Chapter 11, cost differentials on a national basis do not always afford adequate explanation of the movement of goods or transactions in services between any two countries.

As we look on the international map, therefore, we are faced with the very practical issue of national sovereignties, whose differing laws and views on trade practices are in each instance primarily concerned with internal welfare. Nevertheless, action or policies resulting from matters primarily of national interest are of international significance because of their impact on the interdependent, delicately balanced international markets.

Costs and Prices Affected by Many Factors. Consider, for instance, the effect on costs or prices of the following: (1) Raising or lowering of tariff rates; (2) raising or lowering of discount rates of central banks; (3) changing legal reserve requirements of the monetary or banking system; (4) influencing the volume of bank reserves, as by open-market operations or by changing criteria for access to central bank funds; (5) deficit financing programs; (6) raising or lowering of tax rates; (7) quotas or other quantitative limitations; (8) wage and hour legislation or organized labor pressure; (9) agricultural price-support programs or production-control schemes; and (10) legislation pertaining to rights and regulation of business organizations or combinations. Many other similar influences and rigidities may be found, but these will suffice to illustrate the point that governmental economic policy, undertaken for national objectives, will have international repercussions because of the market links constituting the world economy.

Conversely, international activities have their repercussions in the several individual markets. Devaluation of the pound by Great Britain, as an example, had effects on the world which in turn were mirrored in many internal British markets. The International Monetary Fund, the International Bank for Reconstruction and Development, and the Mutual Security Agency will all have substantial effects on individual markets.

It is this interdependence of national economies, themselves being but the aggregate interdependence of individuals in the process of making a living, that gives rise to the need for a code of economic principles acceptable to national governments. What this amounts to is reconciling national and international welfare, just as national policies alone reconcile individual and public welfare.

Price Economy Is One of Continual Adjustment. When markets—supply and demand factors—get out of line, as they always do, since demand is so heavily influenced by subjective valuations, something must give way to adjustment. This may be labor, managerial efficiency, production processes, costs of raw materials, or any of the elements making up the production-distribution-consumption links. If specific costs and prices themselves do not readily adjust because of entrenched rigidity, foreign-exchange rates may have to break; the result of this is a general adjustment of costs and prices at a new level, with a scramble for position on the part of specific cost elements.

The Proposed International Trade Organization

Realizing the golden opportunity to establish a code of economic conduct in international trade following the Second World War, the Department of State, in November, 1945, proposed an international conference on trade and employment. As a beginning, it issued a pamphlet,[1] the opening sentence of which read: "The main prize of the victory of the United Nations is a limited and temporary power to establish the kind of world we want to live in." This was a fine thought and a wonderful opportunity.

These proposals evolved into a *Suggested Charter for an International Trade Organization*,[2] which was submitted for consideration to a number of countries. In the United States, public hearings were held in a few large cities to ascertain public reaction to United States leadership and support of the proposed charter. The suggested charter was submitted to

[1] *Proposals for Expansion of World Trade and Employment*, U.S. Department of State Publication 2411.

[2] U.S. Department of State Publication 2598, September, 1946.

the Preparatory Committee for an International Conference on Trade and Employment, which had been appointed by the Economic and Social Council of the United Nations in February, 1946, and which met in London in October and November, 1946. Out of this meeting arose a *Preliminary Draft of a Charter for the International Trade Organization of the United Nations.*[3]

Further revisions were made by representatives of the members of the preparatory committee who met in New York in January and February, 1947. The "New York draft" was the working document of the preparatory committee at its second session, held at Geneva from April to August, 1947. Representatives of 17 nations participated. Out of this meeting came the *Draft Charter for the International Trade Organization of the United Nations,*[4] which served as the basis for an International Conference on Trade and Employment, called by the Economic and Social Council of the United Nations. This Conference was held in Havana from November, 1947, to March, 1948, and resulted in the *Havana Charter for an International Trade Organization.*[5] The draft was signed by representatives of 53 nations and submitted for ratification to the governments represented.

The proposal was placed before the United States Congress in April, 1949, and the President asked for its ratification. But up to Dec. 6, 1950, United States adherence had not been voted, and on that date the State Department, with approval of the President, reported its intention not to request passage at the current session of Congress but instead to ask for more direct and continuing participation in the General Agreement on Tariffs and Trade. In the meantime, Liberia was the only nation of the 53 signers to ratify the charter, although Australia ratified it conditionally, subject to ratification by the United States. One explanation for the lack of ratification by most of the discussants is that they were waiting to see what the United States would do about it.

Objectives Were Dual: Removal of Trade Restrictions and Harmony of International Full-employment Programs. While the original United States proposals did not specifically incorporate chapters on employment measures and economic-development programs, these features were soon added and were retained throughout. Hence, what started out as apparently international action to reduce restrictions, and thereby to enlarge opportunities for expanded trade, later developed into a proposal for international action and cooperation toward a governmentally planned and controlled international economy, with national interests protected by international discussions prior to action.

[3] U.S. Department of State Publication 2728.
[4] U.S. Department of State Publication 2927.
[5] U.S. Department of State Publication 3206.

Expansion of Trade vs. Expansion of Trade Opportunities. Although trade opportunities and employment rest on each other, there is a wide difference between expansion of trade per se and expansion of trade opportunities. The former may be accomplished temporarily by government action apart from specific market circumstances. The latter presumes trade volumes to be developed and run by free enterprisers. Accordingly, we may look upon the proposed charter as having had two aspects which are totally divergent in operation. One was the charting of a program for the conduct of governments in line with policies and actions taken regarding full employment and economic development under state control. The other was the elimination of national trade barriers, leaving the functioning of the international economy to private enterprise, with government participation generally limited to very broad policies.

Certainly few people can quarrel with the general desire for full and productive employment. The issue is between the types of economic systems under which it may be accomplished. Granted that there is an Employment Act of 1946 on the statute books, it must be noted that this law did not specify *full* employment as an objective. It did declare it to be

. . . the continuing policy and responsibility of the Federal Government to use all practicable means . . . to coordinate and utilize all its plans, functions, and resources for the purpose of creating and maintaining *in a manner calculated to foster and promote free competitive enterprise* [italics added] and the general welfare, conditions under which there will be afforded useful employment opportunities, including self-employment, for those able, willing and seeking to work, and to promote *maximum employment* [italics added], production and purchasing power.

On the other hand, the United Nations Charter calls for adherence to the principle of promoting "higher standards of living, *full employment* [italics added] and conditions of economic and social progress and development." In Art. 56, members of the United Nations "pledge themselves to take joint and separate action" in cooperation with the United Nations for the achievement of its purposes. This *pledge of a full-employment policy,* rather than the wording of the Employment Act of 1946, is the basis for much of the difference of opinion which has developed nationally and internationally regarding the principles of and conditions under which foreign and domestic commerce may be practiced. The importance of interpreting these objectives may be discerned from a report prepared by a committee of experts set up by the Secretary General of the United Nations to report on national and international measures required to achieve full employment. In late 1949, this committee proposed measures to implement obligations under the full-employment clause of the United Nations Charter.

Full employment "Obligations" as They May Affect Foreign Commerce. Of particular interest to the study of foreign commerce were the following three measures:

1. RELATING TO OVER-ALL COMMERCE. Countries should set targets for the main items of their balances of payments in an attempt to eliminate "structural disequilibrium" and should indicate how they hope to restore their over-all financial equilibrium. Presumably, this would mean a certain monetary volume of goods, services, travel, and foreign investments, in order not only to *attain* the planned volumes but also to maintain the proportionate relationships among these volumes. Moreover, countries having deficits in their balances of payments should undertake "reduction of internal inflationary pressures which compromise their ability to export and aggravate their need to import, to adjust their exchange rates when expansion of export is hampered by overvaluation of their currencies, and to adjust their production structure as the external market situation requires."[6] Countries having "surpluses" in their balances of payments should undertake "that a decrease in their exports or a rise in their imports not give rise to internal dislocations which, in turn, generate reduced imports with larger export surpluses," etc.

2. RELATING TO MERCHANDISE. Reasoning that import volumes are subject to fluctuations because of changing business conditions in an importing country, it was proposed that each member (government) should adopt a program of sustaining import volume through turning over to the International Monetary Fund enough of its currency to compensate for a decline in imports arising from its "failure to maintain full employment" and the resulting deflationary developments in the importing country. For, it is reasoned, there is no basis for assuming that people in exporting countries want or need to buy less from those countries to which they export (to the United States, for example) just because people in the United States cease buying from them. But they may not be able to buy as much as they formerly did *in dollar volume* if depressing corrections in price relationships have been permitted to occur in their former market (the United States), as a result of which individuals in the United States temporarily find it necessary or advisable or desirable to reduce their purchases from abroad. Through losing a foreign sales market in whole or in part during its readjustment internally, the former exporting countries (to the United States, in this instance) have lost a source of foreign exchange and can now buy less from the United States because of these developments. This is the cir-

[6] "Full Employment Action," summary by Ruth S. Donahue, *Department of State Bulletin*, Apr. 17, 1950, p. 608. These "correctives" proposed to be taken by countries (governments) are practically the sum total of correctives which businesses must take individually in attempting to remain solvent.

cumstance which would allow governments of the countries formerly exporting to the United States to obtain dollars (provided by the United States government) from the International Monetary Fund, for the purpose of continuing their purchases in the United States. Of course, this would be on a different basis and for a different purpose than that specified in the adopted Articles of Agreement of the International Monetary Fund.

Downward price adjustments and unemployment during the adjustment period are an unnecessary evil to the full-employment disciples. From this idea comes the plan for the government of an importing country to make good the sustaining of full employment in the countries exporting to it, as well as undertaking domestic measures in the direction of full employment, for by this process the erstwhile exporters can in turn continue to purchase from that country and prevent the spread of deflation and unemployment. At the same time, this arrangement will be a guarantee that full-employment measures taken domestically will not be at the expense of a foreign country.

3. RELATING TO INVESTMENT. Each lending country (government) would establish annual targets for new foreign investment, covering both private and public net investment. To the extent that individuals decided not to invest abroad, or to the extent that this was not "compensated" by public lending, the government would make up the "investment deficit" by turning over to the International Bank for Reconstruction and Development the difference between what the "program" called for and the amount of investments actually made. The Bank could then use these funds for loans to other governments, as a new operation, separate from its present functions.

It was these and similar features of international economic planning and direct intervention and control by government—essentials of implemented full-employment policies and of economic development under forced draft—that served to build up mounting opposition to the charter as proposed. One critic states that "the Charter is a master plan for the conduct of international trade by governments," and "there is little, if anything, in the Charter that would indicate a continued belief in private enterprise, whereas throughout the document are the doctrines of a planned economy."[7]

The committee's report was forwarded for study by member governments. The United States reply on these three proposed international measures was as follows:[8]

[7] E. H. Killhefer, "ITO Spells a Planned World," *American Affairs*, January, 1949, p. 35.

[8] "United States Expresses Views in ECOSOC on Full Employment," excerpts from statement by Isador Lubin, United States representative in the Economic and Social Council, *Department of State Bulletin*, Aug. 21, 1950, p. 309.

1. We agree with the recommendation for coinsuration among governments to establish a new equilibrium in world economic relationships but prefer to use the existing machinery of the United Nations for that purpose.[9]
2. We favor a larger and more stable international flow of investment funds, both public and private, but we disagree with the recommendation that such funds should be provided under an automatic or formula scheme.
3. We believe that the International Monetary Fund can play an important part in mitigating the international effects of economic fluctuations, particularly when more countries' balances of payments are in approximate equilibrium. But we do not accept the experts' proposal that countries suffering depression be obligated automatically to deposit their currency and that other countries have automatic drawing rights on such currencies, according to a predetermined formula.

Charter Supported and Rejected. Ratification of the charter was endorsed by some groups. However, qualified positions were usual. For example, among those endorsing adherence, but recognizing and pointing out weaknesses, were the National Council of American Importers, Inc., the Committee for Economic Development, and *Business Week*. Qualifying endorsements pertained to specific features, but the view was that the charter as signed at Havana was the best that could be attained and ratification was desirable "to preserve America's leadership in world trade and to strengthen the forces promoting free trade."[10] Another view was that where the choice lay between having an ITO "where we can thrash out these provisions and work from the inside" and perhaps having no ITO for another decade, the charter as drawn should be adopted.

Among those opposing the charter as drafted were the National Foreign Trade Council, the American Tariff League, the National Association of Manufacturers, the New York Board of Trade, the Chamber of Commerce of the United States, and the Executive Committee of the United States Council of the International Chamber of Commerce. The last of these gave good expression to the wide divergence among economic philosophies involved in the question of adherence. Its report reads, in part:

It is a dangerous document because it accepts practically all of the policies of economic nationalism; because it jeopardizes the free enterprise system by giving priority to centralized national government planning of foreign trade; because it leaves a wide scope to discrimination, accepts the principle of economic insulation and in effect commits all members of the ITO to state planning for full employment. From the point of view of the United States, it has the further very grave defect of placing this country in a position where it must accept discrimination against itself while extending the Most-Favored-Nation treatment to all members of the organization.

[9] Special meetings and an expert advisory commission had been proposed.
[10] *Business Week*, Feb. 25, 1950, p. 136.

Even the dissidents acknowledged good features in the charter, but considered them to be outweighed by the other provisions. Whether one group is extremely naïve and the other overly practical is a matter of opinion. But the supporting groups felt that the charter such as it was was better than none at all and that its imperfections could be ironed out in time through consultations. Some, on the other hand, feel that the best time to have a detailed understanding is before the partnership papers are drawn and not after. Certainly, the action of some members of the United Nations is evidence of the difficulty of coming to an understanding after rather than before the marriage contract is signed.

Charter Could Yield Highly Desirable Objectives. A number of objectives highly desirable to this author could be attained through the proposed charter, these being outlined mainly in that part dealing with commercial policy and restrictive business practices. They appear to lay the groundwork for *expanded trade opportunities* but leave the motivation for expansion to private enterprise. In general, the principles of international conduct expounded are (1) most-favored-nation treatment, (2) the tariff shall be the principal restriction used by member governments, and (3) in the use of others, antidiscrimination is to be the order of the day. Acceptance of these principles is hedged by a great many exceptions, so much so that the exceptions become the rule and the principles receive only lip service. Yet the principles are the best guarantee of expanded trade opportunities through removal of restrictions.

It would seem that if the Havana charter were to be confined to a codification of principles pertaining to commercial policy and restrictive business practices, it would meet little opposition on the part of adherents of the free competitive enterprise system. But when it incorporates numerous exceptions in trade principles to accommodate full-employment measures and accelerated economic-development programs, it seems to go afield from principles of *trade* and to become instead a statement of principles for an international political economy devoted to maintaining full employment.

This conflict of objectives is exemplified in testimony of Secretary of State Acheson, made before the House Committee on Foreign Affairs on Apr. 19, 1950.[11] Regarding the first, he said:

The code of fair trade practices set forth in the charter is a code designed to help achieve an international trading system in which traders may buy and sell where they please—the system economists call "multilateral trade"—the system under which private enterprise and free competition have the best chance to prosper.

[11] "Membership and Participation by United States in the International Trade Organization," *Hearings before Committee on Foreign Affairs, on H. J. R. 236,* U.S. House of Representatives, 81st Cong., 2d Sess. (1950).

At the same time, he said:

In a real and practical way, American action with respect to the International Trade Organization is a test of our leadership. It is a demonstration not only to ourselves but to all other free peoples that we really believe in free enterprise, competition, and multilateral trade.

Later, in the same testimony, he said:

It [the charter] does three things. It establishes a code of principles to guide action in a variety of international economic relations. It creates a mechanism, the International Trade Organization, within the United Nations family, to serve as a forum for the international consideration and solution of trade policy problems. It obligates its members to consult about their international trade policies before they act.

Leaving the question of codification of trade principles and coordination of trade policies for the charter's other objective, the same testimony brought out that "the charter recognizes that action to remove barriers to the movement of goods will be futile unless there are goods to move and purchasing power with which to buy them." This may be interpreted as meaning that reducing trade barriers and leaving the motivation of the economy to private enterprise is not a satisfactory economic system and not acceptable to the "kind of world we want to live in." Accordingly, the testimony continues, the charter "commits the member countries to use their best efforts according to their own constitutional procedures to achieve and maintain full and productive employment within their borders." In any case, one may safely predict that *any* party in power will find it politically expedient to take unprecedented steps (for the United States) to maintain reasonably full employment.

There Is No "National Trade Organization." One may "borrow" the proposal and relate it to the United States instead of to the world. In so doing, one would have to observe the absence of a "national trade organization." What, then, takes the place of such an organization in the United States?

Those things which make the United States a large producing and consuming market are a few economic principles incorporated into law, or at least legislation stating what is *not* to be done. Among these are:

1. A currency which is convertible among the north, south, east, and west. This feature is practically indispensable, both on current and on total account. Successful investment appeal under a philosophy of private competitive enterprise calls for the borrower's (or the investment opportunity's) satisfying the investor sufficiently to develop confidence. Only when satisfactory confidence exists will he voluntarily

part with his funds for this rather than for that, at this time rather than at another, and invest and develop rather than spend for current consumption. Needless to emphasize, the convertibility of currency is fundamental to this and to the conduct of business transactions on credit.

2. Lack of trade barriers among states. Although there have evolved some barriers under the guise of taxation or regulatory measures, there are no tariffs, import quotas, marks-of-origin regulations, import or export licenses, or exchange controls. These obstacles are in large part dealt with in the chapter of the proposed ITO charter titled "Commercial Policy."

3. The cartel issue has been settled in policy by the passage of antitrust laws. The Havana charter's chapter titled "Restrictive Business Practices" attempts to outlaw or at least seriously control these practices.

4. Corporate or business reciprocal privileges are relatively unhindered— this holds for the appointment of dealers and the opening of branch offices, plants, etc. Part of this is, of course, comparable to "direct" investments.

5. Freedom of migration of people among states. This is one feature of economic organization, on both the producing and the consuming side, which lends an adjustability to the United States internal economy and which is practically absent internationally. One would not hesitate to say that there is at present no practical hope for this economic "resource" to become more fluid internationally.

Each of the foregoing and the highly developed banking, communication, and transportation systems, themselves traceable in part to the liberty of business enterprise, play an important part in employment opportunities, which are made easier by the increased possibility of specializing in production and trading. As pointed out in Chapter 11, the extension of trade opportunities is a necessary part of specialization in production; this, in turn, is the best assurance of optimum utilization of the factors of production, lower costs, and higher real incomes.

One of the most commonly observed causes of the high degree of economic development in the United States is the spirit of enterprise, through which advantage may be taken of opportunities which are always arising. True, for a single nation, the United States is blessed with natural resources in advantageous juxtaposition, but many other areas are similarly favored in greater or lesser degree.

To focus all these points on full employment and economic development, it must be said that employment is thereby a result and an opportunity, and not a goal in itself; that economic development is a steady but even then slow, continued last, process. The motivation is linked to the free choice of numerous alternative opportunities, and the choice of these opportunities is the compensation for *insecurity*, as well as the basis for effective political freedom. As may be attested in case after case, in many countries, insecurity has been the spark that started employment and economic development, *as long as there was reasonable hope* that the fruits of labor could be harvested.

Commercial Policy Part of General Agreement on Tariffs and Trade. The picture is not so gloomy, however, as may be suggested by failure of the proposed ITO charter to be adopted. As indicated above, many of its features pertain to trade practices and economic organization; others, which would appear to be separable from these, pertain to government policy and action regarding full-employment and economic-development programs. It is the reasoned view of many that if trade and employment restrictions are modified, especially internationally, employment and economic development will take care of themselves, albeit not according to some governmental blueprint or some predetermined pattern and regulated rate of growth.

In the General Agreement on Tariffs and Trade, signed at Geneva in 1947, the general provisions incorporated a number of features found in the proposed ITO charter. These were substantially that part of the ITO charter having to do with commercial policy provisions and the reductions of trade barriers. Among the principles endorsed were (1) nondiscrimination and most-favored-nation treatment, (2) simplified valuations for customs purposes, (3) simplified and reduced formalities in connection with importation or exportation, these being openly concentrated at the customs frontier, (4) lessened and limited use of subsidies, (5) nondiscrimination in state trading, and conduct thereof according to commercial standards, etc. Some of these, unfortunately, are subject to the same criticism as was the proposed ITO charter—the exceptions and qualifications render the principles ineffectual.

It may be recalled that national adherence to the "principles" outlined in GATT is not merely a matter of negotiation. Legislative action is called for if the obligations undertaken are to be considered an official national pledge. In view of this, the contracting parties undertook to apply provisionally these principles to the fullest extent not inconsistent with existing legislation.

Decision of the President not to press for ratification of the ITO charter, but instead to request fuller participation in the policy objectives outlined in GATT, may be a most helpful compromise. It avoided a situation that might well have become unmanageable and could have resulted in an even wider breach between the political and the business economist. However, little practical good will result if exceptions or qualifications are to be condoned as a matter of principle because they may be tied in with balance of payments "difficulties," which may have been caused by or whose corrections are precluded by full-employment measures. In other words, corrections will have to be permitted in the direction of deflation as well as inflation if the meaning of free competitive enterprise is to have any long-range substance and life.

A continuing organization for consultation and exchange of information, for registration of complaints or violations and hearings thereon, and for over-all supervision of adherence to adopted principles of international conduct is desirable. However, a basic question to be settled, especially if the organization is to have police or sanctioning powers, is fair representation among governments. The ITO charter, for example, proposed one vote per country, with the United States and any of the very small and relatively unimportant countries in international commerce having an equal vote. On matters of principle, of course, the vote of one person who is right may and should prevail in the long run against the votes of many who are wrong. But in matters of degrees of right and wrong, and interpretations, even when honestly based on differing economic philosophies, a different situation would seem to arise, and a lively fight could be expected on the proposal to submit United States or any other country's sovereign rights to pledges or the interpretation thereof by a group of others, several of whom together are relatively weaker than is the larger one.

The proposed ITO charter provided for a continuing body and, in fact, pending consideration of the charter by the governments concerned, there was established an Interim Coordinating Committee of the International Trade Organization. Such an arrangement has been somewhat less satisfactorily provided for by regular meetings of the contracting parties to GATT.

REVIEW QUESTIONS

1. What were the basic economic advantages of the proposed International Trade Organization?

2. What were the basic economic disadvantages of the proposed International Trade Organization?

3. What are some of the factors that affect international prices?

4. Could the proposed ITO have found wider support had it confined its objectives to removal of trade restrictions and not broadened them out to be an international vehicle for full-employment programs? Discuss.

5. Evaluate the discussion regarding expansion of trade vs. expansion of trade opportunities.

6 How may full employment undertakings affect foreign commerce?

7. How may the "obligations" of the United States toward full employment policies, based on membership in the United Nations, affect our future trade in merchandise? In foreign investments?

8. Why was the proposed ITO charter not accepted?

9. Would a "national trade organization" be beneficial if an International Trade Organization were considered to be? Discuss.

10. Explain the commercial policy aspects of the General Agreement on Tariffs and Trade.

Appendixes

APPENDIX A

Application for Export License*

Form Approved Budget Bureau No. 41-R1343.

Instructions (margin annotations):

The address of the Collector of Customs, through whom shipment is to be made, must be entered in this space. Give name of port; if unknown, state "Unknown." If export is to be by mail, so state.

The name and address of the applicant or person authorized by the applicant to receive the license, if issued, must be entered in this space.

Country in which the goods will be consumed—NOT country receiving shipment in transit.

When the *Positive List* does not specify a unit of quantity for an item, the unit commonly used in trade should be shown.

Description for all commodities should be in sufficient detail to permit classification according to Positive List. Do not use general terms. Give additional details for full identification.

In complying with the requirement for fullest disclosure of all parties in interest, names and addresses of other parties (agents, middle men, brokers) concerned in the transaction should be disclosed in Item 9, if space is available, or on an attached sheet.

This number appears in upper portion of the Form IT-116 which is returned to applicant upon receipt of Form IT-419 in OIT.

NOTE: Ultimate consignee must be the person located abroad who will actually use the commodities for the end use designated in Item 12.

Item 8. The intermediate consignee may be a bank, forwarding agent, or other intermediary in a foreign country who participates as an agent in the transaction for the purpose of effecting delivery of the exportation to the ultimate consignee. If no intermediary is to be used, state "None." If unknown at time of application, state "Unknown."

This commodity is erroneously entered on the application form since its processing code or related group number is different from that of the other commodities appearing on this application. A separate application would be required for this item.

---

1. APPLICANT-LICENSE (Exporter) (Instructions on reverse of duplicate)
NAME Foreign Commerce Company
STREET 77 Terminal Street
CITY AND STATE Washington 1, D. C.
CITIZENSHIP American

2. COLLECTOR OF CUSTOMS (Name, port. If unknown, state "Unknown." If export to be by mail, so state.)
New York, N. Y.

3. IF PURCHASER IN FOREIGN COUNTRY IS OTHER THAN ULTIMATE CONSIGNEE, GIVE NAME AND ADDRESS (If same, state "Same.")
Cooperative Airlines, Ltd.
15 Canal St., Seaport, England

4. MAILING ADDRESS (Applicant or person to whom return copy is to be sent)
Deliam Forwarding Company
42 Broadway
New York City 4, N. Y.

5. COUNTRY OF ULTIMATE DESTINATION
Switzerland

FOR OFFICIAL USE ONLY
VALIDATION LICENSE NO
EXPIRATION DATE
OIT CASE NO.

7. ULTIMATE CONSIGNEE IN FOREIGN COUNTRY
NAME AND ADDRESS Fairway Airways
56 Avenue Royale
Dengis, Switzerland

8. INTERMEDIATE CONSIGNEE IN FOREIGN COUNTRY (Give name and address. If same as ultimate consignee, state "Same.")
Atelo Nitram
53 La rue Grande
Reman, France

6. IMPORT PERMIT NO. AND/OR MSA AUTHORIZATION NO.

(a) QUANTITY TO BE SHIPPED	(b) COMMODITY DESCRIPTION AS GIVEN IN SCHEDULE B (Include basic ingredients, composition, type, size, part, grade, horsepower, etc., where applicable.)	(c) SCHEDULE B NUMBER AND PROCESSING CODE	(d) UNIT PRICE	(e) TOTAL SELLING PRICE AND POINT OF DELIVERY (Indicate F. O. B., F. A. S., C. I. F., etc.) TOTAL PRICE
2	Motors, 1200 H.P., Electric, Squirrel Cage type.	704300 ELME 2 - RO	37,210	74,420.00
3 lots	Accessories and parts for motors over 1000 H. P., not including controls for reversible type motors or starting and controlling equipment.	705500 ELME 2 - RO		7,500.00
75	Electronic tubes, commercial and industrial, other than radio and tungar tubes, manufactured by American Tube Co., type N31-B, Catalog No. 211.	709907 ELME - RO	16.75	1,256.25
5	Searchlight mirrors, 60-inch diameter, for use on searchlights of 1,500,000 candle power capacity.	709998 ELME 2 - RO	175	875.00

(Order received from David Black (purchaser's agent), 35 Canal Street, Seaport, England.

(All prices F.A.S. -New York)

FOR OFFICIAL USE ONLY
PRIORITY ACTION
☐ PRIORITY RATING GRANTED ☐ NO PRIORITY ☐ APPROVED

486

10. IS APPLICATION MADE FOR APPLICANT'S OWN ACCOUNT? ☒ YES ☐ NO   IF NOT, STATE NAME AND ADDRESS OF FOREIGN PRINCIPAL AND EXPLAIN FULLY.

11. (a) IS APPLICANT THE PRODUCER OF THE COMMODITIES TO BE EXPORTED? ☐ YES ☒ NO   (b) IF NOT THE PRODUCER, HAVE COMMODITIES BEEN PURCHASED? ☐ YES ☒ NO

(c) IF NOT PURCHASED, HAS ORDER BEEN PLACED WITH SUPPLIER? ☐ YES ☐ NO;   ACCEPTED BY SUPPLIER? ☒ YES ☐ NO;   APPROXIMATE DELIVERY DATE. 9-1-52

NAME AND ADDRESS OF SUPPLIER Aviation Equipment Co., 700 Market St., Edam, North Carolina

12. END USE OF COMMODITIES COVERED BY THIS APPLICATION. DESCRIBE FULLY, STATING WHAT WILL BE PRODUCED OR MANUFACTURED OR WHAT SERVICE WILL BE RENDERED (See Special Instructions, Item 18.)

Commercial airports at Abba, Effe and Ijji, Switzerland urgently need items for airplane repair shops, aviation research laboratories and airfields, to effect safety measures offsetting hazards of sharply increased traffic. Mining industry accessible only by air transport.

13. DATE OF APPLICATION	14. APPLICANT'S PREFERENCE NO.	15. PREVIOUS OIT CASE NO. COVERING SAME TRANSACTION
3-30-52	FC-11	None

16. The undersigned hereby makes application for a license to export and certifies as follows: That all statements herein are true and that (a) he has read the instructions on the duplicate copy of this application and is familiar with OIT export control regulations, (b) this application conforms to such instructions and regulations, (c) all parties to the transaction, the exact commodities and quantities, and all other terms of the order or accepted order-contract and other facts of the export transaction are fully and accurately reflected herein, (d) documents and records evidencing the order (or the accepted order-contract and other facts for this application) and made available to OIT upon demand, (e) any material or substantive changes in connection therewith, whether the export transaction is still under consideration, the application represents a request to export commodities which, subject only to conditions beyond the control of either the applicant or named purchaser, he will be strictly accountable for its use in accordance with the regulations of the OIT.

Foreign Commerce Company
(Applicant) (Same as item 1))

[signature] U. S. Acirena,
Vice President
(Name and title of person whose signature appears on the line to the left)

Signature of person authorized to exercise this application)

This license application and any license issued pursuant thereto are expressly subject to all rules and regulations of the Department of Commerce. Making any false statement or concealing any material fact in connection with this application or altering in any way the validated license issued, is punishable by imprisonment or fine, or both, and by denial of export privileges under the Export Control Act and other Federal statutes.

FOR OFFICIAL USE ONLY

ACTION TAKEN	VALIDITY PERIOD	AUTHORITY		
☐ APPROVED	MONTHS			
☐ REJECTED			(Commodity officer)	(Date)
IS	SC			
			(Review officer)	(Date)

NOTE: Submit acknowledgment card (Form IT-114) and original copy of this application to Office of International Trade, retaining duplicate copy for your files. See Special Instructions on back of duplicate. Reproduction of this form is permissible, providing that content, format, size, and color of paper and ink are the same.

1. ORIGINAL   OIT FILE COPY

Form IT-419
(9-12-50)

EXPORT LICENSE/APPLICATION

U. S. DEPARTMENT OF COMMERCE
OFFICE OF INTERNATIONAL TRADE
WASHINGTON, D. C.

GPO 16—67220—1

487

* Courtesy of U.S. Department of Commerce.

Form of Export License*

In the first part of the license number the date of issuance is incorporated: 1950 (0), fourth month (-4), and fifth day (-5).

All export licenses are subject to revision, suspension, or revocation without notice.

The letter, all the numerals, and the intermediate dashes, jointly comprise the complete license number.

The export license is issued to a named licensee who will be held strictly accountable for proper use of the document.

With these references, licensees can readily associate the export license with his copies of the application and acknowledgment card.

When a unit of quantity is not specified on the *Positive List*, the quantity authorized for export is licensed in terms of the total price.

Purchaser is separately specified as a principal party in interest, when ultimate consignee is not to be held accountable as purchaser.

The export license (Form IT-628) must be presented to and filed with the collector of customs (or postmaster) when the first shipment is cleared for exportation against the license.

On the reverse side of the export license, two endorsements are required:
1. Signature of Licensee, and
2. Signature of Person Presenting License.

SPECIMEN OF FACE OF EXPORT LICENSE

* Courtesy of U.S. Department of Commerce.

488

Form 7525-V (Rev. Nov. 1948)
EXPORT CONTROL
FOREIGN COMMERCE
STATISTICAL REGULATIONS
(See Instructions on Reverse Side)

U. S. DEPARTMENT OF COMMERCE
BUREAU OF THE CENSUS—OFFICE OF INTERNATIONAL TRADE

SHIPPER'S EXPORT DECLARATION

OF SHIPMENTS TO FOREIGN COUNTRIES OR NONCONTIGUOUS TERRITORIES OF THE UNITED STATES

READ CAREFULLY THE INSTRUCTIONS ON BACK TO AVOID DELAY AT SHIPPING POINT

Clearance will not be granted until shipper's declaration has been filed with the Collector of Customs. This declaration shall not be used to effect any exportation after the expiration date of the export license referred to herein, except as specifically authorized by export regulations.

DECLARATIONS SHOULD BE TYPEWRITTEN OR PREPARED IN INK; INDELIBLE PENCIL IS NOT PERMISSIBLE.

FORM APPROVED.
BUDGET BUREAU NO. 41-R297.2.

CONFIDENTIAL

Do Not Use This Area

Do Not Use This Area | District | Port | Country (For customs use only)

FILE NO. (This Space for Use of Customs)

1. EXPORTING CARRIER (if vessel, give name, flag and pier number) | 2. FROM (U. S. Port of Export)

3. EXPORTER (Principal or seller—licensee) | ADDRESS (Number, street, place, State)

4. AGENT OF EXPORTER (Forwarding agent) | ADDRESS (Number, street, place, State)

5. PURCHASER OR ULTIMATE CONSIGNEE | ADDRESS (Place, country)

6. INTERMEDIATE CONSIGNEE | ADDRESS (Place, country)

7. FOREIGN PORT OF UNLOADING (For vessel and air shipments only) | 8. PLACE AND COUNTRY OF ULTIMATE DESTINATION (Not place of transshipment)

(9) MARKS AND NOS.	(10) NUMBER AND KIND OF PACKAGES, DESCRIPTION OF COMMODITIES, EXPORT LICENSE NUMBER, ISSUANCE DATE, EXPIRATION DATE (OR GENERAL LICENSE SYMBOL) (Describe commodities in sufficient detail to permit classification according to Schedule B. Do not use general terms. Insert required license information on line below description of each item)	(11) SHIPPING WEIGHT * (Gross weight in pounds) Not required for truck, rail, and mail exportations	(12) EXPORT "D" OR "F"	(13) SCHEDULE B COMMODITY No.	(14) NET QUANTITY IN SCHEDULE B UNITS (State unit)	(15) VALUE AT TIME AND PLACE OF EXPORT (Selling price or cost if not sold, including inland freight, insurance and other charges to place of export) (Nearest whole dollar; omit cents)

16. WAYBILL OR MANIFEST No. (of Exporting Carrier) | 17. DATE OF EXPORTATION (if Vessel, Date of Clearance)

18. THE UNDERSIGNED HEREBY AUTHORIZES .... (Name and address—Number, street, place, State)
TO ACT AS FORWARDING AGENT FOR EXPORT CONTROL AND CUSTOMS PURPOSES.
(DULY AUTHORIZED
EXPORTER .... BY OFFICER OR EMPLOYEE) ....

▶ 19. I DECLARE THAT ALL STATEMENTS MADE AND ALL INFORMATION CONTAINED IN THIS EXPORT DECLARATION ARE TRUE AND CORRECT.

20. Subscribed and sworn to before me on ...., 19...... | SIGNATURE .... (Duly authorized officer or employee of exporter or named forwarding agent)

FOR ....
(Name of corporation or firm and capacity of signer, e. g., secretary, export manager, etc.)

ADDRESS ....
(TITLE OR DESIGNATION) Notary Public, etc., or those authorized to administer oaths under Sec. 486, Tariff Act of 1930.

Do Not Write in This Area

▶ Declaration should be made by duly authorized officer or employee of exporter or of forwarding agent named by exporter.
* If shipping weight is not available for each Schedule B item listed in column (13) included in one or more packages, insert the approximate gross weight for each Schedule B item. The total of these estimated weights should equal the actual weight of the entire package or packages.
‡ Designate foreign merchandise (reexports) with an "F" and exports of domestic merchandise produced in the United States or changed in condition in the United States with a "D".
NO AUTHENTICATED DECLARATION RELATING TO ANY COMMODITY REQUIRING AN EXPORT LICENSE MAY BE ALTERED, CHANGED OR AMENDED WITHOUT PRIOR WRITTEN AUTHORIZATION FROM THE COLLECTOR OF CUSTOMS OR FROM SUCH OTHER PERSON AS MAY BE EMPOWERED BY EXPORT REGULATIONS TO GIVE SUCH WRITTEN AUTHORIZATION. (See also Instruction 2 (e).) 16-56693-1

489

APPENDIX D

Budget Bureau No. 48-R217.
Approval expires 5-31-50.

Customs Form 7501
TREASURY DEPARTMENT
8.27, 8.51, 10.31, 10.91, C. R. 1943
Aug. 1947

CONSUMPTION ENTRY

UNITED STATES CUSTOMS SERVICE

COLLECTOR'S COPY .... ☐
COMPTROLLER'S COPY .... ☐
STATISTICAL COPY .... ☐

In-Bond Entry No. ....

From Port of ....

Via ....
(Bonded carrier)

DISTRICT No. ....

PORT OF .... DATE ....

Entry No. ....

Term Bond No. ...

Port of lading .... B/L No. .... Date of sailing .... Port of unlading ....
(Above information to be furnished only when merchandise is imported by vessel)

Importer of record ....
(Name)   (Street number, city, and State)

For account of ....
(Name)   (Street number, city, and State)

Imported on the .... Flag .... On .... Via ....
(Name of vessel or carrier and motive power)   (Date imported)   (Last foreign port)

Exported from .... on .... Consular invoice ....
(Country)   (Date)   (Place, number, and date certified)

MARKS AND NUMBERS OF PACKAGES AND ORIGIN OF MERCHANDISE (1)	(2) DESCRIPTION OF MERCHANDISE, NUMBER AND KIND OF PACKAGES (Describe in tariff terms in enough detail to permit classification according to Schedule A)			ENTERED VALUE IN U. S. DOLLARS (see Note 2) (3)	TARIFF		DUTY (6)	
	GROSS WEIGHT IN POUNDS (see Note 1) (2a)	SCHEDULE A COMMODITY NUMBER (2b)	NET QUANTITY IN SCHEDULE A UNITS (state units) (2c)		PARAGRAPH (4)	RATE (5)	DOLLARS	CENTS

Number of invoices .... W. H. Entry No. .... G. O. No. ....

NOTE 1.—In column number (2a), insert "Gross Weight in Pounds" immediately below the description of merchandise. If gross weight is not available for each Schedule A item included in one or more packages, insert approximate shipping weight for each Schedule A item. The total of these estimated weights should equal the actual weight of the entire package or packages.
NOTE 2.—The entered value shown for free or specific-rate merchandise must not include nondutiable charges.

16—17190-5

SIGNATURE ....

PER ....

ADDRESS ....

490

Form of Certified or Consular Invoice

Form 138
FOREIGN SERVICE
(Revised August 1941)

—Attach Additional Sheets Here—

Form Approved.
Budget Bureau No. 47–R003.1.
No expiration date.

INVOICE OF MERCHANDISE

(Before preparing this invoice, read instructions carefully)

(1) PURCHASED ☐   (1) NOT PURCHASED ☐

(Do not include PURCHASED and NOT PURCHASED merchandise in ONE invoice; use SEPARATE invoice for each)

....
(Place and date)

Invoice of .... (2) {purchased from or agreed to be purchased from / shipped by
        (Merchandise)

(3) .... of ....
        (Seller or consignor)   (Address)

by } .... of ....
to }   (Purchaser or consignee)   (Address)

(4) { as per order accepted ....
     { for the account of .... of ....
                            (Name)   (Address)

to be shipped per ....
                                    (Carrier)

(5) MARKS AND NUMBERS ON SHIPPING PACKAGES	(6) MANUFAC- TURER'S OR SELLER'S NUMBERS OR SYMBOLS	(7) IMPORTER'S NUMBERS OR SYMBOLS	(8) QUANTITIES AND FULL DESCRIPTION OF GOODS (N. B.—Always state the cost of packing, and all other costs, charges, and expenses)	(9) INVOICE UNIT (See questions below)	(10) INVOICE TOTAL	(11) CURRENT PRICE (Home consump- tion or export) PER UNIT

(Read carefully instructions 1 and 9 before answering the first three following questions.)

Is this merchandise shipped in pursuance of a purchase or an agreement to purchase? ....
                                                                    (Yes or No)

If answer to preceding question is "Yes," have you entered as item 9 the purchase price of each item in the currency of purchase?

....
(Yes or No)

Is this merchandise shipped otherwise than in pursuance of a purchase or an agreement to purchase? .... If answer is
                                                                                   (Yes or No)

"Yes," indicate below whether you have entered as item 9 the present value for each item in the currency in which the trans-actions are usually made: (a) the value for home consumption including all applicable taxes in the country of exportation; or (b) the export value to the United States if higher; or (c) in the absence of the foreign value and the export value, the price in such currency that the manufacturer, seller, shipper, or owner would have received, or was willing to receive for such mer-chandise if sold in the ordinary wholesale quantities in the country of exportation; or (d) in the absence of all of the fore-going, the cost of production ....
                                            (State whether (a), (b), (c), or (d) is applicable)

Is the currency, entered as item 9, gold, silver, or paper? ....
                                                        (State which)

Have you enumerated all charges and stated whether each amount has been included in or excluded from the above invoice amounts?
.... If the inland freight is included in the invoice price or value, is the price or value of the merchandise the same
(Yes or No)
at the factory as at the point of delivery? ....
                                        (Yes or No)

Have you separately itemized all rebates, drawbacks, bounties, or other grants allowed upon the exportation of the merchandise?

....
(Yes or No)

Is such or similar merchandise offered or sold in the home market for home consumption? .... If so, what taxes are
                                                                        (Yes or No)

applicable? ....
                        (Rate and kind)

(When invoice is signed by an authorized agent the name of his principal must be shown.)

Signature of
Seller or Shipper ....

16—23731-4

By ....
                        (Authorized agent)

APPENDIX E. (*Continued.*)

CONSULAR INVOICE OF MERCHANDISE

Invoice No. _____ Issued in { Triplicate / Quadruplicate

Certified _____
(Date)

FOREIGN SERVICE OF THE UNITED STATES OF AMERICA AT

Date _____

Seller } _____
Consignor }

Purchaser } _____
Consignee }

Carrier _____
(Vessel or railroad)

Port of shipment _____

Destination of goods _____

Port of arrival _____

Port of entry _____

Amount of invoice _____

Kind of goods _____

_____
_____ of the UNITED STATES OF AMERICA.

DECLARATION OF SELLER OR SHIPPER, OR THE AGENT OF EITHER, WHEN MERCHANDISE IS SHIPPED IN PURSUANCE OF A PURCHASE OR AN AGREEMENT TO PURCHASE

I, } _____
We, }

acting in the capacity described below, truly declare that _____

of _____ is { the (seller) or (shipper) } of the merchandise described in the within or attached invoice; that the merchandise is sold or agreed to be sold; that there is no other invoice differing from the within or attached invoice, and that all the statements contained herein and in such invoice are true and correct.

I } further declare that _____
We }

and that it is intended to make entry of said merchandise at the port of _____

in the UNITED STATES OF AMERICA.

Dated at _____ this _____ day of _____

_____
(Seller)

_____
(Shipper)

_____
(Agent of seller)

_____
(Agent of shipper)

CONSULAR CERTIFICATE
Form 140

I do hereby certify that this invoice was this day produced to me by the signer of the above declaration.

I do further certify that I am satisfied that the person making the declaration above is the person he represents himself to be, and that a fee of $2.50 United States currency, equal to _____ (Local currency), has been paid by affixing stamps to the original copy of this document.

Witness my hand and seal of office the day and year aforesaid.

_____
(Date)

_____
_____ of the UNITED STATES OF AMERICA.

DECLARATION OF SHIPPER OR HIS AGENT WHEN THE MERCHANDISE IS SHIPPED OTHERWISE THAN IN PURSUANCE OF A PURCHASE OR AN AGREEMENT TO PURCHASE

I, } _____
We, }

acting in the capacity described below, truly declare that _____

is { the (shipper) } of the merchandise described in the are { (shippers) } within or attached invoice; that the merchandise is shipped otherwise than in pursuance of a purchase, or an agreement to purchase; that there is no other invoice differing from the within or attached invoice, and that all statements contained herein and in such invoice are true and correct.

I } further declare that _____
We }

and that it is intended to make entry of said merchandise at the port of _____

in the UNITED STATES OF AMERICA.

Dated at _____ this _____ day of _____

_____
(Shipper)

_____
(Agent of shipper)

CONSULAR CERTIFICATE
Form 140

I do hereby certify that this invoice was this day produced to me by the signer of the above declaration.

I do further certify that I am satisfied that the person making the declaration above is the person he represents himself to be, and that a fee of $2.50 United States currency, equal to _____ (Local currency), has been paid by affixing stamps to the original copy of this document.

Witness my hand and seal of office the day and year aforesaid.

_____
(Date)

_____
_____ of the UNITED STATES OF AMERICA.

U. S. GOVERNMENT PRINTING OFFICE

492

Bibliography and Selected References

SIGNIFICANCE AND BACKGROUND

America's New Opportunities in World Trade (Washington, The Committee on International Policy of the National Planning Association, 1944).

Condliffe, J. B., *The Commerce of Nations* (New York, W. W. Norton & Company, 1950).

Dietrich, Ethel B., *World Trade* (New York, Henry Holt and Company, Inc., 1939).

Ellsworth, P. T., *The International Economy* (New York, The Macmillan Company, 1950).

Enke, Stephen, and Virgil Salera, *International Economics* (New York, Prentice-Hall, Inc., 1947).

The Foreign Trade of Latin-America since 1913, Pan-American Union, 1952.

Foreign Trade Practice (Reference Sources), Office of International Trade, U.S. Department of Commerce, 1950.

Hansen, Alvin H., *America's Role in the World Economy* (New York, W. W. Norton & Company, 1945).

Harrod, Roy Forbes, *International Economics* (London, Nisbet and Company, Ltd., 1939).

Heilperin, Michael, *The Trade of Nations* (New York, Alfred A. Knopf, Inc., 1952).

Henius, Frank, *Dictionary of Foreign Trade* (New York, Prentice-Hall, Inc., 1947).

Horn, Paul V., *International Trade—Principles and Practices,* 3d ed. (New York, Prentice-Hall, Inc., 1951).

——— and Hubert E. Bice, *Latin-American Trade and Economics* (New York, Prentice-Hall, Inc., 1949).

Lincoln, George A., William S. Stone, and Thomas H. Harvey, *Economics of National Security* (New York, Prentice-Hall, Inc., 1950).

Our 100 Leading Imports (Washington, Foreign Commerce Department, Chamber of Commerce of the United States, 1945).

Patterson, Ernest M., *An Introduction to World Economics* (New York, The Macmillan Company, 1947).

Rosenthal, Morris S., *Techniques of International Trade* (New York, McGraw-Hill Book Company, Inc., 1950).

The United States in the World Economy, U.S. Department of Commerce Economic Series 23, 1943.

Van Cleef, Eugene, *Trade Centers and Trade Routes* (New York, Appleton-Century-Crofts, Inc., 1937).

Balance of Payments Yearbook, International Monetary Fund (annual).

Foreign Commerce and Navigation of the United States, Bureau of the Census, U.S. Department of Commerce (annual).

The International Trader, International Traders' Manual, Inc., New York (annual).

World Economic Survey, League of Nations (serial).

Export Trade and Shipper, Thomas Ashwell and Co., Inc., New York (monthly).

International Financial Statistics, International Monetary Fund (monthly).

Foreign Commerce Weekly, Office of International Trade, U.S. Department of Commerce (weekly).

International Trade Reporter, Bureau of National Affairs (weekly).

ORGANIZATIONAL STRUCTURE AND PRACTICE

Baños, J. Luis, *Comments on Letters of Credit,* (New Orleans, Whitney National Bank, 1949).

Beckman, Theodore N., and Robert Bartels, *Credits and Collections in Theory and Practice,* 5th ed. (New York, McGraw-Hill Book Company, Inc., 1949).

Common Discrepancies in Documents (Irving Trust Company, New York, 1950).

De Haas, J. Anton, *The Practice of Foreign Trade* (New York, McGraw-Hill Book Company, Inc., 1935).

Export and Import Practice, Office of International Trade, U.S. Department of Commerce, 1938.

Foreign Commerce Handbook, Foreign Commerce Department, Chamber of Commerce of the United States, 1946.

Foreign Trade Practice (Reference Sources), Office of International Trade, U.S. Department of Commerce, 1950.

Henius, Frank, *Dictionary of Foreign Trade* (New York, Prentice-Hall, Inc., 1947).

Horn, Paul V., *International Trade—Principles and Practices,* 3d ed. (New York, Prentice-Hall, Inc., 1951).

Huebner, Grover G., and Roland L. Kramer, *Foreign Trade Principles and Practices* (New York, Appleton-Century-Crofts, Inc., 1942).

An Introduction to Doing Import and Export Business, Foreign Commerce Department, Chamber of Commerce of the United States, 1947.

Marsh, Donald Bailey, *World Trade and Investment* (New York, Harcourt, Brace and Company, Inc., 1951).

Modern Export Packing, Trade Promotion Series 207, U.S. Department of Commerce, 1940.

Murr, Alfred, *The Foreign Freight Forwarder* (New York University Bookstore, 1947).

Otterson, J. E., *Foreign Trade and Shipping* (New York, McGraw-Hill Book Company, Inc., 1945).

Parks, Wallace J., *United States Administration of Its International Economic Affairs* (Baltimore, Johns Hopkins Press, 1951).

Pratt, E. E., *Foreign Trade Handbook* (Chicago and London, The Dartnell Corporation, 1948).

A Review of Export and Import Procedure (New York, Guaranty Trust Company, 1946).

Revised American Foreign Trade Definitions—1941 (New York, National Foreign Trade Council, Inc.).

Roorbach, George B., *Import Purchasing* (New York, McGraw-Hill Book Company, Inc., 1927).

Rosenthal, Morris S., *Techniques of International Trade* (New York, McGraw-Hill Book Company, Inc., 1950).

Sánchez, J. Rodríguez, *Foreign Credits and Collections* (New York, Prentice-Hall, Inc., 1947).

Shaterian, William S., *Export-Import Banking* (New York, The Ronald Press Company, 1947).

Southard, Frank A., Jr., *Foreign Exchange Practice and Policy* (New York, McGraw-Hill Book Company, Inc., 1940).

Strong, A. M., *Import Financing by Letters of Credit* (Chicago, American National Bank and Trust Company, 1944).

Syrett, W. W., *Practice and Finance of Foreign Trade* (London, Macmillan & Co., Ltd., 1938).

Ward, Wilbert, and Henry Harfield, *Bank Credits and Acceptances* (New York, The Ronald Press Company, 1948).

Whale, P. Barrett, *International Trade* (London, T. Thornton Butterworth, Ltd., 1932).

Custom House Guide, Import Publications, Inc., New York (annual).

Exporters' Encyclopedia, Thomas Ashwell and Co., Inc., New York (annual).

The International Trader, International Traders' Manual, Inc., New York (annual).

American Import and Export Bulletin, Import Publications, Inc., New York (monthly).

Exporters' Digest, American and Foreign Credit Underwriters Corporation, New York (monthly).

Export Trade and Shipper, Thomas Ashwell and Co., Inc., New York (monthly).

Foreign Commerce Weekly, Office of International Trade, U.S. Department of Commerce (weekly).

International Trade Reporter, Bureau of National Affairs (weekly).

ECONOMIC ASPECTS

America's New Opportunities in World Trade (Washington, The Committee on International Policy of the National Planning Association, 1944).

Beveridge, William Henry, *Tariffs, The Case Examined* (London, Longmans, Roberts and Green, 1932).

Buchanan, Norman S., and F. A. Lutz, *Rebuilding the World Economy* (New York, The Twentieth Century Fund, Inc., 1947).

Condliffe, J. B., *The Commerce of Nations* (New York, W. W. Norton & Company, 1950).

Crump, Norman, *The ABC of the Foreign Exchanges* (London, Macmillan & Co., Ltd., 1951).

Dietrich, Ethel B., *World Trade* (New York, Henry Holt and Company, Inc., 1939).

Donaldson, John, *International Economic Relations* (New York, Longmans, Green & Co., Inc., 1928).

Ellsworth, P. T., *The International Economy* (New York, The Macmillan Company, 1950).

Enke, Stephen, and Virgil Salera, *International Economics* (New York, Prentice-Hall, Inc., 1947).

Graham, Frank D., *The Theory of International Values* (Princeton, N.J., Princeton University Press, 1948).

Hansen, Alvin H., *America's Role in the World Economy* (New York, W. W. Norton & Company, 1945).

Harrod, Roy F., *International Economics* (London, Nisbet and Company, Ltd., 1939).

Hawkins, Harry C., *Commercial Treaties and Agreements* (New York, Rinehart & Company, Inc., 1951).

Heilperin, Michael, *International Monetary Economics* (New York, Longmans, Green & Co., Inc., 1930).

———, *The Trade of Nations* (New York, Alfred A. Knopf, Inc., 1952).

Henius, Frank, *Dictionary of Foreign Trade* (New York, Prentice-Hall, Inc., 1947).

Hoover, Calvin B., *International Trade and Domestic Employment* (New York, McGraw-Hill Book Company, Inc., 1945).

Horn, Paul V., *International Trade—Principles and Practices*, 3d ed. (New York, Prentice-Hall, Inc., 1951).

——— and Hubert E. Bice, *Latin American Trade and Economics* (New York, Prentice-Hall, Inc., 1949).

Gulick, Robert L., Jr., *Imports—The Grain from Trade*, (New York, Committee on International Economic Policy, 1946).

Intergovernmental Commodity Control Agreements (Montreal, International Labour Office, 1943).

Isaacs, Asher, *International Trade—Tariff and Commercial Policies.* (Chicago, Richard D. Irwin, Inc., 1948).

Johnson, D. Gale, *Trade and Agriculture* (New York, John Wiley & Sons, Inc.; London, Chapman & Hall, Ltd., 1950).

Killough, Hugh B., and Lucy W. Killough, *Economics of International Trade*, 2d ed. (New York, McGraw-Hill Book Company, Inc., 1948).

Lewis, Cleona, *America's Stake in International Investments* (Washington, Brookings Institution, 1938).

————, *The United States and Foreign Investment Problems* (Washington, Brookings Institution, 1948).

Lincoln, George A., William S. Stone, and Thomas H. Harvey, *Economics of National Security* (New York, Prentice-Hall, Inc., 1950).

Machlup, Fritz, *International Trade and the National Income Multiplier* (Philadelphia, The Blakiston Company, 1950).

Marsh, Donald Bailey, *World Trade and Investment* (New York, Harcourt, Brace and Company, Inc., 1951).

Mason, Edward S., *Controlling World Trade* (New York, McGraw-Hill Book Company, Inc., 1946).

Our 100 Leading Imports (Washington, Foreign Commerce Department, Chamber of Commerce of the United States, 1945).

Patterson, Ernest M., *An Introduction to World Economics* (New York, The Macmillan Company, 1947).

Pratt, E. E., *Foreign Trade Handbook* (Chicago and London, The Dartnell Corporation, 1948).

Readings in the Theory of International Trade (Philadelphia, The Blakiston Company, 1949).

Rosenthal, Morris S., *Techniques of International Trade* (New York, McGraw-Hill Book Company, Inc., 1950).

Sánchez, J. Rodríguez, *Foreign Credits and Collections* (New York, Prentice-Hall, Inc., 1947).

Shaterian, William S., *Export-Import Banking* (New York, The Ronald Press Company, 1947).

Southard, Frank A., Jr., *Foreign Exchange Practice and Policy* (New York, McGraw-Hill Book Company, Inc., 1940).

Staley, Eugene, *World Economy in Transition* (New York, Council on Foreign Relations, Inc., 1939).

Syrett, W. W., *Practice and Finance of Foreign Trade* (London, Macmillan & Co., Ltd., 1938).

Taussig, F. W., *International Trade* (New York, The Macmillan Company, 1936).

The Theory of International Economic Policy: The Balance of Payments, Vol. 1 (New York, Oxford University Press, 1951).

Towle, Lawrence W., *International Trade and Commercial Policy* (New York, Harper & Brothers, 1947).

The United States in the World Economy, U.S. Department of Commerce Economic Series 23, 1943.

Viner, Jacob, *Studies in the Theory of International Trade* (New York and London, Harper & Brothers, 1937).

Von Haberler, Gottfried, *The Theory of International Trade* (New York, The Macmillan Company, 1936).

Walker, John T., *Foreign Exchange Equilibrium* (Pittsburgh, University of Pittsburgh Press, 1951).

Whale, P. Barrett, *International Trade* (London, T. Thornton Butterworth, Ltd., 1932).

Williams, J. H., *Post-war Monetary Plans* (New York, Alfred A. Knopf, Inc. 1947).

Young, John Parke, *The International Economy* (New York, The Ronald Press Company, 1942).

World Economic Survey, League of Nations (serial).

International Financial Statistics, International Monetary Fund (monthly).

Foreign Commerce Weekly, Office of International Trade, U.S. Department of Commerce (weekly).

POLICIES

Beveridge, William Henry, *Tariffs, The Case Examined.* (London, Longmans, Roberts and Green, 1932).

Commercial Policy in the Inter-war Period (Geneva, League of Nations, 1942).

Condliffe, J. B., *The Commerce of Nations* (New York, W. W. Norton & Company, 1950).

Course and Phases of the World Economic Depression (Geneva, League of Nations, 1931).

Culbertson, William S., *Reciprocity* (New York, McGraw-Hill Book Company, Inc., 1937).

——, *International Economic Policies* (New York and London, Appleton-Century-Crofts, Inc., 1925).

Davis, Joseph S., *International Commodity Agreements: Hope, Illusion or Menace?* (New York, Committee on International Economic Policy, 1947).

Dietrich, Ethel B., *World Trade* (New York, Henry Holt and Company, Inc., 1939).

Ellsworth, P. T., *The International Economy* (New York, The Macmillan Company, 1950).

Enke, Stephen, and Virgil Salera, *International Economics* (New York, Prentice-Hall, Inc., 1947).

Export and Import Practice, Office of International Trade, U.S. Department of Commerce, 1938.

Foreign Marks of Origin Regulations, U.S. Department of Commerce, Economic Series 62, 1947.

Gordon, Margaret S., *Barriers to World Trade* (New York, The Macmillan Company, 1941).

Hansen, Alvin H., *America's Role in the World Economy* (New York, W. W. Norton & Company, 1945).

Hawkins, Harry C., *Commercial Treaties and Agreements* (New York, Rinehart & Company, Inc., 1951).

Heilperin, Michael, *The Trade of Nations* (New York, Alfred A. Knopf, Inc., 1952).

Horn, Paul V., and Hubert E. Bice, *Latin-American Trade and Economics* (New York, Prentice-Hall, Inc., 1949).

Huebner, George G., and Roland L. Kramer, *Foreign Trade Principles and Practices* (New York, Appleton-Century-Crofts, Inc., 1942).

Import Requirements of the United States Food, Drug and Cosmetic Act, (Washington, Food and Drug Administration, Federal Security Agency, 1947).

Intergovernmental Commodity Control Agreements, (Montreal, International Labour Office, 1943).

Isaacs, Asher, *International Trade—Tariff and Commercial Policies* (Chicago, Richard D. Irwin, Inc., 1948).

Killough, Hugh B., and Lucy W. Killough, *Economics of International Trade,* 2d ed. (New York, McGraw-Hill Book Company, Inc., 1948).

Lewis, Cleona, *America's Stake in International Investments* (Washington, Brookings Institution, 1948).

———, *The United States and Foreign Investment Problems* (Washington, Brookings Institution, 1948).

Lincoln, George A., William S. Stone, and Thomas H. Harvey, *Economics of National Security* (New York, Prentice-Hall, Inc., 1950).

Mason, Edward S., *Controlling World Trade* (New York, McGraw-Hill Book Company, Inc., 1946).

Patterson, Ernest M., *An Introduction to World Economics* (New York, The Macmillan Company, 1947).

Rowe, J. W. F., *Markets and Men* (London, Cambridge University Press, 1936).

Stocking, George W., and M. W. Watkins, *Cartels in Action* (New York, The Twentieth Century Fund, Inc., 1946).

———, *Cartels or Competition* (New York, The Twentieth Century Fund, Inc., 1948).

Taussig, F. W., *International Trade* (New York, The Macmillan Company, 1936).

Towle, Lawrence W., *International Trade and Commercial Policy* (New York, Harper & Brothers, 1947).

United States Import Duties (1950) and supplements thereto, United States Tariff Commission.

Villard, Oswald Garrison, *Free Trade—Free World* (New York, Robert Schalkenbach Foundation, 1947).

Young, John Parke, *The International Economy* (New York, The Ronald Press Company, 1942).

Custom House Guide, Import Publications, Inc., New York (annual).

Exporters' Encyclopedia, Thomas Ashwell and Co., Inc., New York (annual).

American Import and Export Bulletin, Import Publications, Inc., New York (monthly).

Export Trade and Shipper, Thomas Ashwell and Co., Inc., New York (monthly).

Exporters' Digest, American and Foreign Credit Underwriters Corporation, New York (monthly).

Foreign Commerce Weekly, Office of International Trade, U.S. Department of Commerce (weekly).
International Trade Reporter, Bureau of National Affairs (weekly).

INTERGOVERNMENTAL ORGANIZATIONS AND AGREEMENTS

Buchanan, Norman S., and F. A., Lutz, *Rebuilding the World Economy* (New York, The Twentieth Century Fund, Inc., 1947).

Commercial Policy in the Inter-war Period, (Geneva, League of Nations, 1942).

Condliffe, J. B., *The Commerce of Nations* (New York, W. W. Norton & Company, 1950).

Ellsworth, P. T., *The International Economy* (New York, The Macmillan Company, 1950).

Foreign Trade Practice (Reference Sources), Office of International Trade, U.S. Department of Commerce, 1950.

Hansen, Alvin H., *America's Role in the World Economy* (New York, W. W. Norton & Company, 1945).

Harrod, Roy Forbes, *International Economics* (London, Nisbet and Company, Ltd., 1939).

Heilperin, Michael, *International Monetary Economics* (New York, Longmans, Green & Co., Inc., 1930).

———, *The Trade of Nations* (New York, Alfred A. Knopf, Inc., 1952).

Hoover, Calvin B., *International Trade and Domestic Employment* (New York, McGraw-Hill Book Company, Inc., 1945).

Horn, Paul V., and Hubert E. Bice, *Latin-American Trade and Economics* (New York, Prentice-Hall, Inc., 1949).

Intergovernmental Commodity Control Agreements, (Montreal, International Labour Office, 1943).

International Currency Experience, (Geneva, League of Nations; Princeton, N.J., Princeton University Press, 1944).

Johnson, D. Gale, *Trade and Agriculture* (New York, John Wiley & Sons, Inc.; London, Chapman & Hall, Ltd., 1950).

Killough, Hugh B., and Lucy W. Killough, *Economics of International Trade*, 2d ed. (New York, McGraw-Hill Book Company, Inc., 1948).

Lincoln, George A., William S. Stone, and Thomas H. Harvey, *Economics of National Security* (New York, Prentice-Hall, Inc., 1950).

Marsh, Donald Bailey, *World Trade and Investment* (New York, Harcourt, Brace and Company, Inc., 1951).

Mason, Edward S., *Controlling World Trade* (New York, McGraw-Hill Book Company, Inc., 1946).

Southard, Frank A., Jr., *Foreign Exchange Practice and Policy* (New York, McGraw-Hill Book Company, Inc., 1940).

Staley, Eugene, *World Economy in Transition* (New York, Council on Foreign Relations, Inc., 1939).

Towle, Lawrence W., *International Trade and Commercial Policy* (New York, Harper & Brothers, 1947).

Walker, John T., *Foreign Exchange Equilibrium* (Pittsburgh, University of Pittsburgh Press, 1951).

Williams, J. H., *Post-war Monetary Plans* (New York, Alfred A. Knopf, Inc., 1947).

Young, John Parke, *The International Economy* (New York, The Ronald Press Company, 1942).

International Financial Statistics, International Monetary Fund (monthly).

Foreign Commerce Weekly, Office of international Trade, U.S. Department of Commerce (weekly).

International Trade Reporter, Bureau of National Affairs (weekly).

Index

A

Absolute advantage, 218–219
Acceptances, bank, for creating dollar exchange, 268
  Federal Reserve limit on, 162, 174–175, 190–191
  under letters of credit, 173–175
  processing of, 182–183
  market for, 106, 162, 183, 277–279, 400
  trade, 170–172
Acheson, Dean, 479–480
Ad valorem duties, 327
Adler, J. Hans, 246n.
Advantage, absolute, 218–219
  comparative, 219–222
  equal, 219
Advertising, 209–211
Advertising Handbook, 211
Agricultural Act of 1948, 345–346
Air mail, 122–123
Air shipment, 109–110
  advantages of, 110
  air-cargo forwarders, 114–115
Aldrich, Winthrop, 316
Ambassadors, United States, 134
American Arbitration Association, 127–128
American Exporter, 207, 211
American Foreign Credit Underwriters Corporation, 166, 188–189
American Import and Export Bulletin, 18n., 207, 208
American National Bank of Chicago, 209
American selling price, 16n., 17
American Tariff League, 478
Analysis of General Agreement on Tariffs and Trade, 345n., 384n., 427n.
Annecy protocol, 384, 386
Arbitrage, 291–294
  exchange, 291–292
  gold, 292
  interest, 292–294
Arbitration and legal services, 126–128

A (continued)

Argentina, IAPI, 356
  multiple-rate system, 369–371
Authority, to pay, 186
  to purchase, 186
Average, marine insurance, 120–121

B

Balance of International Payments of the United States, The, 1946–1948, 28n., 31n., 296n., 298n., 302n., 304n., 309n.
Balance of Payments Yearbook, 10, 61, 263n., 270n., 272
Balances of Payments, 1939–1945, 10, 18
Balances of payments, 243–246, 256–274, 298–299, 312
  adjustments in, 265–269
    deflation, 266–267
    seasonal and cyclical factors, 267–268
  analysis of, 256–274
    compensatory official financing, 270–272
    multiplier, foreign-trade, 272–274
    objectives and limitations, 257–258
    terms of trade, 269–270
  balance and equilibrium, 261–265
  balancing the "balance," 262–265
  and national income accounting, 243–246
  relationship of selected accounts, 258–261
Bank of New York, 171n., 176n.
Banks, central, in foreign-exchange market, 278–279
  commercial, in foreign-exchange market, 277–278
  services performed by, 105–106
  Federal Reserve, in foreign-exchange market, 278–279
  services to foreign commerce, 106
  (*See also* Federal Reserve System)
Becker, Edmund F., 199
Bills of lading, 157, 159–160